BlackRock's Guide to Fixed-Income Risk Management

BlackRock's Guide to Fixed-Income Risk Management

BENNETT W. GOLUB, Editor

WILEY

Published by John Wiley & Sons, Inc., Hoboken, New Jersey.
Published simultaneously in Canada.

For general information on our other products and services or for technical support, please contact our Customer Care Department within the United States at (800) 762-2974, outside the United States at (317) 572-3993 or fax (317) 572-4002.

Wiley also publishes its books in a variety of electronic formats. Some content that appears in print may not be available in electronic formats. For more information about Wiley products, visit our web site at www.wiley.com.

Library of Congress Cataloging-in-Publication Data:

Names: Golub, Bennett W., author. | John Wiley & Sons, publisher.
Title: BlackRock's guide to fixed-income risk management / Bennett W. Golub.
Description: Hoboken, New Jersey : Wiley, [2023] | Includes index.
Identifiers: LCCN 2023007920 (print) | LCCN 2023007921 (ebook) | ISBN 9781119884873 (hardback) | ISBN 9781119884897 (adobe pdf) | ISBN 9781119884880 (epub)
Subjects: LCSH: Financial risk management. | Fixed-income securities—Risk management. | Investments—Risk management.
Classification: LCC HD61 .G644 2023 (print) | LCC HD61 (ebook) | DDC 658.15/5—dc23/eng/20230505
LC record available at https://lccn.loc.gov/2023007920
LC ebook record available at https://lccn.loc.gov/2023007921

Cover Design: Wiley and BlackRock
Cover Image: © Liyao Xie/Getty Images
SKY10055328_091523

"And, of course, stability isn't nearly so spectacular as instability."
~Aldous Huxley, *Brave New World*

Contents

CHAPTER 5

Market-Driven Scenarios: An Approach for Plausible Scenario Construction   **125**

Bennett W. Golub, David Greenberg, and Ronald Ratcliffe

CHAPTER 6

A Framework to Quantify and Price Geopolitical Risks   **145**

Catherine Kress, Carl Patchen, Ronald Ratcliffe, Eric Van Nostrand, and Kemin Yang

Frequently Used Abbreviations

ABS	Asset-Backed Securities
ADV	Average Daily Volume
ANOVA	Analysis of Variance
AP	Authorized Participant
APG	Aladdin Product Group
ARRC	Alternative Reference Rates Committee
ARRs	Alternative Reference Rates
ATM	At-the-Money or Automated Teller Machine
ATR	Alpha Target Ratio
AUM	Assets Under Management
AVaR	Analytical VaR
BGRI	BlackRock Geopolitical Risk Indicator
BLK	BlackRock
BoE	Bank of England
BP	Basis Point
BSRMF	Buy Side Risk Managers Forum
BWIC	Bids Wanted in Competition
CCD	Coupon Curve Duration
CCost	Cost of Carry
CCP	Central Counterparty
CDF	Cumulative Distribution Function
CDS	Credit Default Swap
CDX	Credit Default Swap Index
CIO	Chief Investment Officer
CLO	Collateralized Loan Obligation
CM	Clearing Member
CMBS	Commercial Mortgage-Backed Securities
CMRA	Capital Market Risk Advisors
CP	Commercial Paper
CPR	Conditional Prepayment Rate
CRO	Chief Risk Officer
CSA	Collateral Support Agreement
CTF	Collective Trust Fund
CTR	Contribution to Risk
CVaR	Conditional VaR

DxS	Duration Times Spread
EHVaR	Enhanced HVaR
EM	Emerging Markets
EMH	Efficient Market Hypothesis
ERM	Exchange Rate Mechanism
ES	Expected Shortfall
ESG	Environmental, Social, and Governance
€STR	Euro Short-Term Rate
ETD	Exchange-Traded Derivative
ETF	Exchange-Traded Fund
ETP	Exchange-Traded Product
EWMA	Exponentially Weighted Moving Average
FCA	Financial Conduct Authority
FCM	Futures Commission Merchant
FINRA	Financial Industry Regulatory Authority
FSB	Financial Stability Board
FSOC	Financial Stability Oversight Council
FX	Foreign Exchange
GDP	Gross Domestic Product
GFC	Global Financial Crisis
GNMAII MBS	Ginnie Mae Mortgage-Backed Security
HF	Hedge Fund
HRaR	Historical Redemption-at-Risk
HROR	Horizon Rate of Return
HVaR	Historical VaR
HY	High Yield
IBORs	Interbank Offered Rates
ICTR	Incremental Contribution to Risk
IG	Investment Grade
IM	Initial Margin
IMA	Investment Management Agreement
IOSCO	International Organization of Securities Commissions
IR	Information Ratio
IRMP	Investment Risk Management Paradigm
ISDA	International Swaps and Derivatives Association
ITM	In-the-Money
ITRM	Idiosyncratic Tail Risk Multiplier
KRBC	Key Rate Bucket Convexities
KRD	Key Rate Duration
LCR	Liquidity Coverage Ratio
LDI	Liability-Driven Investment
LIBOR	London Interbank Offered Rate
LTV	Loan to Value
LVNAV	Low Volatility Net Asset Value
MBS	Mortgage-Backed Securities
MCTR	Marginal Contribution to Risk

MD	Mahalanobis Distance
MDS	Market-Driven Scenario
MiFID II	Markets in Financial Instruments Directive
MMF	Money Market Fund
MPO	Multi-Period Optimization
MRAC	Market Risk Advisory Committee
MSQE	Mean-Squared Error
MTB	Mortgage/Treasury Basis
MWCB	Market Wide Circuit Breaker
NAV	Net Asset Value
NBFI	Non-Bank Financial Intermediation
OAC	Option-Adjusted Convexity
OAD	Option-Adjusted Duration
OAS	Option-Adjusted Spread
OAV	Option-Adjusted Value
OCC	Office of the Comptroller of the Currency
OIS	Overnight Index Swaps
OLS	Ordinary Least Squares
OTC	Over-the-Counter
OTM	Out-of-the-Money
OTR	On-the-Run
OTS	Office of Thrift Supervision
OWIC	Offers Wanted in Competition
P&L	Profit and Loss
PCA	Principal Components Analysis
PEPP	Pandemic Emergency Purchase Programme
PFMI	Principles for Financial Market Infrastructure
PQD	Public Quantitative Disclosure
PROC	Portfolio Risk Oversight Committee
PRV	Purchase Redemption Value
PTF	Proprietary Trading Firm
REITs	Real Estate Investment Trusts
RFQ	Request for Quote
RFR	Risk-Free Rates
RPT	Risk and Performance Targets
RQA	Risk & Quantitative Analysis
SAR	Standalone Risk
SARON	Swiss Average Rate Overnight
SEC	Securities and Exchange Commission
SEF	Swap Execution Facility
SOCP	Second Order Conic Programming
SOFR	Secured Overnight Financing Rate
SONIA	Sterling Overnight Index Average
SPACs	Special Purpose Acquisition Companies

STRM	Systematic Tail Risk Multiplier
T-cost	Transaction Cost
TONA	Tokyo Overnight Average Rate
TRACE	Trade Reporting and Compliance Engine
TRS	Total Return Swaps
TSOV	Term Structure of Volatility
TSY	Treasury
UCITS	Undertakings for Collective Investment in Transferable Securities
UMBS	Uniform Mortgage-Backed Securities
UST	US Treasury
VaR	Value at Risk
VM	Variation Margin
WFH	Work from Home
WoW	Week-over-Week
ZV0	Zero Volatility Spread

Foreword

Back in the distant days of the mid-1980s I began my career focused on equity markets. Over the next two decades, the abundance of price and volume data, along with the relatively limited set of variables required to describe equity risk, led to the development of fundamental and statistical equity risk models that are now ubiquitous across the asset management industry.

In due course it became obvious to me that in order to understand investment risk in all its forms, some knowledge of fixed-income markets and products was also necessary. Many years before my association with BlackRock, I came across a book, *Risk Management: Approaches for Fixed Income Markets* (2000) by Bennett W. Golub and Leo M. Tilman. I remember reading it with some fascination. The statistical constructs were, at least in part, similar to those used in equity markets. However, the markets themselves were very different. Nonetheless, the rigor of the discussions and the practicality of the contents were incredibly useful to me back then.

Some years later Ben Golub and I became colleagues when BlackRock acquired Merrill Lynch Investment Management, where I was then the head of its Risk & Quantitative Analysis group in London. This brought me for the first time into contact with BlackRock's fixed-income analytics and risk management teams. My equities background combined with BlackRock's fixed-income expertise made for a good match, and I was appointed the co-head with Ben Golub of a merged Risk & Quantitative Analysis group.

Over the subsequent 16 years, much has taken place in both markets and risk management. The contrasts between equities and fixed-income investing were, in many respects, palpable. Some of the characteristics of fixed-income securities became clearer to me, such as the limited trading and even more limited price data, the lags in the availability of the limited amount of pricing data, the astounding number of individual securities, and the nonstandard terms and conditions of securities. Real-world risk management meant making necessary compromises from the equity ideal.

Currently, changes and reforms are moving fixed-income markets somewhat closer to the more idealized equity markets, making certain types of analyses that were routine in the equity markets partially available for fixed-income securities.

The last 16 years have also contained some major market events, including the Global Financial Crisis and the Coronavirus pandemic, that challenged the notion that even exchange markets operate efficiently all the time. Some of the later chapters in this book that focus on financial crises contain lessons that we learned that are genuinely worth remembering.

This book introduces the notion of an Investment Risk Management Paradigm (IRMP). This is particularly useful as a reminder of the need to enforce consistent levels of rigor across all of the firm's investment processes. Having a formal notion of this standardization has been extremely useful, especially when investment processes change or activities are added.

History will not be kind to some notions of risk management that turn out to be formalized manifestations of self-delusion. Other analytics or frameworks will better last the test of time. But while I am certain that some of the notions described in this book will eventually need to change, just as many were eventually edited out of the first edition, many will stand the test of time. This book presents techniques and practices that are actually used and are actually useful. I recommend it to investors and risk managers who wish to get an insight into how investment risk management is contemporaneously practiced at a major global multi-investment process asset manager.

Ed Fishwick
Chief Risk Officer
BlackRock, Inc.
Summer 2023

Preface

Changing market dynamics, technological advances, and geopolitical stresses have transformed investment risk management. As new and bespoke products have emerged, new risks and additional complexities have driven advances in risk management processes and analytics. Consider, for example, all the forced and rapid innovations that arose from the Coronavirus pandemic. Given the abundance of change, risk managers have had to adapt their processes and tools to address market turbulence, structural bond market changes, product complexity, and increased regulatory oversight. Additionally, risk managers have learned to take advantage of some of these technological advances, resulting in better analytics and the ability to analyze bigger and broader data sets. An intellectually curious risk management culture, coupled with rigorous risk management processes and technological competence, facilitates risk managers' ability to rapidly and effectively adapt to new circumstances.

Recognizing the dynamic nature of investment risk management informs us that it is almost certain that some of the ideas and methodologies presented in this book will inevitably become obsolete themselves. Similarly, there inevitably are important omissions, either intentionally due to the limitations of time or are outside the wisdom and firsthand knowledge of the authors.

This book is a heavily edited and expanded edition of *Risk Management: Approaches for Fixed Income Markets* (2000) by Bennett W. Golub and Leo M. Tilman (the first edition). In the 23 years following the original English language publication, much has happened to reshape the investment risk management landscape. For example, the heightened attention by markets and investors to ESG (environmental, social, and governance) characteristics was never envisioned when the original book was published. The definitive book on ESG risk management has probably not been written yet; this book intentionally omits much of that topic, while the profession awaits a conclusive state-of-the-practice volume. Also, while currently a hot topic and one that certainly has demonstrated the ability to generate multiple risk management failures, this book is intentionally silent on the risk management of cryptocurrencies; we await those markets' risk management processes maturing.

The technological intensity of investment risk management has increased dramatically. Twenty-three years ago, technology was not necessarily at the forefront of most investment management firms. Now, technology is one of the critical success factors—allowing firms to continue to evolve to meet clients' needs, respond to market changes and regulatory requirements, and create operational efficiencies and scale. With improvements in technology, firms are now able to perform tasks that were previously technologically impossible or would take too much time or too much expensive hardware to be useful. When editing sections of the original book for inclusion in this new edition, references to analytic techniques that involved compromising accuracy for computational efficiency were removed from the manuscript; there is much less need to compromise precision for the sake of economizing computational resources. The implications of Moore's Law, broadly speaking, continue to make more and more computational resources economical. Cloud-based applications, for example, can summon massive amounts of computational power on demand. Organizations can store, analyze, manipulate, and synthesize what would have been unimaginable amounts of data more cheaply and quickly than ever before. The sophisticated and creative use of technology, has become an essential part of effective investment risk management. Having the right technology to manage risk is no longer a luxury; it is a necessity.

BlackRock's commitment to innovation and the use of technology has been one of the key drivers of its ongoing robust growth. Developing and evolving Aladdin and leveraging technology has been part of BlackRock's founding vision and has enabled the firm to become a massive scale operator, highly efficient, integrated, and dynamic. As the firm grows and technology evolves, Aladdin continues to be a best-in-class solution, used by BlackRock to operate efficiently at scale. The same Aladdin technology used by BlackRock is also available and heavily used by many major global financial institutions.

The motivation for this book originated due to an inquiry from a BlackRock client about when the first edition would be revised. Initially, this seemed to be a relatively straightforward task, and the project was initiated in 2017. At first, the plan was to update data, tables, and exhibits and remove topics that were no longer relevant. However, after this editing process, it became apparent that simply updating the data and removing obsolete sections would be sorely inadequate given how much markets, products, and risk management have evolved. Instead, it became clear that if the original book were to be properly updated, a substantial expansion of the topics covered would be required. That, of course, made creating the second edition a materially greater task. Given my then current role as chief risk officer of BlackRock, this task would have been beyond my ability to complete. In 2018, I concluded that if we expanded the scope of the book, the only feasible path forward was to ask my fellow BlackRock colleagues to contribute their expertise and enthusiasm and author or coauthor the needed chapters. Unlike the original book, which was written as a unified whole in a single voice, the new edition would include chapters on a wide range of topics written by many authors.

Bringing together BlackRock's leaders in risk management, portfolio management, trading, financial modeling, psychology, and analytics, this successor book to the first edition, now titled *BlackRock's Guide to Fixed-Income Risk Management*, represents a combination of revised and updated chapters from the original book and a collection of new standalone chapters covering a range of investment risk management topics. Each chapter has been authored by BlackRock's current or former senior subject matter experts. While the book focuses primarily on fixed-income practices, analytics, and models, many of the concepts presented are equally meaningful in a multi-asset context. This book can first be considered a practitioner's guide to fixed-income risk management, leveraging BlackRock's overall investment risk management framework for operating a viable risk management program at scale, heterogeneity, and complexity.

ORGANIZATION OF THE BOOK[1]

This book is organized into three sections and covers the following themes:

(I) An Approach to Fixed-Income Investment Risk Management
(II) Fixed-Income Risk Management—Then and Now
(III) Lessons from the Credit Crisis and Coronavirus Pandemic

SECTION I: AN APPROACH TO FIXED-INCOME INVESTMENT RISK MANAGEMENT

In Section I, we describe the pillars of *BlackRock's Investment Risk Management Paradigm (IRMP)*. This paradigm evolved over many years as a tool to bring consistency and structure to BlackRock's risk management activities across its various investment management businesses to ensure that risks are properly identified, measured, governed, and reconciled with actual performance. The IRMP rests upon on the following five pillars:

1. Ex ante risk measurement
2. Risk governance (i.e., having and maintaining agreed upon levels of risks)
3. Portfolio manager risk-return awareness
4. Performance attribution
5. Performance analysis

Each component of the paradigm is discussed in detail in one or more of the following chapters. Given the various risks to which portfolios are exposed and the diversity of measurements available, several chapters expand upon the first pillar, *ex ante risk measurement*. Examples and case studies are incorporated to help illustrate the risk management approaches and analytics presented.

Chapter 1 provides an overview of risk management at BlackRock and discusses several elements that underpin a strong risk management program. The chapter reinforces the importance of governance and oversight and introduces BlackRock's approach to investment risk management. To be clear, though, establishing a comprehensive and pervasive risk management program and culture requires commitment and support from all levels of an organization, starting with senior management. My colleagues and I were fortunate to be able to develop our ideas and methodologies in such an environment. This chapter was coauthored by myself and Rick Flynn, managing director in the Risk & Quantitative Analysis group.

Chapter 2 presents parametric approaches to risk management and was initially included in the first edition. This chapter aligns with the first pillar of BlackRock's IRMP, *ex ante risk measurement*. This chapter includes a discussion of analytical and empirical durations, partial durations, interest rate scenario analysis, and horizon rate of return analysis. The parametric measures of market risk continue to form the backbone of more elaborate and compressive risk methodologies and techniques, which is why we felt that it was an important chapter to revisit and revise in this edition. This chapter has been updated with more recent data. It also includes additional concepts, such as duration times spread (DxS), authored by David Greenberg, former managing director in Technology & Operations—Artificial Intelligence (AI) Labs. Additionally, we added a new section on option usage in portfolio management, which was authored by Jack Hattem, managing director in the Portfolio Management Group. Yury Krongauz, managing director in the Financial Modeling Group, included additional details regarding wave shocks to the Key Rate Duration section. This chapter was updated by Matthew Wang, managing director in the Fundamental Fixed Income Portfolio Management Group.

Chapter 3 reviews the dynamics of interest rate shocks and was also previously published in the first edition. The concepts in this chapter are also part of the first pillar of BlackRock's

IRMP and contain an introduction to principal component analysis as well as an investigation of the probability distribution of interest rate shocks. In this chapter, the relationship between the first principal component and the term structure of volatility is explored and the results are applied to the study of big market move days as well as the historical steepeners and flatteners of the US Treasury curve. This chapter was updated by Matthew Wang.

Chapter 4 focuses on estimating and decomposing portfolio risk and also aligns with the first pillar of BlackRock's IRMP. This chapter reviews portfolio volatility estimation and factor structure, along with the empirical challenges associated with estimating covariance matrices. It contains an overview of Value at Risk (VaR) estimation, including a focus on Enhanced Historical VaR (EHVaR), which is a proprietary approach developed for modeling the forward distribution of asset returns. EHVaR blends the advantages of both parametric and nonparametric forecasting techniques. Finally, the chapter discusses decomposition of realized risk and return. This chapter was coauthored by Amandeep Dhaliwal, managing director in the Financial Modeling Group, along with Tom Booker, director in the Financial Modeling Group.

Chapter 5 introduces the Market-Driven Scenarios (MDS) framework, which is designed to provide structure to the often subjective and ad hoc nature of hypothetical scenario generation. Macroeconomic fundamentals typically drive the general direction of financial market returns. However, tail risks, which can be triggered by geopolitical events, can arise that are difficult to forecast but can have significant adverse effects on fund returns. As an element of the first pillar, this chapter highlights the use of specific econometric techniques and the application of a disciplined multistep process to create Market-Driven Scenarios. The MDS process is inherently multi-asset versus being particularly fixed-income oriented. This chapter was coauthored by myself, David Greenberg, and Ronald Ratcliffe, managing director in the Analytics & Quantitative Solutions team within BlackRock Solutions.

Chapter 6 uses the MDS framework to analyze geopolitical risks and assess their potential market impact in a systematic way. The chapter reviews market responses to unexpected historical geopolitical shocks from 1962–2019. Using one of the top geopolitical risks from 2019 as an example, this chapter demonstrates the application of the MDS framework. This chapter aligns with the first pillar of the IRMP and reinforces the importance of scenario analysis and stress testing portfolios. It was coauthored by Catherine Kress, director and head of Geopolitical Research & Strategy within the BlackRock Investment Institute; Carl Patchen, former vice president in the Risk & Quantitative Analysis group; Ronald Ratcliffe; Eric Van Nostrand, former managing director in the BlackRock Sustainable Investment group; and Kemin Yang, former associate in the BlackRock Investment Institute. Additional contributors include myself, Tom Donilon, chairman of the BlackRock Investment Institute; and Isabelle Mateos y Lago, global head of BlackRock's Official Institutions group.

Chapter 7 presents some approaches for measuring liquidity risk, one of the many investment risks that demands rigorous and continuous oversight. While liquidity risk can have different meanings, this chapter focuses on fund liquidity risk. As a component of the first pillar, this chapter contains a brief history of how liquidity risk management has evolved and covers the various elements of a liquidity risk management framework, including asset liquidity, redemptions, and extraordinary measures. This chapter was coauthored by myself; Philip Sommer, director in the Liquidity & Trading Research Group within BlackRock Solutions; Stefano Pasquali, head of the Liquidity & Trading Research Group within BlackRock Solutions; Michael Huang, managing director in the Risk & Quantitative Analysis group; Kristen Walters, former managing director in the Risk & Quantitative Analysis group; and Nikki Azznara, vice president in the Portfolio Management Group.

Chapter 8 presents approaches for managing market risk in fixed-income portfolios using portfolio optimization techniques. An earlier version of this chapter was previously included in the first edition. However, it has been significantly updated and transformed to reflect new approaches for optimization, including many that are also applicable to multi-asset portfolios. The chapter begins with a discussion of the differences between risk measurements versus risk management and covers typical fixed-income hedges. Then, the chapter transitions to discuss parametric hedging techniques, generalized approaches to hedging, and advanced portfolio optimization and risk management techniques. Various examples are included in the chapter to demonstrate how optimization approaches can be utilized in different situations. This chapter does not necessarily align uniquely with a specific IRMP pillar. Rather, portfolio optimization is a powerful and versatile tool that allows portfolios to be engineered for a variety of reasons. This chapter was primarily authored by Alex Ulitsky, managing director in the Financial Modeling Group. Jack Hattem provided significant updates to this chapter.

Chapter 9 introduces the second pillar, *risk governance,* and also introduces the concept of risk scans to identify potential risk issues. Specifically, properly designed risk and exposure scans can flag portfolios and positions that may not align with client objectives or expectations. Given the increasing size and heterogeneity of investment processes and products, risk managers need to efficiently analyze a multitude of portfolios. This chapter presents a basic univariate risk scan framework that uses simple algorithms to identify potential risk exceptions—what came to be known at BlackRock as Risk and Performance Targets (RPT). I was the primary author of this chapter. Rory van Zwanenberg, director in the Risk & Quantitative Analysis group, significantly contributed to this chapter, along with Katie Day, managing director in the Risk & Quantitative Analysis group.

The third pillar, *portfolio manager risk-return awareness,* focuses on the relationship between portfolio and risk managers. Chapter 10 discusses the importance of risk managers working together with portfolio managers to ensure that risks are properly detected, understood, and then appropriately managed for clients. Effective risk management requires regular interaction with portfolio managers to discuss risk positioning and can include identifying potential adverse behavioral aspects of investing. The chapter concentrates on behavioral finance, an evolving risk management domain, which seeks to identify cognitive blind spots that can impact investment decisions. The chapter includes details on decision-making analytics such as loss aversion, disposition bias, and the endowment effect. The chapter also includes a framework for evaluating behavioral aspects of the investment processes. This chapter was coauthored by Emily Haisley, managing director of the behavioral finance initiatives in the Risk & Quantitative Analysis group, and Nicky Lai, director in the Risk & Quantitative Analysis group.

The fourth pillar, *performance attribution,* decomposes investment returns into their sources of performance, providing portfolio and risk managers with an understanding of the drivers of investment results. Chapter 11 covers approaches and analytical techniques that practitioners can leverage to conduct performance attribution, including Brinson and factor-based methodologies. The chapter provides multiple examples to demonstrate how portfolio returns can be viewed and interpreted. This chapter was coauthored by Reade Ryan, managing director in the Risk & Quantitative Analysis group, and Carol Yu, former vice president in the Risk & Quantitative Analysis group.

The fifth pillar, *performance analysis,* presents a framework to review a portfolio's realized performance relative to its benchmarks, peers, and other comparable accounts. Chapter 12 discusses how to meaningfully measure aggregate platform performance, especially across a heterogeneous set of funds with different benchmarks and risk and performance targets. The chapter covers active performance metrics, such as alpha target ratio, weighted peer percentile, and alpha dollars, along with index performance metrics. Strengths and weaknesses of the various active and index performance measurements are presented. This chapter was coauthored by Mark Paltrowitz, managing director and chief performance officer for BlackRock and the head of fixed-income and multi-asset investment risk; Mark Temple-Jones, former director in the ETF & Index Investments group; Viola Dunne, former managing director in the Risk & Quantitative Analysis group; and Christopher Calingo, director in the Risk & Quantitative Analysis group.

Chapter 13 marks the conclusion of the first section of this book and discusses further evolving the Investment Risk Management Paradigm. Given the dynamic nature of financial risk, continuously evolving a risk management framework to address emerging risks and changing market themes is crucial for a growing investment manager. This chapter starts by covering the characteristics of a traditional buy-side risk management framework and then discusses evolving the framework to better manage a multiplicity of risks at scale. BlackRock Solutions' Aladdin implementation of the Risk Radar system is presented as a tangible example of how risk governance can be successfully executed at scale. This chapter was coauthored by myself; Michael Huang; and Joe Buehlmeyer, director in the Aladdin Product Group.

SECTION II: FIXED-INCOME RISK MANAGEMENT—THEN AND NOW

Despite rapid transformation in other areas of financial markets, for decades, the core transactional underpinnings of bond markets remained largely the same—high touch, over-the-counter markets dependent on dealers' balance sheets with only limited timely price, volume, and order book transparency. However, in the years following the 2008 Global Financial Crisis, significant structural changes in bond markets have occurred. This section briefly discusses some of those bond market changes over the past 20 years.

Chapter 14 discusses the modernization of the bond market and the emergence of fixed-income exchange-traded fund products. The chapter covers the evolution of bond markets, the development of index-based ecosystems, the implications for investing, portfolio management and risk management, and the future state of portfolio construction. This chapter was coauthored by Daniel Veiner, managing director, co-head of Global Trading; Stephen Laipply, managing director, global co-head of Fixed Income ETFs; Carolyn Weinberg, managing director, chief product innovation officer and co-head of the Global Product Group; Samara Cohen, senior managing director, chief investment officer of ETF and Index Investments; Vasiliki Pachatouridi, managing director, head of iShares Fixed Income Product Strategy EMEA; and Hui Sien Koay, director, lead Index Fixed Income Product Strategist for APAC.

Chapter 15 discusses the cessation of LIBOR and the massive undertaking required to shift to Alternative Reference Rates (ARRs). Given the transition's size and scope, the migration away from LIBOR required a significant amount of coordination and organization from various market participants. This chapter also discusses the implications to portfolio management along with risk management. This chapter was written by Jack Hattem.

Chapter 16 covers derivatives reform and the rise of Swap Execution Facilities (SEFs) and central counterparties (CCPs). Following the Global Financial Crisis, market reforms sought to improve transparency in derivatives. Electronification of most trading was required, and counterparty credit risk was reduced by mandating much greater usage of CCPs. This chapter was written by Eileen Kiely, managing director and deputy head of Counterparty Risk in the Risk & Quantitative Analysis group, and Jack Hattem.

SECTION III: LESSONS FROM THE CREDIT CRISIS AND CORONAVIRUS PANDEMIC

Major market disruptions, almost by definition, present the opportunity (and need) to reflect on the necessary changes to risk management practices. The following three chapters were previously published articles that identify some lessons to be learned.

Chapter 17 presents seven specific lessons worth remembering from the Global Financial Crisis of 2007–2008. The credit crisis demonstrated that many widely used risk management techniques relied on critical assumptions that turned out to be profoundly flawed. The Global Financial Crisis changed the risk management profession, with unprecedented extreme market moves and the downfall of well-known financial institutions. Recommendations to enhance risk management practices and beliefs are included in this chapter to correct or mitigate the negative impact of relying on those faulty assumptions.

Chapter 18 highlights the importance of eight principles for buy-side risk management. Chapter 17 and Chapter 18 were initially published in the *Journal of Portfolio Management* and coauthored by myself and Conan Crum, former vice president in the Risk & Quantitative Analysis group.

Finally, the book concludes with a chapter on lessons worth considering from the Coronavirus pandemic. Chapter 19 summarizes 10 key lessons from COVID-19 and considers the implications of the COVID-19 crisis across capital markets. This chapter reviews the key market events from March 2020 and the official sector's interventions. The chapter includes some lessons drawn from COVID-19, identifying what worked and what needs to be addressed further, including policy recommendations and areas for future consideration. This chapter was originally published as a BlackRock *ViewPoint* and was adapted for this book by coauthors Barbara Novick, a co-founder and former vice chairman of BlackRock; Joanna Cound, managing director and global head of Public Policy; Kate Fulton, managing director and head of Americas Public Policy; and Winnie Pun, former managing director within the Global Public Policy group.

BlackRock's Guide to Fixed-Income Risk Management is written for financial services professionals, including chief investment officers, portfolio managers, risk managers, traders, researchers, compliance officers, and modelers. Using BlackRock's approach to risk management as its foundation, the book is particularly intended for buy-side firms. It is also suitable in an academic setting for undergraduate students as well as MBA and PhD candidates.

Bennett W. Golub
New York
Summer 2023

NOTE

1. Several current and former BlackRock subject matter experts authored or coauthored multiple chapters in this book. Their names are listed in the following section and their current (or last) BlackRock titles and team affiliations are provided the first time their names appear. For current BlackRock employees, their titles and team affiliations are representative of their roles as of March 2023.

Acknowledgments

The challenge of measuring and managing the risk of thousands of complex and diverse fixed-income portfolios during periods of both calm and extremely stressed markets offers the ideal setting for developing and applying new ideas. For 34 years, I was fortunate to work in precisely such an environment at BlackRock, Inc., a premier global asset management and risk advisory firm, which served as a state-of-the-practice "laboratory." That laboratory grew in assets under management (AUM) massively during my tenure there, along the dimensions of new products, new asset classes, and new geographies. This environment provided a never-ending and extremely focused demand for practical solutions to real-life problems. Fortunately, because of sophisticated, knowledgeable, and experienced colleagues, who were never shy about providing critiques and feedback, creative and innovative solutions to many risk management challenges developed naturally. The very nature of the problems faced by risk managers—forecasting and mitigating potential severe financial losses—creates the sense of urgency needed to get things done.

BlackRock's risk management philosophy is embedded in the firm's culture and requires the constant development, enhancement, and validation of rigorous techniques for risk measurement and management. Since inception, the firm's commitment to technology and analytics has led to a significant amount of resources being made available for risk management. At the same time, BlackRock's disciplined investment styles and diversity of investment products and services, ranging from mutual funds and institutional accounts to hedge funds, real estate investments trusts (REITs), and collateralized loan obligations (CLOs), created demand for methodologies that are theoretically sound, accurate, intuitive, and computationally feasible. On the other hand, the collaborative approach to portfolio and risk management has led to empirical validation and enhancement of models through constant interaction among financial modelers, portfolio managers, traders, and analysts. This provided a unique opportunity for reconciling theory with reality. Simply put, nothing makes a risk manager's mind focus better than being 20 feet away from a fixed-income trading desk!

The conceptual and computational challenges of risk measurement and management increase exponentially with the size of a financial institution and the diversity of asset classes in which it invests. BlackRock was founded in 1988 as a niche fixed-income investment firm. Since then, it has transformed itself into a global investment company with over \$9 trillion of AUM[1] and independently provides a wide range of risk management services to third-parties. This rapid growth created unique challenges. It was not only critical to develop risk management methodologies universally pertinent to (almost) all classes of fixed-income securities, portfolios, and benchmarks, but to ensure that these approaches were suitable for large-scale practical application in a computationally and operationally feasible manner.

It goes almost without saying that the BlackRock that served as a hothouse for risk management innovations would not have existed as we know it without the leadership provided by Larry Fink and Rob Kapito. Risk management does not have much value if no risks are being taken. Larry, BlackRock's "fearless leader," and Rob provided much of the boldness that, in retrospect, seemed so obvious. Rob Goldstein and Derek Stein kept the shop running, defying the challenges of scale, and Barbara Novick worked hard to keep BlackRock out of political and regulatory troubles.

This book builds on the concepts that were published in the first edition and introduces new methodologies and topics. This book represents the thought leadership, research, and analysis of many BlackRock risk managers, portfolio managers, traders, financial modelers, and other subject matter experts who have helped to advance the field.

No list of acknowledgments would be complete without singling out my colleague and friend, Ed Fishwick. Ed was my partner co-managing BlackRock's Risk & Quantitative Analysis group starting when BlackRock acquired Merrill Lynch Investment Management in 2006. For almost 16 years, we worked together very closely, evolving BlackRock's risk management processes and procedures to ever-changing circumstances. Ed is a world-renowned expert in all matters relating to equity and multi-asset risk management. Yet, this fixed-income-oriented book benefited greatly from his insights and wisdom.

I want to recognize the contribution of my former colleague and friend, Charlie Hallac, who was taken from us before his time, for his extraordinary ability to turn many of the ideas presented in this book into practical reality through robust implementation and infrastructure. Absent his efforts, much that was achieved would have only been academic.

This book is a compilation of writings from numerous current and former BlackRock employees. I would like to explicitly acknowledge the attributed contributions of our past and present colleagues at BlackRock and to apologize for any unintended omissions. Thank you to Chen Ai, Nikki Azznara, Rachel Barry, Arie Belok, Tom Booker, Jacob Brand, Richard Bravery, Joe Buehlmeyer, Chris Calingo, Jennifer Chinn, Samara Cohen, Joanna Cound, Conan Crum, Katie Day, Claire Deng, Samantha DeZur, Amandeep Dhaliwal, Viola Dunne, Michelle Evaul, Stephen Fisher, Rick Flynn, Kate Fulton, David Greenberg, Emily Haisley, Aiting Hanold, Jack Hattem, Michael Huang, Stephon Henry-Rerrie, Adam Jackson, Tracey Jones, Sorag Kabat, Egon Kalotay, Eileen Kiely, Dana Kornbluth, Catherine Kress, Yury Krongauz, Nicky Lai, Stephen Laipply, Jabari Magnus, David McMahon, Meagan Muldoon, Rajat Mukherji, Andrew Narcomey, Barbara Novick, Vasiliki Pachatouridi, Mark Paltrowitz, Martin Parkes, Stefano Pasquali, Carl Patchen, Winnie Pun, Ronald Ratcliffe, Jack Reerink, Alexis Rosenblum, Curtis Ruoff, Reade Ryan, Eugenie Schwob, Tara Sharma, Hui Sien Koay, Antonio Silva, Philip Somers, Mark Temple-Jones, Alex Ulitsky, Onur Uras, Eric Van Nostrand, Rory van Zwanenberg, Daniel Viener, Kristen Walters, Matthew Wang, Carolyn Weinberg, Allison White, Isaac Wittman, Matt Woolley, Kemin Yang, Carol Yu, Helen Zhang, and many other.

Besides attributed coauthors and contributors, many colleagues provided invaluable feedback on the individual chapters. Special thanks to David Belmont, Katie Day, Claire Deng, Chris Fisher, Ed Fishwick, Rick Flynn, David Greenberg, Michael Huang, Vicky Hsu, Arjun Kapor, Yury Krongauz, Ali Nakhle, Barbara Novick, Mark Paltrowitz, Michael Pyle, Alexis Rosenblum, Reade Ryan, Paul Scorer, Kristen Walters, Rory van Zwanenberg, Carol Yu, and many others who reviewed and provided feedback on this book.

Risk management practices have evolved and expanded massively since Leo M. Tilman and I coauthored the first edition. This book follows the developments impacting BlackRock's core businesses by its continued focus on investment risk management practices for liquid securities.

There is, however, a different intellectual path that can be derived from risk management practices and principles. They can successfully be applied in multiple domains and settings, including financial institutions, technology firms, governments, and other organizations. This is the path that Leo M. Tilman has blazed. Leo has applied his extensive experience in investment risk management to the domain of corporate strategy, providing valuable perspectives to major global institutions. Recently, Leo recognized the synergies between business, finance, and military strategy and partnered with former NORAD Commander, General Charles Jacoby (US Army, Ret.), to further explore how risk management can evolve to become risk intelligence, an essential organizational competence that can empower strategy development and execution akin to business and competitive intelligence. This line of thinking is a topic of their book, *Agility: How to Navigate the Unknown and Seize Opportunity in a World of Disruption* (2019). Tilman and Jacoby astutely propose that risk intelligence is the cornerstone of agility—the organizational capacity to successfully navigate disruption and change.

With starts and stops due to the initial bout of Pandemic-driven market shocks, then modifying BlackRock's risk management processes to a work from home model, staff turnover, and my transition from chief risk officer to senior advisor, it has taken almost 5 years to complete this book. Several people were instrumental to driving the book to completion. In addition to her attributed contributions to this book, Kristen Walters helped scope out the pre-Pandemic outline of this book. She helped frame and enlarge the book's breadth. Nikki Azznara also helped to contribute to the book's development and her support is greatly appreciated.

I would especially like to thank Allison White, who remained tenaciously engaged in managing the book's progress from start to finish, for her help. Absent her efforts and dedication, this book would never would have been finished. She has been a pleasure to work with and has gone above and beyond the call of duty.

I would also like to extend my gratitude to Joseph Chalom who has been actively involved and supportive of this project. Thank you to BlackRock's legal team, including Chris Meade, for their assistance. Special thanks and appreciation to Loni J. Sherwin who helped to navigate the various contracts and releases required to publish this book. Thank you to Karen Kim and Colin McFarland for overseeing the data permissions for the exhibits and tables included. Thank you to Laura Zavetz for designing the cover of this book. Thank you to Jim Badenhausen, Andrea Kern, Carolyn Vadino, and Alisa Lessing for reviewing the final manuscript and providing valuable feedback. Thank you to Debbie Polyak for her continuous support in this undertaking.

We are grateful to Bill Falloon, Stacey Rivera, Purvi Patel, Premkumar Narayanan, Samantha Wu, and everyone at John Wiley & Sons, Inc., for their enthusiasm, professionalism, and vision.

Last but certainly not least, I want to thank my wife, Cindy, for her unconditional love, devotion, and support over the years. I dedicate this book to her.

Bennett W. Golub
New York
Summer 2023

NOTE

1. AUM as of March 31, 2023.

An Approach to Fixed-Income Investment Risk Management

CHAPTER 1

An Investment Risk Management Paradigm[1]

Bennett W. Golub
Senior Advisor, BlackRock

Rick Flynn
Managing Director, Risk & Quantitative Analysis, BlackRock

1.1 INTRODUCTION

Risk management analytics and methodologies have evolved significantly over the last 20+ years. Nevertheless, as events continue to demonstrate, putting an effective risk management program and culture into place remains, for some, quite difficult. Doing so requires comprehensive risk management policies and procedures, effective analytics, efficient tools, and people committed to the mission. Each team member, whether a portfolio manager, trader, analytics developer, or risk manager, has an important role to play in managing risk responsibly—risk management only works as a team sport. Effective risk management also requires significant resources and focus.

Establishing an effective risk and control environment typically involves three "lines of defense." As primary risk owners, "the business," i.e., portfolio managers and business managers in the investment management business, are the first line of defense and have the primary responsibility for identifying, managing, and mitigating risk. Risk and control functions, i.e., investment risk, counterparty risk, operational risk, model risk, serve as a second line of defense, acting ideally as independent and trusted advisors to help the business operate more effectively while using its independence to observe and escalate issues of concern. Finally, internal audit is usually thought of as the third line of defense, responsible for reviewing and testing the effectiveness of the control environment as defined by the firm's policies and procedures.

Yet, for all of this effort to be fully effective, a strong and pervasive risk culture across the entirety of the firm is required. Ideally, all employees view themselves as risk managers, regardless of where they fit into the three lines of defense model. This level of engagement will drive the risk management culture forward as well as provide multiple levels of checks and balances.

Aligning the risk management function and culture with the organization's priorities and business model is critical. Different types of financial institutions can have radically different business models which must be fully understood when designing and developing a risk management function. Investment management firms, such as BlackRock, serve clients almost exclusively as fiduciaries. They invest money on behalf of their clients based upon agreed terms and fees. Investment managers do not own (nor ultimately control) the assets managed on behalf of their clients, reducing most (but not eliminating all) conflicts of interest and allowing them to act almost exclusively in their clients' best interests. In this type of organization, risk managers need to ensure that client assets are invested consistently with the explicit or implicit risk tolerance of each client's portfolio, usually, but not always, dictated in prospectuses or written investment management agreements (IMAs). While this can be a complex and challenging endeavor, it entails, for the most part, a close alignment of interests between the investment manager and the ultimate client. This natural alignment of interests, in turn, makes it easier for a positive and committed risk culture to flourish. Failure to thoughtfully align the risk management function to the business model can result in a low performing business with reduced focus on risk-based priorities, lack of trust in management, and low employee morale.

BlackRock has grown from an eight-person organization located in a few small New York conference rooms in 1988, to a global company with more than 19,000 employees managing over $9 trillion of client assets, as of March 31, 2023. As the firm expanded and globalized, BlackRock's core mission has remained the same—serving as a fiduciary to clients. Black-Rock's clients currently include governments, pensions, companies, foundations, insurers, mutual funds, and ETFs, and indirectly, billions of individuals—parents and grandparents, doctors and teachers—who are saving for their future. Risk management is a critical part of helping clients create a better financial future for themselves by meeting their financial goals.

The term "risk management" covers a wide variety of risks including enterprise risks, such as operational, technology, regulatory, model, and other compliance-related risks. While all these risks are important and can significantly impact an organization, this book, similar to the first edition, focuses primarily on investment risk management and the problems specific to portfolio management, trading, financial modeling, hedging, and other areas associated with financial decision-making.

Many investors' priorities appear to be shifting with a rise of interest in sustainability, resulting in the growth of environmental, social, and governance (ESG) products and investment strategies. While BlackRock has made and continues to make significant investments in analytics and processes designed to facilitate risk management through an ESG lens, this important topic is a rapidly evolving domain and deserves a comprehensive review on its own.

This book, as the successor to the first edition, necessarily focuses heavily on fixed-income risk practices, analytics, and models. However, many of the concepts and theories presented can be applied or modified to be applicable to other asset classes. Most of the examples and case studies included in the following chapters are based on BlackRock's risk management approaches, models, and analytics. Heavy reliance has been made on BlackRock Solutions' Aladdin system and its underlying data.

1.2   ELEMENTS OF RISK MANAGEMENT

The following are some critical elements that underpin a strong and effective investment risk management program.

Propagating a risk management culture: Risk management should be a core component of the organization's culture, with senior management recognizing and reinforcing the importance of understanding risk and operating with the highest ethical standards. There must be comprehensive governance and an enterprise risk management framework that evolves to meet business growth, product development, and emerging risks. Internal risk committees and boards should meet regularly to discuss risk management priorities and topics, and risk managers should establish trusted and independent relationships with investors, traders, and other "first line of defense" managers. This culture relies upon high levels of internal transparency regarding the risks being taken by investors and portfolios, subject to regulations and the need to segment certain types of activities.

While practitioners can read about risk management in textbooks, experiencing the risks directly and realizing their consequences provides a different perspective. The financial crash of 1987 had a profound impact on the original founders of BlackRock and demonstrated the consequences of uncontrolled financial risks. As such, high-quality risk management has been a visceral part of BlackRock's culture since the firm's inception. From its very early days, BlackRock has had a dedicated and independent risk management function, ensuring that there is an informed set of independent eyes reviewing portfolio risk and performance to protect clients. As the firm's AUM and product set grew, so too has its risk management team. BlackRock's investment philosophy was founded on always being "risk-aware," and BlackRock's founders and leadership have remained committed to maintaining and disseminating the firm's founding principles and risk management culture.

Knowing the risks: Risk management involves identifying and measuring all material risks, which is far from a static exercise. Markets, technology, competitive pressures, and regulatory regimes are constantly evolving, requiring businesses to continuously respond and adapt. Risk managers should have a deep understanding of how this dynamic process gives rise to new risks and changes existing ones, ensuring that the risks are properly understood across the organization.

The financial crash of 1987 underscored the necessity to understand securities and their nonlinear behavior. Back then, BlackRock focused heavily on the "micro-analytics" of complex securities to have a clear understanding of the characteristics of the portfolios. Further, BlackRock's risk models combine bottom-up and top-down analysis of fund exposures. The risk management team continuously partners with the firm's financial modelers and technologists to create state-of-the-practice risk analytics, continuing the quest to understand portfolios and the risks to which they are exposed.

Relying on one consistent set of information: Everyone—risk takers, risk managers, senior management—should share the same timely information on risk, creating a "virtuous circle" of cleansed data to the fullest extent legally permissible. When everyone relies on one consistent set of information, risk management becomes a transparent and self-enforcing process. Rather than spending time reconciling disparate measures and inconsistencies, team members can concentrate on the substance of fiduciary risk taking: Are the risks deliberate? Are they diversified? Are they appropriately scaled? Are they aligned with client expectations?

BlackRock has a long history of embracing technology and encouraging maximum transparency, which is critical for risk management. Leveraging technology and developing Aladdin were part of BlackRock's founding vision and has enabled the firm to be highly efficient, integrated, dynamic, and scalable. BlackRock started developing Aladdin soon after the firm was founded with the goal of understanding the micro-analytic details of the securities by bringing sell-side analytics to the buy-side. Since the 1990s, Aladdin has been the firm's central operating platform, integrating risk, investment, and client management processes. Aladdin is the foundation of the firm's risk management process, providing sophisticated analytics to enable informed decision making. Each day, risk managers are enabled to review and analyze portfolio risk using a centralized data source.

Risk measures that are "used and useful": Risk management should be a practical exercise aimed at addressing real-world risks—it is not a science project. For risk management to be truly practical and impactful, it is important to employ risk measures that accurately capture risks in meaningful and actionable ways. Armed with these measures, risk managers are positioned to help risk takers understand and manage risks by clearly articulating the issues at hand. BlackRock has continuously believed that assisting risk takers to do "the right thing" is the best way to manage risk. "Policing" risk is a last resort and usually demonstrates a failure to effectively communicate.

Clients come first: As a fiduciary, BlackRock acts as stewards of clients' capital and trust. Putting clients' interests first and working to meet reasonable expectations is important as it serves to protect the firm itself and its reputation. Accurately and consistently measuring and managing risk for clients is paramount for protecting clients' fiduciary interests. Furthermore, risk managers serve a pivotal role in this process by ensuring that clients' investment and risk-taking objectives are properly understood across all stakeholders, that they are accurately reflected in ongoing portfolio management activities, and that the resulting performance is consistent with the risks taken.

1.3   BLACKROCK'S INVESTMENT AND RISK MANAGEMENT APPROACH

Given the importance of risk management to the firm, BlackRock purposefully built a risk framework that touches all aspects of the organization. The process starts at the top with the board of directors and includes a robust governance framework with committees that oversee key risks in the firm. BlackRock's independent risk management team, Risk & Quantitative Analysis (RQA), reports to the firm's president. Structurally, BlackRock's risk management team is independent of BlackRock's various businesses, allowing risk managers to provide an unbiased perspective while working closely with the various risk takers. RQA oversees investment risk, along with counterparty, enterprise, operational, regulatory, technology, third-party, model, and reputational risks. While there is not perfect symmetry and depth in how RQA engages with each of these risk domains, the paradigms are all based on the application of constructive challenge with the ability to independently escalate, as required.

The conceptual model used is intentionally designed not to be intrinsically adversarial. Particularly for an active asset manager, clients are seeking the risk taking and risk management skills of the firm's portfolio managers. Therefore, RQA pursues a *dual mission*. In addition to providing a risk oversight/control role to help manage fiduciary and enterprise risks, RQA uses its deep risk management and analytical subject matter expertise to provide independent consultative advice. Given the subject of this book, what follows will focus specifically on the investment risk management function.

Risk managers at BlackRock are constantly striving to promote a culture of constructive challenge when interacting with investors. The goal is to develop high levels of challenge alongside high trust relationships that result in accuracy in portfolio construction and management. Managing risk requires building close partnerships with investors. Prior to the forced logistical changes that arose due to the Coronavirus pandemic, risk managers were co-located, whenever possible, with investors globally to ensure constant effective communication and trust between risk managers and risk takers. This way, risk managers with significant subject matter expertise are "eyeball-to-eyeball" with portfolio managers. People take risks, not computers or algorithms, so it is important for risk managers to work together with investors and traders to help ensure risks are properly understood and appropriately managed for clients. By partnering with investors, risk management seeks to ensure risk taking is deliberate, diversified, and scaled to meet the reasonable expectations of clients. During the pandemic, we were able to maintain relatively strong connectivity between risk managers and portfolio managers via the necessity for most communications to be through scheduled video calls, as opposed to many impromptu discussions. This arrangement worked much better than (some of us) anticipated. As of March 2023, BlackRock's model operates "at least three days in the office," which seeks to retain the social value of physical proximity while recognizing that working from home provided many advantages to many employees.[2]

BlackRock's portfolio managers oversee thousands of portfolios with many distinct mandates specified by clients or fund constituents. BlackRock's investment process is highly decentralized with well over 100 independent investment teams, responsible and accountable for the decisions and outcomes of the portfolios they manage. BlackRock's portfolio managers have the flexibility to design, implement, and execute independent investment processes, subject to clients' approval, internal transparency requirements, and, more recently, integrating ESG-related characteristics into the actively managed investment process. Portfolio managers can leverage BlackRock's platform-level investment insights, such as those of the BlackRock Investment Institute, while retaining the ability to use their own discretion subject to client constraints. Investment risk managers partner with each investment business to help investors build risk-aware portfolios by advising on portfolio construction, hedging strategies, and managing the risk-return trade-off.

To deliver effective risk management at scale, BlackRock's risk managers employ both top-down and bottom-up approaches as part of their daily risk management processes. This allows risk managers to independently review portfolio composition and determine if the resulting risk profiles are consistent with client guidelines and fund mandates on an ongoing basis. Additionally, risk managers regularly engage with investment teams, both formally and informally, to review risk positioning and performance outcomes.

1.4 INTRODUCTION TO THE BLACKROCK INVESTMENT RISK MANAGEMENT PARADIGM

As a large and complex organization, BlackRock needs to ensure that certain risk management activities occur regularly and consistently across the entire investment platform. To organize this conceptually, BlackRock has developed an Investment Risk Management Paradigm (IRMP) to bring consistency and structure to the myriad of risk management activities and create a coherent and comprehensive approach across all its businesses. This IRMP rests on five pillars, each of which describes a necessary component of an effective investment risk management program. The following chapters in this section of the book will expand upon the five IRMP pillars:[3]

1. Ex ante risk measurement
2. Risk governance (i.e., having and maintaining agreed upon levels of risks)
3. Portfolio manager risk-return awareness
4. Performance attribution
5. Performance analysis

The first pillar is *ex ante risk measurement*, which means ensuring portfolio managers and risk managers have the appropriate tools to identify, measure, and understand important portfolio risks. Multiple risk measures are invariably required and available to provide the most complete picture possible. Risk factors and ex ante risk models are employed (when meaningful) to measure portfolio ex ante volatility and active risk (i.e., ex ante tracking error relative to a defined benchmark) and, where appropriate, Value at Risk (VaR). Among other things, this allows a statistical decomposition of risks. To attempt capturing the inevitable tail risks often missing from statistically driven analytics, Market-Driven Scenarios can be a very useful tool. Numerous "what-if" scenarios can be formulated corresponding to geopolitical events or market factor moves.

Additionally, measures of liquidity risk provide insight on both the liquidity of positions held on the asset side of a fund's balance sheet and the potential for redemptions, driven by the liability side. More recently, an increasing number of exposure metrics are being developed that include not only environmental characteristics but those related to social considerations and institutional governance.

The second pillar is *risk governance*. This is the mechanism by which the appropriateness of the level of risk taking in a portfolio is controlled. To meet clients' reasonable expectations, return and risk objectives for portfolios need to be clearly understood and communicated. This can be specified explicitly or, if necessary due to the nature of the asset owner, inferred implicitly. For instance, based on a client's return objective, an acceptable range of expected ex ante risk for a given fund, consistent with its ability to achieve return objectives, can be determined. Given that level of target risk, a "green zone" can be defined (as part of a two-sided red, amber, green framework) based upon a reasonable range around the targeted ex ante risk level. However clarified, once determined, examining a portfolio relative to the client's expectations and identifying inconsistencies or misaligned risks becomes possible. Above and below this "green zone" represents risk levels that either require heightened attention (low and high "amber zones") or may require timely remediation (low and high "red zones"), indicating that the risks are becoming potentially increasingly inconsistent with prudently achieving the client's identified return objectives. Portfolios can be tracked relative to these ranges. Given the complexity and heterogeneity of investment risk management, a risk scan framework facilitates scalable risk monitoring with improved governance and oversight. Providing a consistent framework to monitor risk across asset classes, a risk scan framework allows for exceptions to be identified, investigated, and escalated, as necessary.

At BlackRock, this process takes place in a regular *Portfolio Risk Oversight Committee*. When exceptions arise and portfolios stray outside the "green zone," risk managers and portfolio managers discuss what remediation, if any, is needed. More complex rules can be constructed that go beyond simply looking at levels of active risk. Following a similar design pattern, acceptable and exception ranges can be determined for any risk exposure of interest, such as liquidity risks or credit concentrations, with exceptions being tracked and actioned, as required.

The third pillar, *portfolio manager risk-return awareness*, ensures that portfolio managers understand and are aware of the types and levels of risks they are taking. Risk managers establish a cadence of interaction with portfolio managers, including regularly scheduled reviews of risk positioning and performance, as well as more informal conversations. The goal is always to collectively understand risk positions in the context of current and expected market conditions, assessing whether the risks are *deliberate, diversified, and scaled* appropriately. Through these interactions, risk managers seek to build trusted relationships with portfolio managers and form their own independent understanding of the investment process, allowing them to constructively challenge portfolio managers, when necessary.

The notion of an emotionally always cool and fully dispassionate portfolio manager is more myth than fact. Over the past two decades, there has been a significant amount of research into how human beings can systematically deviate from purely economically rational decision-making. At BlackRock, some of these insights are incorporated into our risk management process. Portfolio managers can and do benefit from insights from behavioral finance. For example, combining the information provided in trade diaries with actual buy/sell decisions helps to identify potential biases and determine plans for combatting behavioral blind spots. There are also opportunities to improve portfolio manager performance by applying related insights associated with physiological characteristics. Some BlackRock portfolio managers voluntarily choose to wear Oura[4] rings, a biometric sensor, which sends output to a BlackRock psychologist. Analyzing this data can help to identify when these portfolio managers may not always be able to make the best decisions. Managing this may help to improve their effectiveness.

The fourth pillar, *performance attribution*, seeks to understand the drivers of portfolio performance. It turns out that while at 10,000 feet performance attribution seems a rather straightforward analytical task, the reality is that it is often very difficult to execute reliably with a high level of resolution. Attribution requires a reconciliation between portfolio actions, statistical factor decomposition, and accounting profit and loss data.

Risk managers can utilize a variety of performance attribution approaches and analytical techniques to decompose returns. These techniques vary in terms of their operational complexity, precision, and implied decision-making model. Brinson attribution identifies a baseline and analyzes performance based on allocation and selection decisions, while factor-based models are used to also attribute actual performance to underlying market factors. Performance attribution can be used to better understand any number of aspects of the investment process, including the following:

- Consistency between the intended bets in a portfolio and the resulting performance
- Consistency between the portfolio manager's declared style and the resulting performance
- Portfolio manager expertise and style
- Decomposition of market impact from portfolio management decisions

The fifth pillar, *performance analysis*, measures portfolio performance relative to many different benchmarks, such as similar investment mandates, benchmark indices, comparable accounts, and peers' performance. Performance analysis provides insight into the overall market environment and competitive landscape, detailing information about the overall health of a business. Having a performance measurement framework that is consistent, robust, and transparent, lets measures of success be clear to all stakeholders. Important considerations include whether performance is being evaluated gross or net of fees, consistency of share class choice versus peers, and peer group definitions, which vary by vendor. Controlling the ownership of performance analysis at an investment manager is vital because there are necessarily many actors who have extreme self-interests in how the outcomes are measured and reported.

Throughout the remaining first section of this book, each pillar will be discussed in detail, including examples and exhibits to help illustrate the approaches and analytics, as part of BlackRock's comprehensive approach to investment risk management. As a reminder, most of the examples are focused on fixed-income portfolios. However, many of the concepts can be applied across other asset classes.

NOTES

1. Kristen Walters, Allison White, and Nikki Azznara significantly helped to develop this chapter.
2. As of September 2023, BlackRock's model will change to employees working at least four days per week in the office.
3. While the following chapters in this section of the book further develop the IRMP pillars, there is not a one-to-one linkage between pillars and chapters. For instance, several chapters expand upon the first pillar, *ex ante risk measurement*.
4. Oura Ring, 2023.

Parametric Approaches to Risk Management[1]

Bennett W. Golub
Senior Advisor, BlackRock

Leo M. Tilman
CEO, Tilman & Company

2.1 INTRODUCTION

The price of a fixed-income security can be thought of as a function of many interdependent systematic risk factors $F_1, \ldots, F_n$ and time:

$$P = P(F_1, \ldots, F_n, t) \tag{2.1}$$

Parametric approaches to risk management investigate the price sensitivity of securities and portfolios to each risk factor in isolation, with all others being fixed. This task can be best understood by utilizing a Taylor series expansion of the price function around a point—a widely used mathematical technique that provides insights into the local properties of complex nonlinear relationships. Thus, if a function $P(\cdot)$ depends on a single variable x, the Taylor series expansion can be used to approximate the behavior of its percentage changes around an arbitrary point x_0 as follows:

$$\frac{P(x) - P(x_0)}{P(x_0)} = \frac{1}{P(x_0)} \cdot \frac{dP}{dx} \cdot (x - x_0) + \frac{1}{2!} \cdot \frac{1}{P(x_0)} \cdot \frac{d^2 P}{dx^2} \cdot (x - x_0)^2 + \ldots \tag{2.2}$$

where the value of all derivatives is computed at x_0.

In a multivariate setting (Equation 2.1), expression of the Taylor series expansion becomes more complex because of the large number of possible interactions among systematic sources of risk:

$$\frac{dP}{P} = \sum_{i=1}^{n} \frac{1}{P} \cdot \frac{\partial P}{\partial F_i} \cdot dF_i + \frac{1}{P} \cdot \frac{\partial P}{\partial t} \cdot dt + \sum_{i=1}^{n} \sum_{j=1}^{n} \frac{1}{2 \cdot P} \cdot \frac{\partial^2 P}{\partial F_i \cdot \partial F_j} \cdot dF_i \cdot dF_j + \ldots \tag{2.3}$$

Expressions of the form $-\frac{1}{P} \frac{\partial P}{\partial F_i}$ are called partial durations. Option-adjusted duration, key rate durations, volatility duration, spread duration, and prepayment duration (discussed later in this chapter) are examples of partial durations of a security's price with respect to different risk factors. The large number of partial duration measures is due to the many systematic sources of market risk that can affect prices of fixed-income securities, along with the various ways to define them. For instance, this chapter and the following chapter will demonstrate that there are no significant conceptual differences between key rate durations and principal components durations: they simply correspond to alternative ways to describe yield curve dynamics. As far as dependency of prices on time $\left(\frac{\partial P}{\partial t} \right)$ is concerned, it is customary in the derivatives markets to directly compute such partial derivatives. Due to path dependency and other intricacies of fixed-income securities with respect to their evolution through time, we present this aspect of market behavior later in this chapter, not in terms of partial durations, but within the *horizon rate of return* framework (Section 2.8).

With respect to the more traditional (or tractable) sources of market risk, imagination and knowledge of financial markets are required to define an appropriate set of systematic risk factors $F_1, \ldots, F_n$ so that risk management calculations are intuitive and computationally feasible at the same time. In this chapter, a variety of ways to define systematic risk factors is presented and the corresponding first-order terms of the Taylor series expansion (durations) as well as second-order terms (convexities) are computed. The development and utilization of metrics such as these align with the first pillar of BlackRock's IRMP. First, the exposure of portfolios and securities to directional movements in interest rates, the primary source of risk in fixed-income markets, is analyzed.

2.2   MEASURING INTEREST RATE EXPOSURE: ANALYTICAL APPROACHES

2.2.1   Macaulay and Modified Duration and Convexity

Duration and convexity are the most widely used measures of interest rate exposure. They are used by traders in hedging and relative value decisions, portfolio managers when placing directional bets in portfolios relative to benchmarks, and clients and risk managers when formulating guidelines and compliance rules that regulate how closely assets must be managed against liabilities or portfolios against benchmarks. Performance attribution systems utilize durations and convexities when determining if a security has under- or outperformed the market. The first- and second-order terms of the Taylor series expansion are also important back-testing tools used in the price discovery process. While in practice duration and convexity are concepts specific to fixed-income, their analogs can be found in other markets as well. The future valuation of fixed-income instruments depends on the evolution of interest rates and other economic variables over time. Duration and convexity, measures of the price sensitivity to changes in interest rates, are the fixed-income analogs of the "greeks" (delta and gamma) widely used in the derivatives markets.

To derive duration and convexity, the price of a fixed-income security is assumed to be a function of a single risk factor—yield-to-maturity (y):

$$P = P(y) \tag{2.4}$$

Exhibits 2.1 and 2.2 present the price/yield functions of selected instruments[2] and demonstrate that some of these relationships can be substantially nonlinear. As shown in these two exhibits, the price functions of a hypothetical 30-year on-the-run (OTR) Treasury,[3] a put on a US Treasury future, and a swaption are convex while the price functions for a 4% MBS coupon and a callable agency bond are moderately concave, or as conventionally known in

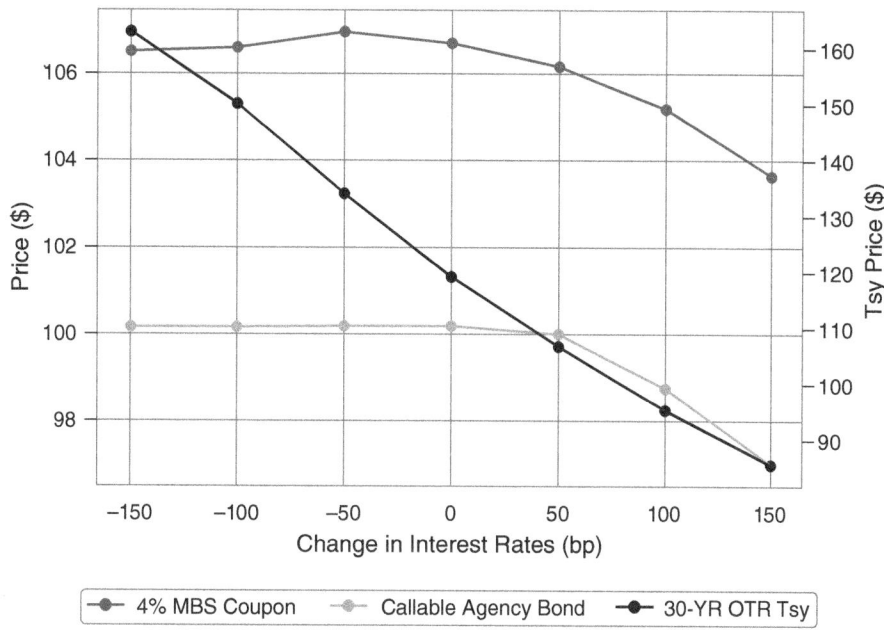

EXHIBIT 2.1 Examples of Price Dependencies on Changes in Interest Rates (as of 1/31/2020)
Source: BlackRock Aladdin, January 31, 2020.

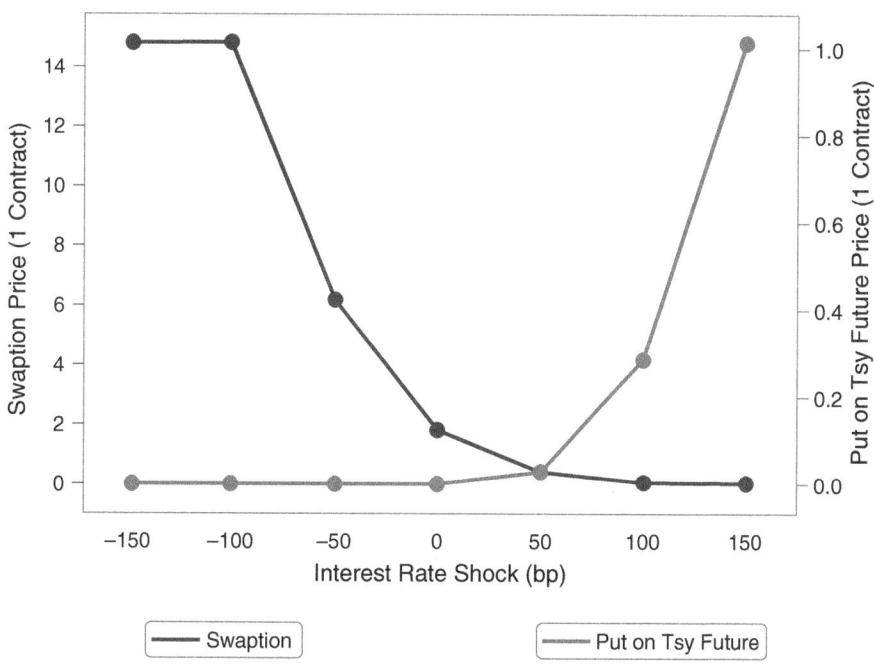

EXHIBIT 2.2 Examples of Price Dependencies on Changes in Interest Rates (as of 1/31/2020)
Source: BlackRock Aladdin, January 31, 2020.

the fixed-income world, *negatively convex*. Intuitively, this means that the price functions exhibit substantially more downside price performance than upside. For example, as shown in Exhibit 2.1, the price function of the 4% MBS coupon does not rally much as interest rates fall, but drops in value substantially as rates rise. The reasons for this characteristic will be discussed later in this chapter.

For a default-free, fixed-income instrument whose cash flows are contractually fixed, do not have any embedded options, and do not depend on the future evolution of interest rates and other risk factors, the price/yield function can be determined analytically. For example, the relationship between the price of an N-year bond that pays fixed annual cash flows $CF_1, \ldots, CF_N$ and its yield-to-maturity is implicitly given by the following simple formula:

$$P = \sum_{t=1}^{N} \frac{CF_t}{(1+y)^t} \tag{2.5}$$

where P is the current price, and y is the annually compounded yield-to-maturity. If the cash flows of a security are not fixed and are a function of interest rates and other risk factors, construction of the price/yield function entails solving the valuation problem. This involves application of numerical methods, including building yield curves, specifying stochastic processes that describe the future evolution of interest rates and other risks, valuing embedded options, forecasting prepayments, if any, and so forth. Explicit construction of price/yield functions for complex portfolios is known as *interest rate scenario analysis* and is discussed in detail later in this chapter.

The need for a simple and intuitive measure of price sensitivity to changes in interest rates resulted in the widespread adoption of the concept (concepts) of duration as a metric. Modified duration, a measure of price sensitivity of a fixed-income security to changes in its yield-to-maturity, is linked to the first-order term of the Taylor series expansion (Equation 2.2). Modified duration is used to locally approximate the relationship between the price P and yield-to-maturity y as a linear function. It is defined as the negative of the percentage change in price, given a 100 basis point change in yield:

$$Modified\ Duration = -\frac{1}{P}\frac{dP}{dy} \tag{2.6}$$

It is easy to see that for securities with deterministic cash flows, modified duration can be derived analytically via Equations 2.5 and 2.6:

$$Modified\ Duration = \frac{1}{P \cdot (1+y)} \sum_{t=1}^{N} \frac{t \cdot CF_t}{(1+y)^t} \tag{2.7}$$

Equation 2.6 represents the way almost all market participants today interpret the term "duration." Originally, however, a slightly different exposure measure was developed. Frederick Macaulay[4] is generally recognized as the first person to develop a formula that quantifies interest rate exposure of fixed cash flow securities. His measure, which is referred to as *Macaulay duration* (also known as unmodified duration), was defined as the average of individual cash flows' terms-to-maturity weighted by the present value of the corresponding cash flows:[5]

$$Macaulay\ Duration = \frac{1}{P} \sum_{t=1}^{N} \frac{t \cdot CF_t}{(1+y)^t} \tag{2.8}$$

It can be verified, both empirically and analytically, that Macaulay duration is directly linked to price volatility:[6] the larger the Macaulay duration, the more volatile the market price of the bond. This measure is also intuitive because it implies higher price risk for securities whose cash flows are concentrated farther in the future. Macaulay and modified durations are obviously closely related:

$$Modified\ Duration = \frac{1}{(1+y)} \cdot Macaulay\ Duration \qquad (2.9)$$

It turns out that if the price of a fixed cash flow bond is written as a function of the continuously compounded rather than annually compounded yield-to-maturity y_C:

$$P = \sum_{i=1}^{N} CF_i \cdot e^{-y_c \cdot t_i} \qquad (2.10)$$

the formula for Macaulay duration is exactly the same as that for modified duration:[7]

$$Macaulay\ Duration = -\frac{1}{P}\frac{dP}{dy_C} \qquad (2.11)$$

The straightforward verification of this fact is left to the reader.

As seen from Equations 2.2 and 2.6, modified duration enables the first-order approximation of the percentage change in price $\frac{\Delta P}{P}$ for a given change in yield Δy:

$$\frac{\Delta P}{P} \approx -Modified\ Duration \cdot \Delta y \qquad (2.12)$$

For example, if a bond's modified duration is 10 years and interest rates rise by 100 basis points, the bond loses about 10% of its value.[8]

The accuracy of the first-order approximation of the price/yield function depends on the degree to which the function is convex or negatively convex (i.e., concave). Therefore, in addition to the first term in the Taylor series expansion, the second term can be used to better capture the shape of the price/yield function:

$$\frac{dP}{P} \approx \frac{1}{P} \cdot \frac{dP}{dy} \cdot dy + \frac{1}{2} \cdot \frac{1}{P} \cdot \frac{d^2P}{dy^2} \cdot dy^2 \qquad (2.13)$$

Convexity, the degree of interest rate exposure measured by the second-order term in the Taylor series expansion in Equation 2.13, estimates the degree and direction of nonlinearity of the price/yield function:

$$Modified\ Convexity = \frac{1}{P}\frac{d^2P}{dy^2} \qquad (2.14)$$

Similar to modified duration, modified convexity of fixed cash flow securities can be derived analytically as well:

$$Modified\ Convexity = \frac{1}{P \cdot (1+y)^2} \sum_{t=1}^{N} \frac{t \cdot (t+1) \cdot CF_t}{(1+y)^t} \qquad (2.15)$$

When used together, modified duration and modified convexity allow for a more precise approximation of changes in price for a given change in interest rates:

$$\frac{\Delta P}{P} \approx -Modified\ Duration \cdot \Delta y + \frac{Modified\ Convexity}{2} \cdot \Delta y^2 \qquad (2.16)$$

Table 2.1 presents an example of the modified durations along with many other metrics for the securities in a sample fixed-income portfolio.

Macaulay and modified durations and convexities were developed to provide more accurate estimates of interest rate price sensitivity for instruments with deterministic cash flows. This necessarily limits their relevance for securities with cash flow variability correlated to interest rates. Thus, in order to attempt to compute something analogous to modified duration and convexity, stochastic cash flows would need to be presumed fixed and generated using a predefined static interest rate scenario, which may lead to inadequate assessment of exposure. In addition to that, by discounting cash flows using a single interest rate (Equation 2.5), modified duration and modified convexity assume that prices of fixed-income securities depend solely on changes in a single risk factor—yield-to-maturity. When computing modified duration of a whole portfolio, it is therefore implicitly assumed that when interest rates change, irrespective of the maturities of the individual securities, their yield-to-maturity moves in the same direction and by the same amount.

Because of these limitations, the increasing complexity of fixed-income instruments created a need to generalize modified duration and modified convexity in a number of important ways:

1. Incorporation of knowledge about the term structure of interest rates
2. Ability to capture cash flow variability with respect to interest rates and other economic variables

Extension of the modified duration methodology in the first dimension can be achieved by modifying Equation 2.5 to discount cash flows of a fixed-income security using the appropriate spot rates[9] rather than a single yield-to-maturity:

$$P = \sum_{t=1}^{N} \frac{E(CF_t)}{(1 + r_t)^t} \qquad (2.17)$$

where r_t is the annualized spot rate at time t, and expected cash flows $E(CF_t)$ are obtained using a single hypothetical scenario that specifies evolution of interest rates and other risk factors over time. In this setting, it is typically assumed that volatility of interest rates is zero; interest rates evolve according to forward rates; and credit spreads, implied volatilities, and other basis risks stay constant. Clearly, the "fair" value obtained via this valuation technique may be different from that observed in the market because of the numerous assumptions built into the generation of expected cash flows. To reconcile theoretical and empirical prices, practitioners have introduced the concept of *zero volatility spread* (ZV0), defined as an additional constant element of discounting (over the yield curve) that forces the "fair" value to equal the market price:[10]

$$P_{market} = \sum_{t=1}^{N} \frac{E(CF_t)}{(1 + r_t + ZV0)^t} \qquad (2.18)$$

TABLE 2.1 Duration Comparison Report for a Sample Portfolio (as of 1/31/2020)

Security Description	Price	Coupon	Maturity	Strike	Mod Dur	OAS	OAD	OAC	Mtg/ Tsy Dur	Vol Dur	Spd Dur	KRDB 2 YR	KRDB 5 YR	KRDB 10 YR	KRDB 30 YR
Treasury Bonds															
OTR 2YR 2	100.09	1.375	1/31/2022		1.96	−1.66	1.97	0.05			0.00	1.96	0.01	0.00	0.00
OTR 5YR 5	100.23	1.375	1/31/2025		4.81	−1.72	4.83	0.26			0.00	0.03	4.80	0.00	0.00
OTR 10YR 10	102.09	1.75	11/15/2029		8.97	0.09	8.97	0.89			0.00	0.05	1.10	7.83	0.00
OTR 30YR 30	108.08	2.375	11/15/2049		21.66	−6.50	21.31	5.66			0.00	0.06	0.68	3.56	17.01
Treasury Futures															
US 10YR NOTE MAR 20 TY 20-MAR-2020	100.00		3/20/2020			−31	8.38	0.6				0.07	8.31		
US LONG BOND MAR 20 US 20-MAR-2020	163.53		3/20/2020			0	12.25	1.82				0.09	1	11.15	
Callable Agency Bonds															
FHLB 2.0 20-FEB-2025	100.00	2.00	2/20/2025		4.74	97	1.06	−3.33		0.01	0.98	0.29	0.77		
Option on Future															
MAR20 TUH0 C @ 106.25 TU 21-FEB-2020	1.93		2/21/2020	106.25		0				0		102.59			
Interest Rate Swap															
SWP: USD 3.167500 09-SEP-2023 IRS		3.17	7/9/2023				3.35	0.14		0		−0.02	3.37		
German Government Bond Future															
EURO-BUND MAR 20 RX 06-MAR-2020	175.04		3/6/2020			0	8.97	0.85					2.92	6.06	

(Continued)

TABLE 2.1 (*Continued*)

Security Description	Price	Coupon	Maturity	Strike	Mod Dur	OAS	OAD	OAC	Mtg/ Tsy Dur	Vol Dur	Spd Dur	KRDB 2 YR	KRDB 5 YR	KRDB 10 YR	KRDB 30 YR
IG Credit															
AMERICAN EXPRESS COMPANY T2 3.625 05-DEC-2024 (SUB)	107.94	3.63	12/5/2024		4.45	142	4.4	0.21		0	4.42	0.09	4.31		
HY Credit															
NINE ENERGY SERVICE INC 8.75 01-NOV-2023 144a (SENIOR)	84.38	8.75	11/1/2023		3.01	1340	3.13	0.13		0	3.15	0.24	2.89		
Agency MBS															
UMBS 30YR TBA CASH 4.0	104.45	4.00	4/25/2049		1.93	88	1.73	−0.96	1.73	0.02	2.36	0.76	0.82	0.16	−0.01
Agency CMBS															
GNMA_16-113-IO 1.1524 16-FEB-2058	8.27	1.15	2/16/2058		3.61	284	4.27	0.38			4.28	0.51	1.95	1.72	0.09
Non-Agency CMBS															
JPMBB_14-C22-XA 0.83511 15-SEP-2047	3.26	0.84	7/15/2047		1.72	190	1.98	0.06			1.98	0.77	1.21		
ABS Credit Card															
NDFT_17-1-C 2.15338 15-JUL-2025 Reg-S	100.11	2.56	7/15/2020		0.04	114	0.04	0	0.44	0	0.44	0.04			

Source: BlackRock Aladdin, January 31, 2020.

2.2.2 Option-Adjusted Framework: OAV, OAS, OAD, OAC

Modified duration and convexity presume that cash flows of fixed-income instruments are deterministic, do not have any embedded options, and are independent of the future evolution of interest rates and other risk factors. For many types of securities, these assumptions are not realistic. For instance, cash flows of a mortgage-backed security depend on the borrowers' decision to prepay all or part of their mortgage loans early, while some of the cash flows of callable corporate and agency bonds may not occur if these bonds are called. Thus, durations and convexities for many securities cannot be computed analytically and require application of numerical methods. Development of the price sensitivity measures that are applicable to all fixed-income securities has been conceptually challenging. Before an operationally feasible methodology could be created, a number of important developments needed to take place. First and foremost, numerical computation of durations and convexities for complex portfolios was contingent on the ability to reverse-engineer derivative fixed-income securities, including collateralized mortgage obligations, asset-backed and mortgage-backed securities, commercial mortgage-backed securities, construction and project loans, futures, options, and so forth. Second, this methodology required dramatic advances in computational technology as well as breakthroughs in option pricing theory, numerical methods, as well as interest rate, yield curve, and prepayment modeling.

Option-adjusted measures—option-adjusted value (OAV), option-adjusted spread (OAS), option-adjusted duration (OAD), and option-adjusted convexity (OAC)—are an important generalization of the modified duration methodology. A rigorous description of option-adjusted spread methodology, which is a valuation rather than a risk management technique, is beyond the scope of this book.[11] The purpose of this section is to give an overview of the concepts underlying the OAS framework and study their applications to risk management.

By explicitly modeling the embedded options and other cash flow uncertainties across a large number of hypothetical interest rate environments, the accuracy of factor exposure metrics improved meaningfully. Among other things, implementation of the option-adjusted methodology involved:

- Obtaining the terms and conditions regarding the way a security is structured
- Estimating and parameterizing yield curves
- Specifying the appropriate option valuation models, econometric prepayment models, stochastic processes that describe the evolution of interest rates and other systematic basis risks over time.

In the option-theoretic sense, *option-adjusted value* (OAV) is simply the expected value of a fixed-income security. It is defined as the mathematical expectation of the discounted future cash flows given the assumption about the future evolution of interest rates and other systematic sources of risk. By virtue of requiring the specification of the current economic environment in addition to conjectures about future behavior of risk factors, OAVs of fixed-income securities are *market-state dependent*: even if assumptions remain unchanged, theoretical values of instruments may vary dramatically with changes in the market environment.

The methods by which OAV is computed depend on the security type. The following are typical choices used by practitioners, although many instruments can be effectively valued using a variety of alternative approaches:

- For path-dependent instruments, including mortgages, mortgage derivatives, and certain OTC options, OAVs are ordinarily computed by sampling interest rate trees using

Monte Carlo simulation. A large number of interest rate scenarios or *paths* are created using random number generators or via stratified sampling (pseudo-random number generation) techniques. For each interest rate path, the present value of the corresponding cash flow is determined using the path-specific spot curve. OAV, which is computed as the average of pathwise prices, is a summary measure that encompasses a vast amount of information. While the entire distribution of pathwise prices can be analyzed directly, it is capable of providing only limited insights.

■ To determine OAVs for path-independent, option-bearing securities (e.g., callable bonds, interest rate caps, floors), backward induction is typically used to value the option on every node of an interest rate tree, capturing a large number of possible interest rate environments generated by the interest rate model. The advantage of backward induction over Monte Carlo simulation lies in substantially faster computations. This method is also not subject to the same type of statistical imprecisions inherent in sampling of interest rate processes.

■ When computing OAVs for interest rate swaps, floating rate notes, and other securities whose cash flows are option-free and path-independent but interest rate dependent, the future evolution of interest rates first needs to be forecasted (via forward rates or otherwise). Given a conjecture about the future behavior of interest rates and other risk factors, cash flows are determined and subsequently discounted using the appropriate spot rates, arriving at OAV of an instrument.

■ OAVs for short-term European options are typically computed using the analytical Black-Scholes-Merton formula or its variants.[12]

The analytical values of fixed-income securities may often differ from market observed prices. At least three alternative interpretations of this phenomenon exist. The first is pretty simple—*money talks and nobody walks*—meaning that the price that one can actually execute is always the final arbiter of value. A second interpretation is that this discrepancy is caused by the inability of theoretical valuation models to fully account for the information contained in market prices due to the numerous assumptions and econometric estimation inaccuracies inherent in these models. Another school of thought interprets the difference between OAV and observed market prices as *market risk premia* embedded in market prices and not captured by theoretical valuation models.[13] A risk premium can be thought of as excess return demanded by investors as compensation for the perceived excess risk of holding a security. It combines market sentiment toward systematic asset class-specific risks as well as idiosyncratic security-specific risks. For instance, the risk premia of noncallable US Treasuries (that are option- and default-free) measure the cost of liquidity and financing assumptions. On-the-run issues exhibit different behavior from virtually identical off-the-run securities; their risk premia are generally negative.[14] For option-free fixed rate corporate bonds, risk premia reflect market sentiment toward credit risk in general, technical conditions, assessment of the issuer's creditworthiness, likelihood of credit quality deterioration or default and implicit forecast of recovery rates in the event of a default. For default-free generic mortgage-backed securities, risk premia quantify the market's sentiment toward credit risk in general, technical conditions, uncertainty with respect to the valuation of the underlying prepayment options, and implied volatility risks.

Option-adjusted spread (OAS) can be thought of as the risk premium associated with holding a fixed-income security. OAS reconciles a theoretical model's assessment of fair price and the empirically observed market price. The concept of OAS is best illustrated via a security that employs Monte Carlo simulation to construct a large number of interest rate paths, each corresponding to a stream of future cash flows ($CF_{i,t}$). OAS is defined as a constant spread over the path-specific spot curve ($r_{i,t}$) that equates the model-based OAV to the market price:

$$P_{market} = \frac{1}{K} \sum_{i=1}^{K} \sum_{t=1}^{N} \frac{CF_{i,t}}{(1 + r_{i,t} + \text{OAS})^t} \tag{2.19}$$

where K is the number of interest rate paths employed in Monte Carlo simulation, $CF_{i,t}$ and $r_{i,t}$ are the cash flow and the spot rate, respectively, corresponding to the i-th path, and N is the maximum possible number of cash flows.

Option-adjusted spreads provide some basis for comparison of securities within and across asset classes. They can be used in risk management or as relative value metrics. For risk management, unexpected changes in OAS is an important risk factor. In portfolio management and trading, if two otherwise seemingly similar securities have different OASs, relative value judgment might drive an investor to go long on the security with the higher OAS. Option-adjusted spreads[15] of securities in a sample portfolio are presented in Table 2.1. Notice that while OASs are positive for the vast majority of securities in the sample portfolio, they can also be negative for certain security types. Examples of instruments with negative OAS include on-the-run government securities in the United States.

Once OAS is determined, option-adjusted duration (OAD) and option-adjusted convexity (OAC) can be computed. These measures of interest rate exposure constitute an important generalization of the modified duration methodology introduced earlier in this chapter. As demonstrated next, by using the OAS methodology when computing price sensitivities, option-adjusted risk measures capture many important properties of fixed-income securities, including various cash flow uncertainties and path dependencies. Recall that modified duration was defined in Equation 2.6 as the negative of the percentage change in price, given a 100 basis point change in yield-to-maturity. This concept was developed with option-free securities in mind and is not generally applicable to instruments with cash flow uncertainty. For this reason, the option-adjusted framework departs from analyzing price sensitivity in terms of yields. Instead of assuming that prices are functions of yields-to-maturity on individual securities, it presumes that changes in prices are caused by *parallel shocks to the term structure of spot rates (r)*:

$$P = P(r) \tag{2.20}$$

By redefining the term *change in interest rates,* the option-adjusted methodology introduces a more generalized analytical framework while preserving the simplifying assumption that price fluctuations of fixed-income securities are primarily driven by a single systematic interest rate risk factor.[16] Option-adjusted duration is defined as follows:

$$\text{OAD} = -\frac{1}{P}\frac{dP}{dr} \tag{2.21}$$

where dr is a parallel spot curve shock. It must be noted, however, that despite being the most widely used one-factor risk management model, approximating yield curve dynamics with parallel shocks is not the most historically plausible alternative. Later in this book (Chapter 3), we use principal components analysis to construct more empirically accurate representations of yield curve movements.

To illustrate the numerical computation of OAD, it is convenient to rewrite Equation 2.21 as follows:

$$OAD = -\frac{1}{P} \cdot \lim_{\Delta r \to 0} \frac{\Delta P}{\Delta r} \tag{2.22}$$

When calculating OAD in practice using Equation 2.22, the following discretization is generally used:

$$OAD = -\frac{1}{P} \frac{P_{up} - P_{down}}{2 \cdot \Delta r} \tag{2.23}$$

where P_{up} and P_{down} are OAVs directly recomputed by shifting the entire spot curve up and down, respectively, by a small parallel shock Δr and keeping option-adjusted spread constant.

Similar to modified duration (Equation 2.12), OAD can be used to approximate price changes resulting from small parallel yield curve movements:

$$\frac{\Delta P}{P} \approx -OAD \cdot \Delta r \tag{2.24}$$

Depending on the security type, the size of the interest rate shock Δr used in Equation 2.23 may influence OAD estimates. This should be intuitive because the larger the shock, the more nonlinearity of the price function is captured when computing OAD. Table 2.2 illustrates the effect of different shock sizes on OAD estimates.

Similar to modified convexity, option-adjusted convexity (OAC) is linked to the second-order term of the Taylor series expansion:

$$OAC = \frac{1}{P} \frac{d^2 P}{dr^2} \tag{2.25}$$

and can be computed using the following discretization:

$$OAC = \frac{1}{P} \frac{P_{up} + P_{down} - 2 \cdot P}{\Delta r^2} \tag{2.26}$$

Table 2.1 presents OADs and OACs of securities in a sample portfolio.

When computed via option-adjusted spread methodology, duration estimates are relatively stable for the majority of fixed-income securities. However, OACs, being the second-order effects, are more difficult to measure accurately. Although in theory they can be computed by shocking the yield curve infinitesimally in either direction via Equation 2.26, this type of analysis depends, to a greater extent than duration, on the size of the spot curve shock. Too small a shock may lead to unstable estimates due to modeling limitations (e.g., valuation issues related to the discretization of continuous-time interest rate processes). Too large a shock may lessen the accuracy of duration estimates and may cause undesirable effects due to interest rate and prepayment models. Both too small and too large a shock may result in unreliable and unstable convexity estimates. These effects are greatly exacerbated by the optionality embedded in the security, especially if backward valuation is used.

By sampling interest rates above and below the current level and computing P_{up} and P_{down} (Equations 2.23 and 2.26), option-adjusted durations and convexities implicitly assume that irrespective of the direction of interest rates, comparable interest rate shocks of opposite signs cause comparable (in absolute value) changes in prices. However, this conjecture is not entirely correct for the so-called cuspy securities—those characterized by highly asymmetric

TABLE 2.2   Effect of Parallel Shock Size on OAD Estimates (as of 1/31/2020)

Shock Size (Basis Points)	12-Year Callable Corporate	Agency CMO	30-Year MBS 2.5%	30-Year MBS 3.0%	30-Year MBS 3.5%	30-Year MBS 4.0%	30-Year MBS 4.5%	30-Year MBS 5.0%
0	8.38	5.87	5.32	2.53	2.61	3.36	2.40	2.70
5	8.38	6.40	5.41	2.61	2.68	3.40	2.44	2.74
10	8.38	6.92	5.50	2.69	2.75	3.45	2.48	2.78
15	8.38	7.43	5.59	2.78	2.82	3.50	2.52	2.83
20	8.38	7.93	5.69	2.88	2.90	3.56	2.56	2.87
25	8.38	8.43	5.78	2.98	2.98	3.61	2.61	2.92
30	8.37	8.92	5.88	3.07	3.06	3.67	2.65	2.96
35	8.37	9.39	5.96	3.16	3.13	3.72	2.70	3.01
40	8.37	9.85	6.04	3.25	3.21	3.77	2.74	3.05
45	8.37	10.32	6.11	3.35	3.28	3.82	2.78	3.09
50	8.36	10.82	6.19	3.44	3.36	3.87	2.83	3.14

Source: BlackRock Aladdin, January 31, 2020.

price sensitivities to changes in interest rates (e.g., at-the-money European options that are close to expiration). In such cases, it can be useful to compute one-sided option-adjusted measures:

$$OAD_{up} = -\frac{1}{P}\frac{P_{up} - P}{\Delta r} \tag{2.27}$$

$$OAD_{down} = -\frac{1}{P}\frac{P - P_{down}}{\Delta r} \tag{2.28}$$

where, as before, P is the current price, and P_{up} and P_{down} are option-adjusted values directly recomputed by shifting the entire spot curve by a small parallel shock Δr and keeping OAS constant. One-sided option-adjusted convexities can be computed in a similar fashion as well.

As compared to modified durations and convexities, option-adjusted measures have clear advantages because they explicitly model options and other cash flow uncertainties embedded in a security and account for its path-dependency and other characteristics. These measures are relatively accurate predictors of future price movements when yield curve movements are small. Needless to say, option-adjusted measures are computationally intensive, especially for complex path-dependent securities, and are sensitive to the assumptions underlying prepayment and interest-rate models. From now on, unless stated otherwise, we will use the terms *duration* and *option-adjusted duration* as well as *convexity* and *option-adjusted convexity* interchangeably.

The aggregate option-adjusted duration and convexity of a fixed-income portfolio is computed as a weighted average of the durations and convexities, respectively, of the individual securities. The weight applied to each instrument's OAD (or, for that matter, OAC) depends on the asset type and is constructed to reflect the actual market exposure to a given systematic risk factor. For non-notional securities, the weight is simply the current market value of the security divided by the total market value of the portfolio. By convention, for notional securities (swaps, forwards, and futures), the weight is a function of the notional amount, the current price, and the premium paid, if any. Thus, the weight applied to parametric risk measures on swaps is $\frac{(1+P)\cdot Notional\ Value}{MV_{portfolio}}$ where P is the current market price of the swap per \$1 of notional and $MV_{portfolio}$ is the total market value of the portfolio. For futures and forward contracts, the weight is $\frac{P\cdot Notional\ Value}{MV_{portfolio}}$. While the approach based on market values can be used for many derivatives as well, it breaks down for swaps with a market value of zero. Therefore, the method that utilizes notional values is more general.

Recall that the OAS of a security can sometimes be thought of as a measure of the risk premium demanded by the market for holding a particular security. In OAD and OAC calculations (Equations 2.23 and 2.26), the securities' OAS is usually kept unchanged when prices P_{up} and P_{down} are recomputed by the valuation model. Therefore, typical formulations of the option-adjusted framework make an implicit assumption about the *absence of spread directionality,* the lack of a relationship between changes in interest rates, and changes in OAS. While this dependency is not always stable, in many market environments, changes in credit spreads are inversely affected by changes in interest rates.[17] Similar to ignoring dependency of changes in spreads on changes in interest rates, many option-adjusted spread models also do not capture the relationship between implied volatility and interest rates (*volatility skew*). Since implied volatility is a function of the in-the-moneyness of the option embedded in a security, implied volatility should change instead of being kept constant when interest rates are shocked and prices are recomputed.

2.2.3 Dynamic Nature of Local Risk Measures: Duration and Convexity Drift[18]

Option-adjusted duration and option-adjusted convexity measure the price sensitivity of fixed-income securities to parallel changes in spot rates. Because OAD and OAC are linked to the first- and second-order terms, respectively, of the Taylor series expansion of the price function, they are, in the language of mathematics, *local* measures of risk. Thus, the actual accuracy of approximating price changes using duration and convexity (Equation 2.16) depends on the nonlinearity of the price/yield function. While accurately predicting price movements for small interest rate shocks, OAD and OAC alone may not be adequate for approximating highly nonlinear price/yield functions when changes in interest rates are large. Interest rate scenario analysis, studied in the following section, provides a direct way to illustrate the *locality* of duration and convexity. As a useful exercise, the reader is encouraged to use OAD and OAC (Table 2.1) to approximate prices corresponding to the various changes in interest rates and then contrast them with the corresponding OAVs computed directly (see Table 2.4).

The locality of OAD and OAC can be directly measured by *duration and convexity drifts*—dependencies of these measures on interest rate movements. Effective hedging requires an understanding of the importance of duration drifts. Since duration hedging is one of the most common methods of managing interest rate exposure, OAD drift estimates the expected mismatch in duration between a portfolio and its hedges if interest rates change. Thus, measuring duration drift is a simple and effective approach to estimating costs associated with rebalancing of hedges. Of course, most of the impact of duration drift can be captured by the timely recomputation of a portfolio's analytics. In most cases, daily updating of duration estimates should suffice, but ideally analytics are recalculated in near real-time. However, since interest rates are known to gap from time to time, analyzing in advance what could happen and designing hedges that are resilient to that possibility creates the most resilient hedge.

Duration drift is defined as the negative of the first derivative of duration with respect to changes in interest rates. It is an estimate of the change in OAD for a 100 basis point parallel change in spot rates, that is:

$$\text{OAD } Drift = -\frac{d\text{OAD}}{dr} \tag{2.29}$$

where dOAD is the change in OAD and dr is a parallel shift in the spot curve. Convexity drift is defined in a similar fashion:

$$\text{OAC } Drift = -\frac{d\text{OAC}}{dr} \tag{2.30}$$

Positive duration drift is a desirable characteristic of a long position in a security since its duration will increase as markets rally, thereby earning itself "over performance." Likewise, as markets sell off, a security with a positive duration drift exhibits shortened duration, reducing the risk of losses if markets sell off even further. In hedging, positive duration drift is a desirable property of the hedged portfolio as well. Typically, due to the mismatch in duration drifts between a portfolio and its hedges, rebalancing is required when the interest rate environment changes. Assuming that the hedged portfolio with a positive duration drift is originally duration neutral, a market rally will result in a lengthening of its duration, and therefore rebalancing will imply selling securities at higher prices. Conversely, if markets sell off and duration of the hedged portfolio becomes negative, rebalancing will require purchasing supplemental hedges at lower prices. Having this additional protection against adverse market movements, securities with positive duration drift will usually imply a give-up in *carry*.[19]

The derivation of expressions for duration and convexity drifts is straightforward. Differentiating duration (Equation 2.21) with respect to changes in interest rates gives:

$$\frac{d\text{OAD}}{dr} = -\frac{1}{P}\frac{d^2P}{dr^2} + \frac{1}{P^2}\frac{dP}{dr}\frac{dP}{dr} \tag{2.31}$$

resulting into the following expression for duration drift:

$$\text{OAD } Drift = -\frac{d\text{OAD}}{dr} = \text{OAC} - \text{OAD}^2 \tag{2.32}$$

Duration drift is a function of both OAD and OAC.[20]

The duration drift of a noncallable Treasury security is always positive, regardless of the interest rate environment. The duration drift of callable corporate agency bonds and generic mortgage-backed securities (MBS) are typically negative. However, as shown in Table 2.3, rising rate interest rate shocks may result in the duration drifts of currently callable corporate agency bonds becoming less negative. This happens because when rates rise dramatically, the call options embedded in corporate bonds becomes deep out-of-the-money, making its risk characteristics similar to those of a fixed cash flow security. Conversely, as rates fall sharply, the price of the currently callable corporate bond approaches the present value of its cash flows-to-call. Thus, until that point, its duration drift becomes increasingly negative due to declining convexity. After that point in the face of a further rally, the duration drift starts increasing, finally approaching zero when the call option becomes deep in-the-money. Similar to the case of callable corporate agency bonds, when the prepayment option of a current coupon mortgage-backed security is deep out-of-the-money, this leads the duration drift of this MBS to resemble that of a fixed cash flow security. In persistently low interest rate environments, MBS that have been exposed to extensive refinancing opportunities become much less sensitive to changes in interest rates as the propensity to prepay "burns out." This results in their duration drifts becoming less negative and, finally, slightly positive. Table 2.3 illustrates these points numerically by presenting duration drifts of selected securities.

Convexity drift is difficult to estimate accurately since it requires the computation of the third-order term of the Taylor series, which is even more difficult to measure precisely than convexity. Similar to the problems with stability and intuitiveness of convexity estimates, the accuracy of convexity drifts worsens with increasing optionality and depends substantially on the size of the utilized yield curve shift. Also, just like durations and convexities, their drifts are first-order approximations and may not be accurate predictors of the actual price behavior when changes in interest rates are large.

2.2.4 Interest Rate Scenario Analysis

Interest rate scenario analysis directly measures the price sensitivity of fixed-income securities to changes in interest rates. As opposed to duration and convexity, which make various *local* approximations of the price/yield function, interest rate scenario analysis better sketches out its analytical shape using numerous direct revaluations (Exhibits 2.1 and 2.2).

Typically, interest rate scenario analysis investigates the price dependency of fixed-income securities to parallel changes in yield or the spot curve. First, a set of *instantaneous* interest

TABLE 2.3 Duration Drifts of Selected Securities in Various Interest Rate Environments (as of 1/31/2020)

		Base OAS (bp)	Parallel Interest Rate Shock (Basis Points)						
			−150	−100	−50	Base	50	100	150
US Treasury	OAV	0	107.86	107.86	106.40	101.75	97.28	93.02	88.97
	OAD		9.04	9.04	9.03	8.98	8.94	8.89	8.84
	OAC		0.91	0.91	0.90	0.90	0.89	0.88	0.87
	Duration Drift		0.09	0.09	0.09	0.09	0.09	0.09	0.09
Callable Agency	OAV	1	100.08	100.08	100.08	100.00	99.61	99.17	98.73
	OAD		0.49	0.49	0.49	0.60	0.87	0.90	0.89
	OAC		−0.53	−0.53	−0.53	−0.81	−0.15	0.01	0.01
	Duration Drift		−0.53	−0.53	−0.53	−0.81	−0.16	0.00	0.00
Generic MBS	OAV	34	104.72	104.78	104.96	104.39	103.30	101.88	100.13
	OAD		1.24	1.23	1.34	1.80	2.42	3.11	3.79
	OAC		−0.39	−0.40	−0.56	−1.13	−1.29	−1.29	−1.17
	Duration Drift		−0.40	−0.42	−0.58	−1.16	−1.35	−1.39	−1.31
Investment-Grade Bond[a]	OAV	59	109.73	109.73	109.73	107.94	105.58	103.27	101.02
	OAD		4.44	4.44	4.44	4.43	4.41	4.40	4.38
	OAC		0.23	0.23	0.23	0.23	0.23	0.23	0.22
	Duration Drift		0.03	0.03	0.03	0.03	0.03	0.03	0.03
CMBS	OAV	41	120.37	120.37	119.40	115.28	111.30	107.48	103.81
	OAD		7.06	7.06	7.05	7.01	6.97	6.93	6.89
	OAC		0.58	0.58	0.58	0.57	0.57	0.56	0.56
	Duration Drift		0.08	0.08	0.08	0.08	0.08	0.08	0.08

Source: BlackRock Aladdin, January 31, 2020.
Note: [a]The Investment-Grade Bond is a non-callable bond.

rate scenarios is specified. Examples in this chapter use parallel spot curve shocks of 0, ±25, ±50, ±75, ±100, and ±150 basis points.[21] OAVs corresponding to each interest rate scenario are then computed using a valuation model. This is similar to the computation of P_{up} and P_{down} in Equation 2.23 (OAD) and Equation 2.26 (OAC). Results of the interest rate scenario analysis of securities in a sample portfolio are presented in Table 2.4. Note, once again, that price/yield functions of fixed-income securities with embedded options can be substantially nonlinear.[22]

Interest rate scenario analysis does not necessarily have to use parallel spot curve shocks. For instance, it could just as easily be performed using parallel shocks to the par curve. In the next chapter, we study other approaches to interest rate scenario analysis that use principal components and other nonparallel interest rate shocks. It must be noted that since evolution of securities through time is ignored by the traditional interest rate scenario analysis formulations, some results can be misleading. For instance, due to the rapid decay of embedded options, rolldown, and carry, the actual performance of fixed-income securities in various interest rate environments can be substantially different from that predicted by interest rate scenario analysis, which uses instantaneous interest rate shocks. Later in this chapter (Section 2.8), the horizon rate of return framework is used to present a more generalized approach to interest rate scenario analysis. This will allow the simultaneous exploration of the price

TABLE 2.4 Interest Rate Scenario Analysis Report for a Sample Portfolio (as of 1/31/2020)

Security Description	Coupon	Maturity	Strike	Option-Adjusted Values for Various Parallel Rate Shocks												
				−150	−125	−100	−75	−50	−25	0	25	50	75	100	125	150
Treasury Bonds																
OTR 2YR	1.375	1/31/2022		100.80	100.80	100.80	100.80	100.80	100.76	100.27	99.77	99.28	98.80	98.32	97.84	97.36
OTR 5YR	1.375	1/31/2025		102.61	102.61	102.61	102.61	102.61	101.56	100.34	99.14	97.95	96.78	95.63	94.49	93.36
OTR 10YR	1.75	11/15/2029		114.82	114.82	114.82	114.49	112.03	109.56	107.11	104.72	102.40	100.13	97.91	95.75	93.64
OTR 30YR	2.375	11/15/2049		157.62	150.61	142.91	135.38	128.16	121.31	114.86	108.83	103.19	97.91	92.96	88.33	83.99
Treasury Futures																
US 10YR NOTE MAR 20 TY 20-MAR-2020		3/20/2020		105.16	105.16	105.16	105.16	104.22	102.12	100.00	97.92	95.88	93.88	91.91	89.97	88.07
US LONG BOND MAR 20 US 20-MAR-2020		3/20/2020		186.42	186.42	183.89	178.99	173.83	168.63	163.53	158.62	153.88	149.31	144.91	140.67	136.58
Callable Agency Bonds																
FHLB 2.0 20-FEB-2025	2.00	2/20/2025		100.20	100.20	100.20	100.20	100.20	100.17	100.00	99.63	99.01	98.21	97.30	96.31	95.29
Option on Future																
MAR20 TUH0 C @ 106.25 TU 21-FEB-2020		2/21/2020	106.25	2.46	2.46	2.46	2.46	2.46	2.43	1.93	1.44	0.96	0.54	0.23	0.07	0.01
Interest Rate Swap																
SWP: USD 3.167500 09-SEP-2023 IRS	3.17	7/9/2023		12.21	12.23	12.26	12.28	12.30	11.48	10.60	9.68	8.77	7.86	6.97	6.09	5.21
German Government Bond Future																
EURO-BUND MAR 20 RX 06-MAR-2020		3/6/2020		175.04	175.04	175.04	175.04	175.04	175.04	175.04	171.16	167.37	163.67	160.06	156.53	153.08
IG Credit																
AMERICAN EXPRESS COMPANY T2 3.625 05-DEC-2024 (SUB)	3.63	12/5/2024		110.04	110.04	110.04	110.04	110.04	109.15	107.94	106.76	105.58	104.42	103.28	102.14	101.02

Sector / Security	Coupon	Maturity													
HY Credit															
NINE ENERGY SERVICE INC 8.75 01-NOV-2023 144a (SENIOR)	8.75	11/1/2023	85.33	85.33	85.33	85.33	85.33	85.06	84.38	83.70	83.03	82.37	81.72	81.07	80.42
Agency MBS															
UMBS 30YR TBA CASH 4.0	4.00	4/25/2049	105.03	105.06	105.13	105.21	105.18	104.87	104.45	103.98	103.42	102.77	102.05	101.25	100.38
Agency CMBS															
GNMA_16-113-IO 1.1524 16-FEB-2058	1.15	2/16/2058	8.52	8.52	8.52	8.50	8.44	8.35	8.27	8.18	8.09	8.01	7.93	7.85	7.77
Non-Agency CMBS															
JPMBB_14-C22-XA 0.83511 15-SEP-2047	0.84	7/15/2047	3.29	3.29	3.29	3.29	3.29	3.28	3.26	3.25	3.23	3.21	3.20	3.18	3.17
ABS Credit Card															
NDFT_17-1-C 2.15338 15-JUL-2025 Reg-S	2.56	7/15/2020		100.14	100.14	100.14	100.13	100.12	100.11	100.10	100.10	100.09	100.08	100.07	100.06
Non-Agency MBS															
ALM_15-16A-A2R 3.33125 15-JUL-2027 144a	3.33	4/15/2024	64.03	64.03	64.03	63.98	63.73	63.27	62.50	61.78	61.07	60.37	59.66	58.96	58.26
Total	2.81														

Source: BlackRock Aladdin, January 31, 2020.

sensitivity of fixed-income securities to changes in interest rates as well as to the passage of time.

2.3   MEASURING INTEREST RATE EXPOSURE: EMPIRICAL APPROACHES

2.3.1   Coupon Curve Duration

Coupon curve duration (CCD) seeks to estimate the price sensitivity of mortgage-backed securities (MBS) to changes in interest rates using an approach very different conceptually from the previously described analytical measures of interest rate exposure. They are perhaps the simplest durations to calculate since they are solely based on the *coupon curve*, the price dependency of MBS of the same agency and term on the coupon. Coupon curves of generic 30-year Ginnie Mae (GNMAII) MBS and Uniform Mortgage-Backed Securities (UMBS) are presented in Exhibit 2.3.[23]

Similar to other interest rate duration measures, CCD is defined as the negative of the percentage change in price, given a 100 basis point change in interest rates (Equation 2.21) and is computed using the generic duration formula (Equation 2.23). However, the difference between CCD and other interest rate durations lies in the determination of P_{up} and P_{down}, which are derived directly from market prices as opposed to being computed by a valuation model such as OAVs. The rationale behind CCD is based on the "similarity" of mortgage-backed securities of the same agency and term in all risk characteristics (credit quality, types of underlying pools, origination guidelines, etc.) but one—coupon. When referring to the in-the-moneyness of the embedded prepayment option, it therefore can be thought that if interest rates increased by 50 basis points, the price of a 3.5% MBS should become equal to that of a 3.0% MBS. Conversely, if interest rates decreased by 50 basis points, the

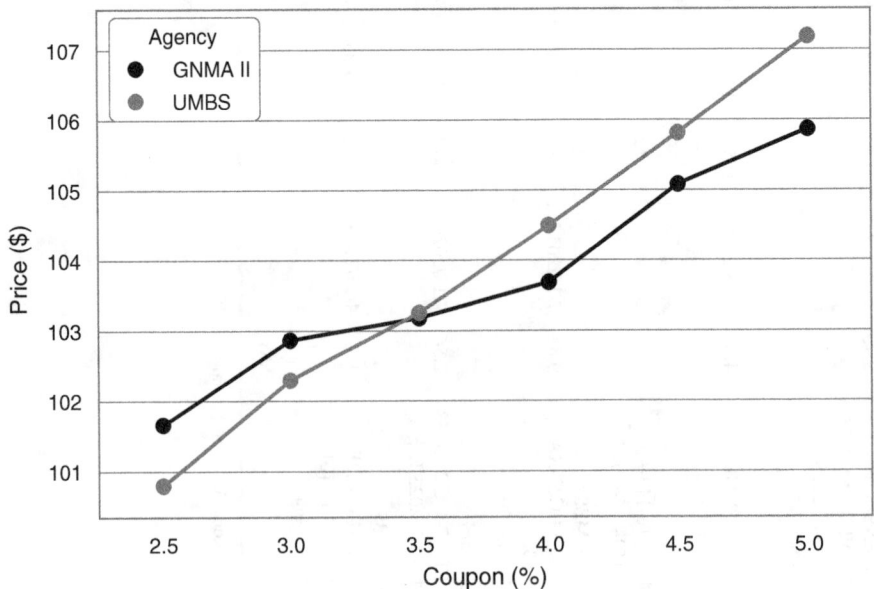

EXHIBIT 2.3   Coupon Curves of Generic 30-Year MBS (as of 1/31/2020)
Source: BlackRock Aladdin, January 31, 2020.

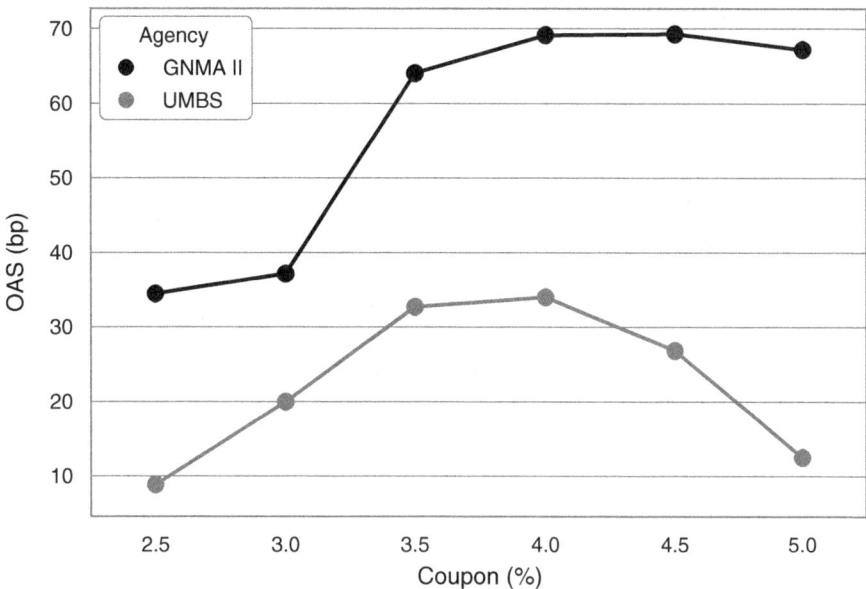

EXHIBIT 2.4 OAS Curves of Generic 30-Year MBS (as of 1/31/2020)
Source: BlackRock Aladdin, January 31, 2020.

price of a 3.5% MBS should become equal to that of a 4.0% MBS. Applying this logic to P_{up} and P_{down} in Equation 2.23 yields:

$$\text{CCD}_{3.5} = \frac{1}{P_{3.5}} \frac{P_{3.0} - P_{4.0}}{2 \cdot 0.005} \tag{2.33}$$

where $P_{3.0}$, $P_{3.5}$, and $P_{4.0}$ are the current prices of 3.0%, 3.5%, and 4.0% MBS, respectively. Since coupons are assumed to be 50 basis points apart, a .005 is in the denominator. CCDs of generic 30-year mortgage-backed securities are presented in Table 2.5. Furthermore, Exhibit 2.4 shows OAS curves for generic 30-year mortgage-backed securities.

CCDs are obviously a crude and simplistic metric, but they can be a useful tool in reconciling analytical measures of exposure with the market's perception of exposure, as reflected in prices of liquid mortgage-backed securities. However, CCDs are only effective when measuring exposure of fairly generic and homogeneous MBSs that are well priced and have similar weighted-average maturities. Extending this approach to other fixed-income asset classes is difficult since identifying groups of instruments that are "similar" in all risk dimensions but one (coupon) is rare.

2.3.2 Empirical (Implied) Duration

As an alternative to computing parametric risk measures by theorizing valuation mechanisms, econometric methods can be used to statistically estimate the price sensitivity of fixed-income securities to a variety of systematic risk factors. Measures of interest rate exposure obtained via applied statistical modeling techniques have come to be known as *empirical* or *implied* durations.[24] While econometrically sophisticated empirical duration formulations can be envisioned, this section illustrates this concept using the simplest and most straightforward approach. Like coupon curve duration, empirical duration seeks to estimate the interest rate exposure through information revealed by market prices and yields. These two methodologies are also similar, as they do not rely on the numerous assumptions built into interest rate, yield curve, and prepayment models. However, in contrast to CCD, empirical duration uses a *historical time series* of prices and changes in yields rather than current market data.

Empirical duration methodologies typically employs regression analysis. As opposed to analytically computing the first derivative of the price function with respect to yield, the statistical relationship between the dependent variable (percentage changes in prices) and the independent variable (changes in interest rates) is estimated. As mentioned before, the term *change in interest rates* can be defined in many different ways. Thus, modified duration characterizes changes in interest rates as changes in yield-to-maturity of option-free bonds. OAD represents changes in interest rates as parallel movements in the spot curve. Empirical duration can be defined as the negative of the slope of the regression line of a bond's percentage changes in price $\left(\frac{\Delta P}{P} \right)$ with respect to changes in its yield-to-maturity (Δy):

$$\frac{\Delta P}{P} = \alpha - Empirical\ Dur \cdot \Delta y + \varepsilon \tag{2.34}$$

where ε is the normally distributed error term. For the majority of fixed-income instruments, the intercept α is typically statistically insignificant in virtually all market environments. Notice the similarity of Equation 2.34 with Equation 2.12 (modified duration). Obviously, Equation 2.34 represents the simplest possible formulation of empirical duration. While other formulations exist, some of them make it difficult to extract the isolated price sensitivity to interest rate movements because of the interaction between interest rates and other systematic risk factors.

A complication arises when computing empirical durations for derivative securities (e.g., mortgage-backed securities) whose yields-to-maturity cannot be meaningfully defined because of the embedded cash flow uncertainties. In this case, it is helpful to assign to each derivative instrument a *benchmark fixed cash flow security* (usually a US Treasury) whose yield-to-maturity is used as proxy for changes in interest rates (Δy) in Equation 2.34. The issues surrounding selection of benchmarks that adequately represent changes in interest rates merit a separate discussion. First, since empirical duration is defined in a univariate setting where price is a function of a single risk factor, selection of the appropriate benchmark should account for the fact that yield curves do not usually move in a parallel fashion. The benchmark must therefore be linked to the characteristics (e.g., OAD or weighted average life) of the derivative instrument whose empirical duration is to be measured. Table 2.5 shows 10-, 20-, and 40-business-day empirical durations of generic MBS securities. Notice that empirical durations across most MBSs are typically shorter than the corresponding OADs. The difference is due to the spread directionality of mortgage spreads and other basis risks ignored by OAD. Notice that the goodness-of-fit (as measured by R^2) is inversely related to the prices of MBSs.

For example, when computing empirical durations, using market prices directly may not be appropriate for all types of fixed-income securities. Prices of forward contracts (e.g., generic to-be-announced [TBA] MBS), have to be adjusted for *carry:* since the price movements of the forwards reflect both market fluctuations of the deliverable asset as well as price movements due to the embedded forward contract approaching expiration. The interest

TABLE 2.5 Parametric Risk Measures for Generic 30-Year MBSs (as of 1/31/2020)

Agency	Coupon	Market Price	OAS	OAD	OAC	Spd Dur	Vol Dur	Prepay Dur	Mtg/Tsy Dur	Emp Dur 10 Day	Emp Dur 20 Day	Emp Dur 40 Day	10 Day R²	20 Day R²	40 Day R²
UMBS	2.5	100.77	82	4.18	−2.74	3.80	0.07	1.01	4.18	3.31	3.37	4.42	83%	89%	88%
	3.0	102.26	84	2.92	−2.04	3.03	0.05	2.39	2.92	1.62	1.83	2.68	79%	84%	79%
	3.5	103.21	92	2.16	−1.42	2.53	0.03	3.54	2.16	0.61	0.64	1.22	52%	49%	58%
	4.0	104.45	88	1.73	−0.96	2.36	0.02	4.91	1.73	0.09	0.2	0.66	1%	6%	29%
	4.5	105.76	78	1.45	−0.61	2.26	0.01	6.38	1.45	−0.01	0.07	0.46	0%	0%	16%
	5.0	107.14	61	1.23	−0.38	2.20	0.01	7.93	1.23	0.18	0.3	0.41	4%	13%	24%
GNMA II	2.5	101.63	108	4.82	−2.03	4.79	0.05	1.22	4.82	0	0	0.06	0%	0%	0%
	3.0	102.83	84	1.95	−3.17	3.07	0.04	2.83	1.95	1.29	1.49	2.39	30%	46%	61%
	3.5	103.15	99	1.16	−1.86	2.41	0.02	3.49	1.16	0.48	0.58	1.29	9%	9%	38%
	4.0	103.65	89	0.53	−0.59	1.87	0.01	4.76	0.53	0.11	0.23	0.74	0%	2%	21%
	4.5	105.05	99	0.83	−0.38	2.07	0.01	6.10	0.83	−0.26	−0.15	0.47	2%	0%	7%
	5.0	105.83	99	0.68	−0.62	1.97	0.00	6.88	0.68	0.36	0.22	0.47	15%	1%	6%

Source: BlackRock Aladdin, January 31, 2020.
Note: Values that are highlighted are not statistically significant.

rate sensitive component of the market prices has to be isolated from the deterministic one. In addition to fluctuations attributed to interest rates, prices of complex fixed-income securities may change due to a variety of other risk factors: credit spread movements, decay of embedded options, prepayments, time, etc. While captured in the time series of percentage price changes of derivative securities, these phenomena are not reflected in the yield-to-maturities of the corresponding US Treasury benchmarks, biasing empirical duration estimates. Due to the market state-dependent nature of many fixed-income securities' risk characteristics, empirical durations may also lead to erroneous conclusions if the immediate market environment changes from the one that supplied the empirical price data used to compute them. For instance, if interest rates changed dramatically after empirical durations on mortgage-backed securities were estimated, empirical durations should be out of date because the in-the-moneyness of the embedded prepayment options has likely changed.

The goodness-of-fit measures (e.g., R^2) and tests for statistical significance of the regression coefficients can be used when judging the quality of empirical durations. Needless to say, empirical durations are very sensitive to pricing errors. They may also be biased due to purely statistical reasons, including the presence of autoregressive behavior, lags in price reaction to changes in yields, and nonnormality of residuals.

In summary, empirical duration is a simple, informative, and intuitive measure of interest rate exposure. By virtue of reflecting the actual empirically observed price behavior, empirical durations provide a valuable "sanity check" when judging the predictive power of option-adjusted and other analytical durations.

2.4 MEASURING YIELD CURVE EXPOSURE

2.4.1 Key Rate Durations[25]

Earlier in this chapter, several conceptually different approaches to measuring the price sensitivity of fixed-income securities to changes in interest rates have been discussed. While the previously described measures of exposure employ very different theoretical and computational techniques, they all rely on the same empirically unrealistic underlying assumption that prices of securities and portfolios are functions of a *single* systematic interest rate factor. Thus, changes in interest rates are represented as changes in yields-to-maturity in the computation of modified and empirical durations and as parallel changes in the spot curve in the calculation of option-adjusted measures. Not surprisingly, while being accurate predictors of price fluctuations resulting from small changes in the *level* of interest rates, modified, option-adjusted, and other durations fail to address the exposure associated with changes in the *shape* of the yield curve.

Consider the following example. When expecting an easing of short-term interest rates by the Federal Reserve, traders often bet on the steepening in the yield curve. To implement their view as a *duration-neutral* relative value trade, they may decide to buy the 2-year on-the-run (OTR) Treasury (TSY) security and sell the 10-year OTR TSY. Using duration alone to judge the interest rate exposure of this trade (which has an aggregate duration of zero by construction) will erroneously indicate that there is no exposure. But while this trade would be insensitive to parallel movements[26] in the spot curve, it is exposed to a different kind of systematic market exposure. The exposure to the flattening of the yield curve cannot be measured by duration alone.

Another example of the limitations of duration with respect to measuring yield curve exposure comes from institutional asset management where a portfolio's investment guidelines often specify a predefined *duration band,* the maximum allowed deviation of the portfolio's duration from that of its benchmark. Similar to the case of duration-neutral trades, an investment mandate may impose a very narrow permissible duration band on a portfolio to limit the magnitude of duration bets, thus constraining an important source of risk (as well as limiting opportunities for outperformance). In search of active return, such a portfolio may be structured to hold longer instruments than those in its benchmark while the excess duration is hedged out using futures, swaps, or other derivatives. This may result in the *gap* between a portfolio and its benchmark having a yield curve bet that is not captured by duration. Obviously, this yield curve bet could be a major source of market risk. These examples demonstrate the need to generalize the concept of duration. To do this, in addition to investigating the price sensitivity to parallel changes in the entire term structure of interest rates, exposure associated with nonparallel yield curve movements must be measured.

Key rate duration (KRD)[27] is an important extension of the option-adjusted framework. The popularity of KRDs is generally attributed to their ability to describe yield curve risk in a visual and intuitive way. KRDs have also proven to be an effective hedging and yield curve risk management tool. They are typically implemented within the option-adjusted framework and can be thought of as partial OADs corresponding to the movements of isolated regions of the yield curve. Key rate durations can provide a visual depiction of yield curve exposure, both at the security and portfolio level. KRD profiles of selected securities are presented in Exhibit 2.5, including a hypothetical 30-year default-free bond to emphasize the different yield curve exposures.

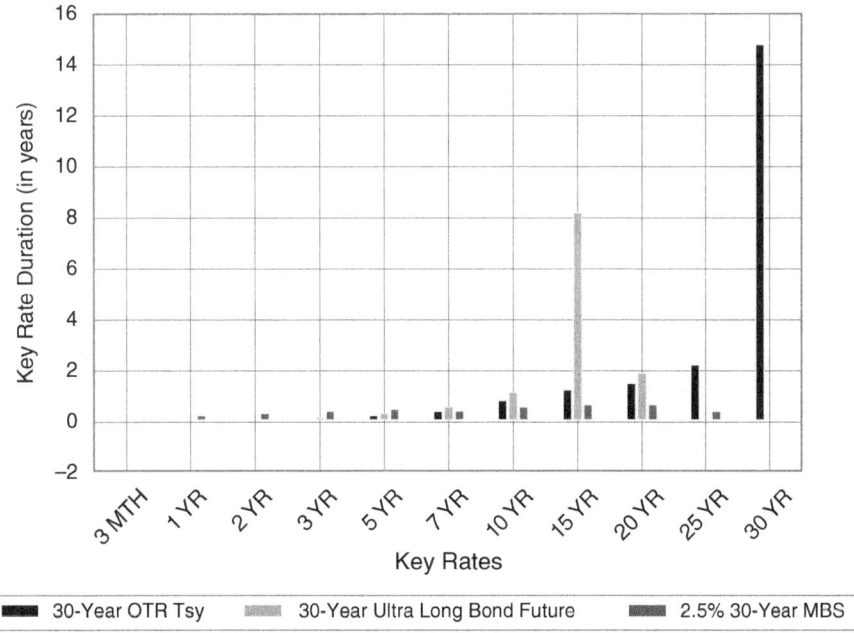

EXHIBIT 2.5 Key Rate Duration (KRD) Profiles of Selected Instruments (as of 1/31/2020)
Source: BlackRock Aladdin, January 31, 2020.

OAD measures the first-order price sensitivity to parallel changes in spot interest rates. KRDs generalize this approach. Instead of assuming that price P is a function of a single random variable (parallel spot curve shock as in Equation 2.20), KRDs present price as a function of n selected spot rates $r_1, \ldots, r_n$ that are known as *key rates:*

$$P = P(r_1, \ldots, r_n) \tag{2.35}$$

KRDs are partial durations that measure the first-order price sensitivity to the isolated movements of different segments of the spot curve:

$$krd_i = -\frac{1}{P}\frac{\partial P}{\partial r_i} \tag{2.36}$$

In this more general setting, because nearly any yield curve movement can be well represented as the vector of changes of properly chosen key rates $(\Delta r_1, \ldots, \Delta r_n)$, a multivariate analog of Equation 2.24 can be used to approximate changes in price using the vector of KRDs:

$$\frac{\Delta P}{P} \approx -\sum_{i=1}^{n} krd_i \cdot \Delta r_i \tag{2.37}$$

Equation 2.37 has important applications and can be used in stress testing and Value at Risk (VaR), individually. KRDs can be computed via the direct analog of Equation 2.23:

$$krd_i = -\frac{1}{P}\frac{P_{i,up} - P_{i,down}}{2 \cdot \Delta r_i} \tag{2.38}$$

Note that $P_{i,up}$ and $P_{i,down}$ in Equation 2.38 are directly computed by a valuation model after the appropriate KRD shock is applied to the spot curve. Just as in the case of OAD and OAC, OAS is kept constant in the calculation of KRDs, again assuming the absence of spread directionality. Despite their conceptual similarity to OADs, the implementation of KRDs within the OAS framework is nontrivial. The construction of KRD shocks therefore merits a separate discussion.

Partitioning the yield curve into segments that correspond to different key rates is somewhat arbitrary, and its implementations vary across financial institutions that employ KRDs in portfolio and risk management. The appropriate number of key rates and their positioning on the yield curve ultimately depend on the composition of a given portfolio. In the examples presented in Exhibit 2.5, the key rates are defined as 3-month and 1-, 2-, 3-, 5-, 7-, 10-, 15-, 20-, 25-, and 30-year points on the spot curve. Alternatively, shorter-term portfolios might require a greater number of key rates at the shorter end of the yield curve. In the extreme case, one might imagine having a separate key rate for every annual, monthly, or even daily spot rate. Unfortunately, only limited practical benefits could arise from this type of excessive granularity. Thus, since certain points of the yield curve are highly correlated and exhibit similar volatilities, investigating the price sensitivity to their changes in isolation, with all other spot rates kept constant is unrealistic. From a mathematical viewpoint, recomputing OAD of a security when a single point on the spot curve is perturbed is also not meaningful:

price is similar to an integral; both are not sensitive to changes in the value of a continuous function at a single point.

Therefore, the following considerations are important for constructing KRD interest rate shocks:

- Spot rates do not move in isolation. If a single spot rate is shocked, an entire *region* of the spot curve around this point should be shocked as well.
- For consistency and other reasons that will become apparent, KRD shocks should aggregate up to a parallel shock, which allows for the intuitive concept that exposure to parallel changes in interest rates (OAD) can be decomposed into exposures to different parts of the yield curve (KRDs).

KRD shocks can be defined in a variety of ways. Initially, KRD shocks were constructed with the previously described rationale in mind, defined using triangular overlapping shocks. For instance, Exhibit 2.6a illustrates that the 7-year KRD shock was defined as having the value of zero basis points for all spot rates with terms less than 5 years, linearly rising to a given number of basis points (Δr) at the 7-year point,[28] declining linearly back to zero at the next key rate (10 year), and staying at zero basis points for all maturities beyond 10 years. As the exception to this rule, the two boundary key rates (3 month and 30 year) were defined slightly differently: the 3-month KRD shock had a value of Δr between zero and 3-month points, linearly declining to zero at the 1-year key rate, and staying at zero for all maturities greater than 1 year. The 30-year KRD shock was defined as zero for all maturities less than or equal to 25 years, linearly increasing to Δr at the 30-year key rate, and staying at Δr for all maturities greater than 30 years.

Alternatively, key rate shocks can be defined as "wave shocks." Exhibits 2.6a and 2.6b illustrate the difference between the classical triangular shocks and the wave shocks.

EXHIBIT 2.6 Difference Between the Classical Triangular Shock and the Wave Shocks

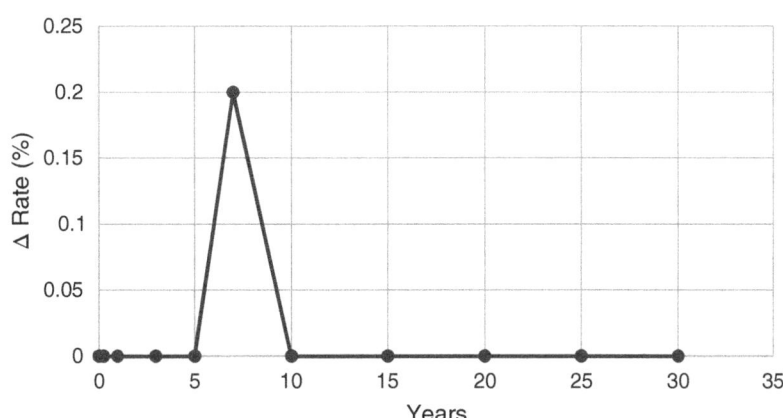

EXHIBIT 2.6a Sample Triangular Shock at the 7-Year Point
Source: For illustrative purposes only.

(*Continued*)

EXHIBIT 2.6 *(Continued)*

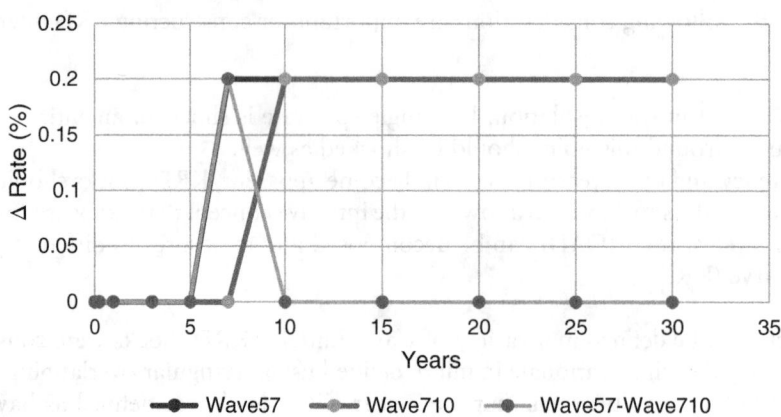

EXHIBIT 2.6b Sample Wave Shocks and Their Difference
Source: For illustrative purposes only.

One can readily see from Exhibits 2.6a and 2.6b that by taking the difference between two subsequent wave shocks, one will obtain a triangular shock. Using wave shocks, the KRDs can be calculated as follows:

$$KRD_{j,ik} = WKRD_{ij} - WKRD_{jk} \qquad (2.39)$$

with the notation $KRD_{j,ik}$ denoting the duration due to a triangular shock peaking at j years and nonzero between i and k years, and $WKRD_{ij}$ referring to the duration to the wave shock, which is zero before i years and rises to its value at j years staying constant thereafter.

If the security price is a linear function of rates, the two approaches for defining the KRD shocks are completely equivalent. However, in practice, certain securities, such as MBS or interest rate options, exhibit strong nonlinearities. In addition, MBS models typically utilize prepayment models that in turn utilize mortgage rate models that are estimated using historical yield curve data. These mortgage rate models produce more accurate results when the simulated yield curve rates are closer to what is plausible based on history.

In order to choose an approach to calculate key rate duration, it helps to go back to why we need them. Key rate durations are primarily used to understand the price change under a realistic curve shift. Therefore, while calculating KRDs, it is important to minimize, to the extent possible, the effects that stem from unrealistic shapes of the forward rate curves under the shocks. A major advantage of using the wave KRD approach is that the implied forward rates of the shocks behave in a more sensible way, with less oscillations in the forward that could affect sensitivity calculations of highly nonlinear instruments. As one can see in Exhibit 2.7a and Exhibit 2.7b, applying a triangular shock results in the trajectory of forward rates where a sharp rise in rates between year 5 and 7 is followed by a sharp decline (going negative) between year 7 and 10. As previously described, when an empirical mortgage model was calibrated, it is unlikely that a similar scenario occurred. Thus, the resulting calculation may not be as reasonable. When utilizing wave shocks, the forward rate changes are less extreme, resulting in a better metric.

EXHIBIT 2.7 Difference in Implied Forward Rates

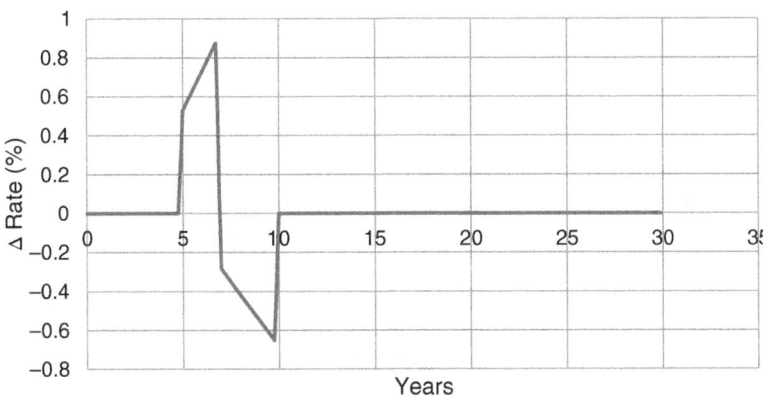

EXHIBIT 2.7a Triangular Shock Implied Forward Rates
Source: For illustrative purposes only.

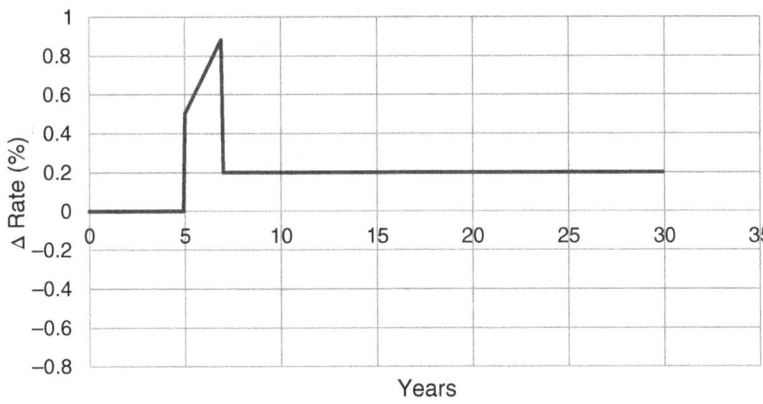

EXHIBIT 2.7b Wave Shock Implied Forward Rates
Source: For illustrative purposes only.

The areas underneath all valid sets of KRD shock definitions exactly add up to a parallel shock, by their construction. However, this does not by itself guarantee that the sum of KRDs is exactly equal to OAD. For securities without interest-rate-correlated cash flow uncertainties, the difference between OAD and the sum of KRDs is usually small. For complex derivative instruments, this difference may be substantial because of the nonlinearity of their value surface. This phenomenon is counterintuitive for many practitioners. Imagine that Equations 2.24 and 2.37 are independently used to estimate the change in price resulting from a given parallel yield curve shock. If KRDs do not sum to OAD, the two methods will arrive at different results. To eliminate this inconsistency, the sum of KRDs can be forced to be equal to OAD. While different ad hoc methods exist, one approach simply adjusts KRDs proportionally by multiplying each KRD by the ratio of OAD and the original sum of KRDs.

The authors are not aware of any published empirical or theoretical validation (or, for that matter, critique) of this method. For all of our future discussions, KRDs should be assumed to have been scaled proportionally in the previously described fashion.

Interpreting KRD profiles can be tricky because they simply measure the *sensitivities* to the different points on the spot curve and ignore the fact that spot rates of dissimilar maturities are not perfectly correlated and may exhibit sometimes dramatically different volatilities. Just like OAD, KRDs also exhibit duration drifts. Finally, the interest rate shocks used to compute KRD have historically implausible shapes and produce nondifferentiable points on the spot curve, implying discontinuous and sometimes even negative forward rates (somewhat mitigated by using wave shocks). This may result in significantly different KRD profiles for very similar securities.

Despite some of these shortcomings, KRDs have proven to be a very popular portfolio and risk management tool. They enable explicit quantitative representation of yield curve exposure and provide insights into absolute and relative yield curve risks embedded in securities and portfolios. In addition to being useful in their own right, KRDs are widely employed by other risk management methodologies, including VaR, stress testing, and hedge optimizations. The KRDs of securities in a sample portfolio are presented in Table 2.6.

2.5   MEASURING AND MANAGING VOLATILITY RELATED RISKS

2.5.1   Volatility Duration

Option pricing theory has taught us that valuation of many derivative securities depends on the assumed future volatility of interest rates and other risk factors. Therefore, it is incumbent upon us to come up with metrics for measuring its impact. In keeping with the conventions associated with interest rate duration, we define the term *volatility duration* as the first-order percent price sensitivity to changes in implied volatility. Readers familiar with derivative markets and option pricing theory will notice that the concept of volatility duration is not new at all and is really only a slight transformation of option *vega*.

In some special cases, volatility duration of interest rate derivatives can be calculated via Black-Scholes-Merton-like formulae analytically. For fixed-income securities with more complex types of cash flow uncertainty, volatility duration is typically estimated numerically within the OAS model framework via the usual partial duration formula:

$$Vol\ Dur = -\frac{1}{P}\frac{P_{vol\ up} - P_{vol\ down}}{2 \cdot \Delta vol} \tag{2.40}$$

Volatility durations of securities in a sample portfolio are presented in Tables 2.1 and 2.5. Since the value of a long option security increases with a rise in implied volatility, fixed-income securities with embedded long options (e.g., options on futures, swaptions, caps, and floors) have been defined to be consistent with interest rate duration as having *negative* volatility durations. Likewise, securities with embedded short options (e.g., MBSs, callable corporates, and agencies) and whose value falls with a rise in volatility have been defined as having *positive* volatility durations. As expected, the more leveraged the embedded option is, the larger is the price sensitivity to changes in implied volatility. Volatility duration is also linked to the in-the-moneyness of the option embedded in a security. Thus, among comparable options on the same index and of the same maturity, the at-the-money (ATM) option has the

TABLE 2.6 Key Rate Duration (KRD) Report for a Sample Portfolio (as of 1/31/2020)

Security Description	Coupon	Maturity	Strike	OAD	OAC	KRD 3 mth	KRD 1 YR	KRD 2 YR	KRD 3 YR	KRD 5 YR	KRD 7 YR	KRD 10 YR
Treasury Bonds												
OTR 2YR 2	1.375	1/31/2022		1.97	0.05	−0.01	0.02	1.95	0.01	0.00	0.00	0.00
OTR 5YR 5	1.375	1/31/2025		4.83	0.26	−0.01	0.01	0.03	0.07	4.72	0.01	0.00
OTR 10YR 10	1.75	11/15/2029		8.99	0.90	0.00	0.02	0.03	0.08	0.16	0.86	7.86
OTR 30YR 30	2.375	11/15/2049		21.62	5.77	0.00	0.02	0.04	0.10	0.20	0.35	20.91
Treasury Futures												
US 10YR NOTE MAR 20 TY 20-MAR-2020		3/20/2020		8.38	0.60	0.00	0.02	0.05	0.12	1.05	7.14	0.00
US LONG BOND MAR 20 US 20-MAR-2020		3/20/2020		12.25	1.82	0.00	0.03	0.06	0.16	0.30	0.54	11.15
Callable Agency Bonds												
FNMA 1.4 30-DEC-2020	1.40	12/30/2020		0.78	−0.63	0.16	0.08	0.04	0.07	0.68	0.02	0.00
Option on Future												
MAR20 TUH0 C @ 106.25 TU 21-FEB-2020		2/21/2020	106.25	0.16	0.62	0.00	0.00	0.00	0.00	0.00	0.00	0.00
Interest Rate Swap												
SWP: USD 3.167500 09-SEP-2023 IRS	3.17	7/9/2023		3.35	0.14	−0.08	0.02	0.04	2.36	1.01	0.00	0.00
German Government Bond Future												
EURO-BUND MAR 20 RX 06-MAR-2020		3/6/2020		8.97	0.85	−0.01	0.00	0.00	0.01	0.02	2.88	6.06
IG Credit												
AMERICAN EXPRESS COMPANY T2 3.625 05-DEC-2024 (SUB)	3.63	12/5/2024		4.40	0.21	0.00	0.03	0.06	0.60	3.71	0.00	0.00

(Continued)

TABLE 2.6 (Continued)

Security Description	Coupon	Maturity	Strike	OAD	OAC	KRD 3 mth	KRD 1 YR	KRD 2 YR	KRD 3 YR	KRD 5 YR	KRD 7 YR	KRD 10 YR
HY Credit												
NINE ENERGY SERVICE INC 8.75 01-NOV-2023 144a (SENIOR)	8.75	11/1/2023		3.13	0.13	0.01	0.08	0.15	1.87	1.02	0.00	0.00
Agency MBS												
UMBS 30YR TBA CASH 4.0	4.00	4/25/2049		1.73	−0.96	0.08	0.33	0.34	0.33	0.28	0.20	0.17
Agency CMBS												
GNMA_16-113-IO 1.1524 16-FEB-2058	1.15	2/16/2058		4.27	0.38	0.04	0.18	0.30	0.53	0.70	0.73	1.81
Non-Agency CMBS												
JPMBB_14-C22-XA 0.83511 15-SEP-2047	0.84	7/15/2047		1.98	0.06	0.05	0.24	0.48	0.90	0.31	0.00	0.00
ABS Credit Card												
NDFT_17-1-C 2.15338 15-JUL-2025 Reg-S	2.56	7/15/2020		0.04	0.00	0.03	0.00	0.00	0.00	0.00	0.00	0.00
Non-Agency MBS												
CSMC_06-3-5A5 6.0 25-APR-2036	3.33	4/15/2024		0.19	0.00	0.05	0.19	0.28	0.48	0.73	0.80	2.14
Total	2.81			5.53	0.73	0.03	0.06	0.28	0.57	1.19	0.18	3.21

Source: BlackRock Aladdin, January 31, 2020.

largest volatility duration (exposure to misestimated as well as changing implied volatility) whereas deep in-the-money (ITM) and deep out-of-the-money (OTM) options have volatility durations that tend to be very small. However, comparing volatility durations of options of different maturities can be misleading since the volatility duration of a short-term ATM option may be substantially smaller in magnitude than that of a long-term ITM or OTM option. Note there is a common misperception of the connection between positive volatility duration (resulting from an embedded short option) and negative convexity. While embedded short options often do cause fixed-income securities to become negatively convex, it is not true that all negatively convex securities have embedded short options. For instance, premium-priced CMBSs (that are effectively prepayment protected) exhibit price compression as their prices rise due to their effective higher level of Loan to Value (LTV). Hence, they are characterized by negative convexity but have no explicit exposure to implied volatility.

Computation of $P_{vol\ up}$ and $P_{vol\ down}$ in the implied volatility formula (Equation 2.40) depends on the valuation model used to value the instrument. More precisely, the means of calculating volatility duration is dictated by the extent to which the utilized interest rate model incorporates the term structure of volatility (TSOV). If an interest rate model (e.g., Black-Derman-Toy, [1990]) is not calibrated to the derivatives market and utilizes only a fixed implied volatility assumption, $P_{vol\ up}$ and $P_{vol\ down}$ are computed by shocking the user-specified implied volatility number and revaluing the security directly.

More elaborate interest rate models (e.g., Brace-Gatarek-Musiela [BGM] model [1997]) calibrate to the term structure of volatility and enable more elaborate exploration of the price sensitivity with respect to changes in implied volatility. After the TSOV is derived from the interest rate derivatives' markets, the simplest approach to computing volatility duration entails shocking the entire term structure of volatility in a parallel fashion and computing $P_{vol\ up}$ and $P_{vol\ down}$. Notice the direct similarity to OAD. A more accurate approach to measuring volatility duration does not utilize the term structure of volatility, a theoretical and unobservable construct, but deals directly with the interest rate derivatives underlying the determination of TSOV. Instead of shocking TSOV in a parallel fashion, implied volatilities of derivative securities used in the calibration are shocked up and down by a given number of basis points. The term structure of volatility is then reestimated, and finally $P_{vol\ up}$ and $P_{vol\ down}$ are directly recomputed by a valuation model. This is particularly well suited for market models, such as BGM or the Forward Market Model by Lyashenko and Mercurio (2019), where the underlying rate modeled is a market observable rate, such as LIBOR while it still exists or the newer benchmarks, such as SOFR.

Volatility duration is computed within the option-adjusted framework, and therefore all traditional advantages and disadvantages of partial duration measures apply. Volatility duration estimates are sensitive to the size of the assumed volatility shock, volatility convexities may not be stable over time, and no relationship is assumed between changes in implied volatility and changes in OAS, which may not be the case in certain market environments. If shocking the term structure of volatility in a parallel fashion is insufficient, volatility KRDs could in theory be computed to explore price sensitivities to the various parts of the volatility surface.

2.5.2 Option Usage in Portfolio Management[29]

Options can be useful portfolio management tools, especially for fixed-income portfolios, serving a variety of purposes in portfolio construction and hedging. Options can introduce a directional risk into a portfolio with limited downside exposure. Utilizing options in a portfolio can provide convex risk exposures or help to manage the overall convexity and volatility levels of a portfolio. Providing the right, but not the obligation, to buy or sell a security at a given price on (or before) a specific date, options are primarily used in portfolio management to do the following:

- *Replicate risk* either more efficiently or with limited downside
- *Hedge* to isolate or remove a particular risk
- *Generate alpha* when optionality is traded as an asset class

Implied volatility can be aggregated across tenors, maturities, and levels of rates to develop a volatility surface to evaluate option positions. As illustrated in Exhibit 2.8, implied volatility can be viewed as a matrix across expiries (terms) and underlyings (tenors) for options on the same instrument. The surface is typically illustrated as two-dimensional, with strikes set at-the-money (ATM). For interest rate options, strikes are based on the forward curve and ATM options are struck at the forward rate. The implied volatility surface is used as a framework to price options in the market and to gauge relative value between options themselves.

While the past helps frame the future, realized volatility is not necessarily the best predictor of future volatility. Hence, there can be significant discrepancies between implied and realized volatility for any given option and underlying security.

Since an option's price is directly related to the implied volatility input into a pricing model, implied volatility itself can be a useful relative value metric when evaluating a position. In the case of most fixed-income options, interest rate volatility is typically measured assuming it is normally distributed and is represented in terms of basis points per day (or annum). This is different from other markets, such as equities, where options are usually traded on a log normal, or percentage volatility, basis. This was not always true, but since interest rates persisted at very low levels for a long time and in some markets actually became negative, the normal distribution became a useful analytical assumption.

Annualized Vol		8/19/16	US Implied Vol						
		Tenor							
		1Y	**2Y**	**5Y**	**7Y**	**10Y**	**15Y**	**20Y**	**30Y**
Term	**1M**	40.1	52.0	65.4	65.6	65.6	64.7	63.9	63.2
	3M	43.0	55.3	70.1	71.1	71.6	71.2	70.9	70.3
	6M	48.5	57.5	71.8	72.9	73.6	73.2	72.6	72.1
	1Y	54.6	62.5	74.6	76.0	77.0	76.1	75.2	74.5
	2Y	66.4	69.6	77.3	78.6	79.6	77.9	76.2	75.1
	3Y	73.7	75.1	79.4	79.8	80.4	77.8	75.5	73.9
	5Y	82.0	81.5	81.8	81.2	80.4	75.8	73.0	71.0
	7Y	81.9	81.4	80.7	79.7	78.1	72.9	69.7	68.0
	10Y	78.6	78.5	77.4	76.1	74.0	68.6	65.5	63.8

EXHIBIT 2.8 At-the-Money Implied Rate Volatility Surface (in Normal BP)
Source: BlackRock. For illustrative purposes only.

Interest rate optionality is predominantly traded in two forms, on government rates (i.e., treasuries and exchange-traded futures on treasuries), or on swap rates, also known as swaptions. Examples of options strategies include the following:

- Introducing a directional exposure conditionally by buying interest rate calls to express a long duration view with limited downside
- Enhancing yield in a portfolio by selling a strangle (range trade) on a particular point on the forward curve
- Seeking relative value alpha by buying or selling two volatility points against each other

Exhibit 2.9 demonstrates both the long straddle payout and the long strangle payout. Portfolio managers may seek to capture the combined premia of both options and execute a long straddle strategy, where the portfolio manager is long both the call and the put at the same strike prices. Alternatively, a long strangle strategy is long both a call and put at different strike prices. Both of these strategies generate improved performance when either markets have a directional move through strike, or implied volatility increases, which impacts the option's value.

Besides implied volatility, other factors must be considered across multiple dimensions when deciding which options to purchase. These include the underlying itself, expiry, moneyness, and cross-section relative value. A call option is out-of-the money (OTM) if its underlying price is below the strike price but is considered in-the-money (ITM) if the underlying price is above the strike price. On the other hand, a put option is OTM if its underlying price is above the strike price and is deemed ITM if the underlying price is below the strike price. When establishing an options position, portfolio managers often consider its breakeven point. This is the level the underlying securities need to move in order to capture the premium spent (or taken in, depending on direction).

When managing the risk associated with options, a portfolio manager will often seek to isolate the volatility metric as the basis of relative value. However, not all volatilities across the surface are the same.

The Greek terms delta, gamma, vega, and theta are often used to describe options exposure. Delta is related to duration and represents the sensitivity of an option's price to changes to the underlying price. Gamma, on the other hand, covers an option's convexity and includes the sensitivity of an option's delta to changes in the price of the underlying instrument.

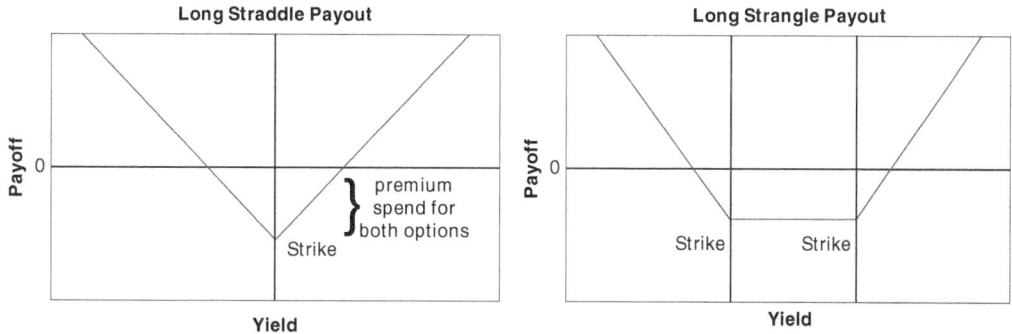

EXHIBIT 2.9 Long Straddle Payout Versus Long Strangle Payout
Source: For illustrative purposes only.

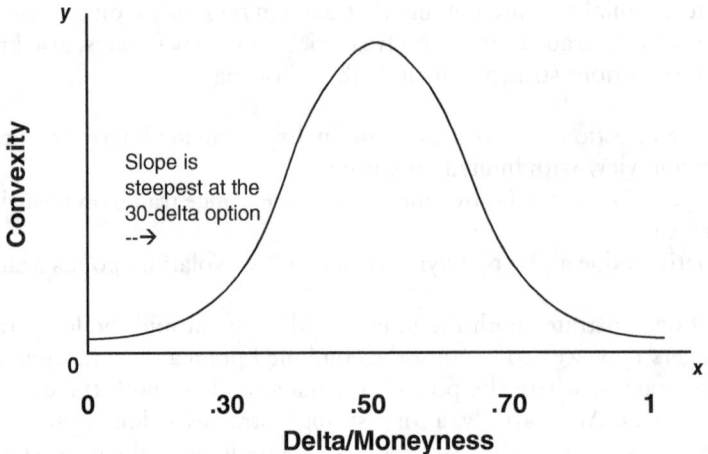

EXHIBIT 2.10   Gamma Versus Delta
Source: For illustrative purposes only.

Convexity is highest for 50-delta options and increases as it nears expiry. Vega is a measure of an option price's sensitivity to changes in volatility, specifically implied volatility, which is the input into an option pricing model. Longer options tend to exhibit greater exposure to volatility risk. Theta, or time decay, is the change in an option's price with respect to time. All things equal, the shorter the tenor of the option, the faster it decays.

As illustrated in Exhibit 2.10, there is an interplay between gamma, vega, and theta. Gamma and vega are both "volatility sensitive" exposures, but the shorter an option gets (i.e., as it ages), it takes on greater exposure, or sensitivity, to gamma (movements in the under-lying) and less to vega (sensitivity to movements in the level of implied volatility). Portfolio managers view the "split point" between gamma and vega differently, depending on which sector they are trading. Nevertheless, when managing a portfolio of options, it is important to be aware of how these risk metrics change as an option gets closer to maturity. Interest rate swaptions are typically initiated off a forward yield point, which will converge to spot upon expiry.

Finally, volatility "skew" is the third dimension of risk associated with options, in addition to tenor (or tail) and term (maturity). A term-tenor pairing is typically quoted for swaptions. For example, the 1-year-10-year swaption straddle represents a 1-year maturity option struck on the 1-year forward 10-year swap rate constructed with both a call and a put. The implied volatility of that structure would generically be based upon that forward interest rate, also known as ATM volatility. As previously illustrated in Exhibit 2.8, the two-dimensional volatility surface represents all ATM options, where puts and calls take on the same volatility level (as to preserve put/call parity), which are struck on their respective forward curve points. Volatility skew is the differential between implied volatilities for the same maturity option at different strikes. This is the third dimension of the volatility surface (the "depth" of a discrete pairing of time and tenor), as illustrated in Exhibit 2.11. Implied volatilities not only vary depending on what they are on and when they expire, but also where on the spectrum of yields they are, relative to the ATM-forward yield.

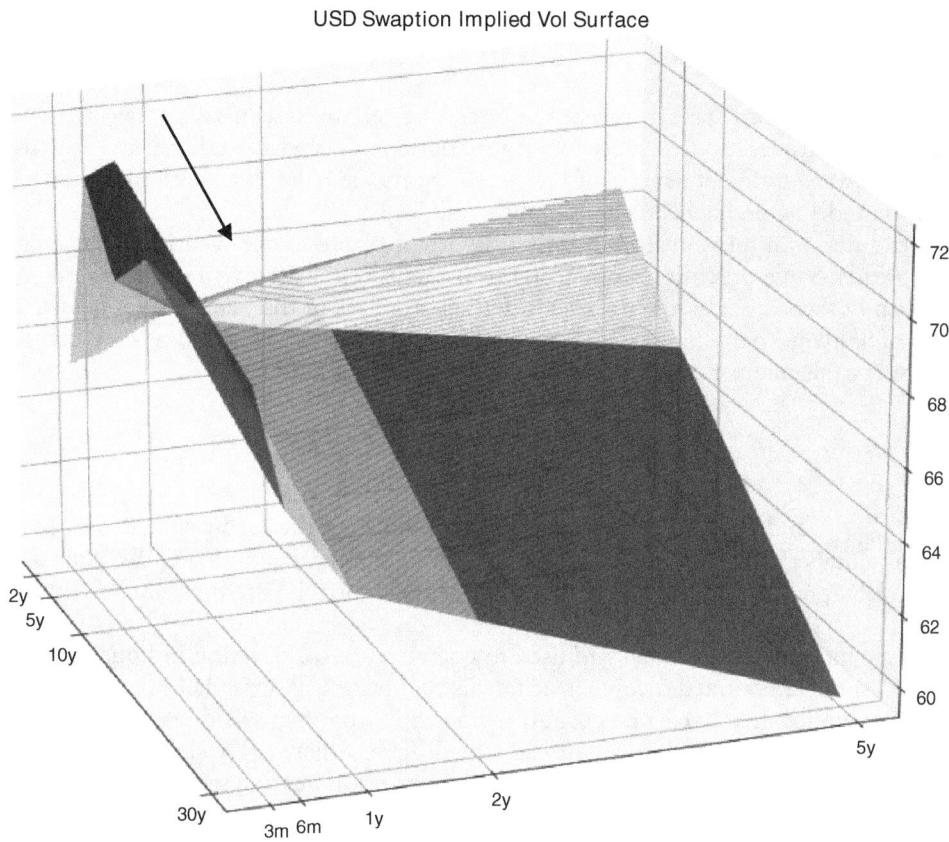

USD Swaption Implied Vol Surface

EXHIBIT 2.11 Adding Skew
Source: BlackRock, January 31, 2020. For illustrative purposes only.

This dynamic of skew exists because the market anticipates realized volatility to be different at different levels of rates. As a consequence, implied volatility is priced differently across yield points, even for the same option maturity. In addition to the spot-vs-forward dynamic of pricing an option, an option position will "roll" down the term structure of volatility as it ages.

2.6 MEASURING CREDIT RISK

2.6.1 Spread Duration

Repeated credit and liquidity crises have clearly demonstrated the extreme importance of understanding the risk associated with systematic movements of credit spreads. As discussed in Section 2.2.2, credit spreads (as measured by option-adjusted spreads or nominal spreads) incorporate several distinct components, including:

- the market's sentiment toward credit risk in general;
- asset class-, issuer-, and individual security-specific credit risk;

- market supply-and-demand conditions; and
- valuation model inaccuracies.

For instance, swap spreads reflect the price of interbank credit risk as well as numerous technical considerations, whereas mortgage option-adjusted spreads reflect the market's sentiment toward different aspects of systematic mortgage risks as well as uncertainty with respect to modeling prepayments and implied volatility.

Spread duration measures the price sensitivity of fixed-income securities to changes in credit spreads. Some practitioners interpret it as the price sensitivity to changes in discount factors, and others see it as the price sensitivity to changes in the market sentiment toward the risk of holding a particular asset class or individual security. Spread duration is computed in the exact same manner as other option-adjusted partial durations:

$$Spd\ Dur = -\frac{1}{P}\frac{P_{spread\ up} - P_{spread\ down}}{2 \cdot \Delta s} \tag{2.41}$$

where $P_{spread\ up}$ and $P_{spread\ down}$ are computed by shocking the credit spread of a security by a small number of basis points (Δs) and computing the corresponding OAVs using a valuation model. Spread durations of securities in a sample portfolio are presented in Tables 2.1 and 2.5.

The definition of the term *spread* used to compute spread duration in Equation 2.41 is asset-class specific. For fixed-income instruments that trade at a spread above a US Treasury benchmark (option-free fixed rate corporate bonds, CMBS, high yield, etc.), *spread* is typically defined as the nominal credit spread (the difference between yield-to-maturity of an instrument and that of its Treasury benchmark). For option-bearing securities valued on the US Treasury curve (MBSs and their derivatives, callable corporate and agency bonds, etc.), *spread* is defined as OAS. For interest rate swaps and their derivatives, *spread* is defined as swap spread. Sometimes market participants choose to calculate spread duration even on US Treasury securities. In this context, spread duration measures the price sensitivity to changes in liquidity premia (OASs) in the US Treasury market.

For a fixed-income security with deterministic cash flows, spread duration is typically close in value to OAD since shocking nominal spread or OAS is virtually equivalent to shocking the spot curve in a parallel fashion. The slight discrepancy between the two measures in these cases is generally caused by the different market conventions with respect to magnitude and compounding of the shocks utilized in option-adjusted duration versus spread duration calculations. Conversely, for fixed-income securities with interest-rate-correlated cash flow uncertainties (e.g., adjustable rate mortgages, floating rate notes, structured notes, IO, PO), spread durations may be substantially different from OADs. While spread duration estimates the price sensitivity to changes in discounting alone, OAD measures the simultaneous price sensitivity to changes in discounting as well as changes in cash flows due to interest rate movements.

Similar to other partial duration measures, it is a common practice to compute spread duration of a fixed-income portfolio as a weighted average of spread durations of the individual securities without questioning the meaning of this aggregate measure. However, the similarity of spread duration to other partial durations is deceiving. As opposed to OADs, KRDs, and other parametric gauges that measure price sensitivity to systematic risk factors that are *universally* applicable to *all* fixed-income securities, spread duration measures the exposure to risk factors that are partially systematic and partially idiosyncratic (asset class, issuer-, or security-specific). For instance, the value of a portfolio invested in US Treasuries, swaps, and MBSs is sensitive to changes in a variety of basis risks: liquidity premia of the US Treasury market, swap spreads, and mortgage spreads, etc. Since these risk factors may not be perfectly correlated and may exhibit drastically different volatilities, exposures to them must be managed separately rather than aggregated into a summarized number. This reality complicates the task of managing credit spread risk of fixed-income portfolios. DxS- and VaR-related metrics attempt to address these limitations.

2.6.2 Duration Times Spread (DxS)[30]

Traditionally, credit risk was largely managed from a rating agency perspective. Hence, credit spread risk had mostly been modeled using a rating-based approach where rating-based spread risk factors were constructed to measure spread movements per rating cohort, with spread duration as exposures. The market turmoil experienced during the Global Financial Crisis, the European Sovereign Crisis, and others have highlighted yet again the limitations of the rating approach and led to alternative modeling mechanisms that are more robust to changing market regimes. The duration times spread (DxS) model, proposed by Ben Dor et al. (2007), has helped to provide a new framework, which has now become the new standard for spread risk management.

Essentially, the DxS approach models the spread movements in a relative fashion. Let R_{spread} denote the spread return of a security and D denote the spread duration and OAS denote option-adjusted spread.

The spread return can be approximated as:

$$R_{spread} = -D \cdot \Delta \text{OAS} \tag{2.42}$$

which can be rewritten as:

$$R_{spread} = -\underbrace{D \cdot \text{OAS}} \cdot \frac{\Delta \text{OAS}}{\text{OAS}} \text{DxS} \tag{2.43}$$

Hence, just as spread duration is the sensitivity to absolute spread change, DxS is the sensitivity to relative spread change. That means that spread volatility is approximated as follows:

$$\sigma_{spread\ return\ vol} \cong \text{DxS} \cdot \sigma_{relative\ spread\ change\ vol} \tag{2.44}$$

The reason why DxS is far superior than the traditional spread duration measure is that, empirically, spreads tend to move in proportion to spread levels. This empirical behavior has been shown to hold surprisingly well over different market regimes and across various market segments. The modeling implications are that relative spread volatilities are more stable than absolute spread volatilities, which makes the job of volatility prediction much easier.

In addition, DxS-based return volatility forecasts combine the stability of relative spread with the more responsive and forward-looking spread level. In detail, spread volatility is modeled as follows:

$$\sigma_{spread} \cong \text{OAS} \cdot \sigma_{relative\ spread\ change\ vol} \tag{2.45}$$

The incorporation of spread information allows the volatility forecast to better reflect cross-sectional differences of spread levels and adjust more quickly to changing market conditions.

DxS works very well for most spread products. However, the linear relationship between spread volatility and spread level tend to break down at very low and very high spread levels, or when spread movements are not credit related (e.g., for mortgage pass-throughs, spread movements are related to prepayment risk instead of credit risk). At very low spread levels, isolating the contribution of the pure credit component from other non-credit components due to illiquidity or mispricing is very hard. Spread volatility tends to flatten out as spread falls below a certain level. Hence, while relative spread becomes unstable, using absolute spread becomes more appropriate. At very high spread levels, securities are "distressed" and they trade on price based on investors' default/recovery projections. In this context, the spread is not very meaningful.

2.7   MEASURING MORTGAGE-RELATED RISKS

In this section, we digress from describing approaches dealing with universal risk factors and focus on systematic sources of market risk that are specific to mortgage-backed securities (MBSs) and their derivatives. Several approaches exist for measuring the exposure of portfolios and securities to prepayments and other mortgage-related risks. Similar to the measures of interest rate and yield curve risk described earlier in this chapter, all of these methods utilize partial durations to estimate the first-order price sensitivity to a given risk factor in isolation, while holding other variables unchanged.

2.7.1   Prepayment Duration

The homeowner's decision to prepay their home mortgage is typically influenced by various economic and borrower-specific variables and considerations, including the prevailing mortgage origination rates, the borrower's mortgage rate, the size of the mortgage loan, the aggressiveness of the servicing entity, the credit score of the borrower, the loan-to-value of the borrower, the origination channel of the borrower (broker originated loans can prepay much faster), the state of the domestic economy, and in particular recent housing market performance. Given that econometric prepayment models attempt to model the sum of the individual decisions by millions of consumers, it is not surprising that they often fail to accurately predict the homeowner's prepayment behavior. Since fair values and risk measures of MBSs and their derivatives depend on prepayment models or assumed static vectors of prepayment speeds, the accuracy of these analytical methodologies is subject to the model's risk that forecasts of future prepayments are materially wrong.

Prepayment duration measures the risk associated with prepayment speeds being systematically slower or faster than those predicted by the user-specified or econometric prepayment model. Computed within the option-adjusted framework, prepayment duration is obtained via the standard duration formula:

$$Prepay\ Dur = -\frac{1}{P}\frac{P_{speeds\ up} - P_{speeds\ down}}{2 \cdot \Delta speeds} \tag{2.46}$$

where $P_{speeds\ up}$ and $P_{speeds\ down}$ require an agreed upon prepayment shock ($\Delta speeds$). One simple approach to computing prepayment duration is to scale the output of a prepayment model up and down by 25% and directly recompute the corresponding OAVs. Prepayment durations of generic 30-year MBSs are presented in Table 2.5. For example, the prepayment duration of a UMBS 3.5% is 3.54. Higher prepayment durations mean that higher prepayment rates will cause the UMBS 3.5% to fall in value. Faster prepayment speeds negatively impact premium and positively impact discount MBSs. The first part of this statement is consistent with Table 2.5, which shows that on 1/31/2020, UMBS and Ginnie Mae have positive prepayment durations. It may seem counterintuitive that prepayment duration for slightly discount MBS (4%) is slightly positive rather than negative, for example, the FNMA 3.5%. This phenomenon can be explained by closely examining the Monte Carlo simulation model used in computing OAVs of MBSs. Recall that the fair value of an MBS is computed by creating a large number of hypothetical interest rate paths. For each path, cash flows are generated using a prepayment model and subsequently discounted on the appropriate (path-specific) spot curve. OAV is the average of all pathwise prices. While almost all pathwise prices of premium mortgages are above par (implying negative sensitivity to prepayments), some of the pathwise prices of discount mortgages are positive and some are negative. This asymmetry results in prepayment duration being sometimes slightly positive for discount MBS coupons.[31]

2.7.2 Mortgage/Treasury Basis Duration

Mortgage/treasury basis (MTB) duration uses a different approach to measuring prepayment risk. As opposed to prepayment duration that estimates the first-order price sensitivity to changes in prepayment speeds as predicted by a prepayment model, MTB duration addresses the borrower's decision to prepay directly. MTB duration estimates the price sensitivity of MBSs to changes in one of the most influential causes of prepayments—the refinancing incentive measured as the spread between the current mortgage origination rate and the 10-year OTR Treasury rate. Description of prepayment risk in terms of spreads to Treasury rates as opposed to nominal mortgage origination rates is due to technical rather than conceptual reasons. Since MTB is an input to many of the existing econometric prepayment models, it is natural to use it in defining the prepayment sensitivity.

Formally, MTB is defined as the spread between the par coupon yield of a conventional (FNMA or FHLMC) MBS and that of the 10-year on-the-run TSY. Par coupon yield is the yield of a theoretical MBS priced at parity. Parity, in turn, is the price that implies the same yield regardless of prepayments while accounting for the MBS payment delay. MTB duration is computed by shifting this spread up and down by a small number of basis points and calculating the negative of the percentage change in price, given a 100 basis point change in the mortgage/treasury basis:

$$MTB\ Dur = -\frac{1}{P}\frac{P_{MTB\ up} - P_{MTB\ down}}{2 \cdot \Delta MTB} \tag{2.47}$$

MTB durations of 30-year generic MBSs are presented in Table 2.5.

It may seem counterintuitive that, as opposed to prepayment durations, which switch the sign approximately near the par coupon mortgage, MTB durations of both premium and discount securities are negative (Table 2.5). This analytical result, which seems inconsistent with the theory that faster prepayment speeds negatively impact premium and positively impact discount MBSs, can be explained by exactly the same analysis of Monte Carlo simulation of interest rate processes as described in Section 2.7.1. The dissimilarity between the two prepayment-related risk factors (MTB duration is more asymmetric than prepayment duration) is due to prepayment duration capturing both the refinancing incentive and prepayments due to housing turnover, whereas MTB duration only addresses the former component. In addition to that, prepayment speeds are shocked directly in the prepayment duration calculation, whereas they are shocked indirectly when MTB is perturbed. The combination of these two effects results in the nonlinear and asymmetric price sensitivity to prepayments. More specifically, MTB duration becomes positive only for discount MBSs whose prepayment options are extremely deep OTM. MTB duration is mostly used for considering hedging of higher coupon MBS, as trading higher coupon OAS requires positioning in the par coupon(s) to hedge the mortgage rate exposure.

2.8   MEASURING IMPACT OF TIME

Changes in prices of fixed-income securities due to their passage through time $\left(\frac{\partial P}{\partial t}\right)$ can be measured using the horizon rate of return (HROR) framework. As an explicit gauge of *ex ante* total return, HROR is an example of a methodology equally advantageous for portfolio management, risk management, and trading. The art of active portfolio management lies in finding optimal trade-offs between risk, return, and various market- and portfolio-specific constraints. As seen from the description of the different risk measures earlier in this chapter, the *risk* aspect of investment decisions is typically approached from a very quantitative angle. In trading, horizon rate of return can be combined with subjective judgments about richness and cheapness of individual securities or entire sectors when making relative value decisions. In risk management, HROR enables incorporating evolution of securities through time into hedge optimizations.

The idea behind HROR is simple. When holding a security over a specified *horizon,* its total return is determined by the following:

- Its current market value
- Its fair value at the horizon date
- The future value of cash flows that are generated by this security over the holding period and are available for reinvestment

HROR is computed using the following formula:

$$HROR = \frac{MV_{horizon} - MV_{today} + Future\ Value\ of\ Cash\ Flows\ at\ Horizon}{MV_{today}} \tag{2.48}$$

where MV denotes market value.

Despite its seeming "objectivity," HROR incorporates a great deal of subjective judgment and views on the market. It is also sensitive to interest rate and prepayment models used to compute the fair value of a security. Let us examine the assumptions underlying the HROR analysis in detail. To determine the fair market value ($MV_{horizon}$) of a security at the horizon (Equation 2.48), the future economic environment, including yield curves, mortgage rates, implied volatilities, and so forth, must be specified, reflecting the user's intuition and views on the market. There are three alternative formulations of HROR—*forward, constant,* and *hypothetical.* The *forward* approach uses the *pure expectation hypothesis* to assume that interest rates between the valuation date and the horizon date evolve as predicted by forward rates. The *constant* method presumes that the economic environment at the horizon is exactly the same as it is today. While the *forward* approach is consistent with the assumption used by the vast majority of valuation models, empirical analyses of historical interest rate movements support the *constant* assumption rather than the pure expectation hypothesis.[32] Various theoretical models (e.g., Heath-Jarrow-Morton, 1992) validate this empirical finding as well, demonstrating theoretically that the conjecture that forward rates are unbiased estimates of future spot rates is generally false. Without going into further detail, it suffices to note that when faced with the choice between the two assumptions, the majority of practitioners prefer the *constant* assumption to the *forward* one. Besides being more historically plausible, the *constant* assumption is very useful and intuitive for market participants because it measures the return of securities associated with aging or "rolling down the yield curve." Finally, the *hypothetical* approach—a way for portfolio managers to explore various what-if market scenarios and their impact on total return—can best be thought of as a potentially highly granular generalized form of interest rate scenario analysis. Thus, in addition to measuring the impact of time, evolution of credit spreads, interest rates, prepayments, implied volatilities, and other risk factors between the valuation date and the horizon date can be hypothesized, and the combined effect on price can be measured. Once the economic environment at the horizon is determined, the path according to which the economy evolves between the date of the analysis and the horizon date needs to be specified. Despite its seeming simplicity, this is not a trivial exercise. However, this step is crucial because values of path-dependent securities as well as values of reinvested cash flows depend on the evolution of interest rates between the valuation date and the horizon. This path has to also be consistent with the assumed economic environment at the horizon. For instance, consider the following HROR scenario:

- at the horizon, interest rates are 100 basis points higher than they are on the valuation date; and
- between the valuation and the horizon dates, interest rates evolve according to forward rates.

This scenario will be inconsistent unless forward rates just so happen to imply that spot rates are exactly 100 basis points higher at the horizon than they are today. Table 2.7 presents HROR scenario analysis of securities in a sample portfolio.

HROR scenario analysis has clear advantages over simplistic, *instantaneous* interest rate scenario analysis. Both approaches provide reasonably comparable results for cases where roll down and option decay are relatively modest. This would be the case for securities with embedded longer-tenor options. However, instantaneous shocks in exposure factors can create material financial illusions. Performing large instantaneous shocks on instruments with embedded shorter-term options (which are characterized by rapid decay)[33] will ignore the option decay and make "lottery ticket" positions look much better than they really are.

The ability to capture the cost of carry as well as the time-dependent nature of risk characteristics can provide valuable insights into the price behavior of fixed-income securities. Table 2.8 presents the OAV of a 6-months call option on a 10-year interest rate swap as a function of both parallel changes in spot rates and time. As the swaption approaches its expiration, the decline in its base OAV (*negative carry*) reflects the progressively lower probability of large interest rate movements between the horizon date and the expiration date and, hence, a lower upside from holding this security. Thus, with 6 months until expiration, gains

TABLE 2.7 HROR Scenario Analysis for the Sample Portfolio (as of 1/31/2020)

Security Description	Coupon	Maturity	Strike	HROR Scenario Analysis (% per year)							
				−150	−100	−50	0	50	100	150	
Treasury Bonds											
OTR 2YR 2	1.375	1/31/2022		1.14%	1.14%	1.14%	1.31%	1.82%	2.32%	2.82%	
OTR 5YR 5	1.375	1/31/2025		1.00%	1.00%	1.00%	1.63%	2.13%	2.63%	3.14%	
OTR 10YR 10	1.75	11/15/2029		0.88%	0.88%	1.47%	1.96%	2.46%	2.95%	3.45%	
OTR 30YR 30	2.375	11/15/2049		1.10%	1.55%	2.00%	2.46%	2.92%	3.38%	3.83%	
Treasury Futures											
US 10YR NOTE MAR 20 TY 20-MAR-2020		3/20/2020		0.67%	0.67%	0.67%	1.18%	1.24%	1.30%	1.35%	
US LONG BOND MAR 20 US 20-MAR-2020		3/20/2020		0.62%	0.94%	1.45%	1.66%	1.70%	1.75%	1.79%	
Callable Agency Bonds											
FHLB 2.0 20-FEB-2025	2.00	2/20/2025		0.60%	0.60%	0.60%	0.74%	1.18%	1.64%	2.80%	
Option on Future											
MAR20 TUH0 C @ 106.25 TU 21-FEB-2020		2/21/2020	106.25	2.39%	2.39%	2.39%	3.47%	8.38%	−75.80%	−200.00%	
Interest Rate Swap											
SWP: USD 3.167500 09-SEP-2023 IRS	3.17	7/9/2023		0.00%	0.00%	0.00%	0.00%	0.03%	0.04%	0.04%	
German Government Bond Future											
EURO-BUND MAR 20 RX 06-MAR-2020		3/6/2020		0.44%	0.44%	0.44%	0.29%	0.34%	0.39%	0.45%	
IG Credit											
AMERICAN EXPRESS COMPANY T2 3.625 05-DEC-2024 (SUB)	3.63	12/5/2024		1.55%	1.55%	1.55%	2.10%	2.60%	3.10%	3.60%	

HY Credit NINE ENERGY SERVICE INC 8.75 01-NOV-2023 144a (SENIOR)	8.75	11/1/2023	13.33%	13.33%	13.33%	13.62%	14.12%	14.62%	15.12%
Agency MBS UMBS 30YR TBA CASH 4.0	4.00	4/25/2049	0.81%	0.80%	0.80%	1.10%	1.69%	2.34%	2.92%
Agency CMBS GNMA_16-113-IO 1.1524 16-FEB-2058	1.15	2/16/2058	2.74%	2.74%	2.84%	3.20%	3.65%	4.09%	4.53%
Non-Agency CMBS JPMBB_14-C22-XA 0.83511 15-SEP-2047	0.84	7/15/2047	1.58%	1.58%	1.58%	1.81%	2.25%	2.68%	3.11%
ABS Credit Card NDFT_17-1-C 2.15338 15-JUL-2025 Reg-S	2.56	7/15/2020	0.73%	0.73%	0.79%	0.79%	1.01%	1.24%	1.46%
Non-Agency MBS ALM_15-16A-A2R 3.33125 15-JUL-2027 144a	3.33	4/15/2024	1.82%	1.82%	1.82%	2.14%	2.64%	3.14%	3.65%
Total	2.83								

Source: BlackRock Aladdin, January 31, 2020.

TABLE 2.8 HROR Scenario Analysis of a 1.47% 6M x 10-Year Right-to-Receive Swaption (as of 1/31/2020)

Time to Expiration	Option-Adjusted Value (Thousands of Dollars)								
	−150	−100	−50	−25	0	25	50	100	150
6 Months	14,395	9,322	4,726	2,927	1,600	754	300	27	1
5 Months	14,414	9,321	4,641	2,795	1,453	632	224	14	0
4 Months	14,432	9,324	4,553	2,649	1,288	502	151	6	0
3 Months	14,448	9,332	4,464	2,480	1,092	357	82	1	0
2 Months	14,456	9,338	4,383	2,291	863	209	29	0	0
1 Month	14,460	9,344	4,325	2,066	555	61	2	0	0
1 Day	14,460	9,345	4,317	1,898	14	0	0	0	0

Time to Expiration	Change in Option-Adjusted Value (Thousands of Dollars)								
	−150	−100	−50	−25	0	25	50	100	150
6 Months	12,795	7,722	3,126	1,328	0	−846	−1,300	−1,573	−1,599
5 Months	12,815	7,721	3,041	1,195	−147	−968	−1,375	−1,586	−1,600
4 Months	12,832	7,725	2,953	1,049	−312	−1,098	−1,449	−1,594	−1,600
3 Months	12,848	7,732	2,864	880	−508	−1,243	−1,518	−1,599	−1,600
2 Months	12,856	7,739	2,783	691	−736	−1,391	−1,570	−1,600	−1,600
1 Month	12,860	7,744	2,726	466	−1,044	−1,539	−1,598	−1,600	−1,600
1 Day	12,860	7,746	2,717	298	−1,585	−1,600	−1,600	−1,600	−1,600

Source: BlackRock Aladdin, January 31, 2020.

TABLE 2.9 Interest Rate Shocks Exceeding Given Thresholds: Cumulative Probability as a Function of Time (as of 1/31/2020)

Time to Expiration	Parallel Spot Curve Shock			
	+/−25	+/−50	+/−100	+/−150
1 Year	76%	54%	22%	7%
6 Months	67%	39%	9%	1%
3 Months	54%	22%	1%	0%
2 Months	46%	14%	0%	0%
1 Month	29%	4%	0%	0%
1 Week	3%	0%	0%	0%

Source: BlackRock Aladdin, January 31, 2020.

corresponding to a sudden 25 basis point decline in interest rates are greater in magnitude than losses corresponding to a 25 basis point rise in interest rates. At this time, the probability of interest rates moving in either direction by 25 basis points or more is approximately 67% with a time horizon of 6 months (Table 2.9).[34] The probability of interest rates moving in either direction by 25 basis points or more in a 1-month time frame is 29%.

NOTES

1. Matthew Wang significantly updated this chapter to incorporate more recent risk management approaches and concepts. Yury Krongauz enhanced the Key Rate Duration section by providing additional details on wave shocks (Section 2.4.1). Jack Hattem authored the section on Option Usage in Portfolio Management (Section 2.5.2). Additionally, David Greenberg authored the section on Duration Times Spread (Section 2.6.2). Finally, Stephen Henry-Rerrie helped to update the charts and graphs included in this chapter.
2. *Interest rates* can be defined in many different ways, including yield-to-maturity (if they can be meaningfully computed), parallel movements of the term structure of spot rates, etc. For the purposes of this discussion, price dependencies on parallel changes in interest rates are used to illustrate the shapes of price/yield functions.
3. For illustrative purposes, a 30-year Treasury was modeled.
4. See Macaulay, 1938, and Weil, 1973.
5. See Fabozzi, 1988.
6. In this book, the terms *price volatility* and *volatility of prices* are used interchangeably.
7. This interesting observation was pointed out to us by our former colleague Irwin Sheer.
8. It has become customary to say "10 years" when referring to duration of 10. This is due to the fact that the first measure of duration, Macaulay duration, was interpreted as the present value-weighted *term-to-maturity*.
9. For an excellent review of different types of yield curves, see Ilmanen, 1995, and Anderson et al., 1997.
10. Zero volatility spread is a special case of OAS discussed in detail in Section 2.2.2. The abbreviation ZV0 is due to the fact that zero volatility spread is often referred to as *zero volatility option-adjusted spread*.
11. For an overview of OAS models, the reader is referred to the chapter by Audey et al., 1995, as well as Chapters 29 and 30 in Fabozzi, 1995a.
12. See Black and Scholes, 1973.
13. See Kao, 1999.

14. This purely technical phenomenon is due to the widely used practice of hedging the primary issuance of spread products with on-the-run Treasury securities as well as to the use of OTR TSY in implementing directional interest rate bets.

15. Throughout the book, unless stated otherwise, OASs are assumed to be continuously compounded and computed off of spot curves. Note that OAS numbers are sensitive to the methods by which spot curves are constructed as well as to the compounding conventions.

16. With respect to spread-sensitive securities, their price sensitivity to Treasury rates (OAD) should be distinguished from price sensitivity to credit spreads as measured by spread duration (Section 2.6.1). For instance, a floating rate note that resets on a quarterly basis has a large sensitivity to credit spreads and a very small sensitivity to Treasury rates.

17. See Kao, 1999.

18. We would like to thank our former colleague Pavan Wadhwa for his help with this section.

19. Carry is the total expected yield (or return) associated with holding a position. Carry incorporates the net coupon, the impact of time, and the cost of financing.

20. Because of fixed-income markets' conventions of reporting duration and convexity, the actual computations in Table 2.3 use the following formula for duration drift: OAD $Drift = \frac{1}{100} \cdot$ (OAC $\cdot$ 100 − OAD^2) = OAC − $\frac{OAD^2}{100}$.

21. Obviously, practitioners need to use their judgment regarding their proposed range of shocks. Certainly, the plausibility of a shock to a given yield curve is not independent from the current level of the yield curve.

22. More advanced and generalized Market-Driven Scenario analysis is discussed in Chapter 5. These scenarios allow numerous variables, such as OAS, to be perturbed along with yield curves.

23. The distinct naming of FNMA and FHLMC mortgage securities was removed with UMBS.

24. See Breeden, 1994.

25. We would like to thank our former colleague Yury Geyman and colleague Yury Krongauz for their contributions to the sections on KRDs.

26. Empirical studies indicate that OAD-neutral yield curve trades are not always entirely insensitive to the directional interest rate movements because parallel shocks can be correlated with various yield curve spreads in certain market environments. In order to eliminate sensitivity to directional market movements more effectively, yield curve trades should be constructed using the first principal component duration as opposed to OAD.

27. See Reitano, 1990, and Ho, 1992.

28. Δr is typically between 20 and 50 basis points.

29. Thank you to Jack Hattem for authoring this section.

30. Thank you to David Greenberg for authoring this section.

31. Investigation of this interesting property of prepayment duration came from our former colleagues Adam Wizon and Irwin Sheer.

32. See Ilmanen, 1995–1996.

33. Tables 2.8 and 2.9 as well as some of the conclusions in this section are based on research by Bill De Leon and Ben Golub.

34. Probability distributions of interest rate shocks were used to compute cumulative probabilities in Table 2.9.

CHAPTER 3

Modeling Yield Curve Dynamics[1,2]

Bennett W. Golub
Senior Advisor, BlackRock

Leo M. Tilman
CEO, Tilman & Company

3.1 PROBABILITY DISTRIBUTIONS OF SYSTEMATIC RISK FACTORS

Changes in default-free interest rates are among the most influential forces affecting prices of fixed-income securities. Fixed-income risk management therefore must be highly concerned with analyzing, understanding, and forecasting yield curve movements. This chapter continues to focus on the first pillar, *ex ante risk measurement*. For simplicity and without loss of generality, this section limits the set of systematic risk factors to those representing interest rates, thus ignoring basis relationships and currency risks. Without substantial methodological changes, the majority of results presented here can be extended to include additional systematic risk factors. For reasons that will be apparent momentarily, this chapter will assume that interest rate movements are described by fluctuations of spot curves and so will use the terms *yield curve* and *spot curve* interchangeably.

When estimating fair values of fixed-income securities, valuation models use spot curves to compute present values of expected future payoffs (Equation 2.17). Different types of spot curves and methods by which they are constructed correspond to a variety of market conventions that assign the appropriate spot curve for each asset class. For instance, US Treasury securities, futures and options on US Treasury securities, agency bonds, and corporate and mortgage-backed securities use the spot curve constructed from the US Treasury market. On the other hand, dollar-denominated interest rate derivatives, including swaps, swaptions, and interest rate caps and floors are usually valued on the spot curve bootstrapped from the markets linked to interbank lending rates or their successors, such as the Secured Overnight Financing Rate (SOFR). Since generalized pricing models need to be able to discount cash flows over a wide range of maturities, representing spot curves as continuous functions is convenient.[3] However, such continuous representations seriously complicate the task of modeling yield curve dynamics, especially using statistical methods. To describe spot curve movements in a simpler and more intuitive setting, spot curves can be *discretized,* and their movements can be represented as vectors of changes of selected points, that is, *key rates* (see Section 2.4.1).

Deterministic measures of interest rate exposure estimate the potential gains or losses resulting from hypothetical what-if interest rate scenarios:

- Option-adjusted duration (OAD) estimates the price sensitivity to small parallel spot curve movements.
- Interest rate scenario analysis calculates price as a function of parallel changes in the spot curve.
- Key rate durations (KRDs) measure the price sensitivity to nonparallel changes in the spot curve.

As an important extension of nonstochastic risk methodologies described in Chapter 2, statistical measures of risk synthesize information about market exposures with assumptions about the probability distributions of systematic risk factors. Of course, this entails the specification of the functional form of these probability distributions and the statistical estimation of their parameters. Recall that when computing fair values of fixed-income securities, valuation models use stochastic processes to describe the evolution of interest rates[4] over time. Some of the earlier interest rate models (e.g., Ho-Lee, Hull-White) presumed changes in interest rates to be normally distributed. Since this assumption may cause interest rates to become negative under certain interest rate scenarios, the next generation of interest rate models (e.g., Black-Derman-Toy, Black-Karasinski) eliminated the possibility of negative interest rates by defining the probability distribution of changes in interest rates as log-normal, at the cost of analytical tractability and absence of volatility skew observed in the markets. Then, global monetary policy chose to make a lie out of the non-negativity assumption, and interest rates fell to near zero and even to negative interest rates, particularly in European markets. This lets us revert to use the normality assumption for interest rates without too many apologies.

In contrast to valuation models that need to project interest rates over the entire life of a fixed-income security in order to compute the mathematical expectation of discounted future payoffs, fixed-income market risk management typically deals with much shorter horizons, for example, 1 day, 1 month, or 1 year. Similar to earlier interest rate models, it is often *analytically convenient* to assume for risk management purposes that changes in systematic risk factors are random variables that follow a joint multivariate normal distribution.[5] Consistent with the majority of interest rate models that presume interest rates to be mean-reverting, risk management typically postulates that the *population mean of changes in systematic risk factors is zero,* ignoring the actual sample mean of the data series that may be reflective of the recent market trends, if any.[6] However, while accurately modeling the business-as-usual part of the empirical probability distributions of interest rates, basis risk factors, and currencies, normal (and, for that matter, log-normal) distributions do not capture the *fat tails* present in the distributions of many financial time series. *From now on, unless stated otherwise, future changes in systematic risk factors are assumed to jointly follow a multivariate normal distribution with zero mean.* To fully define such a distribution, correlations and volatilities (or, equivalently, the covariance matrix) of changes in systematic risk factors need to be statistically estimated from the historical data. In this chapter, the set of risk factors will be limited to the set of key spot rates. Table 3.1 presents correlations and volatilities from Aladdin, which uses 252 exponentially weighted daily observations with a decay factor of 0.98 and 5-day overlap (to mitigate the discontinuities of different markets' time zones).

A closer look at the distribution of US key spot rates (Table 3.1) leads to a number of interesting observations. First, notice that the term structure of volatility (TSOV) of changes in spot rates is not flat: it increases sharply from the 3-month to the 15-year points, and then declines slightly between the 15-year and the 30-year points. Second, note that changes in key spot rates are generally highly correlated. Especially high correlations are exhibited within the following blocks: short (2 and 3 year), intermediate (5, 7, and 10 year), and long (10, 15, 20, 25, and 30 year). The 3-month rate is rather loosely correlated with the rest of the rates, while the 1-year rate is moderately correlated.

Yield curve dynamics can and do change dramatically from time to time. For instance, correlations and volatilities of changes in US key spot rates on 3/16/2020 paint a different picture, as shown in Table 3.2. According to the data and consistent with intuition, due to the Coronavirus pandemic, the US Treasury market was dramatically more volatile in March 2020 than it was in January 2020. In particular, the 2-year spot rate volatility doubled while rates at the intermediate and long end of the yield curve were approximately 70% more volatile compared to January 2020. The correlation matrix similarly reveals changes in the market's dynamics. Correlations increased across the term structure at the front end of the yield curve and then continued to increase at the long end.

The conceptual challenges of forecasting correlations and volatilities of systematic risk factors deserve a separate discussion since statistical measures of risk are very sensitive to the methods used to estimate the parameters of probability distributions. A variety of time series analysis techniques offer methodological flexibility in computing covariance matrices, including detrending, exponential weighting of observations, variable time intervals over which distribution parameters are estimated, and so forth. However, the burden of choosing the most appropriate approach lies on the shoulders of the user and must reflect his or her views on several crucial, almost *ideological,* issues:

- *Relevance of long-term history.* Long-term history (going back, say, 10 years) is applicable to forecasting future events only if the market is believed to have remained fundamentally unchanged over the period. In this context, permanent paradigm shifts (or structural breaks) need to be distinguished from the transitory shocks to the system that have only a temporary effect.
- *Weighting of observations.* From a purely statistical perspective, more recent observations tend to be better predictors of near-term future events than the more distant ones. By applying exponentially declining weights to older observations, transitions from one market regime to another can be captured quickly.

3.2 PRINCIPAL COMPONENT ANALYSIS: THEORY AND APPLICATIONS

3.2.1 Introduction

When yield curve risk is measured via deterministic approaches, characterizing interest rate movements in terms of key rates can be both intuitive and analytically appealing. However, due to their correlation and volatility structure, key rates are less efficient in describing the

TABLE 3.1 Correlations and Volatilities of US Key Rates from Aladdin Daily Dataset (as of 1/31/2020)

	3M	1Yr	2Yr	3Yr	5Yr	7Yr	10Yr	15Yr	20Yr	25Yr	30Yr
Rates/Spreads	1.61	1.51	1.35	1.31	1.35	1.43	1.54	1.79	1.95	2.08	2.18
Vol of Changes in Spot Rates (bp)	33.86	36.19	60.14	66.77	72.42	74.19	75.43	75.49	74.54	73.43	72.62
Correlation Matrix											
Tsy 3M	1.00	0.57	0.35	0.31	0.27	0.25	0.22	0.17	0.16	0.15	0.15
Tsy 1Yr	0.57	1.00	0.87	0.83	0.79	0.76	0.72	0.66	0.64	0.63	0.62
Tsy 2Yr	0.35	0.87	1.00	0.99	0.96	0.92	0.87	0.83	0.81	0.80	0.79
Tsy 3Yr	0.31	0.83	0.99	1.00	0.99	0.96	0.93	0.89	0.87	0.86	0.84
Tsy 5Yr	0.27	0.79	0.96	0.99	1.00	0.99	0.97	0.94	0.93	0.91	0.90
Tsy 7Yr	0.25	0.76	0.92	0.96	0.99	1.00	0.99	0.97	0.96	0.94	0.93
Tsy 10Yr	0.22	0.72	0.87	0.93	0.97	0.99	1.00	0.99	0.98	0.97	0.96
Tsy 15Yr	0.17	0.66	0.83	0.89	0.94	0.97	0.99	1.00	1.00	0.99	0.98
Tsy 20Yr	0.16	0.64	0.81	0.87	0.93	0.96	0.98	1.00	1.00	1.00	0.99
Tsy 25Yr	0.15	0.63	0.80	0.86	0.91	0.94	0.97	0.99	1.00	1.00	1.00
Tsy 30Yr	0.15	0.62	0.79	0.84	0.90	0.93	0.96	0.98	0.99	1.00	1.00

Source: BlackRock Aladdin, January 31, 2020.
Note: Computed based on equally weighted (DLY) BlackRock Solutions values.

TABLE 3.2 Correlations and Volatilities of US Key Rates from Aladdin Daily Dataset (as of 3/16/2020)

		3M	1Yr	2Yr	3Yr	5Yr	7Yr	10Yr	15Yr	20Yr	25Yr	30Yr
Rates/Spreads		0.35	0.51	0.55	0.56	0.65	0.75	0.81	1.08	1.28	1.46	1.60
Vol of Changes in Spot Rates (bp)		169.8	134.4	121.1	117.5	115.6	116.3	121.5	119.9	121.1	122.9	125.4
Correlation Matrix	Tsy 3M	1.00	0.93	0.79	0.74	0.69	0.68	0.71	0.68	0.65	0.61	0.57
	Tsy 1Yr	0.93	1.00	0.94	0.91	0.87	0.86	0.85	0.80	0.76	0.72	0.68
	Tsy 2Yr	0.79	0.94	1.00	0.99	0.97	0.95	0.92	0.84	0.80	0.76	0.73
	Tsy 3Yr	0.74	0.91	0.99	1.00	0.99	0.97	0.93	0.86	0.82	0.78	0.75
	Tsy 5Yr	0.69	0.87	0.97	0.99	1.00	0.99	0.96	0.90	0.86	0.83	0.81
	Tsy 7Yr	0.68	0.86	0.95	0.97	0.99	1.00	0.98	0.93	0.90	0.88	0.86
	Tsy 10Yr	0.71	0.85	0.92	0.93	0.96	0.98	1.00	0.98	0.96	0.95	0.93
	Tsy 15Yr	0.68	0.80	0.84	0.86	0.90	0.93	0.98	1.00	0.99	0.98	0.96
	Tsy 20Yr	0.65	0.76	0.80	0.82	0.86	0.90	0.96	0.99	1.00	0.99	0.98
	Tsy 25Yr	0.61	0.72	0.76	0.78	0.83	0.88	0.95	0.98	0.99	1.00	1.00
	Tsy 30Yr	0.57	0.68	0.73	0.75	0.81	0.86	0.93	0.96	0.98	1.00	1.00

Source: BlackRock Aladdin, March 16, 2020.
Note: Computed based on equally weighted (DLY) BlackRock Solutions values.

dynamics of interest rates from the statistical perspective. Having said that, historical corre-lations and volatilities can still provide useful inferences about the behavior of the different parts of the yield curve. For instance, the 20- to 30-year key spot rates are typically highly correlated and exhibit similar volatilities (Tables 3.1 and 3.2). This knowledge can be effec-tively used in assessing the likelihood of a steepening or a flattening of the spot curve between the 20- and the 30-year maturities. Unfortunately, Tables 3.1 and 3.2 alone do not allow us to address a whole class of questions dealing with the dynamics of the yield curve as a whole; for example, what normally happens to the rest of the yield curve when the 10-year spot rate rallies by a given number of basis points?

Principal components analysis (PCA) is a statistical technique that examines, models, and reveals the variance/covariance structures of multivariate systems. Via a mathematical transformation, PCA can replace a large number of the interdependent variables with a small set of new, uncorrelated *composite* variables called *principal components,* thus allowing for a more parsimonious description of the system's dynamics. Widely employed in geological, environmental, and other natural sciences for many decades, PCA was first applied to equity markets in the 1980s and to fixed-income markets in the late 1980s/early 1990s, and has been of interest to academics and practitioners ever since.[7] Due to the latent statistical nature of principal components and the inability to directly observe them in the market, their use in portfolio management and trading has been relatively limited.[8]

In fixed-income analysis, principal components have a very intuitive interpretation as the most dominant and characteristic yield curve shocks[9] (Exhibit 3.1). Using PCA, researchers identified that the first three principal components, *level, steepness,* and *curvature* typically explain anywhere between 95% and 99% of returns on US fixed-income securities over time. In the language of statistics, it is equivalent to saying that the first three principal components explain the vast majority of the total variability of the yield curve.

In this book, principal components are analytically derived from the variance/covariance matrix of changes in systematic risk factors. This streamlines computations (since no addi-tional regressions or historical fittings are required) and enables principal components to incorporate the assumptions built into the estimation of the underlying covariance matri-ces. For instance, principal components can be based on covariance matrices computed using exponentially weighted observations, creating a tool that captures changes in the market environment virtually instantaneously. At the same time, the shapes of the principal com-ponents' yield curve shocks are determined by the historical data instead of being postu-lated a priori. Namely, the first principal component is not assumed to be a parallel spot curve shock.[10] As demonstrated later in this chapter, the "humped" shape of the first prin-cipal component is an important piece of information that should not be ignored; it can be effectively used when placing yield curve bets or gaining intuition behind extreme market movements. Moreover, when not accompanied by the proper adjustment of other princi-pal components, the assumption that the shape of the first principal component is parallel causes principal components to become correlated. Since in certain instances it is still ana-lytically convenient to assume that the most dominant yield curve movement is parallel, there exists a way to transform the coordinate system, turning the first principal component into the parallel shock and adjusting the shapes of other principal components accordingly (Section 3.3).

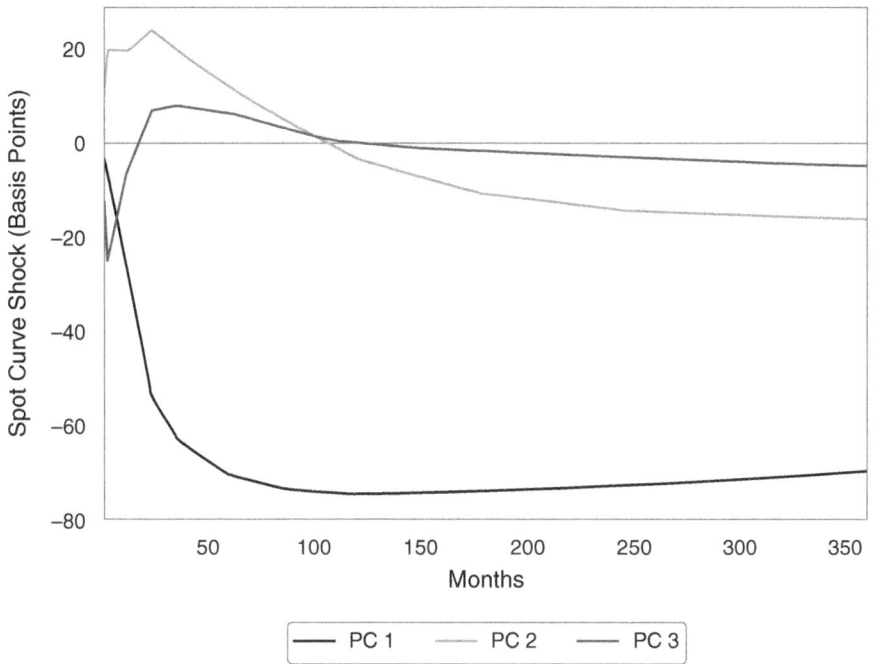

EXHIBIT 3.1 Annualized Principal Components Spot Curve Shocks (as of 1/31/2020)
Source: BlackRock Aladdin, January 31, 2020.

3.2.2 Principal Components Analysis

Changes in systematic risk factors are assumed to follow a joint multivariate normal distribution with zero mean. To fully define such a distribution, it suffices to specify the covariance matrix Σ of changes in risk factors, which, for our purposes, are assumed to be key spot rates. PCA attempts to describe yield curve movements as parsimoniously as possible. It uses the original set of interdependent variables (key rates) to construct a set of new composite variables—principal components. Principal components are, by construction, the linear combinations of changes in the original key rates:

$$p_i = \sum_{j=1}^{n} p_{i,j} \cdot \Delta r_j \tag{3.1}$$

where p_i are principal components (random variables), Δr_j are changes in key rate points on the spot curve (random variables), and $p_{i,j}$ are the principal components' coefficients or *factor loadings*. Note that under the assumption that changes in key rates follow a multivariate normal distribution, principal components are normally distributed as well. Equation 3.1 can be rewritten in matrix terms as follows:

$$\begin{bmatrix} p_1 \\ \cdots \\ p_n \end{bmatrix} = \begin{bmatrix} p_{1,1} & \cdots & p_{1,n} \\ \cdots & \cdots & \cdots \\ p_{n,1} & \cdots & p_{n,n} \end{bmatrix} \cdot \begin{bmatrix} \Delta r_1 \\ \cdots \\ \Delta r_n \end{bmatrix} \tag{3.2}$$

or equivalently

$$\overline{p} = \Omega \cdot \overline{r} \tag{3.3}$$

where $\Omega = \{p_{i,j}\}$ is the matrix of principal components' factor loadings, and $\overline{p}$ and $\overline{r}$ are the vectors of principal components and changes in key spot rates, respectively. While practitioners often use the term *principal components* when referring to random variables p_i as well as factor loadings, $(p_{i,1}, \ldots, p_{i,n})$, the meaning is usually clear from the context.

The system of yield curve movements is n-dimensional. Key spot rates fully describe any spot curve movement and therefore, in the language of mathematics, constitute the *basis* or *coordinate system*. Principal components form a different coordinate system in the space of spot curve changes. The process of constructing principal components can therefore be thought of as a geometrical transformation between the two coordinate systems, schematically presented in Exhibit 3.2.

Equations 3.1–3.3 show the transition from the basis of key spot rates to the coordinate system of principal components. Later in this chapter it will be shown that the matrix of principal components' factor loadings is orthogonal by construction, and therefore the following equations describe the reverse transformation, from principal components to key spot rates:

$$\Delta r_i = \sum_{j=1}^{n} p_{j,i} \cdot p_j \tag{3.4}$$

Equation 3.4 can be written in matrix terms as follows:

$$\begin{bmatrix} \Delta r_1 \\ \cdots \\ \Delta r_n \end{bmatrix} = \begin{bmatrix} p_{1,1} & \cdots & p_{n,1} \\ \cdots & \cdots & \cdots \\ p_{1,n} & \cdots & p_{n,n} \end{bmatrix} \cdot \begin{bmatrix} p_1 \\ \cdots \\ p_n \end{bmatrix} \tag{3.5}$$

or equivalently,

$$\overline{r} = \Omega^T \cdot \overline{p} \tag{3.6}$$

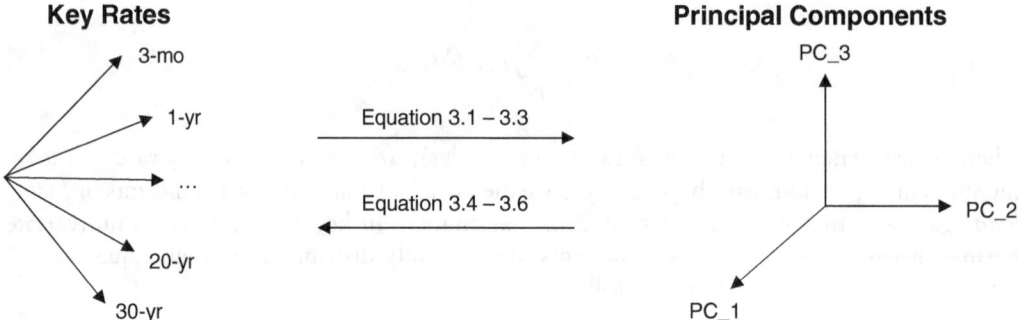

EXHIBIT 3.2 Transition from One Coordinate System to Another: Interdependent Key Rates Versus Uncorrelated Principal Components

Before we proceed to the derivation of principal components' factor loadings, the following important concepts need definition:

- *The total variability* of a given dynamic system is a measure of how *jointly volatile* are all the variables that belong to this system. For instance, during the onset of the Coronavirus pandemic in the United States, the total variability of US interest rates was high, while in January 2020 it was low. The formal definition of total variability will be presented later in this chapter. For now, it suffices to note that total variability can be analytically computed from the covariance matrix Σ of key rate changes.
- *The percentage of the total variability explained* by the given variable is the ratio of this variable's variance to the total variability of the system. By definition, this statistic can take on values between 0% and 100%. In this book, the terms the *percentage of the total variability* explained by a variable and the *explanatory power* of this variable will be used interchangeably.

Principal components can be obtained from the covariance matrix Σ via the following optimization problem. By repeatedly searching through all possible linear combinations of changes in key rates as shown in Equation 3.1:

1. The linear combination of key rate changes that explains the largest percentage of the total variability in the system is determined. The unit-length vector of factor loadings $(p_{1,1}, \ldots, p_{1,n})$ in this linear combination corresponds to the first principal component p_1.
2. The remaining variability in the system, not explained by the previously selected principal components, is computed. The next linear combination of length 1 is then found, such that
   - it explains the largest percentage of the remaining variability in the system and
   - it is uncorrelated with all previously selected principal components.
3. Step 2 is continued until all principal components are determined. By construction, each principal component explains the largest percentage of variability in the system not explained by all previously selected principal components and is uncorrelated with all of them. As mentioned before, the principal components' factor loadings are constructed to be of length 1:

$$\sqrt{\sum_{j=1}^{n} p_{i,j}^2} = 1 \qquad (3.7)$$

While it is intuitive to think about principal components from the previously described optimization viewpoint, in practice, principal components are typically analytically derived from the covariance matrix of key rate changes. It can be shown[11] that the principal components' factor loadings $(p_{i,1}, \ldots, p_{i,n})$ are the eigenvectors of the covariance matrix Σ or, equivalently, the unit-length solutions of the following equation:

$$\Sigma \cdot \begin{bmatrix} p_{i,1} \\ \ldots \\ p_{i,n} \end{bmatrix} = \lambda_i \cdot \begin{bmatrix} p_{i,1} \\ \ldots \\ p_{i,n} \end{bmatrix} \qquad (3.8)$$

The real numbers λ_i are, in turn, the solutions of the following equation:

$$\det(\Sigma - \lambda \cdot I) = 0 \qquad (3.9)$$

where I is the identity matrix and $\det(X)$ is the determinant of a matrix X.

The matrix notation can be used to rewrite Equation 3.8 as follows:

$$\begin{bmatrix} \lambda_i & & 0 \\ & \cdots & \\ 0 & & \lambda_n \end{bmatrix} = \begin{bmatrix} p_{1,1} & \cdots & p_{1,n} \\ \cdots & \cdots & \cdots \\ p_{n,1} & \cdots & p_{n,n} \end{bmatrix} \cdot \Sigma \cdot \begin{bmatrix} p_{1,1} & \cdots & p_{1,n} \\ \cdots & \cdots & \cdots \\ p_{n,1} & \cdots & p_{n,n} \end{bmatrix}^T \qquad (3.10)$$

or equivalently,

$$\Lambda = \Omega \cdot \Sigma \cdot \Omega^T \qquad (3.11)$$

where Λ is a matrix with λ_i on the diagonal and zeros elsewhere, and Ω, as before, is the matrix of principal components' factor loadings. Since the rows of the matrix Ω are by construction linearly independent unit-length vectors, Ω is an orthogonal matrix:[12]

$$\Omega^{-1} = \Omega^T \qquad (3.12)$$

It can be shown that the eigenvalues λ_i of the covariance matrix Σ are the variances of the principal components p_i:

$$\lambda_i = \sigma^2(p_i) \qquad (3.13)$$

As already mentioned, under the assumption that changes in key spot rates follow a multivariate normal distribution, the entire knowledge about the historical behavior of interest rates is contained in the original covariance matrix Σ. PCA provides an alternative description of the yield curve dynamics, transforming the information contained in Σ into:

- the vector $\lambda = (\lambda_1, \ldots, \lambda_n)$ of principal components' variances and
- the matrix Ω of principal components' factor loadings.

The two important concepts introduced earlier in this section can now be formally defined. Since any yield curve movement can be described by the set of *uncorrelated* principal components, the *total variability* of the system is the sum of the principal components' variances:

$$Total\ Variability = \sum_{j=1}^{n} \lambda_j \qquad (3.14)$$

As mentioned before, the percentage of the total variability explained by a given variable is the ratio of its variance to the total variability of the system. The percentages of the total variability of yield curve movements explained by principal components (or their "explanatory powers") can therefore be obtained from the following formula:

$$\zeta_i = \frac{\lambda_i}{\sum_{j=1}^{n} \lambda_j} \qquad (3.15)$$

Explanatory powers of principal components provide important information about the dynamics of interest rates. They can be used to determine how many risk factors are needed to approximate yield curve movements with a sufficient degree of accuracy. For instance, in market environments when the explanatory power of the first principal component is over 95%, describing interest rate movements with a single risk factor is adequate. On the other hand, when the explanatory power of the first principal component is low, two or even three principal components may be required. As mentioned earlier, as an empirical observation, the first three principal components explain almost the entire yield curve variability in the majority of market environments.[13]

The principal components' factor loadings $(p_{i,1}, \ldots, p_{i,n})$ reflect the historical relationship among key spot rates and have a very intuitive interpretation. They visually depict the *shape* of the most dominant yield curve movements, that is, principal components. For reasons that will be described in Section 3.3, the principal components, yield curve shocks can be obtained by multiplying the vectors of factor loadings $(p_{i,1}, \ldots, p_{i,n})$ by the one standard deviation $\sqrt{\lambda_i}$ of principal components.

Table 3.3 illustrates the derivation of principal components on 1/31/2020 from the covariance matrix of changes in US key spot rates obtained from the Aladdin dataset. On 1/31/2020, 92% of the spot curve variability was explained by the first principal component, 97% by the first two, and 99% by the first three. Needless to say, the explanatory powers of principal components are functions of the market environment. Table 3.4 demonstrates PCA on 3/16/2020. Notice that the explanatory power of principal components declined on this date. The first principal component explains only 85%, while the first two principal components explain 95% and the first three, 99%. Tables 3.3 and 3.4 also show the principal components' factor loadings $(p_{i,1}, \ldots, p_{i,n})$ as well as the corresponding annualized interest rate shocks. Notice the change in the shape of the first principal component between the two dates. Looking at January through March 2020, the loading on the front end of the curve is higher than on the back end.

3.2.3 The First Principal Component and the Term Structure of Volatility

The lack of intuition about principal components has limited their use in portfolio management and trading. This section attempts to reduce this obstacle by demonstrating that in the majority of market environments, the shape of the first principal component resembles that of the TSOV of changes in US spot rates. This phenomenon is a consequence of the fact that, except for the very short end of the yield curve, changes in US Treasury spot rates are typically highly correlated during business-as-usual regimes (Tables 3.1 and 3.2). Interest rate movements tend to become even more synchronized during most market crises, resulting in even higher correlations.[14] Exhibit 3.3 compares the shape of the first principal component and that of the TSOV on 1/31/2020. Notice that the two curves are almost identical near the most volatile part of the spot curve (2–10 years) and diverge moderately near both the short and the long ends of the yield curve.

Let $\sigma_i = \sigma(\Delta r_i)$ and $\sigma_j = \sigma(\Delta r_j)$ be the volatilities of changes in key spot rates r_i and r_j, respectively. Recall that by $p_{1,i}$ and $p_{1,j}$, we denoted the factor loadings of the first principal component corresponding to r_i and r_j

The approximation "the shape of the first principal component resembles that of TSOV" can be written as the following approximate relationship:

$$\frac{\sigma_i}{\sigma_j} \approx \frac{p_{1,i}}{p_{1,j}} \tag{3.16}$$

It can be shown that the factor loadings $p_{1,i}$ and $p_{1,j}$ of the first principal component can be obtained via the following regression-like formula:[15]

$$p_{1,i} = \frac{\rho_{1,i} \cdot \sigma_i}{\sqrt{\lambda_1}} \tag{3.17}$$

TABLE 3.3 Principal Components Analysis of Spot Curve Movements (as of 1/31/2020)

			Factor Loadings													
		Tsy 3M	Tsy 1Yr	Tsy 2Yr	Tsy 3Yr	Tsy 5Yr	Tsy 7Yr	Tsy 10Yr	Tsy 15Yr	Tsy 20Yr	Tsy 25Yr	Tsy 30Yr	PC Var	PC Vol	Var Expl	Cvar Expl
Principal Components	1	-3.8	-12.8	-25.7	-29.9	-33.6	-34.8	-35.5	-35.2	-34.5	-33.8	-33.1	4.48	2.12	92%	92%
	2	37.1	37.4	45.3	37.1	22.7	10.0	-6.6	-21.5	-27.5	-30.2	-31.6	0.27	0.52	6%	97%
	3	-85.2	-20.8	22.3	25.2	19.9	10.0	-2.2	-6.9	-10.9	-14.4	-17.2	0.09	0.31	2%	99%
	4	-24.1	50.0	31.5	5.3	-25.5	-38.7	-30.9	-16.8	3.0	24.7	43.5	0.03	0.16	1%	100%
	5	27.3	-72.9	31.2	26.5	2.3	-16.5	-20.8	-21.1	-6.4	12.7	30.1	0.02	0.13	0%	100%
	6	-3.4	10.7	-35.7	-7.7	32.7	36.7	2.0	-52.4	-35.9	4.7	45.4	0.00	0.06	0%	100%
	7	-3.3	-6.0	33.4	-18.7	-43.6	1.7	73.5	-17.1	-26.0	-8.9	11.6	0.00	0.04	0%	100%
	8	-0.2	5.7	-43.7	56.2	10.6	-57.0	38.4	-2.3	-7.3	-3.1	2.4	0.00	0.02	0%	100%
	9	-0.3	1.4	-22.8	52.9	-65.0	47.1	-14.9	-2.4	3.2	1.3	-0.3	0.00	0.01	0%	100%
	10	0.1	-0.2	-0.7	1.5	-1.5	-0.1	-14.1	66.9	-65.2	-15.7	28.7	0.00	0.00	0%	100%
	11	0.0	0.0	0.0	-0.1	0.1	-0.5	-2.0	1.5	40.1	-81.3	42.2	0.00	0.00	0%	100%

Annualized One Standard Deviation Shocks (Basis Points)											
	Tsy 3M	Tsy 1Yr	Tsy 2Yr	Tsy 3Yr	Tsy 5Yr	Tsy 7Yr	Tsy 10Yr	Tsy 15Yr	Tsy 20Yr	Tsy 25Yr	Tsy 30Yr	Var Expl
PC 1 Spot Curve Shock	-8	-27	-54	-63	-71	-74	-75	-74	-73	-71	-70	92%
PC 2 Spot Curve Shock	19	19	24	19	12	5	-3	-11	-14	-16	-16	6%
PC 3 Spot Curve Shock	-26	-6	7	8	6	3	-1	-2	-3	-4	-5	2%
Parallel Spot Curve Shock	128	128	128	128	128	128	128	128	128	128	128	82%

PC Var = Principal Components' Variances times 10,000;
PC Vol = Principal Components' Volatilities times 100;
Var Expl = Percentage of the variance explained;
Cvar Expl = Cumulative percentage of the variance explained.

Source: BlackRock Aladdin, January 31, 2020.

TABLE 3.4 Principal Components Analysis of Spot Curve Movements (as of 3/16/2020)

		Tsy 3M	Tsy 1Yr	Tsy 2Yr	Tsy 3Yr	Tsy 5Yr	Tsy 7Yr	Tsy 10Yr	Tsy 15Yr	Tsy 20Yr	Tsy 25Yr	Tsy 30Yr	PC Var	PC Vol	Var Expl	Cvar Expl
							Factor Loadings									
Principal	1	35.6	32.0	29.5	28.7	28.5	29.0	30.9	29.7	29.3	29.0	28.8	15.07	3.88	85%	85%
Components	2	66.6	36.7	15.2	7.5	-2.8	-8.7	-13.7	-21.3	-27.4	-32.8	-37.1	1.77	1.33	10%	95%
	3	49.6	-1.3	-36.9	-41.0	-38.1	-28.6	-5.9	13.6	22.3	26.3	28.5	0.75	0.87	4%	99%
	4	-25.9	49.8	28.9	4.6	-18.3	-25.5	-25.3	-37.5	-15.1	18.1	49.1	0.05	0.22	0%	100%
	5	-27.4	37.8	16.3	2.3	-24.3	-34.3	-9.1	50.0	36.0	-3.6	-43.5	0.04	0.20	0%	100%
	6	-19.9	60.0	-49.0	-37.2	11.0	39.0	19.6	-2.6	-8.6	-8.1	-6.2	0.01	0.12	0%	100%
	7	-4.6	-2.4	15.9	-0.2	-43.6	-15.6	83.3	-6.4	-21.4	-11.7	2.0	0.00	0.05	0%	100%
	8	1.2	-10.6	57.1	-57.7	-26.0	48.4	-14.3	2.1	5.1	-0.1	-5.6	0.00	0.03	0%	100%
	9	0.4	1.1	-22.5	51.8	-64.1	48.2	-19.3	2.0	1.6	1.3	0.3	0.00	0.01	0%	100%
	10	-0.1	0.1	-1.7	2.4	-1.1	1.4	14.4	-67.1	65.0	15.3	-28.6	0.00	0.00	0%	100%
	11	0.0	0.0	0.0	0.0	0.0	-0.3	-2.1	1.6	39.9	-81.3	42.2	0.00	0.00	0%	100%

	Tsy 3M	Tsy 1Yr	Tsy 2Yr	Tsy 3Yr	Tsy 5Yr	Tsy 7Yr	Tsy 10Yr	Tsy 15Yr	Tsy 20Yr	Tsy 25Yr	Tsy 30Yr	Var Expl
					Annualized One Standard Deviation Shocks (Basis Points)							
PC 1 Spot Curve Shock	138	124	115	111	111	113	120	115	112	113	112	85%
PC 2 Spot Curve Shock	89	49	20	10	-4	-12	-18	-28	-36	-44	-49	10%
PC 3 Spot Curve Shock	43	-1	-32	-36	-33	-25	-5	12	19	23	25	4%
Parallel Spot Curve Shock	387	387	387	387	387	387	387	387	387	387	387	85%

Source: BlackRock Aladdin, March 16, 2020.

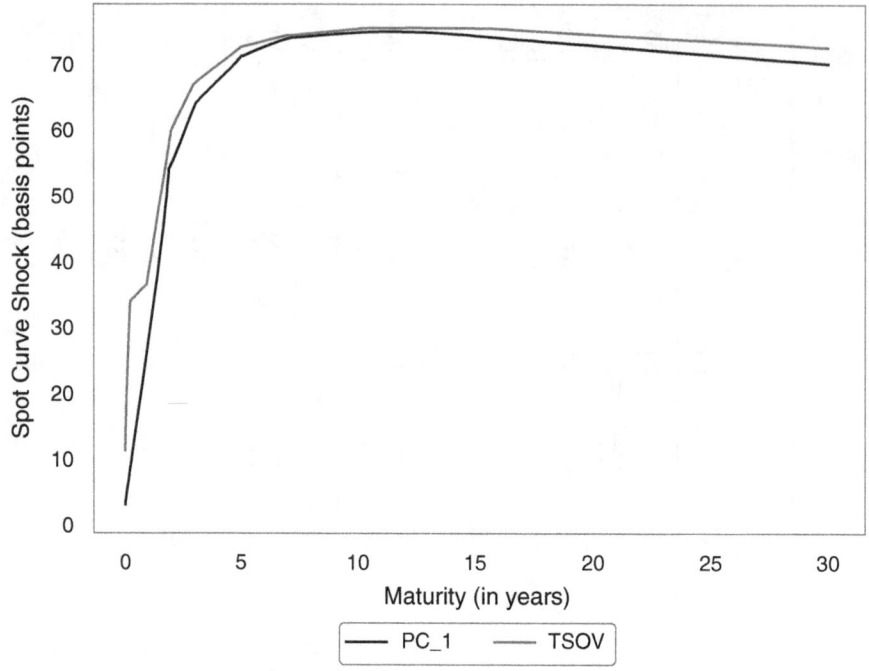

EXHIBIT 3.3 The First Principal Component Shock and TSOV (as of 1/31/20)
Source: BlackRock Aladdin, January 31, 2020.

$$p_{1,j} = \frac{\rho_{1,j} \cdot \sigma_j}{\sqrt{\lambda_1}} \tag{3.18}$$

where $\rho_{1,i}$ and $\rho_{1,j}$ are the correlations between the first principal component and the changes in key spot rates r_i and r_j, respectively.

Because the first principal component is constructed to explain the maximal percentage of the total variability in the system, the high correlation among changes in spot rates makes the first principal component highly correlated with them as well:

$$\rho_{1,i} \approx \rho_{1,j} \approx 1 \tag{3.19}$$

Combining Equations 3.16–3.19 yields

$$\frac{p_{1,i}}{p_{1,j}} = \frac{\frac{\rho_{1,i} \cdot \sigma_i}{\sqrt{\lambda_1}}}{\frac{\rho_{1,j} \cdot \sigma_j}{\sqrt{\lambda_1}}} = \frac{\rho_{1,i}}{\rho_{1,j}} \cdot \frac{\sigma_i}{\sigma_j} \approx \frac{\sigma_i}{\sigma_j} \tag{3.20}$$

Equation 3.20 illustrates that in market environments characterized by highly correlated spot rates, the shape of the first principal component resembles that of TSOV. Since correlations among spot rates typically increase during the periods of market turmoil, practitioners often witness large-move days reflecting "more of a level *[the first principal component and not parallel!]* shift in interest rates."[16] In other words, in the time of crisis all spot rates typically move in the same direction, and the relative magnitudes of their respective changes are determined by their historical volatilities.

Results obtained in this section argue that contrary to some of the existing practices,[17] the first principal component should not be assumed or explicitly forced to be a parallel spot curve shock. Principal components whose shapes are determined by data rather than specified a priori can provide valuable insights into the interest rate movements and also can assist in formulating yield curve bets.

3.2.4 Example: Historical Steepeners and Flatteners of the US Treasury Curve

The similarity between the shape of the first principal component and that of TSOV has a number of implications. The most interesting among them deals with the interest rate directionality of changes in the shape of the yield curve. More specifically, the shape of the first principal component points to a market phenomenon very familiar to fixed-income traders: when the market rallies, the yield curve often flattens, and when the market sells off, the yield curve steepens. In fact, this observation can be reached theoretically as well. Notice that according to the shape of the first principal component, the factor loading of the 2-year rate is smaller than that of the 30-year rate. Therefore, if the market rallies, the 2-year rate will typically decrease less than the 30-year rate, causing the spot curve to flatten.

Two simple experiments dealing with spot and on-the-run US Treasury curves were conducted to investigate whether the market data supports these analytical results. Monthly changes in the level and slope of the US spot and OTR curves were considered. In each experiment, the market was called *bull* if the 10-year key rate (spot or OTR, depending on the experiment) fell more than 15 basis points, *bear* if it rose more than 15 basis points, and *unchanged* otherwise. Likewise, a change in the slope of the yield curve (spot or OTR, depending on the experiment) was defined as a *steepening* if the spread between the 2- and the 30-year rates increased by more than 5 basis points, *flattening* if it decreased by more than 5 basis points, and *unchanged* otherwise. Exhibits 3.4 and 3.5 contain the results of these rudimentary empirical investigations.

Over the 5-year period (January 2015–January 2020), there were six instances of bull flattening and five instances of bear steepening, but only one instance of bull steepening and three instances of bear flattening.

The empirical data seems to support the observation that changes in the slope of the yield curve are consistent with those implied by the shape of the first principal component. Therefore, if a large market movement is expected as a result of an economic data release or any other exogenous event, forecasting the change in the shape of the yield curve using the first principal component seems to be the most historically plausible alternative. However, since the first principal component only deals with the directional yield curve movements, twists and other types of changes in the shape of the yield curve (that correspond to the second and third principal components) were not accounted for by our experiments.

	Flatten	Steepen	Unchanged
Bear	3	5	1
Bull	6	1	1
Neutral	14	7	21

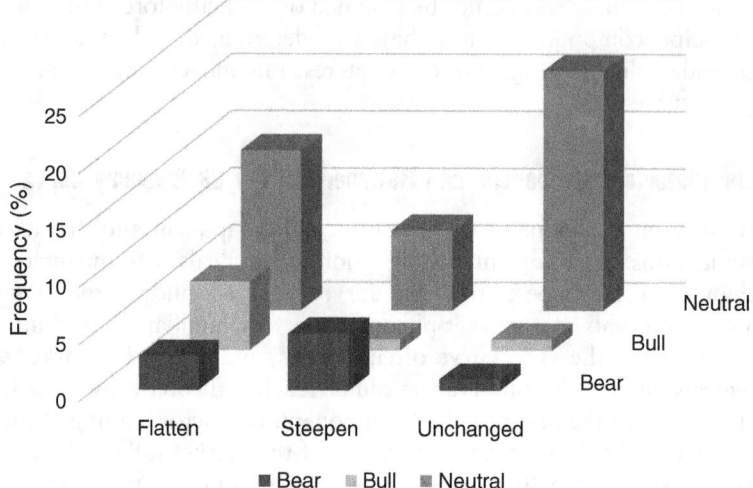

EXHIBIT 3.4   Relationship Between Changes in the Level and the Slope of the US TSY Spot Curve
Source: BlackRock Aladdin, January 31, 2020.

	Flatten	Steepen	Unchanged
Bear	2	5	1
Bull	6	1	1
Neutral	18	7	18

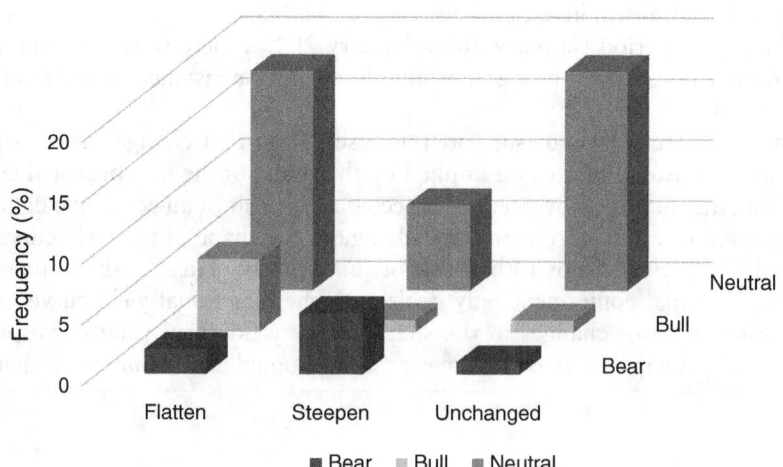

EXHIBIT 3.5   Relationship Between Changes in the Level and the Slope of the US OTR TSY Curve
Slope
Source: BlackRock Aladdin, January 31, 2020.

3.3   PROBABILITY DISTRIBUTIONS OF INTEREST RATE SHOCKS

Many areas of portfolio and risk management make extensive use of hypothetical "what-if" scenarios that describe the evolution of interest rates over time. Analyses of this type are often formulated in terms of spot curve shocks that are expected to occur instantaneously or over a specified horizon. The popularity of these methods is due to the fact that KRDs of fixed-income portfolios and securities allow for the approximation of potential gains and losses associated with a given interest rate movement (Equation 2.37). Earlier in this book (Chapter 2), we discussed approaches to measuring interest rate exposure.

The remainder of this chapter is more suitable for the mathematically inclined reader. This section studies stochastic behavior of interest rate shocks using the framework inspired by PCA.[18] Operating under the assumption that changes in spot rates are normally distributed, it will be demonstrated that any spot curve movement is in one-to-one correspondence with a realization of a standard normal random variable.[19] This allows the likelihood associated with any movement of the yield curve to be judged. For instance, if it is determined that a given interest rate shock corresponds to a three standard deviation realization of the underlying standard normal variable, such a movement of interest rates will be deemed unlikely from a historical perspective. The ability to derive probability distributions of interest rate shocks of arbitrary shapes also enables the construction of coordinate systems other than principal components or key rates. Thus, the coordinate system of principal components can be rotated, turning the first principal component into a parallel shock. This knowledge can be utilized by the risk management methodologies (e.g., interest rate scenario analysis) that model the price sensitivity in terms of parallel spot curve movements or explicitly assume that the first principal component is parallel.

As studied in Section 3.2.2, the dynamics of interest rate movements can be equivalently described via two different coordinate systems: random changes in key spot rates (Δr_i) and random changes in principal components (p_i). In this section, we deal with both historical and hypothetical interest rate shocks—particularly realizations of Δr_i and p_i. If key spot rates and principal components can be thought of as random variables spanning the respective coordinate systems, a given yield curve movement (a realization of Δr_i and p_i) corresponds to a vector of coefficients. We will adopt the following notation. From now on, the subscripts KR and PC next to a vector of coefficients will indicate that this interest rate shock is a realization of key spot rates or principal components, respectively. For instance:

$$\bar{z} = (z_1, \ldots z_n)_{KR} \tag{3.21}$$

denotes an interest rate shock that is written in terms of changes in key rates, where the first key rate is shocked by z_1 basis points, the second key rate by z_2 basis points, and so forth. The *same* spot curve shock $\bar{z}$ can be represented as a realization of principal components as well:

$$\bar{z} = (v_1, \ldots v_n)_{PC} \tag{3.22}$$

Recall that Equations 3.1–3.6 describe the relationship between the coordinate systems of key rates and principal components. Thus, when applied to the interest rate shock $\bar{z}$, Equation 3.5 can be rewritten as follows:

$$\begin{bmatrix} z_1 \\ \ldots \\ z_n \end{bmatrix} = \begin{bmatrix} p_{1,1} & \cdots & p_{n,1} \\ \ldots & \ldots & \ldots \\ p_{1,n} & \cdots & p_{n,n} \end{bmatrix} \cdot \begin{bmatrix} v_1 \\ \ldots \\ v_n \end{bmatrix} = \sum_{i=1}^{n} \begin{bmatrix} p_{i,1} \\ \ldots \\ p_{i,n} \end{bmatrix} \times v_i \tag{3.23}$$

Equation 3.23 reveals that any interest rate shock can be written as a sum of the principal components' factor loadings multiplied by the realization of the appropriate principal component. For any arbitrary change in key spot rates, there exists a unique set of realizations of principal components. Moreover, these realizations can be determined analytically. Conversely, any realization of principal components unequivocally implies a unique change in spot key rates.[20]

Another important corollary of Equation 3.23 lies in the ability to construct principal components' yield curve shocks. Thus, the one standard deviation change in the first principal component has the following representation in the (orthogonal) coordinate system of principal components:

$$\text{One } SD \ PC_1 = \left(\sqrt{\lambda_1}, 0, \ldots, 0 \right)_{PC} \tag{3.24}$$

where $\sqrt{\lambda_1}$, as before, is one standard deviation of the first principal component. When written in terms of changes in key rates, the first principal component shock has the following representation:

$$\text{One } SD \ PC_1 = \begin{bmatrix} p_{1,1} & \cdots & p_{n,1} \\ \cdots & \cdots & \cdots \\ p_{1,n} & \cdots & p_{n,n} \end{bmatrix} \cdot \begin{bmatrix} \sqrt{\lambda_1} \\ \cdots \\ 0 \end{bmatrix} = \left(\sqrt{\lambda_1} \cdot p_{1,1}, \ldots, \sqrt{\lambda_1} \cdot p_{1,n} \right)_{KR} \tag{3.25}$$

When speaking about principal component yield curve shocks, practitioners typically refer to the expressions given by Equation 3.25. Since one standard deviation has a naturally embedded notion of horizon (daily, monthly, or annual standard deviation), the corresponding principal components shocks are defined for the same horizon as well. Annualized principal components of the US Treasury spot curve are presented in Exhibit 3.1.

Before proceeding to deriving the probability distributions of interest rate shocks, consider the following definition. Suppose $\bar{z} = (z_1, \ldots, z_n)_{KR}$ and $\bar{x} = (x_1, \ldots, x_n)_{KR}$ are spot curve shocks represented as vectors of changes in key rates. Interest rate shocks $\bar{z}$ and $\bar{x}$ are said to be of the same shape if one can be obtained from the other via scaling by a real nonzero number c:

$$(z_1, \ldots, z_n)_{KR} = (c \cdot x_1, \ldots, c \cdot x_n)_{KR} \tag{3.26}$$

An example of the two shocks of the same shape is presented in Exhibit 3.6.

As mentioned earlier, the dynamic system of interest rate movements is n-dimensional. It is "spanned" by the vector of n key rates or, alternatively, by the vector of n principal components. While interdependent key rates form a nonorthogonal basis of the space of spot curve movements, uncorrelated principal components constitute an orthogonal basis. Clearly, in any n-dimensional space, an infinite number of different coordinate systems exist, both orthogonal and nonorthogonal.

Suppose $\bar{z} = (z_1, \ldots, z_n)_{KR}$ is a hypothetical interest rate shock presented in terms of key rates. In the beginning of this section, it was claimed that any interest rate shock corresponds to a particular realization of a standard normal random variable. Let us now establish the relationship between an arbitrary interest rate shock $\bar{z}$ and the realization of the underlying random variable. This will allow the probability of $\bar{z}$ occurring to be measured.

Recall that principal components' factor loadings are constructed to be of length 1. Let us start by analyzing the probability associated with $\bar{z}$ by constructing a vector $(\xi_1, \ldots, \xi_n)$ of unit length whose shape is the same as that of $\bar{z}$:

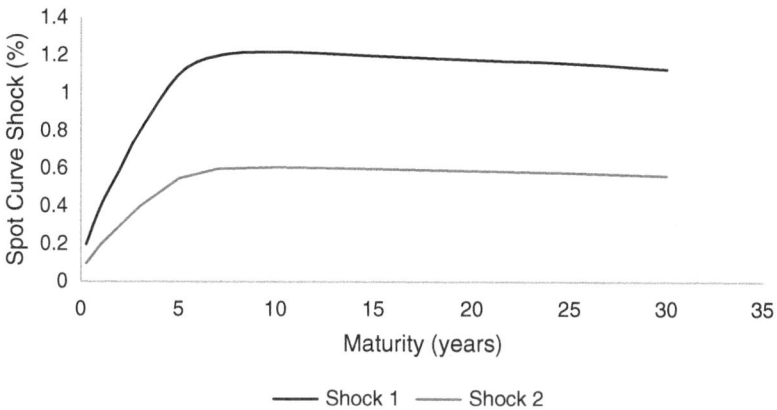

EXHIBIT 3.6 Interest Rate Shocks of the Same Shape
Source: For illustrative purposes only.

$$\overline{z} = |\overline{z}| \cdot (\xi_1, \ldots, \xi_n)_{KR} \tag{3.27}$$

where $|\overline{z}| = \sqrt{\sum_{i=1}^{n} z_i^2}$ denotes the length of $\overline{z}$ as a vector.

Similar to the definition of principal components (Equation 3.1), a new random variable ξ can be introduced as the following linear combination of key rates:

$$\xi = \sum_{i=1}^{n} \xi_i \cdot \Delta r_i \tag{3.28}$$

where Δr_i are changes in key spot rates (random variables). Since ξ is a linear combination of several normal variables, its variance is given by the following formula:

$$\sigma^2(\xi) = (\xi_1, \ldots, \xi_n) \cdot \Sigma \cdot (\xi_1, \ldots, \xi_n)^T \tag{3.29}$$

It is now possible to construct a new orthogonal basis of the space of spot curve changes that is different from the coordinate system of principal components. By design, we will make ξ the first element in this basis. This can be achieved by modifying the principal components' optimization procedure as follows:

1. The percentage of the total variability in the system explained by ξ is determined.
2. By repeatedly searching through all possible linear combinations of key rates, the next linear combination is found such that the following are true:
   - It explains the largest percentage of the remaining variability in the system, not explained by the previously selected variable(s).
   - It is uncorrelated with all previously selected variable(s).
3. Step 2 is repeated until the entire coordinate system is constructed. Each new element explains the largest percentage of the variability in the system not explained by all previously selected variables and is uncorrelated with all of them.

In the space of yield curve movements, the new orthogonal coordinate system (or basis) that is different from that of principal components has just been created. By construction, ξ is the first element in this basis. Just as any interest rate shock can be represented as a function of realizations of principal components (Equation 3.23), the analogous result for the newly constructed coordinate system can be obtained as well:

$$\begin{bmatrix} \Delta r_1 \\ \cdots \\ \Delta r_n \end{bmatrix} = \begin{bmatrix} \xi_1 \\ \cdots \\ \xi_n \end{bmatrix} \cdot \xi + other\ elements\ of\ the\ basis \qquad (3.30)$$

or equivalently,

$$\begin{bmatrix} \Delta r_1 \\ \cdots \\ \Delta r_n \end{bmatrix} = \begin{bmatrix} \sigma(\xi) \cdot \xi_1 \\ \sigma(\xi) \cdot \xi_n \end{bmatrix} \cdot \frac{\xi}{\sigma(\xi)} + other\ elements\ of\ the\ basis \qquad (3.31)$$

It can be seen that

$$(\sigma(\xi) \cdot \xi_1, \ldots \sigma(\xi) \cdot \xi_n)_{KR} \qquad (3.32)$$

is the one standard deviation shock whose shape is the same as that of $\bar{z}$, and $\frac{\xi}{\sigma(\xi)}$ is a standard normal variable.

Equations 3.30–3.31 deal with the representation of arbitrary changes in key spot rates (random variables) in the coordinate system whose first element is ξ. Following, we apply these general results to a particular realization of random key spot rates, that is, the shock $\bar{z}$. Due to the orthogonality, $\bar{z}$ is fully explained by the first element of the basis:

$$\bar{z} = \begin{bmatrix} z_1 \\ \cdots \\ z_n \end{bmatrix} = \begin{bmatrix} \sigma(\xi) \cdot \xi_1 \\ \cdots \\ \sigma(\xi) \cdot \xi_n \end{bmatrix} \cdot \frac{\bar{z}}{\sigma(\xi)} \qquad (3.33)$$

where $\frac{\bar{z}}{\sigma(\xi)}$ is the realization of the standard normal variable corresponding to $\bar{z}$

Equation 3.33 has a number of interesting applications, including the ability to compute a standard deviation of the parallel spot curve shock. This, in turn, allows us to impose a probabilistic context on interest rate scenario analysis (Section 2.2.4) and other methods that estimate the price sensitivity of fixed-income portfolios and securities to parallel yield curve movements. Recall that the traditional approach to interest rate scenario analysis explicitly sketches out the shape of the price function by repeatedly shocking the spot curve by a given number of basis points and recomputing the resulting OAVs using a valuation model (Exhibits 2.1 and 2.2). While it is important to know the magnitude of the potential losses associated with, say, a 150 basis point increase in interest rates over 1 year, it is also useful to know the likelihood of such an event from a historical perspective. Let us illustrate how to compute the annualized one standard deviation of a parallel spot curve shock in a given market environment and then estimate the probability associated with a 150 basis point parallel movement in interest rates over 1 year.

Assuming that the entire set of systematic risk factors is represented as 11 key spot rates as shown in Table 3.1 ($n = 11$), a 150 basis point spot curve shock can be written as follows:

$$\bar{z} = (150, \ldots, 150)_{KR} \qquad (3.34)$$

Clearly, the interest rate shock of unit length whose shape is the same as that of $\bar{z}$ is given by:

$$(\xi_1, \ldots, \xi_{11}) = \left(\frac{1}{\sqrt{11}}, \ldots, \frac{1}{\sqrt{11}} \right)_{KR} \tag{3.35}$$

Using the data from Table 3.1 and Equation 3.29, it can be shown that

$$\sigma(\xi) = \sqrt{(\xi_1, \ldots, \xi_{11}) \cdot \Sigma \cdot (\xi_1, \ldots, \xi_{11})^T} = 199 \tag{3.36}$$

and hence one standard deviation of a parallel spot curve shock on 1/31/2020 is $199 \cdot \frac{1}{\sqrt{11}} = 60$ basis points per year (Table 3.3):

$$(\sigma(\xi) \cdot \xi_1, \ldots, \sigma(\xi) \cdot \xi_{11})_{KR} = (60, \ldots, 60)_{KR} \tag{3.37}$$

Analogous to Equation 3.33, a 150 basis point parallel spot curve shock can be written as follows:

$$\bar{z} = \begin{bmatrix} 150 \\ \cdots \\ 150 \end{bmatrix} = \begin{bmatrix} 60 \\ \cdots \\ 60 \end{bmatrix} \cdot \frac{150 \cdot \sqrt{11}}{199} = \begin{bmatrix} 60 \\ \cdots \\ 60 \end{bmatrix} \cdot \frac{150}{60} = \begin{bmatrix} 60 \\ \cdots \\ 60 \end{bmatrix} \cdot 2.5 \tag{3.38}$$

Equation 3.38 demonstrates that on 1/31/2020, the annualized 150 basis point parallel spot curve shock corresponded to a 2.5 standard deviation realization of the underlying standard normal variable. Since the probability of a continuous random variable taking a particular value is zero, we can use tables of *cumulative* normal distributions to describe the historical likelihood of a given interest rate shock. Thus, on 1/31/2020, the probability of interest rates *increasing by 150 basis points or more* (or 2.5 standard deviations or more) over the course of 1 year was 0.00621. In general, the magnitudes of annualized one standard deviation parallel shocks vary with market environments, ranging between 75 and 110 basis points, in our experience.

The ability to compute probabilities associated with various parallel spot curve movements can be used in a variety of instances. Thus, in analyzing the impact of time on dynamic risk characteristics of fixed-income securities within the HROR framework (Section 2.8), Table 2.9 presented the probability of various interest rate movements as a function of time to option expiration.

NOTES

1. Parts of this chapter are based on Golub and Tilman, 1997a.
2. Matthew Wang significantly updated this chapter to incorporate more recent risk management approaches and concepts. Stephen Henry-Rerrie helped to update the charts and graphs included in this chapter.
3. Construction of well-behaved spot curves that fit data well and do not imply negative forward rates is a complex valuation problem, which is beyond the scope of this book. For an excellent overview of this subject, the reader is referred to Anderson et al., 1997.
4. One-factor interest rate models typically specify the stochastic evolution of the *short rate* over time (see Cheyette, 1997).

5. This being said, many risk management applications can and do employ probability distributions other than normal.

6. Using the population mean of zero as opposed to the actual sample mean when computing historical correlations and volatilities is called *detrending*. For instance, if the 10-year spot rate increased by 10 basis points in each of the 10 consecutive days, the estimate of volatility of changes computed around the sample mean (of 10) would be zero, implying the absence of risk. If the dispersion around the population mean of zero were measured instead, it would properly reflect the actual volatility of the spot rate.

7. See Kuberek, 1990; Litterman and Scheinkman, 1991; and Barber and Copper, 1996.

8. The authors are aware of only a handful of proprietary and government trading desks that use principal components durations in weighting butterfly yield curve trades and in other portfolio management and trading decisions (see Weir, 1996).

9. When creating continuous principal components shocks, their values at the 0-month rate were extrapolated as zero.

10. Because they are more intuitive, the shape of the first principal component is sometimes rotated to be either a parallel OTR or Spot Curve shock (see Wilner, 1996).

11. See Johnson and Wichern, 1982.

12. Assuming that all eigenvalues of the covariance matrix Σ are distinct, orthogonality of principal components' factor loadings implies that principal components are statistically uncorrelated (see Johnson and Wichern, 1982).

13. It is not true, however, that any hypothetical spot curve shift can be explained by the first three principal components. For example, a one standard deviation move in the fourth principal component cannot be explained at all by the first three principal components.

14. See Ronn, 1996.

15. See Johnson and Wichern, 1982.

16. See Ronn, 1996.

17. See Willner, 1996.

18. A technique similar in spirit was also used by Barber and Copper, 1996.

19. By definition, a standard normal variable $N(0,1)$ has a mean of zero and a standard deviation of 1.

20. If the number of principal components used to describe a given yield curve shock equals to the number of key rates, the decomposition is unique and can be obtained analytically. However, approximating an interest rate shock with a smaller number of principal components requires an optimization, and the solution is not necessarily unique.

CHAPTER 4

Portfolio Risk: Estimation and Decomposition[1]

Amandeep Dhaliwal
Managing Director, Financial Modeling Group, BlackRock

Tom Booker
Director, Financial Modeling Group, BlackRock

4.1 INTRODUCTION

Since Harry Markowitz first introduced mean variance analysis in 1952, portfolio volatility has been a primary measure of market risk. Even after the development of more sophisticated measures that more accurately capture tail risk (e.g., various forms of Value at Risk [VaR]), investment risk and performance are usually reported in terms of volatility and Sharpe ratio. While the focus on volatility has its historical roots in the assumption of normally distributed returns and mean variance analysis, empirical asset return distributions are well known to exhibit:

1. fat tails and skewness;
2. time-varying, clustering volatility; and
3. correlation spikes in times of market stress.

As an illustrative example, consider a multi-asset portfolio exposed with equal weighting to the following:

- Equity (MSCI Emerging market and MSCI World total return)
- Currency (GBP/USD)
- Commodity (S&P GSCI Commodity market)
- Fixed-Income (Lehman High Yield and Treasury Yield) indices

A multi-asset portfolio was selected to illustrate that the empirical regularities are neither specific to an asset class, nor eliminated by diversification across the asset classes. Daily returns on the portfolio, presented in the histogram in Exhibit 4.1, exhibit fat tails and negative skewness—clearly inconsistent, as expected, with the normal distribution fitted to the sample using maximum-likelihood estimates. Even casual observation of time series plots of the same portfolio returns in Exhibit 4.2 suggest both time-variation in volatility and the

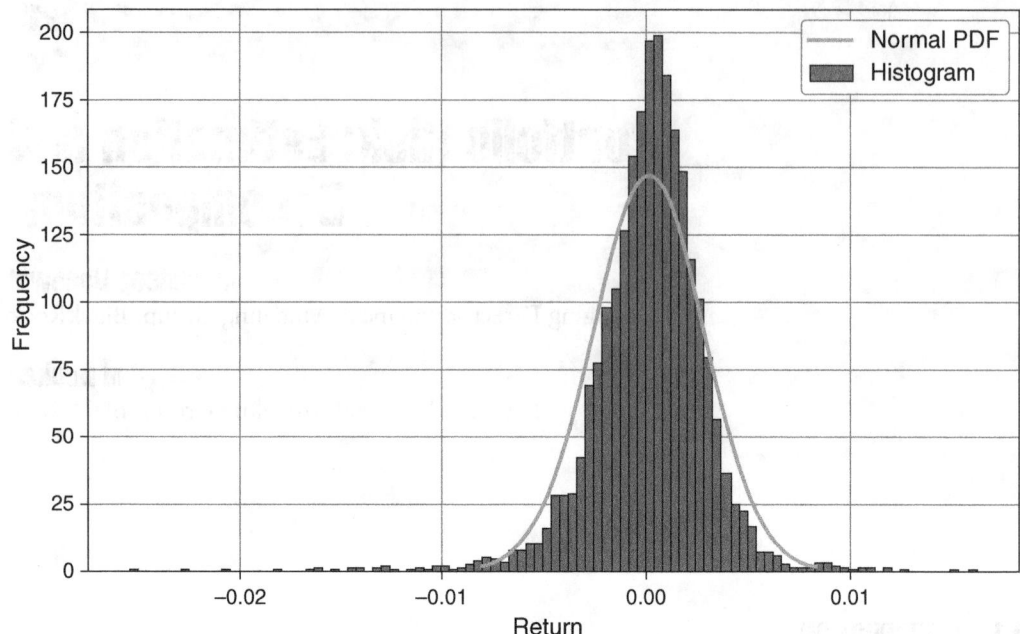

EXHIBIT 4.1   Multi-Asset Portfolio Daily Returns: Normal Versus Empirical[2]
Source: BlackRock Aladdin, January 2001–November 2019.
Note: The histogram summarizes the frequency distribution of daily returns on the sample multi-asset portfolio from January 2001–November 2019. The plot maps the in-sample maximum-likelihood estimate of the normal probability density function.

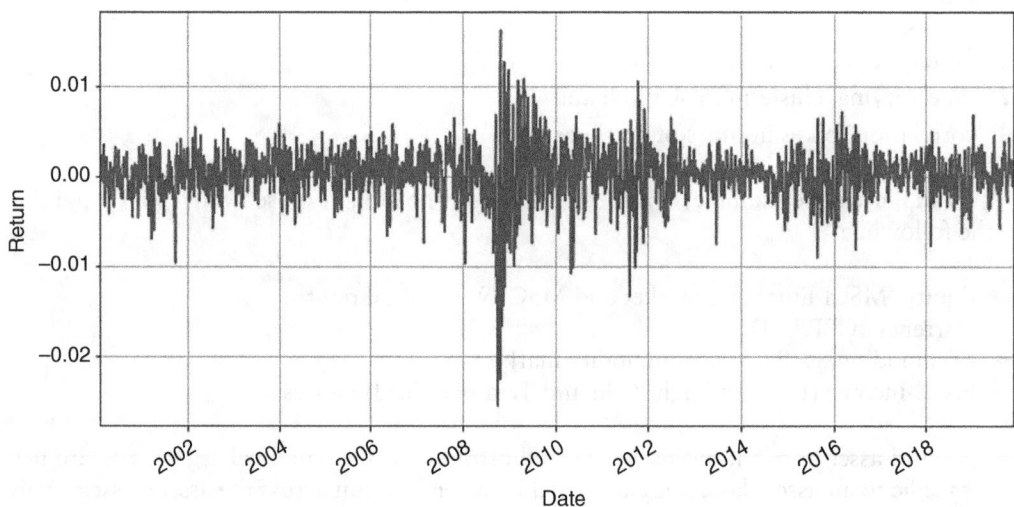

EXHIBIT 4.2   Multi-Asset Portfolio Daily Return Time Series: January 2001–November 2019
Source: BlackRock Aladdin, January 2001–November 2019.

diversity of asset classes notwithstanding, returns cluster in extremes during and immediately following the 2008–2009 crisis period.

Such empirical regularities have spawned an enormous amount of literature seeking to better capture time-series dynamics and thus improve out-of-sample risk forecasts. Much progress has been made—probably best exemplified by the award of a 2003 Nobel Prize[3] to Robert Engle and Clive Granger for pioneering the dominant econometric approach to capturing volatility dynamics. Advances in modeling the dynamics of volatility notwithstanding, the fat tails of return distributions are only partially accounted for by time-varying volatility. While returns scaled by time-varying volatility estimates more closely conform to a normal distribution, such scaling or standardization is not generally sufficient to account for extreme market movements. Thus, even after accounting for forecastable time-variation in volatility, empirical asset return distributions remain too fat-tailed to be considered normal.

Despite these challenges, volatility predominates as a risk metric because, unlike tail risk measures, it is simple to estimate, easily understood, highly persistent, and forecastable. Tail risks are almost by definition unforecastable since they happen too infrequently for any model to be calibrated to predict them. Further, volatility as a risk measure is especially prevalent on the buy-side, where portfolio managers generally do not rely heavily on derivatives and where portfolio returns are measured at long enough time intervals (e.g., monthly) that returns begin to approximate a normal distribution.

As an element of the first pillar of BlackRock's Investment Risk Management Paradigm (IRMP), this chapter commences with a discussion on portfolio volatility estimation, focusing on important empirical challenges to computing covariance estimates. Factor models are introduced in Section 4.2 as a means of modeling the sources of common variation in returns by way of a finite set of characteristics motivated by a combination of theory and empirical evidence. Practical issues of estimation are considered in Section 4.3, ranging from the weighting of historical data and enhancing model responsiveness, to application-specific generalizations of standard factor model specifications.

While total risk, as measured by volatility, is of central importance, the empirical properties of asset return distributions suggest that volatilities do not map simply to downside risk exposures. Section 4.4 thus provides an overview of VaR estimation approaches with a particular focus on enhanced historical VaR (EHVaR)—a proprietary approach to modeling the forward distribution of asset returns, blending advantages of both parametric and nonparametric forecasting techniques.

In Sections 4.5 through 4.9 the focus shifts to the decomposition of realized risk with respect to the characteristics of the portfolio and its factor structure. Factors are not only of econometric importance in portfolio risk forecasting, but they also afford insights to the economic sources of realized risk.

4.2 PORTFOLIO VOLATILITY AND FACTOR STRUCTURE

Portfolio volatility estimation commences with the simplifying assumption that security returns follow a linear factor structure. That is, an N-vector of security returns r can be written as:

$$r = a + Bf + \varepsilon, \text{where } E(f'\varepsilon) = 0 \qquad (4.1)$$

TABLE 4.1   Factor Model Taxonomy

Model Type	Inputs	Estimation Approach	Outputs
Time-series	Security Returns, Macro variables, Factor-mimicking Returns	Time-series regression	$\hat{B}$
Cross-sectional (Fundamental)	Security Returns, Factor Exposures	Cross-sectional Regression	$\hat{f}$
Statistical	Security Returns	Principal Components Analysis	$\hat{B}, \hat{f}$

where a is deterministic, f is a $K \times 1$ vector of factor returns, B is an $N \times K$ matrix of factor exposures, and ε is an $N \times 1$ vector of idiosyncratic returns. The covariance matrix of idiosyncratic returns is diagonal by assumption.[4] The factor structure in Equation 4.1 is general, encompassing three broad classes of models summarized in Table 4.1.[5]

In the terminology of Table 4.1, fundamental (cross-sectional) factor models are predominantly applied in industry. The remainder of this chapter assumes fundamental specifications, wherein factor exposures B are assumed known, and factor returns f are estimated by cross-sectional regression. Most popular academic approaches are based on time-series regressions of security returns on macro variables or returns to characteristic-based portfolios. Such regressions are used to estimate factor exposures to macroeconomic outcomes or portfolios constructed to hedge such outcomes. The choice between the approaches in Table 4.1 depends on considerations of data availability, empirical performance, and interpretability.

Fixed-income securities, defined in terms of readily observable (or computable) characteristics whose links to pricing are well understood, are particularly amenable to modeling by cross-sectional estimation. For example, the US corporate bond model:

$$r_{bond} = \underbrace{r_{time}}_{\text{Time}} \underbrace{- \sum_{i=1}^{11} krd_i \cdot \Delta kr_i + \sum_{j=1}^{4} \sum_{i=1}^{4} \frac{krbc_{i,j} \cdot \Delta kr_i \cdot \Delta kr_j}{2}}_{\text{Interest Rates}}$$

$$\underbrace{- spd\_dur \cdot spd \cdot \left. \frac{\Delta spd}{spd} \right|_{factors}}_{\text{Spreads}} \underbrace{- vol\_dur \cdot \Delta vol}_{\text{Volatility}} + \varepsilon \tag{4.2}$$

captures the exposure of bonds to

- interest rates, as measured by key rate durations krd;
- key rate bucket convexities $krbc$;
- spreads (as measured by spread durations spd_dur, with spread changes modeled as a function of bond characteristics); and
- volatility vol_dur.

While the time, interest rate, and volatility components of return variation are observable, variation in the applicable spread $\left. \frac{\Delta spd}{spd} \right|_{factors}$ is estimated through regression of spread changes on bond characteristics (such as industry, maturity, liquidity, and subordination).

Regardless of the factor structure, the return on a portfolio of N securities can be written as:

$$r_p = w'r \qquad (4.3)$$

where w is the N-vector of portfolio security weights[6] and r is an N-vector of periodic returns.

Given a fundamental factor model, portfolio variance is defined as:

$$\sigma_p = (w'E(rr')w)^{\frac{1}{2}}$$

$$= (w'(BE(ff')B' + E(\varepsilon\varepsilon') + 2E(f'\varepsilon))w)^{\frac{1}{2}}$$

$$= (w'B\Sigma B'w + w'\Omega w)^{\frac{1}{2}} \qquad (4.4)$$

where Σ is the factor covariance matrix and Ω is the block-diagonal covariance matrix of idiosyncratic risk. The last equality holds since the cross-term between factor returns f and idiosyncratic returns ε is zero by the orthogonality assumption in Equation 4.1.

The assumption of a linear factor structure can be motivated in both economic and statistical terms. In economic terms, the assumption attributes systematic covariation to a relatively small number of common, predefined factors—each of which is motivated by a mix of economic intuition and empirical experience. As such, estimates of risk exposure and factor realizations lend themselves to economic interpretation and data-driven insights. For example, apparently disparate assets, or classes of assets, may be more alike in terms of factor risk exposure than simple intuition may suggest, so characterizing assets as bundles of factor risk exposures affords quantitative insights to potential sources of diversification gains.

In statistical terms, assuming a linear factor structure is a pragmatic response to the challenge of estimating a large number of parameters in an unrestricted sample covariance matrix. Assuming a particular linear factor structure is almost certainly an oversimplification; however, estimating a much smaller number of biased parameters with greater precision delivers substantial gains from a statistical perspective.[7]

4.3 COVARIANCE MATRIX ESTIMATION

The covariance matrix is central to almost all portfolio risk analytics. A covariance matrix estimate is necessary and sufficient for forecasting volatility, empirical betas, and conducting implied stress testing. Parametric VaR estimation methods also use the covariance matrix as an input to simulate joint factor realizations. While computing a covariance matrix is trivial, the amount of academic literature devoted to estimating more accurate, responsive, and robust matrices is vast. This section provides an overview of the basic modeling estimation choices: the forecast horizon, the observation window, the exponential decay weighting scheme for historical data, the data frequency (i.e., daily, weekly, monthly), the choice between overlapping and non-overlapping data, and the generalization of factor model assumptions likely to be of particular significance to risk-based optimization of asset allocations.

Commencing with the simplest case of equal time-weighting, the factor covariance matrix $\widehat{\Sigma}$ can be estimated using the sample covariance matrix:

$$\widehat{\Sigma} = \frac{1}{T} \sum_{s=0}^{T-1} f_{t-s}\, f_{t-s}'$$

(4.5)

where the returns to K factors are represented by the $K \times 1$ vector f_{t-s} and T is the length of the estimation window. In order to annualize this covariance matrix, the matrix in Equation 4.5 is multiplied by $252/q$ where q refers to the periodicity of returns in days.[8] For example, if the covariance matrix is constructed from weekly returns, the matrix in Equation 4.5 is annualized by multiplying by $252/5$. More generally, the forecast horizon is set equal to the portfolio holding period, and the frequency of the returns used for estimation is set equal to or higher than the forecast horizon. If, for example, a portfolio is rebalanced monthly then monthly risk forecasts are computed using returns sampled at monthly frequencies or higher.

Notice that the sample mean is not subtracted from the factor returns in Equation 4.5. In periods where markets exhibit strong trending, subtracting the sample mean from returns will introduce a severe downward bias in the estimation of variance.[9] Following industry practice, covariance is computed directly from second moments where sample means are assumed to be zero. Excluding the sample mean results in a slightly conservative risk forecast. Since the factor mean does not need to be estimated in Equation 4.5, the divisor is T rather than $T - 1$.

The following sections provide more detail on special topics concerning calibration of the matrix, i.e., weighting the data, corrections for asynchronicity, as well as enhancements to the responsiveness of the matrix.

4.3.1 Weighting of Historical Data

4.3.1.1 Exponential Decay Weighting In keeping with industry practice, BlackRock's risk models apply exponentially weighted moving averages (EWMAs) to historical observations. An EWMA puts more weight on the most recent observations in the observation window:

$$\widehat{\Sigma} = \frac{1 - \lambda}{1 - \lambda^T} \sum_{s=0}^{T-1} \lambda^s f_{t-s}\, f_{t-s}'$$

(4.6)

Smaller values of the decay rate λ in Equation 4.6 correspond to smaller weights on older observations. Using L'Hôpital's rule, one can show that as $\lambda \to 1$, Equation 4.6 reduces to the sample covariance estimator in Equation 4.5.

Instead of defining λ directly, it is usually more convenient to express the decay rate in terms of half-life. The half-life $t_{\frac{1}{2}}$ is the time elapsed for the weight on historical observations to decay to half the weight on the most recent observation:

$$t_{\frac{1}{2}} = \frac{\log\left(\frac{1}{2}\right)}{\log(\lambda)}$$

(4.7)

For instance, a half-life of 8 days means the weight on observations of squared returns 8 days ago is given half the weight of squared returns today. Such a small half-life quickly

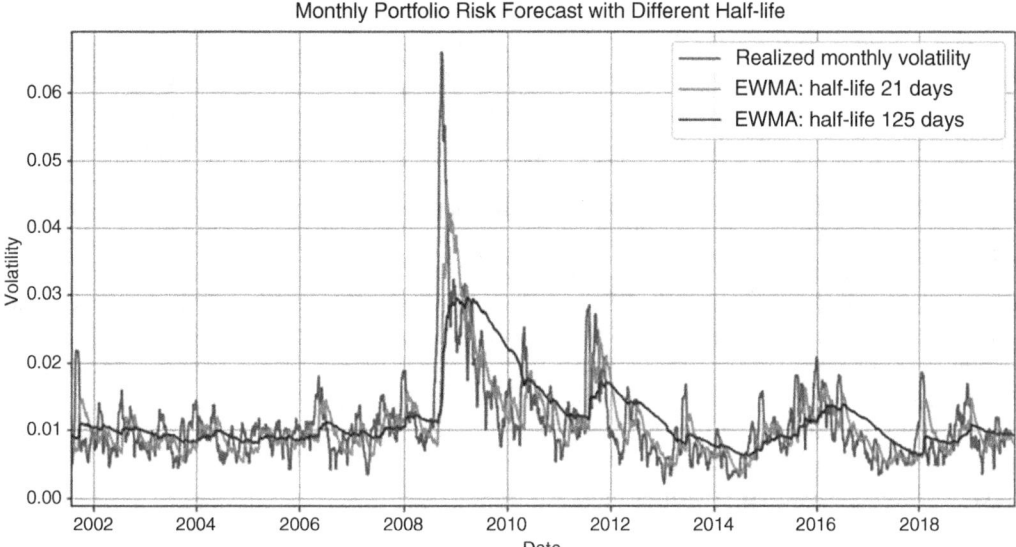

EXHIBIT 4.3 Impact of Half-Life on Multi-Asset Portfolio Risk Estimates
Source: BlackRock Aladdin, January 2001–November 2019.
Note: This exhibit is based on a yearly estimation window with a 21-day half-life, 125-day half-life, and realized volatility. Realized volatility is measured using daily forward returns subsequent to the forecast. Note that the realized volatility estimate itself is subject to error.

decays to zero. Setting too short of a half-life will result in a volatility estimate that fluctuates wildly over time due to purely random noise (sampling error). For example, when using a 252 day window and a half-life of 8 days, the effective number of data points is much smaller than 252 since so little weight is put on the older observations.[10]

$$t_{eff} = \frac{(1 - \lambda^T)^2}{(1 - \lambda)^2 \sum_{s=0}^{T-1} \lambda^{2s}} \approx \frac{(1 + \lambda)}{(1 - \lambda)}, \text{where } T \gg t_{\frac{1}{2}} \qquad (4.8)$$

Combining Equations 4.7 and 4.8, a half-life of 8 days with a 252 day window is equivalent to having only 23 data points.[11]

4.3.1.2 Alternative Weighting Schemes and Stress Scenarios The widespread adoption of EWMA reflects its relative simplicity and robust performance in relatively stable market conditions. However, to accommodate circumstances where the recent past does not adequately reflect changed market conditions, EWMA is unlikely to be the optimal approach to covariance estimation. When volatility suddenly spikes, for instance, static EWMA estimates are likely to underestimate future volatility. Under such conditions, instead of EWMA, regime-weighted covariance estimates may be preferable to estimate a covariance matrix using all periods where the VIX was greater than a specified threshold. As a second example, when conducting implied stress testing, it usually makes sense to construct the covariance matrix using historical observations that are similar to the hypothetical scenario shocks. For instance, if the scenario envisions a second Greek sovereign debt crisis, it makes sense to weight data more heavily around the first Greek debt crisis when calibrating the covariance matrix.

Whether fixes to the shortcomings of EWMA, such as regime-weighted estimation, yield superior risk forecasts depends heavily on how well past crises approximate future crises in terms of the speed, scope, severity, and duration of impacts. Addressing the shortcomings of EWMA using data reweighted to reflect previously observed crises involves judgment and strong assumptions about the structure and dynamics of the future stress scenario.

4.3.1.3 Enhancing Volatility Responsiveness Dynamically The regime or scenario-weighted approaches described in Section 4.3.1.2 rely on judgment or automated triggering with reference to a pre-specified volatility threshold—thus requiring either a timely detection of a shift in volatility regime or specification of an appropriate threshold. A more systematic approach to enhancing the responsiveness of EWMA-based volatility forecasts is to specify an adjustment coefficient that continuously adapts a security-level forecast to current market conditions discerned from the cross-section of realized volatilities.

In particular, a scaling coefficient γ_t may be chosen to minimize the cross-sectional mean-squared error (MSQE) of EWMA volatility forecasts σ_{it}^{EWMA} with reference to most recently observed realized volatilities $\sigma_{i(t-1)}$:

$$\min_{\gamma_t} = \frac{1}{N} \sum_{i=1}^{N} \left[\sigma_{i(t-1)} - \gamma_t \sigma_{it}^{EWMA} \right]^2 \tag{4.9}$$

For a cross-section of size N this yields:

$$\widehat{\gamma}_t = \frac{\sum_{i=1}^{N} \sigma_{i(t-1)} \sigma_{it}^{EWMA}}{\sum_{i=1}^{N} [\sigma_{it}^{EWMA}]^2} \tag{4.10}$$

Note that $\widehat{\gamma} = \frac{\sum_{i=1}^{N} \sigma_{i(t-1)}}{\sum_{i=1}^{N} \sigma_{it}^{EWMA}}$ scales the mean of σ_{it}^{EWMA} to the mean of $\sigma_{i(t-1)}$, and yields very similar results and underscores the intuition of the approach. The coefficient $\widehat{\gamma}$ effectively shortens the EWMA half-life when the cross-sectional average of most recently observed volatilities deviate from the cross-sectional average of current EWMA forecasts. While the time-series mean of $\widehat{\gamma}$ will be unity, it will scale EWMA forecasts estimates up (down) when recently observed realized monthly volatilities are high (low) relative to the longer horizon EWMA estimates.[12]

Exhibit 4.4 illustrates the variation in cross-sectional scaling based on the indices in the multi-asset portfolio example. Even with a small, diverse index-based cross-section, the dynamics reflect a wide range of variation in volatility conditions. The benefit of applying the scaling will be illustrated in the context of EHVaR estimation in Section 4.4.2.

More generally, it is also worth noting that this dynamic adjustment enables a decoupling of the assumptions on the dynamics of volatility and correlations. A correlation matrix derived using a fixed half-life Ω can be rescaled to covariances Σ^* using V, a diagonal matrix of volatilities adapted to recently observed market conditions:

$$\Sigma^* = V\Omega V' \tag{4.11}$$

This adjustment enables fast adaptation to current volatility conditions in the presence of slower moving correlations.

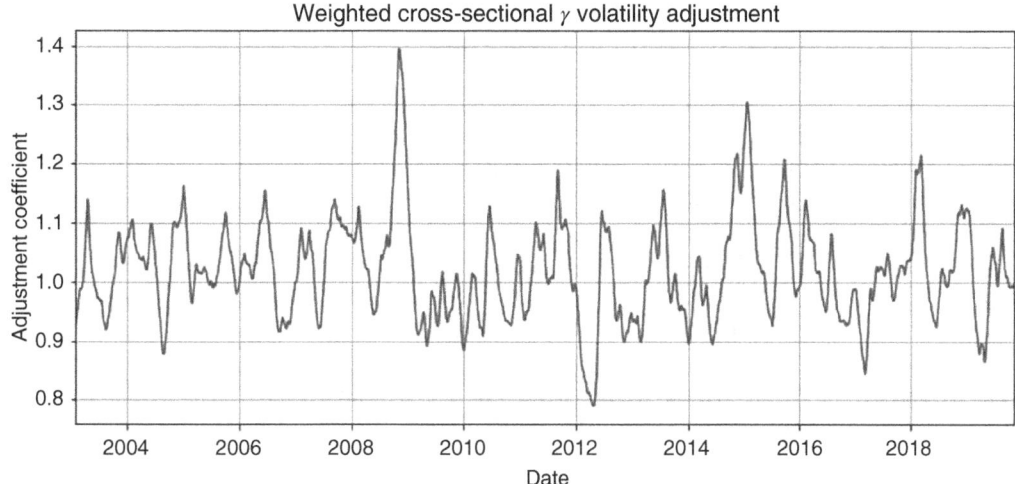

EXHIBIT 4.4 Cross-Sectional Scaling
Source: BlackRock Aladdin, January 2001–November 2019.
Note: The plot maps empirical estimates of $\hat{\gamma}$ based on Equation 4.10. The plotted estimates are smoothed using a 21-day half-life EWMA weighting scheme.

4.3.2 Asynchronicity

When estimating covariance matrices, we often assume we have observable, frequent, and synchronous returns across all assets. In practice, asset returns rarely satisfy these conditions. When returns are not frequent or synchronous, the resulting return volatility and correlation estimates can be severely downwardly biased. This bias can result in higher allocation to sectors with stale prices since those sectors seemingly offer lower volatility and greater diversification. The proximate cause of stale pricing can differ in different contexts, but the underlying cause in most cases is some form of illiquidity. Some causes of stale prices are the following:

- Asynchronous market closing times. Information that impacts markets do not respect market trading hours.
- Thinly traded securities. Securities that do not trade are often matrix priced by vendors or simply flatlined.
- Artificial smoothing of prices by hedge funds; smoothing of prices by real estate appraisers.

The simplest work-around to asynchronicity is to select a sampling frequency that is low enough to eliminate most of the bias. For instance, in fixed-income credit markets, practitioners typically measure risk using monthly data due to severely stale pricing caused by the lack of standardization and transparency in OTC markets.[13]

Using a low sampling frequency introduces problems of its own. Using weekly or monthly data means there are less observations to estimate the matrix. The fewer the number of observations, the more noisy the covariance matrix estimates. In addition, the covariance matrix will be stale between low frequency updates. The covariance matrix will only be current on the day of the matrix update. Further, instead of smoothly updating each day, a low frequency matrix will be flatlined most days and suddenly jump on the day of the covariance matrix update. This jump can make it difficult to disentangle changes in the markets or portfolio from the mechanical process of updating of the matrix.

4.3.2.1 Overlapping Covariance Matrix To mitigate the aforementioned difficulties, BlackRock risk models use overlapping data to simultaneously address the problems of nonsynchronous data and the problem of an infrequently updated matrix. An overlapping matrix updates daily using overlapping lower frequency returns.

For instance, instead of a single 5-day, non-overlapping return, one can construct returns corresponding to Mon–Mon, Tues–Tues, Wed–Wed returns, etc. Instead of using 52 non-overlapping weekly returns, this operation produces 252 overlapping weekly returns to compute the covariance matrix. By introducing overlapping observation windows, the number of effective data points in the estimator increases, lowering sampling variance. The covariance matrix also changes daily, avoiding the sudden jumps in volatility that are introduced when the matrix is only updated infrequently.

The overlapped covariance matrix is computed as:

$$\hat{\Sigma} = \frac{1 - \lambda}{L(1 - \lambda^T)} \sum_{s=0}^{T-1} \lambda^s \sum_{l=0}^{L-1} f_{t-s-l} \sum_{l'=0}^{L-1} f'_{t-s-l'} \qquad (4.12)$$

where L is the *overlap parameter*. In our overlapping weekly example, $L = 5$. When $L = 1$, Equation 4.12 reduces to 4.6.[14]

Although the overlapping time-series in Equation 4.12 has T observations, the number of effective observations is much lower than that. For instance, the overlapped weekly returns share four observations of daily returns with the two adjacent overlapping returns; as a consequence, the overlapped returns will be highly autocorrelated. Since adjacent overlapping data share so many observations, there are fewer than N independent observations.

As shown in Müller (1993), the number of effective observations in overlapped data can be approximated by:

$$t_{eff} \approx \frac{3TL}{2L^2 + 1} \qquad (4.13)$$

For instance, for overlap $L = 5$ with $T = 250$ data points t_{eff}, equals $3 * 5 * \frac{250}{2*25+1} \approx 75$. Compared to the weekly non-overlapping estimator, overlapping has increased the number of effective data points by 50%.

4.3.2.2 Newey-West Estimation As previously described, one way to correct for asynchronicity is to use lower frequency overlapped data. An alternative approach is to still use daily data, but explicitly correct for asynchronicity by estimating the degree of autocorrelation and cross-autocorrelation between returns. Newey and West (1987) is the most popular method used to correct for autocorrelation and heteroskedasticity in factor returns.

Newey-West's original result is a positive semi-definite and consistent estimator $\hat{\Sigma}$ for the L-period sample covariance matrix given by:

$$\hat{\Sigma} = \hat{\Omega}_0 + \sum_{l=1}^{L} \left(1 - \frac{l}{L} \right) [\hat{\Omega}_l + \hat{\Omega}'_l] \qquad (4.14)$$

where $\widehat{\Omega}_l$ represents the matrix of l-th order sample auto-covariances and cross auto-covariances ($l = 1$ gives the contemporaneous case) and $L - 1$ is the number of lagged covariance matrices.[15]

4.3.3 Factor Model Structure: Generalizations

The modeling choices discussed in Section 4.3 are generic to covariance estimation in the sense that they do not depend on the particular form of the factor structure. However, the assumption of a strict factor structure entails a cost-benefit trade-off that is unlikely to be optimal in all use cases. The current section describes two alternatives to the assumption of a strict factor structure:

1. A statistical approach involving explicit optimization of the error-bias trade-off without the specification of an explicit factor structure
2. Empirical augmentation of the covariance structure implied by a factor model

The former approach may be of particular interest in applications such as portfolio optimization when the statistically optimized estimates yield superior out-of-sample properties. Relaxing the assumption of a strict factor structure is likely to be beneficial in risk forecasting applications where it is of particular importance to avoid the underestimation of risk. In each case, the interpretability flowing from the assumption of a strict factor structure is sacrificed to some degree.

4.3.3.1 Optimization of the Error-Bias Trade-Off
As noted earlier, assume the linear factor structure in Equation 4.1 implies that portfolio risk depends on the covariation of K factors rather than N assets. While the unrestricted sample covariance estimate of asset returns is asymptotically unbiased, it involves the estimation of a large number of parameters with low precision, embedding a high degree of estimation error. This imprecision is particularly problematic for asset allocation, when the most extreme parameter estimates, those most likely to contain the estimation error, exert the greatest influence on variance-based optimizers. Assuming a linear factor structure wherein the number of factors K is generally much smaller than the number of assets N is one way to mitigate the impact of sampling error on covariance estimates.

Attributing all covariation in security returns to a small number of factors is almost certainly an oversimplification, so while the implied asset covariance matrix may contain less sampling error, the restricted estimates of covariance are likely to be biased. All else equal, the smaller the value of K, the higher (lower) the bias (sampling error). Recalling that the total mean-squared error associated with a parameter set θ can be decomposed as follows:

$$MSE(\widehat{\theta}) = Var_\theta(\widehat{\theta}) + Bias_{\widehat{\theta}}(\widehat{\theta}, \theta)^2 \tag{4.15}$$

finding the optimal value of K from a statistical perspective involves finding the appropriate trade-off between bias and sampling error.

Given the difficulty of identifying the number and identity of factors to include in a particular specification of Equation 4.1, Ledoit and Wolf (2004) derive an optimal "shrinkage" estimator that does not involve an explicit factor specification. Specifically, Ledoit-Wolf's shrinkage estimator locates the optimal solution δ^* to the convex linear combination:

$$\widehat{\Sigma}_{LW} = \delta F + (1 - \delta)\widehat{\Sigma} \tag{4.16}$$

where $\widehat{\Sigma}$ is the sample covariance matrix, F is a highly structured estimator, and $0 < \delta \leq 1$ is the shrinkage constant. The highly structured estimator F takes a simple form, consistent with a strong simplifying assumption. If, for example, F is set to the identity matrix, then all correlations are shrunk toward zero. The optimal value of the shrinkage constant, δ^*, minimizes the distance between the shrinkage estimate $\widehat{\Sigma}_{LW}$ and the true covariance matrix.

4.3.3.2 Misspecification and Omitted Covariation
Misspecification of the factor risk model may give rise to violations of model assumptions in the form of nonzero covariation between factor returns and idiosyncratic returns or covariation among idiosyncratic returns. Omission of relevant factors is a likely source of model misspecification.

Failure to account for sources of covariation that are zero by assumption only can generate underestimates of risk when they may be of particular significance—such as the computation of VaR or the generation of stress scenarios.

Relaxing the assumptions of a strict factor structure, portfolio risk can be re-expressed as:

$$\sigma_p^2 = w'\widehat{B}\widehat{\Sigma}_F\widehat{B}'w + w'\widehat{\Sigma}_R w + 2w'\widehat{B}\widehat{\Gamma}w \qquad (4.17)$$

where $\widehat{\Sigma}_F$ is the $K \times K$ factor covariance matrix, $\widehat{\Sigma}_R$ is the $N \times N$ idiosyncratic covariance matrix, and $\widehat{\Gamma}$ is the $K \times N$ matrix of covariances between factors and idiosyncratic returns. Equation 4.17 empirically accounts for the potential sources of downward bias associated with the assumption of a strict factor structure. The second term accounts for idiosyncratic covariation (the off-diagonals of $\widehat{\Sigma}_R$ are otherwise assumed zero) and risk attributable to dependence between factors and idiosyncratic returns—zero by assumption otherwise.

4.3.4 Covariance Matrix Estimation: Summary and Recommendations

This section presents an overview of the important considerations in forecasting portfolio risk with reference to factor models. A common theme to the key modeling choices is that they involve trade-offs of one form or another, and, consequently, the appropriate estimation procedure will depend on the intended use case. Representative use cases are summarized in Table 4.2.

TABLE 4.2 Portfolio Risk Estimation Use Cases: Modeling Priorities

Use Cases	Key Considerations
Portfolio Optimization	Accuracy of the covariance matrix (precision matrix) is of greater importance than the covariance matrix itself.
Imposing Risk Limits	Stability may be traded off at the expense of accuracy. An overly responsive matrix used to set risk limits may trigger selling at unfavorable prices when volatility spikes. Alternatively, tight tracking error volatility bands may generate high portfolio turnover and transaction costs.
When the Cost to Understating Risk Is High	A conservatively biased estimate of risk may be preferable to an unbiased estimate. A mean-squared error criteria applies a symmetrical penalty to over- and underestimation of risk. A popular alternative criteria proposed by Patton (2011) applies an asymmetric penalty to over- and under-prediction of risk.

TABLE 4.3 Portfolio Risk Forecasts: Estimation Choices

Forecast Parameter	Guiding Principles
Forecast Horizon	Forecast risk horizon is generally set equal to the portfolio holding period.
Sampling Frequency	Sampling frequency is set to be higher than or equal to the forecast horizon. For example, a monthly risk forecast requires a monthly sampling frequency or higher. In general, higher frequency estimates are associated with lower sampling error.
Observation Overlap	Overlapping returns are generally preferable insofar as they capture intra-period variation in returns that are missed by non-overlapping data. Overlapping returns also provide for a smoother evolution of risk forecasts.
Observation Weighting	Shorter EWMA half-lives (say 40 days, with daily observation frequency) are often optimal at shorter forecast horizons in terms of pure forecasting performance; however, longer half-lives (say 126 days) yield greater stability at the cost of diminished forecast responsiveness. Dynamic adjustment of longer half-life forecasts using the methods discussed in Section 4.3.1.3 may yield a useful compromise between forecasting accuracy and stability.
Window Length	The estimation window length should be chosen with the observation half-life in mind. Given a decay parameter λ, the window length that contains 99% of the weight is log $[0.01/\lambda]$. For example, assuming a 40-day half-life yields a window length of 260 days—slightly longer than 1 year.

Given the use case requirements, Table 4.3 summarizes guiding principles for choosing the estimation settings discussed in this section.[16] Section 4.4 discusses and illustrates the impact of some of the estimation choices summarized in Table 4.3 in the context of formulating tail risk estimates.

4.4 EX ANTE RISK AND VaR METHODOLOGIES

While volatility quantifies risk in terms of variability, portfolio managers are often concerned with more direct measures of exposure to losses in the event of poor performance, where poor performance is defined with reference to a distribution of return outcomes over some horizon. VaR quantifies potential losses in terms of the minimal loss associated with the lower tail of a return distribution, such that the lower tail is defined with reference to a quantile (threshold) of interest, or equivalently, the maximal loss associated with a given level of confidence. More formally, for a given probability α, VaR is defined as the threshold such that the probability that the portfolio return exceeds the threshold return over a given horizon is equal to α. Given a portfolio return cumulative distribution function F, VaR for portfolio p at confidence level α is defined as:

$$\text{VaR}_p(\alpha) = -F^{-1}(1 - \alpha) \tag{4.18}$$

That is, the $\alpha\%$ VaR is computed as the $1 - \alpha$ quantile from the distribution of portfolio returns. Note that by convention, VaR is reported with a positive sign when the $1 - \alpha$ quantile return is negative. For example, a 99% VaR of $100M implies that there is a 1% probability of observing portfolio losses of $100M or greater over the specified horizon. Equivalently, there is a 99% probability that portfolio losses will be lower than \$100M. If returns are normally distributed, the following condition is met:

$$\text{VaR}_{p1+p2}(\alpha) \leq \text{VaR}_{p1}(\alpha) + \text{VaR}_{p2}(\alpha) \tag{4.19}$$

As such, VaR can be said to be sub-additive—a principal tenet of diversification. Sub-additivity states that the risk of two assets combined should be no greater than the sum of the assets' risks. However, it should be noted that the sub-additivity of VaR is not guaranteed when return distributions depart substantially from normality.

Expected shortfall, also known as CVaR (i.e., conditional VaR) satisfies sub-additivity as a risk measure. Whereas VaR represents a threshold that may be violated with probability α, CVaR is the expected value of return conditional on a breach of the threshold. For a given probability α and risk horizon H, expected shortfall is defined as the average portfolio loss conditional on the loss exceeding α% VaR:

$$\text{ES}_p(\alpha) = \frac{1}{\alpha} \int_{a=0}^{\alpha} \text{VaR}_p(a) da = E(-r_p | r_p < -\text{VaR}_p(\alpha)) \tag{4.20}$$

4.4.1 VaR Estimation Approaches

Alternative VaR estimation approaches are classified in terms of their approaches to generating the forward distribution of portfolio returns. There are at least three tractable approaches to calculating VaR: analytical VaR, historical VaR, and Monte Carlo VaR. This section provides a brief overview of each analytic, including their advantages and disadvantages. Enhanced Historical VaR, a proprietary BlackRock analytic, is detailed as a flexible nonparametric framework for VaR estimation that builds on the advantages of HVaR while addressing its most important shortcomings.

Analytical VaR, also known as parametric or delta-normal VaR, assumes that asset returns have linear exposure to a set of risk factors and that the risk factors are normally distributed. Given these two assumptions, VaR reduces to a scalar multiple of tracking error volatility. Given normality, the scalar multiplier is the value of the inverse of the standard normal cumulative distribution, evaluated at a confidence level α. Analytical VaR is defined as:

$$\text{AVaR}_\alpha(\sigma_T) = -\Phi^{-1}(1 - \alpha)\sigma_T \tag{4.21}$$

where $-\Phi^{-1}$ is the inverse cumulative distribution function of the standard normal distribution. So 95% VaR for a portfolio is simply 1.96 times portfolio volatility since 95% of the density of a normal distribution is less than 1.96.

Analytical VaR often misstates risk when there is explicit or embedded optionality (i.e., nonlinearity) since analytical VaR only captures first-order Greeks (e.g., δ, ν). This first-order approximation is only reasonable at very short horizons or when options have little nonlinear behavior. Analytical VaR especially understates risk at high confidence levels since asset returns are often fat-tailed or skewed rather than normal. Both historical VaR and Monte Carlo VaR capture both the nonlinearity of portfolios as well as fat-tailed return distributions.

Exhibit 4.5 plots at weekly frequency the 99% AVaR bound for the equally weighted multi-asset portfolio over a sample spanning 2003–2019. In this example, the 99% bound is based on 375-day estimates of volatility, exponentially weighted, with a 21-day half-life.

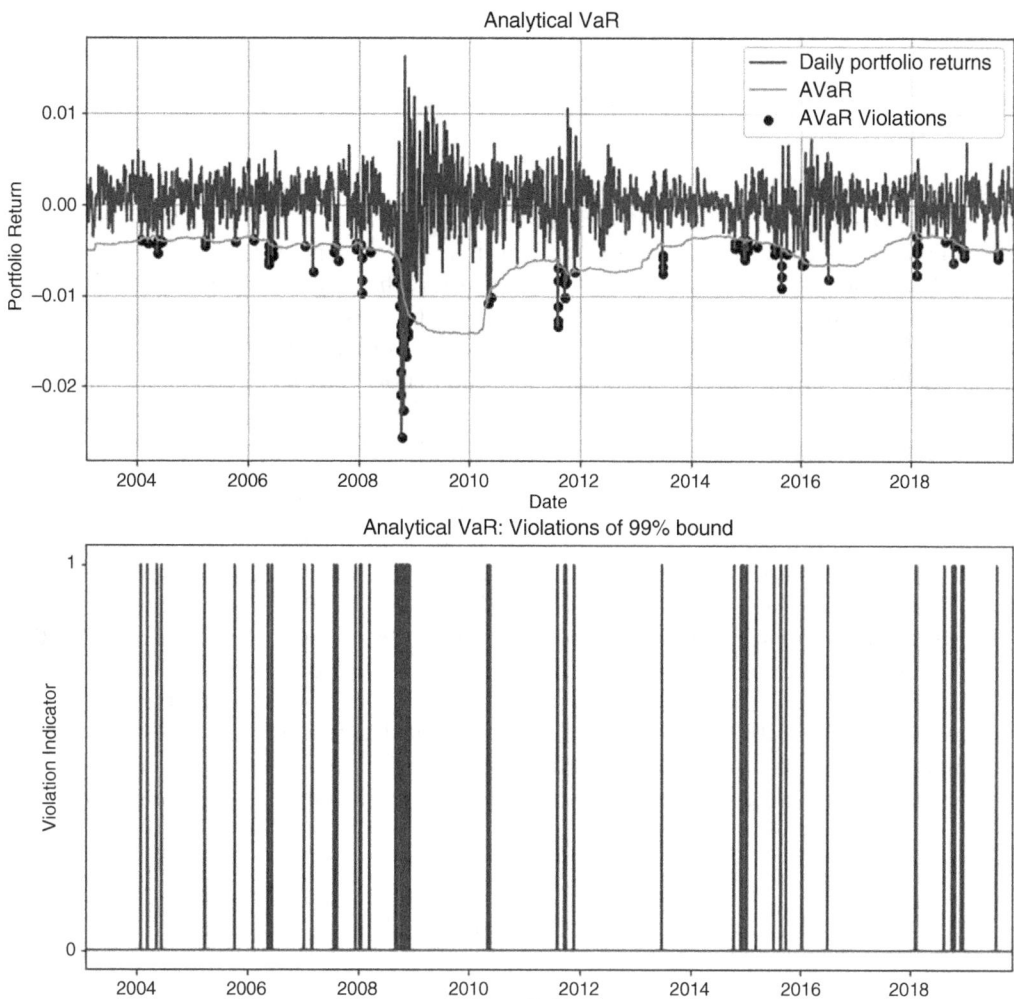

EXHIBIT 4.5 Analytical VaR
Source: BlackRock Aladdin, 2003–2019.
Note: The solid light gray line in the upper panel represents the 99% Analytical VaR bound, estimated using 375-day rolling samples. Black dots in the upper panel indicate return observations that violate the VaR boundary. Each boundary violation is marked by a solid line in the lower panel to enable a clearer visualization of the frequency and pattern of violations.

The 21-day half-life yields relatively responsive risk estimates; however, the 99% boundary exhibits a violation rate[17] greater than 2.9%—consistent with the observation that returns are more fat-tailed than what normality would suggest. The 2.9% violation rate represents a statistically significant exceedance of the 1% expected value, and the violations are not independent, that is, they exhibit statistically significant clustering.[18]

Historical VaR (HVaR) is computed by first generating a history of hypothetical portfolio returns using the current portfolio exposure to risk factors. HVaR sorts portfolio returns from smallest to largest and selects the appropriate quantile α from the nonparametric distribution.

Historical VaR is defined as:

$$\text{HVaR}(\alpha, T) = Percentile\left\{\{r_{p,t}\}_{t=1}^{T}, \alpha\right\} \tag{4.22}$$

where $Percentile\left\{\{r_{p,t}\}_{t=1}^{T}, \alpha\right\}$ denotes the α-percentile of historical portfolio returns r_p over the sample spanning time t to T. Modeling tail events requires a long history of data since, by definition, events in the tails of the distribution do not happen very often. Computing stable HVaR estimates for small α requires using a long history. However, using a long history of data has drawbacks. Specifically, the HVaR estimates may not be aligned to current market conditions. An extreme event far in the past, but still in the observation window, can substantially impact current VaR estimates, a phenomenon known as "ghosting."

Exhibit 4.6 presents the 99% weekly HVaR bound for the multi-asset portfolio based on a 375-day estimation window with constant weighting. The 99% boundary is violated at a rate of approximately 1.6% over the span of the sample—suggesting that forecasts based on the empirical distribution better capture the extremes than the normal approximation. However, the departure from the expected violation rate remains highly statistically significant, and clustering of the violations remain statistically significant. Even though the overall violation rate is much closer to 1% than that yielded by AVaR, the HVaR boundary exhibits sudden shifts triggered by the inclusion or exclusion of extreme observations (such as the 2008–2009 crisis) from the estimation window rather than underlying risk dynamics.[19]

In order to construct HVaR estimates that are more responsive to current market conditions, Hull and White (1999) introduced filtered historical VaR, which involves filtering (i.e., dividing) security or factor returns by ex ante volatility. These filtered historical returns are then rescaled back to the current estimate of volatility. Volatility-scaled (i.e., filtered) historical VaR is defined as:

$$\text{Volatility Scaled HVaR}(\alpha, T) = \sigma_T Percentile\left\{\left\{\frac{r_{p,t}}{\sigma_t}\right\}_{t=1}^{T}, \alpha\right\} \tag{4.23}$$

This augmentation of HVaR is an important element of the enhanced HVaR approach detailed in Section 4.4.2.

Note that HVaR can be viewed as an extension of the analytical VaR (AVaR) metric. AVaR is the VaR forecast derived from portfolio ex ante volatility σ_T under the assumption of normally distributed returns and linear factor exposures. Given portfolio volatility σ_T, $\alpha\%$, AVaR of systematic risk is defined as:

$$\text{AVaR}_{\alpha}(\sigma_T) = -\Phi^{-1}(1 - \alpha) \cdot \sigma_T \tag{4.24}$$

where $-\Phi^{-1}$ is the inverse cumulative distribution function of the standard normal distribution.

To understand the relationship between HVaR and AVaR, recall that we can express the volatility scaled returns $\hat{r}_p$ as the product of z-scores z_p and current volatility σ_T. As mentioned earlier, if the ex ante volatility forecast was unbiased and returns were normally distributed, the z-scores z_p would follow a unit normal distribution. In general, since returns

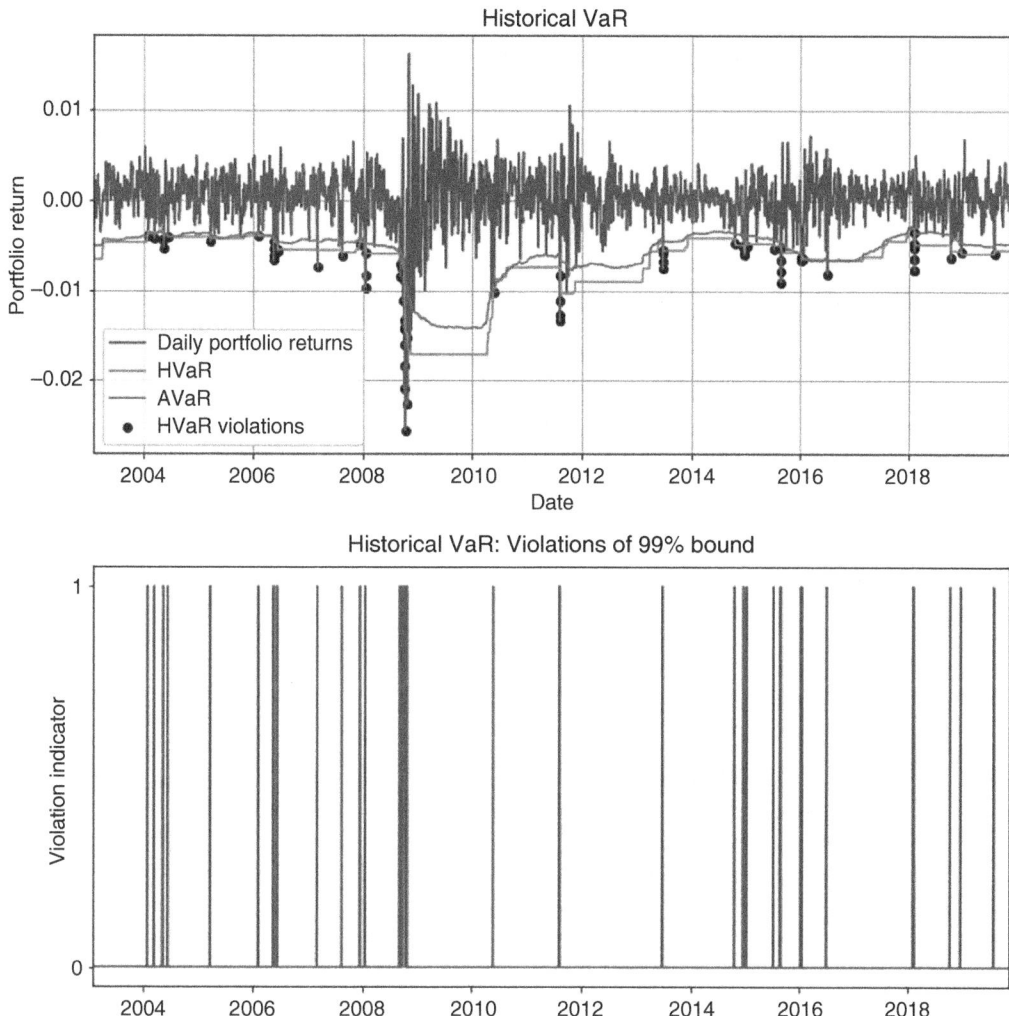

EXHIBIT 4.6 Historical VaR

Source: BlackRock Aladdin, 2003–2019.

Note: The light gray line in the upper panel represents the 99% HVaR bound, estimated using 375-day rolling samples. The dark gray line represents the 99% Analytical VaR boundary. Black dots in the upper panel indicate return observations that violate the HVaR boundary. Each boundary violation is marked by a solid line in the lower panel to enable a clearer visualization of the frequency and pattern of violations.

are fat-tailed and negatively skewed, the VaR of the z-scores will be larger than that implied from the normal distribution. We define an analytic called the Systematic Tail Risk Multiplier (STRM) as the ratio of VaR computed from the empirical z-scores to the VaR from the normal distribution:

$$\text{STRM}_{\alpha} = \frac{\text{VaR}_{p,\alpha}(z_p)}{-\Phi^{-1}(1-\alpha)} \qquad (4.25)$$

Equation 4.26 shows that HVaR forecast can be expressed as AVaR times STRM.[20] This leads to a convenient interpretation of VaR computed under the HVaR framework as a "multiplier" on Analytical VaR:

$$\text{VaR}_{p,\alpha}(\hat{r}_p) = \text{VaR}_{p,\alpha}(z_p \sigma_T) = \left\{ \frac{\text{VaR}_{p,\alpha}(z_p)}{\Phi^{-1}(1-\alpha)} \right\} \cdot \{\Phi^{-1}(1-\alpha) \cdot \sigma_T\}$$

$$= \text{STRM} \cdot \text{AVaR}_{\alpha}(\sigma_T) \tag{4.26}$$

Note that STRM can differ from one either because returns are nonnormal or because the ex ante volatility forecast σ_T is biased.

In *Monte Carlo VaR*, factor returns are simulated from a pre-specified factor return joint probability distribution. Given the simulations of factor returns, securities are repriced in the same manner as described for historical VaR. The primary advantage of Monte Carlo VaR is that it is not limited by history; that is, it can be used to simulate extreme tail outcomes or scenarios with no precedence in the estimation sample. This flexibility of the approach can be a double-edged sword: the more the scenario generation differs from historical data, the greater the importance of the underlying distributional assumptions. A Monte Carlo VaR's efficiency is entirely contingent on the accuracy of the forecasted joint distribution of factor returns.

4.4.2 Enhanced HVaR

The HVaR framework has several drawbacks that limit its applicability. First, because a long historical sample is required to compute a stable VaR forecast (especially for a high confidence level α), HVaR forecasts tend to be relatively static and therefore do not reflect current market conditions. As can be seen in Exhibit 4.6, the 2008 Global Financial Crisis HVaR boundary illustrates an extended period of elevated risk, followed by a sudden decline as extreme observations drop from the sample. The HVaR methodology is constrained into making a trade-off between imprecision in estimating extreme VaR quantiles and insensitivity to current market conditions. Significant clustering of VaR violations occur when VaR forecasts from HVaR do not adjust quickly enough to changes in market risk.

Enhanced HVaR (EHVaR) addresses the tension between the need for a long estimation sample and adaptability to current market conditions by decoupling the calibration of the tail from the calibration of portfolio return volatility. A very fast-moving estimator with a short window is used to calibrate return volatility, while a very long window is used to calibrate the tail. The basic idea is that tail events happen very infrequently and one needs a long history to calibrate them, while volatility is highly time-varying and must be modeled at high frequency.

The second drawback of HVaR, as described to this point, is that it does not incorporate idiosyncratic risk. This is a significant problem for factor models where all unexplained returns are attributed to idiosyncratic risk. VaR on active portfolios that take very little systematic factor risk cannot be accurately measured with HVaR. As described next, EHVaR allows for the incorporation of idiosyncratic risk into the tail risk calculation.

4.4.2.1 EHVaR Systematic Risk Methodology EHVaR estimates, based on the systematic component of risk, are estimated as follows.

1. **Standardization of Factor Returns**
   Historical factor returns $r_{i,t:t+H}^{factor}$ are standardized using ex ante volatility forecasts $\sigma_{i,t}$ such that:

$$z_{i,t:t+H} = \frac{r_{i,t:t+H}^{factor}}{\sigma_{i,t}} \tag{4.27}$$

   Note that ex ante volatility forecasts are obtained using overlapping daily data with a user-specified half-life, overlap, and window scaled to the portfolio return $r_{p,t:t+H}$ horizon H using the "square root of time" rule. For instance, $\sigma_{i,t}$ is computed using a 5-day overlap, 40-day half-life, and 252-day window, with a portfolio return $r_{p,t:t+H}$ horizon $H = 20$, then $\sigma_{i,t}$ is scaled by $\left(\frac{20}{5}\right)^{\frac{1}{2}} = 2$.

2. **Re-scaling to Current Volatility Conditions**
   Standardization in accordance with Equation 4.27 with unbiased volatility estimates $\sigma_{i,t}$ yields an empirical distribution of factor returns with unit variance. Empirical returns consistent with current volatility expectations, $\hat{r}_{i,t:t+H}^{factor}$, are obtained through a rescaling of standardized returns using the current (responsive) volatility forecast:

$$\hat{r}_{i,t:t+H}^{factor} = z_{i,t:t+H}\sigma_{i,T} \tag{4.28}$$

   Portfolio returns are obtained using:

$$\hat{r}_{p,t:t+H} = \sum_j w_j f_j(\hat{R}_{j,t:t+H}) \tag{4.29}$$

   where for security j in portfolio p, w_j is the weight, f_j is the pricing function in full revaluation, and $\hat{R}_{i,t:t+H}$ is the set of scaled factor returns $\hat{r}_{i,t:t+H}^{factor}$ (for each factor i in security j). Full revaluation returns based on the set of factors $\hat{r}_{i,t:t+H}^{factor}$ can be used where applicable for nonlinear securities. BlackRock's implementation of EHVaR allows users to opt for full revaluation or a linear approximation of prices.

3. **Computing VaR and Expected Shortfall (ES)**
   The process of standardization and scaling factor returns to current volatility conditions enables the use of a lengthy sample for nonparametric tail estimation, reflective of current volatility conditions. Estimates of VaR and ES are simply computed from the scaled returns $\hat{r}_{p,t:t+H}$. $\alpha\%$. H-day VaR is computed as the $(1 - \alpha)$ quantile from $\hat{r}_{p,t:t+H}$, the historical sample of synthetic portfolio returns.
   Expected shortfall is computed as the average return in the historical sample that exceeds the $\alpha\%$ H-day VaR confidence level.

Exhibit 4.7 contrasts the empirical 99% HVaR boundary with that obtained through standardization and rescaling to current volatility conditions (as captured by pure EWMA with a 21-day half-life). Standardization and rescaling alleviates the ghosting associated with the pure HVaR, and the overall boundary violation rate drops from 1.6% to 1.2%.

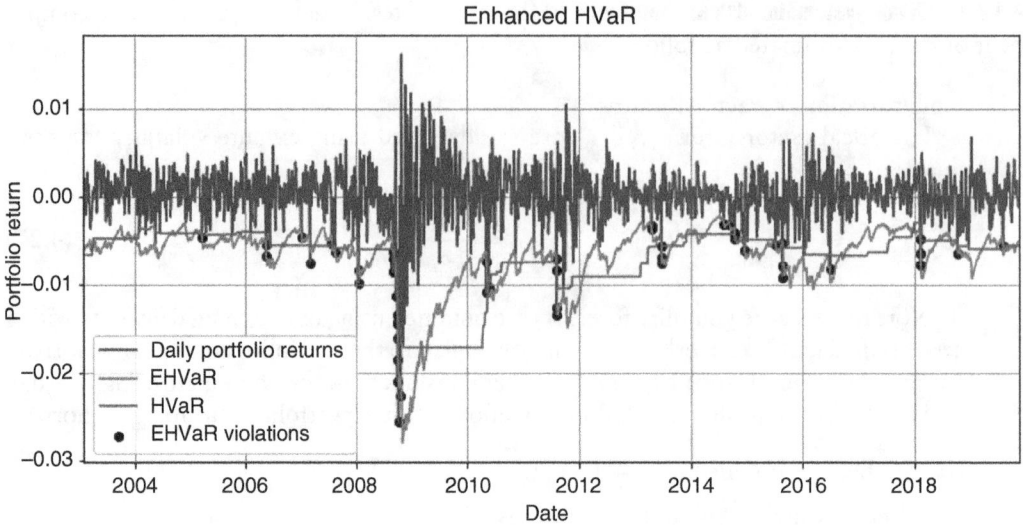

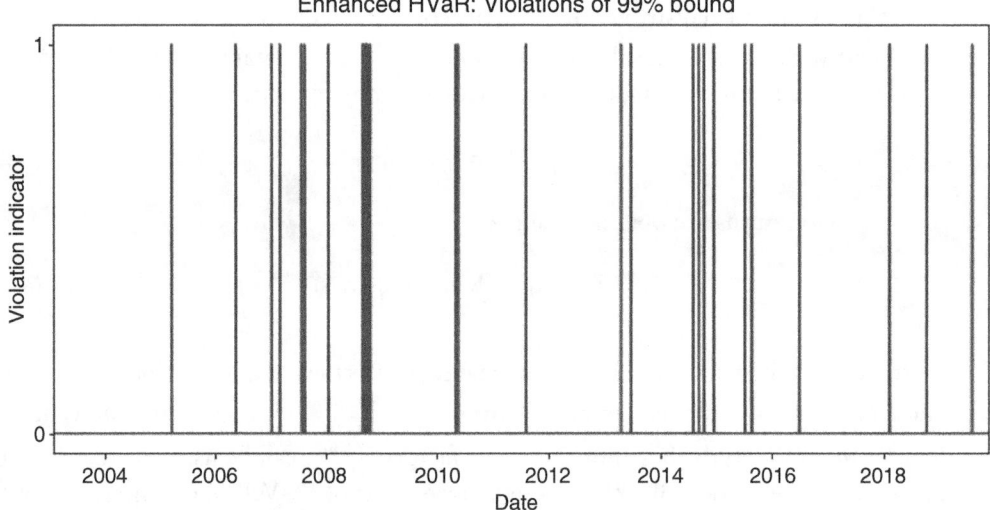

EXHIBIT 4.7   Enhanced Historical VaR
Source: BlackRock Aladdin, 2003–2019.
Note: The light gray line in the upper panel maps the 99% EHVaR bound, estimated using 375-day rolling samples. The dark gray line maps the 99% HVaR boundary. Black dots in the upper panel indicate return observations that violate the EHVaR boundary. Each boundary violation is marked by a solid line in the lower panel to enable a clearer visualization of the frequency and pattern of violations.

Exhibit 4.8 shows that further gains are attainable when returns are rescaled to current volatility estimates incorporating the $\hat{\gamma}$ adjustment described in Section 4.3.1.3: the violation rate is now 1.06% and statistically indistinguishable from 1%. However, rescaling to current volatility conditions, even as measured by an enhanced estimator, leaves room for improvement as the clustering of violations remains statistically significant.

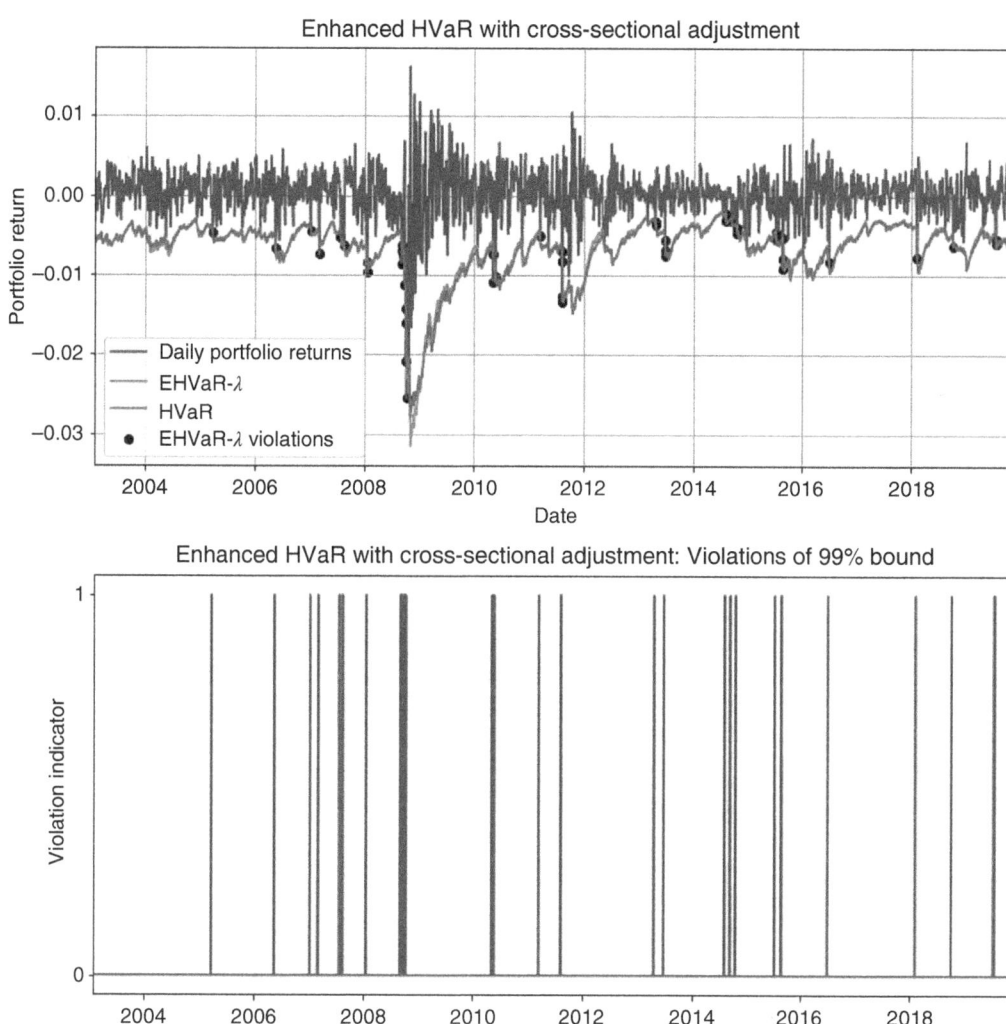

EXHIBIT 4.8 Enhanced Historical VaR with Cross-Sectional Adjustments
Source: BlackRock Aladdin, 2003–2019.
Note: The light gray line in the upper panel represents the $\hat{\gamma}$ - augmented 99% EHVaR bound, estimated using 375-day rolling samples. The dark gray line represents the 99% EHVaR boundary. Black dots in the upper panel indicate return observations that violate the $\hat{\gamma}$-augmented EHVaR boundary. Each boundary violation is marked by a solid line in the lower panel to enable a clearer visualization of the frequency and pattern of violations.

4.4.2.2 EHVaR Idiosyncratic Risk Methodology To accommodate the tail risk effects of idiosyncratic returns on less than perfectly diversified portfolios, EHVaR accommodates the set of following empirical regularities:

1. Idiosyncratic returns tend to be fat-tailed and negatively skewed.
2. Not all instruments exhibit the same degree of fat-tailedness or skew. For instance, the idiosyncratic returns on corporate bonds tend to be highly negatively skewed since these

bonds tend to have a small probability of a very large loss due to downgrade or default. US government guaranteed securities have much lower tail risk since the US government is (hopefully) much less likely to default.

3. The direction of the skew depends on whether the investor is short or long credit risk. The returns of a portfolio that is short credit risk should be positively skewed.

4. Diversified portfolios should have less exposure to tail risk than concentrated portfolios. In a sufficiently diversified portfolio, idiosyncratic returns are approximately normally distributed. In a very concentrated portfolio, idiosyncratic risk can be very skewed and fat-tailed. Portfolios with some level of diversification will fall somewhere in between.

To capture these regularities, the EHVaR model incorporates the simplifying assumption that idiosyncratic returns follow a skewed-t distribution (fact 1), where the parameters of the distribution depend on the asset class (fact 2), the level of issuer diversification (fact 4), and whether the position is long or short (fact 3).

As of March 2023, BlackRock's EHVaR model captures the skew and fat-tailedness of idiosyncratic risk for two asset classes—investment-grade (IG) credit and high-yield (HY) credit.[21] Bonds are bucketed into four cohorts (IG long, IG short, HY long, and HY short) and a different skewed-t distribution is assigned to each cohort depending on the level of diversification within the cohort.

The importance of cohorting long and short positions separately can be highlighted using a simple example. For instance, the diversification score of idiosyncratic risk for an index will generally be quite high—often above 30. The diversification score of portfolio idiosyncratic risk, on the other hand, will often be much lower. Hence, an IG credit portfolio that is actively managed versus a benchmark will be modeled as having an IG long cohort with a low diversification score and an IG short cohort with a high diversification score (as defined in Equation A.2 in Appendix A). The implication is that the benchmark idiosyncratic risk will be more normally distributed, but the portfolio long credit positions will be modeled as being negatively skewed and fat-tailed.

Commencing with determining the mapping of diversification to skewed t-distribution, the idiosyncratic risk contribution to VaR is obtained in two steps, as detailed in Appendix A. Total EHVaR, including both systematic and idiosyncratic sources, is approximated by adding in quadrature as described in Appendix B.

4.4.3   VaR Estimation: Summary

Alternative VaR estimation approaches are distinguishable with reference to how they generate the forward distribution of portfolio returns, and how the methodologies trade-off considerations of simplicity, flexibility, and adherence to historical experience. A more comprehensive coverage of VaR estimation approaches is beyond the scope of a single chapter. This chapter focuses on EHVaR as a means of generating empirically grounded portfolio return distributions, consistent with the factor structure of the constituent assets, and adjusted for the current volatility conditions—important benefits attainable in a framework that can be viewed as an extension of AVaR. EHVaR thus balances the relative simplicity of AVaR with the empirical appeal of HVaR.

4.5 INTRODUCTION TO RISK DECOMPOSITION

The discussion so far has focused on the computation of aggregate measures of portfolio risk. As described in the previous section, such measures often condense vast amounts of information, such as security market values, risk exposures, and forecasts of volatility and correlation, into a single number. This can be helpful in providing a summary view of risk, for example, when assessing levels of portfolio risk against a client's expected return objectives. Of similar importance, however, is the exercise of risk decomposition, where the objective is to understand and contextualize the underlying sources of that risk.

Risk decomposition helps disentangle the influence of any single input with respect to the aggregate risk number, and has important applications in the day-to-day risk management of investment portfolios. As an example, suppose a portfolio breached its pre-agreed risk thresholds; it is natural to question the cause of that breach so that appropriate corrective action can be taken to bring the portfolio back into alignment. Risk decomposition is an important tool to achieve this purpose.

More broadly, risk decomposition analysis is useful for identifying and quantifying the key risk-and-return drivers of a portfolio. This analysis provides the basis for more informed dialogue between risk managers and portfolio managers to ensure that the allocation of risk in portfolios is deliberate, well-diversified, and suitably scaled to the convictions of the investor.[22]

In its traditional form, risk decomposition attributes portfolio risk to individual securities within the portfolio, as these form the basic units of trade and investment activity. The methods in this section generalize and extend this approach in a number of important ways.

The discussion first focuses on aggregating security risk into groups, for example, countries or sectors, which is useful when investment decisions are oriented along these dimensions.

When linear factor models are used for risk analysis, securities' risk can be decomposed into systematic factors and idiosyncratic components of risk. These components can themselves be aggregated *across securities* to give alternative decompositions of portfolio risk grouped by similar kinds of factors. Risk decomposition using a linear factor model can often highlight concentrations of risk that are not obvious from analyzing security-based decomposition alone and so provide a vital, additional tool in providing insight into portfolio diversification.

The previous decomposition modes share one common aspect: they are based upon a single snapshot of portfolio holdings, i.e., a point-in-time. However, it is also instructive and useful to understand how risk decomposition varies over time. In the final section, an approach is presented to quantify the interplay between trading activity and updates to the underlying risk model as market conditions change.

Throughout this section, the aggregate risk measure used to illustrate the decomposition modes is ex ante portfolio risk. However, these methods can be readily extended, with little modification, to the disaggregation of other commonly used risk measures such as parametric VaR. Worked examples are provided throughout to help illustrate the ideas.

4.6 ALTERNATIVE APPROACHES TO RISK DECOMPOSITION

Various approaches to risk decomposition have been adopted in investment and risk management practice. Each has their advantages and disadvantages in terms of underlying assumptions, degree of tractability, and computational cost. In many circumstances, it may be advisable to use multiple approaches to take advantage of their complementary features. However, in recent years, contribution to risk (CTR) has been the most commonly used and has emerged as a standard measure that is implemented by most of the major risk analytics vendors.

The most common risk decomposition measures, together with their strengths and weaknesses, are briefly discussed next.[23]

1. **Standalone Risk (SAR)**

   This measure calculates the risk that arises from holding a security in isolation with the same level of exposure as in the portfolio. It therefore differs from security risk because it is computed as the product of security weights (w) and security risk:

   $$SAR = w \cdot Diag(V)^{\frac{1}{2}} \tag{4.30}$$

   where $V = B\Sigma B' + \Omega$ is the security-level covariance matrix.

   Despite its simple computation, SAR ignores any measured correlation (and diversification) between a particular security and all the other ones in the portfolio. This can easily understate (or overstate) the degree of risk in the portfolio arising from that security depending on whether it is strongly positively correlated (or negatively correlated) to others in the portfolio. The sum of individual security-level SARs is usually not equal to the aggregate portfolio risk (σ_p) as seen in Equation 4.31:

   $$\sigma_p = \sum_{i=1}^{N} SAR_i + Diversification\ benefit \tag{4.31}$$

   The missing component that plugs this difference is due to the omitted cross-security interaction terms and quantifies the degree of diversification across all securities in the portfolio. For this reason, SAR is more commonly used for analyzing investment strategies, such as short-horizon hedge funds, where correlations can be harder to accurately assess and so less reliable for ex ante risk measurement, leading to their explicit separation in the resulting decomposition.

2. **Incremental Contribution to Risk (ICTR)**

   Incremental contribution is calculated as the change in aggregate portfolio risk that arises from liquidating a security entirely and pro-rata redistributing its market value to all other securities in the portfolio. Its computation requires a full revaluation of the portfolio excluding each security held (denoted by $\sigma_{\underline{p}_i}$).

   $$ICTR_i = \sigma_p - \sigma_{\underline{p}_i} \tag{4.32}$$

   For an investment portfolio of N securities, this involves N revaluations. This measure is not additive in that security level incremental contributions do not sum to the aggregate portfolio risk, and so ICTRs need to be recomputed for each layer of granularity used for the analysis. For example, sector-level ICTRs would require separate computation and cannot be recovered (via addition) from security-level ICTRs. The scope of computations can therefore accumulate rapidly when ICTRs are applied to firm-level enterprise risk reporting.

Nevertheless, ICTR gives an accurate assessment of the impact of a security to portfolio risk in the event of its liquidation, which can be valuable when an investor is making large changes to their portfolio or if the security exhibits significant nonlinearity.

3. **Marginal Contribution to Risk (MCTR)**

   Marginal contribution captures the difference in portfolio risk arising from a marginal change in the position of a security. The computation is based on a partial derivative, measuring the change in portfolio risk in response to a small change in a security's allocation, as shown in Exhibit 4.9, and is calculated as:

$$\text{MCTR} = \frac{\partial \sigma_p}{\partial w} = \frac{Vw}{\sigma_p} \tag{4.33}$$

   It represents a (linear) approximation that holds for infinitesimal changes in a security's position, while assuming no changes in all other security holdings. This can present challenges in practice as investors are rarely looking to make such small incremental changes, and any change would typically need to be funded by selling down other securities or cash held in the portfolio. As a result, MCTR can understate (or overstate) portfolio risk changes when investors are looking to make significant trades.

   Nevertheless, the approximation offered by MCTR holds reasonably well for portfolios invested in vanilla securities and comes with lower computational cost as compared to ICTR.[24] It also highlights the overall risk structure of a portfolio.

4. **Contribution to Risk (CTR)**

   This measure attributes a proportion of the portfolio risk to each security. CTR is calculated as the product of the security exposure (w) and the marginal contribution to risk (MCTR), and so has similar benefits and limitations as MCTR in terms of interpretation:

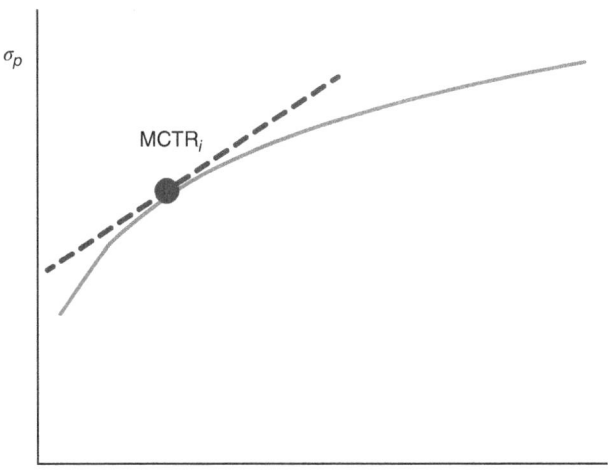

EXHIBIT 4.9 Marginal Contribution to Risk
Source: For illustrative purposes only.

$$CTR = w \cdot MCTR = w \cdot \frac{Vw}{\sigma_p} \qquad (4.34)$$

Unlike the previous measures (SAR, ICTR, and MCTR), CTR also has the intuitive property of additivity, illustrated in Equation 4.35, i.e., the sum of CTRs across all portfolio securities will sum to the aggregate portfolio risk. CTR is also linear in aggregation, i.e., a sector-level CTR is simply the sum of security-level CTRs belonging to that sector, which provides consistency across different decomposition modes and, thereby, enhances its application as an investigative tool for better understanding risk.

$$\sigma_p = \sum_{i=1}^{N} CTR_i \qquad (4.35)$$

The usefulness of these properties is drawn upon repeatedly throughout this section.[25]

4.6.1   A Comparison of the Different Approaches

Exhibit 4.10 compares the different risk decomposition measures for a simple portfolio consisting of corporate bonds, asset-backed securities, and agency debt. An examination of the different contribution values and their differences provides several important insights into the risk profile of this portfolio.

The long duration agency bond, Tennessee Valley Authority (TVA), has the highest individual security risk in the portfolio, but only claims the second highest standalone risk contribution. Instead, the corporate bond issued by PetSmart has the highest standalone risk on account of its moderate security risk, but larger position size. Furthermore, the aggregate portfolio risk is shown as 480 basis points (bp), which is considerably lower than the sum of all standalone risks, which is equal to 797 bp, and quantifies the significant degree of diversification afforded by holding these securities in a portfolio. However, the source of this diversification is not immediately clear by inspecting the standalone risks alone.

When comparing SAR with ICTR, the incremental contributions provide a similar picture of the top contributors, showing the same three bonds—TVA, PetSmart, and Anheuser-Busch—as having the largest impact on portfolio risk based on their magnitude. Unlike SAR, the sign of the ICTR additionally reveals information related to the correlation of each security with the overall portfolio. As an example, the PetSmart corporate bond has the largest ICTR of –194 bp. Liquidating this position and reinvesting the proceeds back into the remaining portfolio positions leads to a sharp increase in aggregate risk. This suggests that the PetSmart bond has a significantly lower (or negative) correlation with the other securities in the portfolio.

Turning to the marginal contributions, at first glance, these appear significantly lower than the alternative contributions. This arises by construction as they are scaled to show the change in portfolio risk due to a 1% change in security weight.

Finally, the last column of the figure shows the CTR for each security, which is calculated as the product of the security weight and the MCTR. The CTRs provide an additive decomposition of the 480 bp of portfolio risk to each constituent security. The top two contributors are TVA and Anheuser-Busch, which reflects their position size, high individual security risk, and correlation with other securities in the portfolio. The MCTRs for both bonds are the highest in the portfolio, indicating that changing their position is the most impactful way to

Security Name	Level 1 Sector Name	Level 2 Sector Name	Weight (%)	Security Risk (bp)	Standalone Risk (SAR) (bp)	Incremental Contribution to Risk (ICTR) (bp)	Marginal Contribution to Risk (MCTR) (bp)	Contribution to Risk (CTR) (bp)
TENNESSEE VALLEY AUTHORITY	Government	Agencies	10	1767	177	109	16	157
ANHEUSER-BUSCH INBEV FINANCE INC	Corporate	Industrial	10	1153	115	60	11	105
CCCIT_07-A3	Securitized	Asset Backed	10	1061	106	43	9	91
FHLMC REFERENCE NOTE	Government	Agencies	10	862	86	29	8	76
CVS HEALTH CORP	Corporate	Industrial	10	519	52	−4	5	46
FORDF_18-2	Securitized	Asset Backed	10	299	30	−29	2	23
GOLDMAN SACHS GROUP INC	Corporate	Financial	10	129	13	−43	1	9
ALTICE FRANCE SA	Corporate	Industrial	10	322	32	−55	0	0
PETSMART INC	Corporate	Industrial	20	928	186	−194	−1	−26
TOTAL			100					480

EXHIBIT 4.10 Risk Decomposition Measures for a Sample Portfolio
Source: BlackRock Aladdin, October 22, 2019.

increase or decrease the aggregate portfolio risk. When combined with their security weight, the resulting CTRs account for more than 50% of the risk in this portfolio. The lowest (negative) contributor is PetSmart, which reaffirms the diversifying effect of this position relative to all others.

These observations will be revisited, and augmented, in the remaining sections of the chapter as each decomposition mode is discussed in greater detail.

4.7 RISK DECOMPOSITION USING CTR

CTR is the primary risk measure underlying the decomposition methodologies presented in the following subsections. It has several useful properties that make it extremely flexible for understanding and quantifying risk along various dimensions of investor interest. In standard risk decomposition analysis, portfolio risk is usually shown at the security-level or at the factor-level. For large investment portfolios, with hundreds of securities, or with exposure to large numbers of factors, risk decomposition reports can be challenging to interpret, particularly when investment decisions are made at the group-level, e.g., when expressing sector or country views. Additionally, group-level metrics often offer a clearer explanation of an investment strategy to senior investors, such as chief investment officers, or to their clients. It is therefore common practice to aggregate these granular contributions in order to summarize risk along dimensions that align with the decision variables utilized by the portfolio's investment management process and also to act as a detection mechanism to guard against unintended risk allocations.

CTR also lends itself to further decomposition for those interested in a more forensic examination of risk. This material is presented after the standard contribution and aggregation modes for securities and factors and covers three principle methods:

- Decomposition of CTRs into atomic contributions that isolate the risk due to a single factor exposure for a single security
- Separation of CTRs into exposure, volatility, and correlation components
- Analysis of variance (ANOVA) which yields a two-dimensional representation of CTRs designed to reveal the interplay between different entities[26] in a portfolio.

4.7.1 Security-Level Contributions and Aggregations

Recall from Equation 4.35, portfolio risk (σ_p) can be disaggregated into security-level contributions (CTR_i^s)[27] as follows:

$$\sigma_p = \sum_{i=1}^{N} \text{CTR}_i^s \tag{4.36}$$

Each security contribution can be re-aggregated to any grouping provided that every security can be mapped to one, and only one, group. The groups are often defined based on security characteristics—for example, sector membership, country membership, benchmark membership, or strategy assignment—and are typically chosen to align with the market views

Level 1 / Level 2 Sector Name	Weight (%)	Contribution to Risk (CTR) (bp)
Government	20	233
Agencies	20	233
Corporate	60	134
Financial	10	9
Industrial	50	124
Securitized	20	114
Asset Backed	20	114
TOTAL		480

EXHIBIT 4.11 Sector Contributions
Source: BlackRock Aladdin, October 22, 2019.

or strategy being implemented in the portfolio. This aggregation gives rise to a group-level contribution and is illustrated in Exhibit 4.11 using sectors as an example.

A sector-level contribution can be calculated by aggregating across all security contributions in a given sector:

$$\text{CTR}_{\text{sec}(j)} = \sum_{i \in \text{sec}(j)} \text{CTR}_i^s \tag{4.37}$$

The portfolio risk can then be recovered by aggregating across all sector contributions as follows:

$$\sigma_p = \sum_{j=1}^{J} \text{CTR}_{\text{sec}(j)} \tag{4.38}$$

To illustrate, the security-level contributions from the sample portfolio in Exhibit 4.10 can be aggregated using the sector mappings to level 1 and level 2 groups (shown in the same exhibit). Exhibit 4.11 presents the resulting sector contributions and shows that the agency bonds dominate the risk profile with a contribution of 233 bp, accounting for nearly half of the overall risk. The agency sector contribution is formed by the summation of the TVA and FHLMC security contributions:

$$233 \text{ bp} = \underbrace{157 \text{ bp}}_{\text{TVA}} + \underbrace{76 \text{ bp}}_{\text{FHLMC}} \tag{4.39}$$

The remaining risk is roughly equally split between the bonds issued by industrials and the asset-backed debt.

4.7.2 Factor-Level Contributions and Aggregations

Factor-level contributions assume the use of an underlying linear factor model that maps security risk to a set of M systematic factors and an idiosyncratic component.

Recall portfolio risk can be expressed in factor terms as:

$$\sigma_p = (w'B\Sigma B'w)^{\frac{1}{2}} \tag{4.40}$$

For ease of exposition, the idiosyncratic term can be incorporated into the systematic term as an additional $M + 1^{th}$ factor.

Analogous to security contributions in Equation 4.34, factor contributions are given by:

$$CTR^f = (B'w) \cdot \frac{\partial \sigma_p}{\partial (B'w)} = (B'w) \cdot \frac{\Sigma B'w}{\sigma_p} \tag{4.41}$$

This provides the required re-aggregation of contributions to aggregate portfolio risk:

$$\sigma_p = \sum_{j=1}^{M+1} CTR_j^f \tag{4.42}$$

As with security decompositions, individual factor contributions can be re-aggregated to any factor grouping (hereafter referred to as factor blocks), providing each factor maps to one, and only one, factor block. Factor block definitions are typically dependent on the specification of the underlying risk factor model. As an example, a risk factor model for US corporate bonds may contain factors to capture interest rate sensitivity to different points on the US government curve, as well as a granular set of spread factors to capture commonality across different ratings (A, AA, ...), maturity (2-year, 5-year, ...) and industry (utilities, financials, ...) cohorts.

Exhibit 4.12 illustrates one possible hierarchy of factor blocks that could be used to create group-level contributions. For the purposes of brevity, a full four-tier expansion is only presented for corporate spread factors for bonds with an IG rating.

Factor block contributions are calculated by aggregating across all factor contributions in a given block:

$$CTR_{blk(k)} = \sum_{j \in blk(k)} CTR_j^f \tag{4.43}$$

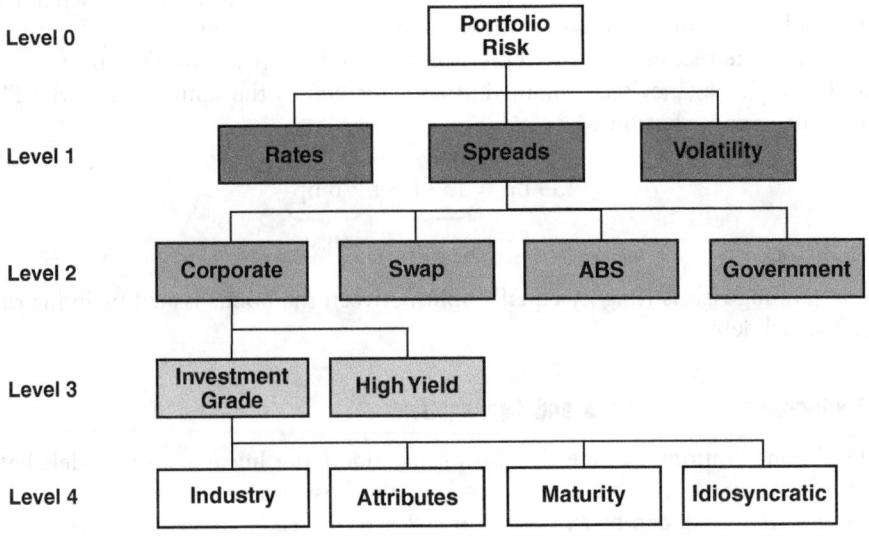

EXHIBIT 4.12   Hierarchy of Factor Blocks
Source: For illustrative purposes only.

Factor Block	Block Level	Contribution to Risk (CTR) (bp)
Rates	1	581
Spreads	1	−99
Swap Spreads	2	5
ABS	2	−6
Government	2	3
Corporate	2	−102
High Yield	3	−77
US Corp HY Industry	4	−88
US Corp HY Attribute	4	−10
US Corp HY Maturity	4	2
HY Idiosyncratic	4	18
Investment Grade	3	−25
US Corp IG Industry	4	−32
US Corp IG Maturity	4	8
US Corp IG Attribute	4	−5
IG Idiosyncratic	4	3
Volatility	1	−1
TOTAL	0	480

EXHIBIT 4.13 Factor Block Contribution
Source: BlackRock Aladdin, October 22, 2019.

The portfolio risk can then be recovered by aggregating across all K factor block contributions:

$$\sigma_p = \sum_{k=1}^{K} \text{CTR}_{blk(k)} \tag{4.44}$$

To illustrate factor block contributions, the hierarchy in Exhibit 4.12 is applied to the sample portfolio of Exhibit 4.10. The resulting block contributions[28] are shown in Exhibit 4.13.

This decomposition yields a very different view of the risk from that provided by the security and sector views. Firstly, all bonds map to US interest rates, and through the accumulation of risk exposures to interest rate factors, this results in a very large, dominant contribution of 581 bp arising from the rates block. This suggests that changes in interest rates are expected to dominate the returns of this portfolio, more so than any other factor. Given this is higher than the portfolio risk of 480 bp, the remaining factor contributions must have a diversifying effect in aggregate. This is primarily driven by the corporate spread factors with an offsetting contribution of −102 bp. Within the corporate spread block, this is mostly attributed to the HY factors, more specifically, industry spread factors.

As a final note, the volatility block, which captures the degree of risk due to embedded optionality, has a minute impact on the risk profile, which aligns with the fact that the majority of the securities in the portfolio bear no explicit exposure to implied volatility movements.

4.7.3 Decomposing Contribution to Risk into Atomic Contributions

Security and factor contributions each give rise to a one-dimensional decomposition of portfolio risk as shown in Equations 4.36 and 4.42. In some cases, a single security may represent

Sector Name	Block Contribution to Risk (CTR) (bp)							
	Rates	HY	IG	ABS	Swap Spreads	Government	Volatility	Total CTR
Government	229					3		233
Agencies	229					3		233
Corporate	237	−77	−25				−1	134
Financial	9							9
Industrial	228	−77	−25				−1	124
Securitized	115			−6	5			114
Asset Backed	115			−6	5			114
Total	580	−77	−25	−6	5	3	−1	480

EXHIBIT 4.14 Atomic Contributions
Source: BlackRock Aladdin, October 22, 2019.

a large proportion of the aggregate portfolio risk, which may prompt an investor to seek to understand the exact factor, or set of factors, that are the underlying source of this risk. Equally, a single factor contribution may dominate the risk profile of a portfolio and may lead to further investigation of which securities are responsible for this contribution. What we call "atomic-level contributions" can help answer these questions. The basic idea is to simultaneously calculate the contribution of each security in the portfolio while also decomposing each securities factor exposure. Exhibit 4.14 shows what this looks like for the sample portfolio.

To understand the calculation of atomic contributions, it is helpful to recall the formulation of portfolio risk from security positions (w), security-level risk exposures (B), and factor covariances (Σ).[29] A simple reordering of summations and some minor simplification yields the definition of atomic contributions:

$$\sigma_p = \frac{1}{\sigma_p}(w'B\Sigma B'w) \tag{4.45}$$

$$= \frac{1}{\sigma_p}\sum_{i=1}^{N}\sum_{j=1}^{M}w_i B_{ij}\underbrace{\sum_{l=1}^{M}\Sigma_{ji}(B'w)_l}_{\text{CTR}_{ij}^{sf}} \tag{4.46}$$

As noted above, atomic contributions (CTR_{ij}^{sf}) can be viewed in two ways:

1. Atomic contributions can be used to split every security contribution into its constituent factor contributions, that is:

$$\text{CTR}_i^s = \sum_{j=1}^{M+1}\text{CTR}_{ij}^{sf} \tag{4.47}$$

2. Alternatively, atomic contributions can be used to apportion every factor contribution into the securities that contribute to that factor (exposure):

$$\text{CTR}_j^f = \sum_{i=1}^N \text{CTR}_{ij}^{sf} \tag{4.48}$$

In both cases, the calculation aggregates by one of the remaining outer summations in the last expression of Equation 4.46 to provide the appropriate resolution.

Aggregations of atomic contributions are also common, either by securities, factors, or both in unison. The latter is typically applied to give a parsimonious decomposition into sectors and factor blocks, which is often easier to comprehend than showing the entire grid of atomic contributions.

Returning to the sample portfolio of Exhibit 4.10, decomposing risk into atomic contributions provides a convenient link between the security-based modes and factor-based modes. Exhibit 4.14 shows the two-dimensional atomic contributions linking the sector decomposition of Exhibit 4.11 with the factor block decomposition of Exhibit 4.13.[30] The row and column aggregate contributions align with the previously shown sector and factor block risk reports.

Each column shows the distribution of block contributions for every sector. As noted previously, the rates contribution is formed from risk exposures across securities in all sectors. Similarly, the row contributions decompose each sector contribution into its underlying factor blocks. This clearly shows that the agency and securitized bonds are predominantly composed of rates risk (with little to no contribution elsewhere), and as to be expected, the corporates block is solely responsible for the IG and HY contributions.

4.7.4 Decomposing Contribution to Risk into Exposure, Volatility, and Correlation

Using Equation 4.34, a security contribution CTR_i^s can be written as:

$$\text{CTR}_i^s = \frac{w_i \sigma_i \sum_j w_j \sigma_j \rho_{ij}}{\sigma_p} \tag{4.49}$$

Under further examination, this expression reveals that three key drivers influence the magnitude of the risk contribution; these drivers are represented by the terms in the numerator: w_i, σ_i, and $\sum_j w_j \sigma_j \rho_{ij}$.

The first term represents the security weight in the portfolio and, more generally, can be thought of as the exposure of the portfolio to a given security. The second term is the risk of the security in isolation, and the third term represents a risk weighted average correlation of that security with all others in the portfolio. The separation of Equation 4.49 into three terms, abbreviated $\text{CTR}_i^s = X_i \sigma_i \rho_{ij}$, was first introduced by Davis and Menchero (2011) under the moniker of X-Sigma-Rho.[31]

This decomposition shows that risk contributions will increase as the security exposure increases, as the security's risk increases, or as the correlation of a given security increases with the remaining positions in the portfolio. As such, it provides an intuitive and easily understood representation of contribution to risk that has gained significant traction with the practitioner community.

It also provides direct linkage with the other risk decomposition measures discussed at the beginning of the chapter, namely SAR and MCTR, which are both embedded in the right-hand side terms. SAR is the product of the first two terms, exposure and volatility, i.e., $\text{SAR}_i = X_i \cdot \sigma_i$ while MCTR is the product of the last two terms, i.e., $\text{MCTR}_i = \sigma_i \cdot \rho_i$.

Security Name	Weight ("X") (%)	Security Risk ("Sigma") (bp)	Correlation ("Rho") (bp)	Standalone Risk (SAR) (bp)	Marginal Contribution to Risk (MCTR) (bp)	Contribution to Risk (CTR) (bp)
TENNESSEE VALLEY AUTHORITY	10	1767	0.89	177	16	157
ANHEUSER-BUSCH INBEV FINANCE INC	10	1153	0.91	115	11	105
CCCIT_07-A3	10	1061	0.86	106	9	91
FHLMC REFERENCE NOTE	10	862	0.88	86	8	76
CVS HEALTH CORP	10	519	0.88	52	5	46
FORDF_18-2	10	299	0.76	30	2	23
GOLDMAN SACHS GROUP INC	10	129	0.73	13	1	9
ALTICE FRANCE SA	10	322	0.01	32	0	0
PETSMART INC	20	928	−0.14	186	−1	−26
TOTAL	100					480

EXHIBIT 4.15 Security-Level X-Sigma-Rho Decomposition
Source: BlackRock Aladdin, October 22, 2019.

Exhibit 4.15 shows the security-level X-Sigma-Rho decomposition applied to the sample portfolio. The additional information provided by X-Sigma-Rho (in comparison to Exhibit 4.10) is the correlation term ("Rho"), which represents the correlation of each security with the rest of the portfolio. This yields the missing piece of information in reconciling the SARs and CTRs and provides explicit validation of the previous remarks relating to which securities are the top-most contributors and which ones diversify. The diversification is clearly provided by the bottom two, high-yield bonds, Altrice and PetSmart, which have low correlations of 0.01 and −0.14 with the remaining positions.

4.7.5 Decomposing Contribution to Risk Using ANOVA

ANOVA is a two-dimensional decomposition, which in contrast to atomic contributions, splits portfolio risk into the same dimensions vertically and horizontally.

In the case of security contributions, ANOVA splits the standalone risk arising from a security from the interaction terms that arise due to this security's correlation with all others in the portfolio. Rather than aggregating the interaction terms into a single number, each correlation term is shown separately. The resulting decomposition is typically represented as a matrix of contribution terms where each row and column corresponds to a single security. In this way, ANOVA exposes how the interaction (both the magnitude and sign) between any two securities contributes to the overall portfolio risk.

The idea is illustrated for a two-security portfolio. The security-level contributions are given by Equation 4.34 as:

$$\text{CTR}_1^s = \frac{1}{\sigma_p}(w_1^2\sigma_1^2 + w_1 w_2 \sigma_1 \sigma_2 \rho_{1,2}) \tag{4.50}$$

$$\text{CTR}_2^s = \frac{1}{\sigma_p}(w_2^2\sigma_2^2 + w_2 w_1 \sigma_2 \sigma_1 \rho_{1,2}) \tag{4.51}$$

Factor Block	Block Contribution to Risk (CTR) (bp)						
	Rates	HY	IG	ABS	Swap Spreads	Government	Volatility
Rates	909						
High Yield	−242	127					
Investment Grade	−81	35	20				
ABS	−12	3	1	2			
Swap Spreads	8	−2	−1	0	1		
Government	2	1	0	0	0	1	
Volatility	−2	1	0	0	0	0	0
TOTAL	580	−77	−25	−6	5	3	−1

Factor Block	Block Correlation						
	Rates	HY	IG	ABS	Swap Spreads	Government	Volatility
Rates							
High Yield	−0.71						
Investment Grade	−0.59	0.69					
ABS	−0.27	0.2	0.19				
Swap Spreads	0.28	−0.21	−0.21	−0.17			
Government	0.06	0.13	−0.01	−0.01	0.2		
Volatility	−0.77	0.66	0.57	0.24	−0.44	−0.13	
	0.88	−0.31	−0.25	−0.17	0.26	0.2	−0.6

EXHIBIT 4.16 Factor Block ANOVA Report
Source: BlackRock Aladdin, October 22, 2019.

This yields the following 2-by-2 ANOVA representation:

$$\frac{1}{\sigma_p}\begin{pmatrix} w_1^2\sigma_1^2 & w_1w_2\sigma_1\sigma_2\rho_{1,2} \\ w_2w_1\sigma_2\sigma_1\rho_{1,2} & w_2^2\sigma_2^2 \end{pmatrix} \tag{4.52}$$

The same set of aggregations and decompositions that apply for standard risk decomposition modes can also be applied to ANOVA, so that each row and column can be mutated to represent a sector, a factor-block, or any other dimension of interest.

Exhibit 4.16 presents the sample portfolio through the lens of a factor block ANOVA report.[32]

The ANOVA report clearly illustrates the interplay between the different factor blocks.

Looking at the magnitudes of the entries, the risk profile is dominated by the contributions from rates and HY, with the remaining factor blocks providing little additional risk contribution. The rates block is shown to have a standalone contribution of 909 bp, which represents the risk arising from this factor block scaled to the aggregate risk. As observed previously, the HY block diversifies this exposure a lot and leads to a sizable reduction in the overall rates block contribution. Generating an ANOVA report at more granular resolutions would allow an investor to hone in on the exact risk factor exposures that give rise to this effect.

The exhibit also shows the implied block correlations between the different factor blocks. These are computed by dividing the row and column entries by the corresponding diagonal entries and is analogous to extracting a correlation matrix from a covariance matrix, where the ANOVA matrix is treated as the covariance matrix. For example, the block correlation between rates and HY is computed as:

$$-0.71 \text{ bp} = \frac{-242 \text{ bp}}{\sqrt{909 \text{ bp} \times 127 \text{ bp}}} \tag{4.53}$$

These correlations allow an investor to scale exposures to different blocks in order to better manage the overall risk of the portfolio while remaining faithful to the existing views expressed in the portfolio.

4.8   RISK DECOMPOSITION THROUGH TIME

The methodologies presented thus far have focused on the decomposition of portfolio risk at a single point in time. In this section, these ideas are extended to examine how risk changes can instead be decomposed through time. Such decompositions have the benefit of yielding insight into how market dynamics and portfolio repositioning separately influence risk levels, thereby enhancing the analytics available to investors for understanding and explaining their strategies. This separation is particularly important as portfolio managers are only able to directly influence the second component (through portfolio repositioning).

The separation of risk changes due to risk forecasts and portfolio repositioning impact distinct components of the risk contribution (CTR), and so it is helpful to adopt the X-Sigma-Rho representation as it facilitates a cleaner separation between these two related effects. Recall the X-Sigma-Rho decomposition of:

$$\text{CTR}_i = X_i \cdot \sigma_i \cdot \rho_i \tag{4.54}$$

It is clear from this expression that portfolio repositioning directly influences the exposure term (X_i), while changes in the risk forecasts are embedded in the last two terms (σ_i and ρ_i). For convenience, it is helpful to aggregate the last two terms as follows $Y_i = \sigma_i \rho_i$ into what is termed the **economy** component. This is in contrast to X_i which we will refer to as the **exposure** component.

The change in risk contribution due to exposure and economy changes between two points in time, t_1 and t_2, is then calculated as follows:

$$\Delta\text{CTR}_{i,t} = \text{CTR}_{i,t_2} - \text{CTR}_{i,t_1} \tag{4.55}$$

$$= X_{i,t_2} Y_{i,t_2} - X_{i,t_1} Y_{i,t_1} \tag{4.56}$$

$$= \underbrace{\frac{1}{2}(Y_{i,t_1} + Y_{i,t_2})(X_{i,t_2} - X_{i,t_1})}_{\text{Exposure change}} + \underbrace{\frac{1}{2}(X_{i,t_1} + X_{i,t_2})(Y_{i,t_2} - Y_{i,t_1})}_{\text{Economy change}} \tag{4.57}$$

$$= \Delta\text{CTR}_{i,t}^{exp} + \Delta\text{CTR}_{i,t}^{eco} \tag{4.58}$$

The last expression provides the desired separation of risk contributions. The first term attributes the change resulting from adjusting only exposures and keeping the economy fixed to its simple average.[33] This term directly answers the question of what changes would be introduced if the underlying risk model was kept static over this time period. The second term reflects the remaining change from adjusting the economy and keeping the portfolio's risk exposures constant, which isolates the change in risk introduced by updates in the underlying risk model's forecasts.

These terms may also be aggregated to provide group-level or portfolio-level decomposition of economy and exposure changes:

$$\Delta\sigma_{p,t} = \sum_i \Delta CTR_{i,t} \qquad (4.59)$$

$$= \sum_i \Delta CTR_{i,t}^{exp} + \sum_i \Delta CTR_{i,t}^{eco} \qquad (4.60)$$

As an example, Exhibit 4.17 shows an economy-exposure risk decomposition of the Barclays Bloomberg Global High Yield Index aggregated by level 1 factor blocks. The example compares two dates: December 2018, when the risk of this index was elevated to 607 bp, and October 2019, by which point the overall risk had fallen to 275 bp. The first two columns provide a point-in-time block decomposition of the index at these dates in accordance with the methodology described in the previous section. The remaining columns show the decomposition into exposure changes, economy changes, and the aggregate of these two effects (labeled "Total Change"). The final row shows that the total change in risk, of –332 bp, can largely be attributed to economy changes, accounting for –266 bp. Within this component, the block decomposition shows that the underlying risk model's estimates of spread factor volatilities and correlations were primarily responsible for this decrease.

A related analysis that often accompanies economy–exposure decomposition is to examine the time-series of portfolio risk under the assumption of constant economy and constant exposure.

In **constant economy** analysis, portfolio risk is recomputed through time using a single, fixed covariance matrix, which is conventionally taken to be the most recent date of analysis. This can indicate the influence of portfolio repositioning on risk forecasts and could be used to determine whether trade sizing is appropriately scaled, for example, when an investor is de-risking or re-risking the portfolio in response to changes in their convictions. Using Equation 4.40, the factor covariance matrix Σ is kept constant, with varying security weights[34] w, and risk factor exposures B.

Factor Block	Contribution to Risk (CTR) (bp)				
	20-Dec-18	22-Oct-19	Exposure Change	Economy Change	Total Change
Rates	−125	−141	44	−60	−16
Spreads	730	410	−111	−209	−321
Volatility	2	6	1	4	4
TOTAL	607	275	−66	−266	−332

EXHIBIT 4.17 Economy–Exposure Risk Decomposition
Source: BlackRock Aladdin, October 22, 2019.

In **constant exposure** analysis, the portfolio's risk factor exposures are assumed to be fixed over time (typically, to the most recent analysis date). The resulting portfolio time-series then isolates changes solely due to updates in the underlying risk model's forecasts of volatility and correlations. This can show how market events propagate through the model and can be used to calibrate an investor's understanding of the responsiveness of their underlying risk model in different market environments.

These ideas are illustrated in Exhibit 4.18, which show the various risk time-series for the same HY index used previously. The black series represents the historical risk of this index for the 2-year period leading up to October 2019. The dark and light grey series represent the constant exposure and constant economy versions, respectively. The graph shows that the dark grey and black series align very closely and, therefore, illustrates that much of the variation in risk for this index has been driven by market changes. The fourth quarter of 2018, in particular, represented a period during which credit spreads widened significantly, reflecting the broad negative market sentiment and the movement of capital away from high-risk assets, such as equities and high yield credit.

From the perspective of a risk manager, the time series decomposition of risk through time between exposure and the economy is a tremendously powerful tool. Day-to-day risk management will necessarily flag current outlier risk levels in portfolios, whether it be portfolio risk or active risk relative to a benchmark. While the level of risk is what it is, careful study of the time series can provide insights for remediation. For example, if a portfolio's risk has risen precipitously and can be primarily attributed to the portfolio manager ratcheting up the portfolio's exposures, the remediation may be as simple as insisting that the portfolio manager dials down exposures. In contrast, if the portfolio's exposure is substantially unchanged over time but the heightened risk arises from increasing economy risk, (i.e., rising correlations and/or volatility), depending on the nature of the portfolio's mandate, the risk manager may

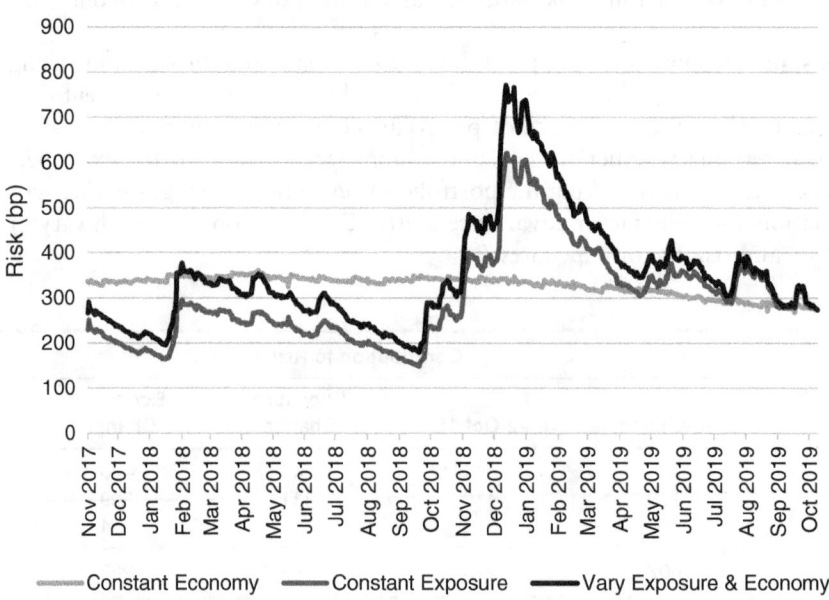

EXHIBIT 4.18   Risk Time-Series for HY Index
Source: BlackRock Aladdin, October 22, 2019.

be more inclined to hear out the portfolio manager and perhaps wait out the market since the risk breach is passive.

4.9 RISK DECOMPOSITION: SUMMARY

The previous section started with a description of alternative measures used to decompose aggregate portfolio risk at a point in time, with an outline of their practical and theoretical strengths and weaknesses. CTR emerges as the most prominent, and widely adopted, measure due to its simplicity, ease of computation, and tractability. The tractability of CTR, in particular, is demonstrated through a variety of decomposition modes that allow practitioners to gain insight into the sources of risk along different dimensions of investor interest as well as over time.

As such, the risk decomposition methods presented in this chapter provide an essential toolbox for practitioners to better understand and manage an investor's risk budget; to create alignment with their investment convictions; and thereby better execute on their client's objectives.

APPENDIX A. EHVaR: IDIOSYNCRATIC RISK ESTIMATION

(1) Calibration of skewed-*t* distributions

The mapping from diversification to skewed-*t* distribution parameters for each asset class is determined by simulating issuer rating transitions using a long-run quarterly historical agency rating transition matrix for all bonds in the Barclays Bloomberg Investment Grade and High Yield indices. The idiosyncratic return associated with each rating transition is then estimated using the difference in average spread level between the initial rating and the final rating times the spread duration of the bond.

To simulate the impact of diversification, portfolios are constructed by drawing bonds at random from the Barclays Bloomberg Investment Grade index; each portfolio consists of N equally weighted bonds where N runs from 1 to 100. The returns on each of the 100 portfolios are simulated 100,000 times by simulating independent rating transitions on each bond in the portfolio, and the resulting portfolio returns are then fit to 100 separate skewed-*t* distributions. An identical exercise is repeated using bonds from the HY index.

The output of the calibration is a mapping from portfolio diversification (defined as the number of bonds N in the portfolio) to a set of parameters that control the degree of skew and fat-tailedness of the skewed-*t* distribution. Exhibit 4.19 shows the fitted high-yield skewed-*t* distribution for different levels of portfolio diversification. The vertical lines indicate 99% Expected Shortfall (ES) for skewed-*t* and normal distributions respectively.

Notice that as the level of portfolio diversification increases, the skewed-*t* distribution starts to converge to the normal distribution. Given a confidence level and skewed-*t* distribution, an idiosyncratic tail risk multiplier (ITRM) is suggested, analogous to the systematic tail risk multiplier (STRM). The tail risk multiplier in Equation A.1 is defined as the ratio of the VaR from the skewed-*t* distribution to the VaR from the normal distribution.[35]

$$\text{ITRM}_\alpha = \frac{\text{VaR}_\alpha(\text{skewed} - t)}{-\Phi^{-1}(1 - \alpha)} \tag{A.1}$$

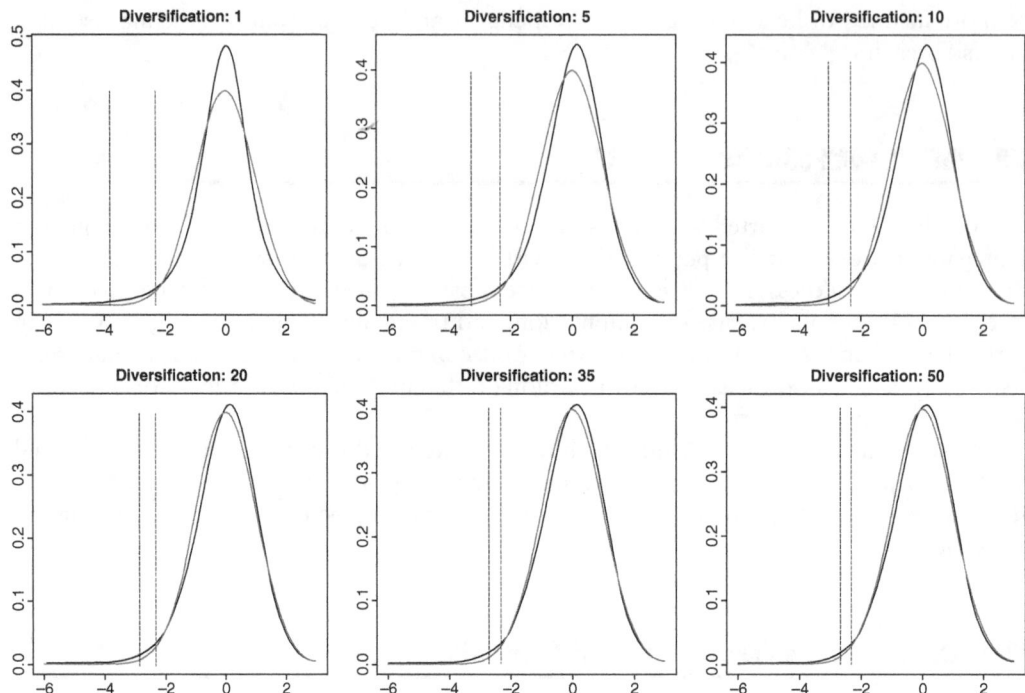

EXHIBIT 4.19 High-Yield Skewed-*t* (dark gray line) Versus Normal (light gray line) Distribution for Different Levels of Diversification (dotted lines represent 99% ES)
Source: BlackRock Aladdin. BBG Barclays USD CORP IG/HY index constituents' OAS as of 12/31/2012. Moody's historical average 1-year rating migration rates, 1983–2010.

Exhibit 4.20 shows the idiosyncratic tail risk multipliers for IG credit and high yield for 95% and 99% VaR and expected shortfall at different levels of diversification. Notice that high yield has higher multipliers than IG, but that both multipliers converge to 1 at high levels of diversification. For a given level of diversification, 99% VaR and 99% ES multipliers are higher than 95% VaR and 95% ES multipliers, respectively; tail risk diverges from the normal approximation further into the tail of the distribution. For a given confidence level α, ES multipliers are higher than VaR multipliers.

(2) Computation of idiosyncratic diversification on portfolio cohorts

The calibration in the previous step provides a map from idiosyncratic diversification and asset type into a particular skewed-*t* distribution. Diversification was defined by the number of bonds in a portfolio. Diversification cannot be defined in a similar way on actual portfolios because two portfolios with the same number of bonds might have very different levels of diversification. For example, a portfolio consisting of three equally weighted bonds issued by Morgan Stanley is clearly less diversified than a portfolio consisting of equal weights in Morgan Stanley, Ford, and GE bonds, respectively. Similarly, a portfolio that has 90% weight in Ford and 5% weights in Morgan Stanley and GE is less diversified than a portfolio that is equally weighted in each. In other words, the definition of diversification in the initial step was straightforward because the portfolios were assumed to consist of equally weighted, uncorrelated securities. However, in practice, idiosyncratic diversification is computed on actual portfolio idiosyncratic cohorts where weights are, in general, unequal, and

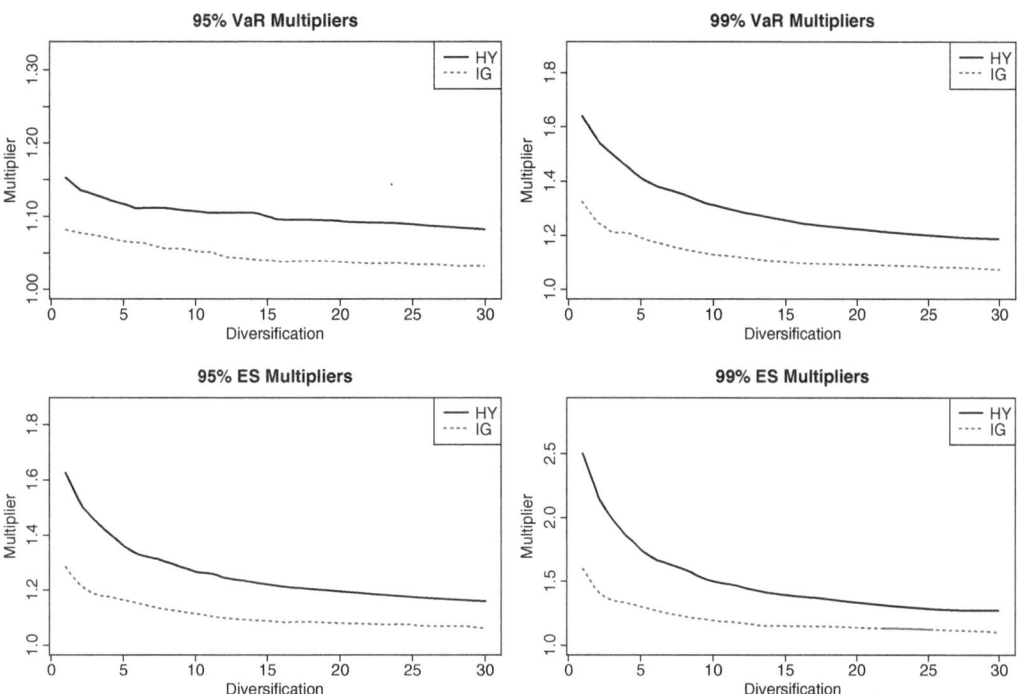

EXHIBIT 4.20 95% and 99% VaR and ES Idiosyncratic Tail Risk Multipliers at Different Levels of Diversification
Source: BlackRock Aladdin, December 31, 2012.

idiosyncratic returns may be correlated. Thus, an algorithm is needed to translate unequally weighted, correlated security weights into the number of equivalent equal weighted, uncorrelated securities. For each cohort, idiosyncratic risk is aggregated at the issuer level. BlackRock risk models impose the assumption that idiosyncratic risk between issuers is uncorrelated. Given a set of notional issuer weights w_i and issuer idiosyncratic volatilities σ_i, the inverse of the Herfindahl index of issuer risk-adjusted weights $w_i \sigma_i$ is used to compute a diversification score for each cohort.[36] The idiosyncratic diversification score reveals the number of equal risk-adjusted issuer bets in the cohort. This diversification score can be used to map each cohort to its own skewed-*t* distribution using the calibration on the equal weighted portfolios described in the previous section.

$$\text{Diversification Score} = \frac{1}{\sum_i \theta_i^2}, \text{where } \theta_i = \frac{w_i \sigma_i}{\sum_j w_j \sigma_j} \qquad (A.2)$$

As described, bonds are first bucketed into four cohorts, and the diversification score is computed for each. The diversification score, asset class, and direction of trade for each idiosyncratic cohort in the portfolio uniquely determine the parameters of the skewed-*t* distribution for the corresponding cohort. The idiosyncratic tail risk multiplier (ITRM) as defined in Equation A.1 is then computed analytically for each cohort based on the confidence level

α and the specific skewed-t distribution. The standalone VaR of each cohort is then defined as the cohort idiosyncratic volatility times the ITRM for the cohort.

$$\text{VaR}_{\alpha,\text{cohort}_j} = \text{ITRM}_{\alpha,j}\sigma_{\text{cohort}_j} \text{ where } \sigma_{\text{cohort}_j} = \sqrt{\left(\sum_j w_j\sigma_j\right)^2} \qquad \text{(A.3)}$$

The standalone VaR of each idiosyncratic is then aggregated with systematic VaR to calculate portfolio total VaR.

APPENDIX B. EHVaR: AGGREGATION

Aggregating VaR from different distributions is generally complex—even in the case when the distributions are statistically independent. In general, it is not possible to combine VaR from different independent distributions directly. A convolution (i.e., sum) of the underlying distributions themselves must be computed, and total VaR must be derived from the convolved distribution. However, in the special case where returns are normally distributed, VaR from different distributions can be added in quadrature to get total portfolio VaR.[37] For instance, analytical VaR is computed by adding systematic and idiosyncratic standalone VaR in quadrature.

$$\text{Analytical VaR}_{\alpha,\text{Total}} = -\Phi^{-1}(1-\alpha)\sqrt{\sigma^2_{\text{systematic}} + \sum_{\text{cohort}_j}\sigma^2_{\text{idio},j}} \qquad \text{(B.1)}$$

Given the complexity in computing the convolution of up to five different distributions (four idiosyncratic cohorts and one systematic cohort), some numerical accuracy is sacrificed for the sake of analytic tractability in computing total VaR. The simplest solution is to follow analytical VaR and add the different standalone VaR components in quadrature even though we know the underlying distributions are nonnormal. This approach embeds a contradiction. Nonnormality is accommodated in computing standalone VaR, and yet the distributions are treated as normal for the purposes of aggregation. However, it can be shown that imposing the assumption of normality in order to aggregate VaR provides a reasonable approximation to the analytically correct method of computing VaR through convolution in most cases: the normality approximation generally provides a slightly conservative estimate of total VaR compared to the analytically correct VaR in the order of 0%–5%. On the other hand, imposing the assumption of normality in computing VaR throughout (i.e., using analytical VaR) will generally result in a significant understatement of VaR, especially at high confidence levels.

EHVaR thus makes the assumption that total portfolio VaR can be computed by adding the systematic VaR and idiosyncratic cohort VaR in quadrature.

$$\text{VaR}_{\alpha,\text{Total}} = -\Phi^{-1}(1-\alpha)\sqrt{(\text{STRM}_\alpha\sigma_{\text{systematic}})^2 + \sum_{\text{cohort}_j}(\text{ITRM}_{\alpha,j}\sigma_{\text{idio},j})^2 + \sigma^2_{\text{idio,other}}} \qquad \text{(B.2)}$$

HVaR can be reinterpreted as simply a rescaled version of analytical VaR where the systematic and idiosyncratic components of AVaR have each been scaled by their own specific multipliers before adding them in quadrature.

NOTES

1. Claire Deng, Egon Kalotay, and David Greenberg significantly contributed to this chapter.
2. With respect to S&P data, S&P GSCI is a product of S&P Dow Jones Indices LLC ("S&P DJI"). S&P® is a registered trademark of Standard & Poor's Financial Services LL; Dow Jones® is a registered trademark of Dow Jones Trademark Holdings LLC. © 2022 S&P DJI. All rights reserved. S&P DJI does not sponsor, market or promote investment products based on its indices, and S&P DJI does not have any liability with respect thereto. Additionally, the MSCI data contained herein is the property of the MSCI Inc. or its affiliates (collectively, "MSCI"). MSCI and its information providers make no warranties. The MSCI data is used under licenses and may not be further used distributed or disseminated without the express written consent of MSCI.
3. Specifically, the Sveriges Riksbank Prize in Economic Sciences in Memory of Alfred Nobel.
4. The deterministic component a represents the horizon rate of return (HROR) where all risk factors are held constant except for the passage of time.
5. The classes of model summarized in Table 4.1 follow Connor (1995). More recent developments, such as Kelly, Pruitt, and Su (2019), integrate statistical and fundamental approaches and estimate characteristics' mappings to loadings on latent factors.
6. In the case where a portfolio has a benchmark, active risk is computed by substituting $w_p - w_b$, portfolio minus benchmark weights, into Equation 4.7.
7. See Section 4.3.3.1 for further discussion of optimizing the bias-precision trade-off. Empirical covariance estimates with less restrictive structural assumptions are discussed in Section 4.3.3.2.
8. Assuming a US holiday calendar.
9. Figlewski, 1997.
10. Given a decay parameter λ, $\log[0.01/\lambda]$ yields the window length that contains 99% of the weight. This rule of thumb can be used to estimate a window length consistent with the chosen half-life.
11. Note that even though the effective number of observations with overlapped data is less than T, the value of T in Equation 4.6 is unchanged. If the returns had been subtracted by the sample mean estimates, then the value of T would decrease to t_{eff} defined in Equation 4.8. Intuitively, if the returns are highly autocorrelated due to overlap, then demeaning will take out most of the variation around the mean, which will result in a spurious low estimate of the volatility of the factor return unless the number of observations is reduced.
12. This adjustment is similar in spirit to the bias-statistic-based approach proposed by Menchero and Morozov (2015).
13. BlackRock risk models allow users to choose daily, weekly, or monthly sampling frequencies to estimate the covariance matrix.
14. Note: The window of unoverlapped (independent) observations needs to increase from N to $N + L$ to compute the N overlapped observations in Equation 4.12.
15. Overlapping and the Newey-West methodology can be shown to be mathematically equivalent under certain conditions.
16. Generalizations of the factor model structure along the lines, discussed in Section 4.3.3, become particularly useful when the covariance matrix is applied to portfolio optimization or when violations of the model assumptions may be of particular significance.
17. "Violation rate" in the current context refers to the rate at which portfolio return observations exceed the 99% VaR boundary over the 2003–2019 sample.
18. Note the forms of the statistical tests of significance.
19. Refer to Section 4.4.1 for an analytical exposition of HVaR as an extension of AVaR.
20. Note that HVaR/ES forecast can similarly be expressed as expected shortfall assuming normality times a tail risk multiplier. STRM for ES is defined as the ratio of expected shortfall of z-scores to ES of the normal distribution.
21. Idiosyncratic risk for all other asset classes is assumed to be normally distributed.
22. The importance of this is described in further detail in Chapter 10.
23. These measures are described in the context of security-level measures.

24. The differences between MCTR and ICTR are somewhat analogous to the use of duration (as a partial, and approximate, measure of interest rate sensitivity) as compared to using full revaluation to understand security price responses resulting from changes in interest rates.
25. CTR can be expressed in basis points or normalized to sum to unity. The latter is achieved by dividing through by σ_p in Equation 4.35.
26. Entities could be securities, factors, or aggregations of either.
27. Superscripts denote a security-level contribution.
28. The coloring corresponds to the factor block hierarchy in Exhibit 4.12.
29. In a system with N securitities and $M + 1$ risk factors.
30. The factor block representation adopts level 1 blocks for rates and volatility, with a mixture of level 2 and 3 breakdowns for the spread factor block.
31. So named after the conventional notation used for exposure, volatility, and correlation in the literature.
32. The matrix is symmetric and it therefore suffices to only show the lower diagonal entries.
33. In theory, many economy-exposure decompositions are possible, on observing that for any constant a: $X_{i,t_2} Y_{i,t_2} - X_{i,t_1} Y_{i,t_1} = (a Y_{i,t_1} + (1-a)Y_{i,t_2})(X_{i,t_2} - X_{i,t_1}) + ((1-a)X_{i,t_1} + aX_{i,t_2})(Y_{i,t_2} - Y_{i,t_1})$. The choice of $a = \frac{1}{2}$ is generally adopted as it assigns equal weight to each component over the time window of the analysis. Other choices of a would bias either the average economy or exposure toward one date over the other.
34. The changing exposure term also reflects variation in risk from changing security weights due to price activity. In practice, this is typically less significant compared to changes arising from portfolio repositioning.
35. An identical computation is done to compute ITRM for expected shortfall.
36. The Herfindahl index is only one among several diversity indices—see for example Meucci (2009). What defines a "good" diversity index in the current context is that the skewed-t distribution parameters resulting from calibrating portfolios with different sets of weights but identical diversity index values are the same. If they are the same, then the portfolio diversity index and the diversification score of calibrated portfolios, which consisted of only equal weighted portfolios, can be treated as equivalent. Monte Carlo simulations suggest that the Herfindahl index was the best among several competing measures of diversity in capturing this particular aspect of diversification.
37. "Combining in quadrature" is a Euclidean (l^2) norm. For instance, x, y, z in quadrature $= \sqrt{x^2 + y^2 + z^2}$.

CHAPTER 5

Market-Driven Scenarios: An Approach for Plausible Scenario Construction[1]

Bennett W. Golub
Senior Advisor, BlackRock

David Greenberg
Managing Director, Technology & Operations – AI Labs, BlackRock (2022)

Ronald Ratcliffe
Managing Director, Analytics & Quantitative Solutions, BlackRock

5.1 INTRODUCTION

Prior to the 2008 Global Financial Crisis, stress testing was typically used as an adjunct to statistical approaches to risk measurement and management (such as Value at Risk [VaR] and ex ante tracking error) to quantify the profit and loss (P&L) associated with potential tail events. While academics and sophisticated practitioners certainly would acknowledge the limitations of statistical risk models based on historical data, the perceived mathematical sophistication of these models as well as the benign nature of short- and medium-term historical experience undoubtedly lulled some risk managers into overlooking the weaknesses of relying on risk models calibrated exclusively with historical data to forecast future market risk.

The extreme market moves exhibited during the Global Financial Crisis exposed the limitations of standard risk models and highlighted the need to augment their insights. Post-financial crisis, market risk has become increasingly difficult to forecast as prolonged monetary policy intervention by central banks and sudden political shocks have arguably overtaken economic fundamentals or technical data in driving financial markets.[2] These policy shocks have triggered sudden regime shifts and breakdowns in historical relationships among market variables.

Given the unpredictability intrinsic in the market, scenario analysis provides a critical complement to VaR and other related statistical risk measures. Serious scenario analysis encourages risk managers to think about what may happen in the future and creates direct and explicit links between changes in the macroeconomic environment, financial markets, and then applies them to portfolio exposures to determine hypothetical investment outcomes. In contrast to purely statistical or risk models, scenario analysis has the singular virtue of being forward-looking even at the risk of being less "scientific." This has led regulators to increasingly emphasize scenario analysis (i.e., stress tests) as an important element of the supervisory process.[3] However, this virtue proved to be a double-edged sword as, unlike more traditional historical approaches, there is no established standard or framework for constructing scenarios. In fact, the greatest challenge in stress testing is how to effectively define and generate hypothetical yet plausible stress scenarios. Further, to our knowledge, there has been only limited research on best practices in scenario generation.[4]

In this chapter, we describe a Market-Driven Scenario (MDS) framework designed to partially mitigate the subjective and often ad hoc nature of hypothetical scenario generation. In the MDS framework, economic forecasts and market views are collected from a wide number of constituencies within an organization, including risk management, investors, and economists. These views are then distilled using a disciplined process that incorporates statistical constraints to form a final set of scenarios.

The MDS framework has some elements in common with the decision-making approach advocated in James Surowiecki's (2004) best-selling book *Wisdom of Crowds*. Surowiecki argues that a decision arrived at by aggregating the information across many individuals is often better than a decision made by any single individual. According to Surowiecki, the aggregation of individual information is likely to be most efficient if three separate criteria are met:

1. Each individual has some private information and specialized knowledge not available to others.
2. Individuals' opinions are independent and not subject to groupthink.
3. There is some independent mechanism for turning the private views into a collective view.

The MDS framework satisfies these three criteria. Namely, scenarios are developed by drawing on input from a diverse set of investment professionals across different asset classes, geographies, and functional units. Each group has specialized knowledge not available to other groups. A firm's risk management team is the central mechanism by which information is aggregated and used to inform the creation of an economic scenario. The entire MDS process is led by this team.

The MDS development procedure starts by having risk managers, investors, and economists periodically identify current issues of focus or concern in the market, such as was the case with the 2016 UK referendum on EU membership ("Brexit"). Once an important issue is identified, a set of idealized economic outcomes are envisioned that seek to span the space of likely outcomes for that event. These outcomes are then translated into instantaneous shocks to a relatively small set of *policy variables*.

The process of translating alternative economic outcomes into sets of policy variable shocks (i.e., moves in major equity, bond, commodity market indices, FX rates) is highly subjective, and the methodologies used by investors for identification and sizing of variable shocks are diverse. Approaches range from relying on the expert opinion of portfolio and risk managers to, at least conceptually, utilizing granular structural macroeconomic models.[5] Since this demands a lot of a structural macroeconomic model, both in granularity and the ability to forecast out-of-sample, in this discussion and in our professional efforts, we have relied upon informed prognostication. We use our imagination and then seek to statistically constrain that imagination. Regardless of the chosen methodology, a set of statistical tools can be developed to help evaluate the plausibility of a specified set of policy shocks, and that sense of plausibility has the potential to shift imaginations away from the implausible (accepting that this may accentuate "Black Swan" biases). Specifically, a multivariate measure called the Mahalanobis distance is used to determine the plausibility and magnitude of a trial policy shock. The distance is then converted to an objective probability or scenario likelihood using a nonparametric approach, which is described later in this chapter.

Once the policy variable shocks are specified, the shocks to all relevant market risk factors are then imputed through a factor covariance matrix. This imputed set of shocks, the *perturbation vector*, is then vetted for plausibility, and the process is iterated several times before convergence upon a final scenario specification. The finalized shocks are then put into a valuation engine, which is run against the portfolios being analyzed, yielding hypothetical P&Ls that can be decomposed into their underlying drivers. From this point, risk managers can assess whether portfolio construction in the face of event risks is consistent with portfolio managers' stated intent and the asset owners' (clients') risk appetite. The risk manager then can ascertain whether the portfolio's positioning is genuinely deliberate, diversified, and scaled.

A wary reader might point out now that the process described is necessarily subjective and only as good as the forecast scenarios. The authors would agree. While a quantitative framework is provided to express those subjective views, they are, ultimately, nothing more than (disciplined) prognostications. While the quality of the forecast is certainly most critical, the formal scenario construction process can add significant additional value by forcing the risk taker and associated risk managers to go through a structured process of quantifying their subjective beliefs and making them transparent to others and therefore subject to critique and challenge. In fact, based on our experience, the process of creating transparency and the resulting challenge forces all participants in the process to think more clearly. And while this does not guarantee that the resulting scenarios are correct, it does guarantee that the involved parties are thinking explicitly and carefully, which can only be a good thing.

As an element of the first pillar of BlackRock's Investment Risk Management Paradigm (IRMP), this chapter highlights the use of specific econometric techniques and the application of a disciplined multistep organizational process of checks and balances in the construction of MDS. The following sections first describe the statistical techniques used to size and evaluate the internal consistency and plausibility of the scenario shocks. The final section walks through the example of constructing a specific Brexit scenario ("Soft Brexit"), which illustrates both the econometrics and subjective aspects of constructing a hypothetical scenario.

5.2 IMPLIED STRESS TESTING FRAMEWORK

5.2.1 Market-Driven Scenario Framework

MDS follows a conditional stress testing approach where a set of policy risk factors are shocked and the remaining risk factors are regressed onto the policy risk factors. The academic literature refers to MDS as conditional stress testing,[6] and the policy and perturbation vector are referred to in the literature as core and peripheral factors, respectively.

Assume there are M risk factors in the system. An implied scenario is conjectured by users specifying their view on a small subset of K policy risk drivers and then letting the shocks to the remaining $M - K$ factors be implied through a multivariate regression:

$$r_j = \sum_{k=1}^{K} \beta_{j,k} r_k + \varepsilon_j \text{ for } j = K + 1, K + 2, \dots, M \tag{5.1}$$

where $\beta_{j,k}$ is the β of factor j to policy factor k. Estimating β coefficients is mathematically equivalent to estimating the covariance matrix of the M risk factor returns. The following sections discuss the calibration of the factor covariance matrix at length since that matrix implicitly pins down all the $\beta_{j,k}$ terms in Equation 5.1. With a perturbation vector r_j in hand, P&L can be calculated based on the factor exposures of the portfolio. Assuming for the moment the returns of the assets are linear in the risk factor returns, the return of any portfolio given shocks to the k policy variables can be computed as:

$$\tilde{R}_{portfolio} = R_{policy} + \tilde{R}_{implied} = \sum_{k=1}^{K} L_k S_k + \sum_{j=K+1}^{M} L_j S_j = \sum_{k=1}^{K} L_k S_k + \sum_{j=K+1}^{M} L_j \sum_{k=1}^{K} \tilde{\beta}_{j,k} S_k \quad (5.2)$$

where L_k represents the portfolio loading on factor k and S_k represents the shock to factor k. Those positions with embedded optionality that exhibit nonlinear payoff functions are usually fully revalued given the entire perturbation vector of factor shocks.

The policy risk factors are typically major market-traded instruments such as S&P 500 returns, bond yields, or factor-mimicking portfolios (e.g., momentum, growth). The goal is to use a small number of policy variables to capture the macro shock to minimize the degree of arbitrariness in the resulting perturbation vector.

5.2.2 Scenario Likelihood

Assume a set of experts propose a vector of policy shocks r to represent a specific economic scenario. How can the plausibility of these shocks be objectively evaluated? An implausible shock is in some sense an outlier. Given current information, an implausible shock is extremely inconsistent with all the data (i.e., it is an outlier). The most popular and oldest method for identifying outliers in the statistics literature is the Mahalanobis distance (MD):[7]

$$MD(r, \Sigma) = \sqrt{(r - \bar{r})' \Sigma^{-1} (r - \bar{r})} \quad (5.3)$$

where r and Σ are the shock vector and covariance matrix of policy variables, respectively.

MD is the multivariate generalization of a standardized return or z-score. To prevent the MD from increasing at rate $\sqrt{n}$ in the number of policy variables, a new variable is defined called the scenario z-score:

$$Z(r, \Sigma) = MD(r, \Sigma) / \sqrt{n} \quad (5.4)$$

Similar to an individual factor z-score, a scenario z-score represents the severity of a given scenario. Provided asset returns follow a certain class of probability distributions known as elliptical distributions (this class contains most distributions used to describe asset returns including the normal and Student t-distribution),[8] scenario z-scores allow users to directly compare the relative likelihood of different scenarios. If Scenario A has a lower scenario z-score than Scenario B, it can be stated that Scenario A is more probable than Scenario B.

The simplest way to calibrate a stress scenario is to compare the scenario z-score with other realized risk events. A "library" of well-known historical scenarios can be created, and a "risk ruler" can be constructed as shown in Exhibit 5.1. It can then be asked where an analyst believes a new hypothetical scenario falls on the risk ruler. For example, if the analyst views the new scenario as less likely than the credit crisis, which is estimated as a 5.3 standard deviation scenario using the selected covariance matrix, the analyst may scale down all policy shocks such that the scenario z-score is less than 5.3. The risk ruler can be thought of as a way to compare a given scenario to other multi-sigma events that ex ante

US Downgrade	Fed Tapering	China Market Crash	Global Financial Crisis	Credit Crisis
July 21– September 20, 2011	May 21– June 24, 2013	June 12– August 26, 2015	September 12– November 3, 2008	July 1, 2007– July 1, 2008
The period starts with 50% chance US downgrade indication from S&P Standards and ends with Operational Twist announcement by Fed. Stock market incurred losses while bonds markets saw gains due to flight to safety.	Tapering talks stirred the market since Congress testimony by Bernanke with both equity and bond markets sold off. Emerging markets suffered badly due to hot money flight back to United States.	Chinese stock market crash beginning with the popping of the stock market bubble on June 12, 2015.	Credit and liquidity crisis and equity market crash set off by Lehman Brothers bankruptcy. Significant credit spreads widening caused by massive deleveraging.	Credit and liquidity crisis stemming from a severe slowdown in the housing market causing significant widening of credit spreads and increased implied volatility.

EXHIBIT 5.1 "Risk Ruler" of Scenario Z-Scores
Source: BlackRock Aladdin, authors' calculations. Data as of July 20, 2011, for US Downgrade, May 20, 2013, for Fed Tapering, June 11, 2015, for China Market Crash, September 11, 2008, for Global Financial Crisis, and June 29, 2007, for Credit Crisis, as cited in Golub, Greenberg, Ratcliffe (2018b.)
Note: Covariance matrices are computed using 5 years of weekly, equally weighted data prior to the scenario dates shown.

were extremely implausible but nonetheless happened. So when prognosticating, the analyst makes a subjective choice about how extreme he or she wants to define the hypothetical event being modeled based on other prior historical outliers. This is purely a judgment call; the risk ruler allows for additional context on making that call.

5.2.3 From Likelihood to Probability

Scenario z-scores measure the *relative* probability of different events provided asset returns follow an elliptical distribution. However, further assumptions are required if converting a scenario z-score to an *absolute* probability. At least two approaches are available: (1) a parametric approach, where one assumes a probability distribution for the z-scores, or (2) a nonparametric approach, where one estimates the empirical distribution of z-scores over a historical observation window.

A nonparametric approach was chosen since estimating the parameters of a multivariate probability distribution can be extremely challenging, especially in the tails of the distribution. Also, market risk is highly susceptible to "fat tails" (i.e., unlikely events).

In the nonparametric approach, T distinct z-scores are computed corresponding to each h-period risk factor return vector (and associated ex ante risk factor covariance matrix) within a historical window of length T. There are T rather than T/h total z-scores since z-scores are computed from overlapping h-period returns. The fraction of these T historical z-scores that are less than the z-score of the proposed policy risk factor shocks are then computed. More formally, we define a cumulative empirical distribution function $\hat{F}$:

$$\hat{F}\left(Z\left(r^*, \Sigma_\tau\right) | \mathcal{F}_T\right) := \frac{1}{T} \sum_{t=1}^{T} 1\left\{Z(r_{t,t+h}, \Sigma_t) \le Z(r^*, \Sigma_\tau)\right\} \tag{5.5}$$

where r^* represents the scenario shocks to the policy risk factors, $1\{\}$ represents the indicator function, $\mathcal{F}_T$ represents the information set as of time T, $Z(r_{t,t+h}, \Sigma_t)$ represents the scenario z-score of the policy variables over a given historical date range and horizon (i.e., the policy variables' historical realizations from time t to $t + h$ scaled by the ex ante covariance matrix Σ_t).

Note that the estimated covariance matrix used to compute the z-score for the policy shocks can use the most recent date or any historical date to begin sampling the data (for this reason this date is labeled τ). It is not immediately obvious that the most appropriate date used is always the most recent date. Once again, this is ultimately a subjective determination. How to go about selecting an appropriate covariance matrix is discussed in more detail later in this chapter.

Having estimated Equation 5.5, one can determine that for a scenario with policy factor shocks r^*, only X% of historical periods had joint returns to policy variables as unlikely as r^*, where $X = 100 * [1 - \hat{F}_{z(r)}[z(r^*)]]$. In other words, an exceedance probability can be defined for any scenario that is the historical probability of observing a z-score greater than that of the scenario given the covariance matrix.

To illustrate these ideas more clearly, the S&P 500 and the 10-year US Treasury spot rate were chosen as the two policy variables in a hypothetical scenario. Exhibit 5.2 shows the rolling scenario z-scores from the realized monthly changes in the S&P 500 and 10-year Treasury rate. The ex ante covariance matrix at each point in time is computed using exponential decay-weighted returns with a half-life of 40 days. The data in Exhibit 5.2 illustrate that there have been three 3σ and higher co-movements in the US equity and bond markets over the last 10 years.

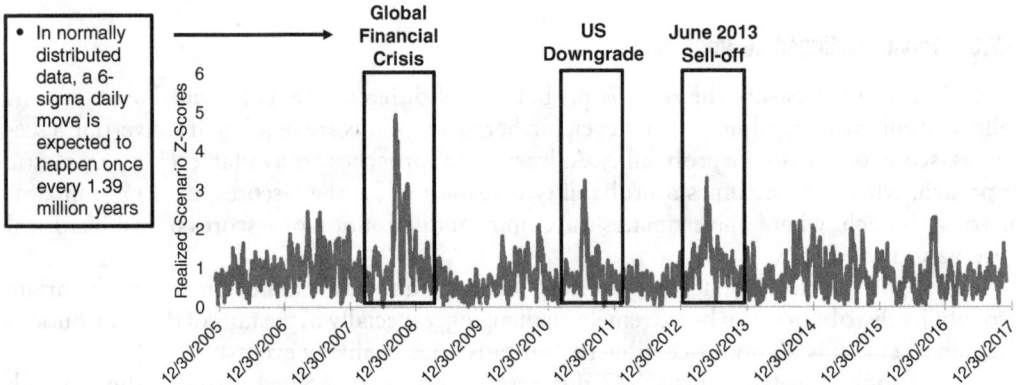

EXHIBIT 5.2   From Scenario Z-Scores to a Likelihood Measure[9]
Source: BlackRock Aladdin, authors' calculations. Data as of December 29, 2017, as cited in Golub, Greenberg, Ratcliffe (2018b).
Note: Scenario z-scores calculated using a 252-day covariance matrix with a 40-day half-life. The empirical time-series of z-scores is generated by computing rolling z-scores across daily return observations.

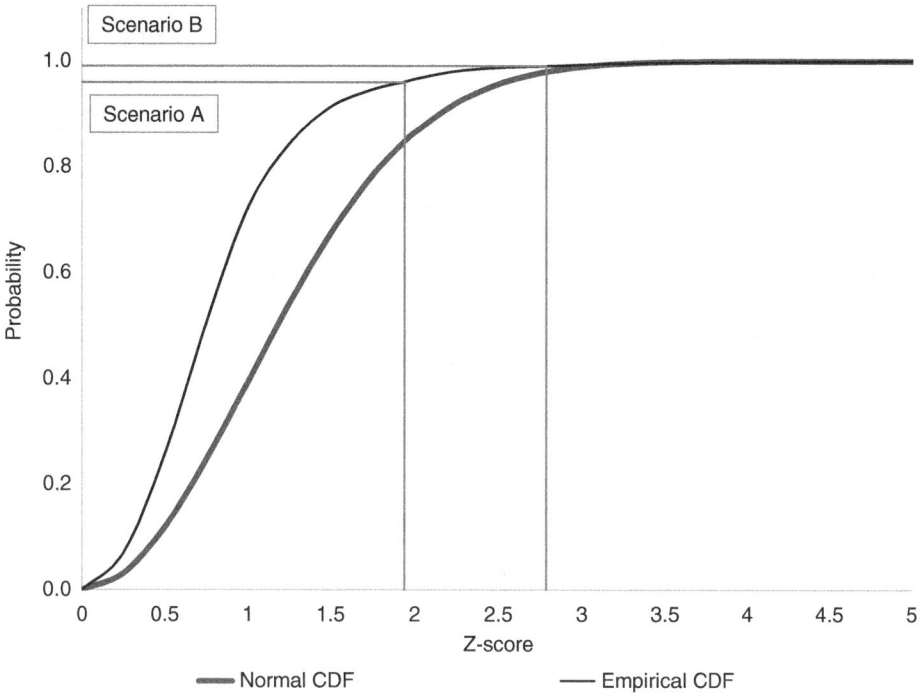

EXHIBIT 5.3 Empirical Distribution of Scenario Z-Scores
Source: BlackRock Aladdin, authors' calculations. Data as of December 29, 2017, as cited in Golub, Greenberg, Ratcliffe (2018b).
Note: CDF is the cumulative distribution function. Scenario z-scores calculated using a 252-day covariance matrix with a 40-day half-life. The empirical distribution of z-scores is generated by computing rolling z-scores across 15 years of daily return observations.

5.2.4 Decomposing the Scenario Z-Score

Using the nonparametric approach, we can now map z-scores into a probability measure. Exhibit 5.3 shows the empirical (black) versus the normal (gray) cumulative probability density of empirical z-scores. The empirical probability lies below the normal probability for extremely high z-scores, indicating that high z-scores are more likely under the empirical distribution.

Continuing with our example, two hypothetical scenarios are constructed using the S&P 500 and the Treasury rate as policy variables, where the magnitude of the conjectured factor shocks is the same in the two scenarios, but the signs differ. These two scenarios are defined in Exhibit 5.4. Scenario A corresponds to a standard "risk-off" scenario where risky assets sell off and there is a flight to quality. Scenario B represents an event similar to the 2013 taper tantrum when both stocks and Treasuries sell off. Exceedance probability refers to the likelihood of observing a scenario more extreme than the proposed scenario as measured by the historical distribution of scenario z-scores. The "risk-off" Scenario A is more than three times as likely as a scenario where both stocks and bonds sell off. Scenarios A and B are labeled in Exhibit 5.3, where the exceedance probability equals 1 minus the cumulative probability on the *y*-axis. Note that the scenario z-score and exceedance probability change through time as the covariance matrix changes. The probability of "risk-off" Scenario A increases, as shown in Exhibit 5.5, in periods of high market volatility.

	A Two-Factor Example Continued: S&P 500 and 10-Year Treasury Yield			
Scenarios	**S&P Price Return Shock (1-month)**	**Tsy Yield Change Shock (1-month)**	**Scenario Z-Score**	**Exceedance Probability**
A	−500 bp	−30 bp	1.94	4.02%
B	−500 bp	+30 bp	2.79	0.96%

EXHIBIT 5.4 Empirical Exceedance Probability—Two-Factor Example
Source: BlackRock Aladdin, authors' calculations. Data as of December 29, 2017, as cited in Golub, Greenberg, Ratcliffe (2018b).
Note: Scenario z-scores are calculated using a 252-day covariance matrix with a 40-day half-life. The exceedance probability of observing an event with a z-score higher than the scenario z-score is generated by computing rolling z-scores across 15 years of daily return observations.

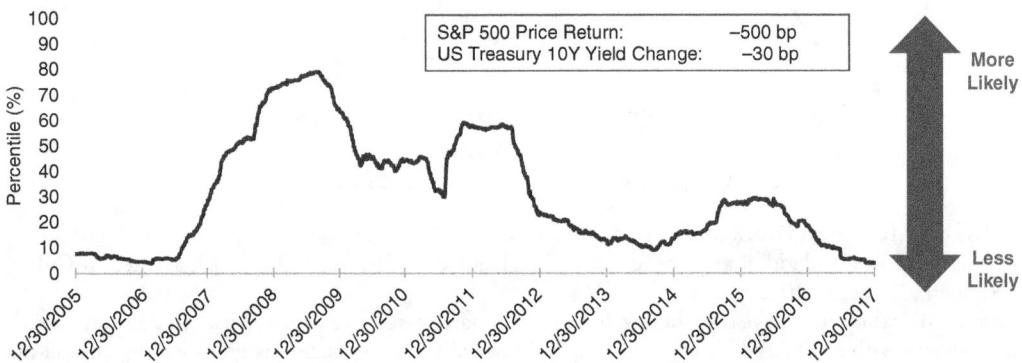

EXHIBIT 5.5 Changes in the Probability of Risk-Off Scenario A Through Time
Source: BlackRock Aladdin, authors' calculations. Data as of December 29, 2017, as cited in Golub, Greenberg, Ratcliffe (2018b).
Note: Scenario z-scores are calculated using a 252-day covariance matrix with a 40-day half-life. The probability of a scenario is calculated as 1 minus the scenario's exceedance probability.

Even though the magnitude of the shocks in Scenarios A and B are identical, Scenario B has a larger scenario z-score. The Scenario B z-score is higher because a sell-off in both equity and bond markets is not as consistent with the December 29, 2017, covariance matrix used to compute the z-score in Exhibit 5.3. Stocks and bond returns have been, in general, negatively correlated during the long secular decline in bond yields since the early 1980s, so Scenario B will usually have a higher z-score than Scenario A (unless the covariance matrix used to measure the two z-scores is estimated under an unusual regime like the taper tantrum in 2013) or future markets exhibit stagflation more frequently than the past.

Kinlaw and Turkington (2014) suggest a method for decomposing the z-score into contributions from the magnitude of the individual shocks and the contribution from the degree of "consistency" of the shocks with the ex ante covariance matrix. The magnitude effect can be isolated by computing the scenario z-score assuming all correlations between policy variables are zero. This quantity can be called the "volatility z-score" $V(z)$:

$$V(z) = \sqrt{\frac{z^T z}{n}} \qquad (5.6)$$

The correlation z-score can then be defined as the scenario z-score $\mathbf{Z}(\mathbf{r}, \Sigma)$ normalized by the volatility z-score $\mathbf{V}(\mathbf{z})$:

$$\mathbf{C}(\mathbf{r}, \Sigma) = \frac{\mathbf{Z}(\mathbf{r}, \Sigma)}{\mathbf{V}(\mathbf{z})} \tag{5.7}$$

As shown in the Appendix, the correlation z-score can also be represented explicitly in terms of the correlation matrix and individual factor z-scores:

$$\mathbf{C}(z, \Lambda) = \sqrt{\frac{z^T}{\sqrt{z^T z}} \Lambda^{-1} \frac{z^T}{\sqrt{z^T z}}} \tag{5.8}$$

where Λ represents the correlation matrix of the policy variables. Notice that the factor z-score vector has been normalized to have unit length. The correlation z-score depends on the relative magnitudes (and signs) of the individual factor z-scores, not on their absolute magnitudes. In other words, the correlation z-score is invariant to the scale of the shocks (i.e., a doubling of shock size will have no impact).

The correlation z-score can be used as a very useful diagnostic to determine whether the sign and relative magnitude of the policy variable shocks are plausible, conditional on a certain covariance matrix. A correlation z-score above one indicates that the policy variable shocks are more inconsistent with the chosen covariance matrix than they are with the same covariance matrix with zero correlations. If the sign of a policy variable shock is accidentally flipped, for example, the correlation z-score will usually be above one, while the volatility z-score will be unchanged.

5.2.5 Specifying a Covariance Matrix

The choice of matrix date and estimation parameters in calibrating the risk factor covariance matrix can have a large impact on the relative ordering of z-scores of different scenarios. Exhibit 5.6 shows the "risk ruler" calibrated in three different ways. The first two "risk rulers" are based on the risk matrix immediately preceding the corresponding risk event, one being "slow," i.e., using a longer half-life, while the other one uses a "fast" decay. The third "risk ruler" interprets the plausibility of shocks using the most recent covariance matrix. Depending on the view of the risk analyst, any of these three risk rulers could become the scale for the new hypothetical scenario being created.

The choice of which covariance matrix to use to compute the perturbation vector and scenario z-score should vary based on the scenario under consideration. If a scenario expresses a stressed market with a sharp sell-off in equities, the covariance matrix should be calibrated with historical data consistent with this kind of market event. Kim and Finger (2000) developed a "broken arrow" stress test where risk factor returns are modeled using a mixture of two normal distributions representing stressed and normal market conditions. The correlation matrix is estimated by measuring the ex post probability that the policy factor shocks come from the stressed regime. A method described by Silva and Ural (2011) is used where the covariance matrix is constructed by weighting observations that are most similar to the proposed scenario. They show that weighting observations based on their similarity to the proposed scenario yields more predictive stress tests. Intuitively this makes sense, since in a major risk-off scenario it would be expected that risky assets are more highly correlated than suggested by a covariance matrix calibrated over normal

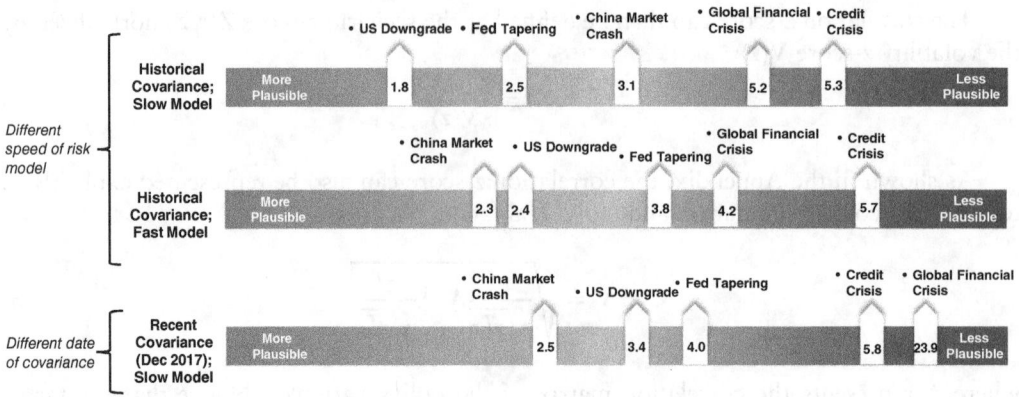

US Downgrade	Fed Tapering	China Market Crash	Global Financial Crisis	Credit Crisis
July 21– September 20, 2011	May 21– June 24, 2013	June 12– August 26, 2015	September 12– November 3, 2008	July 1, 2007– July 1, 2008
The period starts with 50% chance US downgrade indication from S&P Standards and ends with Operational Twist announcement by Fed. Stock market incurred losses while bonds markets saw gains due to flight to safety.	Tapering talks stirred the market since Congress testimony by Bernanke with both equity and bond markets sold off. Emerging markets suffered badly due to hot money flight back to United States.	Chinese stock market crash beginning with the popping of the stock market bubble on June 12, 2015.	Credit and liquidity crisis and equity market crash set off by Lehman Brothers bankruptcy. Significant credit spreads widening caused by massive deleveraging.	Credit and liquidity crisis stemming from a severe slowdown in the housing market causing significant widening of credit spreads and increased implied volatility.

EXHIBIT 5.6   Robustness of Scenario Plausibility
Source: BlackRock Aladdin, authors' calculations. Data for recent covariance as of December 29, 2017, and otherwise using the covariance matrix prior to the scenario dates shown, as cited in Golub, Greenberg, Ratcliffe (2018b).
Note: For the *slow* model, covariance matrices are computed using 5 years of weekly, equally weighted data. For the *fast* model, 1 year of weekly, equally weighted data was used.

periods.[10] Stress scenario losses calibrated using data from other risk-off scenarios will both be more severe (and likely more accurate) than scenarios calibrated using "normal" periods.

5.3   DEVELOPING USEFUL SCENARIOS

5.3.1   Scenario Definition

While constructing an MDS requires the application of subjective judgment, some guidelines and diagnostic tools can constrain some of the subjectivity and rule out unintentionally highly implausible scenarios. Hypothetical scenarios should be defined with sufficient precision and specificity to allow for clear scenario translation into a set of quantitative shocks to market factors. Key risk factors used to define the scenario should not be highly correlated and should be as parsimonious as possible. Scenario z-score metrics can be used to assess scenario plausibility and provide guidance on the magnitudes, signs, and relative sizing of specified shocks. The covariance matrix chosen to generate implied shocks should be consistent with the scenario's specified shocks. Scenario z-score metrics can also be used to identify the historical covariance matrix most consistent with the stress scenario. After the portfolio stress test P&L is computed, statistical criteria can be used to determine whether the scenario needs to be refined by adding or removing risk factors or by restricting the impact of factors to a subset of the portfolios' factors.

Step 1: Define a Market Event or Macro Regime Defining scenarios for potential market events are subject to two levels of uncertainty. There is the uncertainty about whether the scenario will occur, and there is the uncertainty around the impact on asset returns if the scenario does occur. Scenarios should be defined in such a way that removes as much of the second source of this uncertainty as possible. The first step requires defining a hypothetical scenario that will be impacted by financial markets in a reasonably predictable manner.

Any scenario related to a market event should satisfy certain basic criteria:

1. *Scenario probability is small (but not impossible):* A scenario that is viewed as nearly certain will already be fully priced into the markets by investors. Scenarios should be chosen that are severe but perceived to be within the realm of the possible. Additionally, they should not be fully priced into the market, thus still having the potential to have a significant impact on markets. Within the MDS process, we often attempt to summarize the probability space with three scenarios from the perspective of the scenario authors: an upside event, a downside event, and a tail event, with each defined relative to market consensus.

2. *Scenario definition is precise:* The scenario should be defined with sufficient precision such that the scenario impact on markets (both in terms of magnitude and direction) is not subject to interpretation of the scenario definition itself.

3. *Scenario will impact markets that are relevant to the portfolio in a reasonably predictable manner:* This point is related to the previous one. The scenario definition may need to be customized depending on the types of portfolios that are intended to be stressed. For instance, a scenario that involves large foreign exchange shocks may not have any material impact in a single currency portfolio. The impact of a value versus growth shock may not be particularly interesting when applied to a US Treasury portfolio.

4. *Scenario has a well-defined catalyst:* Since the scenario is unlikely, it is helpful to define a catalyst that will likely trigger the scenario.

Step 2: Select Policy Variables Once the scenario has been defined conceptually, specified shocks to policy factors need to be determined. These key risk factors will anchor the scenario and allow shocks to be implied for all the other risk factors through the factor covariance matrix.

The most important maxim in selecting policy variables is to be as parsimonious as possible. The larger the number the variables, the greater the likelihood of unintentionally introducing multicollinearity. Even if all the factors are not collinear given today's matrix, having too many factors increases the likelihood of collinear factors in the future with a different covariance matrix. As a general rule of thumb, adding any candidate policy variable with an adjusted R^2 greater than 90% to the already selected policy variables should be avoided.

In cases where parsimony is impossible and the scenario definition requires using a large number of policy variables, users can restrict by asset block to minimize multicollinearity. Restriction by asset block means that different groupings of implied risk factors are regressed on a different subset of policy variables.

Step 3: Calibrate Shock Sizes to the Policy Variables   One approach to setting initial shock sizes is to look for historical periods that resemble the desired hypothetical scenario. A second way to calibrate initial shock sizes to policy variables is to set a target frequency based on some subjective view of the likelihood of the scenario. Note that the target likelihood does not represent the likelihood of the scenario actually occurring but instead represents the likelihood of observing a scenario at least as extreme as the target scenario as measured by the scenario z-score. The "Brexit" scenario calibration, described later in this chapter, goes into more detail on how to calibrate the shocks to the policy variables.

Step 4: Generate Nonpolicy Factor Shocks from the Policy Factor Shocks   Shocks to all nonpolicy factors are mainly implied through the risk model covariance matrix. The choice of covariance matrix is therefore crucial in determining the implied shocks. When generating implied shocks, an analyst should choose a matrix date where the covariance matrix is consistent with the relationships between the scenario's policy variable shocks. For example, if simulating the end of Quantitative Easing in the United States through a backup at the short end of the curve, it would be appropriate to select a covariance matrix where the key rates at the short end of the curve are more volatile. It is important to note that nonpolicy variable shocks based on the prescribed variance/covariance matrix are not always implied. In some instances, risk managers or investors may have a specific view about the correlation "across" blocks of risk factors, such as equities and credit spreads. Post-financial crisis, the traditional negative correlation between equities and credit spreads has diverged in a number of market environments. Depending on the MDS, risk managers may decide to specify correlations across major market equity factors and credit spreads rather than rely on correlations implied by the covariance matrix. This ability to override correlations at the factor block level provides an important nuance when defining MDS.

Step 5: Generate Portfolio Stress Test P&L   Portfolio stress test P&L over a given time horizon is calculated using the policy and nonpolicy variable factor shocks and the portfolio factor exposures. If there is no embedded optionality in the portfolio, portfolio P&L is simply the product of factor shocks and exposures. Those positions with embedded optionality are often fully revalued given the factor shocks.

5.4   A MARKET-DRIVEN SCENARIO EXAMPLE: BREXIT

5.4.1   Describing Different Brexit Scenario Outcomes

While Brexit was viewed as a low probability event, the referendum on continuing EU membership was one of the key event risks facing the UK in 2016. This risk was identified early in the year and Market-Driven Scenarios were created in February around a vote to "Remain" or "Leave" (known as Brexit), well ahead of the referendum vote in June. The Leave outcome was evaluated through two separate scenarios: (1) "Soft Brexit," where trade relationships with the EU were negotiated and remained intact; and (2) "Adverse Brexit," where there was a negative outcome for the UK with regard to trade relationships when negotiating to leave the EU.

All three of these Brexit-related Market-Driven Scenarios were relevant to any portfolio with exposure to the British real economy or British security markets as well as to the broader European security markets. Specifically, a view for each scenario needed to be articulated on the impact on the British pound, gilts, equity, and credit markets, as well as the broader impact on European equity and fixed-income markets. In an extreme scenario, spill-overs to global markets on panic selling would be expected.

Prime Minister David Cameron, having completed his negotiations for Britain's EU membership, announced in February that the referendum would take place on June 23, 2016. The key negotiation points included sovereignty, migrants, welfare benefits, economic governance, and excessive regulation. In early June, the reaction to the deal was mixed. The "Stay" camp boasted a 10% lead in the polls, while the polls tightened leading up to the referendum. The actual vote to "Leave" ultimately surprised markets despite the narrowing of the polls in the final days before the vote.

The goal of MDS is to identify a range of potential outcomes on all sides of the event risk spectrum. This means defining scenarios that reflect reasonable outcomes of how an event may unfold and impact markets. As previously noted, in this case, the MDS modeled the following: (1) UK Remains in EU, (2) Soft Brexit, and (3) Adverse Brexit. For purposes of exposition, the following discussion will focus on the Soft Brexit scenario, which reflected a decision by the UK to leave the EU while retaining favorable trade and labor agreements. Examples of potential "post-exit" relationships between the UK and EU that informed the Soft Brexit scenario construction included the following: (1) the UK leaving the EU but remaining in the Single Market (e.g., Norway); (2) implementation of a customs union membership (e.g., Turkey); and (3) negotiation of an "EU Single Market-lite" agreement (e.g., Switzerland). Consensus among the investment teams and risk professionals was that a Soft Brexit scenario would be followed by risk-off sentiment in local markets as well as a dovish tone from the Bank of England.

5.4.2 Identifying Key Policy Shocks in Soft Brexit Scenario

To start, policy variables were identified spanning UK markets across asset classes such as the FTSE All Share, 10-year gilt yields, and sterling FX rate. Differentiating this scenario from a generic UK negative economic shock required including additional sector granularity to the policy variables. In the case of Brexit, financial services could be forced to shift to the European continent and property demand would likely slump following an exodus of workers. The added policy variables therefore included shocks to UK banking equity and spreads factors as well as to real estate stocks.

The full set of policy variables are listed in Exhibit 5.7. Notice there were no policy variables specific to Europe. The transmission to European markets was assumed to be captured adequately using implied shocks.

Several shocks were chosen to dampen contagion outside the UK, namely on Italian rates and the Mexican peso. That is, unless these shocks were forced to be relatively small, the covariance matrix would amplify the shocks from the policy variables. Further, the policy variable shocks were restricted to the same asset class (or subset thereof) in most cases, to avoid the effects of spurious correlations.

A Soft Brexit scenario was designed to be more plausible than many of the past stress events shown on the plausibility ruler. Plausibility is evaluated using MD and related multivariate scenario z-scores. The impact of this particular scenario was estimated to be more local in nature than the "US Credit Downgrade," for example (see Exhibit 5.8).

Factor Block	Factor	Shock	Shock (monthly σ)	Applied to	Calibration Comments
Equities	FTSE All Share	−5%	−0.8	ALL-below	UK equity markets fall with financials and real estate sectors hit hardest.
	UK Banks	−2.50%	−0.6		
	UK Real Estate	−2.50%	−1.0		
Rates	GBP 10yr	−10 bp	−0.5	Rates & Inflation Ex Euro Spreads	GBP curve steepens with expectation of dovishness from BoE.
	GBP 2yr	−25 bp	−2.1		
	ITL 10yr	+10 bp	0.4	Euro Spreads	Limited contagion to peripheral rates.
Spreads	UK Credit	+20 bp	1.0	Spreads	UK credit spreads widen with financials underperforming noncyclicals.
	UK Banking	+35 bp	1.1		
	UK Noncyclical	+10 bp	0.7		
FX	GBP/USD	−5%	−2.0	GBP/USD, EUR/USD & EMEA FX	GBP weakens suddenly against USD and depreciates across the board.
	MXN/USD	−1%	−0.2	FX ex-GBP/USD, EUR/USD, EMEA FX	Limited contagion to non-Euro FX.

EXHIBIT 5.7   Soft Brexit Scenario Policy Variable Selection
Source: BlackRock Aladdin, authors' calculations. Data as of February 23, 2016, as cited in Golub, Greenberg, Ratcliffe (2018b).

For sizing the shocks, direct historical comparisons, which are frequently part of the MDS definition process, provided limited guidance. For instance, the British pound's departure from the Exchange Rate Mechanism (ERM) in 1992 was somewhat related to the 2016 vote but was more focused on currency policy alone. The EU referendum was wider reaching. Scotland's referendum was closer in substance but only provided a look at one outcome, the "Remain" outcome. Rather, the relative plausibility of the EU referendum scenarios relative to the scenario z-score of some major economic/financial events needed to be considered, although their relative impact was reasonably assumed. It was expected that the Soft Brexit scenario would have more of an impact than what was expected to be the "Remain" vote and less than an Adverse Brexit scenario where trade and financial relations are damaged. Further, it was expected that a Soft Brexit outcome was more plausible than the US Credit Downgrade, for example.

The initial shocks chosen for policy variables led to a scenario z-score in line with expectations and on the more plausible end of the ruler. Subsequent fine-tuning of the shocks by speaking with asset class experts did not lead to significant changes in this case. By far the most contentious issue was on rates. Would gilts act as a safe haven asset and rally, or would investors flee the UK fixed-income market altogether? In the Soft Brexit scenario, safe haven interpretation prevailed. However, in the Adverse Brexit case, it was assumed that UK yields would rise.

The assumption on the shocks to UK yields had the largest impact on the plausibility of both the Adverse Brexit and Soft Brexit scenarios. Exhibit 5.9 includes a column labeled "Scenario z-score delta," which is defined as how much the scenario z-score would decrease

Plausibility Ruler:

More Plausible — Remain Vote Wins (1.2) • Soft Brexit (1.5) • US Downgrade (1.8) • Fed Tapering (2.5) • China Market Crash (3.1) • Adverse Brexit (3.5) • Global Financial Crisis (5.2) • Credit Crisis (5.3) — Less Plausible

Remain Vote Wins	Soft Brexit	US Downgrade	Fed Tapering	China Market Crash	Adverse Brexit	Global Financial Crisis	Credit Crisis
June 2016	June 2016	July 21–September 20, 2011	May 21–June 24, 2013	June 12–August 26, 2015	June 2016	September 12–November 3, 2008	July 1, 2007–July 1, 2008
Vote to "remain" wins, improving political stability and strengthening the position of the current UK government.	Vote for the UK exiting the EU wins the referendum, but governments still manage to negotiate an agreement.	The period starts with 50% chance US downgrade indication from S&P Standards and ends with Operational Twist announcement by Fed. Stock market incurred losses while bonds markets saw gains due to flight to safety.	Tapering Talks stirred the market since Congress testimony by Bernanke with both equity and bond markets sold off. Emerging markets suffered badly due to hot money flight back to United States.	Chinese stock market crash beginning with the popping of the stock market bubble on June 12, 2015.	The British public vote to leave the EU, and political and economic uncertainty follows. Having backed the vote to stay, the pressure mounts for Prime Minister David Cameron to resign.	Credit and liquidity crisis and equity market crash set off by Lehman Brothers bankruptcy. Significant credit spreads widening caused by massive deleveraging.	Credit and liquidity crisis stemming from a severe slowdown in the housing market causing significant widening of credit spreads and increased implied volatility.

EXHIBIT 5.8 Plausibility Ruler with Brexit Scenarios

Source: BlackRock Aladdin, authors' calculations. Data as of February 23, 2016, for the Brexit scenarios and otherwise using the covariance matrix prior to the scenario dates shown, as cited in Golub, Greenberg, Ratcliffe (2018b).

Note: Covariance matrices are computed using 5 years of weekly, equally weighted data.

Factor Block	Factor	Shock	Factor Z-Score	Scenario Z-Score Delta
Equities	FTSE All Share	−5%	−0.8	0.04
	UK Banks	−2.50%	−0.6	0.08
	UK Real Estate	−2.50%	−1.0	−0.05
Rates	GBP 10yr	−10 bp	−0.5	0.49
	GBP 2yr	−25 bp	−2.1	0.56
Spreads	UK Credit	+20 bp	1.0	−0.07
	UK Banking	+35 bp	1.1	0.08
	UK Noncyclical	+10 bp	0.7	−0.04
FX	GBP/USD	−5%	−2.0	0.09
			Scenario z-score	1.5
			Scenario M-distance	4.5

EXHIBIT 5.9   Soft Brexit Scenario Z-Score
Source: BlackRock Aladdin, authors' calculations. Data as of February 23, 2016, as cited in Golub, Greenberg, Ratcliffe (2018b).

if the policy variable shock for that row was changed from its value as defined in the scenario to its expected value conditional on the value of the shocks to all other policy variables in the scenario. Notice that the scenario z-score delta for all factors except UK rates are near zero in Exhibit 5.9, indicating that all the other factor shocks are consistent with one another, i.e., the scenario z-score cannot be lowered by individually changing any other policy factor. The UK policy factor shocks, however, do express a strong view that is inconsistent with the remaining policy variables as illustrated by the large value of the scenario z-score delta for those factors.

In generating nonpolicy factor shocks, the risk analyst should select a covariance matrix that best models the cross-asset linkages that are expected to occur in the particular scenario. For instance, an analyst who constructs a risk-off scenario may select a regime-weighted covariance matrix estimated using returns that occurred during turbulent economic environments, while a geopolitical risk scenario may call for a covariance matrix estimated using returns from a time that includes dynamic political change. In the Brexit example, given that we lacked reasonably comparable historical events, we mainly relied on the current covariance matrix that reflected a period of rising populist sentiment. Even if we had chosen the exit from the European Exchange Rate Mechanism (ERM) event, the changes over ensuing decades would likely have rendered a matrix from that period not relevant. The perturbation vector reflects the implied factor moves from the shocks to the policy variables, as seen in Exhibit 5.10. The negative shock to the UK equity market is transmitted to other global equity markets, and rates rally broadly. However, the naïve covariance matrix is not relied on to imply shocks across the perturbation vector, which are predicated on the specific regime against which it was estimated. In this case, it was important to note that, while broadly relying on the covariance matrix, the authors had a specific view about the correlation between equity prices and credit spreads in the Soft Brexit scenario. Thus, in addition to applying policy variable shocks to UK and European equity indices, they also implicitly specified a negative correlation between equities and credit spreads in major markets.

Once the full set of shocks were specified, the P&L impact on portfolios could be calculated. Exhibit 5.11 shows the impact of the Soft Brexit scenario on a hypothetical 60/40

Asset Class	Risk Factor	Soft Brexit Implied Shock (bp)	Soft Brexit Implied Shock in σ
Equity Styles	Value	−19	−0.47
	Dividend Yield	4	0.08
	Growth	−36	−0.69
	Momentum	−7	−0.05
Equity Sector	MSCI World Financials	−611	−0.90
	MSCI World Materials	−407	−0.57
	MSCI World Technology	−494	−0.71
	MSCI World Utilities	−231	−0.53
Equity Markets	MSCI EM − MSCI DM	40	0.11
	MSCI Europe (EUR)	−671	−0.86
	FTSE100	−523	−0.76
	S&P500	−383	−0.70
	MSCI World	−422	−0.75
	MSCI Japan	−640	−0.68
	VIX Implied Vol	589	0.69
Rates	Tsy 10Y	−9	−0.46
	GBP 10Y	−10	−0.46
	DEM 30Y	−19	−0.82
	JPY 30Y	−13	−1.27
Muni Spreads	Muni Spread 7Y	6	0.42
	State GO	2	0.60
Spreads	US Cash Bonds IG	12	0.77
	US Cash Bonds HY	26	0.34
	CMBS	3	0.30
	EUR Cash Bonds IG	8	0.49
Sov Spread	EMBI Global (EM)	0	−0.01
	Spain 5y	7	0.32
	Italy 5y	7	0.35
Mortgages	15Y Mtg Basis	0	−0.08
	30Y Mtg Basis	−3	−0.60
Inflation	CPI 10yr	2	0.14
	EUR INF 10yr	7	0.53
	JPY INF 10yr	−10	−0.59
FX	DXY US Dollar Index	−16	−0.07
	AUD/USD	−39	−0.12
	EUR/USD	−292	−0.96
	GBP/USD	−500	−1.99
	JPY/USD	37	0.11
	MXN/USD	−100	−0.23
Commodity	Gold COMEX 1	301	0.56
	Brent Crude Oil	−791	−0.50
	Copper	−179	−0.30

EXHIBIT 5.10 Soft Brexit Perturbation Vector[11]
Source: BlackRock Aladdin, authors' calculations. Data as of February 23, 2016, as cited in Golub, Greenberg, Ratcliffe (2018b).
Note: Cboe Volatility Index® and VIX® are registered trademarks of Cboe Exchange, Inc.

	Hypothetical Portfolio Impact (P&L in bp)		
Potential Outcome	**Index Portfolio Equity**	**Index Portfolios Bonds**	**Index Portfolios Multi-Asset**
	FTSE 100	iBoxx GBP	60% FTSE 100, 40% iBoxx GBP
Soft Brexit The UK also votes to leave, but favorable trade and labor agreements are retailed, leading to some local risk-off sentiment and a more dovish tone from the BoE	−506	+64	−180

EXHIBIT 5.11   Soft Brexit P&L

Source: BlackRock Aladdin, authors' calculations. Data as of February 23, 2016, as sighted in Golub, Greenberg, Ratcliffe (2018b).

portfolio invested in the FTSE 100 equity index and the iBoxx GBP bond index as well as allocations to each index separately. The portfolio losses were driven by the sell-off in equities while the bond exposure acts as a partial hedge.

Notably, the goal of the MDS exercise is not to quantify tail loss and require portfolio managers to reduce risk to any specific MDS and related outcome. The goal is to define MDS in a thoughtful fashion, leveraging and integrating investor, risk manager, and economist insights; to apply the MDS process to portfolios; and quantify the potential set of return outcomes from each scenario. When the portfolio scenario returns are generated, portfolio managers are asked to review the hypothetical returns and confirm that their implied risk positioning is deliberate, diversified, and scaled based on the portfolio manager's level of conviction. Portfolios may very well have varying exposure to any given scenario depending on the respective investment theses of the corresponding portfolio managers. The risk management goal is to ensure that portfolio managers are aware of the risk and potential return from different outcomes associated with a Brexit event and confirm risk is consistent with expectations. Specific funds where portfolio managers had high levels of conviction that Soft Brexit would not occur scaled their positions accordingly.

5.5   CONCLUSION

Never wasting a good crisis, risk management has evolved in the last decade with a more flexible approach to identifying and protecting portfolios against extreme event risk. Historical analysis continues to play a role, but it is possible to entertain a wider range of dangers beyond what has happened in recent years while providing some plausible boundaries on unconstrained speculation about the future. Additionally, analytics and technology developments have made possible faster on-the-fly evaluation of portfolio outcomes, especially where options or other nonlinear securities are involved. Another wave of change may entail wider use of forecasting models, perhaps based on machine learning, for scenario inputs.

The Market-Driven Scenarios approach was illustrated for the UK Brexit referendum, spelling out alternate hypothetical outcomes provided portfolio managers with a guidepost on risk management and hedging decisions. Looming geopolitical risks linked to international trade, for example, provide opportunities for risk managers to apply these techniques. In terms of future developments, the proposed approach should be extended to better take into account the passage of time. While in many cases, positive or negative carry will be de minimus relative to the market impact, for scenarios that are less extreme, the carry impact might be relevant.

APPENDIX: DECOMPOSITION OF SCENARIO Z-SCORE

Kinlaw and Turkington (2014) suggest a method for decomposing MD into contributions from the magnitude of the individual shocks and contributions from the correlation between shocks.

As a first step, MD can be re-expressed in terms of the correlation matrix and factor z-scores:

$$
\mathrm{MD}(r, \mathbf{\Sigma}) := \sqrt{r^T \mathbf{\Sigma}^{-1} r} = \sqrt{r^T (\mathbf{\Sigma}_{\sigma,diag} \mathbf{\Lambda} \mathbf{\Sigma}_{\sigma,diag})^{-1} r} = \sqrt{(r^T \mathbf{\Sigma}_{\sigma,diag}^{-1}) \mathbf{\Lambda}^{-1} (\mathbf{\Sigma}_{\sigma,diag}^{-1} r)/n} = \sqrt{z^T \mathbf{\Lambda}^{-1} z}
$$

(A.1)

where $\mathbf{\Lambda}$ is the correlation matrix and $\mathbf{\Sigma}_{\sigma,\,diag}$ is a diagonal matrix with factor volatilities along the diagonal. The diagonal matrices are then pulled outside the inverse and combined with the shock vector r to construct a vector of z-scores.

Having re-expressed MD in terms of the correlation matrix $\mathbf{\Lambda}$ and z-scores, the scenario z-score can be decomposed in terms of correlation and volatility components.

$$
\mathbf{Z}(z, \mathbf{\Lambda}) = \sqrt{z^T \mathbf{\Lambda}^{-1} z / n} = \sqrt{\frac{z^T}{\sqrt{z^T z}} \mathbf{\Lambda}^{-1} \frac{z^T}{\sqrt{z^T z}}} \sqrt{z^T z / n} = \mathbf{C}(z, \mathbf{\Lambda}) \mathbf{V}(z)
$$

(A.2)

where $\mathbf{C}(z, \mathbf{\Lambda})$ and $\mathbf{V}(z)$ are the correlation and volatility components, respectively.

NOTES

1. This chapter is an edited version of an article authored by Bennett W. Golub, David Greenberg, and Ronald Ratcliffe that was published in the *Journal of Portfolio Management*, Volume 44, Issue 5, 2018. It was adapted with permission for this book.
2. It is also possible to treat monetary policy as part of the economic fundamentals in recognition of the endogeneity. We thank Jean Boivin for providing this insight.
3. While we use the words "scenarios" and "stress tests" interchangeably in this chapter, there is, strictly speaking, a distinction. While scenarios in some cases are designed to represent tail events (the definition of a stress test), they may also encompass more likely events. Quantifying the latter makes it possible to apply to portfolios of assets and evaluate exposures in stable times.
4. One notable exception is an article by Clemens and Winkler (1999) that studies the optimal composition of the team that designs the scenario.
5. The "Lucas critique" would apply to most approaches, with the exception of a model based on micro-foundations. However, most investors would not have available a micro model based on deep foundations where preferences would be invariant to changes in government policy variables.
6. Kupiec, 1999.
7. The Mahalanobis distance used in a financial context can be found in the work of Kritzman et al., 2010.
8. This follows from the fact that the probability density function of elliptical distributions takes the form of the Mahalanobis distance, i.e., $f(x) = k \cdot g(x^T \mathbf{\Sigma}^{-1} x)$.

9. With respect to S&P data, S&P GSCI is a product of S&P Dow Jones Indices LLC ("S&P DJI"). S&P® is a registered trademark of Standard & Poor's Financial Services LL; Dow Jones® is a registered trademark of Dow Jones Trademark Holdings LLC. © 2022 S&P DJI. All rights reserved. S&P DJI does not sponsor, market or promote investment products based on its indices, and S&P DJI does not have any liability with respect thereto.

10. Consistent with the observation by risk managers that correlations spike toward 1 in times of market stress.

11. Cboe Volatility Index® and VIX® are registered trademarks of Cboe Exchange, Inc. With respect to S&P data, S&P GSCI is a product of S&P Dow Jones Indices LLC ("S&P DJI"). S&P® is a registered trademark of Standard & Poor's Financial Services LL; Dow Jones® is a registered trademark of Dow Jones Trademark Holdings LLC. © 2022 S&P DJI. All rights reserved. S&P DJI does not sponsor, market or promote investment products based on its indices, and S&P DJI does not have any liability with respect thereto. Additionally, the MSCI data contained herein is the property of the MSCI Inc. or its affiliates (collectively, "MSCI"). MSCI and its information providers make no warranties. The MSCI data is used under licenses and may not be further used distributed or disseminated without the express written consent of MSCI.

CHAPTER 6

A Framework to Quantify and Price Geopolitical Risks[1,2]

Catherine Kress
Director, BlackRock Investment Institute, BlackRock

Carl Patchen
Vice President, Risk & Quantitative Analysis, BlackRock (2022)

Ronald Ratcliffe
Managing Director, Analytics & Quantitative Solutions, BlackRock

Eric Van Nostrand
Managing Director, BlackRock Sustainable Investment, BlackRock (2022)

Kemin Yang
Associate, BlackRock Investment Institute, BlackRock (2019)

6.1 INTRODUCTION

Geopolitical risks are an important driver of market risk and can have meaningful effects on the global economy, financial markets, and investment portfolios. However, geopolitical risks are often difficult to quantify, and their impacts are notoriously hard to predict. Macroeconomic fundamentals such as economic growth and corporate earnings are typically the major drivers of financial market returns, especially over longer investment horizons. Yet idiosyncratic risks, including those triggered by geopolitical events, can have an outsized impact on markets and individual securities when they occur. The approach we describe in this chapter will focus primarily on a framework for translating ill-defined geopolitical risks into more traditional drivers of risk.

Beginning in 2017, BlackRock launched an effort to better measure and monitor geopolitical risks and their market impact in a systematic way. The approach marries qualitative and macroeconomic analysis with large-scale portfolio analytics and "big data" text mining. As one part of this effort, and further described in Section 6.2, BlackRock undertook a historical analysis of asset price reactions to 68 key geopolitical risk events since 1962. One important finding from this analysis is that the impact of geopolitical shocks has historically tended to be much more acute when the economic backdrop was weak. When the economic environment was strong, the impact of these risk events was more muted.

With the goal of developing meaningful insights that can be applied to the portfolio management process, BlackRock's framework for managing geopolitical risk seeks to leverage the firm's scale and global reach, its in-house expertise in geopolitics, portfolio analytics, and its technological capabilities. To that end, BlackRock developed a Geopolitical Risk Dashboard that identifies the top geopolitical risks that the firm sees as posing a threat to markets and the global economy. This chapter focuses on one of these perceived geopolitical risk scenarios—*Global Trade Tensions*—to illustrate BlackRock's methodology for assessing and quantifying geopolitical risk.

BlackRock's work in this area is necessarily ever evolving, but we believe the framework is an important step forward in helping investors analyze the potential impact of geopolitical risks and how to guard against them in portfolios. As an extension to Chapter 5, this chapter aligns with the first pillar of BlackRock's Investment Risk Management Paradigm (IRMP) and provides an overview of BlackRock's framework and an early example of this ongoing work.

6.2   SETTING THE SCENE

Geopolitical risks are ever present and ever changing. How can investors best monitor these risks and their potential market impact? Subject matter experts from across BlackRock combined forces to find out. As a first step, BlackRock conducted a historical analysis of 68 key geopolitical risk events since 1962, as well as their market impacts. For this purpose, geopolitical shocks were defined as wars, terrorist acts, and other events that increase tensions between states and affect the normal course of domestic politics and international relations.

Such shocks can impact economies and markets in myriad ways. Trade tensions, for example, can lead to the imposition of tariffs that disrupt global supply chains and the flow of commerce. Wars can lead to oil price shocks that boost inflation and hurt consumer spending. And sudden shocks, such as terror attacks, can hurt market confidence, prompting capital flows out of riskier assets and into perceived safe havens.

Three broad classes of geopolitical events were defined: event risks with set dates (such as elections and referenda); exogenous risks (sudden and unanticipated events such as the 9/11 attacks on the United States); and thematic risks (risks that simmer for an extended period, such as tensions between the United States and North Korea). Table 6.1, *A History of Geopolitical Crises,* contains an abbreviated list of the events included in the study. For event risks and thematic risks, markets likely reflected some probability of a destabilizing event before it actually occurred. By contrast, exogenous risks are unanticipated shocks that were most likely substantially not priced in advance by markets.

Note that our event study compared historical episodes of starkly different character and market impact. The goal of the analysis was to identify a set of loose patterns that could inform deeper research into geopolitical risk modeling. We supplemented this proprietary work with a review of the existing academic and private-sector literature on the effects of geopolitical risk on markets. Much of this literature is focused on emerging markets (EMs), which historically have been the epicenter of many geopolitical risks.

Geopolitical risks emanating from developed markets—typified by the United Kingdom's Brexit vote in 2016 and the subsequent twists and turns of the UK exit negotiations—were of rising market relevance and focus.

TABLE 6.1 A History of Geopolitical Crises[3]
Selected key geopolitical events, 1962–2019

Event	Date
Event risks	
Russia declares independence from USSR	6/12/90
German reunification	10/3/90
Brexit referendum	6/23/16
Italy election	3/4/18
US exits Iran nuclear deal	5/8/18
Exogenous risks	
Cuban missile crisis	10/16/62
First oil shock	10/19/73
Fall of Berlin Wall	11/9/89
Iraq invades Kuwait	8/2/90
US embassy bombings in Africa	8/6/98
Sept. 11 attacks	9/11/01
Russia invades Georgia	8/7/08
Arab Spring	1/24/11
Fukushima nuclear accident	3/11/11
Russia annexation of Crimea	2/26/14
WannaCry ransomware attack	5/12/17
Thematic risks	
Vietnam War	8/7/64
Six-day War	6/5/67
Iranian revolution/second oil shock	1/16/79
Iran-Iraq War	9/22/80
Gulf War	1/16/91
Yugoslav wars	6/26/91
Dissolution of Soviet Union	12/26/91
Iraq War	3/19/03
NAFTA renegotiation	5/18/17
US-North Korea tensions	8/8/17
US announces tariffs	2/8/18

Source: BlackRock Investment Institute, June 2019. For illustrative purposes only. Not all geopolitical events were analyzed or included.

6.2.1 Short and Sharp

A key takeaway from our event study was that the average market response to unexpected geopolitical shocks has historically been relatively modest and short-lived. Equity prices tend to take a hit and bonds rally in the immediate aftermath, but these moves often dissipate quickly. For example, the S&P 500 Index fell almost 12% in the first week of trading after the 9/11 attacks of 2001. Yet the stock market had recouped all of those losses by 25 business days after the event.

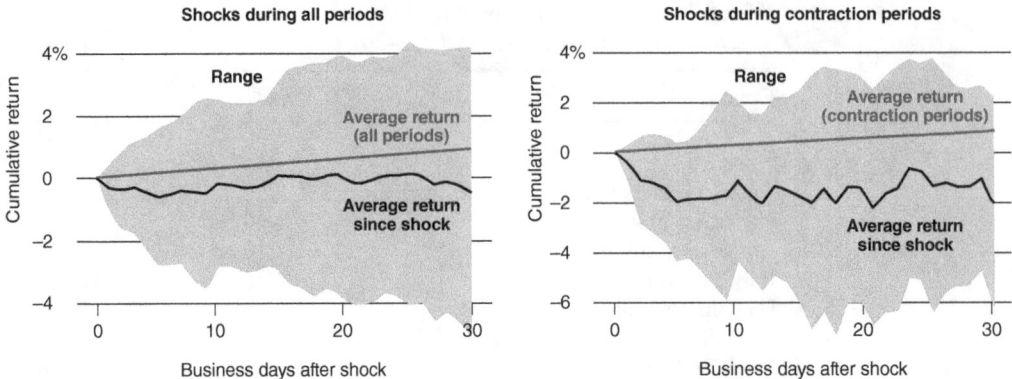

EXHIBIT 6.1 Shock Waves[4]
US equity returns after exogenous geopolitical shocks, 1962–2017
Source: BlackRock Investment Institute, with data from Refinitiv Datastream, an LSEG brand, and Bloomberg, June 2019. Past performance is not a reliable indicator of current or future results. It is not always possible to invest directly in an index.

The average results of the 31 exogenous geopolitical events studied are shown in the chart on the left in Exhibit 6.1 (Shocks during all periods). The S&P 500 stock index was used as a proxy for global risk sentiment. Equity markets show modest losses in the 30 trading days following an event. The negative market reaction has historically been more severe if multiple shocks occur simultaneously or if the economic environment is weak to begin with.

The chart on the right in Exhibit 6.1 (Shocks during contraction periods) illustrates the latter. The average return for all exogenous geopolitical shocks that occurred when the economy was contracting, as defined by US manufacturing PMI as being below 50, are shown. The key takeaway is that equity market losses from geopolitical shocks tended to be of greater magnitude in periods when the economy was contracting.

6.2.2 Shades of Gray

There are several caveats to this analysis. The average asset price responses obscure huge variation across historical events, as the gray error bands in the charts demonstrate in Exhibit 6.1. This reflects the wide variation in the character and implications of the events in the study. However, the primary goal was to identify a few overarching patterns in the relationship between markets and geopolitical events.

Teasing out and modeling the impact of geopolitical events from other market forces is challenging and open to different interpretations. For example, an OPEC embargo led to a near quadrupling of the price of oil during the 1973 oil shock, which came against the backdrop of the Watergate scandal that rocked the United States Administration. At the time, the stock market was reeling and unemployment was on the rise. Another example is the 1998 bombings of two US embassies in Africa, which came in the midst of the Asian financial crisis and Russia's default on its debt, which further precipitated the collapse of a major hedge fund.

Additionally, some geopolitical risks may have muted overall market impacts but outsized effects on specific securities. This can create both risks and opportunities. As examples, think of a financial institution's stock taking a hit after a major cyberattack or a defense contractor benefiting from rising tensions in the Gulf.

6.3 BLACKROCK'S FRAMEWORK FOR ANALYZING GEOPOLITICAL RISKS

Quantifying that historical geopolitical risks have had significant market implications is important, but the greater challenge is assessing the geopolitical landscape and how future risks could play out in markets. BlackRock's framework for assessing and managing geopolitical risks has four key steps:

1. **Identify key geopolitical risks:** First, the top risks across the geopolitical landscape are identified, as well as potential escalation triggers—or catalysts that would cause the risk to materialize—based on the collective insights of experts across the firm.
2. **Analyze the risks:** Second, potential adverse outcomes for each risk are identified, and the relative likelihood and potential broad market impact of each scenario are determined. This includes determining the extent to which each geopolitical risk event is already priced in by markets. We do this using metrics that measure how much market-related discussion is focused on the risk relative to history.
3. **Assess potential market impacts:** Third, potential events are translated into market factor moves for each scenario. These estimates/guesstimates are based on internal analysis of current market conditions and historical data. Once fully specified, we can then apply these scenarios onto portfolios and measure their conditional profit and loss impact.
4. **Take action:** The final step is applying this knowledge to portfolios. Risk-taking needs to be deliberate, diversified, and appropriately scaled. Our geopolitical risk scenarios and estimated asset price responses can be used to help guard against unanticipated adverse portfolio outcomes by allowing the portfolio manager to calibrate his or her exposure.

The process is a blend of qualitative and quantitative analysis. We draw on geopolitical risk experts across the firm to identify scenario themes, while asset class experts across regions help pinpoint the most sensitive assets exposed to a particular risk. Portfolio and risk management experts also contribute their expertise by formulating and analyzing specific geopolitical risk scenarios.

6.4 GLOBAL TRADE DEEP DIVE

The first step in BlackRock's process includes identifying an important geopolitical risk scenario, outlining its rationale, and considering what would happen to relevant financial assets if this scenario were to materialize. As described in great detail in Chapter 5, we call our general approach Market-Driven Scenarios (MDSs).

A precise definition and clear catalysts are key components to the MDS approach. We illustrate this with a deep dive on one specific geopolitical risk, *Global Trade Tensions*. This risk was introduced to BlackRock's Geopolitical Risk Dashboard in June 2018. The backdrop of the scenario was a US Administration that was shaking up the post-war system of global trade and international alliances.

The key rationales for this scenario are the following:

- The United States Administration used protectionist rhetoric and maintained a hawkish position on trade.
- The United States proposed tariffs on $50 billion of Chinese goods in May 2018 and threatened an additional $200 billion (since implemented) if China retaliated.

- The United States invoked national security concerns to impose steel and aluminum tariffs globally, including on the European Union, Canada, and Mexico, renewing fears of a global trade war.

BlackRock identified the following potential catalysts for the *Global Trade Tensions* scenario to materialize:

- The United States imposes sweeping tariffs against China as trade talks break down.
- The United States' allies impose retaliatory tariffs on US steel and agricultural products while airing grievances at the World Trade Organization.
- In response, the United States Administration announces plans to overhaul trade agreements globally, further undermining stability in the global trading system.

Next, we identified the markets most likely to be impacted by the scenario. We then estimated 1-month price shocks to a selected group of financial assets in these relevant markets. These calculations were informed by our analysis of market conditions at the time—including correlations and volatility—and the behavior of asset prices during similar past events.

What specific insights did we apply to the *Global Trade Tensions* scenario? Given our view that rising tensions emanated primarily from the contentious US-China relationship, we began by identifying headline assets in US and Chinese markets. These included equities (S&P 500 and MSCI China), bond spreads (China high-yield credit), inflation (US 10-year inflation-linked debt), and currencies (Chinese yuan) (refer to Table 6.2). As an example, we estimated there would be a 20% hit to Chinese equities. We added granularity by including other risky assets such as EM equities, global high-yield credit, and the Mexican peso to reflect the expected knock-on effects of a surge in protectionism on risky borrowers and EMs.

In this scenario, we expected a global sell-off in equity markets with EM and Chinese equities underperforming over a 1-month horizon. Credit spreads would widen, and economically sensitive commodities, such as copper, would take a hit. Reflecting a flight-to-quality, US Treasuries and gold would rally under the scenario.

6.4.1 Calibrating the Shocks

Estimating asset price shocks under different geopolitical risk scenarios is a highly judgmental process. In our *Global Trade Tensions* example, sweeping protectionist actions initiated by the world's largest economy (and erstwhile champion of free trade) would have significant implications for global growth expectations and financial market returns.

As such, our selected asset price shocks are designed to be more extreme relative to certain historical market events, such as the 2013 "taper tantrum," when then-Federal Reserve Chair Ben Bernanke precipitated a global market sell-off by signaling the end of quantitative easing. We also studied the 2015 Chinese market crash for a historical comparison. Back then, global equities and credit markets—led by China and the broader EM complex—sold off sharply, while perceived safe-haven, such as US Treasuries and the yen, rallied.

To be sure, this scenario required distinct flavors to differentiate it from any historical episode. For example, we specified a shock to EM interest rates (with an 80 bp rise in Mexican 10-year yields) to express a view that EM central banks would have to intervene to stave off currency depreciation in a global trade war environment. Similarly, we modeled a 0.20% rise in 10-year US inflation expectations to reflect the impact of higher tariffs feeding through to US import prices.

TABLE 6.2 A What-If Scenario[5]

Estimated 1-month reactions of selected asset classes to rising Global Trade Tensions scenario, June 2018

Asset class	Sub-asset class	Shock (size)	Shock (standard deviations)	Comments
Equities	China equities	−20%	−3.3	Markets sell off as protectionist rhetoric from the United States escalates, increasing the risk of trade wars with key US trading partners. Chinese stocks suffer the most, and EM assets underperform.
	US equities	−8%	−2.1	
	EM versus DM equities	−5%	−1.9	
Government bonds	Mexico 10-year government bond	80 bp	3.1	Treasuries rally in a flight-to-quality, and EM yields rise as central banks address currency weaknesses.
	US 10-year Treasury	−35 bp	−1.8	
Inflation-protected securities	US 10-year Treasury Inflation-Protected Security	20 bp	2.8	Inflation expectations rise on higher import prices.
Credit	EM debt	80 bp	3.5	Credit spreads widen with global risk-off; China and EM spreads are hit hardest.
Currencies	Mexico peso	−8%	−2.2	EM currencies suffer, while China allows its currency to depreciate. The US dollar strengthens in a flight-to-quality and expectations of a reduction in the US current account deficit.
	US dollar	3%	1.7	
	Chinese yuan	−2%	−1.9	
Commodities	Copper	−10%	−2.3	Industrial metals such as copper fall on expectations of slower global growth. Gold rallies as investors seek safe-haven assets.
	Gold	6%	2.2	

Source: BlackRock Investment Institute, with data from BlackRock's Aladdin Portfolio Risk Tools application, April 2019. For illustrative purposes only. It is not always possible to invest directly in an index.

The next step was selecting the market regime and volatility/correlation structure to apply in the scenario. This facilitates calculating the implied shocks on related asset classes and sectors. In this case, we decided that the market environment at the time of analysis in June 2018 was the most accurate reflection of a period of rising trade protectionism. Lastly, we applied a reality check to assess how plausible our estimated shocks are. We did this using the current market structure and historical episodes of market volatility as a guide. For example, the 20% fall to the MSCI China index represented a move three standard deviations below the asset class's monthly average return. Overall, the analysis showed that our *Global Trade Tensions* scenario was slightly more extreme than the China market crash experienced in 2015, but less severe than the 2008 Global Financial Crisis. This result matched our expectations and research.

After finalizing our selected asset price shocks, we applied them against some 2,000 variables in BlackRock's risk model. Selected results for *Global Trade Tensions* at the time are summarized in Table 6.3. The results demonstrated that negative shocks on US and Chinese

TABLE 6.3   More Shocks[6]
Implied asset-price shocks under trade tensions, June 2018

Asset class		Shock (size)	Shock (standard deviation)
Equity regions	Japan	−7.1%	−1.84
	Europe	−5.5%	−1.76
	UK	−4.3%	−1.38
Equity sectors	Technology	−11.1%	−2.22
	Materials	−8.4%	−2.16
	Financials	−6.5%	−1.81
	Utilities	−1.5%	−0.50
	Implied Volatility	11.4%	1.48
Government bonds	UK 10 year	−30 bp	−1.71
	Germany 30 year	−24 bp	−1.63
	Japan 10 year	−4 bp	−0.98
	Spain 5 year	15 bp	0.81
	Italy 5 year	59 bp	0.86
Inflation-protected securities	Japan 10 year	4 bp	0.62
	Eurozone 10 year	8 bp	1.43
Credit	Euro IG	−0.1%	−0.22
	US IG	0.5%	0.45
	US high yield	−1.9%	−2.40
Currencies	Euro	−3.3%	−1.60
	UK pound	−3.2%	−1.31
	Australian dollar	−2.7%	−1.17
	Japanese yen	−1.7%	−0.82
Commodities	Brent crude oil	1.1%	0.18

Source: BlackRock Investment Institute, with data from BlackRock's Aladdin Portfolio Risk Tools application, April 2019. For illustrative purposes only. It is not always possible to invest directly in an index.

equities would transmit to global equity markets, while perceived safe-haven assets would rally.

6.5   WHAT IS ALREADY PRICED IN?

Markets may or may not be paying attention to a particular geopolitical situation at a given point in time. To assess the extent to which risks are already priced into the market, we needed a short-term estimator. We developed the BlackRock Geopolitical Risk Indicator (BGRI) to measure how much market-related discussion is focused on geopolitical risk generally, along with each of our top risks specifically. Each BGRI tracks the relative frequency of analyst reports and financial news stories associated with specific geopolitical risks. We assign a much heavier weight to the words in contemporaneous brokerage reports than to the other data sources because we seek to measure the market's attention to any particular risk, not necessarily the public's. The higher the index, the more financial analysts and related media are referring to geopolitics versus history. There are two distinct components used to construct each scenario's BGRI Total Score: *Attention* and *Sentiment*.

BGRI Attention: The first component of the BGRI measures how frequently geopolitical topics are discussed in our source material. Specific words related to geopolitical risk in general and to our top risks are identified. Text analysis is then used to calculate the frequency of their appearance in analyst reports and other media. BlackRock identifies anchor words specific to the risk for each BGRI (e.g., trade) as well as related words (e.g., conflict, protectionist, or tariffs). A cross-functional group of portfolio managers, geopolitical experts, and risk managers agrees on keywords for each risk and reviews them regularly to ensure their relevance.

BGRI Sentiment: The second component of the BGRI measures whether the tone of geopolitical discussion is positive or negative. A proprietary dictionary is used, which includes about 150 "positive sentiment" words such as "strong" or "improve" and 150 "negative sentiment" words such as "dip" or "decline." BlackRock then compares the relative frequency with which positive and negative words are used near references to geopolitical topics. A weighted moving average puts more emphasis on recent articles.

$$\text{BGRI Total Score} = \text{BGRI Attention} - (0.2 \ * \ \text{BGRI Sentiment}). \qquad (6.1)$$

Greater weight is placed on the attention score, as the indicator's goal is to fundamentally measure market attention. BlackRock assigns a 20% weight to the sentiment score. This can help mitigate spikes in the BGRI at times when market attention is high but positive sentiment indicates that the risk of a particular scenario may actually be receding.

Conversely, the sentiment component can accentuate increases in the index when sentiment takes a turn for the worse. For example, the rise in our US-China competition BGRI in 2019 was exacerbated by worsening sentiment as both countries escalated their rhetoric around trade and strategic tensions.

Interpretation of the Score: A zero percentile score is defined as the average BGRI level over its history. The contemporaneous score is measured relative to its history, because otherwise it would be difficult to assess what constitutes a "high" or "low" level of market attention to a particular risk.

A score of one is defined to mean the BGRI level is one standard deviation above the historical average or "baseline." Negative scores indicate that market attention is below this historical baseline. We caution against drawing conclusions from small changes in the BGRI (such as moves of 0.1 or less, which we regard as noise).

The average is exponentially weighted, meaning that recent readings are weighted more heavily than those further in the past. This is based on the intuition that markets respond most to shocks to attention levels, and that high levels of attention eventually become "priced in." In other words, the effects of elevated BGRIs wash out over longer periods as investors become more accustomed to the risk.

6.5.1 Is It Priced In?

BlackRock's BGRI scores need to reflect a key property of markets, namely, that geopolitical risk scenarios can and will become partially or fully priced into markets. Markets consume news and recalibrate prices accordingly. The higher the BGRI reading for a particular geopolitical risk, the more financial analysts and media are referring to it, and the more we therefore assume that risk is being priced in by the market. As such, an approach has been developed for adjusting the scenario impact projections for geopolitical risks, using each risk's BGRI.

In Exhibit 6.2, the chart on the right shows how our estimates for the impact of a *Global Trade Tensions* scenario on global equity markets changed over time. The "unadjusted" line does not take into account the level of our BGRI, while the "adjusted" line does. We assume both are equal on the scenario's release date, as each scenario is calibrated to reflect what is not already priced in the market by investors. We then apply a multiplier to the scenario results through time (the dark gray line) to either dampen the estimated impact if market attention toward the risk is elevated versus the release date, or to amplify it if the BGRI suggests market participants may be focusing less on the risk.

6.5.2 Adjusted Impacts

How did this play out in practice? Market attention toward *Global Trade Tensions* quickly rose above the BGRI level observed on the scenario's launch (June 11, 2018), as illustrated in the chart to the left in Exhibit 6.2. This implied the risk was becoming more priced in by

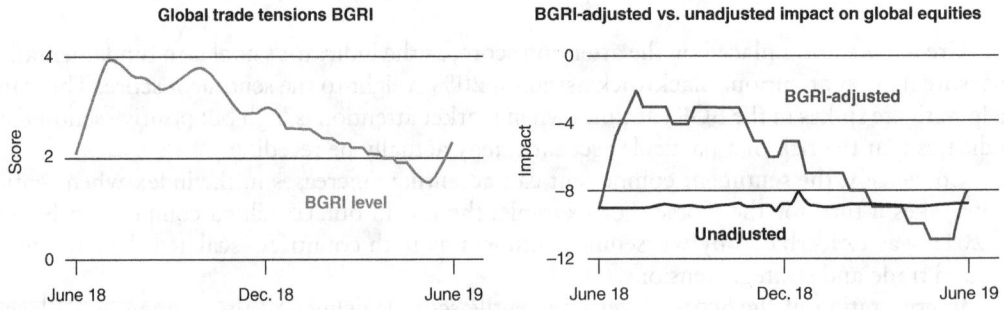

EXHIBIT 6.2 Pricing In and Out[7]
Global Trade Tensions BGRI and estimated global equity impact illustration, 2018–2019
Source: BlackRock Investment Institute, with data from Refinitiv, an LSEG brand, June 2019. The figures shown relate to past performance and are not a reliable indicator of current or future results. Forward-looking estimates may not come to pass. It is not always possible to invest directly in an index.

financial markets. Reflecting this, our BGRI-adjusted scenario impact rose above the unadjusted figure, pointing to less severe potential losses in global equities should the scenario occur.

Yet this trend ultimately reversed. Market attention to the *Global Trade Tensions* risk steadily waned from its July 2018 peak, before an eventual rebound in mid-May 2019. In the latter stage of this prolonged decline, the BGRI-adjusted scenario impact temporarily became more severe than the unadjusted figure, at one point signaling potential double-digit losses in global equities from a trade-related shock.

Note that even the unadjusted impact shown in our chart can change moderately over time. This is due to changes in underlying market conditions such as volatilities and cross-asset correlations. The important takeaway is that the less attention markets are paying to a particular geopolitical risk, the greater the potential market impact may be should a geopolitical shock materialize—and vice versa.

6.5.3   Assessing Likelihood

We combine our estimates of the likely impact of a given geopolitical risk with an assessment of its relative likelihood. Our geopolitical experts—including former policy makers, investors, and strategists across regions—identify escalation triggers for each risk and assess how likely they are to play out over the next six months, relative to the other risks we monitor.

We also estimate an overall gauge of geopolitical risk. Its likelihood score is based on a simple average of our top risks; the market impact is a weighted average by likelihood score. Exhibit 6.3 shows our estimate of the relative likelihood of each of the top risks—against the expected 1-month impact on global equities (at the time the scenario was conceived) should it come to pass. The likelihood scores can help provide a measure of when markets may be over- or underappreciating a particular risk. For example, we kept our *Global Trade Tensions* likelihood score at an elevated level in early 2019—even as market attention to the risk was sharply declining. Why? We saw tensions between the United States and China as structural and likely to persist beyond any short-term disagreements over the bilateral trade deficit. This pointed to rising potential for market volatility should the risk flare up, as it did in May 2019.

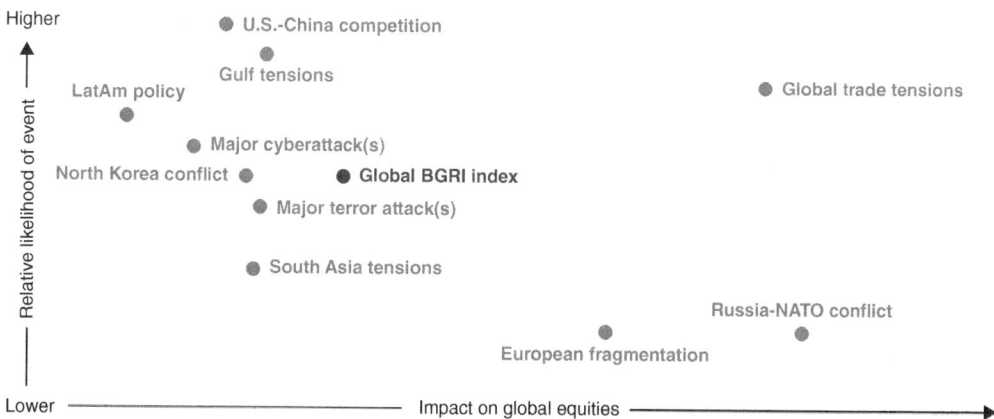

EXHIBIT 6.3   Risks and Impacts[8,9]
Relative likelihood and estimated market impact of selected geopolitical risks, 2019
Source: BlackRock Investment Institute, June 2019. Forward-looking estimates may not come to pass.

6.5.4 Takeaways

At the time the scenarios were conceived, the three geopolitical risks on our top list with the greatest potential market impact included *European Fragmentation, Russia-NATO Conflict,* and *Global Trade Tensions. Global Trade Tensions* was seen as the most likely of these risks to actually play out in the near term.

Gulf Tensions, another risk that was thought to play out, had a relatively modest expected market impact. BlackRock upgraded the likelihood of this risk in May 2019, against a backdrop of increasing tensions between the United States and Iran and heightened pressure on the US-Saudi Arabia relationship. *Major Cyberattacks* (a major cyberattack that disrupts key physical or financial system infrastructure) is an example of a risk with relatively high likelihood but lower expected market impact.

6.6 TAKING ACTION

The primary goal of BlackRock's geopolitical risk framework is to provide investors with insights on those risks with the greatest potential to affect the global economy, financial markets, and portfolio outcomes.

This analysis is an important input for stress testing portfolios. In some cases, the probability of a negative geopolitical event may point to potential losses that are excessively high relative to a portfolio's return targets. This may require hedging or risk-reduction strategies to mitigate downside risk. For portfolio construction, challenges arise as hedging typically comes with a cost. Geopolitical risks need to be weighed against fundamental views and the need to meet return targets.

BlackRock's scenario results can be used to help identify potential impacts on different portfolios. We illustrate with a series of hypothetical portfolios, ranging from a high risk portfolio (100% global equities) to a conservative one (100% bonds), with various blends in between, such as a "60/40" split of the two asset classes.

The Stress Test chart in Exhibit 6.4 illustrates the estimated range of portfolio impacts under various geopolitical scenarios:

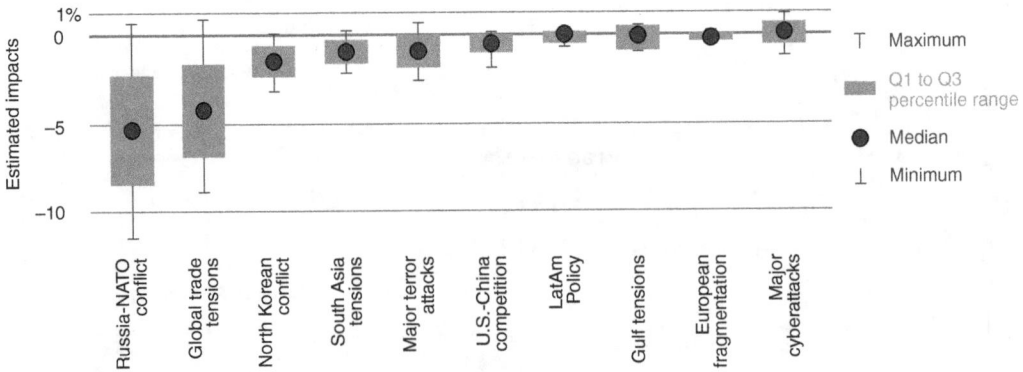

EXHIBIT 6.4 Stress Test[10]
Distribution of estimated BGRI-adjusted impact of geopolitical risk scenarios on hypothetical multi-asset portfolios
Source: BlackRock Investment Institute and RQA, June 2019. For illustrative purposes only.

- The scenario impact figures mostly tilt modestly to the downside, with adverse results for two risks—*Global Trade Tensions* and *Russia-NATO Conflict*—standing out. These two scenarios also show the widest dispersion in results across the hypothetical multi-asset portfolios analyzed.
- A handful of risks, including *LatAm Policy* and *Major Cyberattacks*, have little projected impact on multi-asset portfolios and a narrow dispersion in results. As a point of caution, in the real world, there may be outliers to these results. Think of a concentrated portfolio with heavy exposure to financials under *Major Cyberattacks* or an emerging market fund with heavy exposure to Latin America disproportionately harmed by the *LatAm Policy* scenario.

6.6.1 Key Drivers

BlackRock's scenario analysis is an important input to the risk management process and can be used to stress portfolios. It allows the key drivers of portfolio outcomes under different geopolitical risk scenarios to be identified and estimated. For the *Global Trade Tension* risk, Exhibit 6.5 applies our estimated asset price shocks to a selected group of hypothetical equity/bond portfolios of varying risk levels, ranging from 100% equities to 100% bonds. Exhibit 6.5 shows the estimated performance breakdown by asset class.

The analysis shows that the multi-asset portfolio losses under a *Global Trade Tensions* scenario are driven primarily by their exposure to global equities. In some portfolios, these losses were partially offset by bond exposure ("rates"), reflecting our expectation that the scenario would cause a flight into perceived safe-haven assets. Currency exposures embedded in global equity positions, as well as credit positions within the global bond allocations, detracted from performance. This illustrates the importance of diversification and the search for effective hedges that can help offset losses under differing risk scenarios.

6.6.2 BGRI-Specific Assets

In 2019, we sought to pinpoint assets that have moved significantly along with big changes in individual BGRIs, based on statistically meaningful relationships among them.

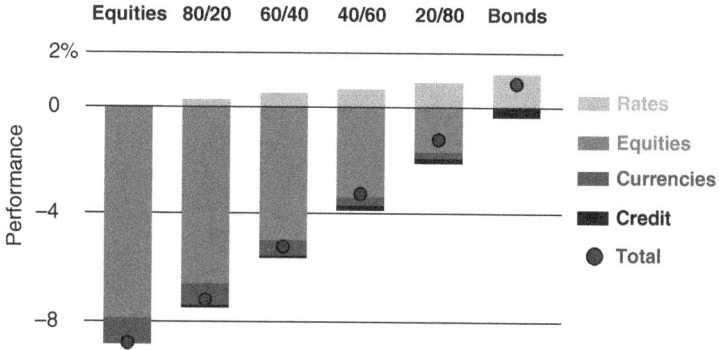

EXHIBIT 6.5 Underwater[11]
Hypothetical portfolio impacts under *Global Trade Tensions*
Source: BlackRock Investment Institute, with data from MSCI and Bloomberg Barclays, June 2019.

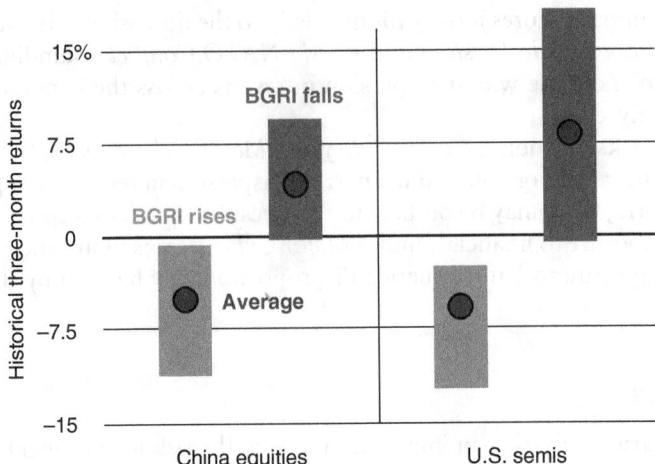

EXHIBIT 6.6   Tied to Trade Tensions[12]
Selected assets' hypothetical reaction to *Global Trade Tensions* BGRI
Source: BlackRock Investment Institute, with data from Refinitiv, an LSEG brand, June 2019.

Exhibit 6.6 examines what happened to selected assets when the *Global Trade Tensions* BGRI rose (the light gray bars) or fell (the dark gray bars) by more than 0.75 standard deviation over a 3-month period. The average 3-month returns and their historical ranges are shown. The analysis focused on 3-dozen assets that were seen as closely related to the *Global Trade Tensions* risk.

Risk assets, such as China equities, on average were hit hard when the *Global Trade Tensions* BGRI was on the rise, but rallied when the BGRI declined significantly. Equities, in the highly cyclical semiconductor sector, showed a similar, and magnified, response. This approach can help tease out assets that may be most sensitive to spikes in market attention to particular scenarios, potentially facilitating risk management.

6.6.3   The Path Forward

As geopolitics is ever evolving, BlackRock continuously seeks out ways to improve our framework. Section 6.7 lists some of the limitations with which the firm is grappling. Among the enhancements we are considering addressing are the following:

- **Multi-period scenario analysis:** The presented approach assumes geopolitical shocks are instant. BlackRock is working on an improvement to our model that would allow for multi-period analysis, or scenarios that would be realized over a time period.
- **Worst-case outcomes:** What happens when multiple tail risk scenarios strike markets at the same time? BlackRock is in the early stages of attempting to answer this question, via modeling a series of worst-case outcomes.

BlackRock's multidisciplinary group of in-house geopolitical experts continuously reviews the list of top geopolitical risks. Scenarios are refreshed as existing risks evolve and new ones emerge. BlackRock's research to quantify geopolitical risks is part of a broader effort to go beyond traditional financial metrics when thinking about risk.

6.7   CAVEATS AND CAUTIONS

While significant progress has been made in applying a framework to quantify geopolitical risks, estimating the impact of geopolitical risks on asset prices and portfolio returns will forever remain a challenging endeavor. Key hurdles include the following:

Fast-moving events: Geopolitical situations can change quickly. Keeping on top of the developments can require a significant commitment of time and resources. For example, tariff levels between major economies can rise in a step-wise fashion in response to incremental news flow or a sudden breakdown in trade talks. And scenarios can quickly become obsolete or morph into different risks. After binary events such as elections, for example, the risk scenario for markets may shift from one in which outsider candidates rise to power, to another in which new leaders implement populist policies.

Time horizon: There can be a disconnect between the time horizons of investors and those of geopolitical risk events. To be sure, the timing of certain geopolitical risk events, such as elections or referenda, is certain. Yet the vast majority are of uncertain duration and occur while markets continue to ingest data and recalibrate prices. The persistence of a market shock also depends on the nature of the event. For example, the negative market impact of a trade war may be quickly unwound in the case of a deal that resolves tensions. Yet an extended trade conflict could have longer-lasting and wider-ranging implications.

Multiple outcomes and triggers: Geopolitical situations can have multiple outcomes, each with wide ranging impacts. Military conflicts, for example, can have many escalation triggers—some hard to foresee. The broad market impact is likely to depend on the extent to which the conflict is contained, or if it draws in major powers.

Of course, geopolitical risks are just one of many factors that impact asset valuations. Broad "risk-on" and "risk-off" shifts in market sentiment—due to changing perceptions around growth, policy expectations, and other fundamental variables—can swamp the impact of geopolitical events on asset prices. Another challenge includes evaluating geopolitical risks independently of each other. Yet in reality, multiple events can occur simultaneously, complicating the analysis.

Early warning: Markets often move ahead of geopolitical risk events. This can dampen the incremental market reactions to the eventual realization of the scenario, at times making for counterintuitive asset price fluctuations. We attempt to address the challenge of markets partially or fully pricing in geopolitical risk events in advance via our BGRI adjustment methodology. Yet we are cognizant that our work in this area is an application of vastly imprecise science. Our market attention indicators, for example, may fail to capture certain relevant keywords.

Bottom line: Geopolitical risks can have a large impact on portfolios, especially in the short term. Investors would do well to keep tabs on them.

NOTES

1. This chapter along with the corresponding dashboards and exhibits represent data from June 2019. Aspects of the analysis have evolved since its initial publication in June 2019.
2. Tom Donilon, Bennett W. Golub, and Isabelle Mateos y Lago assisted in the initial development of this article, which was published in June 2019.
3. The table shows selected geopolitical events from BlackRock's historical study of 68 geopolitical risk events between 1962 and 2019. Risks were bucketed into three groups: event (such as

elections); exogenous (sudden events such as the Sept. 11 attacks); and thematic (a prolonged event such as U.S.-North Korea tensions). Dates refer to the starting date of the event.

4. The charts focus on 31 "exogenous" (unexpected) geopolitical shock events between October 1962 and January 2019. Examples include terrorist attacks and the Arab Spring. The chart on the left depicts average equity returns following the shocks. The S&P 500 was used as a proxy, given its longer available history than global equity indexes. The chart on the right shows equity returns following the eight shocks that occurred in months when the US economy was contracting (ISM US Manufacturing PMI was below 50). The "Average return" lines were calculated based on the closing price of the S&P 500 Index one day before the event date. On the left-hand chart, the average return (all periods) line shows the cumulative average daily return between 1960 and 2019; on the right-hand chart, the average return (contraction periods) line shows the cumulative average daily return between 1986 and 2015 when the US PMI was below 50. The shaded gray "range" is the standard error, or standard deviation, of the historical distribution. With respect to S&P data, S&P GSCI is a product of S&P Dow Jones Indices LLC ("S&P DJI"). S&P® is a registered trademark of Standard & Poor's Financial Services LL; Dow Jones® is a registered trademark of Dow Jones Trademark Holdings LLC. © 2022 S&P DJI. All rights reserved. S&P DJI does not sponsor, market or promote investment products based on its indices, and S&P DJI does not have any liability with respect thereto.

5. The table shows BlackRock's analysis regarding how various assets could react over a 1-month time frame (represented by the "shock (size)" column) to a hypothetical scenario of rising *Global Trade Tensions*. We estimate the severity of each shock based on analysis of similar historical events and current market conditions such as volatility and cross-asset correlations. In line with market convention, fixed-income shocks are expressed as changes in benchmark yields (basis points) and other asset classes as percentage price changes; see the "Implied Stress Testing Framework" section of Chapter 5: Market-Driven Scenarios: An Approach for Plausible Scenario Construction for further details. Indexes used: MSCI China Index for China equities; S&P 500 for US equities; MSCI Emerging Market (EM) Index and MSCI World Index for EM vs. developed (DM) equities; J.P. Morgan EMBI for EM debt; and the US Dollar Index. The Chinese yuan and Mexico peso are represented by their respective exchange rates with the US dollar (USD). Gold and copper are represented by benchmark futures contracts. Scenarios do not reflect all possible outcomes as geopolitical risks are ever evolving. This material represents an assessment of the market environment at a specific time and is not intended to be a forecast or guarantee of future results. There is no guarantee that stress testing will eliminate the risk of investing in any asset class. The MSCI data contained herein is the property of the MSCI Inc. or its affiliates (collectively, "MSCI"). MSCI and its information providers make no warranties. The MSCI data is used under licenses and may not be further used distributed or disseminated without the express written consent of MSCI.

6. The table shows BlackRock estimates of how various assets could potentially react to a hypothetical scenario of rising *Global Trade Tensions*, as defined in our Geopolitical Risk Dashboard. These shocks represent implied 1-month moves from the specific shocks to the assets highlighted in Table 6.2, based on cross-asset correlations and market conditions as of the scenario's inception in June 2018. Calculations assume instantaneous shocks across all risk factors. The shock (standard deviation) column shows the shock size in 1-month volatility terms. Shocks are expressed as price returns for equities, credit, currencies, and commodities; and changes in benchmark yields for non-credit fixed-income sectors. We use benchmark futures contracts for commodities as gauges of market reaction. The indexes for regional equity markets are MSCI World Index, S&P 500 Index, MSCI Emerging Market Index, MSCI Japan Index, MSCI Europe Index, and FTSE 100 Index. MSCI World sector indexes represent the sectors. Implied volatility is represented by the VIX Index. Cboe Volatility Index® and VIX® are registered trademarks of Cboe Exchange, Inc. For credit we use the following Bloomberg Barclays indexes: US Corporate High Yield, US Credit, and European Credit. Scenarios do not reflect all possible outcomes as geopolitical risks are ever evolving. This material represents an assessment of the market environment at a specific time and is not intended to be a

forecast or guarantee of future results. There is no guarantee that stress testing will eliminate the risk of investing in any asset class.

7. The chart on the left shows the BlackRock Geopolitical Risk Indicator (BGRI) for *Global Trade Tensions*. To generate it, specific words are identified related to this geopolitical risk and text analysis is used to calculate the frequency of their appearance in the Refinitiv Broker Report and Dow Jones Global Newswire databases as well as on Twitter. Then adjustments are made for whether the language reflects positive or negative sentiment, and a score is assigned. A zero score represents the average BGRI level over its history from 2003 up to that point in time. A score of one means the BGRI level is one standard deviation above the average. Recent readings are weighed more heavily in calculating the average. The chart on the right shows BlackRock's estimates of the potential market impact of rising trade tensions on the MSCI ACWI Index, a proxy for global equities. The unadjusted line shows the original estimate not adjusted for our *Global Trade Tensions* BGRI and based on the scenario analysis run on June 11, 2018. The adjusted line shows the potential equity impact based on the level of the BGRI. For example, an elevated BGRI level would suggest increased investor attention and therefore a lower BGRI-adjusted market impact. A factor is determined that scales the size of the BGRI move since the date of our original market impact estimate to calculate the BGRI-adjusted market impact. A sigmoid function is used to do so, or a statistical technique that is characterized by an S-shaped curve. We then multiply the original estimate of the market impact by (1 − scaling factor) to reach the BGRI-adjusted market impact score. The scenarios and charts are for illustrative purposes only and do not reflect all possible outcomes as geopolitical risks are ever evolving.

8. The graphic depicts BlackRock's estimates of the relative likelihood (1–10 scale, with 10 most likely) of the risks over the next 6 months and their potential market impact on the MSCI ACWI Index. Market impact estimates are as of the time of creation of each scenario. The Global dot represents our overall assessment of geopolitical risk. Its likelihood score is based on a simple average of our top-10 risks; the market impact is a weighted average the likelihood scores. Some of the scenarios envisioned do not have precedents—or only imperfect ones. The scenarios and the chart are for illustrative purposes only and do not reflect all possible outcomes as geopolitical risks are ever evolving.

9. The impact estimates in Exhibit 6.3 are unadjusted. The BGRI-adjustment process described previously means the estimated market impacts change over time. For example, the *European fragmentation* BGRI spiked from mid-2018 through June 2019, suggesting the risk was more priced in, dampening its expected market impact relative to the estimate displayed in Exhibit 6.3.

10. The charts show the distribution of BGRI-adjusted impact estimates on 11 hypothetical multi-asset portfolios. The portfolios range from conservative (100% bonds) to aggressive (100% equities) with 10 percentile shifts in asset class composition between these extremes. Example: 90% bonds; 10% equities, 80% bonds; 20% equities and so on. Bonds are represented by the Bloomberg Barclays Global Aggregate Index (USD-hedged); equities by the MSCI All Country World Index. The impacts (estimated 1-month performance in US dollar terms following the shock) are shown for each of the top geopolitical risks highlighted on BlackRock's Geopolitical Risk Dashboard. For illustrative purposes only. Estimated impacts do not reflect any management fees, transaction costs, or expenses. Scenarios do not reflect all outcomes as geopolitical risks are ever evolving. This material represents an assessment of the market environment at a specific time and is not intended to be a forecast or guarantee of future results. There is no guarantee that stress testing will eliminate the risk of investing in any asset class.

11. We present the estimated 1-month performance impact in US dollar terms of our *Global Trade Tensions* scenario on six hypothetical portfolios: (1) 100% global equities (MSCI ACWI index), (2) 80% global equities, 20% global bonds (Bloomberg Barclays Global Aggregate index); (3) 60% global equities, 40% global bonds; (4) 40% global equities, 60% global bonds; (5) 20% global equities, 80% global bonds; and (6) 100% global bonds. The BGRI-adjusted estimates are broken down by asset class. Asset class references are for illustrative purposes only and should not be

interpreted as a recommendation. Indexes are unmanaged. Returns do not reflect any management fees, transaction costs, or expenses. Scenarios do not reflect all outcomes as geopolitical risks are ever evolving. This material represents an assessment of the market environment at a specific time and is not intended to be a forecast or guarantee of future results. There is no guarantee that stress testing will eliminate the risk of investing in any asset class.

12. The chart shows the 25%–75% percentile ranges (bars) and average 3-month returns (dots) for selected assets during rolling 3-month periods when the *Global Trade Tensions* BGRI rose or fell by more than 0.75 standard deviations. The MSCI China Index (China equities) and the semiconductor sector subcomponent of the S&P 500 Index are used to calculate returns. Scenarios do not reflect all outcomes as geopolitical risks are ever evolving. This material represents an assessment of a market environment at a specific time and is not intended to be a forecast or guarantee of future results. There is no guarantee that stress testing will eliminate risk in investing any asset class. The figures shown relate to past performance and are not a reliable indicator of current or future results. This information is not intended as a recommendation to invest in any particular asset class or strategy or as a promise—or even estimate—of future performance.

CHAPTER 7

Liquidity Risk Management

Bennett W. Golub
Senior Advisor, BlackRock

Philip Sommer
Director, Liquidity & Trading Research Group, BlackRock

Stefano Pasquali
Managing Director, Liquidity & Trading Research Group, BlackRock

Michael Huang
Managing Director, Risk & Quantitative Analysis, BlackRock

Kristen Walters
Managing Director, Risk & Quantitative Analysis, BlackRock (2020)

Nikki Azznara
Vice President, Portfolio Management Group, BlackRock

7.1 INTRODUCTION

The term "liquidity" is often used ambiguously. In practice, it can have several different meanings—market liquidity, fund liquidity, liquidity premium, and so on.[1] This chapter focuses on fund liquidity risk, the risk that a redeemable multi-fund holder collective fund cannot raise enough cash to meet investor redemptions on a timely basis. Depending on the jurisdiction and legal form of the fund entity, such a failure can be treated as a catastrophic event that results in the termination of the fund and, even more dangerous, leads to an investor "run" on the fund-type or other funds managed by the same fund manager[2].

Managing fund liquidity risk involves evaluating the market liquidity of fund holdings to ensure a fund can convert holdings into cash to meet redemptions in a manner that does not adversely dilute the interests of other remaining shareholders.

Fund liquidity risk issues can often arise as a by-product of other issues, such as poor fund investment performance triggering sustained outflows or reputational scandals associated with the manager leading to redemption shocks. As such, implementing robust top-down governance practices and developing a strong liquidity risk management framework are key to mitigating these potential risks before they create problems. Specifically, to control this risk, fund managers should have a formal and well-defined firm-wide liquidity risk governance framework. The risk management function should be independent of portfolio management

TABLE 7.1 Liquidity Risk Management Elements

Liquidity Risk Measurement	Risk managers identify key liquidity risks and seek to provide accurate and appropriate risk measures for liquidity risk management.
Liquidity Risk Management	Risk managers monitor fund asset liquidity and redemption risks relative to limits.
Portfolio Manager Liquidity Risk Awareness	Risk managers discuss or escalate liquidity risks with decision-makers, as appropriate.
Redemption Toolkit	Risk managers evaluate back-up sources of liquidity and help to ensure operational readiness to employ extraordinary measures, as necessary.

to ensure that all risks, including liquidity risks, are properly managed. In line with the "three lines of defense" model outlined in Chapter 1, individual portfolio management teams should take primary responsibility for managing the liquidity risks associated with their portfolios. As the second line of defense, risk managers should regularly evaluate and discuss risks with portfolio managers, including setting mutually sensible limits on portfolio asset liquidity, both absolutely and relative to redemption risk, with escalation channels to the chief risk officer and chief investment officer, as necessary. Finally, as the third line of defense, audit should independently validate the investment businesses' adherence to key controls and policies. While there can be a variety of approaches, Table 7.1 illustrates key elements of a fund liquidity risk management function, which is grounded on strong governance, standardized processes, advanced analytics, and operational readiness.

This chapter presents an element of the first pillar of BlackRock's Investment Risk Management Paradigm (IRMP). Beginning with a brief history of fund liquidity risk management and its evolution through time, this chapter outlines a liquidity risk framework, describes the role that data (and data scarcity) plays in fund liquidity risk modeling, and finally discusses a few different models and analytics that can be employed to measure and monitor liquidity risk.

7.2 A BRIEF HISTORY OF LIQUIDITY RISK MANAGEMENT[3]

In the wake of the 2008 Global Financial Crisis, structural changes in bond markets coupled with increased regulatory oversight elevated concerns about liquidity risk management. Financial institutions—faced with a reduction in balance sheet capacity, increased capital costs, and heightened regulatory scrutiny—were forced to reevaluate their operating models and adapt to a new market and liquidity regime. To help mitigate the crisis, central banks employed extraordinary means to maintain low interest rates. Presented with accommodative monetary policies that kept interest rates extraordinarily low, many companies seized the opportunity to borrow cheaply. As a result, corporate bond issuance increased, including a proliferation of nonstandard issuance. Exhibit 7.1 shows an increase in US corporate bond issuance, which dipped in 2008 but rebounded post-financial crisis. Concurrently, broker-dealer inventories declined due to regulatory capital requirements and a ban on proprietary trading by banks.

Historically, asset managers were primarily "price takers" in over-the-counter (OTC) markets. When a buy-side trader acts as a price taker, he or she requests quotes from several

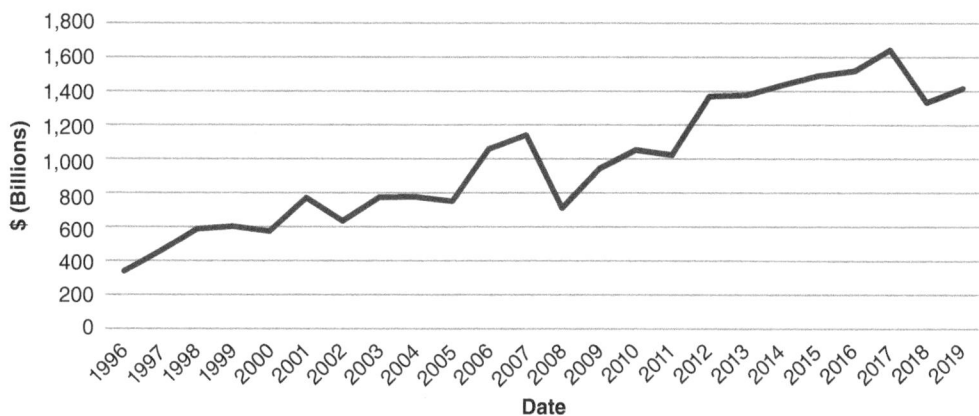

EXHIBIT 7.1 Annual US Corporate Bond Issuance
Source: SIFMA, as of December 2019.

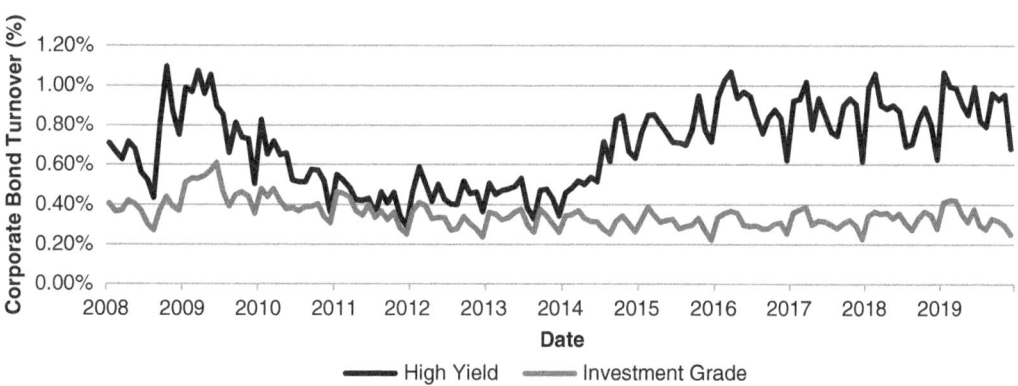

EXHIBIT 7.2 US High-Yield and Investment-Grade Corporate Bond Market Turnover
Sources: BlackRock, FINRA TRACE, as of December 31, 2019.
Note: Turnover measures ratio of monthly average daily trading volumes to the total market value outstanding. We use the Bloomberg Barclays US High Yield and Corporate Bond Indices as proxy for total market value outstanding. Corporate bond cash data sourced from FINRA TRACE.

dealers and takes the best price received. However, following the 2008 Global Financial Crisis, many market participants shifted their trading behavior to become "price makers." As a price maker, a market participant determines the price at which he or she is willing to buy (or sell) a particular security and then actively seeks out that price. This type of trading behavior is predominantly found in equity markets.

While primary issuance remained strong, secondary markets became thinner (e.g., lower turnover and wider bid-ask spreads) post-financial crisis. Specifically, there was a larger price impact for larger transactions in the secondary market, resulting in market participants choosing to increasingly break up secondary market trades into smaller sizes to minimize market impact. Generally, when market participants demand liquidity with immediacy, the cost of liquidity rises, particularly if immediacy is demanded during stressed environments. This can lead to investment losses for some investors and, at the same time, relative value opportunities for those market participants who can buy assets effectively being sold at a discount to fair value.

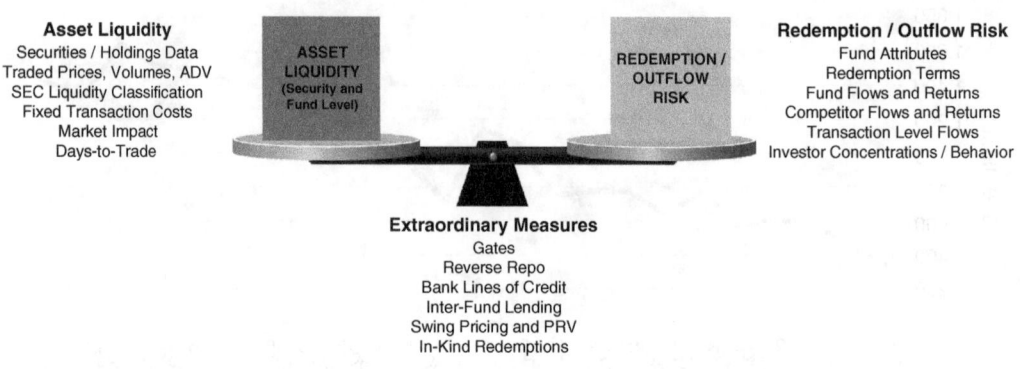

EXHIBIT 7.3 An Effective Fund Liquidity Risk Management Framework[4]
Source: BlackRock. For illustrative purposes only.

Post-financial crisis, market participants needed to modify their approaches. Portfolio managers adapted their portfolio construction process to account for changes to market liquidity, and risk managers built new tools and enhanced their liquidity risk frameworks and portfolio monitoring.

7.3   A FUND LIQUIDITY RISK FRAMEWORK

A comprehensive fund liquidity risk management program measures the liquidity of securities (assets) in funds, analyzes redemption behavior, and seeks to ensure funds are always able to meet reasonably anticipated redemptions on a timely basis. More specifically, the objective of the fund liquidity risk management program is twofold: (1) to help ensure that a fund has sufficient levels of liquid assets to meet a surge of short-term redemptions and (2) to help ensure that a fund does not become illiquid while seeking to meet large sustained levels of redemptions. As illustrated in Exhibit 7.3, the comprehensive fund liquidity risk management framework focuses on balancing asset liquidity with redemption profiles and incorporating the impact of extraordinary measures, as needed, to help meet unanticipated large redemptions in adverse markets.

7.4   ASSET LIQUIDITY

Measuring asset liquidity involves estimating the time required to liquidate positions in a fund in both normal and stressed market environments. Securities markets' trading behavior, structure, conditions, and position size all contribute to determining a given security's asset liquidity. Understanding days-to-trade, transaction costs, and how they fluctuate based on market impact (i.e., the size of trades) are critical to asset liquidity measurement. We begin by discussing the importance of data in measuring and modeling liquidity.

7.4.1   Importance of Data Modeling for Liquidity Risk Management

Portfolio and risk managers have been able to do a decent job modeling liquidity risk in equity portfolios for a long time. Given the nature of equity markets, where securities trade intraday on public exchanges, detailed transparency on trade volumes and pricing at the ticker level is available. This data availability has allowed portfolio and risk managers to measure and model the time and cost required to liquidate positions in normal and stressed markets for equities.

Modeling fixed-income asset liquidity, on the other hand, can be particularly challenging due to the massive number of distinct, tradeable securities in these markets and the generally lower levels of observed transactions for these securities. For instance, thousands of US corporate bonds principally trade OTC. There are approximately 1 million CUSIPs for municipal bonds alone.[5] However, only a small portion of all fixed-income securities trade daily, with trading concentrated in recently issued, large offerings. Yet, despite the low number of transactions per each security, reasonable approaches to assessing liquidity are achievable.

To appreciate how this can be done, consider a particular single family home where the same homeowner has lived for 30 years. During this period, zero transactions are recorded for the house. However, despite the lack of any specific transactional data, the house can and will be sold with a decent estimate of how long it will take and what it will fetch on the market. By reviewing other transaction records in the neighborhood, including houses with comparable attributes (i.e., acreage, number of bedrooms), the value of the house and the time required to sell it can be inferred. In other words, the lack of complete volume data alone does not make it impossible to develop useful information about a bond's liquidity. Other factors may need to be analyzed to properly evaluate liquidity.

Exhibit 7.4, compares daily posted inventory volumes (i.e., dealer axes) to actual TRACE (Trade Reporting and Compliance Engine) transaction data for US investment-grade (IG) corporate bond markets. The dealer axes data indicates that the trading volume observed in TRACE is a lower boundary of what is tradable and suggests that, on average, what can be traded is potentially a multiple of what is actually observed. Similar relationships can be found in the US high-yield (HY) market. Therefore, to effectively model and measure the liquidity of fixed-income securities, additional data need to be incorporated, including dealer axes, dealer runs (essentially bid and offer quotes), and observable data for bonds with similar characteristics.

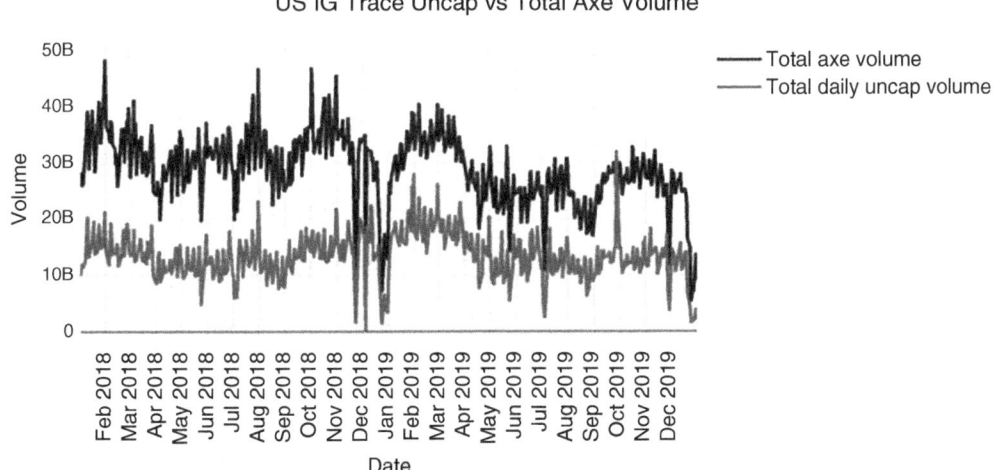

EXHIBIT 7.4   US Investment-Grade Trading Volumes
Sources: BlackRock, FINRA TRACE, Axe Data sent to BLK Brokers, as of December 2019.

The lack of available undithered and contemporary sources of data has often been cited as an impediment to liquidity risk management for fixed-income securities. Due to regulation and increasing demands for transparency by market participants, the availability of fixed-income trading data has markedly improved over the last few years, resulting in enhancements and improved accuracy of price discovery and liquidity risk models. Table 7.2 details some of the improvements in data availability.

7.4.2 Asset Liquidity: Days-to-Liquidate

Improved transactions data facilitates more conventional approaches to developing means for controlling portfolio liquidity. One approach to modeling asset liquidity is to estimate the number of days required to liquidate a position. Days-to-liquidate is calculated as a function of each position's average daily volume (ADV), the size of the trade, and an assumed market participation rate:

$$Days\,to\,Liquidate = \frac{Size\,of\,Trade}{Participation\,Rate * ADV\,Assumption} \tag{7.1}$$

The ADV of a specific security is the value of that security traded, on average, over a specified period, typically daily. ADVs can be measured (e.g., equities and US corporate bonds) using a firm's data, exchanges, and data vendors or modeled (using factor models such as amount outstanding, bid–ask spreads, etc.). Where there is a lack of granular

TABLE 7.2 Improved Transaction Data Availability

Data Source	Recent Enhancements
TRACE	In the United States, TRACE provides daily price and volume data for numerous liquid bond types (including IG and HY), albeit with individual trade volume caps based on trade size. In 2017, the Financial Industry Regulatory Authority (FINRA) introduced more timely access to TRACE corporate bond trade data, including the release of uncapped trading volumes at the CUSIP level on a 6-month lag.
Markets in Financial Instruments Directive (MiFID) II	In Europe, several data vendors provide daily corporate bond trade volumes. As a result of MiFID II regulation, third-party data providers offer detailed "intraday" snapshots of price and volume data at the end of each trading day for liquid bonds and full transparency for less liquid bonds on a monthly lag. Multiple data providers distribute data based on aggregated, nonstandardized feeds from dealers.
Realized Transaction Costs	As a result of MiFID regulation, asset managers are required to report realized transaction costs for European funds, which has improved transparency and encouraged third-party distribution of data to market participants.
Consolidated Pricing Tape	The European Commission is evaluating MiFID II data amendments, including a new consolidated "tape" of pricing data across fixed income and equity markets in a standardized format to improve data consistency and quality. Third-party data providers would be required to report data to a new consolidated tape provider with data tapes for each asset class.

investment-specific data, ADVs can also be estimated based on asset type, sector turnover, or trader insights.

The size of a trade required to be supported can be estimated to varying degrees of confidence based on historical redemption rates, portfolio leverage, derivative exposure, and other fund specific characteristics. Importantly, the liquidity of a fund and its underlying holdings varies depending on the market environment.

The market participation rate is the estimated percentage of a security's ADV that can be liquidated without materially impacting the price. Often in fixed-income markets, the observed trade volume is smaller than the inventory that could possibly trade. Referred to as latent liquidity, volume forecasts based on observed trading data, on average, provide a lower boundary of what could possibly trade. Section 7.8.1 includes more details on modeling trading volumes and outlines a new type of analytics to analyze volume and price data at the individual security level.

7.4.3   Asset Liquidity: Corporate Bond Transaction Costs (T-Costs)

Transaction costs (t-costs) are critical to evaluating asset liquidity. Traders regularly evaluate what bonds and position sizes can be traded without incurring undue t-costs and use t-cost analytics as a measure for best execution. Risk managers leverage t-cost models to review portfolio liquidation costs based on both fixed and variable costs, liquidation times for funds, specific holdings, and the impact of liquidation scenarios (partial or entire funds) and strategies (pro-rata or lowest cost). Since one of the main challenges in modeling fixed-income t-costs is price uncertainty, the expanded pricing and transaction data now available in many global markets have markedly improved the ability for organizations to accurately model t-costs for corporate bonds.

At the most basic level, expected t-costs are the sum of fixed costs (i.e., commissions) and realized market impact. The latter captures the relationship between position size and t-costs. The fixed cost is represented by the bid–ask spread, which can be expressed as the difference between historical bid and ask quotes from dealers, normalized by the mid-price of the benchmark prices.

In practice, there are several challenges in modeling t-costs for fixed-income securities, specifically the limited data available in fixed-income markets (as referenced in Section 7.4.1 and further described in Section 7.8). As an example, implementation shortfall relies on price discovery, which is the process of determining the price of an asset in the marketplace through the interactions of buyers and sellers. Therefore, a key priority is to improve price data quality. Additionally, measurement errors in implementation shortfall set the boundaries of efficiency for functional forms (i.e., the error in the data is large compared to the object being measured). Comparable issues limit the explanatory power of t-cost models, including less reliable bid–ask spreads when bonds are less actively traded. Further, the differentiation of fixed costs and market impact can be "blurry" as the majority of price data provides indicative prices and/or sizes and estimated ADVs. Section 7.8.1 includes more details on modeling t-costs and implementation shortfall.

7.5   REDEMPTION RISK

A critical component when managing a fund's liquidity risk is evaluating its ability to meet redemptions in varying market environments. This involves the ability to respond effectively to unexpected, outsized flows—both short-term surges in redemptions and long-term sustained outflows. Redemption risk is a function of numerous factors, including macroeconomic factors, fund returns, changes in a fund manager's reputation, severe underperformance by similar funds managed by others, and fund attributes (e.g., AUM, investor profile and concentrations). Redemptions may occur under normal or stressed market conditions, which impact a fund in different ways. Under normal market conditions, funds will aim to minimize the cost of meeting subscriptions and redemptions whereas during stressed market conditions, funds might observe large and potentially correlated demands. Approaches to modeling redemption risk are outlined in Section 7.8.2.

7.5.1 Managing Redemptions and Outflow Risk

Portfolio managers should be prepared to utilize a range of tools to meet redemption requests. The "Waterfall" in Table 7.3 would most likely be followed for US open-end 40 Act retail funds. It illustrates a typical sequencing of "all available means" to meet redemptions, including structural fund features, while recognizing constraints based on the fund's mandate and regulatory requirements. Risk managers should review "Waterfall" protocols independently, including the operational feasibility of using back-up sources of liquidity, and assess whether portfolio managers followed appropriate protocols post large redemptions. Not all tools that are legally permissible are, in practice, operationally feasible. The time to learn how to use extraordinary means is NOT during a crisis. Rather, regular drills should be performed to develop and retain operational flexibility.

7.6 LIQUIDITY STRESS TESTING

Liquidity stress testing is an important tool within the liquidity risk management framework, allowing risk managers to ensure a fund can meet redemptions in various environments. To analyze the impact of stressed markets on the liquidity of a portfolio, risk managers should

TABLE 7.3   Key Elements of a Typical Redemption "Waterfall" for US Retail Funds

---

Cash/Highly Liquid Assets are held to provide a highly liquid buffer for a variety of reasons, including (1) the ability to meet small, nontrending "noise" redemptions to minimize the need to incur transaction costs associated with selling a very small pro-rata basket, (2) an investment strategy where risk may be obtained synthetically, and (3) market environments in which the portfolio manager actively chooses to hold excess liquidity. Cash levels in portfolios fluctuate based on these and other factors. Highly liquid assets can include fixed-income ETFs, which can be used by portfolio managers to add daily liquidity to a fund while helping to maintain the risk consistent with the benchmark and fund mandate. Similarly, cash held in a portfolio can be equitized using futures.

Pro-rata/risk constant sale of bonds in a manner that keeps the risk positioning in a fund largely unchanged and consistent with the fund's mandate, including the fund's investment guidelines. Most non-de minimus redemptions in liquid fixed-income funds should be met by the sale of bonds in a pro-rata or "risk constant" fashion. This approach has the valuable feature of treating both the redeeming and remaining investors in the fund equitably.

Short-term borrowings, such as reverse repurchase (repo), overdraft capacity with custodians, and lines of credit, can serve as "back-up" liquidity sources for portfolio managers (to the extent permitted by leverage constraints) when there are large, unexpected redemptions or idiosyncratic redemption behavior in funds. Borrowings for open-end mutual funds are limited in some regulatory jurisdictions. For example, under the 1940 Investment Company Act, borrowing is limited to 33.3% of total fund assets (i.e., the fund must have asset coverage of 300%).

consider the liquidity of the assets in light of redemptions in normal and stressed market conditions. Stressors can be applied to assets, fund redemptions, or both, depending on the intended scenario. Stress testing the asset liquidity profile can be achieved using ADV or t-cost multipliers, applied at the sector or global level that simulate longer times or increased costs to liquidate assets. Applying stress to assets is indicative of volatile markets, but with limited investor redemptions and increased t-costs. Several different stresses can be applied on the redemption side, including investor concentration scenarios to simulate the impact of simultaneous redemptions from a concentrated group of investors, historical redemption scenarios to simulate the impact of historical or hypothetical redemptions, as well as scenarios that simulate the impact of gating a fund. Applying stress to redemptions alone is indicative of increased investor redemptions under normal market conditions. Finally, applying stress to both the assets and redemptions represents a "worst-case scenario" with increased redemptions and challenges in sourcing liquidity leading to expensive transactions or potentially catastrophic fund failure.

Risk managers should consider reverse stress testing, which allows further analysis to determine how additional stresses on the asset liquidity or redemption magnitude impacts a fund's liquidity coverage ratio. It also provides a way of quantifying scenarios that would cause the liquidity coverage ratio to fall below zero over different horizons.

7.7 EXTRAORDINARY MEASURES

In addition to techniques that measure and monitor liquidity risk, other redemption management tools are available in certain jurisdictions in "extraordinary" circumstances to meet unanticipated redemptions. Organizations should perform regular reviews of the redemption tools available to different fund types in varying regulatory jurisdictions. Table 7.4 describes the various extraordinary measures available and details where they are permitted by jurisdiction of fund type. Notably, having access to these measures is only helpful if fund managers know how to put the measures into practice. While these techniques are, by design, rarely used, they could be required with great urgency. It is important to periodically test the ability of the fund manager to utilize these measures to ensure that different parts of the organization understand their role and can put the measures into practice quickly. Various teams, such as legal, operations, risk management, and trading should perform "break glass" testing to ensure that tools can be deployed if needed.

7.8 FIXED-INCOME DATA AVAILABILITY LIMITATIONS

While fixed-income liquidity data has improved, there are still limitations with respect to the granularity of the data reported, as of January 2023. As noted in Table 7.2, TRACE provides daily price and volume data with caps based on trade size. More specifically, HY and IG trading volumes are currently published with individual trade volumes capped at $1 million and $5 million, respectively. Trades are reported 15 minutes following a transaction. If the trade size is larger than the cap, the report indicates the trade was $1 million or over, whereas if the volume is below the cap, the exact volume is reported. Uncapped price and volume data for all trades is published on a 6-month lag. This presents challenges in modeling bond liquidity, as there is no immediate transparency for the bonds trading in excess of their caps. As shown in Exhibit 7.5, based on analysis of 2019 data, 78% and 45% of the total HY and IG trading volumes were capped, respectively.

TABLE 7.4   Examples of Extraordinary Measures[6]

Extraordinary Measure	Description	Permissibility
Temporary Borrowing	Borrowing includes overdraft protection from custodians, repo agreements, inter-fund lending agreements, or bank credit facilities for back-up liquidity purposes. These agreements provide temporary cushions to allow orderly selling of securities while still meeting fund's obligations to clients.	Bank lines of credit are permissible for US retail funds but are ineligible for Undertakings for Collective Investment in Transferable Securities (UCITS) funds.
In-kind Redemptions	In theory, in-kind redemptions can be used, on an ad hoc basis, to meet redemptions for actively managed funds. This reduces liquidity risk as assets can be transferred to fund shareholders rather than having to be sold in a distressed market to meet a redemption.	Allowed by regulation, but only feasible for certain types of funds or large institutional investors due to the electronic platform employed to distribute mutual funds.
Gates	When a fund applies a gate, it only has to meet redemptions up to a certain level (e.g., 10% of net asset value [NAV]). Gates are a mechanism to temporarily stop a hypothetical "run" on a fund. Gates are unlikely to be effective if only applied to certain funds or asset classes.	Allowed for UCITS funds. Not permissible in the United States for retail mutual funds, meaning that a gated fund may need to get fully liquidated.
Pricing Mechanisms	Certain pricing mechanisms, including swing pricing and purchase redemption values (PRVs) allocate transaction costs to redeeming and subscribing investors alike. With respect to redemptions, these mechanisms reduce "first mover" advantage and "run" risk by making redemptions during periods of market stress more expensive.	Swing pricing is allowable and widely used for UCITS funds, and PRV is used for collective trust funds (CTFs) in the United States, regulated by the Office of the Comptroller of the Currency (OCC). Swing pricing is allowable under the US Securities and Exchange Commission (SEC) Liquidity Risk Rule but, as of January 2023, still not feasible given legacy infrastructure supporting fund flows in US retail mutual fund markets.[7]
Suspension	Suspensions act as a more extreme measure by allowing a fund to stop meeting any redemptions. Suspensions can sometimes be in the best interest of clients as an alternative to fire-selling the fund's assets.	Not permissible for US mutual funds without specific allowance from the SEC.

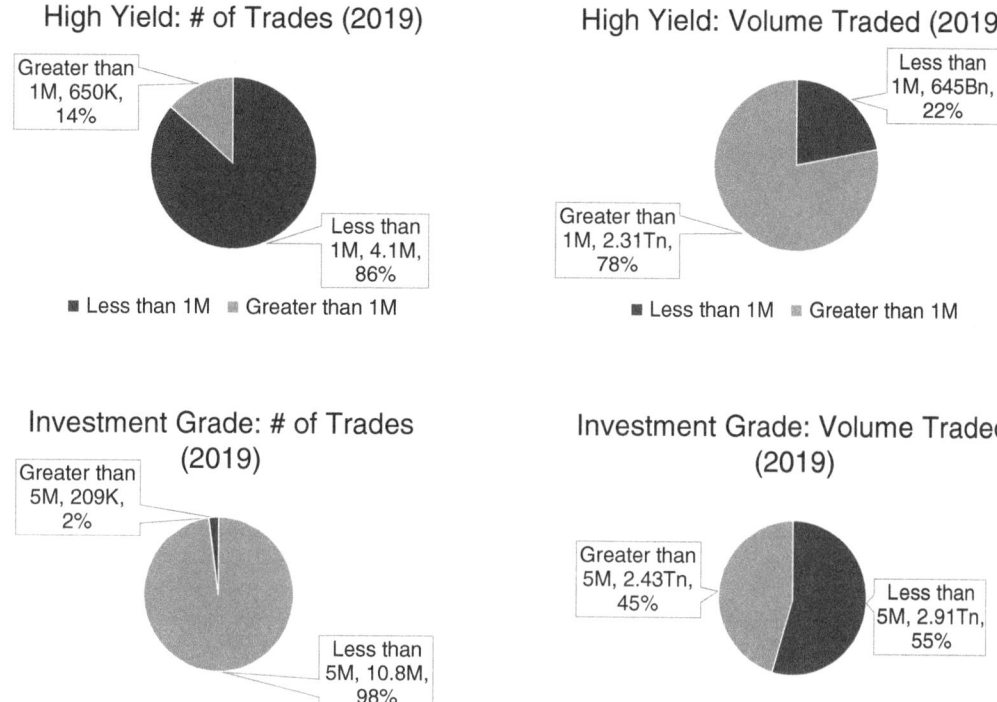

EXHIBIT 7.5 HY and IG Capped and Uncapped Trade Volumes in 2019
Sources: BlackRock, FINRA TRACE, 2019.

Attempting to address this lack of transparency in available data, market participants have developed simplistic approaches based on reported capped and uncapped volumes aggregated at the sector level. By adding together the individual capped volumes for each trade and taking the difference between this amount and the total aggregated volume for the sector, volumes for each of the capped trades can be estimated by distributing the difference to the individual bonds. Using this approach, the traded volumes of the bonds can be mistated, impairing the accuracy of models consuming this data, including transaction cost models.

7.8.1 Modeling Asset Liquidity

Modeling Trading Volumes As described earlier, one way that asset liquidity can be modeled is by computing a position's "days-to-trade" based on a security-level ADV model. Such a model attempts to address the issue of infrequent trade observations by incorporating historical trading data and a broad set of features that reflect the heterogeneity of corporate bond markets. To effectively model trading volumes, the infrequent trading problem can be decomposed into two problems: (1) the probability of the trade occurring and (2) the predicted volume if the bond does trade. Combining both problems creates an unconditional expected value of future tradable volume.

Such a model can be estimated by employing random forest regression, a machine-learning technique. This technique can address nonlinearity and missing data and also deals well with a large set of features.

$$E(V_{t+1}^b) = p_{t+1}^b \cdot E(V_{t+1}^b | TRADE) + (1 - p_{t+1}^b) \cdot \underbrace{E(V_{t+1}^b | NO\ TRADE)}_{0}$$

$$= p_{t+1}^b \cdot E(V_{t+1}^b | TRADE) \tag{7.2}$$

where

b = individual bond
t = time
V_{t+1}^b = bond b's market-wide trade volume at time $t + 1$
$TRADE$ = condition of a trade occurring
p_{t+1}^b = bond b's probability of $TRADE$ occurring at $t + 1$.

$E(V_{t+1}^b | TRADE)$ *predicts "if a bond trades, what is the expected market-wide traded volume?" and lies in the interval* $[min(y), max(y))]$

p_{t+1}^b predicts the probability of a trade occurring tomorrow, and lies in the interval $[0, 1]$

For frequently traded bonds, historical trading activity may provide a good approximation of a bond's future traded volume once it trades. However, for infrequently traded bonds, historical trading activity may be both sparse and not representative of potential traded volume. Using the historical trading activity of similar bonds can help to infer a bond's next day traded volume. Each bond can be characterized by a set of bond features (e.g., amount outstanding, time to maturity) and recent trading activity. Bonds with similar characteristics and similar recent activity likely have similar future traded volumes.

Historical volume data alone do not fully capture a bond's potential tradable volume. Drawing on secondary market data provides insight into dealer inventories (e.g., "axe" or dealer run data), revealing that dealers often post their inventory and their bid prices, almost by definition, assuming that a trade did not yet occur but could have occurred. This approach to modeling assumes that inventory postings serve as an indication that the bond could actually have traded if an investor decided to hit the bid or offer, thus significantly increasing the average estimate for tradability. The trade volume observed in fixed-income securities is often smaller than the inventory that could possibly trade. Referred to as *latent liquidity*, volume forecasts based on observed trading data, on average, provide only a lower boundary of what could possibly trade. When estimating days-to-trade, market volume refers to the amount of securities that are available to sell close to fair value (i.e., at or around the bid price).

For securities with large variance in daily observed trade volume, this can translate into large variance in the estimates for time-to-liquidation. To better account for this, the distribution of daily traded volume can be modeled to quantify the uncertainty in estimating liquidity. For example, *latent liquidity* can be approximated as a tail estimate, pointing to the 90th percentile of the ADV distribution. This allows the security specific range to be quantified between the average daily volume and the more optimistic tail of what is occasionally observed as tradable, possibly at a premium. Put together, such an approach allows the uncertainty of estimating liquidity to be quantified by providing a range for time to liquidation.

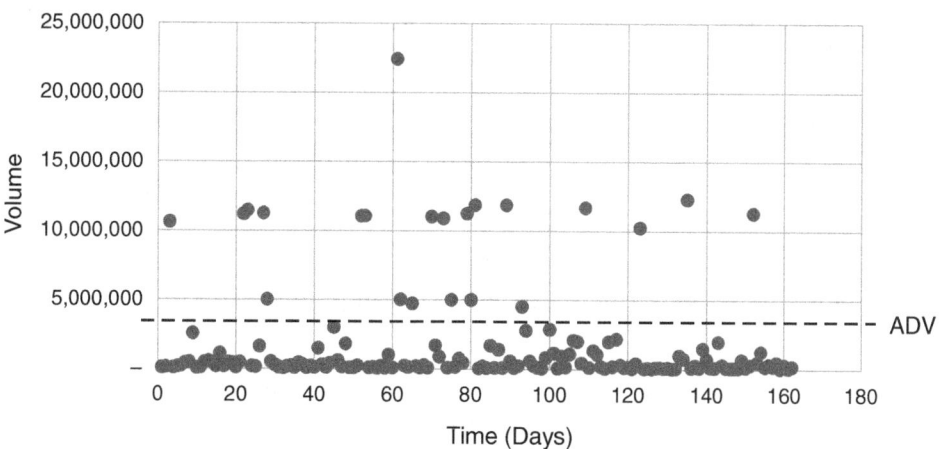

EXHIBIT 7.6 Fixed-Income Bond Latent Liquidity
Sources: BlackRock, FINRA TRACE.

Exhibit 7.6 demonstrates the observed daily traded volume over a 180-day period for an individual corporate bond. This illustrates that the ADV is a conservative measure for liquidity when the variance of observed trading volume is significant.

Modeling Transaction Costs A t-cost model uses empirical transaction data, intraday benchmark prices, and bond attributes to estimate a fixed cost and market impact cost, which varies depending on the size of the trade. Specific to corporate bonds, the purpose of the model is to forecast the liquidity, market impact, and t-cost of trading a corporate bond in the secondary market. The model estimates the t-cost in "price terms."

The following t-cost model uses a standard functional form where the estimated transaction cost is composed of a fixed cost and a market impact component fitted on empirical data as well as corporate bond attributes. The market impact component is a function of the trade notional volume and the estimated ADV, and a regression model can be used to estimate the coefficient.

$$Estimated\ T\text{-}Cost = Fixed\ Cost + Market\ Impact$$

$$= [k_1 \times BAS] + \left[k_2 \times D \times S \left(\frac{Trade\ Notional\ Volume}{ADV} \right)^{\gamma} \right] \quad (7.3)$$

where

- *BAS* denotes percentage bid–ask spread
- k_1 and k_2 are regression coefficients
- *D* is the spread duration of security
- *S* is the option adjusted spread of security[8]
- *ADV* is average daily volume from the most recent version of the ADV model
- γ controls the shape of the market impact

The primary purpose of a t-cost model is to estimate the expected realized cost of a trade, which is expressed as the implementation shortfall against the order arrival price benchmark, or the price in the market at the time the trade order was placed. The implementation shortfall is defined as the percentage difference between traded price and benchmark prices.

$$Implementation\ Shortfall = sign \times (Traded\ Price - Benchmark\ Price)/$$
$$Benchmark\ Price \times 10{,}000 \qquad (7.4)$$

where

- $sign = 1$ for a buy order and -1 for a sell order
- *Benchmark Price* is defined as nearest intraday mid-price at least 5 minutes before the trade

Since the time difference between the execution time and the previous end of day can be several hours, measuring implementation shortfall (with previous end of day prices) as benchmark prices can potentially result in a large return component. The explanatory variables chosen to predict t-cost include implementation shortfall, so the return component adds noise to the end t-cost figures. To minimize this impact, intraday benchmark prices that are sometimes available 5 minutes prior to the execution time can be utilized (when available). The use of a pre-trade benchmark price is considered good practice as it is more difficult to manipulate.

In this example, the model leverages a linear regression to predict t-cost based on fixed cost and market impact. The subscripts i and t indicate that the trades are bond- and time-specific.

Implementation Shortfall$_{i,t}$

$$= [k_1 \times BAS_{i,t}] + \left[k_2 \times D_{i,t} \times S_{i,t} \times \left(\frac{Trade\ Notional\ Volume_{i,t}}{ADV_{i,t}} \right)^{\gamma} \right] + \varepsilon_{i,t} \qquad (7.5)$$

To compensate for the mass of small odd-lot trades, observations can be weighted in the ordinary least squares (OLS) regression by the US dollar amount traded. In this case, the t-cost model is specified to follow the canonical square root shape for the market impact term. There is a vast body of literature in the equity domain supporting this functional form, which is consistent with the trader "rule-of-thumb" that trading one day's volume costs roughly one day's volatility. In a paper by Sommer and Pasquali (2016), the authors summarized the main theoretical and empirical results, which show that square-root-shaped models can be attributed to market microstructure arguments that generally apply similarly for OTC dealer markets. Accordingly, this opens the path for a liquidity analytics framework that is consistently applicable across asset classes, which enables a data driven quantitative liquidity risk management practice.

Similarity and Localization of Models   Analyzing volume and price data at the individual security level is critical for traders and for liquidity optimization (see Section 7.8.3), as it helps to provide a more accurate measure of security-level price and volume data than a model based on sector-level data. To address this need for single-security accuracy, models can be calibrated based on observations of a cohort of similar instruments rather than on the broader sector universe. This can be achieved by overweighting trade observations of fungible securities to maximize the relevance of data at the expense of a reduced number of observations. Developing a "security similarity model" can help to identify securities that share the same liquidity properties as a specified target security, which can be incorporated into asset liquidity and t-cost models.

As an example, given a target security, the model would return a list of similar securities based on user constraints, where similar securities can be broadly defined as those that are "close" or "fungible" to the target security with respect to bond characteristics. Similarity is defined relative to defined "objectives" (e.g., OAS, duration, yield, bid–ask spread). Given these objectives, similarity between any two bonds can be expressed (on a scale of 0–1) based on a set of security characteristics (e.g., industry, sector, country) using machine-learning techniques (i.e., cluster analysis, tree-based approaches, and neural network approaches). In the paper[9] by Jeyapaulraj et al. (2022), the authors propose a supervised similarity learning framework for corporate bonds.

There are several potential use cases for this type of analysis, including but not limited to the following:

- Identifying alternative similar securities where it may be easier to source liquidity
- Providing pricing for illiquid securities where there may be little to no observable data
- Replacing heuristics-based sector categories broadly used in portfolio management by more dynamic data-driven cohorts of similar instruments

7.8.2 Modeling Redemption-at-Risk

Let us now turn our attention to the "demand" for liquidity that arises when fund investors submit redemption requests for timely (typically but not always daily) redemptions. The empirical characteristics of this demand for liquidity defines the redeemable liability that needs to be supported by the fund's assets. Understanding and properly managing this liability is of particular importance for collective funds with multiple investors, some of whom may be redeeming, while others are subscribing, and yet others are just remaining in the fund. Ideally, all three categories of investors are being treated equitably, which depends upon, among others, a thoughtful liquidity-aware portfolio management process.

A good starting point in modeling redemption risk is to measure worst-case redemptions based on historical fund flows (e.g., 99% worst-case 5-day flow over the life of a fund) using a historical "redemption-at-risk" (HRaR) approach. HRaR is a calculated metric based solely on a fund's historical flow and NAV data.

The goal of developing forward-looking "predictive" redemption-at-risk models is to generate signals to help risk managers and portfolio managers anticipate potential large redemptions and proactively adjust positioning to efficiently meet extreme fund flows. While using historical data helps to provide some basis for anticipating forward redemption behavior, historical data do not necessarily "predict the future." As such, forward-looking redemption-at-risk models need to be deeply grounded in macroeconomic data.

In practice, modeling redemption risk is challenging given that some funds may not have experienced outflows historically (e.g., new or rapidly growing funds) and fund redemption behavior may be driven by idiosyncratic fund features (such as investor profile and type of mandate). In addition, for asset managers relying on external platforms to distribute funds, accessing transaction level flows and fund investors' attributes required to fully model idiosyncratic redemption behavior can be difficult. Specifically, the limited observability of granular redemption data is particularly challenging: many mutual funds are primarily distributed by numerous third parties to retail or small investors who can potentially generate thousands of daily subscriptions and redemptions for each fund across all of the distributors. The ability to extract predictive information that drives these flows may be impeded by that information not being made available to the fund manager by the distributors. As a result, flows may only be captured at the aggregate level and, thus, do not provide granularity into the characteristics of the flow (i.e., a single investor versus a platform). Finally, large flow events that result in significant redemptions are typically rare, which presents a modeling challenge when trying to identify patterns that contribute to extreme behaviors from historical experience.

Typically, large outflows are the result of systemic flows (explained by a combination of sector-level flows and macroeconomic factors) as well as idiosyncratic flows (the result of idiosyncratic investor behavior, competitors' performance, discretionary flows, or other event-type risks not observable solely from flow data, such as, insider trading scandals, key personnel departure, etc.). Over the last 30 years, firms or funds that have experienced stressed redemption events were due to extreme events, investment losses/performance issues, regulatory sanctions, reputational issues, or organizational changes, among others, which underscores the challenge of modeling idiosyncratic flows.[10]

Machine-learning-based models attempt to forecast potential investor redemptions by leveraging historical data on realized redemption and subscription requests made by mutual fund investors. These models aim to provide an estimated statistical upper bound on likely redemptions over a given time horizon based on available historical data. These forecasts can subsequently contribute to managing the risks faced by open-end mutual funds and, in particular, can provide insight into liquidity risk by relating observed portfolio redemptions to information about potential future redemptions and enable portfolio managers to prepare for these potential demands. Machine-learning techniques can be appealing given high dimensionality and nonlinearity in the data. However, limitations in data availability and quality present challenges in effectively implementing and applying forecasted redemption risk models.

7.8.3   Modeling Liquidity Optimization

Fund liquidity risk management can be viewed as an optimization problem, where portfolio managers must balance the risk-and-return implications of a portfolio's asset liquidity profile and cash reserves versus expected liquidity obligations. Because the fund shares are redeemable in whole or in part on a daily business day basis, there is a risk that redemptions can be large relative to the size of the fund. Being cognizant of various constraints, such as market capacity, transaction costs, time to access liquidity, and maintaining the appropriate risk profile, a portfolio's liquidation surface can be derived using optimization techniques, which is further explored in Chapter 8.

To meet redemptions under varying market environments, portfolio managers need to be able to access liquidity at the portfolio level. This requires a contemporaneous understanding of the ability and timeliness of extracting cash from each fund. Fortunately, portfolio managers have various means to access liquidity beyond a simple pro-rata liquidation of portfolio assets. Some portfolios explicitly choose to maintain a particular level of cash or ETFs to facilitate unlikely large redemptions. There are, necessarily, trade-offs to be managed, including market capacity, transaction costs, time to access liquidity, and the degree to which non-pro-rata asset liquidations can be permitted to distort a portfolio from its desired risk profile. At the same time, if a portfolio manager liquidates pro-rata assets quickly to avoid taking on market risk, the resulting transaction costs may be excessively high. On the other hand, if

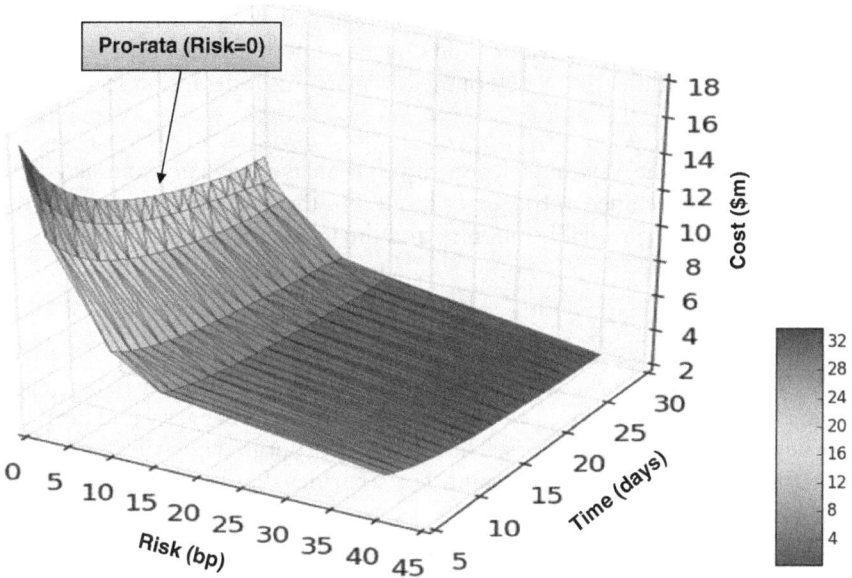

EXHIBIT 7.7 Liquidity Optimization—Balancing Risk Profile, Liquidation Time, and Cost
Source: BlackRock. For illustrative purposes only.

the portfolio manager seeks to limit transaction costs, he or she may space out trading over several days, increasing the market risk to these transactions.

Exhibit 7.7 shows the liquidation profile of a hypothetical corporate bond fund, reflecting the interplay of time, cost, and risk constraints. In the example, given a simulated high-yield corporate portfolio with $20 billion in AUM, a portfolio manager hypothetically needs to raise $1 billion in cash. If he or she decides to sell pro-rata and fast, a much higher cost of liquidation is incurred when risk constraints or liquidation time are relaxed. Changes in market (liquidity) conditions are reflected as transformations of the surface. The example can be extended to incorporate further constraints, such as tracking error, regulatory liquidity thresholds, and the like.

To further demonstrate liquidating a portfolio using optimization, we illustrate how this can be formulated more formally as an optimization problem. Let us assume that a fund comprises securities x_i with market value m_i and notional value n_i. Each security belongs to a unique market sector S_j. If the portfolio manager needs to fully or partially liquidate the fund over a period of time by selling a fraction $p_{i,t}$ of each security on a given day, t, the following relationship must hold:

$$\text{Find the optimal liquidation schedule } p_{i,t} \text{ such that } p_{i,t-1} \leq p_{i,t} \leq 1$$

$$\text{in order to maximize } \sum_i p_{i,t} m_i \text{ subject to constraints} \tag{7.6}$$

Liquidations

In order to achieve a full liquidation, a portfolio must apply this relationship to consecutive days until the fund is fully liquidated (i.e., until $\forall_i : p_i = 1$).

If actual or expected redemption obligations are added as a constraint, such as allowing $\sum_{i,t} p_{i,t} m_i$ to be fixed for a specific value v on a given period (e.g., \$300M in 3 days), a cost efficient liquidation schedule can be determined to meet this redemption scenario.

ADV

For securities with a decent ADV model, security i has an average daily volume volume v_i and a participation rate[11] r_j (defined at the sector level). For these securities, we can constrain the liquidation schedule by the tradable amount, and the following applies:

$$p_{i,t} m_i \leq v_i r_j \tag{7.7}$$

Market Sector Capacity

In the OTC fixed-income markets, large, simultaneous sales of similar paper (e.g., distinct issuers from the same sector) can quickly saturate the market's capacity and keep the market from absorbing more of these securities. This can be incorporated into the optimization problem by formulating an additional constraint. For securities that belong to a sector S_j with an estimate of capacity $c_{j,t}$:

$$\sum_{i \in S_j} p_{i,t} m_i \leq c_{j,t} \tag{7.8}$$

Fixed Time Constraints

Certain securities cannot be liquidated without a time lag, in days, d_i. For example, monthly trading mutual funds do not generate liquidity until 20 days after a redemption request has been submitted. Similarly, IPO lockups cannot be traded until some date in the future. For these securities, the following constraints apply:

$$p_{i,t} = 0 \text{ for } d_i < t \tag{7.9}$$

Risk Constraint

Well-managed portfolios have specific risk constraints, such as being within a specific risk range or below a threshold, which can be presented as R. For example, for index funds, the tracking error must typically be below the defined number of bp. The level of this risk constraint can be set accordingly:

$$\sum_{i,j} [(1 - p_{i,t}) n_i - b_i][(1 - p_{j,t}) n_j - b_j] cov_{i,j} \leq R^2 \tag{7.10}$$

The benchmark position in a security is represented by b_i. Note that for absolute return funds, $b_i = 0$. Note that the sum should be across the union of all securities in the benchmark and portfolio.

Other meaningful optimization constraints can be included, such as cash utilization, tracking errors of the fund, leverage constraints, compliance constraints, etc. By incorporating liquidity analytics and data, a portfolio manager is able to attain more meaningful portfolio allocation/liquidation schedules and can balance a fund's risk profile with liquidation time and cost.

In practice, integrating liquidity analytics into an optimization framework presents several challenges as it requires a higher degree of accuracy of model inputs, broad coverage of consistent liquidity analytics across asset classes, and additional constraints on the functional forms of the models with respect to computational efficiency.

7.9 CONCLUSION

Following the 2008 Global Financial Crisis, there has been considerable market and regulatory focus on liquidity risk along with a shift in the structure of the bond market. The Pandemic scare of 2020, along with idiosyncratic liquidity issues for a number of funds—caused by fundamental lapses in basic governance, valuation, and liquidity risk management—continue to serve as a reminder that there is no substitute for diligent and effective risk management and fund manager judgment.

Effective risk management requires constant portfolio oversight and ongoing enhancement to investment risk management practices. Liquidity risk has required asset managers to improve their liquidity risk management frameworks to align with increased regulation as well as industry best practices. This includes the introduction of improved liquidity datasets and analytics as well as prudent liquidity targets and surveillance tools. The latter are designed to ensure portfolio managers and traders effectively manage short-term, unexpected redemptions as well as sustained redemptions. In addition, portfolios need to be reviewed to ensure that available "back-up" tools (such as redemption gates, temporary borrowing facilities, etc.) are operationally available to help meet redemptions during adverse market conditions or idiosyncratic issues affecting individual funds.

While these advancements have markedly improved the ability to forecast and manage liquidity risk in a consistent fashion across asset classes, this is just the beginning, and much more work is to be done to improve liquidity modeling, analytics, and oversight. Our understanding of liquidity is still rather limited. Paraphrasing Smith (2008): Liquidity is like oxygen. You only become truly aware of its absence.

NOTES

1. See BlackRock's July 2015 ViewPoint, "Addressing Market Liquidity," for additional types of liquidity risks.
2. While the term portfolio manager refers broadly to the execution of an investment strategy for a bundle of securities, we use the term fund manager in this chapter. Specifically, the type of portfolio we are dealing with is a collective vehicle, typically a mutual fund, which has additional burdens other than portfolio management.
3. This section was derived from the Next Generation Bond Market: https://www.sec.gov/spotlight/fixed-income-advisory-committee/blackrock-next-generation-bond-market-fimsa-011118.pdf.
4. This does not represent an exhaustive list of factors considered in assessing fund asset liquidity.
5. MSRB, Federal Reserve, FINRA, SIFMA, S&P Moody's, World Federation of Exchanges, as of 12/31/21.
6. Permissible extraordinary measures by jurisdiction of fund type are based on October 2020 policies and regulations.
7. In November 2022, the SEC proposed regulatory changes to open-end fund liquidity frameworks, including requiring mutual funds to use swing pricing. The proposal would also require a "hard close" for relevant funds, meaning that investor orders would need to be received by the fund, its transfer agent, or a registered clearing agency by the time of the fund's pricing to receive that day's price. A final rule is pending as of January 2023.
8. In other chapters of this book, we refer to S as OAS.
9. Jeyapaulraj et al., 2022.
10. Full list of firm and fund closures, large outflows, and related events in the asset management industry available here: https://www.blackrock.com/corporate/literature/publication/fsb-structural-vulnerabilities-asset-management-activities-092116.pdf.
11. Refer to section 7.4.1 for additional details on participation rate.

CHAPTER 8

Using Portfolio Optimization Techniques to Manage Risk

Alex Ulitsky
Managing Director, Financial Modeling Group, BlackRock

Bennett W. Golub
Senior Advisor, BlackRock

Leo M. Tilman
CEO, Tilman & Company

Jack Hattem
Managing Director, Portfolio Management Group, BlackRock

8.1 RISK MEASUREMENT VERSUS RISK MANAGEMENT

According to the *Merriam-Webster Dictionary*, to "hedge" means to "protect oneself financially by a counterbalancing transaction" or "evade risk of commitment." In finance, hedging is the process of trying to reduce the market risk of a portfolio by buying or selling hedge instruments from a given set of securities (hedge universe). In general, many possible combinations of hedge instruments (hedging strategies) can reduce the systematic risk of a portfolio to a specified level. Therefore, the goal is not to merely identify a hedging strategy that decreases risk in a portfolio to a given risk level, but to do this in an optimal fashion. For a hedging strategy to be optimal, it must be cost-effective, intuitive, stable in different market environments as well as through time, and executable, that is, feasible to implement in practice. The complexity of identifying optimal hedging strategies lies in balancing the hedger's risk-return preferences and market constraints.

Financial disasters have illustrated the crucial importance of hedging. Yet hedging, while reducing potential losses, limits potential gains and may also create substantial model risk.[1] Thus, if parametric measures are inaccurate because of biased interest rate sensitivities, prepayment forecasts, and the like, or if historical correlations and volatilities are forecasting poorly, hedging may fail. In extreme cases, hedging may even make positions and returns more volatile.

In order to think about hedging, consider the following assumptions:

- *Rational economic behavior.* For a given level of expected return, investors are assumed to prefer less risk to more risk. Conversely, for a fixed level of risk, they prefer more return to less return. Given the portfolio holder's preferences, an optimal portfolio can be determined.

- *Availability of accurate quantitative measures of risk and return.* Investors can estimate both risk and return of any security, portfolio, or portfolio vis-a-vis its benchmark.
- *Hedge universe.* The hedge universe is assumed to be sufficiently broad to cover most of the systematic risk in the original portfolio or position.

Conceptually, the task of finding the most appropriate hedge is a portfolio optimization problem. Thus, reduction of risk and enhancement of return can typically be formulated in terms of objective functions, whereas numerous portfolio and market limitations can usually be represented as optimization constraints.

- *Investment guidelines.* Asset management mandates are typically governed by investment guidelines that determine return objectives of the assignment and ensure that the portfolio is managed according to the client's risk preferences. Some portfolios may be explicitly prohibited from owning particular security types or shorting certain asset classes, while other portfolios may have various cash, position size, and asset allocation limits. These investment guidelines must be translated into the language of optimization constraints. For instance, implementing a hedge on a portfolio with no allowed leverage implies the market value of the hedge must be constrained to be less than the total amount of cash currently available in the portfolio. On the other hand, if a portfolio is not allowed to short instruments, hedge optimization should be allowed to only sell securities that are currently held in the portfolio.
- *Market constraints.* When solving for the optimal hedge, numerous market considerations must be accounted for, including liquidity, relative value, and other factors. Thus, the portfolio managers' expectations that certain securities are likely to out- or underperform the market in the future also need to be taken into account, along with knowledge that large transactions in certain securities are likely to move the market,[2] widening bid–ask spreads and increasing hedging costs. Therefore, the active involvement of traders and portfolio managers in hedge instrument selection is especially critical. Hedging is not a purely scientific process!

As is the case with most investment activities, effective hedging must rely on the synthesis of financial modeling and subjective judgment. Success in finding the optimal hedging solution is therefore contingent on the hedger's ability to translate the risk-return preferences and relative value assessments into the parameters of the optimization problem. Thus, hedge optimizations should be formulated in a flexible enough way to allow for extensive interactions with the hedger. The optimal hedge is the one that best matches the goals of the hedger. Technology platforms and the underlying analytical methodologies that construct optimal hedges are merely tools that allow hedgers to explore the alternatives and more effectively search for trade-offs between their objectives and market constraints.

Finding the optimal hedge is a complex iterative process that combines mathematical modeling and market judgment. This chapter illustrates how to use quantitative portfolio construction methodologies to achieve that goal.

Previous chapters have discussed (1) various dimensions of market risk, (2) probability distributions of systematic risk factors, and (3) different risk measures. However, risk measurement is not risk management: the mere ability to quantify risk embedded in fixed-income securities and portfolios does not protect one from financial catastrophes. Practical yet theoretically sound approaches to explicitly reduce market risk to a predefined level in a timely manner are required. The task of hedging exposures to potentially hundreds of interdependent systematic risk factors via back-of-the-envelope-type computations is, in many cases, virtually impossible. Complex hedging problems that lend themselves to formal objectives and constraints can best be solved via portfolio optimizations—techniques that formalize and balance trade-offs between risk and other investment objectives with market constraints. Portfolio optimization is a powerful tool that allows portfolios to be engineered for a variety of reasons; hence, it is not specifically aligned to only one of BlackRock's Investment Risk Management Paradigm (IRMP) pillars. For example, it could be used as a tool to help actively measure risk. It could also be used as a tool to help actively adjust the levels of risk and exposures.

8.2 TYPICAL FIXED-INCOME HEDGES

Hedging objectives, as well as the type of market risk embedded in a security or portfolio, determine the appropriate hedge instruments. Hedges can be used to optimize performance, mitigate portfolio risks, and improve a portfolio's convexity in an adverse market scenario. The universe of fixed-income hedge instruments has evolved and includes the following:

- Interest rates
  - Risk-free rates across currencies (i.e., Gilt, Bund, and Treasury nominal cash securities and their associated futures and options)
  - OIS curve hedges
  - Alternative Reference Rate products (LIBOR benchmark replacements, which include SOFR, SONIA, and ESTR)
  - Swap spreads (across multiple curves including OIS and new alternative reference rates)
  - Options on swaps curves (swaptions)
- Credit products
  - CDX & iTraxx indices, tranches, and options
  - Sovereign CDS
  - Single name CDS
- Currencies
  - FX forwards and options
  - Forward volatility agreements
- Commodities
  - Energy, metals, inflation futures, and swaps

To determine which hedging instruments are appropriate, the hedger first must have a comprehensive understanding of the portfolio's objective and underlying risks. By decomposing the risks, hedges can then be applied purposefully. The application of a hedge can be constructed by considering a wide range of asset classes to mitigate risk for diversified portfolios and maximize hedge effectiveness, which is a gauge of how well the intended risks will be offset. Once a set of hedges have been identified, the hedger should conduct various analyses to identify the correlations between the risks and hedges to isolate risks. Finally, by applying a relative value volatility framework, hedgers can identify the most appropriate hedge based on a combination of risk offset and pricing.

To demonstrate this process, consider a fixed-income portfolio that contains mortgages. As illustrated by Exhibit 8.1, a mortgage-backed security has several inherent risks that can be substantially mitigated through hedging. In this case, by applying a pay-fixed swap and long options exposure via swaptions, the hedger mitigates interest rate and "swap spread" risk, convexity risk, and volatility risks. At the end, the hedger is left with the risk he or she is happy to bear or simply cannot hedge—mortgage prepayment risk, i.e., the uncertainty of when the mortgage-backed security will pay down its principal amount.

Adverse tail risk events can have a negative impact on any portfolio but can potentially be catastrophic for portfolios with concentrated risk. Hedging provides solutions to isolate risk and protect a portfolio against adverse market conditions.

Other hedging considerations to be aware of include the following:

1. Hedging can only reduce residual risk; the only perfect offset is to sell the asset itself.
2. Exposure to model risk changes as volatilities and correlations change or underlying probability distributions change.
3. Option risk metrics change as positions age.
4. Hedge effectiveness can be optimized, in some cases, via active management and monetization of the positions themselves.

The remainder of the chapter focuses on using hedges for portfolio optimization.

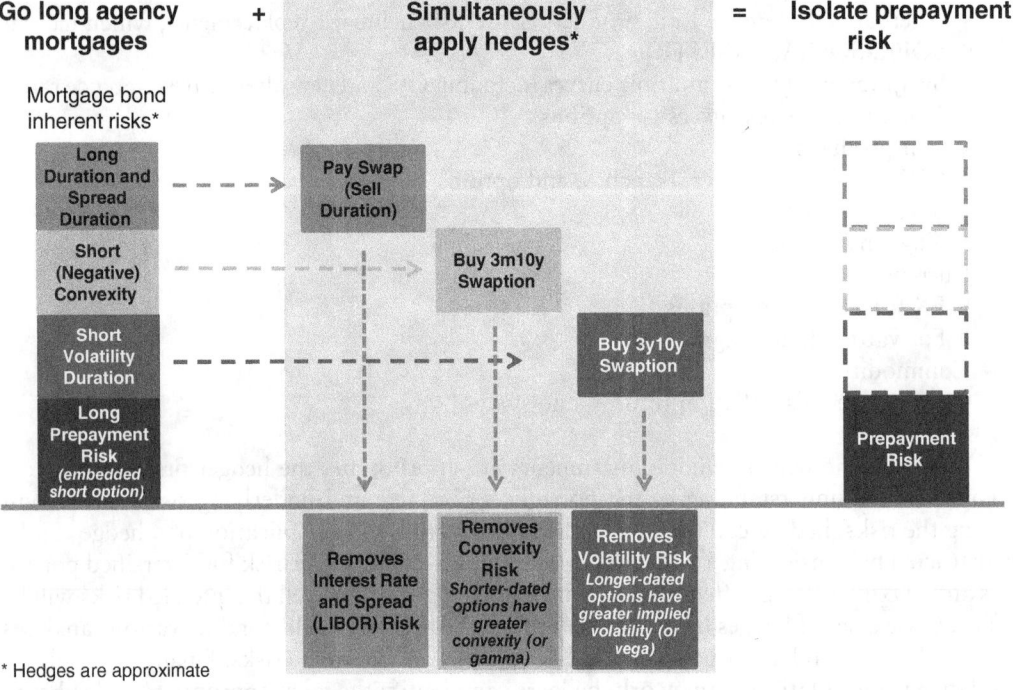

EXHIBIT 8.1 Applying Hedges to Isolate Risk
Source: BlackRock. For illustrative purposes only.

8.3 PARAMETRIC HEDGING TECHNIQUES

Similar to many risk measurement methodologies that estimate risk of fixed-income portfolios by approximating price changes using Taylor series expansions (Chapter 2), traditional approaches to hedging utilize various parametric measures in trying to reduce market exposures in one of several dimensions. For most fixed-income instruments, whose returns are reasonably highly correlated, parametric approaches to hedging described here are practical and effective. However, these techniques may become inadequate in more general cases when no assumptions can be made about the high correlation among returns on the original portfolio and those on its hedges (Section 8.4).

The simplest approach to risk reduction, *delta* or *duration* hedging, is widely used both in option pricing theory as well as in practice. Hedging exposure to small parallel changes in the yield curve is the most typical use of duration hedging in fixed-income markets. Because it uses option-adjusted duration, this technique provides effective protection against small parallel changes in the yield curve but may fail to address the risk associated with large or nonparallel interest rate movements.

Consider a fixed-income portfolio with market value V_P and option-adjusted duration OAD_P. By using duration to hedge the interest rate risk of this portfolio, one *degree of freedom* is assumed, and therefore, a single hedge instrument is required. Suppose that the selected hedge instrument has the price P_H and duration OAD_H. Hedging requires estimating the proper size in this security (i.e., unknown face value F_H) that would offset the interest rate risk to the first-order approximation. For both the portfolio and the hedge instrument, use Equation 2.24 to write the first-order approximation of price changes for a given parallel yield curve movement:

$$\Delta V_P = -OAD_P \cdot V_P \cdot \Delta r \tag{8.1}$$

and

$$\Delta V_H = -OAD_H \cdot P_H \cdot F_H \cdot \Delta r \tag{8.2}$$

where ΔV_P and ΔV_H are changes in the market values of the portfolio and the hedge instrument, respectively, and Δr is an arbitrary parallel change in the spot curve. To hedge the portfolio for any parallel interest rate movement is, by definition, equivalent to determining the face value F_H of the hedge instrument such that any change in the portfolio's market value is offset by the equal in magnitude but opposite in sign change in market value of the hedge instrument, i.e.,

$$\Delta V_P = -\Delta V_H \tag{8.3}$$

Combining Equations 8.1–8.3 yields:

$$-OAD_P \cdot V_P \cdot \Delta r = OAD_H \cdot P_H \cdot F_H \cdot \Delta r \tag{8.4}$$

or equivalently,

$$-OAD_P \cdot V_P = OAD_H \cdot P_H \cdot F_H \tag{8.5}$$

The expression given by Equation 8.5 is typically referred to as *matching dollar durations*. Solving for F_H yields:

$$F_H = -\frac{OAD_P \cdot V_P}{OAD_H \cdot P_H} \tag{8.6}$$

Despite the fact that duration hedging does not require application of numerical methods, it possesses all the properties of a hedge optimization problem. The analytical solution is simply due to the fact that matching dollar durations has only one degree of freedom. The optimality of this solution can be judged via the properties of the hedge instrument, including its duration drift (and, hence, rebalancing costs), relative value, liquidity, expected return, and so forth. In the case of duration hedging, the numerous considerations that determine optimality of the hedge are implicit in the selection of the hedge instrument.

The multivariate analog of duration hedging involves simultaneous risk reduction along several dimensions and is typically formulated in terms of partial durations. Similar to the previous example, consider a domestic fixed-income portfolio with a market value V_P. Assume that the market exposure of this portfolio to $n + 2$ systematic risk factors can be described (to the first-order approximation) by the following vector of partial durations:

$$Exposure_P = krd_{1,P}, \ldots, krd_{n,P}, Vol\,Dur_P, Spd\,Dur_P \tag{8.7}$$

where $\{krd_{1,P}, \ldots, krd_{n,P}\}$ are the portfolio's key rate durations, $Vol\,Dur_P$ is volatility duration, and $Spd\,Dur_P$ is spread duration. In order to exactly match all $n + 2$ systematic exposures of the original portfolio, an equal number of hedge instruments is needed. Each of these securities is characterized by a vector of market exposures as well:

$$Exposure_i = krd_{1,i}, \ldots, krd_{n,i}, Vol\,Dur_i, Spd\,Dur_i \tag{8.8}$$

The exact hedging of all $n + 2$ individual exposures is equivalent to solving the following system of linear equations:

$$\begin{bmatrix} krd_{1,P} \cdot V_P \\ \cdots \\ krd_{n,P} \cdot V_P \\ Vol\,Dur_P \cdot V_P \\ Spd\,Dur_P \cdot V_P \end{bmatrix} = -\begin{bmatrix} Exposure_1 \\ \cdots \\ Exposure_{n+2} \end{bmatrix}^T \cdot \begin{bmatrix} F_1 \\ \cdots \\ F_{n+2} \end{bmatrix} \tag{8.9}$$

where $F_1, \ldots, F_{n+2}$ are the unknown face values of the hedge instruments that are to be determined. In the vast majority of practical situations,[3] the system of linear equations in Equation 8.9 has a unique solution.

In hedging various market exposures, parametric risk measures other than partial durations can be employed as well, including scenario option-adjusted values (OAVs), option-adjusted convexities, and key rate convexities. While writing analogs of Equation 8.9 for these cases is straightforward and left to the reader, note that simplistic parametric approaches to hedging that attempt to account for the nonlinearity of value surface frequently result in unstable and nonintuitive hedges.

Although a multivariate methodology that focuses on matching multiple partial durations is better than one-dimensional duration hedging, it is not always effective. Firstly, hedging strategies calculated as exact solutions of systems of linear equations (Equation 8.9) do not account for transaction costs, making them notoriously unstable. As a result, these strategies may not only require frequent rebalancing but may also lead to excessive transaction costs. Secondly, other risk factors, such as sector or industry exposures, may contribute to the overall portfolio risk. In this case, focusing on duration hedging via Equation 8.9 may lead to amplification, rather than reduction, of the resulting portfolio risk.

Finally, an investor may have additional requirements for portfolio construction. In this case, hedging risk becomes just one of the competing portfolio objectives. For example, if complete hedging will result in higher trading costs or insufficient hedging instruments are available, the investor may settle on a partial hedge. In this case, the determination of the best portfolio construction strategy cannot be addressed by solving Equation 8.9. Instead, it becomes an optimization problem, which is further discussed in the next section.

8.4 GENERALIZED APPROACH TO HEDGING

While effective in constructing simple hedging strategies, the techniques presented in Section 8.3 have only limited capabilities. In addition to risk hedging objectives, the hedger often needs to consider other goals and constraints, such as liquidity, internal fund policy, and regulatory requirements. This, in turn, requires hedgers to have greater flexibility in representing their objectives by incorporating market-driven and other portfolio level considerations in the language of hedge optimizations.

What is the goal of hedge optimization? Hedge optimization attempts to translate the hedger's preferences into the language of mathematics, incorporating market knowledge so that the resulting solutions are intuitive, cost-effective, executable, and stable. In the end, however, successful fixed-income risk management relies heavily on the hedger's ability to make conscious and rational trade-offs. As a result, hedging to manage risk requires a synthesis of rigorous modeling and subjective market-based judgment.

This section presents various applications of risk hedging, including exposure hedging, benchmark risk, and stress scenario hedging. These use cases can be described within the framework of constrained portfolio optimization.

8.4.1 Hedging as Constrained Portfolio Optimization

In this section, the various stages of hedging are considered in detail. In the first stage, the hedging target or objective must be clarified and expressed mathematically. In the case of exposure hedging, targets are typically formulated in terms of desired risk characteristics of the hedged portfolio, such as total duration, various partial durations, OAVs, convexity, etc. The hedger can also incorporate other state-dependent outcomes that focus not on average portfolio properties, but rather on tail risk measures such as Value at Risk (VaR), conditional VaR, and so forth. The goal of hedging, therefore, is to determine the optimal combination of hedge instruments, namely, the ones that bring the risk parameters of the hedged portfolio as close as possible to those of the target.

The second stage involves formalizing the various investment preferences and utilities as objective functions and optimization constraints. This includes identifying market risks, hedging costs, and other penalties that are subject to minimization as well as measures of expected benefits that are subject to maximization. The corresponding characteristics, such as risk and cost, have to be modeled not only for the original portfolio but for all of the instruments in the hedge universe as well.

However, models may be insufficient for defining an effective and meaningful objective function. Rather, this knowledge must be supplemented with information about the *relative importance* of various optimization goals to the hedger. For instance, a hedger may believe that in order to achieve his or her objectives, it is more important to minimize tracking error rather than minimize the up-front hedging costs. (Note: Relationships of this kind can be obtained heuristically and subsequently formalized.)

Finally, the third stage of hedging calls for a rigorous yet flexible mathematical formulation of the hedge optimization problem. Besides being an effective tool for dealing with the explicit goal of risk reduction, hedging can be formulated as a constrained portfolio optimization approach that enables the hedger to combine effective risk management with other investment objectives.

As emphasized earlier, developing the most appropriate hedge is a complex and iterative decision-making process. By varying the relative importance of different optimization objectives, like balancing efficiency and cost of hedging, the investor can investigate the impact of various trade-offs and arrive at the solution he or she deems optimal. Examples are provided to illustrate these points later in the chapter.

In the next section (Section 8.4.2), mathematical formulations for several common portfolio construction approaches are presented. While they are all based on portfolio optimization, each focuses on different use cases involving risk hedging. In Section 8.4.3, these quantitative techniques are illustrated using two examples. The first example deals with a risk-controlled environmental, social, and governance (ESG) tilting in a fixed-income benchmark replicating portfolio (Section 8.4.3.1). The second example focuses on reducing the potential negative impact of a stress scenario on portfolio performance (Section 8.4.3.2).

8.4.2 Mathematical Formulation

Two groups of models are commonly used in defining portfolio optimization objectives to achieve optimal risk hedges:

1. Models of market risk
2. Models of cost associated with hedging

Models of Market Risk: A variety of methodologies exist for dealing with different aspects of systematic market risk in fixed-income portfolios. Thus, the exposure to movements of default-free interest rates can be measured via option-adjusted duration and convexity, key rate durations, principal component analysis, interest rate scenario analyses, variance/covariance, VaR, and the like. On the other hand, prepayment durations, mortgage/treasury basis durations, coupon and OAS curve durations, spread durations, and volatility durations can be used to estimate the first-order price sensitivity to a variety of basis risks. Finally, VaR presents the overall exposure to interest rate, basis, and currency risks as one summarized measure.

Multifactor risk models have become the most common approach to measuring the market risk of fixed-income securities. These models[4] incorporate a collection of risk factors that are most important for fixed income, such as duration and credit spread, as well as other risk factors, such as inflation proxies and industry exposures. In this section, multifactor risk models will be used to illustrate various portfolio construction methodologies that may be employed for optimal hedging.

Models of Cost: Hedge optimizations that do not consider hedge cost are usually unrealistic since large quantities of hedge instruments can seemingly be bought and sold without penalty to improve the objective function; such hedges are impossible to implement in practice. To ensure that the sizes of the proposed hedges are feasible, a transaction cost objective must be defined. Transaction cost (t-cost) models for fixed-income securities were discussed previously in Chapter 7, in the context of a liquidity risk management framework. In their most common form, these models incorporate two main drivers for trading costs. The first driver—the linear component of trading costs—is characterized primarily by bid–ask spreads, which are assumed to scale linearly with trade size. The second driver measures the effects of trading on the price—namely the price response to large trades—which is the market impact transaction cost component. As a result, the cost of trading in larger sizes becomes progressively higher and causes a nonlinear dependence of trading costs on the trade size.[5] These cost penalties measure the immediate trading cost of establishing the hedge and do not measure, for example, the cost of carry associated with alternative hedging strategies, which will be addressed later in this chapter.

In the next subsections, we describe how these models become integral components in optimization-based hedging strategies. To illustrate, several common investment objectives were selected, which include exposure hedging, managing a portfolio to a benchmark, and limiting losses under stress scenario conditions.

8.4.2.1 Exposure Hedging When both market risk, reasonably represented by a covariance matrix with factor loadings, and transaction cost models are available, finding the best hedging strategy to meet the target can be formulated in the context of portfolio optimization. Before providing a mathematical description for the hedging optimization problem, the following notations are introduced:

w = a vector of dimension $N \times 1$;

> the i-th element of this vector is the weight in the portfolio of security i (where $i = 1, \ldots, N$) for the N assets in the universe (which includes both portfolio holdings and available hedge instruments).

w_0 = a vector of dimension $N \times 1$;

> the i-th element of this vector is the weight of security i in the initial portfolio composition. Securities that are not present in the initial portfolio have zero weight.

F = factor exposure matrix of dimension $N \times K$;

> $F_{i,k}$ is element (i, k) of the F matrix that measures the exposure (sometimes termed the factor loading or the "beta") of security i to factor k (where $k = 1, \ldots, K$). In this case, K is the number of factors used to model security returns.

F_T = a vector of dimension $K \times 1$;

> the k-th element of this vector is the target exposure to k-th factor.

V_F = a covariance matrix of systematic risk factors of dimension $K \times K$.

V_s = a covariance matrix of idiosyncratic risk of dimension $N \times N$.

λ_F = factor risk aversion, a nonnegative scalar penalty on factor risk.

λ_S = idiosyncratic risk aversion, a nonnegative scalar penalty on idiosyncratic risk.

Using these notations, the multifactor risk for a portfolio can be expressed as follows:

$$Risk(b) = w^T V_s w + (F^T w)^T V_F (F^T w) \tag{8.10}$$

Simply put, the objective of optimization is to identify the hedging instrument weights based on the portfolio's holdings. In practice, however, it is common not only to focus on finding an optimal mix of hedge instruments but to concurrently allow for adjustments in the portfolio holdings. This is especially beneficial when acceptable changes in original portfolio positions make the resulting hedge less expensive.

The transaction cost is composed of security-specific linear and market impact terms. Commonly, it can be expressed as follows:

$$T\text{-}Cost\,(w - w_0) = \sum_{i=1}^{N} \left(a_i \left| w_i - w_{0,i} \right| + b_i \left(\frac{\left| w_i - w_{0,i} \right| * PV}{ADV_i} \right)^q \left| w_i - w_{0,i} \right| \right) \qquad (8.11)$$

where

a_i = a linear cost coefficient
b_i = a market impact or nonlinear cost coefficient
PV = the total portfolio value
ADV_i = the average daily trading volume for i-th security
q = describes dependence of the market impact on trade size

The objective for hedging can be formally written as a constrained optimization problem whose goal is to minimize deviation from the target exposures in the presence of the trading cost control.

In the simplest form, consider a long-only portfolio that has a hedging target based on factors included in the risk model. The vector of desired holdings h can be computed as a solution to the following optimization problem:

$$Minimize_w[\lambda_F * (Fw - F_T)^T V_F(Fw - F_T) + T\text{-}Cost(w - w_0)]$$

$$\Sigma_i h_i = 1$$

$$w_i \geq 0, \;\; i = 1, \ldots, N \qquad (8.12)$$

The first constraint is a weight normalization condition that ensures that trading is self-financed (when no borrowing is required).[6] The other N constraints enforce a long-only, or "no short," condition for the portfolio holdings.

In the absence of a transaction cost control, hedging instruments should be selected to ensure that these assets are not perfectly correlated with each other. Otherwise, optimization will not result in a unique solution. Desired hedging efficiency can be achieved by any combination of these totally correlated securities as long as the combinations result in the same net exposure.[7] The presence of a linear trading cost component in optimization can break the tie, but only when correlated securities have different trading costs. In that case, optimization will select the lowest cost hedge and most unique solution. The market impact component of the transaction cost penalty plays an important role in ensuring unique solutions for hedging in all possible scenarios. Because of its nonlinear form, the market impact term in the transaction cost model forces the hedger to identify the lowest cost hedge and diversify across available hedging instruments to achieve the objective.

By varying the risk penalty strength λ_F and re-optimizing, the hedger can adjust the trade-off between the tighter tracking of the target exposure and the transaction costs required

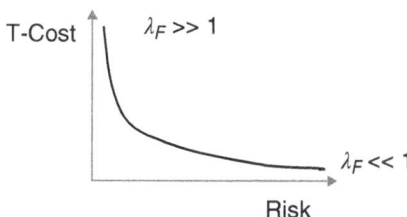

EXHIBIT 8.2   Illustration of the Risk Versus Transaction Cost Trade-Off
Source: BlackRock. For illustrative purposes only.

to reach the solution. Clearly the lowest risk solution ($\lambda_F \gg 1$) corresponds to the highest transaction costs, as demonstrated by Exhibit 8.2 where each point on the curve corresponds to an optimal solution with a pre-specified risk aversion. The hedger may therefore prefer to find a portfolio that achieves the closest match to target exposures given the transaction cost budget.

Alternatively, to identify a specific level of hedging, the initial optimization approach can be reformulated to minimize trading cost with a hedging efficiency control. In this case, the optimization objective can be expressed as follows:

$$Minimize_h[T\text{-}Cost(w - w_0)]$$

$$(Fw - F_T)^T V_F (Fw - F_T) \leq \varepsilon$$

$$\sum_i w_i = 1$$

$$w_i \geq 0, \quad i = 1, \ldots, N \tag{8.13}$$

where ε is the upper bound for factor volatility of the optimal portfolio with respect to the hedging target.

Optimization, described by Equation 8.12, requires the portfolio to be rebalanced every time when hedging provides even slightly more risk reduction benefits compared to the cost of trading required to achieve them. Equation 8.13 leads to a different investment policy. In this case, the portfolio rebalance is triggered only when the initial portfolio exposure is misaligned with the hedging target, such that the volatility constraint is not satisfied. However, Equation 8.12 and Equation 8.13 will yield the same results at the same risk level.

In practice, the portfolio construction approach to hedge optimization is formulated in the presence of different constraints. For convenience, these constraints can be classified as *structural, mandatory,* or *optional.*

> *Structural constraints* ensure that the optimization problem is correctly formulated from a mathematical perspective. As an example, weight normalization can be classified as a structural constraint, ensuring that optimization will preserve the total portfolio value and that all trading is self-financed.[8]

> *Mandatory constraints* reflect the investment policy of the portfolio. A long-only condition is considered a mandatory constraint, which prohibits the inclusion of short positions in the portfolio.

Optional constraints reflect the hedger's preferences, such as trading restrictions for portfolio exposures and position sizes, etc. The incorporation of these optional constraints in portfolio construction is commonly viewed as either a convenience, to avoid small nonmaterial trades, or as a protective measure against unexpected market moves that are not captured by the risk model. It is important for the hedger to calibrate these optional constraints. Overly tight bounds will require constant portfolio readjustments and the hedger may not be fairly compensated for that turnover. In the case of market stress, overly relaxed constraints may not provide sufficient portfolio protection. Consequently, a hedger needs to find the right balance.

The complexity of the resulting portfolio optimization problem is highly dependent on the hedger's choice of constraints. Several of these optional constraints force decision variables (e.g., portfolio holdings or exposures) to fall *within* pre-specified ranges. These constraints preserve convexity of the original problem[9] and, as a result, are neither computationally expensive nor difficult to implement using modern optimization packages.[10] Examples of such constraints include the following:

- Trading universe restrictions—only a prescreened set of hedging assets from an available pool can be included into the portfolio.
- Trade restrictions—no buy, no sell, or no trade lists are specified.
- Trade size restrictions—trades may not exceed perceived market availability for a given security.
- Factor exposures—constraints placed on maximum deviation in factor exposures, like KRDs, OAVs, etc., in relation to the target.

Another category of constraints consists of conditions that require a "multiple choice" or, equivalently, "either-or" formulation. Some practical examples of these constraints for fixed-income portfolios include the following:

- Minimum trade size condition—each trade size must be *either* zero *or* above the threshold.
- Minimum holding size condition—each position must be *either* zero *or* above the threshold.
- Maximum number of trades condition—number of trades can be *either* 0, *or* 1, *or* 2 or ... but should not exceed user-specified value.
- Maximum number of holdings condition—number of holdings can be *either* 1, *or* 2 or ... but should not exceed user-specified value.
- Trade round-lot condition—trading of each security should be in predefined sizes, e.g., in increments of $100K of notional value.

These constraints make the corresponding optimization problem nonconvex and support a multitude of possible solutions. As a result, finding the absolute best solution for hedging optimization, in the presence of these "multiple choice" constraints, is extremely expensive from a computational point of view—even with the best available commercial solvers in today's market. Consequently, practitioners focus on developing heuristic algorithms that are capable of building high-quality portfolios that satisfy formal constraints but do not guarantee to offer the absolutely lowest risk solution.

The portfolio optimization approach described for hedging risk is a common strategy. However, there are a number of variations to this methodology. The hedger can always extend the list of objectives besides explicit risk minimization and include control of the portfolio's exposure to factors that are outside of the risk model. For example, a corporate bond investor might want to manage industry exposures based on an alternative industry classification or allocate capital to bonds with different investment ratings. This goal can be achieved by adding constraints or penalties on corresponding portfolio exposures to the basic framework described by Equation 8.12.

Another common extension of the basic optimization model incorporates idiosyncratic risk into portfolio construction. Inclusion of an idiosyncratic risk control into optimization leads to the following formulation:

$$Minimize_h[\lambda_F * (Fw - F_T)^T V_F(Fw - F_T) + \lambda_S * w^T V_S w + T\text{-}Cost(w - w_0)]$$

$$\sum_i w_i = 1$$

$$w_i \geq 0, \ i = 1, \ldots, N \tag{8.14}$$

Now both penalty coefficients (for factor and idiosyncratic risk) are subject to variation. The resulting trade-off (factor volatility versus idiosyncratic volatility versus trading cost) can be used to identify the preferred strategy.

In addition to transaction costs, other cost components may be associated with maintaining the hedge. One common example is the *cost of carry* (CCost), which is typically defined as the total cost resulting from holding a hedge instrument over the life of the hedge. When the model is calibrated for the cost of carry, the cost element can be incorporated into the portfolio construction to make it more realistic and help to differentiate between alternative hedging instruments. In the presence of cost of carry, the hedge optimization problem can be expressed as:

$$Minimize_h[CCost^T * w + \lambda_F * (Fw - F_T)^T V_F(Fw - F_T) + \lambda_S * w^T V_S w + \gamma * T\text{-}Cost(w - w_0)]$$

$$\sum_i w_i = 1$$

$$w_i \geq 0, \ i = 1, \ldots, N \tag{8.15}$$

where *CCost* is a vector of cost of carry returns for individual securities and γ is the weight of the transaction cost penalty component.[11]

Investors can also incorporate a measure of security attractiveness, such as an ESG score, to find optimal hedges. In this case, a portfolio optimization objective includes maximizing (good/high) ESG and minimizing risk and transaction costs, which can be written as follows:

$$Maximize_h[E^T w - \lambda_F * (Fw - F_T)^T V_F(Fw - F_T) - \lambda_S * w^T V_S w - \gamma * T\text{-}Cost(w - w_0)]$$

$$\sum_i w_i = 1$$

$$w_i \geq 0, \ i = 1, \ldots, N \tag{8.16}$$

In this formulation:

E = a vector of dimension $N \times 1$; the i-th element of this vector is the ESG score for i-th asset.

In all previous examples, optional constraints, such as asset bounds, factor exposure bounds, etc., can also be included to accommodate a hedger's specific investment objectives. Modern portfolio construction platforms support this wide range of constraints and penalties. As a result, these platforms offer a broad spectrum of risk hedging portfolio construction approaches to investors.

So far this chapter has focused on various portfolio construction and optimization approaches that enable us to target desired hedging efficiency. Next, other common hedging applications that can also be solved as constrained portfolio optimizations will be discussed.

8.4.2.2 Managing a Portfolio Against a Benchmark In addition to hedging various components of risk embedded in a portfolio, the previously described approach to hedge optimization is also used to manage fixed-income portfolios relative to their benchmarks. One particular example of this investment strategy is often called *index* or *benchmark replication*. This strategy is commonly employed to build a practical portfolio that is similar to the desired index or benchmark.

For benchmark replication, the optimization objective is to minimize ex ante active risk with respect to the portfolio benchmark. If there are no trading restrictions or transaction costs, active risk minimization can be expressed as follows:

$$Minimize_h \left[\begin{array}{c} \lambda_F * ((F(w - w_b))^T V_F(F(w - w_b)) + \\ \lambda_S * (w - w_b)^T V_S(w - w_b) \end{array} \right]$$

$$\sum_i w_i = 1$$

$$w_i \geq 0, \quad i = 1, \ldots, N \tag{8.17}$$

where w_b is the vector of benchmark holdings.

$$\sum_i w_{b,i} = 1 \tag{8.18}$$

When all benchmark names are easily investable, optimization results in a full benchmark replication. However, this is not necessarily a practical solution. In contrast to equity markets, complete benchmark replication is almost impossible in the fixed-income security universe due to liquidity constraints and availability limitations. Many bond issues end up in "bond heaven," long-term buy and hold portfolios. Consequently, benchmark replication is commonly achieved in the presence of investable universe restrictions and liquidity considerations.

In the presence of transaction costs and a maximum number of holdings constraint (for an example), the resulting optimization objective function can be written as follows:

$$Minimize_h \left[\begin{array}{c} \lambda_F * ((F(w - w_b))^T V_F(F(w - w_b)) + \\ \lambda_S * (w - w_b)^T V_S(w - w_b) + T\text{-}Cost(w - w_0) \end{array} \right]$$

$$\sum_i w_i = 1$$

$$\sum_i \delta(w_i) \le M < N$$

$$w_i \ge 0, \quad i = 1, \ldots, N \tag{8.19}$$

where $\delta(w_i)$ equals 1 if the holding for i-th asset is nonzero and zero otherwise. User-defined parameter M specifies the maximum number of names allowed in the optimal portfolio. It is also a common practice to add constraints on individual asset and risk factor exposures to augment basic risk and transaction cost minimization. These constraints provide investors with more granular control to construct a portfolio that mimics the benchmark.

A different replication problem is commonly faced by fixed-income exchange-traded fund (ETF) managers, who also need to specify the security basket composition that will be used during create and redeem processes. Optimization can be leveraged to solve for these baskets in a systematic, auditable, and repeatable manner.[12]

Index replication methodologies, described in this section, rely on the presence of highly calibrated risk models. However, what should an investor do in the absence of a reliable risk model, while individual security parameters, like duration, ratings, OAS, etc. are available? Clearly, in this case a risk minimization approach is no longer applicable.

For benchmark replication, there is frequent objection to overly relying on risk minimization as described by Equations 8.17 and 8.18. While the overall goal may be to match exposures at the portfolio level (durations, ratings, or OAS), hedgers may also prefer to match exposures on a more granular level (security groupings) to avoid unintended biases. For example, absent a concerted effort, an index ETF portfolio can end up with an unintended bias with respect to liquidity.

To address these concerns, stratified sampling has been proposed as a non-optimization-based approach to build portfolios that match a predefined benchmark across a set of user-specified characteristics.[13] While this approach "can do the job," common implementation is marked by shortcomings, which are further illustrated in this chapter. First, we will describe a stratified sampling algorithm and then introduce *Optimized Stratified Sampling* as a comprehensive and robust solution to address conventional stratified sampling limitations.

A conventional stratified sampling heuristic algorithm can be described using the following three-step procedure:

Step 1. Select a set of portfolio attributes. For example, select duration and credit rating as two attributes (A_1, A_2) of importance.

Step 2. Choose a bucketing scheme for all attributes. For example, $A_{1(i)}$ describes bucket i-th for attribute A_1; if we select e.g., quintiles to bucket A_1, then "i" varies between 1 and 5.

Step 1 and Step 2 create a multidimensional grid. In this example that includes two attributes and quintile-based buckets, the resulting two-dimensional grid would have $5 \times 5 = 25$ cells.

Step 3. Determine security weights from a universe of available assets such that the resulting portfolio weight from each cell closely matches the benchmark. A typical approach is to "fill in buckets" sequentially by going one-by-one through the list of available securities.

Stratified sampling results in a quick solution to an exposure matching exercise. Sequential portfolio construction, however, makes it difficult to adopt changes to the attribute selection or to the grid after completing the exercise. In addition, there may be multiple choices for security selection within each cell of the predefined grid. Thus, the resulting portfolio is not uniquely specified. Moreover, if a portfolio level attribute—such as liquidity—is not incorporated in the grid definition, the resulting portfolio may score poorly on this metric. To address these shortcomings, we can reformulate the security selection process associated with stratified sampling as an optimization procedure.

Similar to Step 1 and Step 2 of the conventional stratified sampling approach, we propose using a factor or attribute-based grid definition based on investor preferences. However, the process diverges at Step 3, by applying a penalty to the difference in exposures between the portfolio and the benchmark within each cell of the grid. These differences are aggregated, and minimization of the resulting function with (optional) additional constraints results in a portfolio that most effectively satisfies exposure targets within all cells.

This methodology can be easily generalized by reformulating it as a *minimization of the distance between multivariate distributions of portfolio attributes*. This distance can be expressed as a weighted sum of absolute deviations or, alternatively, as a weighted sum of squared differences between the portfolio attribute and its target value within each cell.

To illustrate this proposal, consider a long-only portfolio construction that aims to mimic the benchmark. In its basic form with just two attributes (A_1 and A_2), the optimized stratified sampling approach can be described in the following way:

$$Minimize_{\{h\}} \left[\sum_{i,j} \gamma(i,j) \left[\sum_k w_k \delta(A_{1,k}, i)\delta(A_{2,k}, j) - \sum_n b_n \delta(A_{1,n}, i)\delta(A_{2,n}, j) \right]^2 \right]$$

$$\sum_k w_k = 1$$

$$w_k \geq 0, \quad k = 1, 2, \ldots, N$$

$$\gamma(i,j) \geq 0, \text{ for all } i,j \tag{8.19}$$

Equation 8.19 represents the following:

w_k = the weight of k-th asset in the portfolio (an optimization variable).

b_n = the weight of n-th asset in the benchmark or target portfolio.

$A_{i,k}$ = the exposure of k-th asset to i-th attribute.

$\delta(A_{1,k}, i)$ = an indicator that is equal to 1 when exposure of asset k to attribute A_1 corresponds to i-th bucket; otherwise, it has a value of 0.

$\gamma(i,j)$ = a user-defined coefficient that penalizes deviation in exposures between the portfolio and the benchmark for a cell defined by its attribute values $[A_1(i), A_2(j)]$.

Equation 8.19 matches the aggregate portfolio weight in each of the buckets to that of the benchmark. This approach can be generalized beyond capital allocation or weight matching within each bucket. It can also include matching of other attributes, like yield or OAC. Furthermore, the investor can try to match multiple attributes across strata simultaneously. In the case of single linear attribute θ (e.g., yield to worst) matching, the resulting optimization can be written as follows:

$$Minimize_{\{b\}} \left[\sum_{i,j} \gamma(i,j) \left[\sum_{k} \theta(k) w_k \delta(A_{1,k}, i) \delta(A_{2,k}, j) - \sum_{n} \theta(n) b_n \delta(A_{1,n}, i) \delta(A_{2,n}, j) \right]^2 \right]$$

$$w_k \geq 0, \text{ for all } k$$

$$\sum_{k} w_k = 1$$

$$\gamma(i,j) \geq 0, \text{ for all } i, j \qquad (8.20)$$

When a risk model is also available, the basic index replication approach described in the beginning of this section can be augmented with an optimized stratified sampling objective to achieve more granular exposure matching in conjunction with risk and liquidity control of the resulting portfolio.

8.4.2.3 Stress Scenario Hedging In previous examples, portfolio optimization was applied to risk management and risk hedging in the then current market conditions. What if the hedger's objective is to assess the portfolio's performance in a stress scenario? What if the potential loss under that scenario exceeds permissible tolerances? This section illustrates how to adjust for stress exposure in portfolio construction by leveraging constrained portfolio optimization.

Consider a hypothetical stress scenario that results in potential losses to each asset. In order to control aggregate portfolio loss, the conventional framework (Equation 8.18) is extended by adding a linear constraint on total or benchmark-relative (active) portfolio loss that can be realized under the selected scenario.[14] In the case of a long-only portfolio, the resulting portfolio hedging approach can be formulated as follows:

$$Minimize_b \begin{bmatrix} \lambda_F * ((F(w - w_b))^T V_F (F(w - w_b)) + \\ \lambda_S * (w - w_b)^T V_S (w - w_b) + T\text{-}Cost(w - w_0) \end{bmatrix}$$

$$w^T L \leq \varepsilon_1$$

$$(w - w_b)^T L \leq \varepsilon_2$$

$$\sum_{i} w_i = 1$$

$$w_i \geq 0, \quad i = 1, \dots, N \qquad (8.21)$$

where

L = the vector of security level stress scenario loss estimates
ε_1 = the stress scenario loss threshold
ε_2 = the active stress scenario loss threshold

Alternatively, an investor can decide to control both loss and risk under a stress scenario simultaneously. This results in the following optimization formulation:

$$Minimize_b \left[\begin{array}{c} \lambda_F * ((F(w - w_b))^T V_F(F(w - w_b)) + \\ \lambda_S * (w - w_b)^T V_S(w - w_b) + T\text{-}Cost(w - w_0) \end{array} \right]$$

$$w^T L \leq \varepsilon_1$$

$$(w - w_b)^T L \leq \varepsilon_2$$

$$(F_s w)^T V_{Fs}(F_s w) + (w)^T V_{Ss}(w) \leq \delta_1$$

$$(F_s(w - w_b))^T V_{Fs}(F_s(w - w_b)) + (w - w_b)^T V_{Ss}(w - w_b) \leq \delta_2$$

$$\sum_i w_i = 1$$

$$w_i \geq 0, \quad i = 1, \ldots, N \tag{8.22}$$

where

δ_1 = the stress scenario risk threshold
δ_2 = the stress scenario active risk threshold

In this formulation, the first two constraints provide an upper bound for total portfolio loss and loss relative to the original portfolio or benchmark. The second two constraints set an upper bound on total and active risk computed using the risk model associated with the stress scenario.

However, the benefit of controlling the stress exposure by introducing additional constraints comes with a price. The hedger, therefore, should consider conducting a cost-benefit analysis to assess when hedging stress exposure is indeed beneficial. Multiple metrics can be utilized.[15] Bilgili, Ferconi, and Ulitsky (2017) suggested a metric that was based on a risk-scaled deviation from the original portfolio holdings, which more accurately reflects the investment objective of the portfolio. The hedger then computes how much loss reduction can be accomplished through hedging at various levels of deviation from the initial portfolio composition. This methodology is of a general nature and can be extended to simultaneously control exposure to multiple stress scenarios.

What if, however, the hedger is not certain about the accuracy of the asset loss estimation or of the stress test risk model? One reason for this uncertainty may be just the rarity of such events. Alternatively, the hedger may attempt to avoid modeling stress scenarios based on historic events or make explicit assumptions about potential losses and other parameters describing the stress scenario. The presence of uncertainty creates challenges. Without explicitly defined loss values and a stress risk model, the hedger is not able to apply any of the stress hedging portfolio construction approaches outlined previously. However, Bilgili, Ferconi, and Ulitsky presented a practical portfolio construction solution that accommodates uncertainty in the stress scenario parameters.[16] The authors considered both uncertainty in losses and in asset correlations in cases that involved the stress scenario assumptions and proposed a robust optimization methodology based on reformulating the stress hedging problem into a soluble worst-case scenario control problem.

Traditional approaches to stress testing, like the ones outlined previously, first define the stress scenario and then assess the impact of that scenario on a portfolio. For example, we might examine the impact of a particular rise in US interest rates on an international bond portfolio. Reverse stress testing, on the other hand, starts with assigning a specific condition, such as the loss level or risk level for the portfolio, and proceeds to identify the scenarios that generate the most negative portfolio performance.[17] With that information in hand, the portfolio manager can decide if these particular scenarios are probable and decide whether a hedge should be established. In the latter case, the techniques outlined above can be applied to optimally rebalance a portfolio.

To summarize, this section illustrated a general framework for formulating different hedging and risk mitigation strategies as various forms of constrained portfolio optimization. The ultimate specification of relevant investment objectives for a specific hedging scenario, as well as the selection of constraints and penalties, is always the responsibility of the hedger. Optimization then incorporates these portfolio construction components in a way that is consistent, scalable, and well measured.

The next section describes the application of portfolio construction methodologies to risk management and risk hedging.

8.4.3 Examples of Optimized Risk Management Strategies

This section illustrates how to apply portfolio optimization methodologies to risk management and risk hedging using two case studies. Section 8.4.3.1 shows how an investor can incorporate an ESG tilt into a portfolio while constructing a fixed-income index product. Section 8.4.3.2 illustrates optimal hedge design against potential losses under a stress scenario.

8.4.3.1 Creating an ESG Tilt While Managing a Fixed-Income Portfolio Relative to a Benchmark Sustainable investing has become one of the fastest growing investment themes in recent years. This section demonstrates one way to create an index replicating fixed-income portfolio consistent with a specific investor's preference toward companies that have higher ESG ratings, as provided by a specific ESG data provider. ESG "ratings" may vary significantly across different data providers.

The standard portfolio construction process for a nonoptimized passive product focuses on closely matching benchmark risk measures such as duration, convexity, spread, spread duration, sector, and issuer exposures. This is commonly achieved via a combination of the conventional stratified sampling approach (Section 8.4.2.2) and selection rules specified by the portfolio manager.

In an optimization-based index replication, the investment objective combines risk minimization and a variation of optimized stratified sampling to control risk exposures that are not fully captured by the risk model. In this example, optimized stratified sampling is based on sector-based security bucketing with constraints on key rate durations (KRDs) and duration times spread (DxS) within these buckets.

A portfolio manager can introduce a positive ESG tilt while continuing to control the active risk and active exposures across a stratification grid. Transitioning to this new ESG tilt may be best achieved via optimization. To illustrate this approach, consider designing an ESG enhanced index product benchmarked against the Bloomberg Barclays Euro Aggregate Corporate Index.[18] Assume a portfolio has an NAV of EUR 970mm and EUR 10mm in spendable cash. The initial portfolio comprised of 2,838 holdings, ~90% of the Index's holdings, to ensure close tracking to the benchmark (~1bp annualized) and to preserve the desired liquidity profile. In this setup, both the initial and benchmark portfolios have BBB rating on the ESG scale while the active ESG score for the portfolio is 0.01 (see Exhibit 8.3).[19]

To introduce an ESG tilt, ESG scores need to be incorporated in the objective, e.g., as an "alpha" term (refer to Equation 8.16). The optimization engine will seek to maximize the weighted average of ESG, and a hedger can specify a scaling value to control the ESG impact relative to other objectives. In this basic setup, transaction costs were not included. Therefore, the optimization balances ESG maximization versus active risk minimization in the presence of the following investment constraints:

- Overall active duration within 0.02 years
- Active KRDs contributions to each sector within ± 0.02 bp
- Active DxS contribution to each sector within ± 0.5 bp
- Active issuer exposure within ± 10 bp
- Utilize 10mm of spendable cash
- Maximum number of trades below 150

When the ESG scaling is weighted to be more impactful than active risk, the resulting constrained optimization increases the total portfolio ESG score to 5.49 and active risk score to 0.20 (refer to Exhibit 8.4). The new portfolio satisfies all constraints and has only a minor increase in annualized active risk (from 1 to 2 bp).[20]

Optimization-based portfolio construction also allows the investor to analyze to what extent ESG improvement is achievable at different levels of active risk. In addition, the portfolio manager may be interested in what the maximum achievable ESG score for the portfolio

Benchmark Full Name	Portfolio Avg ESG Rating	Benchmar... ESG Rating	Benchmar... ESG Ratin...	Portfolio Avg ESG Rating Num	Active Avg ESG Rating Num	Active Risk
BBG Barc Euro Aggregate Corporate Index	BBB	BBB	5.29	5.30	0.01	1

EXHIBIT 8.3 Portfolio Summary Screen
Source: BlackRock Aladdin, 2020. For illustrative purposes only.

Benchmark Full Name	Portfolio Avg ESG Rating	New Portfolio Avg ESG Ra...	Benchmar... ESG Rating	Portfolio Avg ESG Rating N...	New Portfoli... ESG Rating ...	Benchmar... ESG Ratin...	Active Avg ESG Rating Num	New Active Avg ESG Rating Num	Active Risk	New Active Risk
BBG Barc Euro Aggregate Corporate Index	BBB	BBB	BBB	5.30	5.49	5.29	0.01	0.20	1	2

EXHIBIT 8.4 Portfolio Optimization Results
Source: BlackRock Aladdin, 2020. For illustrative purposes only.

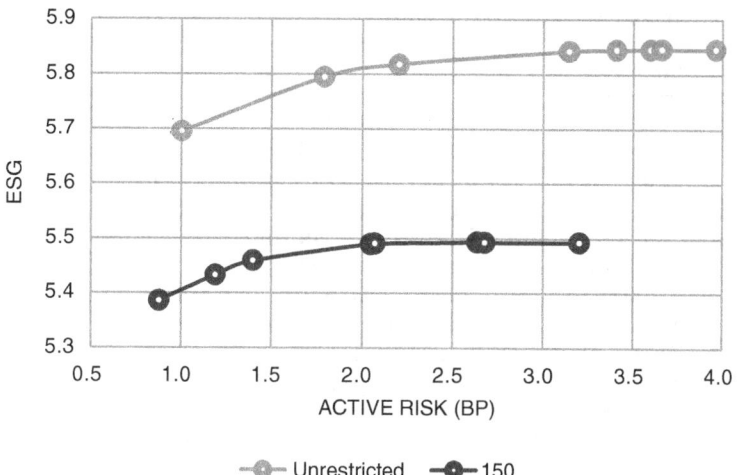

EXHIBIT 8.5 ESG Versus Active Risk for a 150 Trade Rebalance and for a Rebalance Without Trade Number Restrictions
Source: BlackRock Aladdin, 2020. For illustrative purposes only.

is when no restrictions are placed on the number of trades. Results of these exercises are presented in Exhibit 8.5. As expected, adding a constraint on the number of trades reduces the maximum achievable ESG compared to the unconstrained case. Going from left to right along the horizontal axis, each point on this chart is a result of individual portfolio optimization with increasing weight on the ESG term relative to risk. The higher slope on the left part of the curve indicates that a measurable ESG gain can be achieved even at a relatively small increase in active risk. The flattening of the curve to the right indicates diminishing improvements as we push harder for higher ESG scores.

As demonstrated in Exhibit 8.5, the optimizer trades off between active risk and ESG ratings, the stronger the tilt toward a higher ESG score, the higher the active risk, relative to the benchmark.

The portfolio manager must decide how to balance increases in ESG scores relative to an acceptable level of portfolio active risk. In this example, if the annualized active risk limit is ~1.4 bp, the portfolio manager can increase the ESG score from 5.30 to ~5.46, which is more than 80% of the maximum amount achievable with 150 trades. However, it should be emphasized that this is just a point-in-time analysis. In order to adopt the objective as an investment policy, the portfolio manager should consider how persistent these results are and how the selected strategy will perform under different market conditions. Back-testing and stress testing are common approaches available to further explore the relationship between the introduced ESG tilt and the realized performance of the strategy.

8.4.3.2 Hedging Stress Scenario Exposure To illustrate stress scenario exposure hedging, an "Inflation Rise" example is used.[21] This "crisis" is defined by a 30 bp monthly rise in 10-year US inflation, as measured by the difference between nominal and real interest rates. Reviewing the previous 10 years of data and considering historical events, the probability of such an increase in inflation is approximately 1%.

TABLE 8.1   Bond ETF Strategies

Strategy	Name
Strategy 1	US Aggregate Bond ETF
Strategy 2	Emerging Bonds ETF
Strategy 3	High-Yield Corporate Bond ETF
Strategy 4	Muni Bond ETF
Strategy 5	Investment-Grade Corporate Bond ETF
Strategy 6	Agency Bond ETF
Strategy 7	International Inflation Linked Bond ETF
Strategy 8	Euro Government Bond ETF
Strategy 9	Canadian Corp Bond ETF
Strategy 10	Global Government Bond ETF

Source: BlackRock, 2020. For illustrative purposes only.

For this example, a long-only bond portfolio consisting of 10 equally weighted strategies via bond ETFs is used. (See Table 8.1.)

Table 8.2 contains each bond ETF strategies' correlations and volatilities under normal market conditions. The initial, equal-weighted, portfolio has an ex ante portfolio risk of 303 bp per year. To construct the stress test profit and loss (P&L), a historical scenario-weighting approach is used that is similar to the one described by Silva and Ural (2011) and Ruban and Melas (2010). P&L results for each bond ETF strategy in the "crisis" are listed in Table 8.2. For example, the US Aggregate Bond ETF, Strategy 1, would lose 208 bp were the inflation scenario shock to occur.

As a next step, the total portfolio is subjected to this Inflation Rise scenario. Exhibit 8.6 demonstrates that under this stress test, the portfolio loses 96 bp. As discussed in Section 8.4.2.3, the hedger's objective is to determine the optimal portfolio reallocation for different levels of loss reduction while minimizing tracking error to the initial portfolio.

In this example, six optimizations were run to identify the minimum ex ante risk versus the initial portfolio to achieve loss reductions from 96 bp to 90 bp, 80 bp, 70 bp, and 40 bp. The resulting portfolio holdings at each level of loss reductions are illustrated in Table 8.3. The objective is to demonstrate a stress scenario hedging methodology and focus on the qualitative assessment of results; this section does not go into the detailed analysis of the corresponding portfolio holdings.

The hedger needs to balance the cost of portfolio adjustments, as measured by tracking error to the initial holdings, against the benefit of hedging, as measured by the reduction in loss. The required portfolio construction approach is described by Equation 8.21. In this case, the hedger solves for portfolio holdings that have minimal tracking error to the initial holdings at different levels of reduction in the stress P&L. Results of this analysis are presented on Exhibit 8.6.

As illustrated by Scenario A in Exhibit 8.6, if the hedger can tolerate up to 22 bp of tracking deviation (TE) from the initial holdings, then the loss can be reduced by 16 bp. If that trade-off is acceptable, hedging will be beneficial, and the methodology outlined previously will help to determine the required portfolio rebalancing strategy. The resulting trade into Scenario A reduces exposure to higher loss assets such as Aggregate Bond, Muni Bond, and Investment-Grade Bond ETFs. For risk-control purposes, the strategy increases exposure to

TABLE 8.2 Inputs for Inflation Rise Stress Test Scenario

	Initial Allocation (%)	Inflation Rise P&L (bp)	Volatility (bp)	Strategy 1	Strategy 2	Strategy 3	Strategy 4	Strategy 5	Strategy 6	Strategy 7	Strategy 8	Strategy 9	Strategy 10
Strategy 1	10%	−208	398	1	0.4	−0.45	0.83	0.96	0.99	−0.42	0.61	0.6	0.93
Strategy 2	10%	−38	425	0.4	1	0.3	0.38	0.43	0.35	0.1	0.46	0.42	0.43
Strategy 3	10%	90	266	−0.45	0.3	1	−0.47	−0.29	−0.52	0.46	−0.03	0.02	−0.37
Strategy 4	10%	−141	269	0.83	0.38	−0.47	1	0.76	0.84	−0.45	0.5	0.42	0.8
Strategy 5	10%	−254	581	0.96	0.43	−0.29	0.76	1	0.93	−0.34	0.61	0.66	0.89
Strategy 6	10%	−160	321	0.99	0.35	−0.52	0.84	0.93	1	−0.44	0.59	0.56	0.92
Strategy 7	10%	340	1115	−0.42	0.1	0.46	−0.45	−0.34	−0.44	1	−0.07	−0.01	−0.34
Strategy 8	10%	−260	722	0.61	0.46	−0.03	0.5	0.61	0.59	−0.07	1	0.62	0.82
Strategy 9	10%	−93	471	0.6	0.42	0.02	0.42	0.66	0.56	−0.01	0.62	1	0.66
Strategy 10	10%	−240	549	0.93	0.43	−0.37	0.8	0.89	0.92	−0.34	0.82	0.66	1

Source: BlackRock, 2020. For illustrative purposes only.

TABLE 8.3 Portfolio Holdings Following Optimization

Strategy	Name	Initial holdings, Loss = 96 bp	Scenario A.					
			Optimized holdings, Loss = 90 bp	Optimized holdings, Loss = 80 bp	Optimized holdings, Loss = 70 bp	Optimized holdings, Loss = 60 bp	Optimized holdings, Loss = 50 bp	Optimized holdings, Loss = 40 bp
Strategy 1	US Aggregate Bond ETF	0.10	—	—	—	—	—	—
Strategy 2	Emerging Bonds ETF	0.10	0.11	0.11	0.11	0.11	0.11	0.11
Strategy 3	High-Yield Corporate Bond ETF	0.10	0.11	0.15	0.18	0.21	0.24	0.26
Strategy 4	Muni Bond ETF	0.10	0.08	0.04	0.00	—	—	—
Strategy 5	Investment-Grade Corporate Bond ETF	0.10	0.11	0.08	0.05	0.03	0.02	0.00
Strategy 6	Agency Bond ETF	0.10	0.17	0.15	0.13	0.10	0.09	0.07
Strategy 7	International Inflation Linked Bond ETF	0.10	0.10	0.10	0.11	0.11	0.11	0.11
Strategy 8	Euro Government Bond ETF	0.10	0.08	0.05	0.01	—	—	—
Strategy 9	Canadian Corp Bond ETF	0.10	0.10	0.10	0.11	0.11	0.12	0.13
Strategy 10	Global Government Bond ETF	0.10	0.15	0.22	0.29	0.32	0.31	0.31

Source: BlackRock, 2020. For illustrative purposes only.

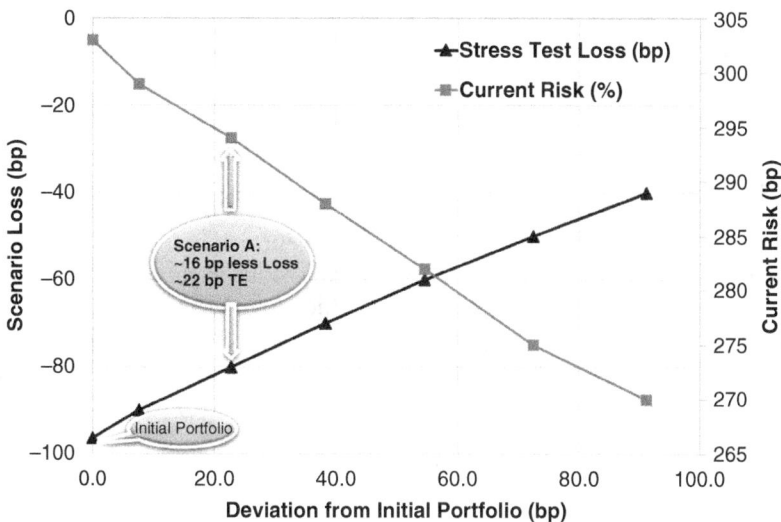

EXHIBIT 8.6 Stress Test Loss Reduction[22]
Source: BlackRock, 2020. For illustrative purposes only.

portfolios that have high correlation to the sold names. The Inflation Linked Bond Fund has strong positive performance under this scenario, but this portfolio also has the highest volatility, so its allocation did not change. As a side-benefit, the hedged portfolio exhibits a lower total risk—something that can be attributed to repositioning into less risky assets.

To summarize, a generalized approach to risk hedging with different risk hedging objectives can be translated into constrained portfolio optimization. The formulated solutions were based on employing parametric risk and transaction cost models, which commonly lead to mean variance style single portfolio, single period constrained optimization problems. While this framework is quite useful in practice, it is not the only choice. In the next section, several alternative methodologies are covered.

8.5 ADVANCED PORTFOLIO OPTIMIZATION AND RISK MANAGEMENT TECHNIQUES

As previously discussed, "mean variance" style portfolio construction solutions can provide hedgers with insights on optimal capital allocation across securities to identify optimal hedging strategies and achieve a range of investment objectives.

This section covers several examples of quantitative portfolio construction solutions for risk hedging and risk management that go beyond the traditional "mean variance" approach. These include

- a risk budgeting/parity solution (Section 8.5.1),
- strategies that permit investors to efficiently hedge risk in multiple portfolios simultaneously (Section 8.5.2.1),

- hedging across extended time horizons (Section 8.5.2.2),
- incorporating forward looking economic scenarios and/or outcomes (Section 8.5.2.3), and
- risk budgeting for factor-based investing (Section 8.5.3).

8.5.1   Risk Budgeting/Parity

Diversification is one of the core tools used for investment risk management, helping to control non-systematic risks. The management of portfolio concentration is a necessary but not sufficient condition for achieving a form of diversification. While achieving diversification is one of the main contributions of mean variance optimization, this methodology is by no means unique. Recently, due to their robustness and diversification properties, the inclusion of risk budgeting conditions has become a regular component in portfolio construction.

Interestingly, there is no standard interpretation of risk budgeting among investment practitioners. While selecting risk targets is a common practice in all approaches, the underlying condition may be defined in different ways. In some cases, it is just a set of linear constraints that control exposure to risk-related factors, such as duration. This is a particularly simple choice and one that can be easily handled within a conventional mean variance framework, as discussed in the previous section. Another common option is to specify the upper bound of risk for some asset groups and/or factors in the portfolio. In practice, this can be implemented using additional quadratic constraints.[23]

This section focuses on risk budgeting constraints that are described as *risk contributions*.[24] We will start by illustrating how risk contribution constraints can be integrated in fixed-income portfolio construction. Let us consider an example of a long-only fund of funds that allocates between managers with different fixed-income styles.[25] In these settings, total portfolio risk can be written as:

$$\sigma_p = \sqrt{w^T V w} \qquad (8.23)$$

where w is an N-vector of manager allocation weights and V is the corresponding covariance matrix between managers. Using these notations, the risk contribution for i-th portfolio can be calculated:

$$RC_i = w_i \frac{\partial \sigma_p}{\partial w_i} = w_i \frac{(Vw)_i}{\sqrt{w^T V w}} \qquad (8.24)$$

and when every individual portfolio has a positive risk contribution to the resulting fund of funds, these constraints can be written as:[26]

$$RC_i = \varepsilon_i \sigma_P$$

or, alternatively,

$$w_i \sum_j V_{ij} w_j = \varepsilon_i \sum_{ij} w_i V_{ij} w_j, \quad i = 1, \ldots N$$

where

$$\sum_i \varepsilon_i = 1$$

$$\varepsilon_i \geq 0, \forall i$$

$$\sum_i w_i = 1$$

$$w_i \geq 0, \forall i \tag{8.25}$$

Risk parity is a particular example of this approach where the hedger requires the risk contribution from each portfolio to be the same. In this case:

$$\varepsilon_i = \frac{1}{N} \tag{8.26}$$

The common approach to compute holdings that satisfy risk contribution conditions is to transform these constraints into a single equation:

$$\sum_{ij} \left(\frac{1}{\varepsilon_i} w_i \sum_j V_{ij} w_j - \frac{1}{\varepsilon_j} w_j \sum_i V_{ji} w_i \right)^2 = 0 \tag{8.27}$$

or, equivalently, minimize the resulting quartic expression as suggested in Maillard et al. (2010). Consequently, in contrast to mean variance optimization, a portfolio construction solution, in the presence of risk budgeting conditions, cannot be achieved using conventional quadratic programming. As a result, initial approaches were based on developing various heuristic algorithms.[27]

The minimization problem for a long-only portfolio with total risk contribution constraints was shown to have a unique solution.[28] Building on this initial observation, the question arises as to whether an alternative method can be designed that is capable of solving the problem directly—without heuristics. The answer is yes—by reformulating risk contribution constraints using conic programming.[29]

In order to illustrate this approach, a set of additional variables proportional to the marginal risk contribution of each asset are introduced:

$$y_i = \frac{1}{\varepsilon_i} \sum_j V_{ij} w_j, \ i = 1, \dots, N \tag{8.28}$$

Then, the risk contribution problem can be written as "risk minimization" with quadratic constraints:

$$
\begin{aligned}
& \underset{w,y,\theta}{Minimize}[\theta^2] \\
& w_i y_i \geq \theta^2, \forall i \\
& \sum_{ij} w_i V_{ij} w_j \leq \theta^2 \\
& \sum_i w_i = 1 \\
& w_i \geq 0, \forall i \\
& \theta \geq 0
\end{aligned}
\tag{8.29}
$$

where θ is an auxiliary variable that takes the value of the total portfolio risk after above minimization is solved. To satisfy both quadratic constraints, the solution has to be consistent with selected risk-budgeting requirements. That can be accomplished if each y_i variable has a positive value so that the resulting quadratic constraints are of the second-order conic programming (SOCP) type.[30] However, that is indeed the case since we target the following condition:

$$w_i y_i = \theta^2, \forall i$$

and for long-only portfolio we have

$$w_i \geq 0, \forall i$$

As a result, the total value of every y_i variable must be positive, and the resulting quadratic constraint will satisfy the SOCP requirements.

Easily generalized, the constrained optimization solution described previously results in an allocation across managers that satisfies the risk contribution condition. For example, instead of solving for manager selection or risk-based allocation into a mix of fixed-income ETFs, a risk-budgeting approach to factor investing can be applied. In that case, portfolio construction can be described as a two-step approach. In the first step, risk-budgeting conditions help to determine capital allocation between factors. In the second step, portfolios are constructed from individual securities that will match the predetermined factor allocations. The second step can be formulated as a separate optimization problem where the objective is to match factor exposures using a pre-specified investment universe.[31]

8.5.2 Going Beyond a Single Fund/Single Period in Portfolio Risk Management

In previous sections and examples, the focus was on hedging risk and portfolio construction methodologies for a single fund within a single rebalance scenario. In practice, however, portfolio managers often have to manage multiple funds simultaneously. For instance, a portfolio manager may be responsible for the management of multiple similar, but not identical, funds. As a fiduciary, the portfolio manager must attempt to treat the funds as equally as possible. That means that if the portfolio manager's market views have changed and he or she is repositioning the strategy, he or she needs to implement those views across his or her book of similar business.

While it is possible to accomplish this task by treating these funds on an individual basis, it is important to be wary of oversimplification. For another example, in the presence of cross-fund constraints on security or sector exposures, which can be imposed by regulators, solving for each fund individually does not guarantee that these cross-fund constraints will be satisfied. Solutions may require iterative refinements, which can be costly. Yet another limitation of not considering simultaneous multi-fund rebalancing is apparent when taking into account the market impact component of transaction costs. When trading in the same security occurs in multiple funds, the total value of the resulting market impact costs will be underestimated if the market impact is calculated and then aggregated on a fund-by-fund basis. This is because of the nonlinear nature of market impact, represented by the nonlinear functional form of the market impact function (see Equation 8.11).

Another assumption to consider when implementing the previously described hedging strategies is whether or not all trading can be completed in a single rebalance. This trading strategy may not be practical. Liquidity limitations in fixed-income markets may prevent investors from completing the hedging exercise within a single rebalance.

In the next section, we formally describe how to extend our conventional mean variance framework. First, we discuss risk hedging approaches that accommodate simultaneous multi-fund portfolio management. We then describe portfolio construction and risk hedging in a multi-period context. Clearly, there is an even greater level of generalization where investment objectives can span multiple funds over multiple horizons. Solutions that are discussed in this section can be extended to accommodate this larger optimization problem.

8.5.2.1 Multi-Fund Portfolio Construction and Risk Management Several options are available for specifying the objective function for a simultaneous multi-fund optimization. A common approach is to define the objective in a way that ensures that all funds are treated "fairly" and no fund can serve as a "liquidity provider" for another member of the group.[32] In this case, the objective function aggregates the sum of all the individual fund objectives, except for transaction costs, which are then added based on aggregating trading across funds. As a result, while each fund may have different investment universes, benchmarks, and hedging objectives, it is important that all funds in a multi-fund optimization have the same transaction cost model.

This multi-fund investment objective function for an N-fund family can be schematically written as:

$$U_{MF} = \sum_{i=1}^{N} U_i + T\text{-}Cost \tag{8.30}$$

where U_i includes all investment objectives for the i-th fund and the *T-Cost* term describes aggregate trading across all funds. Various investment constraints and penalties can be specified on a fund-by-fund basis and included in the multi-fund optimization.

The solution simultaneously identifies an optimal set of trades and resulting holdings for all of the funds in the family. This multi-fund framework enables the investor to accommodate arbitrary cross-fund constraints and establish an optimal rebalance strategy aimed to hedge undesired risk exposures or create desired active exposures on an individual fund basis. In addition, the investment objective can be extended to include risk and exposure control for the aggregate holdings across the fund family.

Another extension of the traditional mean variance based approach is to consider how to optimize hedging and risk control when, due to excessive market impact costs or availability limitations, it cannot be realized in a single rebalance. In the next subsection, the methodology is presented using parametric risk models first, and then using a different approach based on scenario optimization.

8.5.2.2 Multi-Period Portfolio Construction and Risk Management When markets are illiquid or thin relative to expected trade sizes, effective hedging or portfolio repositionings may be difficult to establish in a single rebalance, thus requiring a different approach. The multi-period optimization (MPO) methodology is based on a solution proposed by Grinold and Kahn (1995) and Almgren and Chriss (1999). The objective is to compute an optimal multi-period trading strategy that accounts for risk, transaction cost, and all other investment constraints that can be specified on a period-by-period basis. Users of this framework can also capture various deterministic multi-period effects, like benchmark changes, risk model changes, liquidity variations, etc. When risk and transaction costs are the only important components to the investor, the resulting MPO objective function can be written in the following generalized form:

$$U_{MPO} = \sum_{t=1}^{T} (\lambda * Risk(t) + T\text{-}Cost\,(t)) \tag{8.31}$$

where *Risk*(*t*) is an expected variance of the portfolio return and *T-Cost* (*t*) is the cost of trading for the period "t." The variables are hold or buy-sell quantities for each asset and period. The resulting optimization solves for the complete multi-period trading strategy. This approach accommodates period-specific conditions, such as different factor exposure or holding limits. It is also able to integrate period-specific investment preferences, like different risk aversions for different periods, which makes it a very general framework for handling multi-period trading. Duration of the rebalancing process (*T*) is typically determined by the hedger on the basis of the overall liquidity characteristics of the trade.

One common application for this methodology is in transition management, where the goal is to establish an optimal risk-controlled trading strategy for moving from a legacy portfolio to the target portfolio.[33] Other applications include defining risk-managed trading strategies to raise cash during a partial or total fund liquidation as well as cash inflow accommodation. In the partial liquidation example, the objective is to raise sufficient funds to satisfy a redemption request while preserving fund characteristics for remaining investors. In the case of cash inflow, the objective can be to identify an optimal schedule of acquiring futures or ETFs to reduce the cash drag and hedge the risk in the early periods while allowing for the unwinding of these synthetic positions at a later stage.

The MPO framework described in this section relies on parametric models to measure risk at different horizons. In the next section, a different approach based on scenario optimization strategies is presented.

8.5.2.3 Risk Management Using Scenario Optimization Reliance on parametric risk models, even in the presence of uncertainty, was common for the hedging strategies that have been discussed so far in this chapter. Scenario optimization is a well-known alternative approach introduced by Ron Dembo in the early 1990s.[34] Rather than building up these parametric models based on historical data, one can search for the portfolio that satisfies investment objectives under multiple different forward-looking single- or multi-period economic scenario realizations. Furthermore, given explicit scenario definitions, full security repricing can be accommodated, if needed. Clearly, the robustness of this approach is critically dependent on the quality of the scenario simulation engine.

As with the conventional portfolio construction framework described earlier in this chapter, a hedger can structure a scenario optimization approach to accommodate different objectives. These objectives can be further characterized as *horizon-based* or *trajectory-based*.

> *Horizon-based objectives* focus on the portfolio's property at the same time horizon (or cross-section) for all scenarios. For example, finding a portfolio allocation that will minimize portfolio credit risk over a pre-specified period given a set of loss scenarios is an illustration of a "horizon-based" objective.[35] Another example is hedging a portfolio's option-adjusted volatility (OAV), given a set of interest rate scenarios.[36]
>
> *Trajectory-based objectives* focus on portfolio characteristics for each scenario across multi-period scenarios. Controlling for portfolio volatility along each scenario is an example of a "trajectory-based" objective.

In the multi-period case, the hedger can further combine these "horizon-based" and "trajectory-based" objectives with other investment constraints to find a portfolio that is best "on average" across all scenarios.

Scenario optimization objectives can also be conveniently cast in terms of a regret framework, which can be illustrated using the following two-step approach. First, the hedger will determine the best possible outcome given the objective for each available scenario. Then, the hedger must identify portfolio holdings that will minimize the deviation from the best outcome across all scenarios.

For example, in the case of interest rate hedging, optimization starts with specifying OAVs that correspond to various interest rate scenarios that function as hedging targets ($OAV_{target,i}$). The resulting objective function $U_{scenario}$ measures the extent to which the hedged portfolio's scenario OAVs resemble those of the target. This can be formulated as a weighted sum of squared differences:

$$U_{scenario} = \sum_{i=1}^{N} w_i * (OAV_{hedged,i} - OAV_{target,i})^2 \qquad (8.32)$$

where w_i is the probability of the i-th scenario as selected by the investor and N is the number of scenarios. This represents an example of a quadratic regret function. Minimization is applied to the average of quadratic differences, thus minimizing the dispersion of outcomes.

In some cases, linear regret, which aims to minimize average differences, can be an appropriate measure. As an example, in a credit risk minimization study,[37] the target for each scenario is the minimal loss amount. Scenario optimization solves for the portfolio that has the smallest average deviation from that ideal loss value for each scenario. Because the target values for each scenario are constants, scenario optimization with a linear regret formulation—in contrast to quadratic regret—is equivalent to the optimization of the scenario-averaged objective.[38]

The hedging of interest rate scenarios unveils a very interesting conceptual dilemma about selecting scenario weights. Given that the probability of interest rates moving by 200 bp or more over 1 year is substantially smaller than that of interest rates moving by, say, 50 bp, it is unclear whether losses corresponding to a 200 bp interest rate move should be hedged as tightly as those corresponding to a 50 bp move. In other words, it is up to the hedger to decide if it is reasonable to place equal emphasis on hedging different scenarios given the fact that the probabilities of the underlying events are drastically different. The answer depends on whether the hedging program is designed as protection against catastrophic events or business-as-usual market movements. For instance, in managing mortgage servicing and insurance portfolios, all interest rate scenarios are typically hedged in a similar fashion, implicitly assigning equal probabilities to the underlying interest rate moves. In practice, the weights $w_1, \ldots, w_n$ in Equation 8.32 can be either specified by the user or computed using the probabilities associated with various interest rate scenarios.

To summarize, in this section, extensions of the mean variance approach were discussed in order to handle multiple funds in a single rebalance or to optimally trade a single fund across multiple periods. While we will not go into detail here, it should be noted that it is certainly possible to combine these objectives in a comprehensive optimization across multiple funds and multiple periods—the integration of scenario and mean variance approaches for risk management and risk hedging included. The component-based approach to quantitative portfolio construction as applied to risk management and outlined in this chapter provides full flexibility for an investor to select and achieve desired objectives.

8.5.3   Example: Risk Budgeting for Factor-Based Investing

The objective of factor-based investing is to target preselected exposure or capital allocation to investment risk factors that the investor believes generate attractive long-term returns.[39]

Here, as an alternative, we describe a portfolio construction approach based on targeting factor risk contributions. Our solutions are based on the methodology outlined in Section 8.5.1.

For illustrative analysis, the following three macroeconomic factors have been selected: *Real Rates*, *Inflation*, and *Credit*. The estimated correlations among these factors and factor volatilities are shown in Table 8.4.[40]

In order to better illustrate the risk parity approach, we consider minimum volatility and equal weighting allocations as benchmarks. These, in turn, will be compared to a risk parity portfolio:

$$\text{Weight Concentration} = \frac{\sum_{i=1}^{N} w_i^2 - 1/n}{1 - 1/n}$$

$$\text{Risk Concentration} = \frac{\sum_{i=1}^{N} RC_i^2 - 1/n}{1 - 1/n} = \frac{\sum_{i=1}^{N} \left[\frac{(Vw)_i}{\sqrt{w^T V w}} \right] - 1/n}{1 - 1/n} \qquad (8.33)$$

where w_i denotes the weight of i-th factor, V denotes the overall covariance matrix so $(Vw)_i$ is the i-th element of the marginal risk contribution vector.

As shown in Table 8.5, although the minimum volatility portfolio provides a solution with the lowest portfolio risk (108 bp), it has the highest weight concentration.[41]

As illustrated in Table 8.5 and Exhibit 8.7, the equal weighting approach achieves maximum diversification at the weight level but has a high portfolio risk of 173 bp and the highest risk concentration. As expected, the risk parity approach achieves equal risk contributions among all factors, as shown on Exhibit 8.8. It has 109 bp portfolio risk with better diversification, as measured by weight concentration, than the minimum volatility benchmark. Thus, the risk parity method offers an attractive compromise between the low risk and low weight concentration benefits of the two benchmarks. Of course, that observation is dependent on the stability of the factor risks. Experience has shown that during periods of severe market stress, correlations often do not remain stable and can dramatically increase risk.

TABLE 8.4 Volatility and Correlation Among Factors

Factor Name	Factor Volatility	Factor Correlations		
Real Rates	4.6%	1.00	0.40	−0.61
Inflation	3.9%	0.40	1.00	−0.65
Credit	2.8%	−0.61	−0.65	1.00

Source: BlackRock, 2020. For illustrative purposes only.

TABLE 8.5 Portfolio Risk, Weight, and Risk Concentrations for All Strategies

	Portfolio Risk (bp)	Weight Concentration	Risk Concentration
Minimum Volatility	108	0.12	0.12
Equal Weight	173	0.00	0.81
Risk Parity	109	0.09	0.00

Source: BlackRock, 2020. For illustrative purposes only.

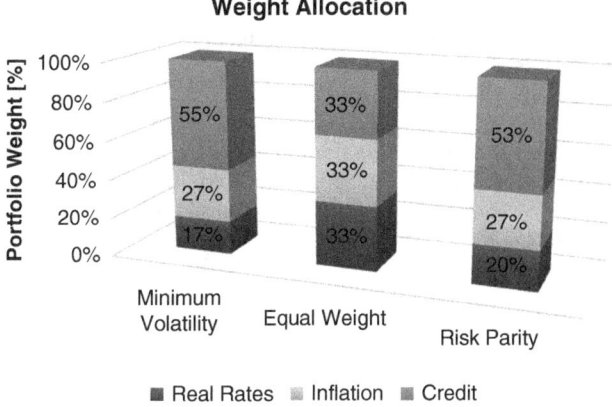

EXHIBIT 8.7 Weight Allocation for Different Strategies
Source: BlackRock, 2020. For illustrative purposes only.

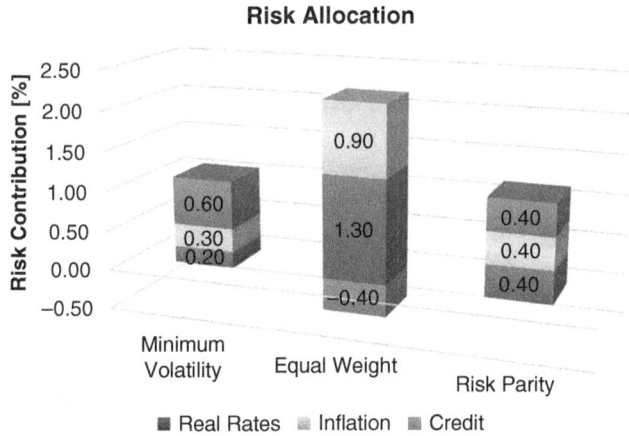

EXHIBIT 8.8 Risk Allocation for Different Strategies
Source: BlackRock, 2020. For illustrative purposes only.

To summarize, risk budgeting conditions offer an intuitive and practical way to incorporate an investor's views on risk allocation. Risk parity is just an example of such views but illustrates the benefit of a risk budgeting methodology. As a result, risk parity and its generalizations can become the foundation for building diversified, risk-managed portfolios. As an alternative, these constraints can also be included as components within a conventional mean variance approach for risk hedging and portfolio construction.

NOTES

1. See uses of VaR by LTCM in Jorion, 1999.
2. To "move" the market means to change the existing bid–ask spreads by performing large transactions.

3. For this system of linear equations to have a unique solution, it is sufficient that no two hedging instruments have identical or proportional exposures to all systematic risk factors and that for each risk factor there exists at least one hedging instrument that is exposed to it.

4. See, e.g., Fama and French, 1993; Ferson and Harvey, 1991; Ang, 2014; this book.

5. See Grinold and Kahn, 1999; Kissell, 2003. Market impact costs can be further classified as temporary or permanent costs (Kissell, 2003). Temporary market impact describes our influence on price that is expected to subside after trading is completed. In contrast, permanent market impact will persist and influence asset price after completion of the trade. For simplicity, we will focus on temporary market impact in this chapter.

6. This objective can be extended to include minimization of the external cash inflow when the use case is to finance the hedge.

7. In practice, an investor can eliminate perfectly correlated hedging instruments prior to optimization or post-process optimization results.

8. For many fixed-income securities, it is important to distinguish between their market and notional values and between corresponding weights. Market value simply refers to the price of a security. Market-value-based weights, therefore, must be normalized to ensure that the trade is self-financed. Notional weights determine security exposures to risk factors and may be subject to a different normalization.

9. Cornuejols, G., & Tutuncu, R. (2007).

10. See, e.g., www.cplex.com, www.mosek.com, www.gurobi.com.

11. In this example, hedging was accomplished as a self-financed transaction. When hedging is financed through an up-front investment, the market value of that inflow can be described as an additional cost and should be minimized.

12. Illustrated in Golub, Ferconi, Madhavan, and Ulitsky, 2018.

13. See Dynkin et al., 2006.

14. See, e.g., Ruban and Melas, 2010; Bilgili et al., 2017.

15. See, e.g., Ruban and Melas, 2010.

16. See Bilgili et al., 2017.

17. See, e.g., Cotoi and Stamicar, 2018.

18. Bloomberg Barclays Euro Corporate index consists of euro-denominated securities with a minimum of EUR 300mm amount outstanding, a fixed-rate.

19. There are a great and wide variety of ESG data providers and methodologies. In this example, we utilize MSCI ESG scores, which are the weighted averages of the three components—environmental, social, and governance—computed using industry-specific weights. Using MSCI definitions, an aggregate portfolio score can be mapped into a letter rating. In this example, both the initial and benchmark portfolios have BBB ratings. The MSCI ESG Ratings Methodology can be found at https://www.msci.com/documents/1296102/21901542/ESG-Ratings-Methodology-Exec-Summary.pdf. The MSCI data contained herein is the property of the MSCI Inc. or its affiliates (collectively, "MSCI"). MSCI and its information providers make no warranties. The MSCI data is used under licenses and may not be further used distributed or disseminated without the express written consent of MSCI.

20. In this case the improvement in ESG score from 5.30 to 5.49 is insufficient to change the ESG letter rating. Despite the uplift in the new portfolio ESG score, the overall ESG rating (BBB) remains unchanged based on the MSCI definitions because of the integrality of MSCI's letter grading methodology.

21. This section is based on a paper published by Bilgili, Ferconi, and Ulitsky, Risk, 2017.

22. This chart illustrates how much ex ante tracking deviation from the initial portfolio is required to achieve different hedging efficiencies as measured by reduction in portfolio loss. The horizontal axis indicates ex ante tracking deviation from the initial portfolio holdings starting at zero (= initial portfolio) to 100 bp. The left vertical axis sets the scale for hedging efficiency measured by scenario loss achievable at different levels of tracking. The corresponding results are shown by the green line. The blue line illustrates the total ex ante risk for portfolios at different hedging levels. The corresponding risk scale is set on the right vertical axis.

23. See Scherer, 2015.
24. See Bridgewater, 2010; Qian, 2006.
25. Finding a solution that satisfies risk-budgeting constraints with respect to a noncash benchmark, i.e., in active space, is a significantly more challenging problem. See Bai et al., 2016.
26. The case when selected portfolios are set to have negative risk contribution can also be handled using this approach.
27. See Chaves et.al, 2012; Feng and Palomar, 2015; Griveau-Billion et al., 2013; Kaya, 2012.
28. See Maillard et al., 2010.
29. See Siu, 2014.
30. This approach is extensible also to cases when individual portfolios holdings are positive, while some of the portfolios are expected to have negative risk contribution.
31. See, e.g., Greenberg et al., 2016.
32. Scherer, 2015.
33. See Blake et al., 2003.
34. Dembo, 1991.
35. See Mausser and Rosen, 1999.
36. See Golub and Tilman, 2000.
37. See Mausser and Rosen, 1999.
38. Quadratic regret sets a higher penalty on larger deviations, which can determine the investor's preference for selecting it over linear formulation.
39. See Ang, 2014; Greenberg et al., 2016.
40. Details of factor definitions and factor properties are given in Greenberg et al., 2016.
41. To measure factor weight concentration, we use normalized Herfindahl index. For more details on these measures, see, e.g., Maillard et al., 2010.

CHAPTER 9

Risk Governance[1]

Bennett W. Golub

Senior Advisor, BlackRock

9.1   INTRODUCTION

Continued growth in the number of distinct and complex portfolios have challenged historical investment risk management approaches. While regular reviews of portfolio characteristics by independent risk managers with specific subject matter expertise remains the core of an effective risk management paradigm, this model does not scale elegantly. Risk managers, evaluating a group of quantitative risk metrics using heuristics, who raise issues directly to geographically co-located portfolio managers as they arise, works exceedingly well with a manageable number of portfolios. However, given the increasing size and heterogeneity of investment processes and products, risk managers need to be able to efficiently analyze a multitude of portfolios and monitor a broader range of risk metrics. *A handful of smart people visually scanning increasingly numerous and long columns of risk analytics with a metal ruler as their guide won't cut it in the future!*

Combining advanced workflow technology with algorithmic processes, machine-driven risk scans can improve the precision and comprehensiveness of risk management and enable risk managers to operate more accurately, efficiently, and effectively at greater scale. The second pillar of BlackRock's Investment Risk Management Paradigm (IRMP), *risk governance*, involves engaging with risk takers to help define risk appetites, achieve appropriate levels of risk, and ensure risk taking is aligned with client expectations. Exception-based risk scans can be used to identify portfolios or positions that may not align with client objectives or expectations. Risk scans are calibrated by different portfolio types and allow risk managers to analyze and identify a variety of potentially risky situations. In this chapter, we review the risk scan framework and provide an example of a particular univariate risk scan that uses *ex ante active risk*, which BlackRock calls Risk and Performance Targets (RPT). [2]

9.2   RISK SCAN STANDARD FRAMEWORK

Risk scans are algorithmic processes that identify predefined risk exceptions and define workflows for their resolution. These risk scans enable risk managers to manage investment risk at scale across portfolios by systematically flagging potential issues that may require further attention. Risk scans do not replace the role of a risk manager or human judgment. Instead, they enable risk managers to operate at scale in a robust manner with a high degree of rigor. By defining resolution and escalation procedures for potentially problematic scans, the risk scan framework also facilitates proper governance and oversight, which is a critical component of an effective risk management process. No risk management process will ever be perfect, but having in place rigorous and auditable processes and procedures can allow an extreme adverse performance event to be distinguished from a failure by an investment management firm to prudently discharge its fiduciary duties.

Risk scans generate risk exceptions based upon predetermined thresholds. Different scans can be tailored based on the different portfolio types and can span ex ante active risk, factor exposures, issuer concentration, and liquidity risks, as examples. The risk scan ingests those specific risks, applies thresholds, and specifies associated logic to ascertain which of those portfolios or positions should be flagged as potential exceptions requiring further attention. For example, an algorithmic scan that flags large week-over-week (WoW) changes in active duration, active spread duration, active risk, and P&L in a particular fixed-income portfolio could require attention from a risk manager. For instance, a WoW active duration change of 1.5 standard deviations relative to the portfolio's history of changes might signal the need for further investigation.

Multiple risk scans can be applied to an individual portfolio. For instance, each asset class could have different risk scans defined to ensure appropriately comprehensive oversight. Thresholds that can flag exceptions from each risk scan must be defined, along with scan frequency (i.e., daily, monthly). Risk scans must also have well-documented resolution steps, including commentary on the exception, escalation, and rules for when a long-standing exception should be re-reviewed.

Risk exceptions are generated when there is a breach above a predetermined threshold. The exceptions then feed directly into a standardized and streamlined end-to-end workflow, ensuring well-defined time frames for oversight and resolution. At BlackRock, risk managers review and analyze exceptions and, depending on the situation, discuss the exception with senior risk managers and portfolio managers. If there is a true exception, risk managers and portfolio managers must communicate to understand the concern and the appropriate resolution. Based on this oversight, the risk may be accepted or may, if there is a disagreement, require additional escalation.

When the flow of risk exceptions is reviewed, some, even many, exceptions may be deemed false positives, suggesting that algorithm enhancements may be required. At the same time, when tuning the algorithm to reduce the number of false positives, care must be taken to avoid permitting too many false negatives to go unattended. There is little science to precisely guide how to balance the burdens of running down false positives versus the consequences of having a false negative hurting clients' portfolios and the reputation and long-term commercial damage to the manager. Experience teaches that a wise manager learns to accept the cost of escalating some false positives rather than letting a true risk management problem go unattended.

Diligent risk managers should memorialize commentary regarding risk exceptions within a defined time frame that is aligned with the frequency of the scan. Typically, risk managers at BlackRock provide commentary 5 business days following the flagging of an exception. While issues may persist, risk scans have a period for which the commentary associated with an identified exception expires. After an exception comment expires, commentary is refreshed within a defined time frame. The defined period is utilized to avoid overburdening the risk managers while at the same time recognizing that just because a risk exception may be allowed to persist, conditions can be dynamic, and the assessment of the exception needs to be periodically reviewed.

In the event that a risk manager and portfolio manager cannot agree on how to handle an exception, escalation protocols need to be put in place to address the issue with senior management, including the head of the investment business or chief investment officer (CIO), the chief risk officer (CRO).

While algorithmic scans will never replace the need for subject matter expertise or human judgment, they do have the ability to enhance the breadth and depth of risk management. By algorithmically scanning thousands of portfolios and detecting risk anomalies across a wide range of criteria, risk managers can efficiently expand their scope and the accuracy of their surveillance. With the proper software and work flows, risk managers can efficiently identify and investigate risk exceptions through a consistent global framework, which feeds into a standardized process to investigate, mitigate, and resolve exceptions. The following section focuses on a specific risk scan framework—the RPT framework.

9.3   RISK AND PERFORMANCE TARGET (RPT) FRAMEWORK

The RPT framework is a particular type of risk scan that can be used to identify an important class of risk exceptions. It has been employed at BlackRock for many years. Providing a structured approach to calibrate risk, the RPT framework aligns portfolio risk-taking with clients' investment objectives and reasonable return expectations. The framework uses a standardized process that compares ex ante risk estimates to predefined risk targets.

At BlackRock, risk ranges are developed through a collaborative process between portfolio managers, risk managers, and, when appropriate, client businesses. Risk managers are responsible for determining whether portfolios should be included in the RPT framework and then defining the appropriate risk ranges.[3] Alpha targets are an integral input for setting risk ranges, as they seek to align actual risk taking to client performance expectations. Alpha targets are agreed upon by the client businesses and portfolio managers, with input from risk managers, as needed. Additionally, RPT risk ranges are determined based on a portfolio's investment objectives and, in some cases when client's provide specific quantitative risk expectations, set in accordance with those specific requirements defined in the IMA, fund prospectus, or regulatory guidelines.

Depending on how the ex ante risk compares to the predefined risk ranges, at a given point in time, portfolios are classified as being in different "risk zones" that help to determine whether risk-taking is aligned with client expectations and guide risk management actions. There are three risk zones in the RPT framework, which are defined as follows:

1. *Target (Green Zone)*—This zone is considered the "normal" or "target" range of risk-taking for portfolios. Portfolios within the green zone require no action. In normal market conditions, a risk manager should not be surprised to see a portfolio's risk fluctuate within the green zone.

2. *Risk Alert High and Risk Alert Low (Amber Zone)*—This zone suggests that risk-taking may have diverged from levels considered to be "normal" but does not necessarily require action. Risk managers should monitor risk levels and engage in regular discussions with the respective portfolio managers, as appropriate.

3. *Risk Watch High and Risk Watch Low (Red Zone)*—This zone indicates that portfolios have entered a region of risk-taking that is potentially inconsistent with the portfolio objectives. This can occur at both the high (risk watch high) and low (risk watch low)

risk-taking levels. Portfolios in the RPT red zone are considered risk exceptions and require investigation and follow-up when they remain in the red zone for longer than predetermined time frames. Experience has taught that there needs to be a certain level of asymmetry to risk watch *low* and risk watch *high* exceptions. For example, a portfolio that is in the risk watch low zone for a prolonged period increases the probability of not achieving its alpha target. However, a portfolio that is in the risk watch high zone may result in a total return loss in excess of a client's reasonable expectation. While both types of exceptions need to be addressed, more immediacy is required for a risk watch high exception.

There are different approaches for setting risk zone ranges. Ultimately, this is a heuristic. For example, risk managers can determine the risk zones based on what they believe is an achievable information ratio (IR)[4]. The expected IR of a portfolio may, for example, be limited by the presence of binding portfolio constraints, available investment opportunities, historical IRs earned on otherwise similar portfolios, or results of systematic backtests. The approach used to determine the target IR also depends on the product and data available.

Historical IR, when available, may provide a good initial estimate of the expected future IR of a product. When both historical and back-test data are unavailable, the IR of the product may be guesstimated based on the ability of the portfolio to modulate risk and the investment universe and constraints. The IR can then be used to set achievable risk-and-return targets dependent on any specific client objectives. Equations 9.1 and 9.2 can be used to determine IR and expected reasonable risk level ranges:

$$Information\ Ratio\ (IR) = \frac{Active\ Return}{Active\ Risk} = \frac{a}{\sigma} \qquad (9.1)$$

$$\sigma = \frac{a}{IR} \qquad (9.2)$$

Once a risk manager has determined the expected risk range for a portfolio, he or she then needs to set appropriate thresholds. Exhibit 9.1 provides one example of a heuristic methodology that can be used to calculate risk zone ranges by applying fixed multipliers to the portfolio's risk target. Employing a standardized methodology helps promote consistency across portfolios. However, portfolio objectives, investment universe, and constraints may influence risk ranges. Therefore, the exact range of calibration may not be applicable for all portfolios.

Any particular portfolio's risk may move through risk zones over time, as market conditions and portfolio manager conviction levels vary. (Scientific active equity portfolios, which optimize their holdings subject to a given level of risk, are rarely outside their risk zones.) When a portfolio is in the red zone for a predefined period, risk managers investigate using various risk measures to determine the root cause and what actions are needed. Tail risk measures can be evaluated to determine if risk levels fail to capture event/tail risks. Ex ante and

Risk Watch Low	Risk Alert Low	Target Risk	Risk Alert High	Risk Watch High
30–40% * Target	50–70% * Target	Determined by IR	130–150% * Target	160–200% * Target

EXHIBIT 9.1 An Example of Risk Zone Ranges
Source: For illustrative purposes only.

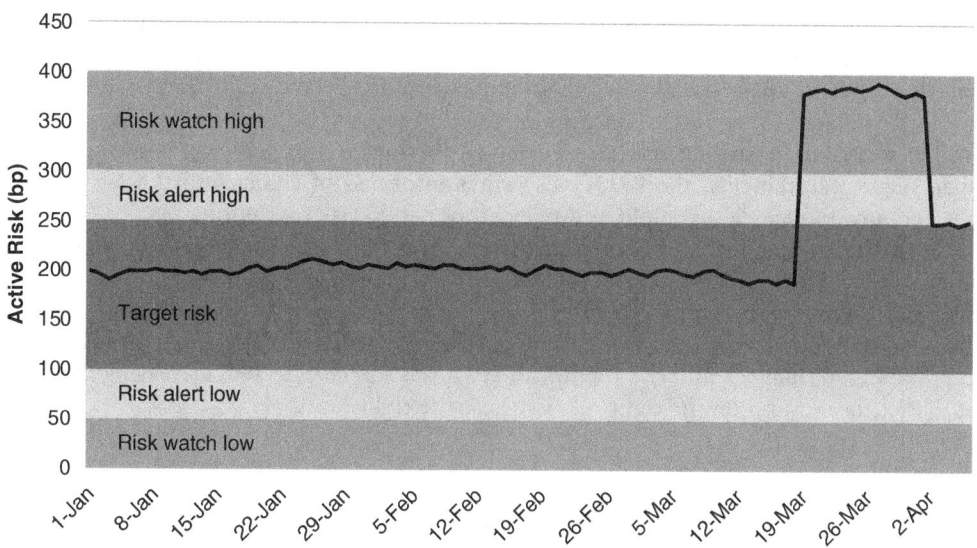

EXHIBIT 9.2 An Example of RPT
Source: For illustrative purposes only.

ex post risk levels are also evaluated relative to alpha targets and realized returns to determine if a portfolio is taking too much risk or too little risk.

Exhibit 9.2 provides an example of the RPT framework applied to a particular fixed-income portfolio. As illustrated, a portfolio was in the green zone for over 2 months. However, on March 19, 2022, the portfolio manager actively increased risk substantially by increasing a high conviction position. This generated a risk exception through the RPT process and was escalated and discussed with the portfolio managers, risk managers, and CIO. Following those discussions, the portfolio manager reduced the position and the portfolio's ex ante risk was brought down to the upper levels of the green zone. This example illustrates how risk managers and portfolio managers can interact through the RPT Framework to ensure that portfolio risk positioning and performance is consistent with client expectation and that portfolio managers are following established supervisory investment processes.

9.4 GOVERNANCE

As previously discussed, a strong governance and control framework is necessary to oversee a firm's risk management practices. BlackRock has established a *Portfolio Risk Oversight Committee* (PROC) that oversees the implementation of pillar two (*risk governance*) of the IRMP. Focusing on broad themes in risk taking, the committee is responsible for reviewing the risk scan exceptions tagged by risk managers, including risk scans and RPT exceptions. The end-to-end workflow established by the risk scans allows exceptions to be prioritized and for the committee to focus on the most critical issues. The committee identifies and evaluates risk exceptions across portfolios and monitors that appropriate escalation, follows up and resolution occurs. The committee also reviews portfolios that have been added to and removed from the universe of in-scope risk scans as well as any notable threshold changes. This is done to make sure that administrative processes (or things even worse) do not inadvertently disarm risk oversight.

At BlackRock, the PROC is chaired by the CRO and meets monthly to review risk exceptions and ensure proper follow-up occurs. Asset class leaders from the Risk & Quantitative Analysis (RQA) group are members of the committee and are responsible for providing details regarding escalated exceptions. The committee addresses any internal policy issues, regulations, or questions regarding risk monitoring. Adhering to any new or revised investment management requirements, the PROC also stays informed of changes to the scope of risk scans and any applicable threshold and relevant portfolio risk exceptions.

Given the complexity and heterogeneity of investment risk management, a risk scan framework facilitates scalable risk monitoring with improved governance and oversight. Providing a consistent approach to monitor risk across asset classes, the risk scan framework allows for exceptions to be identified, investigated, and escalated, as necessary. High severity exceptions can be flagged, and risk themes and patterns can be detected, increasing the chance that there is laser focus on the right risk issues at the right time.

NOTES

1. Rory van Zwanenberg and Katie Day significantly helped to develop this chapter.
2. While this chapter focuses on fixed-income portfolios, risk scans and Risk and Performance Targets can be applied to actively managed liquid portfolios across asset classes.
3. As a market value/total return concept, the RPT Framework may not be applicable for portfolios managed to other objectives, such as income-oriented portfolios that are highly gain/loss constrained.
4. Sharpe ratios are typically used with absolute return products.

CHAPTER 10

Risk-Return Awareness and Behavioral Finance[1]

Emily Haisley
Managing Director, Risk & Quantitative Analysis, BlackRock

Nicky Lai
Director, Risk & Quantitative Analysis, BlackRock

10.1   INTRODUCTION

Ideally, risk managers act as independent and trusted advisors, ensuring key controls are embedded in the investment process and followed. Rather than simply policing controls, effective risk managers help portfolio managers *understand* their risk exposures, return drivers, and the benefits of a disciplined investment process. Behavioral finance—the intersection of finance and psychology—complements traditional risk management methods to achieve these goals, serving as another arrow in the risk manager's quiver. It flags psychological or unintentional motivations for risk-taking and can help portfolio managers be aware of biases that can systematically degrade return.

This chapter focuses on the third pillar of BlackRock's Investment Risk Management Paradigm (IRMP), *portfolio manager risk and return awareness*, with a focus on behavioral finance. Effective risk management requires regular interaction with portfolio managers to discuss risk positioning and should include evaluating potential behavioral aspects of investing. People take risks—not computers. Therefore, it is critical for risk managers to work together with portfolio managers, in close proximity, to ensure that the risks are properly detected and understood and appropriately managed for clients. As such, risk managers need to have a detailed understanding of the investment processes and portfolio management teams to be able to articulate the risks and highlight cognitive blind spots or behavioral biases.

Deliberate, Diversified, and Scaled Risks

To help portfolio managers understand and manage portfolio risks and exposures, risk managers use quantitative analytics and constructive challenge to assess whether risk taking is *deliberate, diversified, and scaled*.

Risk managers need to help ensure that portfolio managers' risks are *deliberate*, meaning that the risk exposures in a portfolio are clearly intentional. The behavioral literature helps inform risk managers to be on guard for common errors in risk comprehension, which can lead to unintended risk taking. If there are unintended bets, risk managers need to suggest changes to the portfolio. For example, they can help the portfolio manager reduce exposures or identify hedging strategies and other quantitative techniques to better manage portfolio risk.

Risk managers should also help ensure that portfolios' risks are *diversified*. Portfolios should seek to be invested in a variety of securities with uncorrelated systematic factor exposures as viewed through the lens of a risk model. Numerous behavioral biases such as over-confidence, the illusion of control, and groupthink can lead to under-diversification. When risk managers are involved in portfolio construction, they help portfolio managers to build "risk-aware" portfolios that diversify risks.

Finally, risk managers help ensure portfolio bets and positions are *scaled* and aligned with client expectations. As mentioned in Chapter 9, Risk and Performance Targets define acceptable ranges of risk for a specific portfolio as a whole, but there may be situations where the risk in a portfolio is either too low or too high relative to the client's objectives. This may be a result of a research view; however, risk preferences have been shown to be highly unstable and can often shift due to causes outside of conscious awareness. Risk managers challenge investors to scale risk up or down depending on how much risk the portfolio is taking relative to targets. Another perspective on the implications of properly scaled bets is that the highest conviction ideas should be the largest drivers of risk and return in a portfolio.

10.2 PORTFOLIO AND RISK MANAGER PARTNERSHIP

Effective risk management requires close communication between portfolio and risk managers. Therefore, it is essential for risk managers to establish trust and credibility with the investment teams. Additionally, the relationships with individual portfolio management teams needs to be adapted based on the portfolio management team member's temperaments, the team's investment strategy, clients' objectives and expectations, along with behavioral risks. To gain credibility, risk managers need to have subject matter expertise and a detailed understanding of the investment processes, portfolio exposures, and the market environment.

Crucially, risk managers must maintain their independence—they are responsible for ensuring that the risks are properly understood and managed without bias or inappropriate influence from the portfolio management team. Risk managers need to provide constructive challenge on both portfolio decisions and the process through which those decisions are made. Ultimately, risk managers should strive to cultivate a relationship with the portfolio management team that combines high trust and high challenge.

Risk managers and portfolio managers should meet regularly to discuss the portfolio's risk positioning and performance. The meeting frequency should be aligned with the investment strategy and process—riskier portfolios and higher turnover products need more frequent portfolio and risk manager interaction than those that are less risky and have longer horizons. To keep portfolio managers informed, risk managers should develop and use a standard set of analytics and stress tests to discuss portfolio exposures under varying market conditions. Increasingly, behavioral analytics are incorporated into this standard set of analytic tools. Additionally, risk managers need to stay closely connected to markets to provide comprehensive and impactful insights into the portfolio. As translators of information, risk managers use data and analytics to demonstrate potential portfolio impacts, even when the focus is behavioral influences on decisions.

By cultivating a trusted and close relationship with portfolio managers, risk managers are uniquely suited to evaluate behavioral biases and blind spots. Since these are, by their very nature, mistakes, it is natural for portfolio managers to feel defensive when they are identified in an investment process. Through their regular interactions, knowledge of the investment strategy and process, and by highlighting the shared goal of being a fiduciary to clients, risk managers can cultivate the trust and respect of portfolio managers needed to enable them to address and overcome their biases. Through the use of standardized analytics, debate, and a bit of introspection, the goal is to deepen the understanding of actual risk-taking and drivers of return.

10.3   BEHAVIORAL RISK MANAGEMENT FOR FIXED INCOME

While it may not seem to be the case given the highly technical and increasingly quantitative nature of investment management, investing is a psychologically intensive endeavor. Discipline, courage, and an ability to prevent emotions from corroding a sound intellectual framework are keys to success according to Benjamin Graham and Warren Buffett. The British economist John Maynard Keynes deduced that effective investing requires *anticipating the anticipations* of other market actors. Truly a psychologically complex task.

Most professional investors will readily agree that psychology moves markets and matters for their success.[2] However, the question of how to address this psychological component is perplexing. Risk management provides a scientific approach to help address this challenge by applying the behavioral literature, in which there has been substantial advances on two questions integral for sound risk management:

1. What are the typical mistakes made in decisions under uncertainty?
2. When mistakes are identified, how do we facilitate learning or reduce the likelihood of mistakes through the design of the decision-making environment?

The scale and variation of these "typical" mistakes, or biases, identified in the literature are immense. While learning about biases is a good first step, the literature suggests that education is not sufficient to *change behavior*. Instead, it is necessary to embed the insights into investment processes and analytics to feed into everyday decisions and oversight.

The vast majority of this rapidly expanding field is devoted either exclusively to equities or to allocation decisions between equities and fixed income.[3] In 2016, an editor of the *Journal of Behavioral Finance* estimated that more than 90% of behavioral research relates to equities or other asset classes other than fixed income.[4] As of January 2020, of the nearly 2,000 results to a search on "behavioral finance" in the Social Science Research Network[5] only 28 citations also contained the word "bonds," 6 contained "fixed income," and 23 contained "interest rates."

Though one could argue that the assessment of fundamental value is clearer cut for a bond compared to a stock, the paucity of research in fixed income likely reflects the challenges of studying this asset class rather than the lack of bias in fixed-income investing. One of the challenges associated with studying biases in fixed income is availability and access to data. Academic researchers generally have greater access to the trading history of retail investors, but retail investors have limited access to buying bonds directly compared to the access they have to numerous online equity brokerages. A more profound challenge is the multidimensional nature of fixed-income investing. Research on equity fund managers typically analyzes decisions at the level of stock selection and return. In contrast, a single decision to purchase a fixed-income instrument by a professional fund manager may reflect a decision regarding the issuer, duration, exposure to broader credit market spread, or currency. Typically, there are separate decision-making processes for macro exposures and for credit selection. It is therefore important to reflect this multidimensionality in behavioral analysis. Any plausible effort in this area will therefore rely on a robust fixed-income risk-and-attribution model.

In this chapter, we present a set of analyses to identify potential behavioral biases by fixed-income portfolio managers and provide case studies that illustrate that they are not immune from these biases. This is accomplished by leveraging a suite of analytics that quantifies the classic behavioral biases identified in equity investing, translated into a fixed-income context. For example, to analyze credit selection, we focus on the spread risk component of each issuer. More precisely, we analyze the portfolio's active duration times spread (DxS) to each issuer and each issuer's performance over the portfolio's benchmark in terms of percentage change in spread. When macro exposures are analyzed, we aggregate the portfolio's duration exposures, currency exposures, and spread exposures. These relevant exposures are decided based on the investment universe of the portfolio, e.g., duration exposure typically is separated out by country. We then set a delta threshold to infer an active decision from a change in exposure.

Unlike the case of a traditional equity portfolio, which is oriented toward stock picking, most fixed-income portfolios are constructed with a strong portfolio orientation. To the extent that a stock is bought or sold by a traditional equity portfolio, it is safe to assume that a buy or a sell signals the outcome of the portfolio management process, including biases, if any. In contrast, it is harder to infer a portfolio management processes' bias from the buy or sell of any particular instrument in isolation. Typically, many fixed-income trades tend to involve the simultaneous buy and sell of multiple securities. Therefore, trying to infer portfolio management intent (including trying to identify biases) by looking at them on a single security trade basis is nearly pointless. Thus, behavioral analyses of fixed-income portfolios need to rely on heuristics to infer the true intents of sets of trades, hence the establishment to delta thresholds. In short, the analyses of fixed-income portfolios are likely to have less resolution compared to their equity portfolio counterparts.

Guarding against blind spots, these fixed-income analytics reveal potential subconscious influences on decisions that can lead to risk aversion or risk seeking that is *not deliberate, diversified, and scaled*. Moreover, the analytics provide a competitive edge to the portfolio management process to help understand its strengths and weaknesses.

The second approach to behavioral risk management goes beyond analysis of the decisions themselves and examines the *process* by which decisions are made. Group dynamics inevitably come into play, as most decision processes have a team context. Secondly, the process should include guardrails to defend against bias resulting from knee-jerk reactions. Finally, without proper feedback on mistakes, there will be no evolution over time. These components make up the three main criteria for a framework to evaluate the investment process:

1. Does the process fully employ the collective intelligence of the team?
2. Does the process include safeguards to diffuse the influence of *"fast thinking"* on decisions?
3. What are the mechanisms to deliver feedback for continuous learning?

10.4 DECISION-MAKING ANALYTICS

Decision-making analytics seek to quantify biases identified by behavioral finance using a portfolio's historical positions, exposures, and performance. When a bias is identified and presented to the investment team, several postmortems on the decisions that underlie the bias are included. Open positions that reveal a pattern consistent with a bias can be flagged for further review. In addition to pointing out opportunities for improvement, these analytics can help reinforce aspects of the investment process that are working well, including where portfolio managers can potentially take on more risk. Recommendations can be revisited in regular risk meetings.

There are a range of biases to explore, but this chapter focuses on two biases that stem from the phenomenon known as loss aversion—the disposition bias and the endowment effect.

10.4.1 Loss Aversion

A core tenet of behavioral finance is that utility is derived from *gains and losses* relative to a neutral reference point rather than over total absolute levels of wealth, return, praise, etc. This is illustrated through Kahneman and Tversky's (1979) prospect theory value function.[6] Exhibit 10.1 demonstrates that a loss is perceived as roughly twice as painful as an equivalent gain is pleasurable. As a result, people tend to be risk averse for gains and risk seeking for losses. We like to lock in gains because there is less marginal upside in further gain, yet we are more willing to take risks to avoid the intense pain of loss.

Naturally, risk managers may question whether a string of poor performance puts the portfolio manager "in the domain of losses" and thus induces a degree of irrational risk

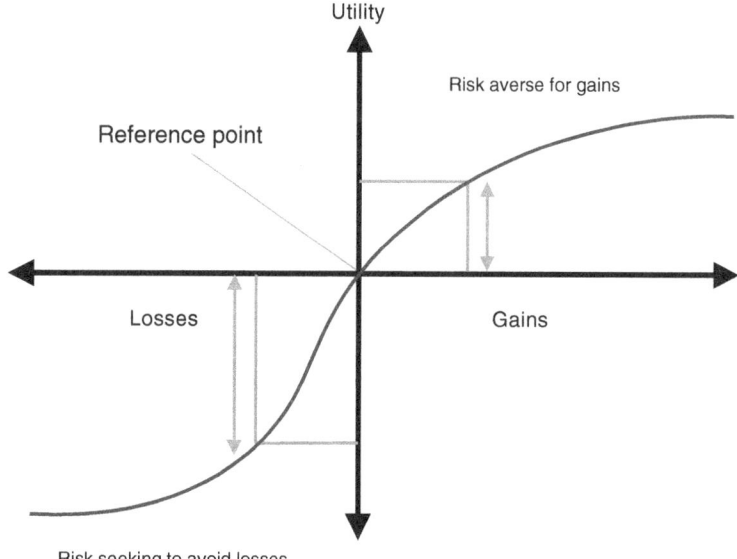

EXHIBIT 10.1 Prospect Theory Value Function
Source: BlackRock. Based on concepts in Kahneman, D. and Tversky, A. (1979) Prospect theory: An analysis of decision under risk. *Econometrica* 47(2), 263–291. https://doi.org/10.2307/1914185.

seeking. In this situation, risk managers should offer constructive challenge if the portfolio manager "doubles-up when down" or takes an extreme "Hail Mary" risk in an attempt to turn around performance. However, risk managers may also observe the converse—after a string of poor performance, the portfolio manager may struggle to find conviction in any investment thesis. These two distinct patterns of behavior may seem inconsistent but can be reconciled by considering whether the loss has been *realized* or not. Controlled lab studies[7] show that paper losses tend to result in risk-taking in order to avoid the loss and go back to the neutral reference point. In contrast, losing positions that have already been closed out tend to be internalized, resetting the reference point, and are associated with subsequent risk aversion.

Complicating the issue of reference dependence further, people may arrive at different decisions depending on which reference point is most salient at the time of the decision. At a single point in time, the reference point for a portfolio manager may be the status quo (i.e., current portfolio performance), an initial value (price when position was opened), a metric to evaluate performance (a benchmark), a goal one would like to achieve (alpha target), or even a social comparison (for example, the return achieved by an overconfident peer).

In the subsequent analyses of the disposition effect, an incarnation of loss aversion that is the tendency to hold losing positions too long, the reference point is determined by the initial value of the position. Gains or losses are determined based on the active return of the position relative to the cost of opening it. To analyze the endowment effect, overvaluing positions already in the portfolio, the reference point is the current portfolio holdings. In this case, reducing a position is considered a loss.

In the next section, case studies are introduced that demonstrate decision-making by fixed-income investors across foreign exchange (FX) exposures, multiple macro exposures, and credit selection. These case studies were chosen to illustrate the multidimensional nature of fixed-income investing. However, we want to caution risk managers not to get lost in the detail of individual exposures and to maintain ongoing communication with portfolio managers to discuss their high-level perception on performance, particularly when performance is challenged. Experience has taught us that irrational decision-making may arise when the portfolio manager feels like he or she is behind, trying to catch-up, or has dropped out of the race.

10.4.1.1 The Disposition Bias One of the implications of loss aversion is the tendency to hold losing positions for too long. Losing positions may be held for emotional reasons—to avoid admitting defeat and experiencing the pain of a realized loss when closing the position. Moreover, the tendency to take risks to avoid losses can encourage "doubling down" in the hope of getting back to the neutral reference point. Exhibit 10.2 illustrates three case studies that demonstrate the disposition bias in FX exposures, macro-exposures, and investment-grade credit selection.

The first case study is for a portfolio that takes a significant amount of risk on emerging market currencies. Decisions are inferred based on changes to the FX exposure of the portfolio through time. Once a decision threshold is defined, the associated P&L of each position can be calculated to determine whether it is a gain or a loss relative to the fund's benchmark. The bias is measured by calculating the daily probability of realizing a paper gain and the daily probability of realizing a paper loss. Realizing a paper gain is defined as taking profit by trimming or completely closing a position with a positive return relative to the benchmark. Similarly, realizing a loss is defined by reducing or stopping out completely a position that has a negative active return. The 6-month rolling average for realized gains versus losses based on FX exposures is shown in Graph 1.A in Exhibit 10.2. In this example the portfolio

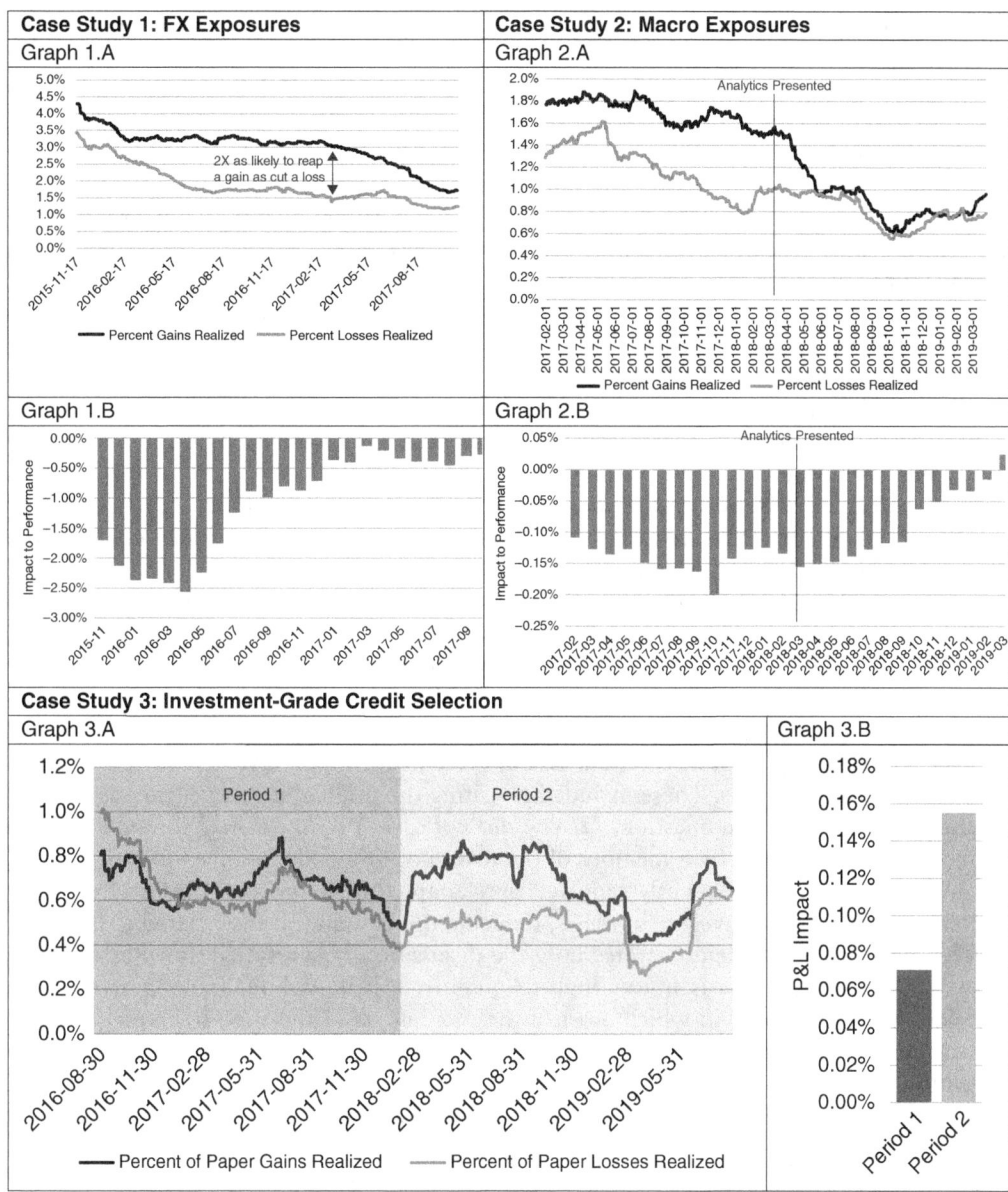

EXHIBIT 10.2 Case Studies on the Disposition Bias
Source: BlackRock. For illustrative purposes only.

manager has a stable tendency to reap winners (black line) and run paper losses (gray line). At the most extreme point, the probability of reaping a gain was two times the probability of cutting a loss.

In itself, there may not be anything wrong with the pattern illustrated in Graph 1.A in Exhibit 10.2. Maintaining conviction in losing positions is the right approach if the investment thesis is still valid. However, there are two reasons for caution. First, decisions should be based on future-looking expectations, not the price paid in the past, creating this gain/loss reference point. Secondly, holding onto losers and reaping gains can take the momentum out of a portfolio, which in some circumstances can be a potential source of positive return in foreign exchange markets. Whether or not the bias is costly for a portfolio manager and for different types of trades is an empirical question.

Thus, the next step is crucial—seeing whether the pattern consistent with the bias actually has an impact on performance. To determine whether the bias is costly, the *subsequent return* of losing positions held and winners reaped is reviewed. If the losers held underperformed the winners reaped, it can be concluded that the bias has a cost. In this example we look at subsequent performance over a 3-month window, but this can vary based on the typical time horizon of the fund. The performance differential between losers held and winners reaped is then weighted by the size of the positions to calculate the P&L impact of the bias. We take a 6-month rolling window of the P&L impact in Graph 1.B in Exhibit 10.2, revealing there is a cost to the bias through time (which reached a maximum cost of 2.5%). In this case study, an intervention was not necessary as the cost of the bias had already reduced to a negligible level in line with an effort to reduce the fund's turnover. However, the use of the analytics generated productive discussion with the portfolio manager on how a mindset of "switching" into a position with better future expectations, rather than "crystalizing" a loss, could reduce the likelihood of the bias from reoccurring.

The second case study examines a fund that has a significant risk exposure to macro bets, such as different countries' duration and fixed-income asset classes (investment grade, high yield, emerging market debt) as well as FX exposures. Since the gains realized exceed the losses realized in Graph 2.A in Exhibit 10.2 and the P&L from the trades shown in Graph 2.B is persistently negative, the graphs demonstrate that prior to April 2018, there was evidence of the disposition bias with sizable cost. The risk management team intervened in April, offering strategies to reduce the bias. These included revisiting the original investment thesis to see if it was still valid, asking the question, *"If you did not own it today, would you buy it?"* and having the thesis reviewed by a member of the team not originally involved in the position. The investment team subsequently reported they adapted their process to more frequently underwrite their original investment thesis, reducing the bias and the associated cost.

The third case study demonstrates how the disposition bias resulted in a P&L benefit, serving as a caution that it is not enough to quantify a bias without looking at the cost. This example is for a fund in which most of the risk budget is allocated to credit selection. In investment-grade credit markets in particular, risk managers should not assume that a disposition bias imposes a cost. Since vanilla corporate bonds have a specified cash flow with relatively low risk of default, the valuation of the security is less subjective compared to that of, say, a technology stock. If the investment process is strong in screening out the issuers with a high probability of default, a mean-reversion style of investing could be at times beneficial to take advantage of short-term market mispricing.

Upon the behavioral analytics identifying the disposition bias, the portfolio manager was not surprised and commented on his strong track record of trading against market over-reaction. The portfolio manager's preference to bet on mean-reversion translated to a tendency to cut winners and hold on to losers. The disposition bias appears strongest in 2018 (shaded light gray in Graph 3.B of Exhibit 10.2) when the benefit to bet on the mean reversion of losing positions was most pronounced.

10.4.1.2 The Endowment Effect The endowment effect is defined as the tendency to overvalue something that one already owns. The endowment effect is another bias that relates to loss aversion. The pain of giving up something one already owns requires a higher hurdle than the (imagined) benefit of acquiring something new. This bias resonates with anyone who finds decluttering a house to be a tortuous task.

In the initial laboratory demonstration,[8] an experimental group was "endowed" with some object, such as a coffee mug. Next, they were asked to report the lowest amount of money they would be willing to accept to sell the mug.[9] Their prices were compared to a control group who reported the highest price they would pay to acquire a mug. The market did not clear—the prices people were willing to accept to sell far exceeded the prices people were willing to pay. While this finding indicates the endowment effect can be induced instantaneously, other work finds the effect strengthens the longer the ownership history.[10]

In the context of investing, the endowment effect refers to the tendency of a portfolio manager to overvalue positions already in their portfolio—simply because they own them. While this bias can be tricky to quantify, we apply the finding that the endowment effect tends to increase with the length of ownership history and look for evidence that positions are held even after the investment thesis has come to fruition.

Specifically, we look at the returns generated throughout the lifetime of each trade by aligning each trade at the inception date and observing the return generated within the first 3 months. For all trades held longer than 3 months, we then observe the return generated in the next 3 months and so on. Because the amount of capital in each bucket diminishes as time goes on, it is important to compare the annualized standalone return (return per unit of time and weight) rather than the cumulative P&L contribution. In Exhibit 10.3, Graph 10.3.A displays a pattern consistent with the endowment effect for a credit portfolio manager. In this example, the analysis focuses on the return contribution from the spread component only (active option-adjusted spread [OAS] return). Note that in credit markets, the impact of the new issue premium can distort the results. If it is quite substantial, it can mimic the pattern of the endowment effect. Therefore, we identify newly issued bonds and isolate the returns generated in the first month of the issuance. Graph 10.3.A (Exhibit 10.3) demonstrates that the new issue premium has minimal impact on the overall pattern, as highlighted in the light gray portion of bar.

The behavioral research suggests that people are more likely to recall anecdotes rather than analytics.[11] Going through particular examples not only helps explain the analysis, but it also encourages portfolio managers to re-live the decision as a postmortem exercise. The key question that relates to this exercise is to understand whether the position was held even after the investment thesis had come to fruition.

Graphs 10.3.B and 10.3.C in Exhibit 10.3 show two postmortem examples from the case study with the credit selection portfolio manager. The DxS of the position relative to the fund benchmark is used to show the weight of the position in the portfolio. (The face value of the bond issuer is also shown in order to differentiate changes in weight due to active decisions and due to market movements.) Additionally, active OAS return is shown through time. Graph 10.3.B (Exhibit 10.3) illustrates a clear example where the bond performed well and then rolled over approximately 10 months later. The portfolio manager considered whether the position was held even after the investment thesis had materialized. Graph 10.3.C (Exhibit 10.3) shows a more complicated example. The position was trimmed but held at a substantial active weight until a credit event occurred. The team sold the position at a sizable loss. This position was one of the long-term core holdings of the fund intended to replicate the characteristics of the benchmark, typically of higher quality and with decent carry. Here the portfolio manager reflected on adapting the investment process to more frequently review core holdings. Like the disposition effect, the endowment effect is a bias which can be reduced by asking oneself, *"How much would I pay to own this?"* rather than asking, *"How much do I want to sell it for?"*

Graph 10.3.A Evidence of the Endowment Effect

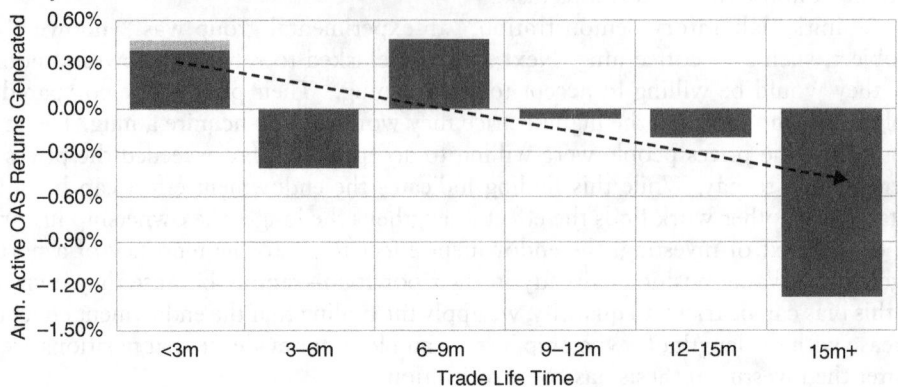

■ Ann. returns excluding new issue premium ■ New issue premium effect

Graph 10.3.B Post-Mortem 1

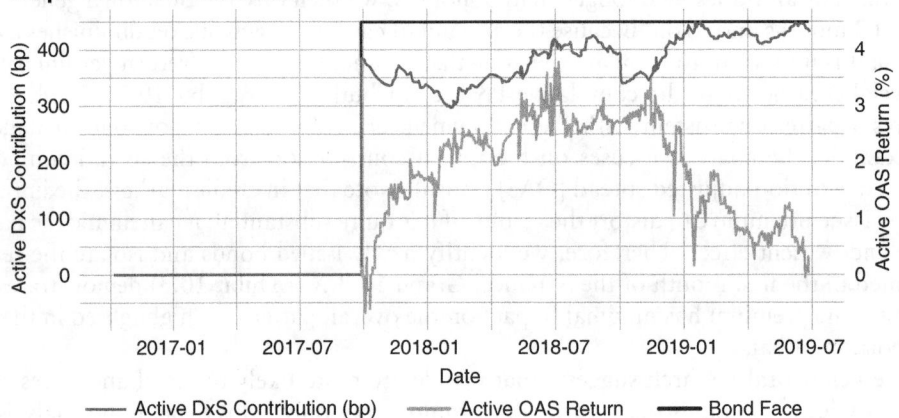

—— Active DxS Contribution (bp)   —— Active OAS Return   —— Bond Face

Graph 10.3.C Post-Mortem 2

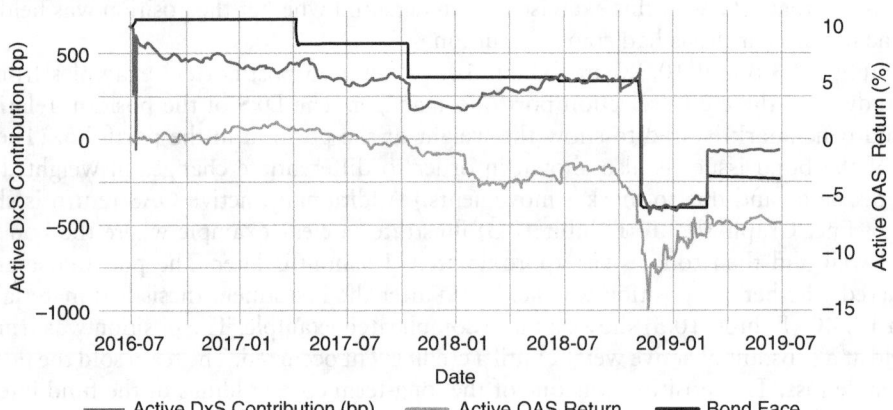

—— Active DxS Contribution (bp)   —— Active OAS Return   —— Bond Face

EXHIBIT 10.3   The Endowment Effect in Investment Grade Credit Selection
Source: BlackRock. For illustrative purposes only.

10.5   INVESTMENT PROCESS

At BlackRock, risk management plays an important role in the oversight and evolution of investment processes. As an independent function, risk managers can freely call out risks or inefficiencies in the investment process. As a centralized function, risk managers are positioned in the center of the network of investment teams, facilitating the transfer of best practices from team to team. As an oversight function, risk managers can architect and enforce disciplined processes that help ensure risk taking is deliberate, diversified, and appropriately scaled.

Taking risks requires understanding the paths that result in the best outcomes *in expectation*. A good investment process is not going to result in a good outcome all of the time nor even most of the time. However, a sound investment process should *tilt the investment outcome in favor of success*. The inherent uncertainty and efficiency of markets precludes perfect prediction. Investors recognize that they cannot get every call right, but inevitably market volatility, a run of poor performance, or even personal or professional distractions can derail confidence and focus. Under increased stress, the investment process is more likely to be misapplied or overridden. This is an opportunity for the risk manager to step in to renew the portfolio manager or team's faith in the process and draw them back to the necessary discipline. There are several properties of an investment process that potentially biases outcomes toward success. Risk managers can conduct an audit of the investment process based on a framework that flags risks and highlights opportunities for improvement (see Table 10.1). While this is illustrated through a fixed-income lens, the framework is applicable across asset classes.

TABLE 10.1   Framework for Evaluating Behavioral Aspects of Investment Processes

	Opportunities	Risks
I. Leverage the Wisdom of the Crowds	Diversity	Groupthink Only discuss shared information/views
	Independence	Anchoring Conformity
	Decentralization	Echo chambers
II. Bolster Deliberate System II Thinking	Speed bumps	Lack of documented trade rationales
	Action plans	Lack of premortems
III. Continuous Learning	Proper, frequent feedback	Cannot separate individual and group input Cannot separate accurate predictions from luck
	Growth mindset	Lack of postmortems Leaders unwilling to examine mistakes

10.5.1   Leveraging the Wisdom of the Crowds

Many, if not the majority, of investment decisions in organizations are made in a group context. Even if an investment process is primarily a solo operation, the individual portfolio manager receives information through social, industry, and company networks. Therefore, the first criteria, leveraging the wisdom of crowds, focuses on how well the investment process leverages the *collective intelligence* of the team and the firm. Collective intelligence is particularly important for fixed-income portfolios as different investment processes within the same firm rely on forecasts of common macroeconomic variables (i.e., interest rates, GDP growth, inflation), which have profound effects on returns.

As introduced in Chapter 5, James Surowiecki's *wisdom of the crowd* phenomenon suggests that the aggregated view of multiple individuals is typically more accurate than any single individual in the crowd. There are numerous empirical validations of the wisdom of crowds, ranging from decontextualized laboratory tasks to forecasts of real-world geopolitical and macroeconomic events.[12,13] One natural experiment on a casino "count the crystals" task found taking five estimates over time from a single individual is only as good as taking estimates from 1.5 individuals. Extrapolating from the data, infinite estimates from a single individual is not as accurate as taking single estimates from two individuals.[14]

The error canceling function of diversity. There is mounting evidence on the importance of diversity (in the sense of different perspectives and/or points of view) and active fund management is no exception. In addition to the empirical evidence, it can be shown mathematically that diversity improves the accuracy of forecasts because diversity can cancel out errors in individual forecasts. The overall error in the forecasts across a group of individuals can be reduced by pooling their forecasts ($E[x_i]$). Assuming the individual forecasts (x_i) are uncorrelated, the variation in individual estimates ($Var[x_i]$) reduces the error in the forecast. If θ is the true value, then we have the following identity:

$$(E[x_i] - \theta)^2 = E[(x_i - \theta)^2] - (Var[x_i]) \tag{10.1}$$

$(E[x_i] - \theta)^2$, the error in crowd forecast, is always lower than the average error of individual estimates $E[(x_i - \theta)^2]$, so long as there is variation in the views and some knowledge in the crowd.

In the case of active fund management, suppose we have five equally skilled analysts generating forecasts for a particular issuer. If no other information is available, then a portfolio manager is better off betting on the average estimate of all five analysts versus betting on the forecast of any one analyst that may be randomly selected through time.[15] If there is information in the population and enough diversity and independence in opinions, the errors in each of the views will cancel out to result in a more accurate forecast. While it is often conventionally accepted wisdom that making good collective decisions focuses on consensus building and compromise, surfacing dissent and the aggregating heterogeneous views will result in better outcomes.

Unfortunately, aspects of our psychology make surfacing and processing diverse views challenging. It is harder to communicate with and trust someone who does not share your background, assumptions, and beliefs. Therefore, homogenous teams benefit from being able to share complex information and reach decisions faster. However, numerous risks fall under the umbrella of *groupthink*. When group harmony is valued above accuracy, there is a lack of challenge and sense-testing ideas. While individual team members may have relevant and unique information, information that is "common knowledge" is typically discussed because it feels good to agree. Finally, since it appears on the surface that everyone is in violent agreement, there is excess optimism in group decisions.

Risk managers can work with investment teams to adopt processes to ensure that unique views are aired in team discussions. For example, by administering a regular survey in which each team member reports his or her current conviction on trades and market views prior to meetings, the risk managers can lead a team discussion guided by the responses, with particular attention paid to team members with diverse views. Surveys supplement and structure debate, which is the typical aggregation mechanism used by investment teams.

Independence is blind. Diversity can cancel out errors so long as the errors of the individuals are uncorrelated. Thus, team members must maintain independent thought and have the psychological safety to express it. This sounds simple enough, but again, psychology can get in the way. For example, our aversion to sticking out from the herd can lead those who have nonconsensus views to keep quiet. Conformity and deference to authority are other strong forces that can lead team members to adopt the view of the team leader, particularly if he or she is a dominant or highly revered leader.

Here again, administering surveys prior to team discussions can help ensure team members are forming independent views rather than self-censoring when others voice their opinions. Risk managers can use surveys to collect market views and then *blind* these views before presenting survey responses to the rest of the team. In this way, people remain unbiased by the source of the view, whether it be a junior analyst or a senior investor.

It is important for an individual to maintain independence of thought *even within oneself*. Yet our psychology punishes inconsistency. We view people who are inconsistent in their views as "flip floppers" who lack integrity. Within ourselves, we have a strong desire to see ourselves as consistent as well. As a result, we may believe that changing our mind is a sign of weakness. However, elite forecasters with persistent track records of exceptional performance strongly disagree with these statements and strongly agree with statements like, *"Allowing oneself to be convinced by an opposing argument is a sign of good character."* This attitude, termed *active open-mindedness*, allows people the freedom to have a series of views that are more independent through time than the average forecaster.[16]

Emergent benefits of decentralization. Markets are the ultimate example of a decentralized aggregation mechanism. Price emerges from information aggregated across areas of expertise and geographies. In order to cultivate the wisdom of the crowds in a local team environment, mechanisms should encourage decentralized information gathering and specialization of expertise.

Evaluation of the team's network structure is an indication of how permeable the membrane of the team is to decentralized ideas and information or whether the team is at risk of being in an echo chamber. An echo chamber forms in a network when a single idea is repeated again and again because everyone in the highly connected network speaks to each other. People come to believe the view due to repetition rather than on the merits of the argument.[17]

The risk of echo chambers can be assessed through discussion with the team or if network data on team communication is available. Risk managers can use network analytics, such as the *clustering coefficient*. Exhibit 10.4 shows the end points of the continuum of the clustering coefficient. In the star configuration, the target team (in black) tends to speak to teams (in dark gray) who do not speak much to each other. In the clique configuration, a team is more at risk of being in an echo chamber. A decentralized network structure promotes both diversity of thought and independence, while also increasing the chance of accessing expertise and localized knowledge. These elements are crucial in cases in which the crowd is "wicked," that is, when the central tendency of the distribution of views is dead wrong.

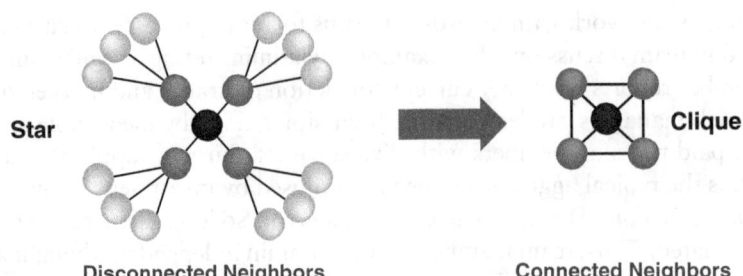

Star   **Clique**

Disconnected Neighbors   **Connected Neighbors**

EXHIBIT 10.4   Network Configurations for Evaluating Decentralization
Source: BlackRock. Based on concepts in Yang, S., Keller, F. B., and Zheng, L. (2017). *Social network analysis: Methods and examples.* Thousand Oaks, CA: SAGE. https://dx.doi.org/10.4135/9781071802847.

10.5.2   Bolster System II Thinking

One of the many roles of a risk manager is to ensure that the risks taken are deliberate. In his book *Thinking, Fast and Slow*, Daniel Kahneman (2011) adopts a model that distinguishes deliberate thinking from automatic, intuitive heuristics. These heuristics or rules of thumb are thought to serve us well most of the time but can sometimes steer us into systematic, predictable mistakes. "Automatic System I" is fast and effortless, as it executes coordinated mental programs in parallel. "Deliberate System II" is slow and serial, requiring self-control and draining cognitive resources as it serially processes mental programs. Both systems can learn and contain information. A good investment process harnesses both systems, but the first step is to bridle System I thinking to stave off its associated behavioral biases.

Self-imposed speed bumps. A good investment process will introduce "speed bumps" to curb System I's *fast* thinking. System II needs time to process and reflect on information, which can be achieved by simply writing down the reasons for the decision. Most investment teams document the investment thesis and accompanying analysis as part of their process. However, the documentation is often extensive during the research phase and sparse during the execution and position management phase, which is when time pressure is more intense and emotions are heightened for a live trade.

To introduce "speed bumps" into the investment process, an investment team can document the rationale for every trade, including top-ups and trims. Further, some teams use a shared "trade diary" for each position, where team members can pose questions and reflections and offer ongoing analysis.

For investment teams that want more from their documentation, *verifiable predictions* can help by tying forecasts to a verifiable reality. Verifiable predictions tie the investment thesis to something observable that elucidates whether the thesis is valid or not. Instead of saying "the spread on the bond will tighten," verifiable probabilistic predictions detail whether the bond will tighten over a specified time horizon and for what reasons, resulting in better feedback and analytics that help the team identify the team's unique sources of alpha and their limits.

Hold the reigns on uncertainty with plans. In the behavioral literature, a distinction is made between "hot" and "cold" state decision-making, which maps loosely to System I and System II thinking. People tend to underestimate the influence of *affect* or visceral factors, such as emotion, pain, hunger, temptations, on their decisions. As behavioral economist George Loewenstein noted, "*Affect has the capacity to transform us as human beings, profoundly; in different affective states, it is almost as if we are different people. Affect influences virtually every aspect of human functioning: perception, attention, inference, learning, memory, goal choice, physiology, reflexes, self-concept, and so on."*

The performance of a live trade triggers "hot" state decision-making for portfolio managers, while thinking through how to manage an investment idea before it has been executed is characterized as "cold" state decision-making. A portfolio manager is typically less encumbered with emotions when researching a view. However, emotions are normally triggered based on how the idea performs. By documenting a trade action plan, a portfolio manager or researcher can plan how he or she will manage the trade under different future states. Of course, this plan requires updating as new information arises but provides a sound roadmap to draw portfolio managers back to their original views that were untainted by visceral factors. If creating plans at the trade level is not feasible, the plan can be constructed at the portfolio level, e.g., triggers to re-risk or de-risk the portfolio.

While hot and cold thinking both have their benefits and limitations, there is some debate about whether acting on instinct has its advantages. While conventional wisdom states it is only through experience that intuition is formed (e.g., trained chess players recognize a pattern and form a strategy instantaneously), the latest research finds emotions are essential for decisions.[18] The *emotion as information hypothesis* competes with the more conventional wisdom and suggests emotions contain information, particularly about risks or threats in the environment.

When faced with uncertainty, action plans arm the portfolio manager with the benefit of "cold state" or System II thinking, which involves planning, mental simulations of future states. Action plans also help portfolio managers to consider who is on the other side of the trade. Since group debates can become heated, one way to deal with different points of view is to record potential reactions to different circumstances (e.g., what you will do if you are wrong and your colleague is right?). Disagreements can turn from a debate of whether to execute the trade to how the trade will be managed if different team members' views turn out to be a reality.

Risk managers can encourage teams to record action plans in order to document what should be monitored to understand whether the investment thesis is still working. For example, risk managers may assess perspective valuation by tracking the OAS of new issues. Thresholds could be set to trigger required actions, such as adding, trimming, taking profit, or stopping out the trade. For a single trade, several factors may be monitored, each with several predefined triggers for action. If a trigger is breached, the team can meet to decide whether to execute the plan. It may be that new information has invalidated the previous plan. Thus, action plans are not simply triggers to act, they are also triggers to update or re-underwrite the investment thesis.

Risk managers may have a rebellion on their hands for suggesting any form of additional documentation, especially since action plans can be particularly complex. However, it is worth discussing action plans at least for the most concentrated positions or the most influential factors that influence performance, such as duration. A good investment process will set up decision-makers to have access to two different *types of thinking* when they must make a decision. The risk manager must draw the investor back to the previously agreed plan, particularly in times of extreme risk events.

10.5.3 Facilitate Continuous Learning

Learning flourishes when frequent and unambiguous feedback is available. However, investment time horizons are often measured in years, making statistically meaningful input sparse.

TABLE 10.2 Ego-Protective Barriers to Learning from Mistakes

Attribution bias	Success is attributed to skill, and failure is attributed to bad luck. Similarly, success is attributed to oneself, and failure is attributed to others.
Overconfidence	Most people, including experts, think they know more than they actually do. Overconfidence can lead to excessive risk-taking and big surprises when confidence intervals are too narrow.
Hindsight bias	Once we know the outcome of an uncertain event, we have the sense that it was inevitable and misremember our prior predictions in line with what actually happened, aka, the "knew it all along effect."
Outcome bias	It is tempting to judge decisions by their outcome rather than the process by which the decision is made or by taking into account the role of chance.
Choice-supportive bias	The tendency to ascribe positive characteristics to a choice after it has been selected. The post hoc rationalizations we make for decisions are often different and more optimistic than the logic that was the basis for the decision.
Confirmation bias	The tendency to selectively attend to evidence and generate reasons that support your prior belief. This can lead to an unwillingness to change one's mind when new evidence presents itself; an inability to update based on new information.

Even when time horizons are shorter, feedback is extremely noisy due to the stochastic nature of markets. Further, it is difficult to make time for postmortems as portfolio managers' time is dominated by forecasting the future, not reliving the past. Even when time is carved out for reviewing decisions, numerous biases that protect our egos may get in the way (see Table 10.2).

Risk managers and professional athletic coaches oftentimes play similar roles. Professional athletes will watch replays of bad plays in order to improve, but they cannot succeed without the help of a good coach. Similarly, risk managers can help portfolio managers identify their blind spots. Documentation is important, not just to stop "fast thinking," but also to create the "replay" of the decision process. A good coach will conduct the review focusing not only on what happened, but also on the logic and the mindset driving the behavior.

Close feedback loops. Behavioral economist Richard Thaler offers simple yet sage advice: "Write stuff down."[19] This helps ward off the hindsight bias, the tendency to misremember one's prior predictions in line with the actual outcome. If the hindsight bias interferes with us knowing "when we got it wrong," we are doomed to repeat the same mistakes over and over and enter new decisions overconfidently. Further, the outcome bias leads us to judge decisions by whether the outcome was positive or negative rather than the process by which the decision is made or by taking into account the role of chance. Thaler asserts, *"Any firm that can distinguish skill from chance has a leg up."* By simply recording and revisiting the decision rationale and prior predictions after a successful trade is closed, portfolio managers benefit by seeing if they were right or if they were lucky. Reviewing after an unsuccessful trade tells them if they were right but exogenous factors got in the way or if they were just plain wrong.

In addition to supporting System II thinking, documenting speed bumps and action plans can help to support continuous learning. It creates a record that brings color to postmortems and can even be codified for analysis. Verifiable predictions enable hit rates to be calculated across different types of ideas. Verifiable *probabilistic* predictions keep the outcome bias in check—if you are 60% confident, you should be right 60% of the time. Investment forecasts must always be probabilistic due to the challenges of predicting the future and the stochastic nature of markets. Aggregating across probabilistic forecasts helps give the portfolio manager due credit for well-calibrated conviction and keeps overconfidence in check.

As previously discussed, most investment decisions are made in a group context. Here, the attribution bias can get in the way, as people tend to attribute good outcomes to themselves and bad outcomes to others. Further, since only the group investment decision is implemented, individual team members have no way to track how a trade would have performed based on their individual judgments. Hence, valuable learning opportunities are lost. This can be rectified by completing a daily conviction survey on trades, where the risk managers are able to compute the hypothetical P&L of the trade managed to each team member's reported conviction at the time.

Cultivate a growth mindset. When presenting analytics or conducting postmortems, risk managers should be aware that for almost any human with a pulse, getting feedback on one's mistakes is painful. Just as important as the accuracy of the information is the subtext of the conversations, because how well people learn from mistakes depends on their beliefs about learning and intelligence.

A growth mindset[20] is the belief that talent is just the starting point and that abilities can be developed through dedication and hard work. People who have a growth mindset can overcome ego-protective biases when they believe that mistakes are opportunities to learn and improve. In contrast, a fixed mindset leads people to view failure as evidence of an immutable lack of ability and disengage. Empirically, those with a growth mindset show greater allocation of attention to mistakes and show better subsequent performance.

In the context of risk management, this highlights the importance of refraining from labeling portfolio managers as "skilled" or "talented." Instead, risk managers should focus on the sophistication of the process, dedication, hard work, progress up the learning curve, and a willingness to examine mistakes. Language should emphasize future performance, using words like "yet/not yet." Bad investments should be recast as a learning experience. Difficult situations, such as periods of prolonged volatility and drawdowns, should be recast as opportunities to improve investment processes and build personal coping strategies that will be useful later in careers. Looking at behavioral analytics that reveal systematic mistakes need not be a painful experience if the identification of bias is framed as an opportunity. Random, unsystematic mistakes are much more unfortunate as they are harder to correct.

Finally, risk managers should ensure portfolio managers have a protected learning environment. Risk management should be independent from talent selection and compensation decisions. This type of environment appeals to investors who are curious and willing to evolve their process.

10.6 CONCLUSION

At BlackRock, risk management involves establishing a close but independent relationship with portfolio managers. A great risk management function should engage closely with the investment management process, but never lose its objectivity. This is much easier said than done. By having in-depth knowledge of the investment process, risk managers generate informed views of the investment teams' strengths and weaknesses. Risk managers identify risks, exposures, and concentrations that the portfolio team may not be focused on, helping to ensure that investment activities are consistent with client objectives and portfolio management strategies. Risk managers review the investment process with an objective lens and provide a different perspective to portfolio management.

The portfolio manager and risk manager relationship intensifies with the application of behavioral finance. It shifts the microscope from risks in markets and portfolios to risks in the psychology of the portfolio managers themselves, resulting in more intense scrutiny of systematic biases with decision-making analytics. It means moving the investment team away from unilateral decisions from their lead portfolio manager. It means urging portfolio managers to invest time in documentation and planning. It means holding portfolio managers to their investment process even when extreme performance triggers overconfidence on the upside and denial on the downside. Behavioral finance offers strategies to supplement traditional risk management with tools that take human behavioral risks into account.

Ultimately, risk managers must cultivate a culture of trust and constructive challenge with the portfolio management team. The trust derives both from the competence of the risk manager and the sense that the risk manager "has the portfolio manager's back." Through this perspective, challenge can be viewed as additive rather than a threat. Risk managers should question rather than instruct, interpreting analytics as a team with a recognition that constraints rather than bias may be driving the pattern. The art is deciphering post hoc rationalizations or defensiveness from legitimate alternative explanations in order to drive continuous improvement for clients.

NOTES

1. Matthew Wang and Katie Day contributed to the initial development of this chapter.
2. In an informal poll of active, nonsystematic BlackRock investors, more than 95% agree with the statement, "My job has a lot of emotional highs and lows."
3. The predominant bias in allocation decisions is *myopic loss aversion*: an excess allocation to fixed income due to a short-term focus on the possibility of losses in equity markets.
4. Bruce, 2016.
5. https://www.ssrn.com/index.cfm/en/.
6. Kahneman and Tversky, 1979.
7. Imas, 2016.
8. Kahneman et al., 1990.
9. Preferences were elicited in an incentive-compatible fashion to prevent participants from giving a high number as a negotiation tactic. They had to record for each price point whether they would sell or keep, and then one price point was selected at random to count.
10. Strahilevitz and Loewenstein, 1998.
11. See, for example, Heath and Heath, 2008.
12. For a review see Clemen, 1989.
13. For details on real-world forecasts see Tetlock and Gardner, 2016.
14. van Dolder and van den Assem 2018.
15. Of course, time and resource is finite so every team member cannot form an informed view on every decision, but surely, there are some crucial elements of the process that would benefit from a crowd view.
16. See Tetlock and Gardner, 2016.
17. See Pentland, 2013.
18. See Damasio, 1994.
19. Javetski and Koller, 2018.
20. Dweck, 2009.

CHAPTER 11

Performance Attribution[1]

Reade Ryan
Managing Director, Risk & Quantitative Analysis, BlackRock

Carol Yu
Vice President, Risk & Quantitative Analysis, BlackRock (2022)

11.1 INTRODUCTION

Portfolio managers, especially those who are managing portfolios relative to a benchmark or "benchmarked portfolios," typically make investment decisions based on three questions:

1. How much of performance is generated from risk-on or risk-off positioning?
2. What part of performance is generated from specific sector exposures or asset class allocation bets?
3. How much of performance is generated by selection decisions within an asset class?

Performance attribution analysis decomposes investment returns into their sources of performance, providing portfolio and risk managers with a comprehensive understanding of the drivers of performance and investment results.

Performance attribution has evolved to become a critical tool for risk managers. As the fourth pillar of BlackRock's Investment Risk Management Paradigm (IRMP), *performance attribution* allows for the degree of consistency between intended bets and actual performance to be determined. Over the last 30 years, various performance attribution models and techniques have emerged, which can yield different results. Regardless of the approach, performance attribution combines quantitative and qualitative measures to decompose investment results and helps portfolio managers understand the impact of various drivers on their performance.

When determining the appropriate performance attribution approach, risk managers first need to distinguish between portfolios that track a benchmark and those that do not. Benchmarked portfolios tend to have more options to conduct performance attribution. However, effective performance attribution can also be achieved for portfolios that do not explicitly track a benchmark. A portfolio without a benchmark is a cash or hurdle-rate account, and risk managers can perform effective attribution leveraging factor-based attribution, which is discussed later in this chapter. While there are a multitude of performance attribution approaches and analytical techniques, this chapter focuses on Brinson and factor-based methodologies.

11.2 BRINSON ATTRIBUTION AND BEYOND

Investment managers and their clients always look for insights into the efficacy of their actions. What drove performance? Were managers' actions consistent with their purported investment styles? Introduced in 1986, Gary Brinson, Randolph Hood, and Gilbert Beebower developed a framework to determine how distinct investment decisions impacted portfolio returns over a specific period.[2] The market value Brinson model uses a weighting scheme to assess positions and decomposes a portfolio's active returns relative to a passive benchmark. Originally, the Brinson model included three terms—allocation, selection, and a residual cross-term. However, practioners have typically simplified the original model and analyze portfolio performance based on allocation and selection measures.

Fixed-income benchmarked portfolios can leverage the Brinson framework to identify a baseline and analyze performance based on allocation and selection decisions. Practitioners can and generally do use *Brinson attribution* on returns that have been risk-adjusted, meaning that the level and change in reference interest rates are stripped away to better quantify the value-add from allocation and selection decisions.

Let us assume that the portfolio's return over a certain period of time is R_p, while R_b represents the benchmark return over the same period of time. Given that $w_{p,i}$ ($w_{b,i}$) is the portfolio (benchmark) weight in sector i and $r_{p,i}$ ($r_{b,i}$) is the portfolio's (benchmark's) return in sector i, the portfolio's active return, the differential return between a portfolio and its benchmark, in a given period can be expressed as:

$$R_p - R_b = \sum_i w_{p,i} \cdot r_{p,i} - \sum_i w_{b,i} \cdot r_{b,i} \tag{11.1}$$

Using algebra, the right-hand side of Equation 11.1 can be rewritten:

$$= \sum_i (w_{p,i} - w_{b,i})(r_{b,i} - R_b) + \sum_i w_{p,i}(r_{p,i} - r_{b,i}) \tag{11.2}$$

The first term in Equation 11.2 measures a portfolio manager's skill at allocating market value to different sectors. It measures the performance generated by being over- or underweight different sectors relative to the benchmark's weights across an interval of time. If the portfolio's return in each sector equals that of the benchmark, then the portfolio's total active performance is equal to this first term. The second term in Equation 11.2 is the portfolio-weighted difference in the sector returns of the portfolio versus its benchmark. It measures the performance generated by a portfolio manager's skill at selecting different securities within a given sector. These selection decisions generate potentially different returns in each sector for the portfolio relative to its benchmark. If the portfolio's sector weights are the same as its benchmark, then the portfolio's total active performance is equal to this second term.

Exhibit 11.1 is an intentionally simplistic example of market value Brinson attribution with only two sectors in which the portfolio and benchmark can be invested.

Exhibit 11.1 shows a case where a portfolio manager only made allocation decisions, and thus, the performance of Sector A and Sector B in the portfolio is the same as in the benchmark. Using Equation 11.1, the portfolio sector return is 12.50%, compared with the benchmark returns of 10%, demonstrating that the active performance is 2.50%. In this example, portfolio returns were generated from allocation decisions only—the portfolio was

	Market Value %		Sector Returns		Sector Allocation	Security Selection
	Port	Bench	Port	Bench		
Sector A	50%	33%	20.0%	20.0%	1.67%	0.0%
Sector B	50%	67%	5.0%	5.0%	0.83%	0.0%
TOTAL	**100%**	**100%**	**12.50%**	**10.00%**	**2.50%**	**0.00%**

EXHIBIT 11.1 Market Value Brinson Attribution
Source: BlackRock. For illustrative purposes only.

overweight the outperforming sector, generating a return of +1.67%, and underweight the underperforming sector, generating a return of +0.83%.

Now consider an example where the portfolio and benchmark performance are not identical. In Exhibit 11.2, the portfolio manager makes the same allocation decisions within the portfolio as he or she did in Exhibit 11.1. However, the portfolio's securities in Sector A underperform those in the benchmark (15% versus 20%), while the portfolio and benchmark securities in Sector B perform the same.

Based on these assumptions, the active performance in Exhibit 11.2 is also 0.00%, as the total return for both the portfolio and benchmark is 10.00%. However, in this example, while positive returns were generated by the same allocation decisions (+2.50%) as in Exhibit 11.1, these were offset by the negative selection in Sector A (–2.50%), which underperformed the benchmark's securities.

Brinson attribution allows a portfolio's return to be viewed from multiple dimensions by drilling down into sector and selection performance. Brinson is straightforward to calculate and easy to interpret. As demonstrated, only market values and sector returns relative to a benchmark are needed to analyze the impact of sector allocation and security selection. However, Brinson cannot meaningfully be used outside of the context of a benchmark and can be too coarse a method if the decisions analyzed are not material to the actual portfolio performance. Additionally, basic Brinson does not analyze the impacts of being overweight or underweight to the market. There is a limiting assumption associated with classic Brinson attribution that goes beyond the lack of "market." Brinson implies that the sectors and sub-sectors reflect the scope of allocation decisions, and it assumes that securities were chosen in the context of the sectors, which may not necessarily be true.

In practice, portfolios tend to have more than two sectors. Exhibit 11.4, while still relatively simplistic, demonstrates Brinson attribution in a sample portfolio (Exhibit 11.3) that contains three sectors and nine securities. At the sector level, Exhibit 11.4 illustrates

	Market Value %		Sector Returns		Sector Allocation	Security Selection
	Port	Bench	Port	Bench		
Sector A	50%	33%	15.0%	20.0%	1.67%	−2.50%
Sector B	50%	67%	5.0%	5.0%	0.83%	0.0%
TOTAL	**100%**	**100%**	**10.00%**	**10.00%**	**2.50%**	**−2.50%**

EXHIBIT 11.2 Market Value Brinson Attribution
Source: BlackRock. For illustrative purposes only.

	Portfolio Weight (%)	Benchmark Weight (%)
Corporate	60	50
ALTICE FRANCE SA	15	10
ANHEUSER-BUSCH INBEV FINANCE INC	15	10
CVS HEALTH CORP	10	15
GOLDMAN SACHS GROUP INC	10	15
PETSMART INC	10	0
Government	25	15
FHLMC REFERENCE NOTE	10	5
TENNESSEE VALLEY AUTHORITY	15	10
Securitized	15	35
CCCIT_07-A3	5	20
FORDF_18-2	10	15
TOTAL	100	100

EXHIBIT 11.3 Sample Portfolio and Benchmark Weights
Source: BlackRock Aladdin. For illustrative purposes only.

that the portfolio is overweight corporate and government positions and underweight securitized positions. The portfolio sector return is 275 bp, compared with the benchmark of 198 bp, resulting in 77 bp of active performance. In Exhibit 11.4, the portfolio manager's decision to be overweight corporates was positive, resulting in one-third of returns generated from allocation decision and two-thirds of returns were generated from security selection.

Brinson attribution can be extended beyond the simple market value case by using risk-adjusted weights and returns for each sector. In the remainder of the section, several beta-adjusted attribution examples are reviewed, but first we will briefly discuss how to conduct risk-adjusted attribution and how the formulas change.

Let us define the beta $\beta_{p,i}$ ($\beta_{b,i}$) as portfolio's sector i beta to the benchmark, which can be calculated:[3]

$$\beta_{p,i} = \frac{Cov(r_{p,i} \cdot R_b)}{Var(R_b)} \tag{11.3}$$

	Market Value %		Sector Returns		Sector Allocation	Security Selection
	Port	Bench	Port	Bench		
Corporate	60	50	441	351	35	54
Government	25	15	15	10	1	1
Securitized	15	35	45	62	(12)	(3)
TOTAL	100	100	275	198	24	53

EXHIBIT 11.4 Brinson Attribution in Sample Portfolio
Source: BlackRock. For illustrative purposes only.

Using these betas, Equation 11.1 can be rewritten:

$$R_p - R_b = \sum_i \beta_{p,i} w_{p,i} \cdot \frac{r_{p,i}}{\beta_{p,i}} - \sum_i \beta_{b,i} w_{b,i} \cdot \frac{r_{b,i}}{\beta_{b,i}} = \sum_i \widehat{w}_{p,i} \cdot \check{r}_{p,i} - \sum_i \widehat{w}_{b,i} \cdot \check{r}_{b,i} \qquad (11.4)$$

where $\widehat{w}_{p,i} = \beta_{p,i} \cdot w_{p,i}$ and $\check{r}_{p,i} = \frac{r_{p,i}}{\beta_{p,i}}$ represents the sector's beta-adjusted weight in the portfolio and sector's return per unit of beta respectively.

The total beta for the portfolio is:

$$\beta_p = \sum_i \widehat{w}_{p,i} = \sum_i \beta_{p,i} w_{p,i} \qquad (11.5)$$

Note that by definition $\beta_b = \sum \beta_{b,i} w_{b,i} = 1$.

If the portfolio and the benchmark moved exactly according to their betas, then the active performance of the portfolio will be equal to $(\beta_p - \beta_b) * \widehat{R}_b$, where $\widehat{R}_b = \frac{R_b}{\beta_b}$, which equals R_b. In such an example, returns would be generated from the amount that the portfolio is overweight or underweight the benchmark in beta terms.

Performing a similar arithmetic slight of hand on Equation 11.3 that we used on Equation 11.1, we get the following:

$$R_p - R_b = (\beta_p - \beta_b)R_b + \sum_i (\widehat{w}_{p,i} - \widehat{w}_{b,i}) (\widehat{r}_{b,i} - R_b) + \sum_i \widehat{w}_{p,i} (\widehat{r}_{p,i} - \widehat{r}_{b,i}) \qquad (11.6)$$

The first term on the right-hand side of equation is the active performance generated from being overweight or underweight the benchmark in beta terms. The remaining terms represent the standard attribution model, where the weights and returns are "beta-adjusted."

To demonstrate beta-adjusted attribution, consider Exhibit 11.5, where the portfolio manager makes the same allocation decisions as he did in Exhibit 11.1. However, now we have the additional information that Sector A is four times riskier than Sector B, as measured by their betas, 2.0 and 0.5, respectively.

In Exhibit 11.5, as in Exhibit 11.1, the portfolio outperformed the benchmark and the active performance is 2.50%. Market value Brinson attribution suggested that the allocation decisions drove this outperformance. However, now we consider the market beta associated with each sector. Thus, we need to calculate the beta-adjusted market values along with the beta-adjusted returns to understand the impacts of sector allocation and security selection. Since Sector A and Sector B performed in line with their betas, beta-adjusted attribution demonstrates that there was no sector allocation or security selection returns. The outperformance was, in this method, solely the result of the overall portfolio-level decision to be long the market relative to the benchmark. Thus, the total active return equals the active beta 0.25 multiplied by the benchmark's return 10%, which is equal to 2.50%.

Now consider another beta-adjusted attribution example (Exhibit 11.6), where the portfolio manager makes the same allocation decisions as he did in Exhibit 11.5. However, in this scenario, the portfolio's returns in Sector A are assumed to underperform the benchmark, resulting in no active performance. The fund-level beta allocation is 2.50%, demonstrating that portfolio returns were generated due to exposure to a rising market. Using the beta-adjusted weights and returns, there is no sector allocation, as the benchmark beta-adjusted returns are identical to the overall return on the market. However, the portfolio lost money due to security selection (–2.50%) because the portfolio's beta-adjusted return in Sector A is less than that of the benchmark.

	Market Value %		Betas		Sector Returns		Beta-Adjusted MV%s		Beta-Adjusted Returns		Sector Allocation	Security Selection	Fund-Level Beta Allocation Return
	Port	Bench	Port	Bench	Port	Bench	Port	Bench	Port	Bench			
Sector A	50%	33%	2	2	20.0%	20.0%	100.0%	66.7%	10.0%	10.0%	0.00%	0.0%	
Sector B	50%	67%	0.5	0.5	5.0%	5.0%	25.0%	33.3%	10.0%	10.0%	0.00%	0.0%	
TOTAL	100%	100%	1.25	1.00	12.50%	10.00%	125%	100%	10.00%	10.00%	0.00%	0.00%	2.50%

EXHIBIT 11.5 Beta-adjusted Attribution

Source: BlackRock. For illustrative purposes only.

	Market Value %		Betas		Sector Returns		Beta-Adjusted MV%s		Beta-Adjusted Returns		Sector Allocation	Security Selection	Fund-Level Beta Allocation Return
	Port	Bench	Port	Bench	Port	Bench	Port	Bench	Port	Bench			
Sector A	50%	33%	2	2	15.0%	20.0%	100.0%	66.7%	7.5%	10.0%	0.00%	−2.5%	
Sector B	50%	67%	0.5	0.5	5.0%	5.0%	25.0%	33.3%	10.0%	10.0%	0.00%	0.0%	
TOTAL	100%	100%	1.25	1.00	10.0%	10.0%	125%	100%	8.00%	10.00%	0.00%	−2.50%	2.50%

EXHIBIT 11.6   Beta-adjusted Attribution

Source: BlackRock. For illustrative purposes only.

11.2.1   Comparing Market Value Brinson Attribution to Beta-Adjusted Attribution

If we compare market value Brinson attribution with beta-adjusted attribution, the drivers of performance yield different results. Consider a portfolio manager who makes allocation decisions by being overweight and underweight the benchmark, but both the portfolio and benchmark returns are identical (10%). In Exhibit 11.7, the standard Brinson attribution results suggest that there is no active performance, along with no sector allocation nor security selection returns generated.

However, if we take risk into consideration and add the betas, Exhibit 11.8 demonstrates that Portfolio A is four times riskier than Sector B. Therefore, if the market is up, the portfolio manager should expect that Sector A returns would be four times greater than Sector B. Using the beta-adjusted weights and returns, there is no active performance. However, fund-level beta allocation is 2.50%, indicating that the portfolio generated returns from the up market, but lost money due to sector allocation (–2.50%).

Comparing Brinson versus beta-adjusted attribution models, Exhibit 11.9 demonstrates that the portfolio manager makes the same allocation decisions within a portfolio as he did in Exhibit 11.7, by being overweight and underweight the benchmark. However, Sector A underperforms the benchmark (15% versus 20%), while Sector B performs in line with the benchmark (5%). Based on the results, there would be no active performance. Since the portfolio is overweight the overperforming sector, performance was generated from sector allocation (2.50%). However, these returns were offset by security selection (–2.50%), as the portfolio returns in Sector A were less than the benchmark.

Exhibit 11.10 shows that the portfolio manager made the same allocation decisions as he did in Exhibit 11.9. However, Sector A's beta in the portfolio is 1.5, instead of 2. Again, if the market is up, it would be expected that Sector A's returns would be three times the amount of Sector B. Therefore, even though Sector A underperformed the benchmark in absolute terms, both Sector A and Sector B returns were in line with beta, and there was no attribution to either sector allocation or security selection.

Performance attribution strives to analyze portfolio returns, relative to a benchmark, in a way that is aligned with how the portfolio manager takes risks. Performance attribution focuses on understanding the portfolio returns relative to the risks taken. There are many risk measures that can be used to perform attribution. If a portfolio manager makes decisions based on asset class, then performance attribution should be analyzed through an asset class lens. Similarly, if the portfolio manager makes decisions based on ratings, then rating buckets should be used to analyze performance. Ultimately, performance attribution should be aligned with the way investors make decisions.

| | Market Value % | | Sector Returns | | Sector | Security |
	Port	Bench	Port	Bench	Allocation	Selection
Sector A	50%	33%	10.0%	10.0%	0.00%	0.0%
Sector B	50%	67%	10.0%	10.0%	0.00%	0.0%
TOTAL	100%	100%	10.0%	10.0%	0.00%	0.00%

EXHIBIT 11.7 Brinson Attribution
Source: BlackRock. For illustrative purposes only.

	Market Value %		Betas		Sector Returns		Beta-Adjusted MV%s		Beta-Adjusted Returns		Sector Allocation	Security Selection	Fund-Level Beta Allocation Return
	Port	Bench	Port	Bench	Port	Bench	Port	Bench	Port	Bench			
Sector A	50%	33%	2	2	10.0%	10.0%	100.0%	66.7%	5.0%	5.0%	−1.67%	0.0%	
Sector B	50%	67%	0.5	0.5	10.0%	10.0%	25.0%	33.3%	20.0%	20.0%	−0.83%	0.0%	
TOTAL	100%	100%	1.25	1.00	10.0%	10.0%	125%	100%	8.00%	10.00%	−2.50%	0.00%	2.50%

EXHIBIT 11.8 Beta-adjusted Attribution

Source: BlackRock. For illustrative purposes only.

	Market Value %		Sector Returns		Sector Allocation	Security Selection
	Port	Bench	Port	Bench		
Sector A	50%	33%	15.0%	20.0%	1.67%	−2.5%
Sector B	50%	67%	5.0%	5.0%	0.83%	0.0%
TOTAL	**100%**	**100%**	**10.0%**	**10.0%**	**2.50%**	**−2.50%**

EXHIBIT 11.9 Brinson Attribution
Source: BlackRock. For illustrative purposes only.

11.3   FACTOR-BASED ATTRIBUTION

An alternative approach, factor-based attribution, breaks down portfolio returns across multiple factors, providing portfolio managers with a rich set of return factors to understand their investment thesis and mandate. Factor-based attribution leverages the risk models that are used to calculate ex ante risk to describe performance of benchmarked or nonbenchmarked portfolios. As the converse of ex ante risk calculations, factor-based attribution data are derived from historical time series of the factors and their returns. Ex post attribution can be performed given exposures and returns over a given period.

Factor-based attribution can be used to decompose portfolio performance into different components to determine whether or not investment returns are aligned with the portfolio manager's investment thesis. A fixed-income portfolio and each underlying securities' returns within the portfolio can be evaluated based on factor and idiosyncratic risk exposures. Factor-based attribution allows portfolio performance to be broken down into a parametric component (i.e., returns due to factor exposures) and an idiosyncratic component. Additionally, the factor model can be used to further break down the parametric component into (1) returns from the overall market exposure (i.e., returns from beta) and (2) returns from factor exposures that are orthogonal to the market (i.e., residual factor returns).

Factor-based attribution calculates how much market risk a portfolio assumes on its own or relative to a benchmark and can be used to determine how much of the return comes from the market beta. Generating a comprehensive set of decomposed returns, factor-based attribution demonstrates the impact of being overweight or underweight factor exposures, such as industries, maturities, or style-factors.

Using the sample portfolio and benchmark weights from Exhibit 11.3, Exhibit 11.11 illustrates factor-based attribution. Table 11.1 shows the individual returns for each security by factor, while Table 11.2 demonstrates how those factors contribute to active portfolio return. Table 11.3 aggregates performance results at the sector level, which can be used as a point of comparison to Brinson attribution.

In Exhibit 11.11, the portfolio is overweight corporates and government positions and underweight securitized positions. Factor-based attribution indicates that during the time period, the portfolio generated positive returns from corporate spreads (84 bp), carry (18 bp), and asset-backed securities (ABS) spreads (4 bp). However, these returns were offset primarily by negative idiosyncratic returns (−24.9 bp).

If we compare the Brinson attribution results from Exhibit 11.4 with the factor-based attribution results (Exhibit 11.11–Table 11.3), different stories emerge as to what is driving performance. In both cases, the results indicate that the portfolio generated returns from being overweight corporate positions and lost money for being underweight securitized positions.

	Market Value %		Betas		Sector Returns		Beta-Adjusted MV%s		Beta-Adjusted Returns		Sector Allocation	Security Selection	Fund-Level Beta Allocation Return
	Port	Bench	Port	Bench	Port	Bench	Port	Bench	Port	Bench			
Sector A	50%	33%	1.5	2	15.0%	20.0%	75.0%	66.7%	10.0%	10.0%	0.00%	0.0%	
Sector B	50%	67%	0.5	0.5	5.0%	5.0%	25.0%	33.3%	10.0%	10.0%	0.00%	0.0%	
TOTAL	100%	100%	1.00	1.00	10.0%	10.0%	100%	100%	10.00%	10.00%	0.00%	0.00%	0.00%

EXHIBIT 11.10 Beta-adjusted Attribution
Source: BlackRock. For illustrative purposes only.

However, by taking a closer look at how much of performance is attributed to allocation and selection, there is a difference between the two examples.

In the Brinson attribution example, the portfolio generated returns by being overweight corporate positions, i.e., allocation to corporate positions generated 35 bp of return while selection decisions generated 54 bp. However, factor-based attribution analyzes the results differently, by looking at the different factors to determine whether selection or allocation contributed to returns. In Exhibit 11.11, the portfolio's performance was largely driven from corporate spreads, which resulted in 85 bp of return. However, idiosyncratic returns were quite weak in the portfolio. Specifically, the largest idiosyncratic loss came from PetSmart (18 bp).

Diving further into the example, the factor-based attribution results indicated more positive performance from being overweight corporate spreads than the Brinson attribution results. Factor-based attribution considers how risky and exposed individual securities are to the factors. The PetSmart corporate bond was a particular risky bond. During a period of strong performance for corporates, the factor-based model would expect significant performance from the bond. However, PetSmart underperformed resulting in negative idiosyncratic risk. Market-value Brinson attribution did not take the riskiness of the security into consideration.

Portfolio and risk managers can use the contribution by individual security (Table 11.2) to gain more insight into allocation and selection decisions. While the portfolio generated returns, the factor-based attribution analysis indicated that the portfolio lost money due to selection (idiosyncratic) decisions. As illustrated, both Brinson attribution and factor-based attribution can be used to analyze performance drivers. However, the approaches generate different results due to their methodologies. Analysts must be very thoughtful when drawing inferences from these different approaches.

EXHIBIT 11.11   Factor-Based Attribution. This Exhibit 11.11 comprises of Tables 11.1, 11.2 and 11.3.

TABLE 11.1   Security Return Breakdown by Factors

	Carry	Rates	Corporate Spreads	Agency Spreads	ABS Spreads	Idio	Total (bp)
TENNESSEE VALLEY AUTHORITY	32	34	0	−43	0	(38)	(15)
ANHEUSER-BUSCH INBEV FINANCE INC	48	39	279	0	0	38	404
CCCIT_07-A3	37	54	0	0	−21	22	92
FHLMC REFERENCE NOTE	29	54	0	−14	0	(9)	60
CVS HEALTH CORP	40	48	273	0	0	24	385
FORDF_18-2	28	20	0	0	−17	(10)	21
GOLDMAN SACHS GROUP INC	30	8	86	0	0	24	148
ALTICE FRANCE SA	74	35	467	0	0	(27)	549
PETSMART INC	193	17	650	0	0	(179)	681

Source: BlackRock Aladdin. For illustrative purposes only.

TABLE 11.2 Active Portfolio Return Contribution by Security

	Portfolio Weight	Benchmark Weight	Active Weight	Carry Contribution	Rates Contribution	Corporate Spreads Contribution	Agency Spread Contribution	ABS Spreads Contribution	Idio Contribution	Total (bp) Contribution
TENNESSEE VALLEY AUTHORITY	15.0	10.0	5.0	1.6	1.7	—	(2.2)	—	(1.9)	(0.7)
ANHEUSER-BUSCH INBEV FINANCE INC	15.0	10.0	5.0	2.4	2.0	14.0	—	—	1.9	20.2
CCCIT_07-A3	5.0	20.0	(15.0)	(5.6)	(8.1)	—	—	3.2	(3.3)	(13.8)
FHLMC REFERENCE NOTE	10.0	5.0	5.0	1.5	2.7	—	(0.7)	—	(0.5)	3.0
CVS HEALTH CORP	10.0	15.0	(5.0)	(2.0)	(2.4)	(13.7)	—	—	(1.2)	(19.2)
FORDF_18-2	10.0	15.0	(5.0)	(1.4)	(1.0)	—	—	0.9	0.5	(1.1)
GOLDMAN SACHS GROUP INC	10.0	15.0	(5.0)	(1.5)	(0.4)	(4.3)	—	—	(1.2)	(7.4)
ALTICE FRANCE SA	15.0	10.0	5.0	3.7	1.8	23.4	—	—	(1.3)	27.5
PETSMART INC	10.0	—	10.0	19.3	1.7	65.0	—	—	(17.9)	68.1
TOTAL	100.0	100.0	—	18.0	(2.1)	84.4	(2.9)	4.0	(24.9)	76.5

Source: BlackRock Aladdin. For illustrative purposes only.

(Exhibit 11.11 Continued)

TABLE 11.3 Active Portfolio Return Contribution by Sector

	Active Weight	Carry Contribution	Rates Contribution	Corporate Spreads Contribution	Agency Spreads Contribution	ABS Spreads Contribution	Idio Contribution	Total (bp) Contribution
Corporate	10	22	3	84	—	—	(20)	89
Government	10	3	4	—	(3)	—	(2)	2
Securitized	(20)	(7)	(9)	—	—	4	(3)	(15)
Total	—	18	(2)	84	(3)	4	(25)	77

Source: BlackRock Aladdin. For illustrative purposes only.

11.4 EQUITY FUNDAMENTAL FACTOR-BASED ATTRIBUTION

Just as factor-based attribution can be performed for fixed-income securities, so too can it be calculated for equity portfolios. In Table 11.4, for simplicity, we consider an equally weighted five-stock portfolio with a one-stock benchmark. We will examine the attribution of the market's return over a 1-day period.[4] In this case, we set the benchmark to be 100% Apple.

Using market-value factor-based attribution (Table 11.5), factors considered include style (e.g., growth, value), industry, country, and currency. Every security in the universe has exposures to these factors calculated from fundamental and statistical data. The sum product of each security's exposures vector and the universe's factor returns yields the factors-only mode of equity factor attribution. The remaining return that is not attributable to factors is defined as "stock specific," or the idiosyncratic portion of a security's return that is unexplainable by factors. These may include company specific events such as earnings, mergers, acquisitions, and the like.

Similar to beta-adjusted factor-based attribution for fixed-income securities, we can perform the same attribution for equities. This involves attributing a portion of return to the security's beta, then beta-adjusting factor returns to avoid double counting the beta component.

Table 11.6 demonstrates that over the 1-day period, Apple was a major contributor to the portfolio's performance. Using market-value factor-based attribution, much of the outperformance can be explained by style factors (Exhibit 11.12). However, the beta-adjusted

TABLE 11.4 Five-Stock Portfolio with Apple as the Benchmark

Security	Portfolio Weight (%)	Benchmark Weight (%)	Active Weight (%)	Return (%)	Beta to Benchmark
Apple	20	100	−80	−4.44	1.00
AT&T	20	0	20	0.50	0.16
Chevron	20	0	20	−1.08	0.52
Tesla	20	0	20	1.52	0.68
Walmart	20	0	20	−1.80	0.20

Source: BlackRock Aladdin, January 31, 2020. For illustrative purposes only.

TABLE 11.5 Market-Value Factor-Based Attribution

Security	Style Contribution (%)	Industry Contribution (%)	Country Contribution (%)	Currency Contribution (%)	Stock Specific Contribution (%)	Contribution to Active Return (%)
Apple	1.73	0.80	0.04	0.00	0.98	3.55
AT&T	−0.35	0.21	−0.01	0.00	0.24	0.10
Chevron	−0.36	−0.10	−0.01	0.00	0.26	−0.22
Tesla	−0.40	0.16	−0.01	0.00	0.55	0.30
Walmart	−0.33	0.03	−0.01	0.00	−0.05	−0.36

Source: BlackRock Aladdin, January 31, 2020. For illustrative purposes only.

TABLE 11.6 Beta-Adjusted Factor-Based Attribution

Security	Beta Contribution (%)	Style Contribution (%)	Industry Contribution (%)	Country Contribution (%)	Currency Contribution (%)	Stock Specific Contribution (%)	Contribution to Active Return (%)
Apple	3.55	0.03	−0.25	0.02	0.00	0.20	3.55
AT&T	−0.15	−0.10	0.11	0.00	0.00	0.24	0.10
Chevron	−0.47	0.02	−0.12	0.00	0.00	0.36	−0.22
Tesla	−0.60	0.13	0.22	0.00	0.00	0.55	0.30
Walmart	−0.18	−0.08	−0.06	0.00	0.00	−0.05	−0.36

Source: BlackRock Aladdin, January 31, 2020. For illustrative purposes only.

factor-based attribution provides additional information into securities' exposure to the market. The market, Apple, was down 4.4%. Given that the portfolio held 20% Apple, the portfolio is 80% underweight Apple relative to the market. The large negative exposure to the market explains a much larger portion of outperformance in the beta-adjusted mode (Exhibit 11.13) compared to the market-value mode (Exhibit 11.12).

Consider AT&T and Tesla. The former has the lowest beta to the market, whereas the latter has the highest. Accordingly, using beta-adjusted factor-based attribution, beta detracted the least in AT&T and the most in Tesla (Exhibit 11.13).

Beta-adjusted factor-based attribution provides additional risk information into securities' market exposure in addition to factor exposures. Without considering beta-adjusted factor-based attribution, it would appear that the outperformance from Apple is driven primarily by style; however, most of the outperformance can be explained by market exposure being more intuitive given the portfolio's rather large negative exposure to the market. As previously illustrated, different approaches to performance attribution generate different results due to their methodologies. To be as relevant as possible, performance attribution should be aligned with the way investors make decisions. Alternatively, in some cases, the rigor of particular attribution methodology can become compelling to portfolio managers and, over time, can become a major element in how portfolio managers come to think about how they add or subtract risk from a portfolio. In these cases, the attribution methology becomes, in effect, the language that describes key aspects of the portfolio management process itself.

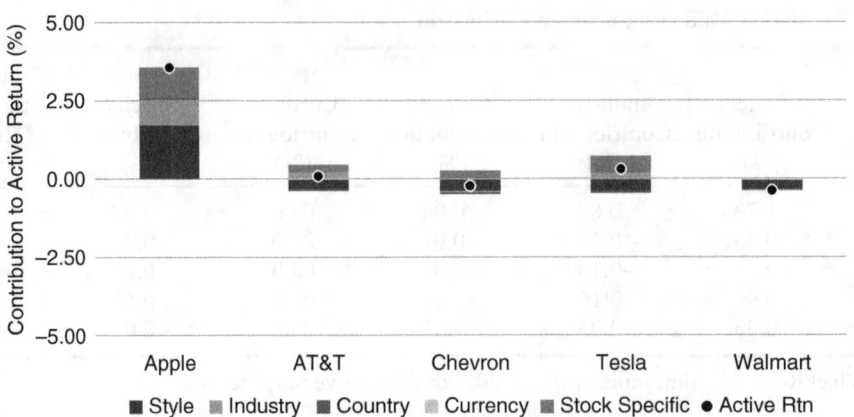

EXHIBIT 11.12 Market-Value Factor-Based Attribution
Source: BlackRock Aladdin, January 31, 2020. For illustrative purposes only.

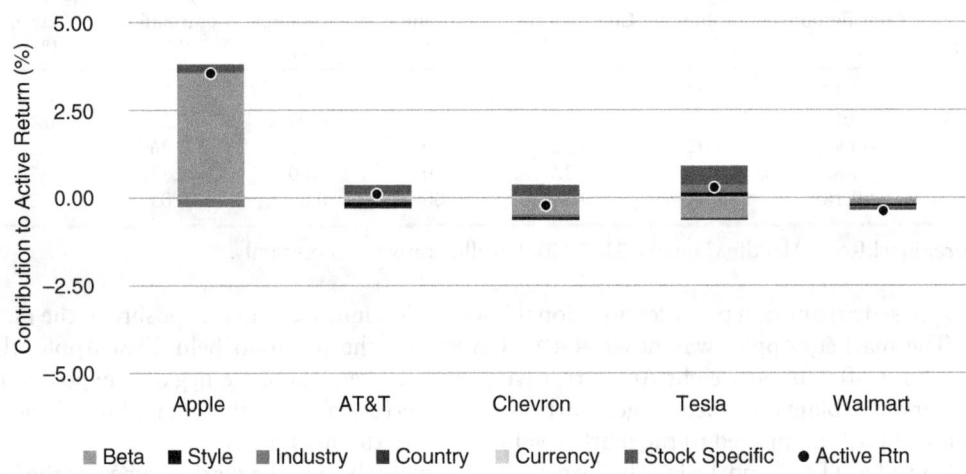

EXHIBIT 11.13 Beta-Adjusted Factor-Based Attribution
Source: BlackRock Aladdin, January 31, 2020. For illustrative purposes only.

NOTES

1. Vess Tomin, managing director in the Financial Modeling Group, has been leading the development of performance attribution for BlackRock Solutions.
2. Brinson, July/August 1986.
3. Note that one does not have to use beta to risk adjust the Brinson methodology. In place of beta in the analysis, spread duration or duration times spread (DxS) could also be used.
4. January 31, 2020.

CHAPTER 12

Performance Analysis

Mark Paltrowitz
Managing Director, Risk & Quantitative Analysis, BlackRock

Mark Temple-Jones
Director, ETF & Index Investments, BlackRock (2023)

Viola Dunne
Managing Director, Risk & Quantitative Analysis, BlackRock (2023)

Christopher Calingo
Director, Risk & Quantitative Analysis, BlackRock

12.1 INTRODUCTION

The world of investing has become increasingly competitive and complex, which necessarily drives investment management firms to deliver superior value to clients, shareholders, and employees. To this end having a performance measurement framework that is consistent, robust, and transparent is critical. BlackRock's fifth Investment Risk Management Paradigm (IRMP) pillar, *performance analysis*, focuses on reviewing a portfolio's performance relative to the benchmark, peers, and other comparable accounts. While helpful at a manager level, some traditional performance measures, such as percentage of assets under management (AUM) outperforming the benchmark, lack necessary granularity. Other measures, such as the information ratio, are useful on a portfolio-by-portfolio basis but can be difficult to interpret when aggregated across various products.

This chapter focuses on how to meaningfully measure aggregate platform performance in active and index investment processes, especially across a heterogeneous set of funds with different benchmarks and risk and performance targets. Performance analysis complements and sits on top of fund-level performance attribution, which focuses on bottom-up analysis and was previously discussed in Chapter 11.

In the active space, the industry standard methodology, calculating the percentage of AUM outperforming the benchmark or a peer group median, has several drawbacks, including its binary nature, embedded survivorship bias, and failure to account for the varying risk-return profiles of different portfolios. As an alternative, this chapter introduces the concepts of alpha target ratio, weighted peer percentile, and alpha dollars as attempts to address these limitations.

In the index space, as a metric, the percentage of AUM within or above predefined performance tolerances is binary in that it does not differentiate between meaningful performance improvements or issues over time across exposures, regions, or vehicles even if a portfolio is within tolerance. Similarly, this approach often does not necessarily differentiate between tracking error contributions that are within a portfolio manager's control and tracking error attributable to exogenous factors. These limitations are addressed using direct tracking basis points, which are detailed later in the chapter.

Performance analysis is a critical component of the investment process. An appropriate performance analysis framework needs to balance applicable metrics that provide sufficient granularity while retaining the ability to meaningfully aggregate measurements across products.

12.2 PERFORMANCE GOVERNANCE

Performance governance requires an independent and objective review of investment teams, portfolio managers, and the performance of the individual portfolios managed. Organizationally, ideally, the team responsible for officially measuring performance should be separate and independent from the investment teams. But while independence of the performance governance function is preferable, the measurement function cannot be done in a vacuum. A strong partnership among stakeholders, including investors, product managers, and risk managers, and financial control should be established.

To be effective, the performance governance function must ensure investment performance is measured consistently, using standard metrics wherever possible. A coordinated and consistent approach enables the ability to conduct "product health reviews," which are not limited to performance metrics (measured on an absolute, active, and risk-adjusted basis) but can also include business objectives (e.g., profitability, sales growth, and operating efficiency). A detailed product health review will also include competitor analysis and industry dynamics that may influence the portfolio under review.

12.3 PERFORMANCE METRICS

Performance measurement can be divided between active versus index managed portfolios. Understanding these metrics provides risk managers with the ability to generate comprehensive and detailed performance analysis. However, the strengths and weaknesses of both active and index performance measures need to be understood.

12.3.1 Active Performance Measurement

While actively managed portfolios can be evaluated using a variety of metrics, the two most common are (1) performance versus benchmark and (2) performance versus an appropriate peer group. Each of these metric helps to inform a different aspect of a portfolio's performance.

An active *portfolio's performance relative to its benchmark*, or a portfolio's active performance, shows the return a portfolio generates relative to its benchmark. Active performance can be measured on a gross or net of fee basis and across various periods, with the most common periods being 1 month, year to date, 1 year, 3 years, and 5 years.[1] Active performance is frequently also measured against an alpha target.[2] A general rule of thumb suggests that a portfolio's gross alpha target be three to four times its fees, though depending on the risk characteristics and objectives of the portfolio, the target may slightly differ. Maintenance of this margin aims to let clients receive an adequate amount of alpha above what is contractually paid out to portfolio managers.

An active *portfolio's performance versus its peers* can be measured as a percentile rank, or peer percentile, within an appropriate peer group. For example, a portfolio with a peer percentile of 25 has underperformed 25% of its peer group, outperforming 75% (a lower percentage is by convention better). Multiple factors impact the peer percentile calculation, including the peer group vendor, methodology, share class, return type, and filtering.[3] Peer percentile methodologies should ideally be aligned internally, but this is not always possible given the complexity of portfolio strategies and varying suitability of vendor-defined peer groups. For instance, some peer groups are rather heterogeneous, such as outcome-oriented, liquid alternatives, or cross-border categories. Due to these differences, a different vendor-defined peer group or a custom-defined peer group may need to be used. In certain cases, a proper peer group may not be available at all.

When used together, a portfolio's active performance and peer group percentile can reveal important information concerning the market environment and competitive landscape, in addition to the portfolio manager's effectiveness. As an example, during highly volatile market periods when asset class correlations are high and systematic risk primarily drives returns, portfolios within a peer group may exhibit clustering. That is, a small difference in returns may cause a significant difference in peer percentiles. Consider a case where a particular portfolio has poor active returns but a strong peer percentile, which implies that while the general strategy of the portfolio may be challenged within the universe of managers competing in that particular strategy, the portfolio is doing well. Such a finding might lead investors to question the value of investing in the strategy while retaining respect for their particular manager. Aligning and comparing gross and net active performance and peer percentiles can result in better insights for clients into performance returns. Peer percentiles and active performance complement each other, and both are important tools when seeking to develop an understanding of performance.

Techniques exist to allow active performance and peer percentiles to be aggregated to describe a portfolio's overall performance when measured across multiple time horizons. The following sections discuss three types of actively managed portfolios performance metrics.

12.3.1.1 Alpha Target Ratio

The alpha target ratio (ATR) is a measure of the percentage of an alpha target a portfolio has generated over a corresponding period. The inclusion of the ATR ratio in portfolio review discussions can incentivize portfolio managers to engage in appropriate risk taking by not excessively penalizing or rewarding them for outlier returns.

The ATR can be transformed into a composite derived from a weighted average of multiple time horizons. As an example, one could use the trailing 1-year, 3-year, and 5-year ATRs (e.g., 20% on 1 year, 50% on 3 years, and 30% on 5 years). However, the ATR depends on the number of years since a portfolio's inception, t_{incept}, and as such, other time horizon combinations can be considered:

$$ATR_{comp} = \begin{cases} \dfrac{w_1}{w_1 + w_3 + w_5} \times ATR_1 + \dfrac{w_3}{w_1 + w_3 + w_5} \times ATR_3 + \dfrac{w_5}{w_1 + w_3 + w_5} \\ \times ATR_5 \text{ if } t_{incept} \geq 5 \\[2mm] \dfrac{w_1}{w_1 + w_3} \times ATR_1 + \dfrac{w_3}{w_1 + w_3} \times ATR_3 \text{ if } 5 > t_{incept} \geq 3 \\[2mm] \dfrac{w_1}{w_1} \times ATR_1 \text{ if } 3 > t_{incept} \geq 1 \\[2mm] N/A \text{ if } 1 > t_{incept} \end{cases} \quad (12.1)$$

The various ATRs can also be floored or capped to enhance aggregation and to limit the incentive for taking on excessive risk. Assuming alpha targets and benchmarks are set consistently and appropriately, the ATR can be aggregated across multiple portfolios and portfolio mandate types with the user's preferred aggregation method, such as AUM-weighted average, simple average, etc.

12.3.1.2 Weighted Peer Percentile The weighted peer percentile is similar to the ATR in that it is derived from a weighted composite of the trailing 1-year, 3-year, and 5-year peer percentiles. However, unlike the ATR, the peer percentiles of each period underlying the weighted peer percentile are bounded by 1 and 100. The efficacy of this metric is highly dependent on the selection of an appropriate peer set, similar to how the value of the ATR metric depends on benchmark and target setting. Note that the P_{comp} also depends on the number of years since a portfolio's inception, t_{incept}:

$$P_{comp} = \begin{cases} \dfrac{w_1}{w_1 + w_3 + w_5} \times P_1 + \dfrac{w_3}{w_1 + w_3 + w_5} \times P_3 + \dfrac{w_5}{w_1 + w_3 + w_5} \times P_5 \text{ if } t_{incept} \geq 5 \\[2mm] \dfrac{w_1}{w_1 + w_3} \times P_1 + \dfrac{w_3}{w_1 + w_3} \times P_3 \text{ if } 5 > t_{incept} \geq 3 \\[2mm] \dfrac{w_1}{w_1} \times P_1 \text{ if } 3 > t_{incept} \geq 1 \\[2mm] N/A \text{ if } 1 > t_{incept} \end{cases}$$

$$(12.2)$$

12.3.1.3 Strengths and Weaknesses of the ATR and Weighted Peer Percentile ATR and weighted peer percentile measures aim to improve upon one of the most commonly reported performance metrics in the investment management industry today: the percentage of current AUM that is above the benchmark or above the peer median.

For three reasons, the percentage of current AUM above the benchmark or peer median is necessary but not necessarily sufficient for understanding performance:

1. *The metric is susceptible to survivorship bias,* in that it only considers the trailing performance of current AUM.

2. *The metric is binary,* demonstrating that a product can only be above or below the benchmark. The information on the *amount of alpha* is ignored.

3. *The metric does not consider the varying risk-return profiles of different types of portfolios.* Not all of the AUM is equally risky, but under this metric it is treated as such.

ATR and weighted peer percentiles metrics help to address two of the three limitations of the "AUM-above-the-benchmark" metric. First, they are not binary. Second, they incorporate a portfolio's alpha target, thus recognizing its particular risk-return profile. However, neither of these metrics address survivorship bias. This challenge can be mitigated by presenting these metrics alongside a measure of alpha dollars, which is further discussed in section 12.3.1.4.

Another strength of the ATR and weighted peer percentiles metrics is that their weighting of historical returns can be adjusted toward longer-term performance, consistent with the importance of focusing on creating long-term alpha. For instance, a reasonable weighting scheme might be 20% / 40% / 40% over 1, 3, and 5 years, which seemingly appears to focus on the 3-year and 5-year time horizons. But with a little arithmetic, we can see the underlying weightings. In this example, the 1-year time horizons are 100% of the 1-year component, 1/3 of the 3-year component, and 1/5 of the 5-year component, making the actual total weight being placed on the 1 year returns as 20% × (1/1) + 40% × (1/3) + 40% × (1/5), which is approximately 41%.

Despite these advantages, these metrics also have limitations. First, these metrics do not take risk-adjusted returns into account. Second, they do not consider outcome-oriented measures (such as internal rated return). Third, the metrics do not address drawdown control. Ultimately, the ATR and weighted peer percentiles do not delineate the distribution of returns. Instead, they show a portfolio's realized performance, not the contributing elements to the portfolio's performance.

12.3.1.4 Alpha Dollars We have found one particular dollar-weighted metric, alpha dollars, that can help to evaluate a product's performance and the total value across multiple portfolios and portfolio types. The alpha dollars metric measures the value created for clients in dollar terms and is a necessary complement to the ATR. Alpha dollars can be calculated on a regular basis (e.g., monthly) by multiplying a portfolio's beginning-of-month AUM[4] by the gross or net active return. While shortening the length of the period to a time frame as granular as daily could theoretically improve the precision of the metric, data frequency, data quality, and computational requirements may make monthly periods the optimal frequency for this metric.

The monthly alpha dollars can then be summed across months and platforms to calculate total firm-wide alpha dollars created. For comparison, the alpha dollar target can be calculated similarly using a portfolio's monthly alpha target instead of the gross active return:

$$Alpha\ Dollars = \sum_{i=1}^{n} AUM_i \times R_i \text{ for } i \text{ months}$$

$$Alpha\ Dollars\ Target = \sum_{i=1}^{n} AUM_i \times \alpha_{tgt,i} \text{ where } \alpha_{tgt,i} \text{ is the monthly alpha target} \quad (12.3)$$

12.3.1.5 Strengths and Weaknesses of Alpha Dollars Alpha dollars provide additional context and insight because the metric is dollar-weighted instead of time-weighted. Alpha dollars complement the ATR and weighted peer percentiles when describing performance at the platform level. The ATR and weighted peer percentiles are useful metrics at the portfolio level, but there are some shortfalls when aggregated up into a suite-level or platform-level score.

For example, the overall ATR of a product suite can be calculated by determining the ATR of the underlying portfolios and then calculating the AUM-weighted average. Since this approach weights ATRs using current AUM, it suffers from survivorship bias. Alpha dollars neutralizes this survivorship bias by including terminated accounts in its calculations. Additionally, because alpha dollars represent a dollar figure, summing the alpha dollars of multiple portfolios into a single number is a clean and efficient way to consider suite-level or platform-level performance. It may be more logical to consider alpha dollars at the suite or platform level as opposed to the portfolio level, given that portfolios oftentimes share alpha sources. Additionally, alpha dollars address the fact that for performance analysis purposes, not all AUM is created equal. Alpha dollars help to draw out differences between portfolios with higher versus lower alpha targets.

For example, suppose two portfolios have the same AUM; one is a fixed-income institutional portfolio with a 200 bp alpha target and the other is a long/short fixed-income hedge fund with a 500 bp alpha target. All else equal, if both portfolios met their alpha targets, they would have the same ATR. The alpha dollars metric would reflect the difference between these two portfolios: the long/short fixed-income portfolio's higher alpha target and higher realized return translates into higher alpha dollars.

With that said, there are a few methodological weaknesses of alpha dollars:

1. As a dollar-weighted metric, the formula places greater weight on performance in periods where AUM is higher. The reverse is also true. The ATR and weighted peer percentiles correct for this limitation by isolating a portfolio's investment performance and neither reward nor penalize flows that may be out of the portfolio manager's control.

2. Alpha dollars do not directly account for risk-adjusted returns because risk is not included in the calculation.

3. Alpha dollars do not explicitly account for the fees that were paid for the alpha that was generated. However, this limitation can be mitigated simply by comparing alpha dollars to the dollars of fees generated. All things equal, the ratio of the alpha dollar to dollars of fees can give the analyst a good sense of the distribution of total alpha generated. The aforementioned rule of thumb on setting alpha targets at three to four times fees also provides a reference point to evaluate the appropriateness of the level of fees charged.

Alpha dollars can play an important role in informing decisions around capacity management. The ability to generate alpha is a scarce resource; as a portfolio's AUM increases significantly, it can become increasingly difficult for a portfolio to meet its alpha target. The same alpha target with a higher AUM translates into a higher amount of alpha dollars that must be extracted from the market. The alpha dollars metric helps investment teams understand their alpha target in dollar terms and can help identify capacity management decisions should the alpha dollars target seem too high. In this way, alpha dollars helps with the understanding of capacity constraints. But in summary, the primary value of the alpha dollars approach is the ability to sum alpha dollars also across heterogeneous products, allowing total platforms or books of business to assess their overall success or failure.

12.3.2 Index Performance Metrics

Given that the primary objective of index portfolios is to mirror the performance of their benchmark, index portfolio performance metrics are primarily concerned with the tracking error between a portfolio's return and the return of its benchmark. Because these tracking errors can be rather small, the resolution of the performance metrics process needs to be much higher.

Significant tracking error can arise from the many factors in the index space that preclude portfolio managers from fully replicating a benchmark precisely. Some, like the inability to source all the securities in the benchmark, would show up in the types of analysis used with active portfolios. Others, like the presence of securities lending income or the actual timing of administrative fees, require access to additional data. In the following sections, we assume that it is the portfolio management process that is being analyzed, which does not necessarily include all the elements of period by period returns.

12.3.2.1 Direct Tracking Basis Points (BP) A portfolio's direct tracking bp seeks to measure tracking error more precisely by measuring only the return components the portfolio manager has control over. While some degree of tracking error is a result of indirect (exogenous) factors outside of a portfolio engineer's control (e.g., tax treatments, pricing methodology differences), direct factors can still be mitigated (e.g., operating inefficiencies or errors).

Fixed-income direct tracking bp ($FDTB_t$) is simply the sum of all index fixed-income return attribution components that a portfolio engineer has control over for a certain time period t:

$$FDTB_t = D_t + C_t + CR_t + RD_t + T_t + FX_t + Excess_t$$

where:

$$D_t = \text{duration}$$
$$C_t = \text{convexity}$$
$$CR_t = \text{curve risk free}$$
$$RD_t = \text{roll down}$$
$$T_t = \text{trade contribution}$$
$$FX_t = \text{foreign exchange}$$
$$Excess_t = \text{any excess factors}$$

12.3.2.2 Strengths and Weaknesses of Direct Tracking BP The direct tracking bp metric is a simple and tangible measurement of the total impact a portfolio manager has on a portfolio. The strength of the metric lies in the ability to aggregate it across all index portfolios on an AUM-weighted basis into a single number for the platform. As direct tracking bp are computed monthly, the trend over time can reveal whether the platform is improving on the components a fund company has control over.

A weakness of the metric, similar to the ATR or weighted peer percentiles, is that the direct tracking bp metric may be subject to survivorship bias on an aggregated level as it is weighted using the latest AUM figures. Another potential weakness is that the metric relies on the quality of the underlying attribution, which makes it susceptible to inaccurate attribution of tracking components.

12.4 CONCLUSION

Performance analysis and measurement requires a multidimensional approach, as no single metric can tell the full performance story of a portfolio over time. Measuring performance of an active manager can be a challenging exercise. No single performance metric is perfect, and a fair amount of performance volatility can be generated by a portfolio over any given period. In light of this, performance measurement and analytics that are flexible but have standardized inputs are required. In addition, the independent performance measurement team needs to maintain a close partnership with stakeholders to implement robust processes and controls, which help to ensure portfolio performance is measured rigorously. Over time, an existing performance governance framework will need to evolve to continue adapting to changing product types, markets, and client needs. However, its objective should remain consistent—to help portfolio managers improve and to help their clients evaluate the efficacy of their investments.

NOTES

1. The use of performance metrics in marketing material is subject to local regulatory guidelines. For example, the SEC marketing and advertising rule (amendments to Rule 206(4)-1 and Rule 206(4)-3) requires marketing material to show 1, 5, 10 year, and since fund inception returns.
2. An alpha target is an active return target a portfolio manager seeks to generate above its portfolio's relevant benchmark.
3. Filtering refers to how share classes are grouped together.
4. Beginning-of-month AUM is also known as AUM prior month-end.

CHAPTER 13

Evolving the Risk Management Paradigm[1]

Bennett W. Golub
Senior Advisor, BlackRock

Michael Huang
Managing Director, Risk & Quantitative Analysis, BlackRock

Joe Buehlmeyer
Director, Aladdin Product Group, BlackRock

13.1   INTRODUCTION

This section (Chapters 2–12) has discussed in detail the conceptual pillars that underpin a strong investment risk management function. Those pillars were presented as being parts of a coherent and comprehensive Investment Risk Management Paradigm (IRMP). To review, that paradigm consists of five pillars:

1. Ex ante risk measurement
2. Risk governance (i.e., having and maintaining agreed upon levels of risks)
3. Portfolio manager risk-return awareness
4. Performance attribution
5. Performance analysis

As investment managers' books of business become increasingly numerous, heterogeneous, and complex, the need for a coherent paradigm is vital in order to have a template to apply to the investment manager's distinct activities. The precise tools used to execute each pillar of the IRMP is, of course, a function of a particular point in time. Financial systems evolve due to the dynamic nature of financial risk. The inherent adaptive characteristics of financial systems leads to evolution, often seeking to exploit weaknesses in the "defense" undertaken by investors and their risk managers.

Constantly reviewing how the tools are used to operate the IRMP is crucial. At its simplest, forecasts from the risk model used to govern risk-taking need to be reconciled with realized returns. If there is a mismatch, the model's structure needs to be reviewed and possibly redesigned. Specifically, new attempts by market participants to obfuscate well-known risks need to be made transparent. Similarly, new emerging risks need to be identified, and risk managers need to incorporate those changing characteristics into their program.

Effective risk management functions need to constantly evolve as the risk environment changes over time. Investment risk management processes also have to regularly change and evolve to meet the ever changing needs of clients, changes in tax laws, and regulatory innovations.

In line with a changing investment landscape, investment processes, asset classes, and products have increased in number, size, complexity, and heterogeneity. An organization's risk management function needs to keep pace with these developments, leveraging advancements in technology to manage across a growing variety of risks and portfolios. This chapter outlines a vision that is quickly becoming a reality by creating a much more scalable framework for investment risk management. This involves the efficient identification and resolution of a broad range of understood risks across heterogeneous portfolios through the use of extensive formal risk governance combined with new applications of investment risk management technology.

13.2 TRADITIONAL BUY-SIDE RISK MANAGEMENT FRAMEWORK

Traditionally, a buy-side risk management "best practice" framework has been characterized by teams of independent risk managers, with substantive subject matter expertise and a bevy of risk management tools, engaged in continuous communication with portfolio managers, ideally in close proximity. For decades, that has been the BlackRock model.

The COVID-19 pandemic and subsequent expedited adoption of "work from home" put elements of that legacy approach to the test, and the verdict seems to be that effective risk management can indeed be done on a (partially) virtual basis, although how well that holds up over an extended time frame has, fortunately not been tested. High levels of direct engagement with portfolio managers, preferably in person or, if not feasible, virtually, helps risk managers develop a visceral understanding of the investment management process and the positioning of underlying portfolios. This permits the risk managers to raise and discuss substantive issues with portfolio managers as they arise through time. If necessary, it also provides a rationale for escalation.

Portfolio risks and exposures are evaluated using a combination of quantitative metrics and heuristics against predetermined thresholds. Exceptions levels are defined in advance for each portfolio. The (virtual/hybrid) proximity allows risk managers to have real-time connectivity and enhances their ability to assess portfolio manager risk-and-return awareness.

While this traditional framework can be highly effective, it does not necessarily scale efficiently. Scaling occurs primarily by increasing the number of people—more risk managers with highly specialized subject matter expertise are needed as more distinctive product types in more locations are being managed. More and more highly trained risk managers will be required to maintain the level of surveillance and constructive challenge given increases in the heterogeneity of investment processes, the number of investment management locations, coupled with increases in the number of asset classes managed, non-securitized private assets and other product types.

13.3 EVOLVING THE IRMP: IN PURSUIT OF INVESTMENT RISK MANAGEMENT AT SCALE

Risk managers need to be able to consistently and effectively identify, understand, and resolve risk issues across a wide range of risks, exposures, and distinct portfolios. We believe that the challenges of scale and complexity can be partially addressed by increasing the use of system-generated "risk exceptions" that are managed through a rigorous workflow, particularly if there is a pervasive high touch risk management program in place. While there is no replacing the value of the subject matter expertise of independent risk managers, the use of systematic multivariate algorithmic scans of risk, exposure, and return metrics can significantly enhance the thoroughness and precision of investment risk management while improving scalability.

In reality, at high-quality/high-integrity investment managers, the number of severe and obvious risk problems likely to pop up is typically rather low (but not zero!). Most likely, those problems are going to be the proverbial "needles" in the haystack. But as an organization continues to scale, the increasing number of distinct portfolios creates more potential "haystacks" for problems to hide in. Even the most dedicated risk manager will eventually find it mind-numbing to constantly and thoroughly search out these rare events. Decades of experience have taught us that the most intellectually creative people, who are vital for effective investment risk management, are just not all that good at executing repetitive surveillance functions. They either get bored and miss things or become disillusioned about a career in risk management and quit.

On the other hand, computers are superb at reliably executing repetitive tasks. The risk management system of the (near) future can be configured with multiple automated risk scans, tailored to the type of mandate. For instance, risk and exposure scans can be programmed to flag the following:

- Changes through time on factor exposures
- Levels of realized returns
- Differences between risk and exposures of cohort accounts versus representative accounts[2]
- Levels and changes in portfolio liquidity
- Changes in portfolio redemption risk
- Large portfolio inflows or outflows
- Issuer concentration risk targets
- Portfolios where back-testing indicate poor predictive accuracy of a risk model
- Levels and changes in portfolio stress testing
- Trades with abnormally large market impact
- Portfolios that do not meet client-directed ESG requirements

These portfolio characteristics can be configured into sophisticated risk scans. In such a world, risk managers can develop algorithms to more systematically scan their books and identify potential risk and exposure issues. Algorithms can range from the simple to very complex and can be tailored to help detect specific risk and exposure concerns defined by risk managers. Over time, sets of these scans can evolve into a formal quantification of the cumulative organic wisdom of an organization's risk management team.

Additionally, algorithms can be applied more broadly, top-down, across the investment platform or can be fine-tuned, bottom-up, for a specific team or process. A chief risk officer of an asset management firm might mandate that all portfolios globally must ensure that the active risk-taking is in-line with funds' return targets and clients' risk appetite, that sufficient liquidity is maintained to ensure funds' can meet both redemption requests and margin calls, and that portfolios are not overly concentrated in any single name. A senior investment risk manager charged with overseeing a credit hedge fund might be more focused on the hedge fund's credit beta to the Barclays High Yield Index and whether performance and risk is derived primarily from credit trades. Scans can be developed to monitor many of these other portfolio requirements.

The use of algorithmic scans is not necessarily limited to identifying investment risk. Scans can be developed to help control other types of risks, including counterparty credit risk exposure, operational risk statistics, and so on. The objective of these algorithms is to systematize *the natural intelligence* of risk managers to improve the identification of potential real risk concerns. The term natural intelligence is meant to describe the wisdom and experience risk managers have developed over time. It is specifically meant to be understood as distinct from artificial intelligence or machine learning. Such methodologies, in theory, could seek to "learn" by analyzing risk managers' behavior in response to changing results from the risk and exposure scans. While there may be ways to use such techniques, at this point in time,[3] the ability to glean insights remains limited, given the low number of "true positive" risk issues in the BlackRock data set.

13.4   RISK GOVERNANCE

Risk governance and risk oversight are distinct but related elements of an investment manager's risk management process and are critical to a firm's ability to meet its fiduciary obligations to clients. Risk governance can be thought of as the systematic and structured practice of risk oversight combined with a set of structured actions that ensure that portfolios' risks and exposures are being appropriately controlled.

But in addition to actually performing governance and oversight, risk managers need to be able to demonstrate that such a process is actually being performed diligently. Even good investment managers occasionally have portfolios that incur extreme adverse performance. When this happens, there is almost always an inexorable desire, either internally or externally (or both), to find a villain. When this happens, risk managers are inevitably high on the list of "usual suspects." To protect against the accusation that investment managers were not supervised "prudent men," a structured risk and exposure surveillance process with a full audit trail permits the investment manager to demonstrate that while investment performance may have indeed been bad, it was bad for the right reasons. Properly designed software can provide such a risk management audit trail.

Combining algorithmic scans with a comprehensive workflow process, risk managers can efficiently analyze and provide feedback on flagged exceptions and work to distinguish between false positive and true positive risk exceptions. An optimized workflow will allow risk managers to systematically review portfolio exceptions, provide commentary, either sign off on an observed risk exception or escalate, as appropriate. Specialized workflow tools, designed by and for risk managers, can allow risk exceptions to be transparently actioned to ensure and evidence that appropriate processes are in place and being followed.

Ultimately, the primary value of employing a more systematic risk exception review and workflow process is that it will allow risk managers to be able to spend more time on real true positives or other issues requiring their subject matter expertise.

13.5   SUPPORTING RISK GOVERNANCE THROUGH TECHNOLOGY

The risk management process requires disciplined risk governance. By the term risk governance, we are referring to the organizational processes that constrain and calibrate the risk-taking that takes place throughout an investment manager's book of business. This incorporates governing levels of risk, processes for reviewing exceptions, a defined range of remediation steps that can be brought to action, and clarity regarding who within the organization can put those remediation steps into action. Reputable investment managers need such governance processes, although they may or may not think of them as a formal set of procedures. However, the degree to which they are supported through technology can vary significantly across firms. At one end of the spectrum, a portfolio's risk-and-return measures may be occasionally tracked in spreadsheets, with significant deviations being escalated and triaged verbally or via email. At the other end of the spectrum, purpose-built investment risk management solutions provide integrated workflows that seamlessly connect limit management, exception detection, sign-off, reporting, and auditing.

While spreadsheet-based solutions may have proved sufficient in the past (refer to Section 13.2 "Traditional Buy-Side Risk Management Framework"), for rapidly growing investment managers, spreadsheets may be ill-suited to support the kind of scale, breadth, and transparency required. Ultimately, spreadsheet systems scale reliably only with additional people, and typically with limited efficiency. Purpose-built investment risk solutions, such as Aladdin's "Risk Radar," in contrast, are designed with flexible rulesets and surveillance tools to specifically meet the requirements for a robust risk governance framework described previously (refer to Section 13.4 "Risk Governance").

13.6 IMPLEMENTING A RISK GOVERNANCE FRAMEWORK THROUGH ALADDIN

As the industry and risk management practices have evolved, so too has Aladdin. Enabling both BlackRock and Aladdin clients to implement a robust and scalable risk governance framework, "Risk Radar" was developed through close collaboration between BlackRock's Aladdin Product Group (APG) and Risk & Quantitative Analysis (RQA) group.

Risk Radar's premise is simple: to allow investment risk managers to specify, detect, analyze, and resolve potential portfolio issues in an effective, efficient, and transparent way. Improving investment risk management was the initial focus of Risk Radar. As previously mentioned, heuristic surveillance approaches are vulnerable to the inevitable loss of focus, by even the best risk managers, when requiring them to repeatedly seek out low frequency events. However, it soon became obvious that Risk Radar's capabilities were much more generalizable, allowing it to be configured to easily address a broad variety of risks, from liquidity and operational risk to environmental, social, and governance (ESG) and climate metrics. Further, Risk Radar evolved in line with the emergence of new technologies and rapidly changing skillsets—such as the emergence of the citizen developer[4]—to achieve new levels of scale by allowing risk managers to interact with the system not just through manual means but also through programmatic means.

The following section provides a tangible example of how a solution, such as Risk Radar, can help investors implement a comprehensive, robust and transparent risk governance process.

13.7 ALADDIN'S RISK RADAR EXAMPLE

13.7.1 Aladdin's Risk Radar Overview

Risk Radar is a risk management solution that provides exception-based risk governance and reporting workflows. Users create rules that track one or more risk or return indicators, subscribe portfolios to those rules, and then manage exceptions that are created if portfolios trigger their respective rule evaluations. Managing an exception may entail classifying and accepting an identified risk for a given period, escalating a risk, or in some cases, marking an exception as a false positive. All elements of a risk event, including rule limit calibrations, evaluation results, and risk manager actions, are captured over time and can be used for reporting and audit purposes. This makes it easy to revisit a particular risk manager's decision-making or evidence that appropriate risk management processes were in place after the fact. This capability can be particularly valuable precisely at a time when there is a severe negative realization in a portfolio, which is nearly inevitable at some point due to the very nature of investment risk-taking. After the fact, a lot of angst may be generated, and it is not unheard of for clients to challenge the effectiveness of the manager's risk management process. While Risk Radar cannot eliminate every severe negative realization, it can provide precise and auditable evidence that a risk was known and within appropriate boundaries. Of course, there is the other edge of the knife, namely, if the risk management process was lax or ineffective, Risk Radar will also memorialize those weaknesses.

13.7.2 Rules and Portfolio Subscriptions

Risk exceptions arise when a portfolio triggers a preprogrammed rule, i.e., the portfolio's risk metrics exhibits a behavior that falls outside the pre-specified limits programmed into the rule(s). Therefore, the exception-based process invariably starts with defining a set of rules and aligning the applicable portfolios to those rules.

Risk Radar allows risk managers to create rules across large numbers of risk-and-return metrics and at various levels of granularity—from the portfolio level to the sector level, all the way down to the individual security level. Additionally, multiple metrics can be combined to create complex rules that capture the interplay of multiple dimensions at once and stand a better chance of identifying true positive exceptions compared to simple univariate rules. Example use cases include monitoring both the market value exposure and contribution to risk of a single issuer, or taking into consideration a portfolio's realized return when assessing whether the portfolio manager's risk-taking is appropriate given the portfolio's alpha target.

Once a rule has been created within the system, it can then be subscribed to by one or more portfolios, which in turn, will result in the portfolio being regularly evaluated in Risk Radar.

13.7.3 Exceptions and Tasks

Once one or more rules have been defined within the system, risk managers can then turn more of their attention to responding to the risk events that get triggered. Each risk event creates a task for the risk manager to review and act upon.

There are many ways to specify a risk event. For instance, in addition to flagging the level of a key metric, such as portfolio beta or duration, a risk manager may have concerns about how a metric evolved through time. History matters. Sharp changes in exposures could simply reflect the repositioning of a portfolio. But it could also be problematic. For instance, it could be unintentional. It might indicate a poorly understood convexity effect from an (embedded) options position. It could also be indicative of a portfolio manager acting in a manner inconsistent with his or her normal behavior. It could be style drift. The risk event could be evidence of a massive surge in overconfidence or a sudden bout of fearfulness. For those reasons, a good risk manager will always ask and want to know "what has changed" so he or she can figure out the "why." Upon reviewing a risk exception, Risk Radar provides a summary of both the underlying metrics that are tracked and of any previous risk management actions. This helps risk managers reduce the detection-to-action cycle time, with less time spent chasing after data and more time spent on analyzing true risk events.

Exhibit 13.1 displays a triggered risk event. In this example, the portfolio is substantially underweight its holdings of Wells Fargo & Company, measured by active risk contribution. The time series of risk contributions for this issuer shows that the underweight has been

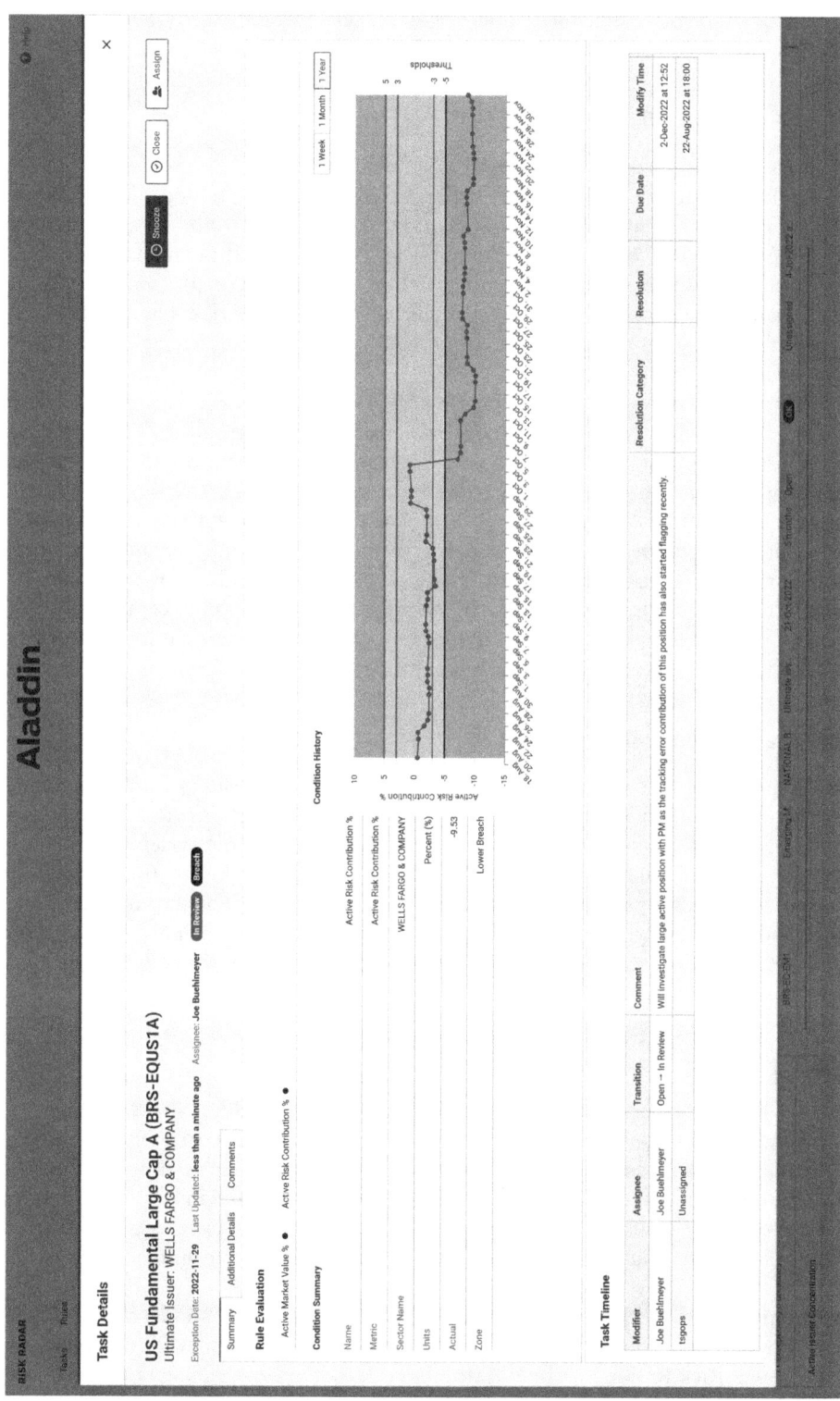

EXHIBIT 13.1 An Example of Task Detail

Source: BlackRock Aladdin, 2022. For illustrative purposes only.

known for almost 3 months. Additionally, the risk manager's recognition of the event and his action plan was recorded.

13.7.4   Exception Classification

Following the risk manager's review of an exception, which may entail a conversation with the relevant portfolio manager, the risk manager will need to decide what actions, if any, to take. In Exhibit 13.2, the risk manager records that he spoke with the portfolio manager about the large active underweight in Wells Fargo & Company and that the portfolio manager indicated that the position was deliberate. The risk manager then chose to "Snooze" the exception for 1 month, after which the exception will trigger again and require the risk manager to review the underweight and stay on top of the situation. Risk Radar will not let the risk event fall between the cracks.

Should the risk persist beyond the acceptable period or change beyond a given threshold, the task will be brought back to the risk manager's attention. As a result, risk managers are no longer required to review the same exceptions every day and instead can focus on new issues or reopened issues that have been flagged by the system based on a predefined policy.

Lastly, Risk Radar provides a *customizable* classification mechanism that allows risk and investment managers to tailor classifications to a specific type of rule. For example, liquidity risk exceptions might be acknowledged and "risk accepted" because the portfolio has inter-fund lending arrangements in place. Similarly, an issuer concentration exception might be "risk accepted" because it arose from a passive breach caused by a material jump in price of an issuer's securities due to some positive idiosyncratic news.

13.7.5   Risk Exception Reporting and Audit

Using Risk Radar, as opposed to spreadsheets and emails, as the repository for an investment manager's risk governance rule sets and risk events, along with their risk management resolutions, greatly facilitates regular risk reviews or audits. By design, the system captures any changes that are made to rules or portfolio subscriptions, persists all exceptions that occur, and retains all actions and commentary added by risk managers. This ensures maximum transparency and auditability and makes it easy to answer questions such as, "*Which funds are in scope for a given governance process?*" or "*What actions did the risk manager take when this issue last occurred?*"

13.7.6   What Is Next for Technology-Enabled Investment Risk Oversight?

As of Summer 2023, the rule sets used by BlackRock and other Aladdin clients are the result of leveraging the *natural intelligence* of portfolio and risk managers. In theory, one could imagine using machine-learning techniques to empirically identify which risk metric histories allow robust forecasting of future portfolio disasters. However, as previously alluded to, the limited number of severe unattended "true positives" (fortunately) limits the extent to which the at-scale classification of unattended risk exception can be used to train machine-learning processes.

A less ambitious possibility is using machine-learning techniques to model risk managers' responses to different risk events. With every day that passes, and with every exception that is classified through Risk Radar, a potential training data set grows. This data might be able to be used to model the actions of risk managers and present the machine's guess on how to action a particular risk exception. Initial results are proving promising, the objective being that these techniques will be able to complement existing governance processes and help

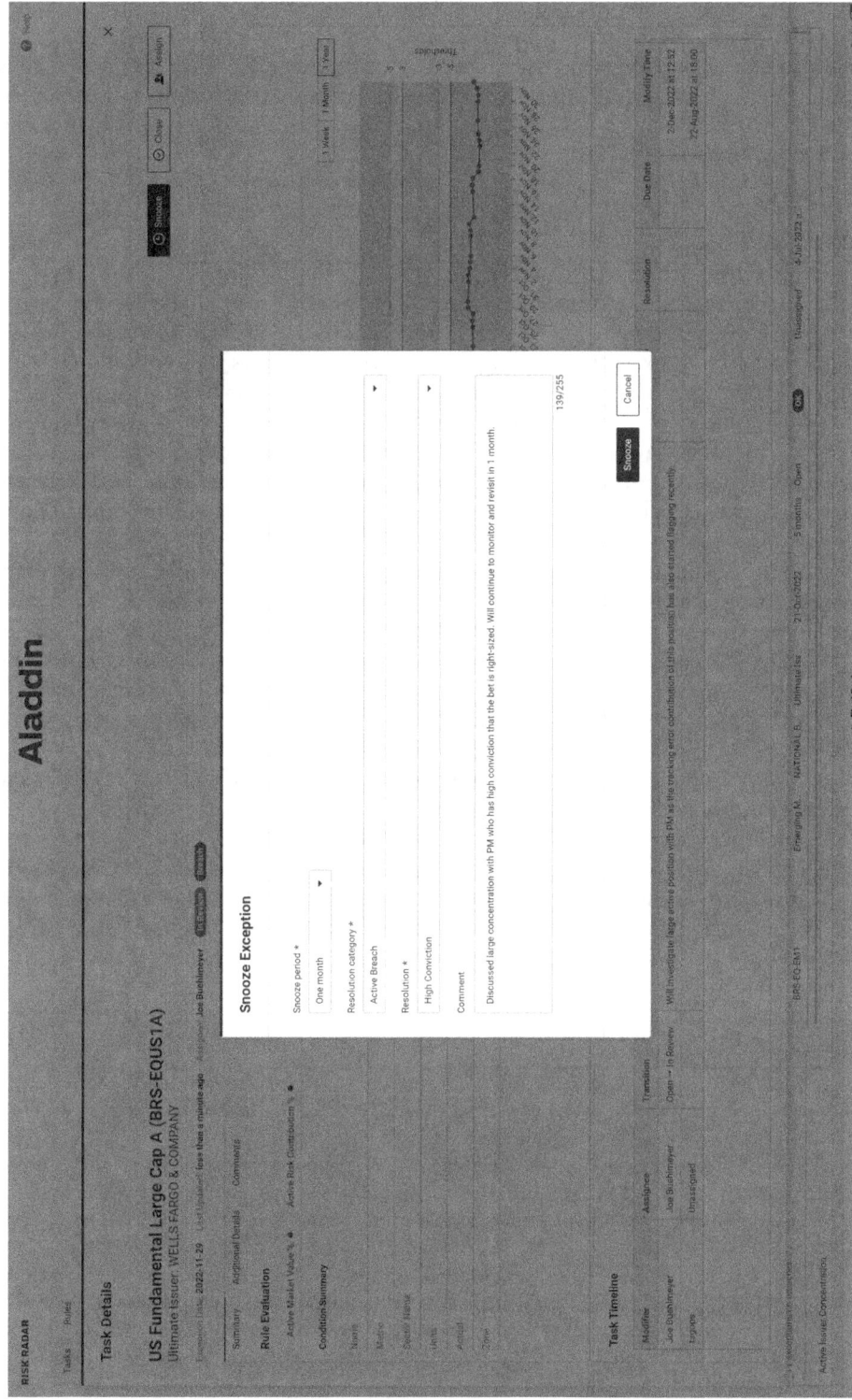

EXHIBIT 13.2 An Example of Exception Classification
Source: BlackRock Aladdin, 2022. For illustrative purposes only.

further improve the signal-to-noise ratio and help weed out false positives. The machine's guesses have also been used to identify potential instances where the risk manager may have incorrectly actioned a risk exception, oftentimes the result of an inexperienced risk manager attempting to determine the most appropriate course of action. Of course, emulating the practices of human risk managers, no matter how hard we hope, is not necessarily the same thing as optimally managing risk.

13.8 CONCLUSION

Increasing scale and complexity creates investment risk management challenges for investment managers. Those challenges can be significantly addressed through increasing the use of system-generated "risk exceptions" predefined by risk managers and combined with a workflow that leverages the risk manager's time, experience, intelligence, and productivity.

To be as clear as possible in the English language, this discussion does NOT say or advocate that completely automated investment risk management tools can be created. To the contrary, deploying this new approach to risk governance hopefully creates a more efficient and thorough process to let risk managers effectively apply their subject matter expertise and wisdom where it is needed the most.

Risk Radar may facilitate evolving the geographic distribution of investment risk managers. The initial oversight of risk exceptions generated daily is, most likely, location agnostic. Managing that first level of surveillance may be able to generate economies of scale or lower operating costs. For instance, the initial oversight of surfaced risk exceptions could be reviewed at centers of excellence physically distinct from actual portfolio management. It does, however, remain critical that on-location risk managers continue to maintain close connectivity to their assigned portfolio manager teams and continue to act as "risk translators" and communicators of increasingly complex risk metrics and stay closely connected to portfolio managers, portfolios, markets, and traders.

While technology will continue to evolve and advancements will be made to further systematize and enhance investment risk management, a resilient world-class risk management function will always need independent subject matter experts and objective risk managers constructively challenging portfolio managers to ensure risk-taking remains deliberate, diversified, and scaled.

NOTES

1. Nikki Azznara, Kristen Walters, Katie Day, Rick Flynn, and Rory van Zwanenberg significantly contributed to the development of this chapter.
2. BlackRock developed a framework to help oversee a heterogeneous universe of portfolios. A representative account, which is also referred to as a "rep account," serves as a model for other similar portfolios. Those similar portfolios are known as cohort accounts.
3. As of June 2023.
4. The term "Citizen Developer" is an emerging term in the industry that is used to refer to investment professionals outside the technology domain that have acquired certain programming skills that allow them to perform large-scale data analysis, automate selected activities, and so on, without being formally recognized as software engineers. Refer to https://www.gartner.com/en/information-technology/glossary/citizen-developer.

Fixed-Income Risk Management—Then and Now

CHAPTER 14

The Modernization of the Bond Market[1]

Daniel Veiner
Managing Director, Global Trading, BlackRock

Stephen Laipply
Managing Director, iShares Fixed Income ETFs, BlackRock

Carolyn Weinberg
Managing Director, Investment Product Management, BlackRock

Samara Cohen
Senior Managing Director, ETF and Index Investments, BlackRock

Vasiliki Pachatouridi
Managing Director, Indexed Fixed Income Portfolio Management Group, BlackRock

Hui Sien Koay
Director, Indexed Fixed Income Portfolio Management Group, BlackRock

14.1 CHARTING THE EVOLUTION OF BOND MARKETS

For decades, the conventions and practices of the bond markets remained largely unchanged, despite rapid transformation in other areas of the US financial markets and those around the world. However, in the years following the 2008 Global Financial Crisis, there have been a number of important structural shifts in bond markets, with modernization firmly underway and change accelerating.

14.1.1 The Current State of Bond Market Liquidity

The pre-crisis market was characterized by greater risk-taking capacity, larger balance sheets for risk warehousing, and lower funding and capital costs.[2] Post-crisis, regulatory oversight was enhanced, dealer balance sheet capacity was significantly reduced, funding and capital costs increased, and operating models were rationalized accordingly. Banks and broker-dealers shifted from primarily principal-based trading to more of a hybrid model consisting of both principal and agency trading with increasing reliance on electronic trading and all-to-all platforms.

Initially, post-crisis liquidity was poor in both depth and breadth. However, as operating models adjusted to the post-crisis environment, liquidity improved somewhat, although

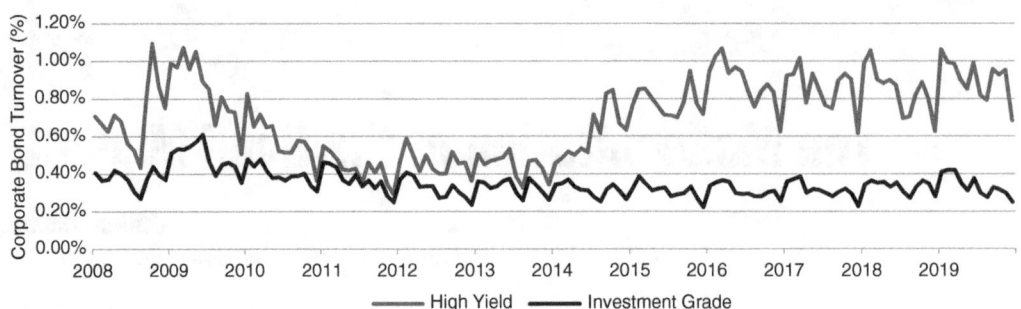

EXHIBIT 14.1   US High-Yield and Investment-Grade Corporate Bond Market Turnover
Sources: BlackRock, FINRA TRACE, as of December 31, 2019.
Note: Turnover measures the ratio of monthly average daily trading volumes to the total market value outstanding. The Bloomberg Barclays US High Yield and Corporate Bond Indices are used to proxy total market value outstanding. Corporate bond cash data is sourced from FINRA TRACE.

unevenly. Since 2012, while the US high-yield (HY) corporate bond market daily turnover has improved, the US investment-grade (IG) bond market has stagnated, as shown in Exhibit 14.1.

Looking back, dealer inventories have declined dramatically, largely driven by regulations implemented following the crisis. Over this time, the size of credit markets has significantly expanded. As illustrated in Exhibit 14.2, dealers held ~11.8% of the high-yield and investment-grade markets on their balance sheet in 2007; they now hold <0.1%. This decline has significantly impacted liquidity, as dealers are not "making markets" in material size and instead seek to match buyers and sellers.

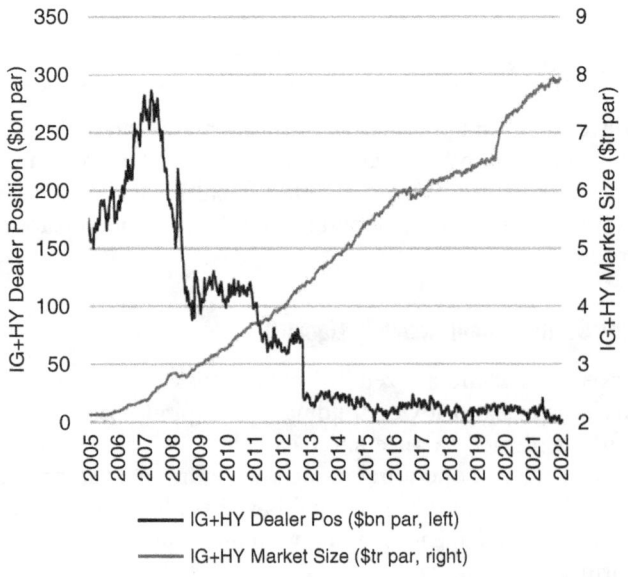

EXHIBIT 14.2   Investment-Grade and High-Yield Dealer Positioning Versus Market Size
Sources: BlackRock, Bloomberg, as of August 31, 2022.

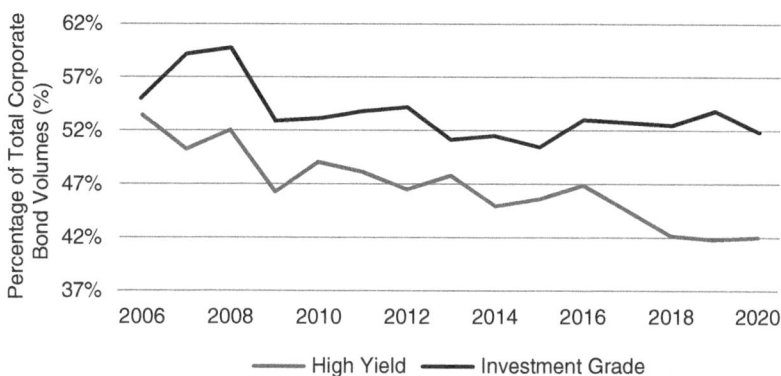

EXHIBIT 14.3 Share of the Top-Decile Most-Traded Bonds as Percentage of Total Corporate Bond Volumes
Source: Goldman Sachs, as of March 31, 2019.

In US IG and HY, market breadth has improved post-crisis, as liquidity is less concentrated with greater trading activity across a wider subset of bonds, as shown in Exhibit 14.3.

Exhibit 14.4 illustrates that the average trade size in US IG and HY markets has reduced over time, as facilitating larger trades remains challenging given the reduction in principal inventory. The acceleration in electronic trading is also likely driving this trend, as market participants typically break larger trades into smaller blocks on electronic platforms to gain better execution.

14.1.2 The Modernization of Bond Market Structure

Fixed-income exchange-traded funds (ETFs) proved to be an important catalyst for accelerating the modernization of the bond market. As fixed-income ETF adoption ramped up, it was

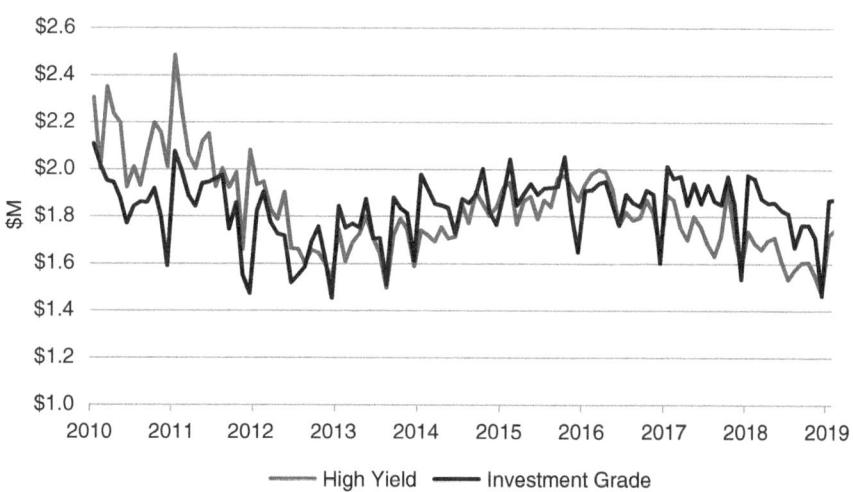

EXHIBIT 14.4 US Investment-Grade and High-Yield Markets—Average Trade Size Excluding Trades Less Than $100k
Sources: MarketAxess, BlackRock, TRACE, as of January 1, 2020.

necessary for market makers and broker-dealers to develop robust, real-time pricing models to evaluate potential arbitrage opportunities between the ETF's exchange price and the NAV (Net Asset Value—the market value of its underlying bond basket). Over time, market makers have increasingly utilized the ETF primary mechanism to accommodate the increased demand for institutional ETF block trading (i.e., *creations* in which ETF shares are created out of baskets of bonds or *redemptions* in which baskets of bonds are exchanged for ETF shares).

The growth in ETF primary activity, alongside the development of more robust algorithmic bond pricing, enabled dealers to develop technology to facilitate over-the-counter (OTC) trading of baskets of bonds (e.g., "portfolio trades"). Often, fixed-income ETF market makers use fixed-income index derivatives to hedge their risk as they assemble baskets of bonds for ETF primary activity. The fixed-income ETF creation mechanism is a tool available for market maker to manage inventory and hence reduce balance sheet utilization. Dealers may have several bonds on their balance sheet that they are seeking to submit toward the creation of a fixed-income ETF. They can then sell the ETF in the secondary market on an equity exchange using equity trading algorithms.

The growth in all of these activities drove the consolidation of trading desks across cash bonds, ETFs, and index derivatives (i.e., CDX and TRS). The most sophisticated players have been able to increase trading and risk management synergies by effectively linking market making activity in credit flow desks with their market making fixed-income ETF desk to reduce costs and increase the provision of liquidity.

Advancements in technology and data processing capabilities have enabled market participants to leverage the ever-growing amount of electronic trading data to allow for automated real-time bond pricing on thousands of CUSIPs. Growth in ETF primary activity increased the depth and quality of transaction level data, creating a feedback loop that allows for constant refinement in automated pricing models. Algorithmic credit pricing is transforming the way participants source, hedge, and manage fixed-income portfolios. As a result, broker-dealers are able to efficiently facilitate portfolio trades for investors, leveraging algorithmic pricing and ETF primary trading.

Additionally, the growth of alternative electronic trading platforms improved trading velocity and price discovery, aided by the quality of real-time bond pricing. Various electronic venues offer innovative trading protocols from open or all-to-all trading, streaming quotes that allow for click-to-trade and auto-execution in credit. The rise in all-to-all trading has allowed nonbank market makers (proprietary trading firms) to provide institutional liquidity alongside traditional banks, increasing intermediation capacity and liquidity overall. All of these advancements have been beneficial to liquidity and transparency and have contributed to substantial efficiency gains across both the buy-side and sell-side.

The growth of fixed-income ETFs, portfolio trades, and electronic trading are all interrelated and can be seen as an inevitable by-product of banks and broker-dealers using technology to better navigate markets in a "balance sheet constrained world."

Bond market structure is transforming rapidly, along with the speed of execution. Exhibit 14.5 provides a schematic illustrating pre-crisis and more current bond market structures. Fixed-income investors and traders have a wider array of options than ever before to optimize venue selection and execution tactics. Depending on order size and risk profile, investors can determine if a given trade would be best executed through a high touch (i.e., voice) or low touch (electronic trading venue or auto-execution) approach, and if execution could be enhanced by portfolio trading. Harnessing fixed-income beta exposures

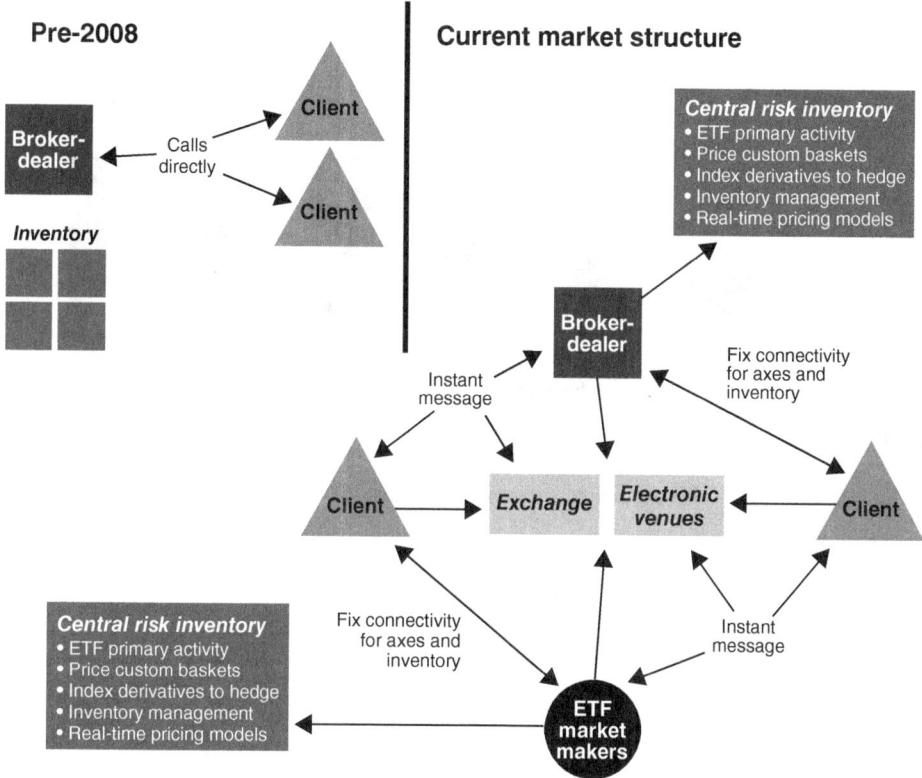

EXHIBIT 14.5 Evolution of Market Structure
Source: BlackRock. For illustrative purposes only.

to manage the risk and liquidity of large-scale portfolio transactions is an increasingly viable option. These enhanced options help to improve the liquidity of bond markets, reducing implementation time, and minimizing execution slippage. The next section goes into each of these market structure developments in more detail.

14.1.3   Continued Growth in Electronic Bond Trading

Electronic trading continues to grow rapidly across all asset classes. As demonstrated in Exhibit 14.6, on the MarketAxess and Tradeweb trading venues, global electronic average daily volumes in credit increased to over $10bn per day in 2019, exhibiting a three time growth rate since 2014. In 2019, US IG and HY volumes executed on the MarketAxess platform represented 20% and 10% of total TRACE IG and HY trading volumes, respectively, up from 12% and 4% in 2013 (see Exhibit 14.7).

The liquidity of both IG and HY credit were impacted more significantly by the Global Financial Crisis and its aftermath than less risky asset classes. Accordingly, the market had to adapt, turning to electronic trading and the use of fixed-income ETFs to help manage risk and inventory levels.

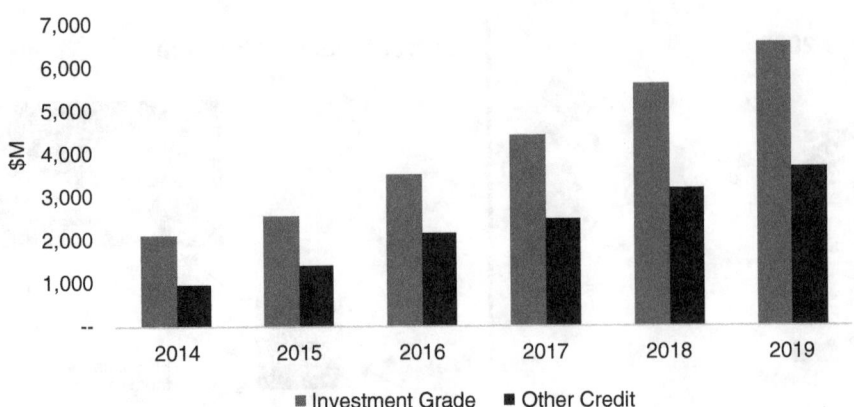

EXHIBIT 14.6   Growth in Electronic Trading
Sources: MarketAxess and Refinitiv, an LSEG Business, as of December 31, 2019.
Note: Other credit includes US high yield, emerging markets, Eurobonds, and municipal bonds.

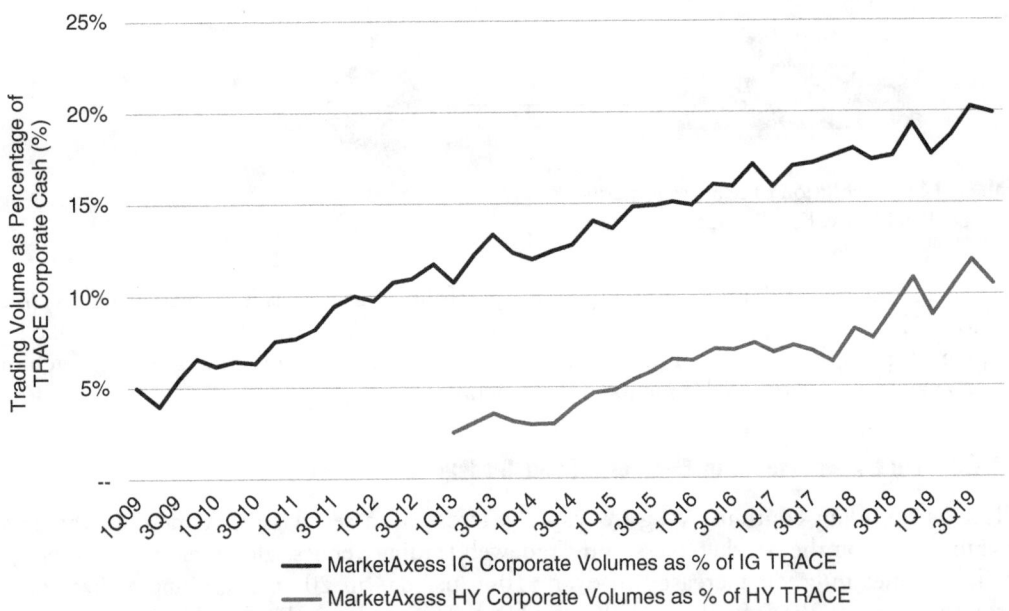

EXHIBIT 14.7   MarketAxess US Corporate Trading Volumes as Percentage of TRACE Corporate Cash
Volumes
Sources: MarketAxess, SIFMA TRACE, as of December 31, 2019.
Note: For IG, includes an adjustment for the increase in reported affiliate back-to-back trades by certain
market participants to FINRA for the period from April 2014 through October 2015.

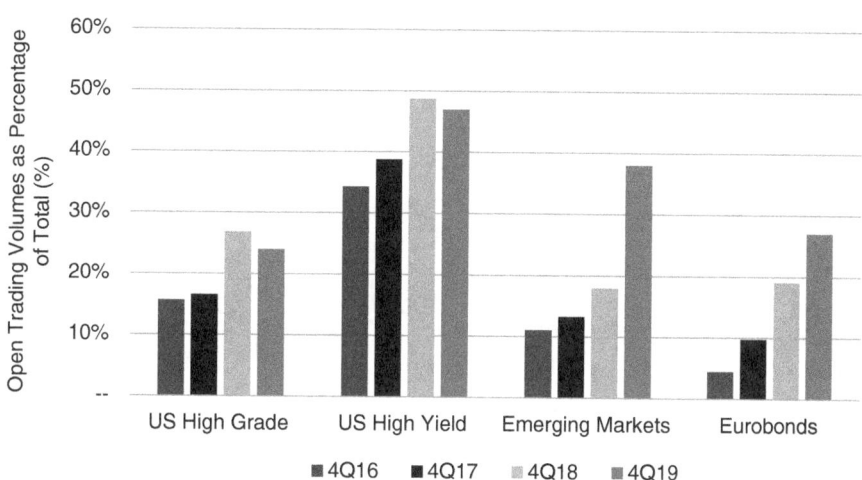

EXHIBIT 14.8   MarketAxess Open Trading Volumes as Percentage of Total Volume
Source: MarketAxess, as of December 31, 2019.

As the pre-crisis principal trading paradigm evolved into more of an agency-driven model, centralized marketplaces promoted diversity of market participants and price discovery. On the MarketAxess platform, Open Trading Volumes in IG and HY bonds represented 24% and 47% of total volumes in Q4'2019, respectively, as shown in Exhibit 14.8.

14.2   THE DEVELOPMENT OF AN INDEX-BASED ECOSYSTEM

14.2.1   Fixed-Income ETFs: Continued Strong Growth and Adoption

Fixed-income ETF adoption has surged across both institutional and wealth channels. In 2017, LQD (BlackRock's iShares IG bond ETF) was the largest ETF holding at insurance companies across all asset classes.[3] Fixed-income ETF AUM and trading volumes have continued to increase, with trading volumes in particular growing at an accelerated rate, as shown in Exhibit 14.9. While fixed-income ETF AUM rose by 16.2% from 2020–2021, fixed-income

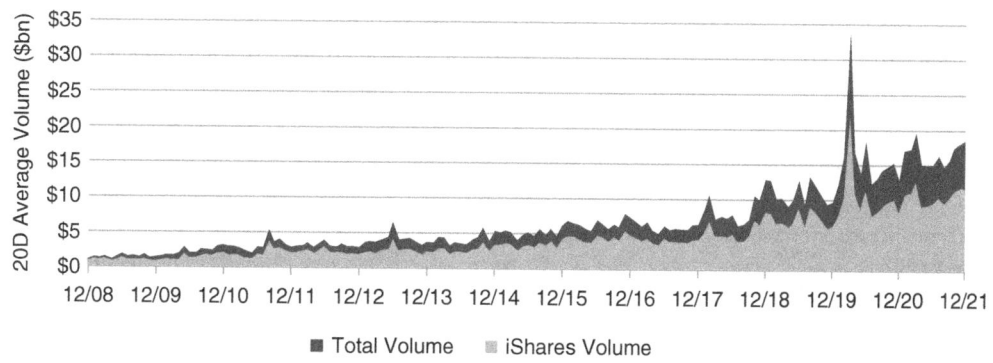

EXHIBIT 14.9   US Fixed-Income ETF Average Daily Volume (ADV)
Sources: BlackRock, Bloomberg, as of December 31, 2021.

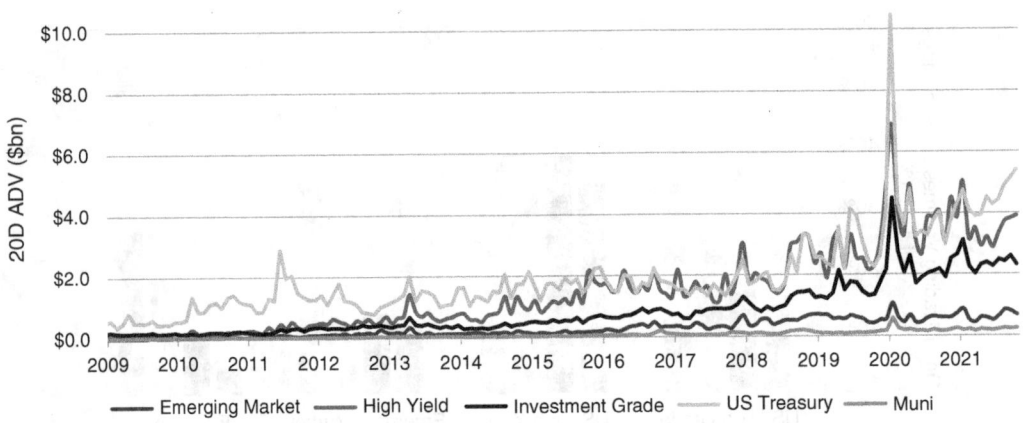

EXHIBIT 14.10 US Fixed-Income ETF Average Daily Volume (ADV) by Sector
Sources: BlackRock, Bloomberg, as of December 31, 2021.

ETF trading volume grew by 3.3%.[4] Trading volume in credit products increased at a particularly brisk rate (see Exhibit 14.10), in part due to growing activity in related derivatives and cash bond trading associated with credit portfolio trading.

US HY ETF and US IG ETF volumes are also growing relative to HY OTC and IG OTC cash volumes, particularly in times of heightened volatility. For example, as shown in Exhibit 14.11, in December 2018, US HY ETF secondary volumes represented 45% of OTC HY cash volumes, an all-time high, as HY spreads widened by 108 bp.[5]

14.2.2 Portfolio Trading and Fixed-Income ETFs

To appreciate the extent to which fixed-income ETFs have proliferated in the post-crisis fixed-income ecosystem, the notion of a portfolio trade needs to be understood. A portfolio trade is a transaction in which a counterparty bids or offers a portfolio of multiple line items simultaneously as a single trade. Such a transaction differs from traditional Offers Wanted in Competition (OWIC) and Bids Wanted in Competition (BWIC) in that the portfolio trade is executed in an all-or-none fashion. (Note, however that significant pre-trade line item negotiations may still occur between the counterparty and end client to adjust the portfolio.) Portfolio trades can be highly customized to client needs and risk profiles.

Approximately $75 billion in IG and $38 billion in HY portfolio trades occurred in 2019, accounting for more than 1% of trading activity in each market and more than double the overall activity relative to 2018.[6] In 2019, the average portfolio trade size was approximately $53 million with an average of 89 unique CUSIPs per transaction.[7] Accordingly, individual positions in portfolio trades remained fairly small (i.e., less than $2 million). Trading costs for portfolio trades can vary substantially depending on size, number, and composition of the line items, market conditions, and correlation of the basket to a liquid credit ETF. If executed strategically, portfolio trades can lead to substantial efficiencies in both cost and execution time. Exhibit 14.12 provides a schematic of a typical portfolio trade.

The growth of portfolio trading is another reflection of investor demand for utilizing baskets of bonds, as opposed to individual line items, for investment and risk management purposes. Electronic trading at the single name level offers investors ease of execution, but there are practical limitations on size. ETFs allow investors to gain exposure to specific asset

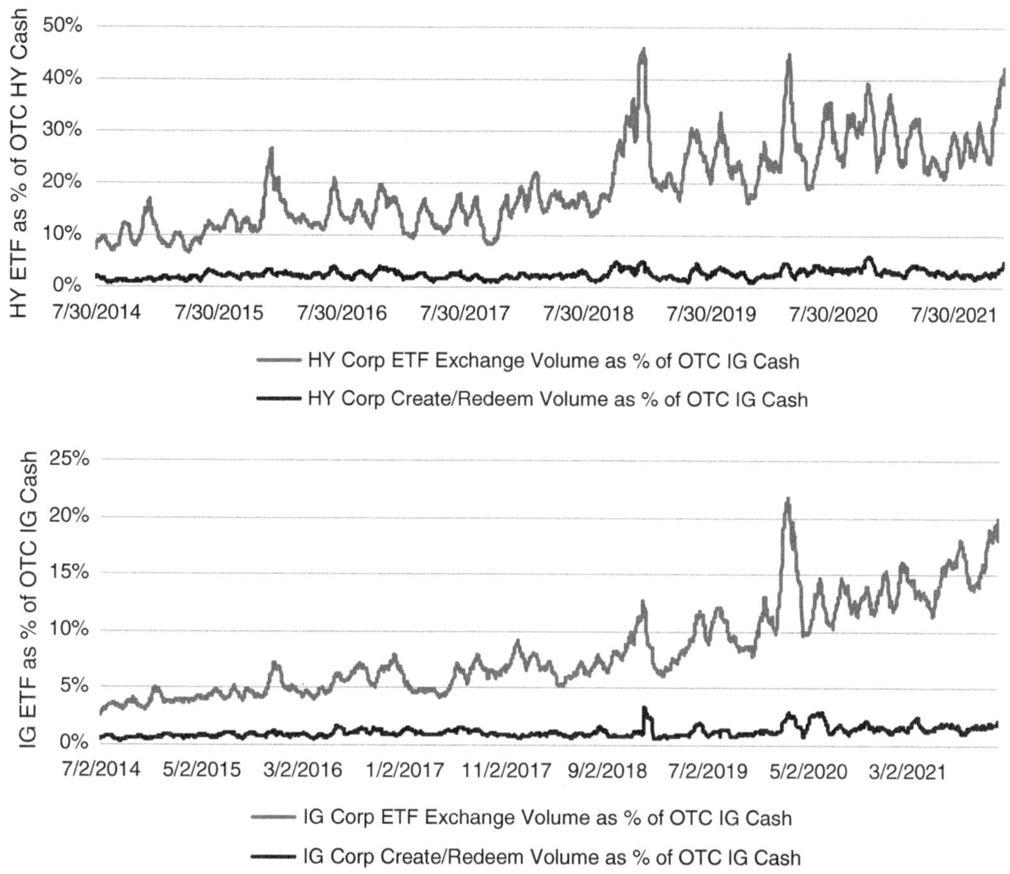

HY ETF as % of OTC HY Cash

—— HY Corp ETF Exchange Volume as % of OTC IG Cash

—— HY Corp Create/Redeem Volume as % of OTC IG Cash

IG ETF as % of OTC IG Cash

—— IG Corp ETF Exchange Volume as % of OTC IG Cash

—— IG Corp Create/Redeem Volume as % of OTC IG Cash

EXHIBIT 14.11 High-Yield (HY) and Investment-Grade (IG) Corporate ETFs Trading Volumes as Percentage of OTC Cash Volumes
Sources: BlackRock, Bloomberg, as of December 31, 2021.
Note: Inclusive of all US IG Corporate ETFs, based on BlackRock's database. There can be no assurance an ETF's trading or liquidity will be maintained.

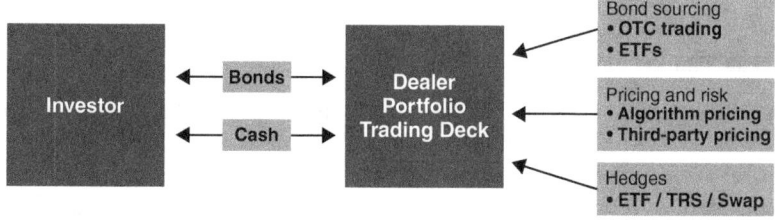

EXHIBIT 14.12 Portfolio Trade Example
Source: BlackRock. For illustrative purposes only.

classes in large sizes, but constraints exist if investors desire more bespoke bond portfolios that are not currently offered in an ETF format. Fixed-income ETF liquidity can be utilized to help the portfolio trading protocol bridge this gap.

Portfolio trades are also a result of dealer counterparties adapting their business models to the post-crisis environment by investing in and harnessing both technology and the ETF ecosystem.

Ultimately, fixed-income ETFs have contributed to the growth in portfolio trading in two important ways:

1. *Risk Management*—Dealer counterparties use fixed-income ETFs to hedge the inventory that is being aggregated for a portfolio trade or use the creation/redemption mechanism to source or liquidate resulting bond inventory from such transactions. The equity exchange liquidity of fixed-income ETFs provides dealer counterparties with an efficient inventory and risk management tool.[8]

2. *Valuation and Transparency*—Fixed-income ETF creation/redemption baskets may contain hundreds of bonds, which need to be purchased or sold. As the volume of creation/redemption activity has sharply increased, so has trading activity across a larger number of bonds, resulting in greater market transparency. Coupled with investments in technology, such data enable dealers to more efficiently price portfolio trades. Counterparties can now algorithmically price thousands of bonds simultaneously, something that was previously extremely time consuming and not always easily done. Finally, through the trading of fixed-income ETFs on an exchange, market participants are able to observe the value of the portfolio being formulated as well as the implied value of the underlying securities, which is especially powerful during times of stress when single name corporate bonds' liquidity tends to be diminished.

14.2.3 Continued Growth in Bond Index Derivatives Markets

While portfolio trading directly impacts the cash bond market, the ongoing growth in the fixed-income index derivatives markets has also helped to increase activity, improve liquidity, and enhance the overall robustness of the ecosystem. Hedging activity, which can drive volumes in fixed-income ETFs and cash bonds, may aid in additional price discovery and drive relative value opportunities across similar instruments (e.g., total return swaps [TRS] versus ETF). Currently, the most actively used index derivative instruments include credit default swaps (CDX) and options, fixed-index TRS, and fixed-income ETF options.

14.2.4 Fixed-Income ETF Options

The option markets for fixed-income ETFs, particularly credit ETFs, have been growing even more rapidly than ETFs themselves. Like the underlying fixed-income ETFs, fixed-income ETF options are exchange traded and are cleared instruments with a robust, broad market-making community. This gives them a substantial access and liquidity advantage over bilateral OTC option products. Fixed-income ETF options also have the advantage of being more closely aligned with the underlying cash bond markets—a highly desirable feature for exposure and risk management.

14.3 IMPLICATIONS FOR INVESTING, PORTFOLIO MANAGEMENT, AND RISK MANAGEMENT

Rapid increases in primary volumes and portfolio trading, continued broadening in secondary exchange trading volumes, and the explosive growth in fixed-income ETF derivatives markets have converged to form a powerful ecosystem that has become an integral part of bond markets. The following sections discuss how investors are harnessing this toolkit to seek better investment and risk management results.

14.3.1 Use Cases for Fixed-Income ETFs and Other Index Exposures

Broadly speaking, there are six general use cases for fixed-income ETFs, though these use cases could also apply to other index/basket forms of exposure as well.

1. **Strategic Asset Allocation**
   Fixed-income ETFs provide low-cost, efficient access to bond market exposures for core beta and/or factor positions. Portfolio managers may find that low-cost index instruments such as fixed-income ETFs can form the core of their beta and/or factor tilts more efficiently than individual OTC bonds.

2. **Tactical Asset Allocation**
   Index products can provide opportunistic exposure to specific asset classes, geographic regions, and maturity ranges. An example would be a portfolio manager with a near term but high conviction view on a specific fixed-income asset class, but not at the sector or security level. The manager could go long or short an ETF or associated index exposure to rapidly and efficiently implement this view.

3. **Liquidity Management**
   Index products can provide a liquidity sleeve or buffer that maintains portfolio yield and beta exposure. Given ongoing post-crisis challenges in single-name bond liquidity, managers are less inclined to rely upon liquidating multiple single names to meet liquidity needs. Using a fixed-income ETF or other index exposure could be better for this purpose.

4. **Cash Management**
   Fixed-income ETFs can provide potential yield enhancement and instrument diversification for longer-term cash allocations. Several fixed-income ETFs now provide exposure across shorter maturity treasury, corporate, multisector, and floating rate exposures.

5. **Portfolio Transitions**
   Portfolio managers can harness the liquidity of the fixed-income ETF ecosystem to change the allocation mix in a bond portfolio. As an example, a pension fund may want to shift its allocation from IG to HY. Rather than trying to liquidate the IG allocation bond-by-bond, the manager could in-kind the IG portfolio into one or more fixed-income ETFs (depending on maturity and index eligibility) and use the exchange to sell the exposure more rapidly and efficiently than the OTC market. This is a classic example of a portfolio trade.

6. **Derivative Complement / Substitute**
   A wide range of index tools provide investors and portfolio managers with the ability to either gain or hedge exposure in both funded and synthetic form depending on objectives, liquidity, and cost efficiency. As an example, a high-yield manager may wish to

temporarily reduce their overall market beta. Rather than sell down individual securities, the manager could buy protection on high-yield CDX, borrow and short a high-yield ETF, short a TRS or future, or buy a put option on a high-yield ETF. The choice of exposure will depend upon the correlation between the given instrument and their bond portfolio, the liquidity of the instrument relative to the desired size of the position, and the cost of the instrument on both an absolute and relative value basis.

14.4   THE FUTURE STATE OF PORTFOLIO CONSTRUCTION

Looking ahead, ongoing changes in bond trading protocols and technology should continue to have profound implications for bond markets, investors, and portfolio construction.

14.4.1   Portfolio Engineering and Construction

Fixed-income portfolio managers will increasingly recognize that index exposures, such as fixed-income ETFs, can serve as the beta and factor components of bond portfolios. Nearly all diversified bond portfolios and strategies contain elements of beta and factor exposure, and the cost of these exposures at the individual bond level can be quite high.

As an example, consider a "core plus" bond strategy that contains elements of both IG and HY exposure. One such exposure contains thousands of bonds, yet is highly correlated to a simple 90/10 blend of the Bloomberg Barclays US Aggregate Bond Index and the ICE BAML High Yield Index.[9] The blended index exposure has a comparable level of return volatility and an annualized total return within 20 bp of the actively managed strategy.

This is not to suggest that a simple blended index strategy could replicate an alpha seeking, core plus strategy. Rather, it demonstrates the presence of a high level of beta and factor exposure in the form of a static tilt to high-yield exposure. Rather than building up these exposures with individual bonds, a portfolio manager may benefit from improved liquidity, cost, and operational efficiencies by employing the use of low-cost index products.

14.5   CONCLUSION

Bond markets are modernizing at a breathtaking pace. Continued adoption of fixed-income ETFs and bond index derivatives, continued growth in electronic trading and all-to-all protocols, the surge in portfolio trading of cash bonds, advances in algorithmic pricing, and dramatic improvements in technology are changing the way investors trade and create and manage fixed-income exposures.

These developments will likely only continue to accelerate, and market participants on both the buy-side and sell-side will need to continue to rapidly evolve their operating models, trading infrastructure, and technology in order to keep pace.

Ultimately, all of this rapid change accrues to the benefit of investors. Liquidity and transparency should continue to improve, and fixed-income portfolio managers are now able to more rapidly construct and more efficiently and precisely manage bond portfolios than ever before.

NOTES

1. This chapter was originally published by BlackRock in 2019 and adapted for this book. Special thanks to Daniel Veiner, Stephen Laipply, Carolyn Weinberg, Samara Cohen, Vasiliki Pachatouridi, Hui Sien Koay, and Matt Wooley for their thought leadership and help in adapting the chapter.
2. Refer to 2017 Next Generation Bond Market: https://www.sec.gov/spotlight/fixed-income-advisory-committee/blackrock-next-generation-bond-market-fimsa-011118.pdf.
3. S&P, as of 12/31/2017.
4. BlackRock, Bloomberg, as of 12/31/21.
5. BlackRock, Bloomberg. HY spread widened measured by changed in the Bloomberg Barclays US HY Index OAS change from 11/30/2018 to 12/31/2018.
6. JP Morgan, as of 12/31/2019.
7. Morgan Stanley, as of 12/31/2019.
8. Shares of iShares ETFs may be bought and sold throughout the day on the exchange through any brokerage account. Shares are not individually redeemable from the ETF; however, shares may be redeemed directly from an ETF by Authorized Participants in very large creation/redemption units. There can be no assurance that an active trading market for shares of an ETF will develop or be maintained.
9. Laipply et al., 2019.

CHAPTER 15

The LIBOR Transition

Jack Hattem

Managing Director, Portfolio Management Group, BlackRock

15.1 INTRODUCTION

Interest rate benchmarks serve many purposes across the market ecosystem. Following the 2008 Global Financial Crisis, significant changes have been made. When the first edition of this book was initially published, the London Interbank Offered Rate (LIBOR) was the primary reference index for US interest rate derivatives markets and commonly used as a valuation benchmark for the US mortgage market, floating rate securitizations, and much of the asset-backed securities markets. LIBOR continued to be present throughout financial systems for decades and served as an interest rate benchmark for hundreds of trillions of dollars of financial instruments. However, LIBOR's credibility came into question due to manipulation allegations, and after extensive review, the Financial Conduct Authority (FCA)[1] determined that it would no longer compel panel banks to submit quotes after year-end 2021.

As of December 2021, Sterling LIBOR, along with several other global interbank offered rates (IBORs), ceased to exist. Cessations dates were established for LIBOR settings, including USD LIBOR, which will continue to be set until June 30, 2023. As a result, multiple Alternative Reference Rates (ARRs) were defined for major currencies, as shown in Exhibit 15.1, and transition efforts have been underway. However, the migration to the ARRs has been very complex given the global reach and multiple asset classes impacted. Additionally, markets for ARRs have been at different stages of development and adoption.

An Alternative Reference Rates Committee (ARRC) was established by the Federal Reserve Board and the New York Fed to help guide the United States, transition away from LIBOR benchmarks. BlackRock participates in the ARRC in the United States to help identify transitional challenges and collaborate with other institutions for solutions. BlackRock was invited to participate in an advisory capacity in 2017 and as a full member upon the ARRC's expansion in 2018. BlackRock advocated for a legislative solution for tough legacy products and the SOFR First initiative, which strengthened market liquidity. Additionally, BlackRock participates in the Risk-Free Rates (RFR) working group in the UK. The ARRC estimated that $223 trillion of exposure remained outstanding to USD LIBOR as of March 2021,[2] while GBP LIBOR exposures were estimated at $30 trillion at the end of 2018.[3] Clearly, the scope of the transition was immense.

Since the LIBOR cessation was announced, benchmark reform required awareness, assessment, and action from various market participants spanning portfolio managers, risk managers, traders, financial modelers, and technologists. Portfolio and risk managers needed

Currency	Rate	Description	Type of Rate	Products	Began Publishing
US Dollar	Secured Overnight Financing Rate (SOFR)	Repo-based index to reflect overnight funding rates (calculated as volume-weighted median based on tri-party repo data from Bank of New York Mellon and general collateral financing repo data from DTCC)	Secured	Futures Cleared Swaps FRNs	New York Fed began publishing the overnight rate in April 2018 and SOFR Averages and Index in March 2020.
Sterling	Sterling Overnight Index Average (SONIA)	Effective overnight interest rate for unsecured GBP bank transactions	Unsecured	Futures Cleared Swaps FRNS	Bank of England reformed SONIA in April 2018, and it began publishing a compounded daily index and averages from July 2020.
Euro	Euro Short-Term Rate (€STR)[4]	€STR reflects the wholesale euro unsecured overnight borrowing of euro area banks	Unsecured		European Central Bank began to formally publish the €STR rate in October 2019.
Swiss Franc	Swiss Average Rate Overnight (SARON)	Repo-based index to reflect overnight funding rates	Secured	Futures Cleared Swaps	SARON introduced in August 2009, with historical data available from June 1999.
Japanese Yen	Tokyo Overnight Average Rate (TONA)	Transaction-based benchmark for the uncollateralized overnight call rate	Unsecured	Futures Cleared Swaps	Study Group on Risk-Free Reference Rates identified TONA in 2016 as the risk-free rate.

EXHIBIT 15.1   Alternative Reference Rates

to assess portfolios and identify instruments that referenced LIBOR, such as interest rate swaps, asset-backed securities, loans, and floating rate notes. Additionally, client portfolio guidelines and fund performance benchmarks that referenced LIBOR needed to be addressed. Changes from the unsecured LIBOR curve to risk-free rate curves impacted risk models, including historical analyses. Thus, the transition effort required detailed examination of existing exposures, along with a detailed understanding of the impact of the differences between the ARRs and LIBOR. Legacy exposures in each portfolio and investment strategy were different, which meant that different portfolios faced different trade-offs.

As a large asset manager, BlackRock manages thousands of fixed-income accounts on behalf of retail and institutional clients. These portfolios are managed on a fiduciary basis. Every account is a separate legal entity with individual prospectuses or client mandates. Each portfolio management team has an independent investment process that is monitored by the firm's risk management group. At BlackRock, transitioning to the new ARRs initially required a detailed analysis of existing LIBOR exposures across the fixed-income account universe and their related risks. BlackRock then developed tools and processes to enable investment teams to assess and manage LIBOR exposures and their related risks. Additionally, BlackRock incorporated new data into models and tools and began actively trading new ARRs. Workflows were modified to incorporate the new reference rates into Aladdin, while continuing to manage existing positions that referenced LIBOR. Furthermore, BlackRock established internal working groups that met regularly with representatives from the risk, investments, trading, client relations, legal, accounting, and operations teams to coordinate the transition.

15.2 IMPLICATIONS TO PORTFOLIO AND RISK MANAGEMENT

Upon the FCA's announcement of LIBOR's cessation dates, the rules-based "fallback spreads" became fixed, meaning that the fallback spread for 3-month USD LIBOR is 26.2 bp. For products that adopt the fallback plus spread methodology, there is no longer ambiguity with respect to valuation or risk on these contracts at the time of transition.[5] With this information, portfolio management decisions, along with valuation and risk models, can incorporate the timeline and application of fallback spreads.

Further, the FCA indicated that there should be no new transactions referencing US LIBOR beyond the end of 2021. While new issuance in the cash markets have been transitioning away from LIBOR, portfolio managers are still able to transact in LIBOR-based instruments as hedges for existing positions. While there has been concern that the transition from IBORs may create market disruption, fixing fallback spreads and further clarity on methodology should mitigate this risk and help facilitate an orderly transition. US federal legislation was passed in 2022 creating a pathway forward for "tough legacy" exposures (those that had no fallback or whose fallback referenced LIBOR) to transition to a "SOFR plus Spread" methodology. As cessation approaches, the cleanest portfolio solution is to transition exposures actively away from LIBOR.

15.3 SHIFT FROM LIBOR TO SOFR

SOFR was not selected with the expectation that it would be a direct equivalent to LIBOR. Rather, it is intended to be a representative risk-free benchmark that is transparent and backed by high transactional volume in the United States. The ARRC endorsed a forward-looking

Term SOFR rate, representing another positive step for a segment of the market (specifically, loans) that had been delayed in transitioning. The SOFR First initiative, similar to the UK's Sonia First, has led to growth in liquidity and daily volumes of SOFR swaps. These initiatives aimed to help switch trading conventions in the interdealer market from LIBOR to SOFR. They have also helped to promote behavioral changes and the growth of liquidity.

Exhibit 15.2 shows several figures that demonstrate SOFR's growth and adoption. As shown in Exhibit 15.2, Figure 2, SOFR swaps have accounted for more than 90% of daily volumes on average of interest rate risk traded in the outright linear swaps market in September and October 2022, while LIBOR swaps accounted for less than 4% of the overall volume in October 2022.[6]

There are key differences between SOFR[7] and USD LIBOR. Specifically, SOFR lacks a credit component, as SOFR is a secured funding rate derived from the repo market. This differs from LIBOR, which is unsecured and incorporates an element of credit risk. When managing a credit basis risk, like any other, portfolio and risk managers must be mindful of portfolio objectives and constraints alongside market depth and liquidity. Unlike LIBOR, SOFR is an overnight rate. Where LIBOR is typically quoted at forward points (1-month, 3-month, 6-month), a 3-month SOFR rate for interest rate products is derived by compounding the overnight rate in arrears. This is consistent with the conventions for interest rate swaps using overnight index swaps (OIS).

Figure 1: Daily Average Interdealer Outright Linear Swaps Risk Traded

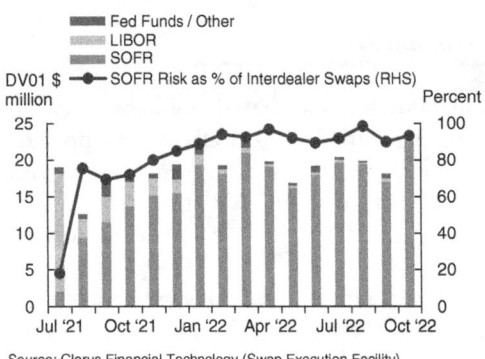

Source: Clarus Financial Technology (Swap Execution Facility)

Figure 2: Daily Average Total Outright Swaps Risk Traded

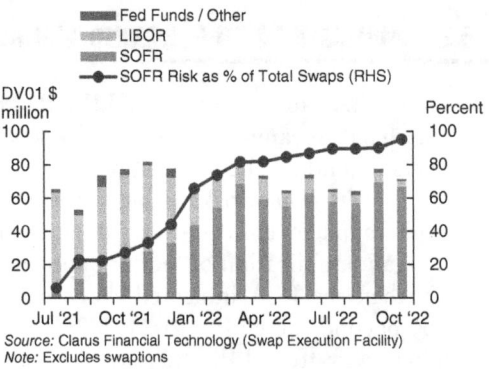

Source: Clarus Financial Technology (Swap Execution Facility)
Note: Excludes swaptions

Figure 3: SOFR Linear Swaps Open Interest

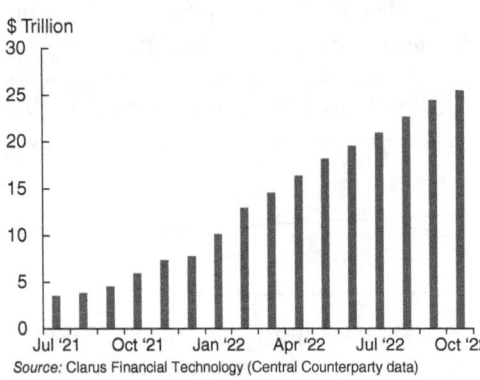

Source: Clarus Financial Technology (Central Counterparty data)

Figure 4: Monthly SOFR OTC Derivatives Volumes

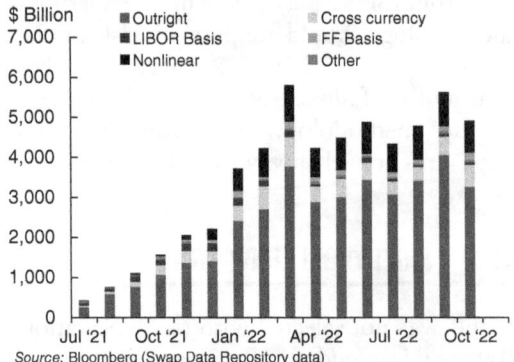

Source: Bloomberg (Swap Data Repository data)

EXHIBIT 15.2   Linear Swaps

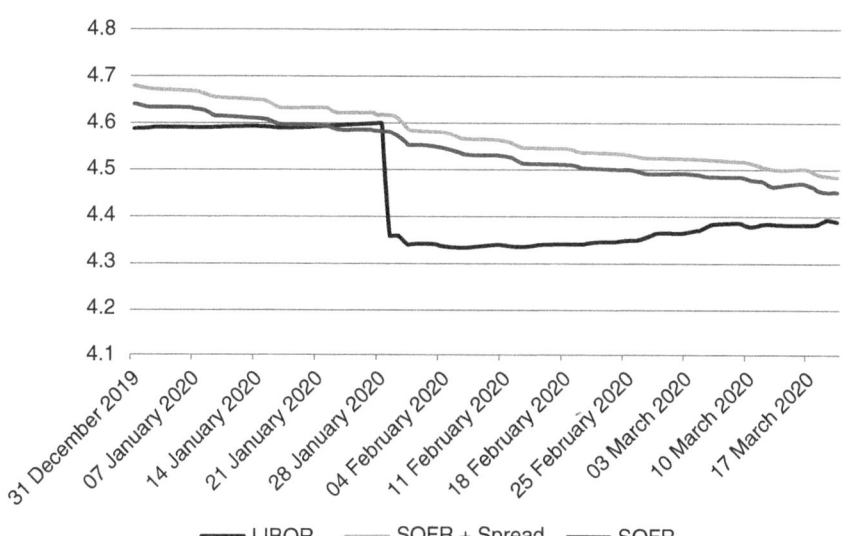

EXHIBIT 15.3 3M LIBOR Versus SOFR Versus SOFR Plus Spread Parent Leg Durations
Source: BlackRock.

While much of the LIBOR transition focused on the adoption of new instruments and changing market conventions, the analytical impact on LIBOR instruments that mature beyond 2021 has also received extensive scrutiny. Exhibit 15.3 illustrates the impact of transitioning from a USD LIBOR instrument to SOFR on three 5Y interest rate swaps—3-M LIBOR, SOFR, and SOFR +34 bp spread (Deferred Spread).

As shown in Exhibit 15.3, the duration profile of the swaps between LIBOR and SOFR differs quite significantly. The duration of the LIBOR swap drops sharply around the payment date of the floater, whereas the SOFR swaps exhibit a smoother downwards trend. While the duration profile of the SOFR swap may sometimes be more preferable in certain cases, (e.g., duration hedging), recognizing that a SOFR swap behaves differently is important.

A significant jump in the duration of the LIBOR floating leg, which is aligned with the drop seen from the parent leg (duration is approximately the net of the two legs) is seen in Exhibit 15.4. SOFR with 0 spread has a duration approximately equal to 1 day. The SOFR leg with a spread applied has a slightly higher duration. Adding a spread forces it to behave more like a fixed-rate instrument.

15.4   RISK MANAGEMENT IMPACT AND COORDINATION

The LIBOR transition reinforces the importance of having a deep understanding of products and how they are interconnected. From a risk management perspective, overall basis risks will increase in the market with the introduction of products that reference these new ARRs. These basis risks vary by construction, given the substantive difference between a reference rate that contains a dynamic credit component versus a riskless credit funding curve. Similarly, basis risks can arise due to the nuanced differences in compounding differences.

Three-month LIBOR was a standardized reference rate incorporated into both securities and derivatives; there has been growth of ARRs along with increased usage of

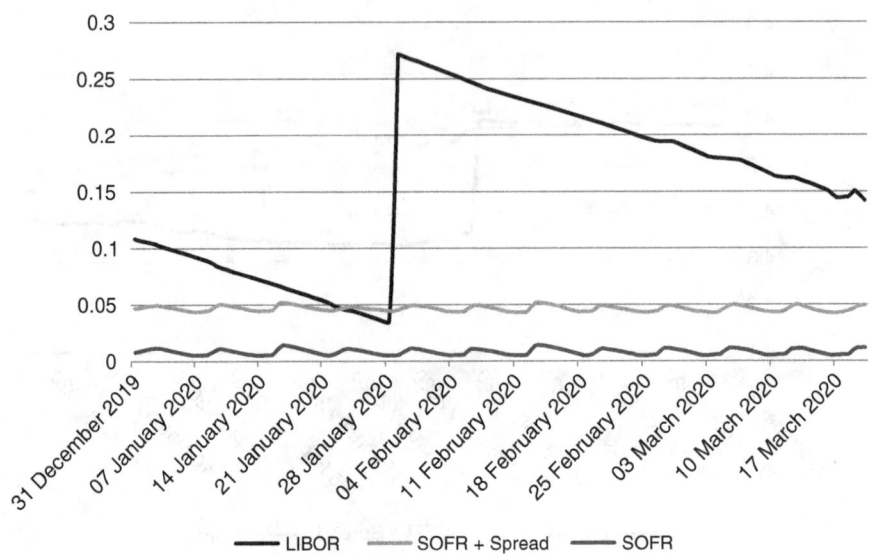

EXHIBIT 15.4   LIBOR vs SOFR vs SOFR Plus Spread Floating Leg Durations
Source: BlackRock.

OIS and CMT curves contributing to potential mismatches between an asset (or former-LIBOR-now-converted assets) and its associated hedges. However, with appropriate preparation and attention to detail, these risks can be managed, alongside the many other risks that currently exist in markets.

As liquidity grows in the ARRs, some products may change; differences in benchmarks must be carefully understood as products and solutions evolve to meet end-user needs. Understanding portfolio objectives and risk guidelines will be foundational to selecting a performance or risk benchmark replacement. There is no one-size-fits-all solution for every portfolio managed. Different investment teams by design manage their clients' portfolios differently. This means that across a multi-investment team manager, like BlackRock, there will likely be disparate holdings of LIBOR-based instruments at varying maturity points across the aggregate book. The same investment team may have managed portfolios for different periods, increasing the likelihood that portfolios may retain different vintages of securities. Every investment management team with remaining exposure to LIBOR needs to assess its current exposure and determine the appropriate transition plan.

Risk management systems need to be flexible to incorporate new data and conventions as market structure evolves. While the transition is still in progress, reflecting on the past several years of benchmark reform, global coordination was a key factor in mitigating any widespread systemic risk. Great effort was made to secure the stability of these alternative reference rates in the future. The process continues to evolve. However, we can be sure that floating rate markets and market structure for both cash and derivatives will continue to evolve to meet the needs of clients.

15.5   REFLECTIONS ON A BENCHMARK REFORMS

LIBOR, as a reference rate and benchmark, was deeply embedded throughout global financial markets. LIBOR not only served as an index for trillions of dollars of exposures across the cash and derivatives markets, it was also used as a floating swap reset rate and a benchmark index for floating rate securities. Beyond serving as a reset index, LIBOR was used as a portfolio and risk benchmark throughout portfolio management. The size and scope of benchmark reform was massive. Market participants initially were resistant to embrace the change, noting both the uses and interdependencies of LIBOR within the global bond markets as challenges. The transition required a significant amount of global collaboration and organization, as LIBORs are different globally and did not migrate at the same pace nor into the same type of rate.

From a portfolio management perspective, benchmark reform occurred in three stages: *awareness, assessment, and action.* Education was a key element throughout the process to understand the nature of the transition, the reasons behind it, the new reference rates chosen, and the process by which the transition would occur. The United States chose SOFR as LIBOR's replacement given the high daily volumes in the overnight repo markets, giving confidence to the stability of the rate going forward and in the quality of the process by which it was derived.

However, there were key differences between LIBOR and the newly selected rates. Understanding these differences was an important step to helping ensure a smooth transition. As discussed, USD LIBOR and SOFR have different conventions (compound overnight versus term) and represent different things (notably, there is no dynamic credit component embedded within SOFR). Basis risk was not necessarily a hurdle to the transition; it just needed to be understood.

Assessment of positions involved aggregating exposures across maturity, asset class, and by fallback rate. Some legacy cash securities did not even contemplate a cessation of LIBOR. Such "tough legacy" securities were originally left in limbo until a concerted effort was put forth to pass legislation at both the New York state and federal levels to provide a pathway forward for these securities. Assessing portfolio-level exposures to LIBOR occurred as well; in some cases, a replacement risk or performance benchmark had to be chosen. Commonly used fixed-income risk metrics had to migrate as well, such as LIBOR OAS.

Finally, an action plan needed to be developed. Industry forums and trade associations worked to establish timelines and protocols for contractual transition of contracts. In many cases there was a preference for "active transition," where end users could be deliberate about when and how to migrate existing LIBOR-based exposures to a new reference rate. Initiatives such as "SOFR First" in the United States were announced by a subcommittee of the CFTC's Market Risk Advisory Committee (MRAC), which helped drive liquidity growth in the newly established SOFR markets. The establishment of this liquidity began in futures and then swaps and then options. Active transition required surveillance of liquidity developments in the new rates while being mindful of the potential liquidity deterioration of the old. Notably, there has not been a one-size-fits-all approach to the transition. Certain segments of the market, notably business loans, required a forward-looking term rate. Thoughtful collaboration created a solution while not bifurcating markets at too early a stage, which would threaten the viability of overnight SOFR, compounded in arrears.

The LIBOR transition can be reflected on as a monumental task that required tremendous efforts from the official sector and market participants. Markets will continue to evolve and innovate to meet the needs of end users. And the benchmark reform efforts are paving a path toward the future with more stable, honest, and reliable reference rates for the financial system.

NOTES

1. The FCA is the UK regulator of the LIBOR administrator who publishes the rate.
2. ARRC, March 2021.
3. Working Group on Sterling Risk-Free Reference Rates, 2018.
4. €STR is the new interbank rate slated to replace EONIO Euribor.
5. This includes nearly all new issuance since the beginning of benchmark reform and all derivate products, both new and legacy, adhering to the ISDA protocols.
6. ARRC, "Meeting Readout," November 9, 2022.
7. ARRC announced in June 2017 its choice of SOFR as an alternative to USD LIBOR.

CHAPTER 16

Derivatives Reform: The Rise of Swap Execution Facilities and Central Counterparties

Eileen Kiely

Managing Director, Risk & Quantitative Analysis, BlackRock

Jack Hattem

Managing Director, Portfolio Management Group, BlackRock

16.1 THE CALL FOR CHANGE: 2008 GLOBAL FINANCIAL CRISIS

For many, the defining moment of the 2008 Global Financial Crisis (GFC) was the Lehman default, which exposed a complex and opaque web of over-the-counter (OTC) derivatives contracts among dealers and clients across the globe. Soon after this default, it became evident that many of these derivative trades were insufficiently collateralized or not collateralized at all, and many were subject to ongoing valuation disputes. In contrast, the disciplined risk mitigation techniques used in the exchange-traded and centrally cleared markets proved to be more resilient. Global regulators actively sought to leverage this central trading and clearing architecture, ultimately producing the first step toward derivatives market reform at the 2009 G20[1] summit in Pittsburgh, Pennsylvania. The following recommendation initiated structural market reforms across the globe:

> *All standardized OTC derivative contracts should be traded on exchanges or electronic trading platforms, where appropriate, and cleared through central counterparties by end [of] 2012 at the latest.*[2]

The G20 recommendations targeted two distinct functions of the derivatives markets: trading and clearing. Trading is the process of agreeing upon the structure and price of a trade. Prior to the GFC, derivatives were negotiated, priced, and traded between two parties, with little transparency to the market and regulators. Similarly, derivatives were financially serviced between the same two parties, including exchanging ongoing payments and collateral when required. Subsequent market reforms sought to (1) enhance transparency and competition in derivatives through mandating electronification of trading through exchanges or Swap Execution Facilities (SEFs) and (2) reduce counterparty credit risk by mandating the use of central counterparties (CCPs). The result of these changes has been a significant market-wide shift from voice/phone trading to electronic execution facilities and from bilateral trade servicing to CCPs.

16.1.1   SEFs[3]

Initially, OTC derivatives (often referred to generically as "swaps") traded on a decentralized basis, and price discovery occurred bilaterally between buyers and sellers. These markets did not generate the same price discovery benefits as those from central limit order books as seen in listed derivatives markets. Post-GFC reforms sought to move OTC derivative trading activity toward centralized electronic platforms to enhance efficiency and provide transparency. Serving as a similar function as an exchange, SEFs are strictly price discovery utilities and, therefore, rarely create credit exposure in trade execution. Trade settlement and clearing functions, like margin requirements, payments, and delivery, are delegated to a CCP. SEFs also provide trade confirmations that reflect legally agreed upon terms.

16.1.2   CCPs

A CCP's core purpose is to provide credit intermediation. Taking trades from exchanges, SEFs, or OTC participants, a CCP serves as the buyer to each seller and the seller to each buyer. A CCP sits between the two parties in order to guarantee financial performance over the life of the trade. Operating on a market risk neutral basis, a CCP only faces market risk upon the default of one (or more) of its members. In order to manage the risk of a defaulting counterparty, the CCP uses collateral and other mechanisms, which will be discussed in more detail later in this chapter.

A CCP has members (generally dealers) who represent the ultimate buyer/seller in the trade settlement and clearing process. These members are regulated financial institutions and are subject to additional rules and oversight by the CCP, including minimum capital requirements, operational proficiency in trade processing, and managing the risks therein. A member generally provides a deposit to the CCP, which backstops any potential shortfall in collateral collected.

Exhibit 16.1 highlights the success of the G20's efforts to move derivatives into central clearing. The graph shows the notional value of outstanding interest rate swap trades (as reported by dealers) from 2008 to 1H 2021. The "Dealer" line shows the steady decline of bilateral trades, while the "CCP" line shows a commensurate increase in cleared trades since the 1H 2016, when the CCP data was officially broken out from the broader Other Financial Institutions ("Other FI") category. As shown, prior to 1H 2016 CCPs track so closely to Other FI that it can serve as a proxy for trends in cleared trades back to 2008.

16.2   THE VALUE OF DERIVATIVES IN FIXED-INCOME PORTFOLIOS

Derivatives are a critical tool for portfolio management, both for hedging purposes and synthetic positioning. They can be broadly categorized into two segments: exchange-traded derivatives (ETD) and OTC derivatives. ETDs are traded and priced on exchanges and are highly standardized contracts, usually in the form of futures or options. Their standardization facilitates liquidity and necessarily limits their customizability. In contrast, OTC derivatives are typically priced either bilaterally or on SEFs. OTC derivatives, which are most frequently

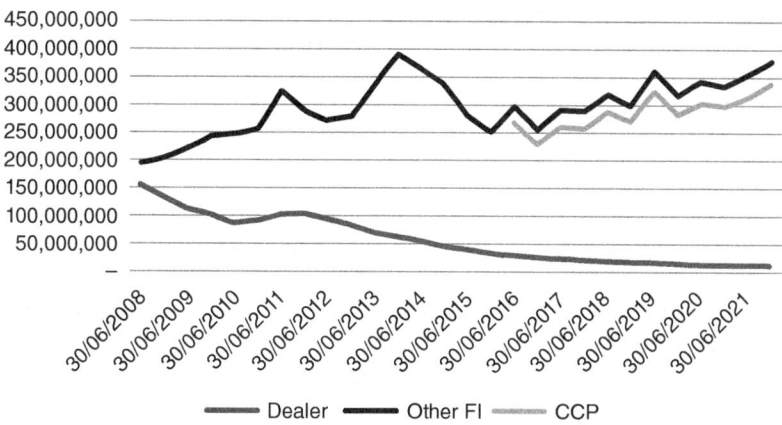

EXHIBIT 16.1   BIS OTC FI Swaps

Source: BIS OTC Derivatives Statistics: Interest Rate Swaps Notional. Available at https://stats.bis.org/statx/srs/table/d7.

swaps, are not constrained by standardized parameters, making them capable of being much more flexible investment instruments and customizable for bespoke hedging or investing activities.

ETD and OTC derivatives usage in portfolios range from managing duration and yield curve exposure (government futures and interest rate swaps) to convexity and volatility management (interest rate options of varying maturities). Basis risk can be taken or managed using derivatives to take deliberate exposure between cash instruments and futures or to establish a risk position between different yield curves (i.e., treasuries versus Fed funds or OIS). Importantly, basis risk can be managed using derivatives where a manager may choose to hedge out or isolate a particular exposure. The flexibility that OTC derivatives provide in a portfolio, along with a systemic need to hedge interest rate risk, has made the interest rate swap market the largest measured by total notional exposure.

OTC interest rate swaps can be customized to match particular dates, payment, or amortization schedules, or floating rate indices (also known as the funding leg). Swaps can be structured to match dates and hedge cash flows or isolate a spread between asset and hedge, which is known as an asset swap. The corresponding options complex, derived off of the interest rate swaps market, is known as the swaptions market. Unlike options traded on an exchange, this OTC market also has great flexibility in both strike price and maturity and generally has good depth. For example, a mortgage prepayment model may use both short-dated and long-dated volatility as inputs. The swaptions market allows a portfolio manager to create positions that isolate both gamma and vega exposures of the model's valuation of mortgages by constructing hedges using specific options.

The OTC derivatives market has grown by product type as well. Traditional use of interest rate swaps and their corresponding options has grown alongside usage of caps, floors, variance swaps, credit default swaps, volatility locks, contingent options, and a variety of other exotic derivative products. These products have seen volume increases and usage in portfolios over the past several years, as they help managers achieve particular risk objectives in terms of hedging or alpha creation.

16.3   TRADING FIXED-INCOME DERIVATIVES: THE RISE OF SEFs

Derivatives have been available to market participants for centuries,[4] with the foundation of ETDs dating back to the 1900s.[5] Over the last 100 years, ETDs were primarily traded in pits around the world, with human traders making markets in various derivatives and options. Today, only a few trading pits are active, as exchanges have replaced human traders with proprietary technologies, providing enhanced execution through better pricing and liquidity.[6] Of note, this transition has been market-driven, with market participants responding to improved trading structures.

In contrast to the market-driven changes in ETD execution, the change in OTC derivative execution was driven by the G20 recommendations. Before the G20 recommended reforms, an OTC derivative was negotiated, priced, and executed as a contract between two counterparties, such as an asset manager and broker-dealer. The exchange of risk was completed via phone and details confirmed (sometimes days later) on paper. Electronic trading via SEFs has eclipsed this trading method, dominating the bulk of OTC derivatives trading. As shown in Exhibit 16.2, at the end of the third quarter in 2022, more than 70% of interest rates swaps executed in the United States were transacted on SEFs, with risk transfer, certainty of trade, and confirmation occurring near instantly.

Making markets more efficient, this shift to electronic trading has increased pricing transparency. When interest rate swaps were traded over the phone, price discovery occurred through those phone calls because inter-broker pricing screens were not always accurate. Today, an investor can see the depth of the derivatives markets on-screen within order books. While brokers are currently standing behind the trades, it does seem inevitable that at some point the traditional end-user-to-broker (agency relationship) will become an all-to-all market, where end users may ultimately even exchange risk with each other.

While the shift to electronic trading was already underway and would likely have continued its natural progression, many of the specifics of *how* derivatives are traded were mandated by global regulators to address the market's shortcomings that were laid bare by the GFC. While each jurisdiction introduced its own rules, they were generally consistent in intent. The most transformative trading mandate was that most swaps must be traded on a SEF. On SEFs, a trade inquiry is sent to multiple parties, with the goal of providing price transparency and price discovery to the end user. The rules specify how many broker-dealers need to see a given inquiry, depending on its size.

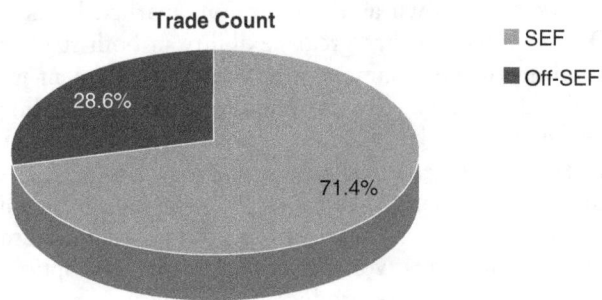

EXHIBIT 16.2   SEF Execution (Q3 2022)
Source: ISDA SwapsInfo Quarterly Review (Q3 2022, p. 12). Available at https://www.isda.org/a/ wMcgE/ SwapsInfo-Third-Quarter-of-2022-and-Year-to-September-30-2022-Review-Full-Report.pdf.

16.4　CLEARING FIXED-INCOME DERIVATIVES: THE RISE OF CCPs

In addition to trade execution requirements, regulators introduced rules that govern the ongoing financial servicing of swaps, which is referred to as clearing. Specific mandates required parties to a swap transaction to "give up" the risk management of the trade to a CCP, significantly changing the counterparty risk dynamics in the OTC derivatives markets.[7] While this section describes the basic structure of clearing, Section 16.5 details the specific tools CCPs use to manage counterparty risk and provides some recent examples of how CCPs have failed to operate as expected. Section 16.6 describes how the rise of CCPs has impacted market participants' risk profiles and risk management strategies, highlighting some key areas of vulnerability in current CCP structures.

Bilateral OTC trades result in a direct exchange of funds between the execution parties. Each counterparty pair has its own legal agreement with potentially different risk management terms, including collateral requirements and default processes. Typically, each party regularly values the price movement of the contract, also known as mark-to-market, and pre-agreed contractual details dictate the required movement of funds to cover these valuation changes. If a counterparty nears default, the legal agreement specifies the rights of the other party to exit the trade and demand payment.

The bilateral derivatives market is often depicted as an interconnected field of entities whose complex system of payments is streamlined by the introduction of a CCP (refer to Exhibit 16.3). This macro level view clearly demonstrates the efficiencies brought by a central counterparty, particularly through multilateral netting, where a multitude of payments can be reduced to just a few. It also highlights the systemic importance of the CCP who sits at the center of all the market's trades.

The CCP is not just a conduit for the payments; it also establishes and enforces the risk parameters that govern trades, which will be discussed later in this chapter. When we look at an individual trade at a micro level, the CCP's role becomes clear (refer to Exhibit 16.4), and the level of complexity introduced to the end-investor when a simple fixed-to-floating bilateral trade is transformed into a cleared trade can be understood.

The introduction of the CCP is only part of the story as the vast majority of end-investor's cleared trades are managed through an intermediary, called a clearing member (CM). Payments and margin are sent through the CM, creating a node of risk for the end-investor, who must ensure the CM has sufficient credit and operational standing to manage their funds. The arrows in Exhibit 16.4 demonstrate the transfer of credit risk across the parties. Importantly,

From non-centrally cleared to centrally cleared exposures

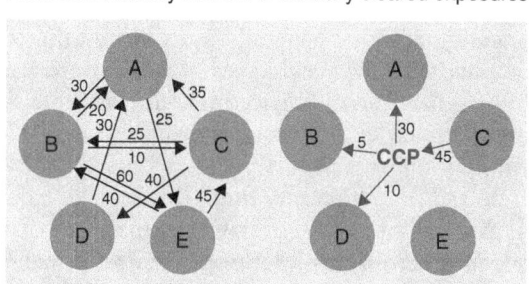

EXHIBIT 16.3　Bilateral Derivatives Market
Source: From BIS Quarterly Review, December 2015. Available at https://www.bis.org/publ/qtrpdf/r_qt1512g.pdf.

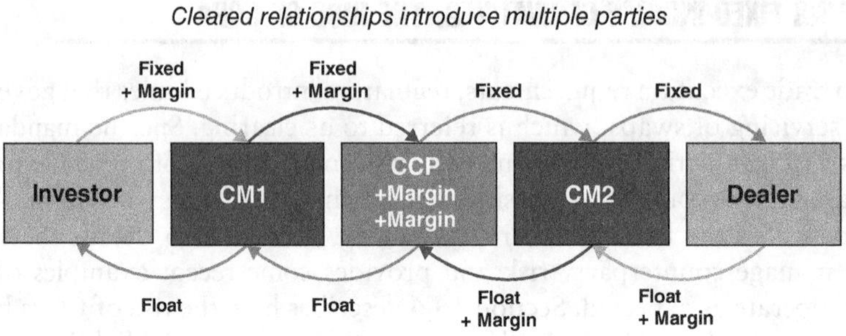

Cleared relationships introduce multiple parties

EXHIBIT 16.4   CCP Role in a Trade
Source: BlackRock. For illustrative purposes only.

the CMs do NOT assume the CCPs credit risk. Instead, the risk is transferred (contractually) to the end-investor, resulting in the end-investor having residual counterparty credit exposure to both the CM and the CCP.

16.5   CCP RISK MITIGATION TECHNIQUES

While counterparty credit risk is materially reduced through the use of CCPs, it is not entirely eliminated. Additionally, some of that counterparty risk reduction results in incremental liquidity risks and operational risks. CCPs have established a detailed and complex series of risk mitigation techniques that serve to significantly reduce the counterparty credit risk in the derivatives markets.[8] Some of the most important risk mitigation techniques that are used by CCPs include the following:

- *CM requirements and surveillance.* CCPs establish financial and operational requirements for its CMs to ensure that its membership is and remains financially and operationally sound.
- *Margin requirements.* One of the most visible and effective risk management tools is the collection of margin, also referred to as collateral. There are two different forms of margin:
  1. Variation margin (VM) is collected on a daily basis to cover the prior day's market moves, or mark-to-market.
  2. Initial margin (IM) is collected up front to protect against a potential failure of a counterparty to pay the VM when due. The calculation of IM is done through sophisticated mathematical models that generally use a blend of historical and hypothetical assumptions to predict the extreme changes in value over a specific amount of time, typically at more than a 99% confidence interval. The precise assumptions that are used to determine this metric may vary according to each CCP; the level of IM is ultimately at the discretion of the CCP.
- *Default fund.* Also referred to as guaranty fund, this layer of capital is meant to protect against the potential shortfall of IM to cover VM in the event of a counterparty default. In theory, though not in practice, this level of protection is meant to cover the tail risk not covered by the IM model. In practice, the size of the default fund is set to cover the potential loss incurred by the default of one or two of the largest CMs in extreme but plausible market conditions. However, the default fund may not be sufficient to cover an

IM shortfall. CMs contribute the vast majority of resources to the default fund, with most CCPs contributing a modest amount, which is often referred to as the CCP's "skin in the game." End-investors rarely contribute to a default fund and instead pay fees to CMs to compensate them for their contributions.[9] In addition to the prefunded resources, CMs are often subject to assessments of up to one or two times their original contribution. CMs are often contractually obligated to fund additional contributions if the total combined default fund is insufficient to cover a counterparty default. Default funds, by design, mutualize risk, meaning that each CM is ultimately underwriting some of the credit risk of the other CMs.

The totality of the financial resources the CCP has to use in a default is referred to as the waterfall, the default waterfall, or the financial safeguards package (refer to Exhibit 16.5). While most CCPs have billions of dollars in their financial safeguards packages that cover a myriad of extreme market conditions, CCPs cannot anticipate every market stress event. What happens if the resources are insufficient to cover the default? Once the waterfall is exhausted, the CCP switches to loss allocation tools, which can directly impact the end investor. These key loss allocation tools include the following:

- *Margin haircutting* is present in most major CCP's post-waterfall plans. It is usually referred to as gains haircutting or variation margin gains haircutting. A CCP can confiscate a portion of the profit from the in-the-money trades to cover remaining losses.

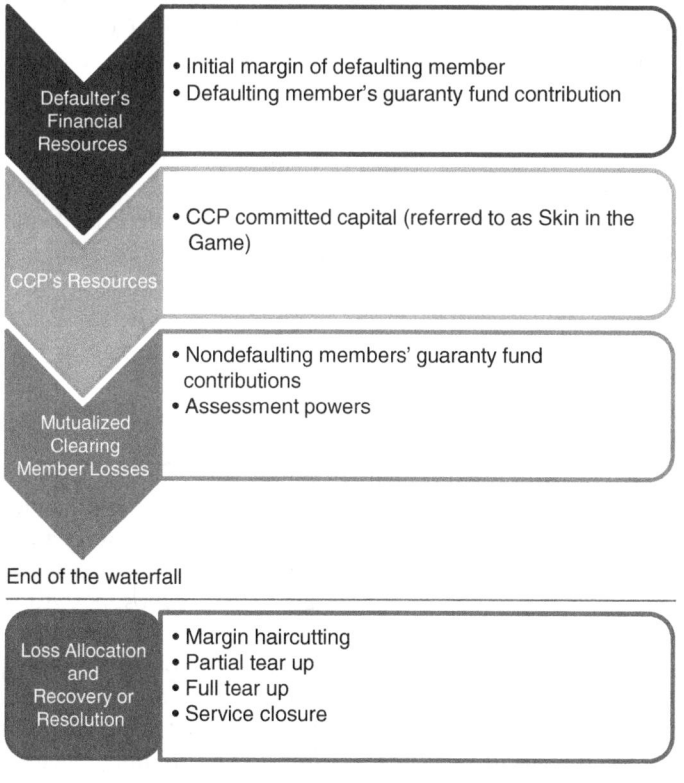

EXHIBIT 16.5   CCP Default Waterfall
Source: BlackRock. For illustrative purposes only.

- *Partial tear up* can be used to address a market dislocation in a defined subset of trades by canceling the affected trades, thus removing the obligation of the CCP to further service them and putting the end-investor's trade value to zero.
- *Full tear up* is a partial tear up on a larger scale where an entire asset class or even all trades at the CCP are canceled.

16.5.1 CCP Risk Mitigation Techniques: What Could Go Wrong?

Even the best laid plans can go astray, and a CCP's risk structure is no exception. While there have not been any actual CCP failures in many decades, there have been events that highlight some of the potential weaknesses in CCPs' risk structures. For example, a problem with an Asian CCP's technology system allowed an incorrect trade to flow through to clearing, resulting in a loss allocation to CMs upon its ultimate liquidation. In addition, a Nordic CCP had lax membership standards and failed to accurately model the risk in some of its trades, resulting in a sizable mutualized loss allocation to its CMs. Lastly, a UK CCP failed to monitor the buildup of risk among a handful of its CMs in a particular asset class, and when large price moves resulted in the inability for some CMs to meet VM payments, the CCP opted to bypass the waterfall and cancel trades instead (employing partial tear ups). While the Asian and Nordic CCP examples resulted in losses that were contained within the CCP and its CMs, the UK CCP example had a direct impact on end-investors.

These examples demonstrate areas where the CCP structure came close to breaking down. Specifically, operational failures and margin insufficiency led to the losses that ensued. These are examples of a CCP externalizing losses to the market. The CCP's operational controls and its financial safeguard package failed, allowing them to push the resulting losses on to the market.

CCPs design, manage, and sell risk management systems to the market. Just as a buyer of goods and services expects a quality seller to back its product, a financial investor should expect the same from the CCP. If the CCP fails to design its business controls and loss waterfall in a way that provides the service as advertised (e.g., virtually zero probability of loss), that CCP and its shareholders should be held accountable for the costs of its failure. Unfortunately, that is not how the market is currently constructed, and an increasing number of market participants believe this should change.

16.6 THE CALL FOR CHANGE: MARKET PARTICIPANTS ASK FOR STRONGER CCPs[10]

As more and more trades have moved to CCPs to comply with global clearing mandates, market participants have seen their credit risk exposures shift from traditional banks and broker dealers to CCPs. For many banks, CCPs are the largest credit exposures recorded on their books; for end-investors, CCPs dominate derivatives exposures. All the while, evaluating and mitigating CCP risk is challenging. Evaluating CCP risk is constrained by current limited disclosure standards, and mitigating CCP risk is constrained by monopolistic markets that are buoyed by global clearing mandates. Market participants have raised concerns across jurisdictions, highlighting how disclosures should be improved and advocating for higher regulatory standards to better insulate the market from a CCP failure, given the concentration of systemic risk central clearing introduces. Advocacy has included direct engagement with CCPs and regulators, participation in government-sponsored round tables, working collectively through trade associations, and publishing white papers and open letters to socialize concerns. Some of the key issues raised include the following:

Disclosures. There are two key pieces of CCP disclosure: (1) the Principles for Financial Market Infrastructure Disclosure Framework (PFMIs)[11] that was introduced in 2012 and (2) the Public Quantitative Disclosure Standards for Central Counterparties (PQDs),[12] introduced in 2015. These two disclosures underpin the risk analysis undertaken by the vast majority of market participants. Nevertheless, these disclosures lack key elements that would allow the market to better assess a CCP's risk profile.

For example, the PFMIs are qualitative and provide high-level, general descriptions of numerous CCP risk topics. In addition, guidelines suggest the disclosures should be released every other year, which makes the relied upon information fairly stale for market participants who operate on a more frequent review cycle. The PQDs provide more specific information on a quarterly basis, though some data are provided on an aggregate basis, limiting its usefulness. Importantly, there is no external audit requirement for either the PFMIs or the PQDs, which undermines the market participants' confidence in their accuracy and consistency.

"Skin in the game." The purpose of a CCP's contribution to the default waterfall is to align its incentives with prudent risk management. For example, if a CCP's contribution to the waterfall is first in line to cover excess loss after a CM default, the CCP will be incentivized to implement conservative IM models in order to minimize the risk to its own capital. Similarly, a CCP contribution that is tapped after the default fund is exhausted incentivizes the CCP to appropriately size its default fund. How much "skin in the game" is needed to optimally align these incentives is a question that remains unanswered.

Too much "skin in the game" could operate like a subsidy to excessive risk takers and lead to a moral hazard situation. Too little "skin in the game" creates the potential for excessive returns to CCP owners who are able to increase risk (through less rigorous risk mitigation) without bearing the responsibility for potential losses. While the optimal number has not been widely studied by academics or regulators, market participants are largely united in the view that what CCPs have today is insufficient.

Figure 16.6 shows default fund and "skin in the game" data for four major swaps clearinghouses, using each CCP's PQD disclosure for Q4 2021, converted to USD at 2021 exchange rates: Japan Securities Clearing Corporation, ICE Clear Credit, CME (IRS), and LCH Swapclear. Default fund sizes range from more than $2 billion to almost $8 billion, while all "skin in the game" contributions are materially less than $200 million, with LCH's (the largest interest rate CCP in the world) and ICE Clear Credit's (the largest credit CCP in the world) contributions comprising less than 2% of the default fund. Many market participants are highlighting this disparity as a vulnerability to the safety and soundness of CCPs and are asking regulators to require a better balance between the default fund (contributed by CMs) and the "skin in the game" (contributed by CCPs).

Loss allocation. As previously discussed, most CCPs have the ability to allocate losses to CMs and, in extreme circumstances, to end-investors. Additionally, the current incentive structures could lead to skewed loss allocations, with a CCP able to externalize its business losses to the market. For the end-investor, the issue of loss allocation is particularly guiling because the end-investor pays fees for a CCP's service, which is credit risk mitigation. If that

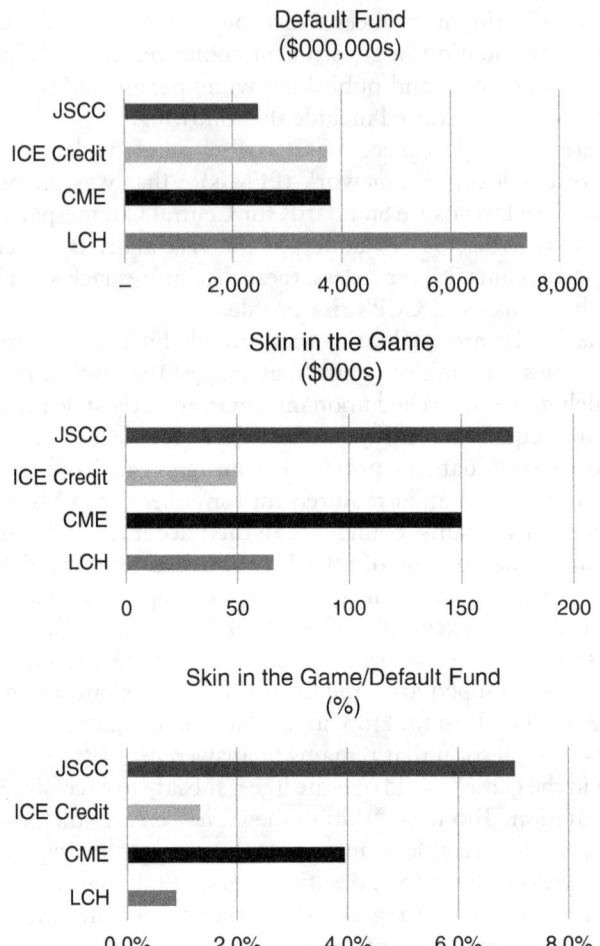

EXHIBIT 16.6 Default Fund Member Contributions (Q4 2021)
Source: Public Quantitative Disclosures (available on each CCP's website).

CCP incurs losses due to mispricing of its services or due to mismanagement of products, basic principles of equity would argue that the loss should be allocated to the CCP's owners, not its customers.

Governance. If a CCP is allowed to allocate losses to its customers, then the customers should have a say in decisions that impact the CCP's risk mitigation techniques. The risk management incentive structure is a delicate balance, and governance structures should be employed to maintain that balance. Most governance structures at CCPs require participants to act in the interest of the CCP, which could be at odds with market participants' interests and, even more importantly, at odds with market stability. In addition, end-investor participation in a CCP's governance structure is inconsistent. Optimal structures should allow input from market participants, including end-investors, and provide transparency to regulators on divergent views. Enhanced transparency for regulatory authorities would help to prioritize systemic stability over other interests.

16.7 CONCLUSION

CCPs are complex financial institutions that play an increasingly important role in derivatives risk management. Providing credit risk mitigation and transparent aggregate risk information, most CCPs are well structured with financial safeguard packages that would withstand most imaginable market scenarios. However, seasoned risk managers know that not all market scenarios are imaginable, and chances are that markets will exhibit future disruptions that will not have been envisioned. Hence, conservative financial structures are important. While the probability of a CCP default is low, the severity of loss from a CCP default would be material. Therefore, despite the disclosure challenges, risk managers should continue to assess the worst-case solvency of the CCPs that stand behind derivatives trades.

Furthermore, many CCPs are for-profit institutions and are incentivized to generate returns to owners, often public shareholders. Absent sufficient governance, these incentives may conflict with prudent risk management. Structuring CCPs to properly align their incentives, including sufficient capital requirements and regulatory oversight, is paramount. The global regulatory community continues to evaluate and address the issues raised, and some progress has been made and continued progress is expected. CCPs have also voluntarily engaged with market participants to address disclosure issues, in particular. In the arc of financial market history, the prominence of CCPs is relatively nascent. As critical market participants, CCPs and global regulators need to continue engaging on the issues, and market participants should be able to observe ongoing improvements.

NOTES

1. www.g20.org, n.d.
2. Leaders' Statement the Pittsburgh Summit, 2009, p. 9.
3. SEFs are referred to as Multilateral Trading Facilities (MTFs) in global markets.
4. Boerse-frankfurt.de, 2023.
5. Commodity Futures Trading Commission, n.d.
6. Market veterans mourn slow death of historic trading pits, 2021.
7. While a substantial portion of inter-dealer fixed-income derivatives were already being cleared at CCPs before the GFC, the mandate brought more participants, including end-investors, into the clearing ecosystem.
8. Most CCPs adhere to international risk standards, the Principles for Financial Market Infrastructures (https://www.bis.org/cpmi/info_pfmi.htm), though there is meaningful variability in how the standards are interpreted and adopted.
9. The clearing market is structured such that end-investors pay fees to access clearing services, and these services include loss mutualization among the service providers. In fact, end-investors are frequently unable to contribute to default funds due to regulatory constraints or structural impediments.
10. For further details and reading on BlackRock's views on central clearing please refer to *A Path Forward for CCP Resilience, Recovery and Resolution*, authored by 20 global financial institutions (2020), https://www.blackrock.com/corporate/literature/whitepaper/path-forward-for-ccp-resilience-recovery-and-resolution.pdf; *An End-Investor Perspective on Central Clearing Looking Back to Look Forward* (2018), https://www.blackrock.com/corporate/literature/whitepaper/

viewpoint-end-investor-perspective-central-clearing-looking-back-to-look-forward.pdf; and *Resiliency, Recovery, and Resolution: Revisiting the 3 R's for Central Clearing Counterparties* (2016), https://www.blackrock.com/corporate/literature/whitepaper/viewpoint-ccps-resiliency-recovery-resolution-october-2016.pdf.

11. Committee on Payment and Settlement Systems and Board of the International Organization of Securities Commissions, 2012.

12. Committee on Payments and Market Infrastructures and Board of the International Organization of Securities Commissions, 2015.

Lessons from the Credit Crisis and Coronavirus Pandemic

Risk Management Lessons Worth Remembering from the Credit Crisis of 2007–2009[1]

Bennett W. Golub
Senior Advisor, BlackRock

Conan Crum
Vice President, Risk & Quantitative Analysis, BlackRock (2013)

17.1   INTRODUCTION

The credit crisis of 2007–2009 necessitated a rethinking of financial markets, in general, and risk management practices, in particular. Many investors took losses well in excess of their expectations, and the subsequent rebound in risk assets that began in the spring of 2009 resulted in significant underperformance for those with conservative allocations. More distressing was the near complete loss of liquidity and transparency as large segments of the market literally ground to a halt. Traditional fundamental and technical drivers of risk and return were overwhelmed by the impact of malfunctioning markets and dramatic changes in government policy. The paramount importance of managing liquidity was demonstrated decisively, and the hypothesis of market efficiency as the sole defining paradigm for modeling and measuring institutional risk had been demonstrably falsified by experience. In light of these observations from the credit crisis, best practices in risk management needed to be retooled for a world in which global financial markets cannot be assumed to always be open and efficient and the rules of the game can be dramatically in flux.

The purpose of this chapter is to present several specific lessons worth remembering from the credit crisis. The credit crisis demonstrated that many widely used risk management techniques relied on critical assumptions that turned out to be flawed. Recommendations on the future practice of risk management are made to correct or mitigate the negative impact of relying on these faulty assumptions. Our discussion of these specific lessons worth remembering from the credit crisis aims to enhance our understanding of why economic theory and quantitative methods in risk management failed and to offer recommendations for what can be done to try to correct for these failures in the future.

This chapter does not provide a mathematically oriented review of specific methodological modeling flaws, a topic covered by others. For instance, Taleb (2007b) argued against "the use of commoditized metrics such as 'standard deviation,' 'Sharpe ratio,' 'mean variance,' and so on in fat-tailed domains where these terms have little practical meaning" (p. 1).[2] But neither is this chapter a Luddite creed about abandoning quantitative risk management for a more "common sense" risk management process.[3] The goal of this chapter is to provide detailed analysis of six lessons worth remembering from the credit crisis of 2007–2009.

Numerous lessons can be gleaned from the credit crisis, and undoubtedly, this period will be researched for many years. In this chapter, the following six specific lessons worth remembering from the credit crisis are explored in-depth. First, institutions must recognize the paramount importance of liquidity. Second, investors in securitized products need to look through data to the behavior of the underlying assets. Third, institutions must always be cognizant that financial certification is useless during systemic shocks. Fourth, market risk can change dramatically, and institutions need to manage their level of risk rather than letting it be determined by the market. Fifth, institutions must adapt to the increasing importance of policy risk. And sixth, institutions must always remember that by the time a crisis strikes, it is too late to start preparing for it. Undoubtedly many other lessons can be extracted from this period of unprecedented financial disruption and volatility, but remembering and addressing these six lessons from the credit crisis will be important for the future success of institutional risk management.

17.2   THE PARAMOUNT IMPORTANCE OF LIQUIDITY

The Basel Committee on Banking Supervision (2008) used the phrase "the paramount importance of liquidity" based upon the observation that "a liquidity shortfall at a single institution can have system-wide repercussions" (p. 7). In this chapter, however, our focus is solely on the survival of a particular institution. Liquidity is the lifeblood of commerce, and the ability of institutions to meet their immediate cash obligations is critical to their financial survival. There are at least two distinct, but relevant and interconnected, definitions of liquidity. As articulated by the Basel Committee on Banking Supervision (2008),

> *[f]unding liquidity risk* is the risk that the firm will not be able to meet efficiently both expected and unexpected current and future cash flow and collateral needs without affecting either daily operations or the financial conditions of the firm. *Market liquidity risk* is the risk that a firm cannot easily offset or eliminate a position at the market price because of inadequate market depth or market disruption. (p. 1)

During the credit crisis, funding and market liquidity evaporated from large segments of the fixed income and commercial paper markets for extended periods of time. In many cases, liquidity returned to these markets primarily as a result of specific government programs. These programs provided either explicit credit guarantees or incentives to certain investors to purchase assets. Examples of these programs in the United States included the Term Asset-Backed Securities Loan Facility (TALF), Money Market Investor Funding Facility (MMIFF), Term Securities Lending Facility (TSLF), Temporary Liquidity Guarantee Program (TLGP), Commercial Paper Funding Facility (CPFF), Asset-Backed Commercial Paper Money Market Mutual Fund Liquidity Facility (ABCP-MMMFLF), and the Public-Private Investment Partnership (PPIP).

Leading up to the credit crisis, many market participants lost sight of the paramount importance of liquidity and, as a result, suffered greatly. To some extent the failure of institutions to manage liquidity was due to complacency and irresponsibility; however, the lack of appreciation for the importance of liquidity was also due in large part to an inadequate conceptual framework. Markets have generally exhibited increasing degrees of liquidity as improvements in financial modeling and theory, market infrastructure, and the dramatic fall in the costs of computation, data storage, and data communications have made transactions quicker and easier.[4] For instance, exchange-traded equities have moved from trading in eighths to trading in sixteenths and then in decimals, and the abundance of short-term funding liquidity allowed leverage at investment banks to rise from less than 12 to 1 to as high as 40 to 1 in the run-up to the credit crisis.[5] Nevertheless, the credit crisis of 2007–2009 proved that without the necessary liquidity, nothing else matters. Forecasting the synchronous shortening of investment horizons, which drove much of the liquidity crisis, is a difficult if not impossible task; hence, the need for institutions to actively plan for the potential loss of liquidity is vital. As such, we will discuss five distinct lessons worth remembering from the credit crisis specifically related to the issue of liquidity.

17.2.1 Price ≠ Intrinsic Value Unless Special Conditions Hold

The cornerstone of academic finance for a long time has been the efficient market hypothesis (EMH), as described by Fama (1965) and Samuelson (1965). In well-functioning markets, the search for arbitrage opportunities should generally lead prices to approach the market's best assessment of intrinsic value.[6] The argument first put forward by Friedman (1953) was that prices cannot substantially deviate from intrinsic value for long because arbitrageurs will always step in to exploit any such mispricing until it disappears. The arbitrageurs are assumed to ultimately prevail over the naïve investors because the naïve investors are assumed to eventually go broke due to their poor investment decisions.

More recently, however, research in finance has focused on the "limits to arbitrage" (see, for example, DeLong et al. [1990], Lakonishok et al. [1991], and Shleifer and Vishny [1997]). This strand of research argues that funding liquidity constraints will force arbitrageurs to go broke long before market prices return to intrinsic value. These constraints include the inability to sell short; short investment horizons; and the existence of systematic, directional noise trading.

During the credit crisis, several seemingly obvious arbitrage opportunities failed to be exploited. Such opportunities included pre-refunded (tax-exempt) municipal bonds trading at higher yields than (taxable) US Treasuries of similar maturities, and special purpose acquisition companies (SPACs) that had not yet made a single acquisition but traded at a significant discount to the cash on their balance sheets.[7] Although an argument can certainly be made that these examples of unexploited arbitrage opportunities (i.e., liquidity premia, asymmetric information, and so on) are not necessarily definitive violations of the EMH, the credit crisis demonstrated that markets can break down so dramatically that market prices simply do not even exist for extended periods of time! If there is a sustained lack of bids on a valuable asset, the nuances of claims of market efficiency become somewhat irrelevant.[8]

Many missed arbitrage opportunities occurred in the over-the-counter markets where the vast majority of fixed-income assets are typically traded. There are literally millions of tradable fixed-income securities. On a given "typical" (i.e., pre- or post-crisis) day, some of these securities, such as on-the-run Treasuries, will trade thousands of times a day. Others, corporate bonds for example, might trade sporadically over the course of a day. Yet others might trade only every few days, while some might never trade at all.[9] As a result, it is rarely the case that fully synchronous prices exist for the bond markets.

Typically, most bonds are priced intraday "off" one or more liquid instruments, such as an on-the-run Treasury or an interpolated Treasury curve, an interest rate swap or swap curve, a credit default swap, or an interest rate option or implied volatility surface. Thus, when seeking the value of a bond, investors generally rely on direct quotes from broker/dealers, "indications" of value from broker/dealers who are not making a firm offer to buy, or a third-party pricing service that "prices" bonds by determining an indicative pricing matrix garnered from discussions with broker/dealers about bond spreads off more liquid sectors of the market. During the credit crisis, through our interactions with industry peers, we became aware of the increased use of "pricing" or "valuation" committees by asset managers as the veracity of "published" prices broke down. What is the market value of an asset that does not trade? During the credit crisis, published prices from third-party pricing vendors for many securities were materially greater than the levels that could actually be obtained from the markets, assuming any price was executable at all.

The valuation problem is not as simple as it might appear to those who view the financial world through the lens of large capitalization stocks on the New York Stock Exchange and other public exchanges. In fact, the accounting profession felt the need to provide detailed guidance on how to value assets precisely when markets are not active. In a real-time market for securities with lots of available information, it is, of course, hard to reconcile the EMH with an inactive market. In the United States, the Financial Accounting Standards Board (FASB) Statement of Financial Accounting Standards (FAS) No. 157 issued in September 2006 required 128 pages to explain a framework for valuing assets in inactive markets. The FAS Staff Position (FSP) FAS 157-3 issued on October 10, 2008, right in the middle of the credit crisis, "clarified" the notion of price (i.e., fair value) "when the market for that asset is not *active* (italics added)," as follows:

> A fair value measurement represents the price at which a transaction *would occur* between market participants at the measurement date. As discussed in Statement 157, in situations in which there is little, if any, market activity for an asset at the measurement date, *the fair value measurement objective remains the same, that is, the price that would be received by the holder of the financial asset in an orderly transaction (an exit price notion) that is not a forced liquidation or distressed sale at the measurement date.* Even in times of market dislocation, it is not appropriate to conclude that all market activity represents forced liquidations or distressed sales. However, it is also not appropriate to automatically conclude that any transaction price is determinative of fair value. Determining fair value in a dislocated market depends on the facts and circumstances and may require the use of significant judgment about whether individual transactions are forced liquidations or distressed sales. (p. 3)

The position of the FASB is that, even in an inactive market with forced liquidation and/or distressed sales, the notion of "fair" value still exists and that value may be materially different than observed market prices. The FASB also asserts that the existence of a market dislocation does not necessarily invalidate the information content of observed prices. It is fair to say that the need for such "clarification" from the FASB demonstrates the level of turmoil and disorder in the markets.

The FASB groups assets into three categories depending on the confidence associated with their valuation. Level 1 assets are assets that are readily traded and whose prices are directly observable, Level 2 assets are assets that are priced based upon readily observable market quantities, and Level 3 assets are assets for which no observable or comparable market prices exist. To put the magnitude of the valuation problem into context, consider the massive growth of Level 3 assets during the credit crisis. As of the fourth quarter of 2008, financial companies in the S&P 500 had nearly $537.4 billion of Level 3 assets. For a sense of perspective, note that the total market capitalization of S&P 500 financial companies at the end of 2008 was $598 billion. It is certainly true that the value of these assets could be much less than their reported value of $537.4 billion. It is also true that the value of these assets is certainly not zero, yet these assets have no readily observable price. Without a market price, financial markets cannot clear and asset sales cannot be used to turn wealth into cash regardless of their intrinsic value. The failure to account for the risk of an asset's value becoming unobservable can be devastating.

Therefore, while it is not appropriate to abandon the concept that on many, if not most, occasions markets will exist with pricing that is a decent estimate of the intrinsic value of an asset, it is equally inappropriate and downright imprudent to permit a financial institution's objectives and viability to become hostage to the assumption that an open and efficient market will be waiting for it at all times. Institutions need to pay close attention to their vulnerability to a failing market and take concrete steps to limit this exposure. Being highly attuned to the cash flow requirements of liabilities to creditors and beneficiaries is one of the best ways to limit this kind of vulnerability.

17.2.2 Cash and Cash Flow Are the Only Robust Sources of Liquidity

Arguably one of the best analogies used to describe a liquidity crisis is that "liquidity is like oxygen—you really notice how much you need it once it is gone."[10] If an institution's assets and liabilities are perfectly structured, securities do not need to be sold to raise cash. Regardless of market conditions, positions could always be held to maturity and funding liquidity risk would cease to be an important concern. The credit crisis revealed, however, that many institutions had not structured their portfolios with sufficient attention to the cash flow requirements of their liabilities, meaning that portfolios needed to access markets in order to sell assets and generate cash. But, as discussed previously, the risk of relying solely upon the market mechanism can at times be so onerous as to put an institution in jeopardy. The only consistently reliable way to meet demands for cash is through portfolio cash flow, reserves of cash, or highly liquid securities.

The liquidity crunch experienced by many institutions does not mean that the institutions did not make forward cash flow projections, but rather that those projections may not have properly distinguished the certitude of the forecasted asset cash flow that was being generated. Not all portfolio holdings have equally reliable cash flows, and the credit crisis highlighted the dangers of confusing projected cash flows with well-defined and reliable cash flows. An example of a security that can generate consistent and reliable cash flows is a high-quality bond with fixed coupon and principal payments. Other forms of portfolio cash flows, such as cash dividends or distributions from private partnerships, were revealed to be much more variable. This lesson is embodied to a large extent in Principle 1 of the "Principles of Sound Liquidity Risk Management and Supervision" issued by the Basel Committee on Banking Supervision (2008). It is appropriate to substitute the phrase "financial institution" for "bank" because this sound principle is universally applicable. Principle 1 states that

[a] bank is responsible for the sound management of liquidity risk. A bank should establish a robust liquidity risk management framework that ensures it maintains sufficient liquidity, including a cushion of unencumbered, high-quality liquid assets, to withstand a range of stress events, including those involving the loss or impairment of both unsecured and secured funding sources. (p. 9)

The credit crisis demonstrated unequivocally that it is folly to assume that markets will always be available to provide required liquidity. Just as running a critical care medical facility without a backup electrical generator would constitute gross imprudence, it is imprudent, bordering on malfeasance, to run a financial institution in a manner dependent on continuously available market liquidity. Many investors, who grew complacent and assumed market liquidity would always be available, learned this lesson the hard way.

One way to think about the conceptual problem faced by many institutions is that their asset allocation and risk models did not sufficiently penalize illiquid securities. These models do not generally make a distinction between the prices of securities that can be easily converted into cash using the market and those that cannot.[11] Anyone who has gone through the process of obtaining month-end marks for fixed income and alternative securities knows that widely quoted prices are more like appraisals than actual conversion-to-cash prices. Moreover, standard techniques in multi-asset portfolio optimization tend to compound problems. Portfolio optimizers typically recommend placing sizable allocations in illiquid securities because state-of-the-practice risk models are unable to distinguish between prices for US Treasuries, which actually are conversion-to-cash prices, and dealer marks for illiquid securities, which are more like appraisals and can differ substantially from conversion-to-cash prices.

A prime example of this problem is the endowment investment model that had been popularized by David Swensen, the head of Yale University's endowment. Swensen (2009) advocated large allocations to illiquid asset classes such as real assets, hedge funds, and private equity. A breakdown of the Yale endowment's asset allocation is provided in Exhibit 17.1. Over a 5-year period, the Yale endowment averaged allocations of only 12.3% and 4.4% to the traditional, liquid asset classes of US equity and fixed income, respectively. However, Yale's allocation to the illiquid absolute return, real asset, and private equity strategies averaged 67.2% over the same 5-year period. Moreover, by 2008, the Yale endowment was even running a slightly leveraged portfolio with a −3.9% allocation to cash.

Swensen (2009) advocated large allocations to illiquid strategies for two basic reasons. First, investors typically "overpay" for more-liquid securities. Second, finding top managers in illiquid asset classes is easier and offers greater returns than searching for top managers in liquid asset classes.[12] The ability of the Yale endowment to generate above-market rates of return cannot be questioned. On June 30, 2008, the Yale endowment had earned a 15.9% annual return over a 20-year period and a 16.3% annual return over a 10-year period.[13] These large returns enabled the endowment's revenue contribution to grow from $45 million

	June 30, 2008	June 30, 2007	June 30, 2006	June 30, 2005	June 30, 2004
Liquid Assets	**25.4%**	**31.0%**	**32.5%**	**34.6%**	**40.5%**
US Equity	10.1	11.0	11.6	14.1	14.8
Fixed Income	4.0	4.0	3.8	4.9	7.4
Non-US Equity	15.2	14.1	14.6	13.7	14.8
Cash	−3.9	1.9	2.5	1.9	3.5
Illiquid Assets	**74.6**	**69.1**	**67.5**	**65.5**	**59.4**
Absolute Return	25.1	23.3	23.3	25.7	26.1
Private Equity	20.2	18.7	16.4	14.8	14.5
Real Assets	29.3	27.1	27.8	25.0	18.8

EXHIBIT 17.1 Yale Endowment Asset Allocation
Source: The Yale Endowment (2008), as cited in Golub and Crum (2010a).

and 10% of total revenues in 1985 to a projected $1.15 billion and 45% of total revenues in 2009.

During the credit crisis, illiquid assets unfortunately experienced large negative returns. The Yale endowment ran into difficulty generating cash at exactly the same time that demands for cash from the Yale University budget were at their highest. Thus, the Yale endowment, as well as the other asset managers that subscribed to the Swensen endowment model, found that high paper returns do not necessarily correspond to adequate liquidity. As Bhaktavatsalam and Wee (2009) noted, "investment losses since September have forced colleges such as Harvard and Yale to freeze salaries, delay construction projects or borrow money to meet their budgets" (p. 1).

It is unlikely that the cost of this real financial distress will be deducted from the posted returns of the Yale endowment or the endowments of other universities, colleges, and nonprofits; however, given that Yale University and other institutions were forced to become the de facto providers of liquidity in place of their endowments, some performance adjustment is most likely warranted in trying to realistically assess the performance of the Swensen endowment model relative to other investment strategies. The market will not always be available to turn wealth into cash, especially for illiquid asset classes. Risk managers must always remember that cash, reliable cash flow, and unencumbered highly liquid assets are the only robust sources of liquidity.

17.2.3 Complexity and Opacity Matter More Than You Think

In well-functioning markets, arbitrage should push price toward intrinsic value. However, arbitrage relies upon the presence of expert investors who actually know the intrinsic value. An interesting result of price being near intrinsic value is that many investors can gain the benefits of diversification by taking positions in a security without having to be an expert in the security. In essence, market efficiency enables non-expert investors to free ride expert investors. The result is that liquidity will tend to be higher when price hovers around intrinsic value for sustained periods of time as non-expert investors enter to take advantage of diversification opportunities.[14]

When severe market dislocations occur in a particular asset class, many concentrated expert investors will be knocked out of the market because they typically have the largest exposures to the assets in question. In complex and opaque markets, the number of expert investors tends to be small. Many of the asset classes most severely impaired during the credit crisis were exceedingly complex. They required sophisticated analytics and large databases that were regularly refreshed with the current state of the collateral underlying each of the complex assets. In addition, expert investors would use statistical models to drive intricate cash flow models, which were, in turn, inputs into Monte Carlo valuation engines. Infrastructures like these can take years and cost millions of dollars to build and millions more to maintain. Finally, for these models to have an impact, large pools of capital are needed to take positions of sufficient size to justify the substantial fixed investment in analytics. Without these expert investors, the price arbitrage process can quickly break down. Without arbitrage, price will inevitably deviate from intrinsic value and liquidity will collapse as expert investors are forced to sell, while non-expert investors refuse to enter the market given the uncertainty in pricing. The result is that prices must fall to "stupid cheap" levels in order to bring new buyers to the market who can participate without similar investments in analytics.[15] One indirect way to observe this phenomenon is to look at the kurtosis of complex assets relative to simple assets. The monthly mean, standard deviation, and kurtosis of returns for several fixed-income indices since August 31, 1999, are displayed in Exhibit 17.2.

Moment	US AGG	TSY	AGY	CORP	MBS	ABS	CMBS
Mean	0.52%	0.51%	0.51%	0.54%	0.53%	0.44%	0.52%
Standard Deviation	1.09	1.42	1.08	1.81	0.84	1.27	3.08
Kurtosis Pre-Lehman	1.55	1.24	1.91	1.41	0.29	0.04	1.33
Kurtosis Full Sample	1.47	1.46	1.88	5.50	2.53	9.86	17.67

EXHIBIT 17.2   Fixed-Income Monthly Return Moments, August 31, 1999–September 31, 2009
Sources: Monthly index return data from Barclays Capital and authors' calculations, as cited in Golub and Crum (2010a).

Exhibit 17.2 shows that kurtosis in complex securitized assets, such as commercial mortgage-backed securities (CMBS), is more than 12 times the kurtosis of simple assets, such as US Treasuries and US agency debt, and even of a broad fixed-income index, such as the Barclays Capital US Aggregate.[16] Furthermore, prior to the bankruptcy filing of Lehman Brothers, the kurtosis of complex securitized assets was actually less than that of the Barclays Capital US Aggregate. But when the liquidity crisis really hit after the Lehman bankruptcy, the kurtosis of complex securitized assets increased several-fold while the kurtosis of simpler assets barely moved. In other words, the potential for prices of complex assets to gap so substantially could not have been inferred from past data. Only the recognition that these markets were intrinsically more fragile, because only a few entities were truly experts in complex assets, would have alerted risk managers to the potential for large negative tail returns.

As a result, all investors, and risk managers especially, need to use common sense and to be cognizant of the complexity of the markets in which they operate. Risk managers should not view all new assets as Rubik's cubes that have to be solved, nor should they fear being deemed unsophisticated if they find certain assets exceedingly complex and therefore inappropriate investments. If smart risk managers cannot wrap their arms around a new idea after a reasonable amount of focused time, it may be that only very few people can. It is precisely these types of products that are susceptible to fragile market behavior. Complex markets will have fewer genuinely expert investors, and hence, any market dislocation can cause liquidity to quickly disappear. Risk managers must heighten their awareness of an asset's level of complexity. For risk management purposes, complex assets should be grouped with illiquid holdings when attempting to measure total portfolio exposure to liquidity risk. Complex assets must be assumed to always have the potential to become illiquid, even when trading is robust and pricing is consistent with intrinsic value, because in a stressed scenario these types of holdings are likely to be the first ones adversely affected.

17.2.4   Collateralization Can Be a Two-edged Sword

The credit crisis demonstrated decisively that counterparty exposure is not just a theoretical risk. Many firms incurred large counterparty losses for the first time as Lehman Brothers failed, and the immediate aftermath of the failure was handled in such a dysfunctional manner.[17] This financial catastrophe caused market participants to attempt to improve their control over counterparty risk by, among other approaches, aggressively extending collateral agreements to cover situations where uncollateralized exposures remained. In general, collateralization can significantly reduce counterparty risk, but even with collateralization many risks remain, although some are more obvious than others.

First, institutions must remain vigilant. For instance, they need to be alert to errors purportedly due to "computer problems" or "mistakes" and other signs of dealer stress when collateral transfers are due. Second, the collateral valuation process must be aggressively managed, and counterparties need to be ready to challenge dealers when appropriate, pushing back against opportunistic repo desks. It is not uncommon for actual executable levels in the fixed-income markets, particularly for less-liquid securities during periods of market stress, to be worse than the pricing from third-party pricing services. But during the credit crisis, we observed many situations in which repo desks used significantly more adverse prices than the prices provided directly from the trading desks of their own firms! Third, institutions need to carefully scrutinize the quality and value of collateral being delivered to them. The terms of collateral support agreements (CSAs) need to be read carefully to make sure that the type of collateral and the haircuts are reasonable. Absent this detailed review, institutions may discover that for over-the-counter securities, the terms of trade do not sufficiently protect borrowers from being subject to forced liquidations at highly disadvantageous prices. Fourth, the CSAs need to be reviewed very carefully with respect to the process by which haircuts can be changed; at a minimum, notice periods should be required before any adverse changes in haircuts go into effect so that the borrower has time to either move his financing or to raise the necessary additional collateral or liquidity. Last, institutions need to run stress tests on collateralized positions—particularly illiquid ones—that incorporate both extremely adverse market outcomes and adverse changes in the level of haircuts. Institutions that borrow against these positions must ensure that they have adequate liquidity to meet the contingent demands for liquidity.

A more subtle issue, though, is that institutions with limited liquidity must recognize that most collateral support agreements require two-way flows. Hence, while collateral support agreements reduce counterparty risk, they can also greatly increase funding liquidity risk. Stricter market standards typically require cash or high-quality, liquid securities to meet collateral requirements. This means that collateral calls can easily force illiquid portfolios into a funding liquidity crisis even if there are no other external demands for cash, such as investor redemptions. In such a situation, the noble objective of trying to reduce credit exposure to counterparties could exacerbate funding liquidity risk. In cases where hedging is used to manage market risk, the same type of trade-off may need to be made. And while credit risk and market risk may prove to be very damaging, the inability to meet collateral calls can often prove to be fatal. We are aware of a number of liquidity-impaired institutions that, when faced with this trade-off, chose to either leave certain derivatives on a non-collateralized basis or to lift market hedges designed to reduce risk in order to avoid the likelihood of bankruptcy if they were presented with collateral calls. The inability to meet demands for collateral can set off rapid downward spirals in the ability to access liquidity. Risk managers of institutions must be aware of this trade-off and be prepared to balance normal risk management processes with the liquidity pressures that collateral agreements can create.

Perhaps the most famous downward "death" spiral of the credit crisis caused by collateral support agreements is the near collapse of AIG. Mollenkamp et al. (2008) described the counterparty risk associated with the credit risk models provided to AIG by consultant Gary Gorton:

> Mr. Gorton's models harnessed mounds of historical data to focus on the likelihood of default, and his work may indeed prove accurate on that front. But as AIG was aware, his models didn't attempt to measure the risk of future collateral calls or writedowns, which have devastated AIG's finances.... The problem for AIG is that it didn't apply effective models for valuing the swaps and for collateral risk until the second half of 2007, long after the swaps were sold.... The firm left itself exposed to potentially large collateral calls because it had agreed to insure so much debt without protecting itself adequately through hedging. (p. A1)

Date	Event	Collateral Posted	Cumulative Total
September 5, 2007	AIG posts $450 mil after GS demands $1.5 bil in collateral.	$450 mil	$450 mil
November 1, 2007	AIG posts $1.5 bil after GS demands $3 bil in additional collateral.	$1.5 bil	$1.95 bil
November 1, 2007–March 28, 2008	AIG discloses cumulative collateral posts of $5.3 bil.	$3.35 bil	$5.3 bil
March 28, 2008–June 8, 2008	AIG discloses cumulative collateral posts of $9.7 bil.	$4.4 bil	$9.7 bil
June 8, 2008–September 9, 2008	AIG discloses cumulative collateral posts of $16.5 bil.	$6.8 bil	$16.5 bil
October 15, 2008	AIG forced to raise $14.5 bil in additional collateral after S&P downgrade.	$14.5 bil	$31 bil
October 15, 2008–December 10, 2008	AIG discloses $37.3 bil in cumulative collateral posts and new government bailout of $150 bil.	$6.3 bil	$37.3 bil

EXHIBIT 17.3   AIG and the Two-Edged Sword of Collateral
Source: Kiel (2008), as cited in Golub and Crum (2010a). GS is Goldman Sachs.

Exhibit 17.3 details the numerous collateral calls that eventually forced the US Treasury and the Federal Reserve to commit $182 billion to prevent AIG's collapse. It is very likely that the AIG insurance units were worth more than the losses incurred on CDS protection written by its Financial Products Group, AIGFP. However, the liquidity demands triggered by the downgrades of AIG were so great that they quickly overwhelmed the company's ability to raise cash by selling assets. The near collapse of AIG is an extreme example of the consequences of failing to account for the liquidity demands of collateral support agreements.

17.2.5   Liquidity Is a Common Risk Factor

The liquidity of an investment can have a material impact not only on the ability to raise cash by selling an asset, but also on the level of market returns. Conceptually, it stands to reason that investors need to be paid a premium to hold illiquid positions because market liquidity represents a valuable option available to exercise. Pastor and Stambaugh (2003) and Amihud and Mendelson (1986) demonstrated that more-illiquid securities have, in fact, earned higher rates of return over time. The existence of this premium creates, either directly or indirectly, a common risk factor. The direct impact of market liquidity on asset returns is fairly well known. In periods where returns to liquidity are large, both liquid and illiquid securities will show sharply negative correlations. For instance, in the fourth quarter of 2008, returns to liquidity were very high. The liquid Barclays Capital US Treasury Index earned its highest quarterly return (8.75%) since the first quarter of 1986, while the illiquid Barclays Capital Asset-Backed Securities (ABS) and Barclays Capital Commercial Mortgage-Backed Securities (CMBS) indices earned their lowest quarterly returns ever, –6.82% and –13.52%, respectively.[18]

The credit crisis has shown that risk managers need to monitor the liquidity risk on all their securities, even those that appear very liquid. Exhibit 17.4 displays the cumulative

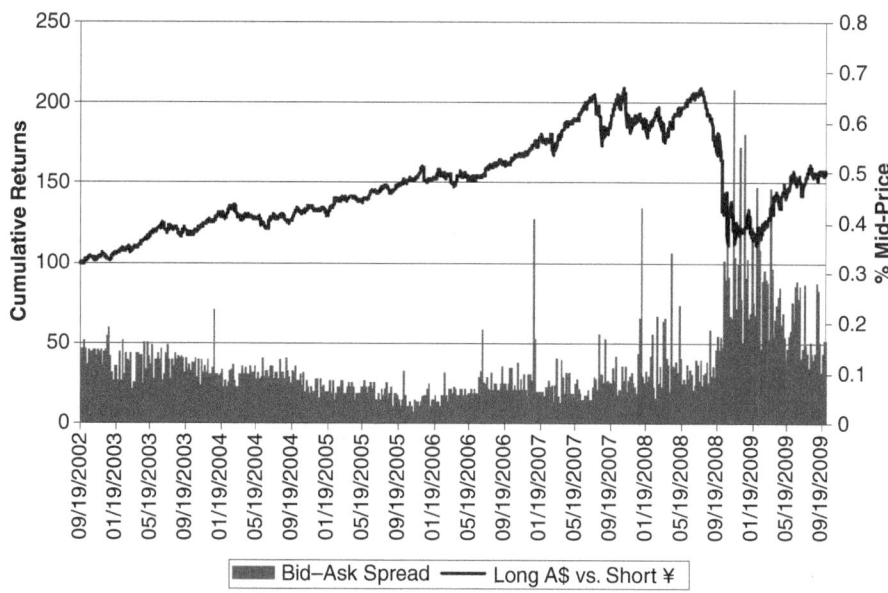

EXHIBIT 17.4   A$/¥ Carry Trade Cumulative Returns and Bid–Ask Spread
Source: Bloomberg and authors' calculations, as cited in Golub and Crum (2010a).

returns of going long the Australian dollar (A$) and short the Japanese yen (¥) from September 2002 to June 2009. The long A$/short ¥ carry trade was an extremely popular position in the run-up to the credit crisis, and according to any state-of-the-practice risk model, the trade should not have been exposed to liquidity risk. Foreign exchange markets are among the most liquid markets in the world, and both Japan and Australia are developed market economies making them relatively immune to the "sudden stops" in capital flows that can strike developing economies.

In reality, however, this trade had very large exposures to liquidity risk. As a commodity exporter, Australian growth is much more exposed to illiquid, emerging market countries. Furthermore, this particular trade was extremely popular among market participants who used leverage to enhance returns. These market participants were also exposed to liquidity shocks, similar to those that afflict emerging market countries.

Market participants that exposed themselves to the liquidity risk of the long A$/short ¥ carry trade enjoyed several years of consistently strong returns. Between the fall of 2002 and summer of 2008, this position more than doubled in value. In less than a few months, however, in the fall of 2008, nearly all those gains were wiped out. Liquidity shocks sent emerging markets economies and trade finance into a tailspin, putting pressure on commodity exporters such as Australia. Liquidity shocks also impaired funding to leveraged players just when trades, such as the long A$/short ¥ carry trade, were going against them. This forced many market participants to liquidate positions at exactly the same time. Hence, returns to the liquidity-exposed carry trade became extremely negative and bid–ask spreads spiked more than eight times.[19]

The preceding analysis demonstrates how even extremely liquid foreign exchange markets are exposed to the common risk factor of liquidity. It is interesting to note that in the initial stages of a liquidity crisis, the more-liquid securities can actually be the hardest hit because liquidity-poor investors often have little choice but to sell their most-liquid positions first in order to minimize transaction costs. In fact, liquid portfolios of all sorts become the "ATM machines" for many liquidity-strapped market participants. This common characteristic of various securities will, on occasion, create atypical correlations in the market where liquid positions suffer declines together. As a liquidity crisis progresses, though, the adverse market impact on more-illiquid securities appears to propagate more slowly. This occurs because the ability to measure changes in market values for these securities is more limited as the markets are themselves less transparent. However, declining liquidity will eventually lead to forced sales as lenders refuse to take illiquid securities as collateral for market value-based loans. In the later stages of a liquidity crisis, the value of illiquid securities will fall spasmodically with observed executions. At this stage in a crisis, liquid positions will significantly outperform as they retain more value relative to illiquid securities.

This is likely the exact phenomenon that generated the "quant crisis," which struck large-capitalization equity stocks in August 2007. Khandani and Lo (2008) found evidence that the quant crisis resulted from the rapid unwinding of equity portfolios with large exposures to the equity value risk factor or stocks with high earnings-to-price, cash flow-to-price, and book-value-to-price ratios. Furthermore, Litzenberger and Modest (2008) argued that the quant crisis started as "losses in the sub-prime credit market, extreme movements in credit spreads, and the steep declines in prices of many buy-out-related equities led to deleveraging by several large hedge funds and proprietary trading desks and ultimately to forced liquidations of positions held by many market-neutral quantitative equity strategies" (p. 5).

As is well known, most equity value stocks quickly bounced back by the end of August 2007, and the liquidity crisis moved on to devastate the securitized products from which the crisis originated. The quant crisis of August 2007 demonstrated the large losses that indirect exposure to liquidity risk can generate even in extremely liquid positions such as large-cap equity. Quantitative equity funds wanted exposure to the equity value risk factor due to its history of consistent, strong returns. Unfortunately, this pure play on equity value became a sizable exposure to liquidity factor risk as the strategy became increasingly crowded by leveraged players.

The lesson worth remembering from the credit crisis is that liquidity is a common risk factor that can at times generate very large positive and negative returns. Risk managers need to carefully monitor positions with direct exposure to liquidity risk, such as securities with large bid–ask spreads, limited trading volume, or high complexity, as discussed earlier. Risk managers must also monitor the indirect liquidity risk in their liquid positions. Unfortunately, indirect exposures to liquidity risk are difficult to measure quantitatively, but crowded trades and embedded exposures to illiquid positions, such as bank stocks with embedded exposure to complex securitized assets, are warning signs that risk managers must closely monitor in addition to traditional quantitative measures of liquidity risk.

17.3 INVESTORS IN SECURITIZED PRODUCTS NEED TO LOOK PAST THE DATA TO THE UNDERLYING BEHAVIOR OF THE ASSETS

As is generally well accepted, the genesis of the credit crisis was in complex and, in retrospect, poorly understood securitized US mortgage products.[20] Many market participants were subsequently caught off guard by their inability to substantively assess the underlying exposures in those products. One lesson certainly worth remembering from the credit crisis is that investors and risk managers need to be more hands-on and to develop a deeper and direct understanding of the underlying assets, including an understanding of the behavior, incentives, and current practices of borrowers, servicers, and originators. Furthermore, this hands-on knowledge needs to be adequately incorporated into risk analytics and models. The original attraction of securitization was that it provided ways for investors to easily and efficiently invest in new asset classes and obtain portfolio diversification through ownership of different types of market beta. Ideally, securitization permits information costs to be greatly economized. Securitization should in theory lead to the standardization of investment vehicles and enhanced liquidity for the underlying assets being securitized.

Many distinct players are involved in the securitization process. Originators make loans to individual borrowers for varied needs: residential mortgages, credit cards, auto loans, and commercial real estate mortgages. Some originators immediately sell all of their loans and others act solely as agents for portfolio lenders. Others might warehouse loans prior to selling them for securitization. Investment bankers assemble deals by bundling the underlying assets into pools and then provide the initial data on pool characteristics to investors. Rating agencies initially assess the credit risk of deals, rate them, and then continue to monitor risks throughout the life of the product. Servicers then provide ongoing information on the performance of the underlying asset pool. Finally, broker/dealer trading desks make markets in the different tranches of the securities as well as provide investors with the regular market valuations they require. They also stand by, willing to commit their capital to provide investors with market liquidity by making reasonably tight secondary markets.

The net result of these endeavors was to increase investor access to new asset classes and to drive rapid growth in the issuance of securitized assets in the run-up to the credit crisis as displayed in Exhibit 17.5. After years of relative success, combined with the development of increasingly sophisticated analytical and statistical modeling, these efforts also began to encourage a sophisticated style of "analytically intensive armchair management" that relied

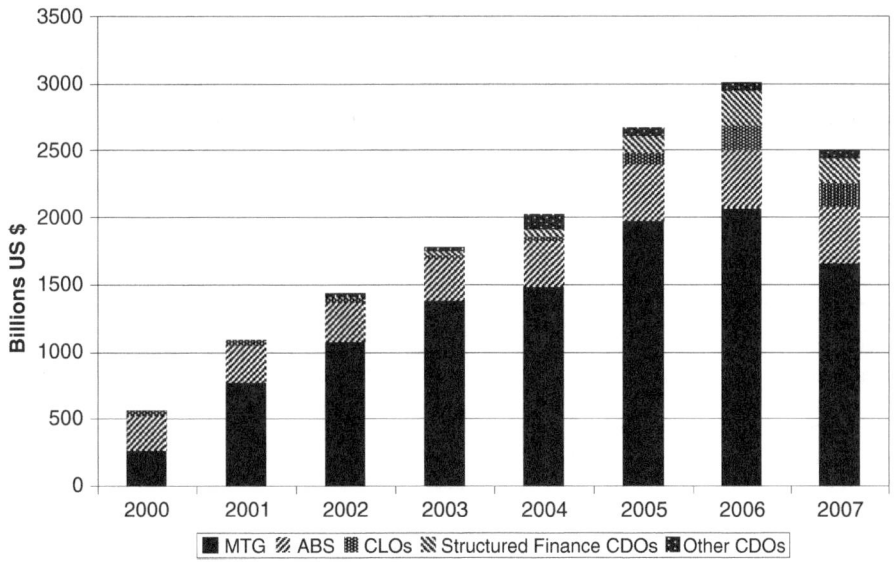

EXHIBIT 17.5 Growth in Issuance of Securitized Assets
Sources: Securities Industry and Financial Markets Association (2008) and authors' calculations, as cited in Golub and Crum (2010a).

on data, statistical models, and technology to perform surveillance over portfolios versus "boots on the ground." The credit crisis demonstrated the limitations of this investment process as many securitized products were racked by severe defaults, delinquencies, and loss severities completely outside the realm of expectations. The quality and performance of the underlying assets turned out to be materially worse than expected. The integrity of the actual underwriting standards and of borrower behavior is now known to have been much worse than what many investors could have anticipated. These revelations, however, were probably not as big a surprise to many loan brokers, originators, and servicers. In many cases, behavior by borrowers and lenders was borderline fraudulent and was not something that any amount of armchair data analysis or modeling could ever have uncovered.[21]

A key lesson of the crisis is that investors seeking to participate in complex securitized products need to be deeply involved in the information cycle. A method for assessing the quality, completeness, and relevance of data must be developed. In many cases, there is no substitute for direct due diligence by investors. In the run-up to the credit crisis, for instance, data showing low default and delinquency rates masked deteriorating borrower and collateral quality as home equity cash-outs increased aggregate leverage in the household sector. Collecting and analyzing more default and delinquency data alone would never have revealed the significant slide in lending standards. The standard data on securitized products had lost its substantive information content. Only field-level research and the collection of additional nonstandard data on the underlying assets would have alerted investors to growing problems. A perfect example of this is the Countrywide Home Loan Mortgage Pass-Through Trust 2007-HY7 (CWHL 2007-HY7) detailed in Exhibit 17.6.[22]

As Exhibit 17.6 shows, this particular non-agency residential mortgage-backed security has collateral characteristics that appear to be very favorable. The mortgage loans are to prime borrowers with a weighted average FICO score of 738.58.[23] The mortgages are first-lien loans and borrowers are well above water with a weighted average loan-to-value (LTV) ratio of less than 72%. CWHL 2007-HY7 consists of conventional hybrid adjustable-rate mortgages, and the weighted-average fixed rate period is more than 6 years. CWHL 2007-HY7 does have a high percentage of California loans at 45.72%, but in recent years California was one of the strongest housing markets. CWHL 2007-HY7 was securitized into 34 certificates, of which 27 were offered and 7 were not. Both Moody's and S&P rated 24 of the 27 offered certificates AAA. The remaining three certificates were rated Aa2, A2, and Baa2 by Moody's and AA+, AA, and A by S&P. Therefore, all of the offered certificates were rated at least investment grade by Moody's and S&P.

	Loan Group 1	Loan Group 2	Loan Group 3	Loan Group 4	Total Pool
Principal Balance	$63,330,778	$219,914,897	$177,522,952	$99,209,739	$559,978,366
Principal Balance (%)	11.31	39.27	31.70	17.72	100.00
Fixed Rate Period (months)	36	60	84	120	75.52
CA Mtg. Loans (%)	36.56	43.65	40.47	65.55	45.72
Loan to Value (%)	72.44	70.85	71.30	72.40	71.45
Avg. Current Mtg. Rate (%)	6.09	6.62	6.66	6.77	6.60
Avg. FICO Score	738.00	735.00	743.00	739.00	738.58

EXHIBIT 17.6 CWHL 2007-HY7 Pool and Loan Group Characteristics
Sources: Countrywide Home Loans Servicing (2007) and authors' calculations, as cited in Golub and Crum (2010a).

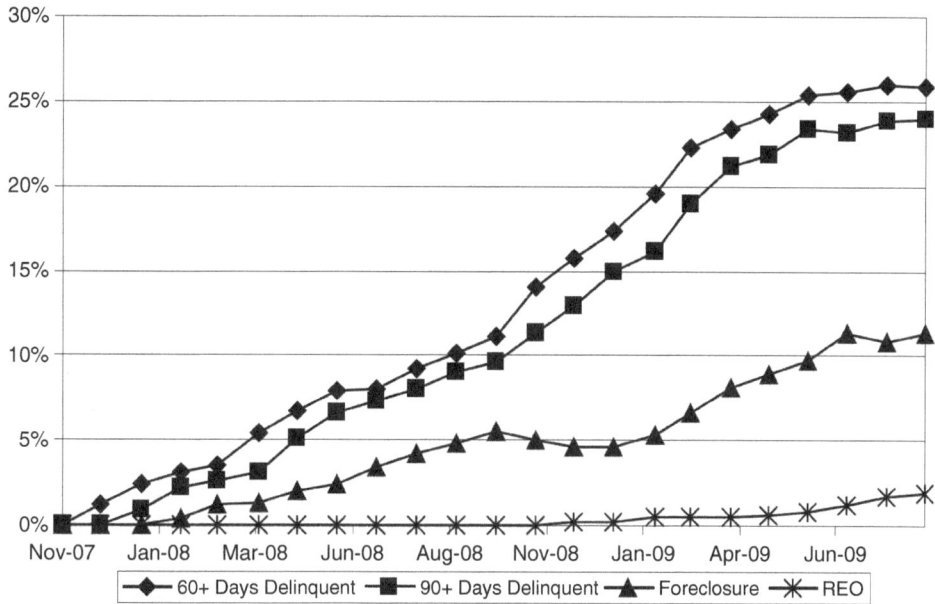

EXHIBIT 17.7   CWHL 2007-HY7 Collateral Performance
Source: Bloomberg, as cited in Golub and Crum (2010a).

Exhibit 17.7 shows the actual credit performance of CWHL 2007-HY7 since its issuance in late 2007. The delinquency and foreclosure rates indicate that the deal had been a total disaster. Only 20 months after issuance, more than 25% of the pool was 60 days delinquent, and nearly 10% was in foreclosure. Investors and rating agencies thought that CWHL 2007-HY7 was a high-quality deal with prime borrowers who had an average 739 FICO score and 72% LTV. Unfortunately, these statistics had lost their information content as the housing bubble progressed and the nature of the collateral changed.

As the housing bubble progressed, more borrowers sought loans with more favorable repayment terms, added leverage, and relaxed underwriting standards, including higher-quality prime borrowers. In order to meet the demands of borrowers and to satisfy strong investor demand for mortgage-backed securities backed by loans to borrowers with high FICO scores and low LTVs, originators began to issue a very different kind of mortgage. The new mortgages included the increased use of interest-only features, higher combined LTVs through the use of second-lien mortgages and home equity loans, and relaxed underwriting standards, such as increased issuance of less than full documentation loans. Returning to the CWHL 2007-HY7 deal, had an investor actually known what characteristics to look for, information from the loan prospectus would have revealed that CWHL 2007-HY7 contained riskier mortgages than even the contemporary pools of prime mortgages. For example, as shown in Exhibit 17.8, 95% of the loans were not fully amortizing compared with 84% of the 2007 prime cohort, and 80% of the borrowers did not fully document their income compared with 63% of typical 2007 prime mortgages. In fact, the change in the mortgage origination market was so pronounced that even these additional statistics did not fully capture the slide in lending standards. For instance, Missal and Richman (2008) noted that some employees at subprime lender New Century "measured

	CWHL 2007-HY7	2007 Prime Hybrid Cohort
Combined LTV	77%	74%
Less than Full Documentation	80	63
Interest Only	95	84
60+ Days Delinquent (% Current Balance)	25	8

EXHIBIT 17.8 Deteriorating Quality of Underlying Assets
Sources: Countrywide Home Loans Servicing (2007), Bordia et al. (2009), and authors' calculations, as cited in Golub and Crum (2010a).

loan quality by whether the loan could be sold, not whether it was likely that the borrower would meet his or her obligation" and the Federal Bureau of Investigation stated that 63,713 mortgage fraud reports with possible losses of more than $1.4 billion were filed in fiscal year 2008 (see endnote 21). In light of this information, it is not surprising that one-quarter of the CWHL 2007-HY7 pool was seriously delinquent compared with "only" 8% of similar vintage loans. The seismic shift in collateral risk over time had made it difficult for models relying on previously sufficient summary statistics to accurately capture the dramatic rise in delinquencies and defaults that would later be realized.

Borrowers and originators knew the collateral characteristics that investors and rating agencies demanded, and they worked hard to supply that demand. Unfortunately, investors and rating agencies were not intimately involved in the underlying origination process and could not look through the securitized products they were investing in and rating in order to see the flaws in the collateral; they could not see beyond the standard summary statistics they had come to depend on. As a result, when collateral statistics, such as FICO score and LTV ratio, failed to predict collateral performance, market participants were continually negatively surprised as collateral losses well exceeded estimates provided by armchair risk management.

Another way to think about this problem is through the paradigm of managing model risk. Traditionally, this has been thought of as a highly quantitative process to determine if the mathematics and computational implementation of a model is robust and correct. Another dimension of model risk exists, however, and that is the risk that although the computations in the model may be correct, the phenomena being modeled may be incomplete or even irrelevant. From this perspective, the "risk" that needs to be managed is that the analytical model or statistical characterization of risk may simply be missing the relevant and ever-changing nature of the actual behavior of the underlying assets. Therefore, if an institution has investments in securitized assets, then not only must it acquire the analytical capability to understand the risks of its investments, but it must also invest in a process to ensure that the models it is relying on remain relevant to what is happening with the underlying assets.

Statistically, a failing model can be identified by observing its mistakes, but a much less expensive way to identify a failing model is to maintain a better understanding of the underlying behavior of the assets. The latter task does not necessarily lend itself to the degree of (false) analytical precision as many quantitatively oriented finance practitioners might like, but the credit crisis demonstrated that it is folly to assume that highly dispersed economic phenomena can always be managed by a misguided faith in the law of large numbers. It is the nature of every economic system that if large entities are relying on a particular type of model, other participants in the system will opportunistically adapt their behavior to take advantage of the model reliance. It certainly could be argued that investors in AAA-rated tranches thought their investments were sufficiently "out-of-the-money" to any reasonable estimate of model risk so that this level of expertise was not required. Billions of dollars lost has taught us that this assumption was wrong. Risk managers must either make sure that their institutions are managing their model risk or are choosing not to participate in these markets.

17.4   CERTIFICATION IS USELESS DURING SYSTEMIC EVENTS

The credit crisis revealed the fallacy of relying upon thinly capitalized "certifiers" of financial products. Bond insurers, auction managers, Fannie Mae, Freddie Mac, and even the value-added provided by rating agencies have all been substantially washed away by the credit crisis. While investors can and should access third-party information providers, prudent investors need to rely more upon their own credit analysis and surveillance capabilities to understand the underlying credits that are ostensibly being "wrapped" by other institutions. If institutions are not willing or able to do this, then they should probably choose not to invest in those particular classes of assets.

Risk managers also need to be extremely skeptical of any purported form of insurance against systemic risks. Exhibit 17.9 details how many structured products and insured municipal bonds were rated AAA by rating agencies prior to the credit crisis. In 2006, only nine US corporations received the top rating, but more than 37,000 structured finance deals and 22,324 insured municipal bonds were rated AAA. The amazing proliferation of AAA ratings and the little attention that such proliferation received at the time demonstrates the extent to which market participants had become reliant on certifiers to protect them from systemic risks.

Ironically, the overreliance on certifiers by market participants was so pervasive that it became a systemic risk in its own right. The situation was so bad that much of the market became totally dependent on the government to provide direct guarantees and recapitalizations that market participants had previously believed would be provided by certifiers. Most notable among these were the various capital injections and debt guarantees extended to banks by governments around the world after AAA-rated securities began to default and

Entity	Number of AAA Ratings	AAA Ratings as Percent of Total
Structured Finance	37,000	60
Insured Municipal Bonds	22,324	47
Non-Insured Municipal Bonds	2,292	5
Sovereign Nations	19	17
US Corporations	9	<1

EXHIBIT 17.9   Pre–Credit Crisis AAA Ratings by Security Type
Sources: Data on structured finance are from Coval, Jurek, and Stafford (2008) and corresponds to ratings as of mid-2007, as cited in Golub and Crum (2010a). Data on corporations are from Salas (2006) and date to August 7, 2006, as cited in Golub and Crum (2010a). Data on sovereign ratings are from McCormack (2006) and date to October 6, 2006, as cited in Golub and Crum (2010a). It should be noted, however, that unlike corporations, sovereign nations, and municipalities, every structured finance deal will include and offer some AAA-rated securities. In fact, the purpose of structured finance is to restructure the cash flows of the underlying assets in a way that a range of risk levels from AAA-rated to equity tranches as well as varying maturities can be created to suit investor needs.

bond insurers failed to protect the principal guaranteed in insurance contracts.[24] A key lesson worth remembering from the credit crisis is that systemic risks really are systemic, and risk managers must be extremely skeptical of any entity that attempts to protect their institutions from such risks. Risk managers must closely monitor and control the absolute size of all systemic risk exposures excluding certifier protections. Assuming that certifier protections will shield institutions from systemic risk exposures can have catastrophic results when those risks are realized.

17.5 MARKET RISK CAN CHANGE DRAMATICALLY

The run-up to the credit crisis saw compression in almost all measures of risk premia. The collapse of the term premium caused former Federal Reserve Chairman Alan Greenspan to make his famous bond market conundrum comments in February 2005, and the search for yield caused real estate cap rates, credit spreads, and liquidity premia to fall to record lows.[25] Volatility also declined and many market observers remarked that economies and financial markets had become more flexible and diversified and, hence, more resilient to unexpected shocks. These developments were dramatically reversed, however, when numerous measures of risk premia abruptly rose from record lows to record highs.

The fact that market risk appetite can swing up and down over short periods of time has been previously documented. For instance, Shiller (1981) showed that stock price volatility is as much as 13 times greater than the volatility of real dividends. Although it is well known that risk appetite is volatile, it is still easy for risk takers to overestimate the persistence of risk appetite regimes. A lesson worth remembering from the credit crisis is that risk managers must be very vigilant about investments that require continuity in risk appetite or in the ability to foresee risk appetite changes.

Risk managers should develop tools to help track changes in risk appetite. Exhibit 17.10 details the construction of a market risk appetite index.[26] The goal of the risk appetite index is to aggregate factors that are reliable measures of global market risk. As discussed by Park, McCormick, and Jiltsov (2007), the factors used to create the aggregate risk appetite index have three characteristics: (1) the direction of factor movement is consistent with economic intuition, (2) the factor shows significant responsiveness to changes in market risk, and (3) a factor change has low cross-sectional correlation. The arrows in Exhibit 17.10 indicate which direction the factor moves when markets become more risk loving or risk averse.

Each risk factor detailed in Exhibit 17.10 is given a percentile rank for the sample period. Rankings are sorted so that high percentiles are indicative of high-risk-appetite markets and low percentiles are indicative of low-risk-appetite markets. Percentiles are then averaged together to determine the overall level of the market risk appetite index for a particular time frame. An example of the BlackRock Short-Term Risk Appetite Index for a 3-month horizon is displayed in Exhibit 17.11. The short-term risk appetite index is meant to capture high-frequency changes in risk appetite. Extending the risk appetite time horizon to 1 year or more can help capture long-term changes in market risk appetite. The aggregate risk appetite index is displayed in the upper-right panel of Exhibit 17.11, and the index components are displayed in the lower panel of Exhibit 17.11. The upper-left panel of Exhibit 17.11 displays the change in index components over 3 months, 1 month, 1 week, and 1 day as well as diagnostics on the aggregate risk appetite index.

Along with large changes in risk appetite, the market's level of risk, as measured by volatility, can also change dramatically. Asset and risk factor volatilities that previously had

Risk Factor	Description	Risk Loving	Risk Averse	Interpretation
Market Volatility				
G3 Implied Vol	Implied volatility from EUR, GBP, and JPY	↓	↑	Uncertainty in the FX market
Equity Implied Vol	S&P Volatility Index—VIX	↓	↑	Uncertainty in the equity market
EM Risk				
EM CDS	Emerging Markets Spreads: Brazil, Russia, and Turkey 5-yr CDS contract	↓	↑	Credit risk in high-beta emerging markets
EM Equity to Vol Ratio	Brazil, Mexico, Turkey, India Stock Exchange Indices: Index level divided by realized volatility	↑	↓	Sovereign risk in volatile emerging markets
Risk Appetite Ratios				
S&P 500 P/E	S&P Adjusted Price Earning Ratio	↑	↓	Confidence in corporate profits growth
Equity Bond Ratio	FTSE World Index over Treasury, Bund, and JGB bond prices	↑	↓	Flight to quality, movement in global equities vs. government bonds.
Gold Price to Global Gold	Gold spot price over S&P Gold Index	↓	↑	Gold as safe haven manifests when gold equity sector does not follow gold spot.
Market Liquidity				
TED Spread	3-mo. LIBOR-3mo. T-bill rate	↓	↑	Liquidity risk

EXHIBIT 17.10   Risk Appetite Index Components
Source: BlackRock, as cited in Golub and Crum (2010a).

been low can quickly spike up. Moreover, correlations also tend to increase when market risk rises. As a result, portfolio risk can increase even faster than individual market risks as diversification falls. In addition to changes in the market's level of risk, the composition of risk can also radically change. Certain assets and risk factors that at one time had low volatilities can become highly volatile when crises erupt. Historically volatile assets are often closely watched by investors and risk managers because their ability to create large losses and gains is well documented. Risk management techniques and resources are often devoted to track and manage these known volatilities. As Exhibit 17.12 demonstrates, formerly low-volatility assets can quickly become major sources of risk.

The graph in Exhibit 17.12 displays the risk decomposition of a fixed-income portfolio actively managed against the Barclays Capital US Aggregate Index, whose active risk factor exposures were held constant for 5 years. Before the credit crisis of 2007–2009, interest rate risk and corporate credit risk were clearly the largest contributors to active risk. Once the credit crisis began, however, the level of risk increased sharply and the composition of risk changed dramatically. Exposures to securitized assets suddenly became the dominant sources of risk whereas previously they contributed very little to overall risk. Risk managers must be prepared for the changing level and composition of market risk.

Risk management, in its most literal form, is about managing the risk of a portfolio, which means not only optimizing the active decisions of portfolio managers, but also preventing the level of portfolio risk from being carried away by the market and beyond

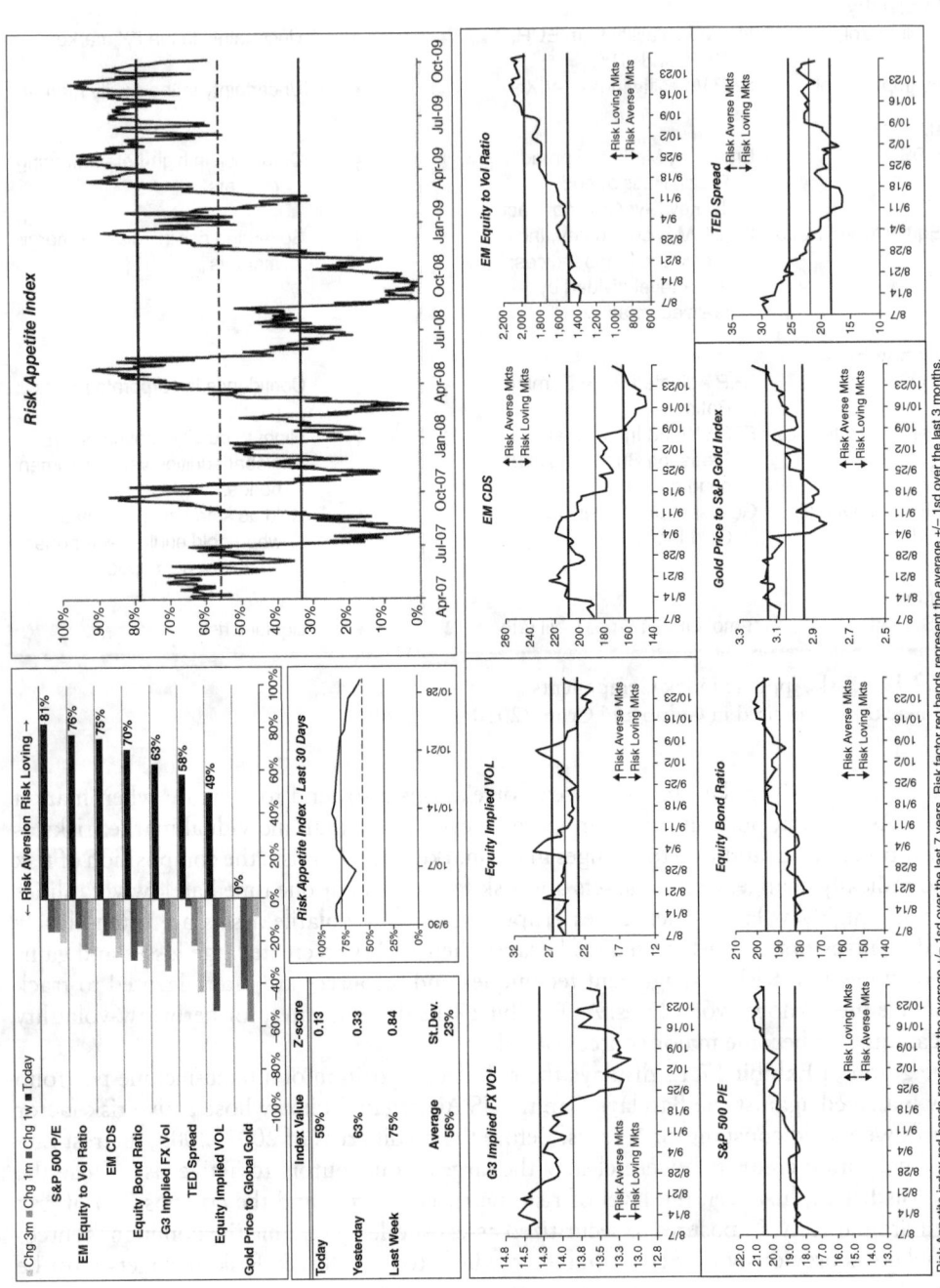

EXHIBIT 17.11 Short-Term Risk Appetite Index, 3-Month Horizon

Sources: Underlying data are from Bloomberg and calculations were done by BlackRock, as cited in Golub and Crum (2010a).

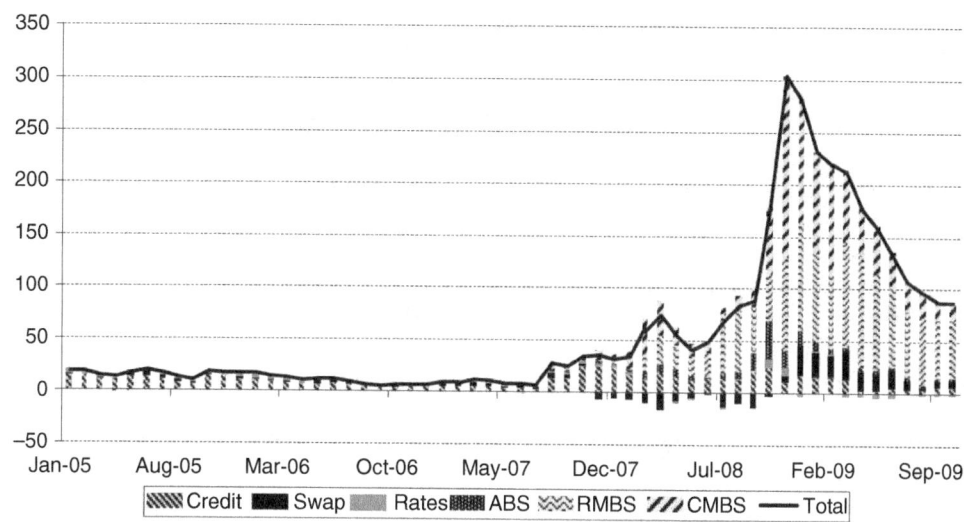

EXHIBIT 17.12 Active Risk for Constant Exposure Portfolio, January 2005–October 2009 (in annualized bp)
Source: BlackRock, as cited in Golub and Crum (2010a). Data are for illustrative purposes only and do not represent the actual positions of any BlackRock portfolios.

acceptable boundaries. While markets recovered much of their losses, financial history has clearly demonstrated, time after time, that it is not always possible to hold desired long-term positions through all market conditions. As Keynes famously said, "The market can stay irrational longer than you can stay solvent."[27] Risk managers not only need to have cutting-edge knowledge of the latest models and techniques, but also a historical perspective of how bad financial crises can actually get.

As discussed earlier, the level and composition of market risk can quickly change and active decisions need to be made about how to respond to changes in market risk. Note that a portfolio manager's ability to manage down the increased level of risk may be constrained as many relevant trading markets shut down. Unfortunately, managing the level of risk may lead to being a seller at precisely the wrong time. The risk of being whipsawed by V-shaped recoveries in financial markets is real and can negatively impact returns. Best practices would be to proactively constrain levels of risk based on predetermined risk tolerances, so that the risk of being whipsawed is more limited. Moreover, the alternative of doing nothing means that risk levels will be determined by the market. Ultimately, the level of risk should be consistent with the institution's fiduciary responsibilities.

The worst situation, but unfortunately all too common, is for institutions to get "risk management religion" right after a dose of excessive risk. Once the horse is out of the barn, the risk of being whipsawed is the greatest. But even in such challenging situations, the ultimate arbiter of the appropriate level of risk is the institution's ability to bear risk. Institutions with large, near-term liquidity demands may not be in a position to ride out the storm, whereas an institution with a stable base of funding and capital can much better afford to try to wait for the market to revert to more stable, long-run valuations. Market fluctuations do not respect the risk tolerances of individual institutions, and only active risk management can protect them from undesired levels of risk as market volatilities change.

17.6   THE CHANGING NATURE OF MARKET RISK

Across the globe, power and control over the financial system is shifting from financial to political capitals. The scale of intervention by governments around the world is truly without precedent. Increasingly, policy changes are becoming major drivers of market dynamics. In many markets, policy risk has surpassed economic fundamentals and market technicals as the primary source of risk. In some ways, markets in the developed world are behaving in a fashion that is consistent with the policy risk typically assumed to exist in emerging markets. The risk management teams of the future may come to rely somewhat less on economists and statisticians and lean more on politically oriented analysts. Standard quantitative techniques are not well equipped to deal effectively with policy risk because changes in policy often result in a structural break in the covariance of economic variables.

For example, Exhibit 17.13 shows the average monthly conditional prepayment rate (CPR) for 30-year Fannie Mae mortgage-backed securities (MBS) by coupon, from January 2009 to September 2009. Despite having larger incentives to refinance, 6.5% and 7.0% coupon MBS are actually prepaying at a slower rate than 6.0% and 5.5% coupon MBS. There is, of course, an obvious economic reason for this relationship. Borrowers in high-coupon mortgages tend to have higher LTVs and lower FICO scores than borrowers in low-coupon mortgages, and due to the stress in the banking system, mortgage lenders are currently reluctant to refinance low-credit-quality borrowers. This dynamic could very easily change if legislation was passed to make it easier for low-credit-quality borrowers to refinance. If such a policy change were to occur, then the prepayment risk in higher-coupon MBS would instantly increase. This spike in prepayment risk would represent an obvious structural break in the economic relationship between prepayments and borrower credit quality that no econometric model of prepayments could be expected to forecast.

The US federal government passed legislation, such as the Housing and Economic Recovery Act, which in part aims to reduce foreclosures by making refinancing into Federal Housing

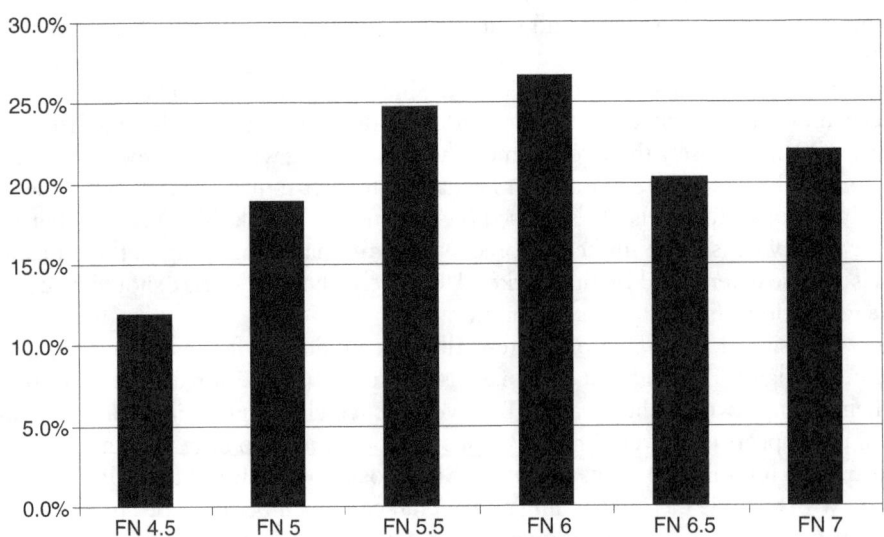

EXHIBIT 17.13   Average Monthly CPR, January 2009–September 2009
Source: BlackRock and authors' calculations, as cited in Golub and Crum (2010a).

Administration loans easier.[28] Currently the program would cover at most 400,000 borrowers, but if the program were expanded, the bar graph in Exhibit 17.13 could change dramatically. Furthermore, the announced buy-outs of delinquent loans by Fannie Mae and Freddie Mac could easily spike monthly CPRs on high-coupon mortgages several-fold. In such an environment, the qualitative analysis of savvy political analysts might result in a better read of the factors most likely to drive markets than the analysis of traditional risk managers.

Cho, Mufson, and Tse (2009) reported on the beginning of this transition, as a number of financial institutions spoke openly about the growing importance of getting better plugged into the political process:

> As financial firms navigate a life more closely connected to government aid and oversight than ever before, they increasingly turn to Washington, closing a chasm that was previously far greater than the 228 miles separating the nation's political and financial capitals.... In response, senior executives of major financial companies are traversing the Beltway to meet lawmakers in person for the first time. Firms such as Fidelity Investments, BNY Mellon and even Goldman Sachs, which has prospered in the crisis relative to many other banks, are opening additional offices or bulking up their staffs in the capital. (p. A1)

Risk management organizations will also need to invest in acquiring the human capital that can provide the qualitative analysis demanded by the heightened importance of policy risk.

17.7 BY THE TIME A CRISIS STRIKES, IT'S TOO LATE TO START PREPARING

An effective and robust risk management process requires a material and sustained commitment of resources. It is a very expensive undertaking, and it requires a long-term investment in people and technology. Generally, very few financial professionals will say that they are against the concept of risk management. It is the actions that matter, however, not the sentiment.

Senior management must buy into and constantly demonstrate their support for a vigorous independent risk management group if the risk management process is to succeed. A team of professional risk managers with substantial subject matter expertise and strong communication skills is critical in order for the risk management process to have the desired impact. Risk managers need to have the skills required to garner the respect of their institution's risk takers and senior managers, and organizational career paths need to be created to provide necessary rewards to attract and retain top-level talent.

A significant investment in analytics and information management technology is also required to develop the appropriate risk metrics, leverage risk managers, and create a reliable information utility that can be trusted across the organization. Institutions need to avoid multiple systems that create internal information wars and result in the inability to make and enforce decisions. Inevitably this will require strong support by senior management; in many instances, the value of a nuance of improvement in accuracy or theoretical elegance to the immediate users often seems exceedingly important, even though maintaining a "Tower of Babel" degrades an organization's ability to be decisive. Accessing and using information must be fast and easy in order for it to be useful on a regular basis. Having a risk management team with an efficient information infrastructure in place will allow an organization to respond to unanticipated issues and challenges.

The lesson of the credit crisis worth remembering is that while it is impossible to anticipate every potential contingency that may arise, having a professional risk management team and a comprehensive database of portfolio holdings and characteristics will facilitate a fast response when a crisis does strike. Although the black swans of Taleb (2007a) are, by definition, unknowable, a strong risk management team can help institutions mitigate the consequences of unforeseen events.

17.8   CONCLUSION

The credit crisis of 2007–2009 forced market participants to rethink current state-of-the-practice methods in risk management. This chapter highlighted six lessons worth remembering from the credit crisis. These six lessons need to be incorporated into an institution's risk management process if it is to weather or even prosper in the next financial crisis. Many institutions were forced to learn some of these lessons the hard way when efficient market–based risk models and operational assumptions failed to reveal sizable sources of risk, and illiquid markets impaired the ability to raise cash from asset sales. Furthermore, policy risk is a major contributor to market volatility, and resources need to be developed to identify and manage these risks as well.

The goal of this chapter is not to design more complex analytical models, nor is it to attack quantitative risk management in general. Rather the purpose of this chapter is to clearly articulate the lessons worth remembering from the credit crisis and outline the steps risk management organizations need to take to be successful in the future. Finally, while the financial markets have recovered from the lows of March 2009 to higher valuation levels, more normalized liquidity, and increased stability of major counterparties, market participants should not be lulled into believing that the problems associated with the credit crisis were a one-time event. It is our hope that the risk management lessons discussed in this chapter will help institutions to persevere when such problems arise again.

Originally, we intended to title this chapter "Risk Management Lessons Learned from the Credit Crisis of 2007–2009." As suggested by Andrew Lo in an email quip, however, titling any chapter about the financial markets as "lessons learned" would probably be unduly optimistic. Unfortunately, Andrew Lo's remark contains a lot of wisdom and reflects an accurate read of the history of financial markets. The historical record is not encouraging (see, for example, Kindleberger [1978], Galbraith [1997], Bruner and Carr [2007], or Lowenstein [2000]). In fact, the very existence of several detailed histories of financial crises demonstrates the repeatability of these crises across time. The writings during and about the Crash of 1907, the Great Depression, or even the more recent Long-Term Capital Management crisis seemed very contemporary when read during the credit crisis of 2007–2009. Perhaps it is thus an ambitious, but reasonable, aspiration to hope that the financial community—or at least its current living and practicing members—does retain the memories of this bout of turbulence, rather than being forced to suffer again at perhaps an even greater cost to society. If we are fortunate enough to skip a generation before reliving a period like the credit crisis of 2007–2009, then all the work done by the numerous commentators and analysts of this period shall not have been in vain.

NOTES

1. This chapter was originally a paper by Bennett Golub and Conan Crum (2010a) that was published in the *Journal of Portfolio Management*, 36(3). The chapter has been slightly modified from the original publication with permission.
2. Akerlof and Shiller (2009) made a more fundamental critique of efficient market–based models in general by arguing that most economic fluctuations are the result of "animal spirits" and not the result of optimizing behavior by rational, self-interested economic agents.
3. See Wood (2008) for additional discussion on the debate between those advocating a return to "common sense" risk management and those in favor of traditional quantitative risk management.
4. Arguably, the collapse of Long-Term Capital Management (LTCM) in 1998 demonstrated how quickly liquidity could collapse, although that phenomenon also showed how quickly the markets recovered. For whatever reason, it does not appear that markets remembered the lessons of LTCM.
5. See Satow (2008) for additional evidence that changes in Security and Exchange Commission regulations also contributed to increased leverage at financial institutions.
6. Sometimes, the term *fundamental value* is also used to refer to the underlying value of an asset that might be different from the value assigned to the asset by the market. Fox (2009) provided an entertaining history and debate about the critiques and defenses of the EMH.
7. See Van Eck Global (2009) and LaCapra (2009) for additional details on the dislocation in market prices for pre-refunded municipal bonds and SPACs.
8. We had firsthand exposure to the "no bid" aspect of many markets during the credit crisis. As the old adage goes, seeing is believing, and we are able to bear witness to this type of market breakdown.
9. These bonds are said "to have gone to bond heaven."
10. Smith, 2008, p. 1.
11. See Lo, Petrov, and Wierzbicki (2003) for an example of one of the few models that explicitly includes liquidity in the portfolio optimization process.
12. See Swensen (2009, pp. 53–77) for additional details.
13. By comparison, the S&P 500 had earned an annual total return of 10.4% from June 30, 1988, to June 30, 2008, and 2.9% from June 30, 1998, to June 30, 2008.
14. See Copeland and Galai (1983) and Glosten and Milgrom (1985) for examples of models that explicitly studied the interaction of informed investors, liquidity traders, and market makers on bid–ask spreads.
15. Market gyrations that significantly impair expert investors are usually correlated with other factors, such as increased volatility, increased risk aversion, and a breakdown of widely used models, which result in asset underperformance. The purpose of this section is not to deny the existence of these other factors, but rather to emphasize the large impact that expert investors have on the liquidity of complex markets.
16. "Excess" kurtosis is a statistical measure of the peakedness, and hence the fatness of tails, of a distribution relative to the normal distribution. As shown here, large values are consistent with a high degree of extreme upside and downside moves in returns.
17. See, for instance, Bullock (2008), Fortado and Cahill (2009), Desmond (2008), Goldstein (2008), and Hyuga et al. (2008) for details on the various counterparties and legal problems that plagued the Lehman Brothers' bankruptcy.
18. From July 31, 1999, to August 31, 2009, the monthly return correlation between the Treasury index and ABS and CMBS indices was 0.25 and 0.23, respectively.
19. In addition to liquidity, other factors compounded the negative performance of the A$/¥ carry trade. For instance, the flight-to-quality trade of fall 2008 saw many investors move into lower-yielding, but more shock-resistant currencies such as the ¥ and US$.
20. Several market observers, including Hurtado (2009), Voreacos and Kary (2008), and Mnyanda and Pan (2008) have cited the July 2007 collapse of two Bear Stearns hedge funds, the High-Grade

Structured Credit Fund and the High-Grade Structured Credit Enhanced Leveraged Fund, as marking the start of the credit crisis of 2007–2009.

21. The Federal Bureau of Investigation Mortgage Fraud Reports provide an excellent review of the various mortgage-related crimes that became increasingly prevalent in the run-up to the credit crisis of 2007–2009. The 2006 report is available at http://www.fbi.gov/publications/fraud/mortgage_fraud06.htm#6; the 2007 report is available at http://www.fbi.gov/publications/fraud/mortgage_fraud07.htm#6; and the 2008 report is available at http://www.fbi.gov/publications/fraud/mortgage_fraud08.htm#6.

22. See Hernandez (2008) and Mildenberg and Freifeld (2008) for additional information on mortgage fraud investigations involving Countrywide Financial Corporation.

23. FICO scores are a metric developed by the Fair Isaac Corporation to help measure the creditworthiness of a borrower. FICO scores range between 300 and 850. Borrowers with FICO scores above 720 are generally considered to be prime borrowers, those with FICO scores above 680 are considered near-prime or Alt-A borrowers, and those with FICO scores below 620 are typically classified as subprime.

24. Please see Pittman (2008), Glover (2008), Moses (2008), and Trowbridge and Mider (2008) for additional information on some of the losses incurred by banks due to bond insurer downgrades and defaults.

25. See Greenspan (2005) for more details.

26. This particular risk index is used internally at BlackRock and is a slightly modified version of the Market Risk Sentiment Index of Park, McCormick, and Jiltsov (2007).

27. Finkelstein, 2006, p. 63.

28. See Lynch (2008) or US Department of Housing and Urban Development for additional details on the Housing and Economic Recovery Act at http://www.hud.gov/news/ recoveryactfaq.cfm.

CHAPTER 18

Reflections on Buy-Side Risk Management After (or Between) the Storms[1]

Bennett W. Golub
Senior Advisor, BlackRock

Conan Crum
Vice President, Risk & Quantitative Analysis, BlackRock (2013)

18.1 INTRODUCTION

The purpose of this chapter is to highlight the importance of eight specific principles on the organization and objectives of a buy-side risk management process. The risk principles elaborated upon in this chapter are certainly neither exhaustive nor necessarily new. In particular, many of these principles were incorporated into the report "Risk Principles for Asset Managers" published by the Buy Side Risk Managers Forum (BSRMF) and Capital Market Risk Advisors (CMRA) in 2008,[2] which included a systematic enumeration of risk management principles developed by and for a group of buy-side risk managers.[3,4] While many of these principles were generally acknowledged prior to the credit crisis, ensuing events have raised doubts about the depth of adherence to them in practice. This chapter highlights, emphasizes, and elaborates on some of those principles as well as identifies additional principles, with the overall intent being to emphasize each risk principle's particular importance to buy-side risk management.[5]

The following eight risk management principles are developed in greater detail in subsequent sections. First, risk management requires institutional buy-in. Second, the alignment and management of institutional interests is critical to risk management. Third, institutions need to get their portfolio managers to think like risk managers. Fourth, risk management organizations need to be independents with strong subject matter expertise. Fifth, institutions must clearly define fiduciary obligations to clients. Sixth, while a top-down perspective is necessary, a bottom-up risk management process is vital. Seventh, risk models require constant vigilance (and skepticism). Eighth, risk management does not mean risk avoidance.

18.2 RISK MANAGEMENT REQUIRES INSTITUTIONAL BUY-IN[6]

For risk management to be successful over the long term, it must become an integral part of an institution's governance and culture. Inevitably, this can only happen if it is strongly supported at the top of an organization. In the auditing literature, this is often referred to as the "tone at the top."[7] The particular circumstances of every organization and its management will differ. Senior management teams across different institutions may be more or less conservative, experienced, financially sophisticated, long-term oriented, or concerned about the financial livelihoods of their employees or shareholders. To some, risk management is simple common sense. To others, it is seen as a path to value maximization, as an ethical principle driven by a sense of duty, or as the only way to sleep at night. To yet others, it may be driven by the desire to avoid reliving previous professional and personal nightmares.

Regardless of the ultimate source of motivation, a demonstrable commitment from the top is required for even the best risk management process to be successful. In practice, this means that an institution will make risk informed decisions even if they conflict with other pressing objectives. Institutional behavior inconsistent with a risk oriented mindset will not be rewarded, and hard decisions will be made when the risk culture framework is violated. For instance, if a risk manager is in conflict with a large revenue producer, the actions taken by senior management in resolving the conflict will speak a hundred times louder than mouthing slogans but not backing them with action. This does not mean that senior management always has to fully back the views of its risk managers. Situations will necessarily differ, but the manner in which the various considerations are weighed is critical. Through consistent actions over time, senior management must demonstrate that risk management concerns will be taken very seriously and that the institution will not be governed solely by short-term considerations.

Senior management also has to articulate its commitment to and enforce clear policies on the role of risk management. Despite the long history of risk management failures, we are unaware of senior management teams that have openly advocated against risk management. This is reminiscent of Mark Twain's famous quote, "Actions speak louder than words but not nearly as often." To turn words into action, effective risk management requires significant organizational resources, equitable compensation between risk takers and risk managers, support for the development and enforcement of risk limits, full and open dialogue across internal organizational boundaries delineating responsibilities and authorities, and full internal transparency of risk-taking activities. Senior management also must demonstrate their buy-in through less formal means, such as explicitly recognizing and reinforcing the role of risk management through internal and external communications and making sure that the importance of the risk management process is broadly recognized within the institution. Even relatively minor internal signals, such as the allocation and location of office space, will speak loudly by making sure that the official ideology is reflected along the various dimensions of the institution's internal pecking order. Without institutional buy-in, even a talented risk management organization will be able to play only a peripheral role and is likely to achieve limited impact.

18.3 THE ALIGNMENT AND MANAGEMENT OF INSTITUTIONAL INTERESTS

Although it is beyond the scope of this chapter to explore in detail the subtleties and nuances of designing organizational incentive structures, to ignore the relationship between the alignment of interests and the effectiveness of risk management would be to ignore a material aspect of what drives success or failure in risk management. In many cases, the best risk manager might not be able to make important contributions to the welfare of an institution because, despite the commitment of senior management, the institution does not act with a common set of goals. At such institutions, powerful constituencies are not necessarily incentivized to look out for the long-term welfare of the institution. The microeconomic and cultural aspects of institutional alignment are briefly discussed in this chapter. A broader topic—the impact of corporate governance models and regulation—is not addressed, although it is also clearly very important. Because the specifics of these issues vary quite dramatically across institutions, our focus will be only on those aspects of an institution that are generally within the direct control of its management.

One of the key challenges for an institution is finding ways to maximize individual performance while also maximizing the institution's overall long-term effectiveness and welfare. Institutions often have a variety of internal stakeholders, and each stakeholder has interests that may not necessarily align completely with each other or with the firm as a whole. Compensation methodologies with narrowly focused goals tailored to individuals or to organizational subunits will, by design, tend to encourage the behaviors incentivized by those goals. Although incentive-focused compensation structures inspire individuals to work hard and produce, these efforts can potentially be detrimental to an organization's long-term interest. For instance, it might not be realistic to expect a salesman who is compensated solely on a commission basis to provide the best support to smaller accounts, absent some element of the institution's culture or control structure, even if the institution declares that it aims to provide the highest degree of client service.

Similarly, portfolio managers compensated solely on their performance may not choose to participate in the broader objectives of the institution, such as sharing ideas or energetically training junior professionals, again, absent some element of the institution's culture or control structure. When an institution is organized by narrowly focusing incentives to the specific tasks and goals of different internal stakeholders, it is economically rational and highly predictable that internal stakeholders will tend to pursue those different agendas even when they conflict with each other and the institution's long-term welfare. In these types of institutions, the risk manager's job will be much more challenging because the risk manager will have to design a range of processes to manage the (potentially) excessive pursuit of these objectives to the detriment of the overall institution's welfare.

In contrast, when internal policies and incentives channel behavior in a common direction, the task of the risk manager is greatly simplified. Equitably shared common bonus pools, compensation programs that reward long-term performance, and employee equity ownership are all steps that encourage synchronized behavior. Although many details need to be carefully tuned to optimize a particular institution's activities, by pursuing this path, the institution will tend to have less internal dissonance. The lack of internal dissonance alone does not necessarily map to the long-term welfare of the institution; for instance, a single-minded focus on sales or earnings growth may lead to excessive levels of risk being taken by portfolio managers. In such a case, the common goal is clear to all internal constituents but may lead the institution in lockstep off a cliff.

The ideal case is when the common direction of individual constituents is also rationally aligned with the long-term welfare of the institution itself. This requires a careful balancing of individual and collective incentives to generate the optimal trade-off between individual performance and collective interests in order to make the institution both efficient and robust. There is no obvious formula for achieving this. Executive management's job is to constantly strive to balance these two conflicting institutional incentives. When this is (approximately) achieved, the risk manager's job becomes significantly easier because the various internal constituencies are heading in the same general direction and that direction is sober and prudent.

The previous discussion focused on the microeconomic incentives inside an institution. Perhaps this is the area where traditional economists are intellectually most comfortable. Experience has shown, however, that an institution's culture can provide an exceedingly powerful force for the alignment of efforts that can mitigate the inevitable internal dissonance resulting from competing interests. To be succinct, different cultures will lead to different degrees of focus on either increasing the "size of the pie" or fighting about how big a slice of the existing (or even smaller) pie goes to each stakeholder. An institutional culture that earns the respect and loyalty of employees becomes an extremely powerful means for aligning individual and institutional interests.

From this perspective, an institution's culture should ideally create a common sense of purpose, interests, and values among all the internal stakeholders. That common sense of purpose may arise from a well understood common set of values, a long operating history with emphasis on critical decisions that exemplify commitment to those values, or even a powerful "founding myth" that provides a particular view of how and why the institution came into existence. This necessarily goes beyond the repetition of empty platitudes and, to be effective, must be consistent with how the institution is run and treats people on a day-to-day basis. When the operation of an institution and the treatment of its people are consistent with a common sense of purpose, an institution can move in a generally unified direction even if that direction is at times inconsistent with the individual stakeholder's narrow interests.

A common set of values, however, only has efficacy if the institution can effectively execute them. Thus, being well run is a necessary condition for an institution to be the vehicle for the transmission of those values. From a risk management perspective, the following characteristics are valuable:

- Relatively flat hierarchy—senior management is seen as being aware of what is actually happening across the institution.
- Trust/credibility—stakeholders believe in the intentions of the institution.
- Nonbureaucratic—stakeholders believe that things can get done.
- Nonpolitical—stakeholders believe that the institution is a meritocracy and that individuals will be fairly judged based on their contributions.
- Good internal communications—stakeholders must believe what the institution says; to the extent that the institution is perceived to be disingenuous or incompetent, cynicism will arise.
- Common information and transparency—to the maximum extent appropriate and permissible, stakeholders should be able to obtain information about the institution's operations. By educating stakeholders, they can understand the trade-offs faced by the institution. This culture of openness will facilitate the surfacing of bad news from the bottom up in an expedited manner. An open and honest institution will empower information to percolate up throughout its ranks.

By demonstrating over time and under a range of challenging situations that it is committed to doing the right thing and to treating its internal stakeholders fairly, an institution builds respect, loyalty, and a common sense of purpose. This does not mean that the institution cannot or should not make hard decisions. For instance, economic distress may require that an institution downsize. The way this is handled, including the fairness of the process for determining which employees are to be let go and the manner in which they are then treated, both financially and as individuals, will create the basis for the respect required to encourage stakeholders to put their faith in the institution's values. To the extent that this is done, bonds of loyalty are created that will motivate stakeholders to place the institution's values above their own narrow, near-term self-interests and to act in the interests of the institution's long-term welfare. If stakeholders believe in an institution, then they will have a greater motivation to preserve and protect it and that, in a nutshell, is the same mission as risk management.

18.4   GETTING RISK TAKERS TO THINK LIKE RISK MANAGERS

Ultimately, risk management needs to focus on increasing the overall effectiveness of portfolio managers. In order to do this, risk management principles and assessments must be integrated into the investment processes of the risk takers. Both risk takers and risk managers are in the forecasting business—risk takers forecast returns, and risk managers forecast return distributions.[8] Risk takers constantly adjust portfolio positioning as their return forecasts change. Similarly, an appropriately informed risk taker should also adjust portfolio positioning as the risk manager's return distribution forecasts change. Thus, successful risk managers help push forward the institution's "first line of defense."

Focusing on strengthening the first line of defense can be thought of as "the lazy risk manager's approach" to risk management because, if the risk takers are thinking about their own risks properly, then the risk managers should ideally not have that much to do. If the risk managers effectively communicate how they see the world, then the risk takers can work to make the appropriate risk–return trade-off. Conceptually, this is a trivial point. In practice, it can be quite challenging. First, the risk manager must make sure that all the relevant risk drivers have been identified. Then, the risk manager needs to make sure that the portfolio manager has access to accurate, timely, and comprehensible ex ante metrics so that the portfolio manager has an appropriate risk dashboard.

While the existence of such a dashboard is a necessary condition for success, it is not sufficient. In practice, it may turn out that absent direct involvement by risk managers, portfolio managers may not be able to fully and appropriately use the dashboard. The goal is to help portfolio managers construct efficient portfolios. By efficient, we mean that the portfolio reflects the portfolio manager's views of the market, but does not contain inadvertent risk. To help achieve this, risk managers must own the burden of translating their insights into actionable items. As well stated by a senior investment professional, "It is essential that the experts, who understand the necessary complexity of the risk that big and diversified firms take, can somehow manage to communicate their messages effectively to people who have other responsibilities."[9]

18.5   INDEPENDENT RISK MANAGEMENT ORGANIZATIONS[10]

The fourth principle that needs to be highlighted addresses both the need for a risk management orientation within an investment operation and how a risk management organization should be set up within an institution. Even if a risk organization succeeds in "getting risk takers to think like risk managers," in order to provide effective checks and balances, from an organizational perspective it needs to be truly independent of the risk takers. This holds true even when dealing with explicitly quantitative investment processes that mathematically optimize expected return subject to formal risk constraints. Experience has taught that even these investment processes do not always work as planned.[11] To provide an independent perspective, the risk manager needs to be able to look at the entire investment process with the critical eye that can only come from organizational independence. That independence means having the ability to raise issues that might go to the root of current processes or positions.

The credit crisis of 2007–2009 clearly demonstrated the necessity of having a strong, independent risk management function. For instance, there have been accusations that Washington Mutual, Inc. (WaMu), which was seized by the Office of Thrift Supervision (OTS) in September 2008, ignored, marginalized, and possibly even fired risk managers who raised concerns about the bank's mortgage lending practices.[12] We are aware of numerous instances where risk management teams exist primarily because clients, auditors, or regulators have demanded that they exist, although in practice these risk organizations are, at best, peripheral or, in some cases, totally irrelevant to the investment processes of their institutions. In contrast, Walker (2009) argued that commitment to a strong risk management process on the part of JP Morgan's chairman and chief executive, Jamie Dimon, helped the firm weather the credit crisis much better than many other financial firms.

Independent risk management means, at a minimum, that the risk management group reports directly to the top of the institution and is not subordinate to the investment functions. The head of an independent risk management organization should ideally report to the chief executive officer or president of the organization rather than to its chief investment officer. The risk organization's compensation structure should also be configured so that risk managers are incentivized by the long-term success of the organization and not by the short-term performance of the investment portfolios.

Independent risk management functions need not mean that the risk managers function primarily as internal institutional "policemen" who monitor and constrain the behavior of the risk takers. Although organizations need to have "eyes and ears" into their risk-taking activities, and events may arise when inappropriate behavior that requires remediation is uncovered, we argue that there is often much more efficacy in having the risk managers working closely and collaboratively with the risk takers. This approach has two significant advantages. First, the risk manager's efforts are primarily directed toward improving the risk awareness of the investment process rather than functioning in a detached and explicitly confrontational role. This increases the risk manager's value to the investment team as a source of subject matter expertise in addition to being another resource dedicated to problem solving. The second advantage of this approach is that it necessarily puts the risk manager more directly into the flow of the investment team's decision-making process and, as a result, much more aware of what is actually happening. Thus, rather than being off at a distance and struggling to understand the context of the investment process, the independent, but embedded, risk manager is directly involved in the process.

For this approach to work, the embedded independent risk manager must have substantive subject matter expertise, good interpersonal skills, and be a strong self-starter. These skills will aid the embedded independent risk manager in gaining the respect and acceptance of investment management colleagues and, hence, the creditability to influence their thinking. This is the desired outcome. However, if in spite of these skills and vantage point, the embedded independent risk manager is ultimately unsuccessful in educating or persuading the risk takers about material concerns associated with the risk of their portfolios, they are well placed to provide input up the line of the risk management organization. These concerns can then be addressed either by bringing in more senior risk managers to work with the risk takers or, if still unsuccessful, to escalate the concern further up the institution to a final resolution.

Nevertheless, this type of risk management organizational structure is not without its own challenges. The independent reporting line and compensation structure should, in theory, permit embedded risk managers to retain their independence. In reality, however, the day-to-day environment in which risk managers operate can capture their "hearts and minds." There is a risk that the embedded risk manager becomes just another quant serving the investment team rather than a provider of an independent perspective on portfolio risk. This, of course, defeats a significant element of the role of the risk manager, that is, to serve as a check and balance.

This challenge must thus be actively managed by the independent risk management organization. Competitive compensation, regular risk team meetings, a strong risk culture, and attentive oversight of the risk organization's line managers are all critical techniques to ensure that the embedded risk manager does not become, in effect, just another member of the investment team. For instance, the advantages of deeper subject matter expertise and strong interpersonal relationships gained from longer tenures working with a particular portfolio management team need to be balanced against the advantages of rotating individual risk managers between different investment teams in order to facilitate and maintain independent perspectives. Similarly, the desire to have independent embedded risk managers seated with the investment teams needs to be balanced against the increased risk of "capture" that occurs when risk managers do not sit with their (independent) risk management colleagues. For this reason, some senior managers of independent risk organizations choose to keep the members of their risk management team in close physical proximity to mitigate capture (and to increase risk team synergy), whereas others seek to have small embedded pods of independent risk managers working within a sea of portfolio managers. It is hard to draw specific guidelines to achieve the optimal level of embeddedness, but the trade-off between the enhanced knowledge of positions and risks arising from close intellectual and physical proximity versus the risk of capture must be a constant focus of the senior managers of independent risk organizations. As such, a strong and effective independent risk management organization is also an essential element required to ensure individual risk managers are operating successfully.

18.6 CLEARLY DEFINE FIDUCIARY OBLIGATIONS[13]

An investment manager is obligated to manage its client portfolios in the client's best interest and in accordance with the explicit or implicit instructions received. Without clearly understanding the objectives of every portfolio and the portfolio beneficiary's return requirements and tolerance for risk, the investment process cannot be managed properly. Moreover, no solace is to be found for managers who simply note that their fund's lack of clarity in its fiduciary responsibility is no more egregious than that of other funds. In the midst of the Great Depression, Stone (1934) clearly articulated this principle and his words are a testament to their permanence:

> [W]hen the history of the financial era which has just drawn to a close comes to be written, most of its mistakes and its major faults will be ascribed to the failure to observe the fiduciary principle, the precept as old as holy writ, that 'a man cannot serve two masters'.... [F]inancial institutions which, in the infinite variety of their operations, consider only last, if at all, the interests of those whose funds they command, suggest how far we have ignored the necessary implications of that principle. The loss and suffering inflicted on individuals, the harm done to a social order founded upon business and dependent upon its integrity, are incalculable. (p. 1)

As the credit crisis and past crises have shown, the impact of neglecting fiduciary responsibilities is exposed most dramatically when risks are at their highest.

For investment managers, the following basic questions must be answered: What is the target return of the portfolio? What level of risk can the portfolio tolerate? Which classes of securities are appropriate, and what limits should be placed on portfolio construction? Often, the answers to these questions can be formally structured through the selection of an investment benchmark combined with active return targets and expected risk levels. The questions themselves are simple, but acquiring, understanding, and sharing the answers to these questions requires time and resources, particularly if the manager is responsible for multiple clients whose assets are managed for differing purposes. For effective risk management, sufficient time and resources are required to define fiduciary responsibilities and to structure an investment and operational process that maintains an ongoing focus on those goals. Without clear definitions and goals, it is nearly impossible to manage the exposures and events that put at risk the assets of those clients to whom institutions owe their primary fiduciary responsibility.

18.7 BOTTOM-UP RISK MANAGEMENT

In a world of increasingly complex and diverse investment securities and derivatives, effective risk management must incorporate a bottom-up approach. Effective risk management requires that the organization intellectually "gets its hands dirty." Many risks lurk in the details, especially those that arise suddenly. Risk management organizations must invest in the subject matter expertise required to identify the risks of each security or derivative and then aggregate those exposures up to the portfolio level. A primarily top-down risk management approach generates risk assessments based on gross assumptions that may mask critical risk attributes of securities or derivatives. Such approaches necessarily must rely either on stylized facts or integrative risk models. As such, they work only when the underlying assets behave either as believed or as modeled. In some cases, top-down risk management can actually become almost aspirational, as the expectations of the institution begin to shape its view of investment risks. Unfortunately, these expectations can be naïve or just plain wrong, and there have been more cases than bear repeating in which institutions simply did not understand the true risks of their portfolios. Hence, effective risk management requires assessments based on highly granular facts. Bottom-up risk management based on intensive subject matter expertise is the only way to deliver accurate assessments.

In order to conduct bottom-up risk management, an institution needs to know what it owns and where it owns it. This is common sense and easy to simply assume. The reality for many institutions is that constructing an enterprise-wide inventory of positions and exposures remains a significant challenge due to the limitations of internal information systems. In addition, the specific details of the assets must be known. Even in the case of explicitly top-down asset allocation investment strategies, the risk manager needs to understand the details of the instruments chosen to implement the top-down views. For example, if futures contracts or derivatives are used, the precise terms and conditions of those instruments as well as their basis risks need to be studied carefully. Simply knowing the general characteristics of a class of securities will not suffice, because under stressed conditions the nuances of each particular product can have profound implications. Securities need to be reverse-engineered so that the parts that make up the whole are understood.

In the equity space, bottom-up risk management includes traditional fundamental research combined with close attention to market, style, industry, and idiosyncratic risk exposures. In fixed income this includes not just monitoring factor exposures and fundamental credit analysis, but also the financial engineering on top of it. Assets and liabilities associated with a portfolio need to be modeled in a microanalytically correct manner. Only after individual securities are appropriately defined and their exposures modeled and measured, can those exposures be aggregated to portfolio-level risks. Deriving aggregate risks from a bottom-up risk management process is difficult, takes time, and is expensive, but such a process results in risk assessments that are based on facts rather than assumptions.

18.8   RISK MODELS REQUIRE CONSTANT VIGILANCE

Principle 6.8 of BSRMF and CMRA (2008) states that "no one statistic suffices to describe complex investment risk.... [I]t therefore may be advisable for asset managers to avoid over-reliance on any single statistic" (p. 20). This is good advice; it implicitly presumes, however, that any of the available risk statistics might be useful at a given point in time. In a market environment that is rapidly changing, this simply may not be true. The credit crisis of 2007–2009 challenged most, if not all, available risk metrics at various times, rendering many of them inaccurate or useless. For instance, looking at the partial derivatives of market value with respect to changing market risk factors for a portfolio whose holdings have no bid quickly becomes a theoretical exercise. When markets stop trading, there is very little point in looking at the theoretical sensitivity of the nonexistent market value of a security, and it would almost certainly be catastrophic to try to hedge such a position with liquid market instruments.

In order to be tractable and useful, risk models necessarily must simplify the characteristics of a very complex and fast-changing world, but that simplification comes at the cost of accuracy and structural integrity under stress. Hence, given their known limitations, risk models and financial analytics should always be continuously monitored for their effectiveness and relevance. The underlying assumptions of the models should be constantly assessed to see if they still hold true, and if not, models should be reevaluated to see how robust they are to the violation of those assumptions.

Market risk models are necessarily sophisticated heuristics because the underlying system being modeled is economic and, hence, adaptive to the economy's knowledge of the model and its use by market participants. Moreover, most models are an abstraction of an infinitely more complex reality, and the phenomena being modeled may only represent a small part of the potential losses. Taleb's ludic fallacy highlights the dangerous tendency of objectifying a risk through a particular paradigm that cannot capture its true risks.[14] In plainer language, the risk is that the risk manager may effectively confuse the expected behavior of the model with the realities of the market. Financial markets do not represent a giant game where the actions and relationships are predetermined by a finite set of known rules. Staring at computer screens all day and analyzing models that are governed by static code can easily lead to a level of detachment and false sense of confidence that the artificial world created in our risk models adequately captures the real world we are seeking to understand.

Risk managers, therefore, have no choice but to create models fully knowing that they will be incomplete, inaccurate, and ultimately disposable. Therefore, they must make an ongoing effort to understand when and why models stop working. Too often, model complexity is increased to address interim shortcomings, when it is the model's basic assumptions that need to be re-examined. Risk managers must be very conscious of the cult of science and expertise that can radiate from the use of mathematically sophisticated risk models because it is easy to apply them in circumstances that exceed the models' predictive powers.

Yet even though the models may at times be imperfect, if properly used they can often provide insights into market behavior. Although seasoned risk practitioners generally understand many of the limitations of their models, a challenging balance remains to be maintained. That balance involves not overselling the certitude available from using these models, while identifying the models' weaknesses, which can then provide grist for those who are either uncomfortable with the reliance on domains of knowledge outside their own expertise or, more likely, those who have a vested interest in diminishing the constraints associated with the use of the models. To the extent that the institution has a constructive culture and an alignment of interests, this challenge can be managed, but it requires constant attention and balancing.

Financial markets are constantly changing. The very existence of a widely understood risk model will necessarily change the overall characteristics of the system. Hence, risk analytics and processes need to be constantly reviewed and reinvented. Risk managers will continually be fighting the last war if models are only reevaluated after they catastrophically break down. Risk managers must, therefore, also devote appropriate resources to staying abreast of current research and practices.

18.9   RISK MANAGEMENT DOES NOT MEAN RISK AVOIDANCE

A necessary condition for generating active returns in the absence of arbitrage is risk-taking. The goal of risk management is thus twofold: first, making sure that only desired types and levels of risks are taken while undesired risks are avoided; and, second, making sure that the sizes of the risks taken make sense given the size of the target return and the client's tolerance for risk. If these conditions can be achieved, investors will have increased confidence to position their portfolios more decisively. In particular, risks can be more precisely positioned to incorporate the particular bet the investor seeks without creating ancillary exposures that have the potential to pollute the original insight driving the investment decision. This point is best captured by BSRMF and CMRA (2008): "understanding the relationship between risk and reward enhances all aspects of the asset management business" (p. 6). This perhaps is the point most worthy of highlighting and emphasizing.

This chapter has reflected on the importance of eight specific principles of buy-side risk management. They were acknowledged before the 2007–2009 credit crisis and will undoubtedly be rediscovered after the next crisis. These eight principles should be incorporated into the design of buy-side risk management organizations. The credit crisis raised questions about institutional commitment to risk management in practice. It is our hope that the principles outlined in this chapter will help buy-side institutions persevere, and perhaps even prosper, when market turbulence rises again.

NOTES

1. This chapter was originally a paper by Bennett Golub and Conan Crum (2010b) that was published in the *Journal of Portfolio Management*, 36(4). The chapter has been slightly modified from the original publication with permission.

2. The Global Association of Risk Professionals (GARP) beame the sponsor of the Buy-Side Risk Managers Forum in 2011. The Risk Principles for Asset Managers were updated 2015.

3. Golub was a member of BSRMF and participated in that group's (and CMRA's) preparation of the report, which is organized into sections on governance, investment, operational, and other risk principles.

4. The reflections on buy-side risk management discussed in this chapter evolved in the context of helping manage risk during the credit crisis of 2007–2009 and during the writing of Golub and Crum (2010a).

5. Many of these principles certainly apply to other types of financial institutions, but their relative importance may differ. For instance, the existence of material proprietary trading books at broker/dealers may create the need for different types of intra-organizational relationships between risk takers and the firm's risk managers. See BSRMF and CMRA (2008, p. 7) for a more complete discussion.

6. This principle broadly aligns with principle 5.7 (BSRMF and CMRA [2008, p. 14]).

7. See, for instance, Institute of Internal Auditors, 2005.

8. This insight was provided by Kenneth Winston.

9. From an email sent to the authors by Quintin Price.

10. See principles 5.4 and 5.5 (BSRMF and CMRA, 2008, p. 13).

11. See, for example, Khandani and Lo, 2008.

12. See Thomas and Pearle (2008) for additional details on insider claims that executives at WaMu repeatedly ignored warnings raised by internal risk managers.

13. See principles 5.6 and 6.6 (BSRMF and CMRA, 2008, pp. 14 and 18).

14. Sicart (2007) summarized the ludic fallacy of Taleb (2007) as "the misuse of games to model real-life situations." The misused game in this context is the risk model.

CHAPTER 19

Lessons Worth Considering from the COVID-19 Crisis[1,2]

Barbara Novick
Co-Founder, Former Vice Chairman, BlackRock

Joanna Cound
Managing Director, Global Public Policy Group, BlackRock

Kate Fulton
Managing Director, Global Public Policy Group, BlackRock

Winnie Pun
Managing Director, Global Public Policy Group, BlackRock (2023)

19.1 INTRODUCTION

The COVID-19 crisis posed unprecedented challenges for global economies. While the public health and humanitarian crisis is ongoing, select lessons can be drawn from the March 2020 market turmoil. The outbreak of the pandemic resulted in a liquidity crisis that was different from the credit crisis experienced during the 2008 Global Financial Crisis (GFC). Market volatility increased sharply, and market liquidity deteriorated significantly, including in markets traditionally seen as liquid and low risk. As many countries moved into lockdown to contain the pandemic, issuers, banks, and investors concentrated their actions on reducing their risk exposures and retaining their liquidity. The COVID-19 outbreak became an extreme stress event that, fortunately, demonstrated the effectiveness of the many improvements to financial market resilience made over the past decade and highlighted areas that require attention.

This chapter summarizes 10 key lessons from COVID-19 and considers the implications of the COVID-19 crisis across capital markets. Additionally, this chapter reviews the key market events from March 2020 and the official sector's interventions. The chapter includes some lessons drawn from COVID-19, identifying what worked and what needs to be addressed further, and addresses policy recommendations and areas for future consideration.

19.2   BACKGROUND

The capital markets ecosystem is dynamic and diverse, involving numerous types of market participants and products. Market participants include banks as well as nonbanks such as insurers, pension plans, sovereign wealth funds, asset managers, foundations, endowments, and family offices. Within each of these categories is a variety of participants. There is also a wide range of products in which they originate, create, trade, or invest. Asset management products, for example, are diverse both in terms of asset class (e.g., equity, fixed-income, derivatives, cash, real estate, private equity) and entity (e.g., open-ended mutual funds, including exchange-traded funds [ETFs] and money market funds [MMFs], hedge funds, real estate investment trusts, collateralized loan obligations, and private funds for equity and credit and real estate).

In the decade since the GFC, policy makers focused significant attention on the functioning of the banking system and capital markets, along with the roles played by various market participants and products. Numerous changes were made to improve financial stability. For example, new rules mandated central clearing of over-the-counter (OTC) derivatives in place of bilateral agreements, which has led to standardization, more transparency, and better risk management—but has necessarily also concentrated risk in a handful of central clearing counterparties (CCPs).[3] Equity market structure enhancements, many of which were industry-led, included more objective standards, mechanisms to manage extraordinary volatility, enhanced technology infrastructure requirements, and regulatory reporting.[4]

After an extensive review of the asset management industry, the Financial Stability Board (FSB) and International Organization of Securities Commissions (IOSCO) concluded that a products- and activities-based approach was needed to reduce systemic risks in market finance. A products- and activities-based approach can be thought as being in contrast to an entities-based approach, which focuses regulatory attention primarily at the type of entity who is managing a particular product. Fund reforms included specific rules for MMFs, an expansion of liquidity risk tools, detailed liquidity risk management and stress testing for mutual funds, and new rules on the use of leverage and derivatives in funds. Likewise, a host of new rules increased data collection from asset managers, providing transparency to regulators and others. These rules include the registration of private funds, the reporting of MMF and other mutual fund portfolio data, the reporting of the use of derivatives in separately managed accounts and funds, and the reporting of data on ETFs and their authorized participants (APs).[5]

19.3   CORE PRINCIPLES UNDERPINNING RECOMMENDATIONS

First, policy making should be data driven. Post-GFC reporting requirements and multiple market events have created a wealth of new data and case studies, allowing policy makers to evaluate past hypotheses. One such hypothesis was that ETFs would increase market volatility, and that market makers and APs would step away in times of market stress. The pandemic presented ETFs with their most significant test to date. Contrary to the hypothesis, more APs became active in ETF primary markets, ETFs were a source of liquidity as investors increasingly turned to them to adjust their asset allocations, and ETFs became a source of real-time price discovery.

Second, policy making must be guided by a holistic view of the ecosystem and connectivity among its various elements. The actions of banks, nonbanks—including CCPs, exchanges,

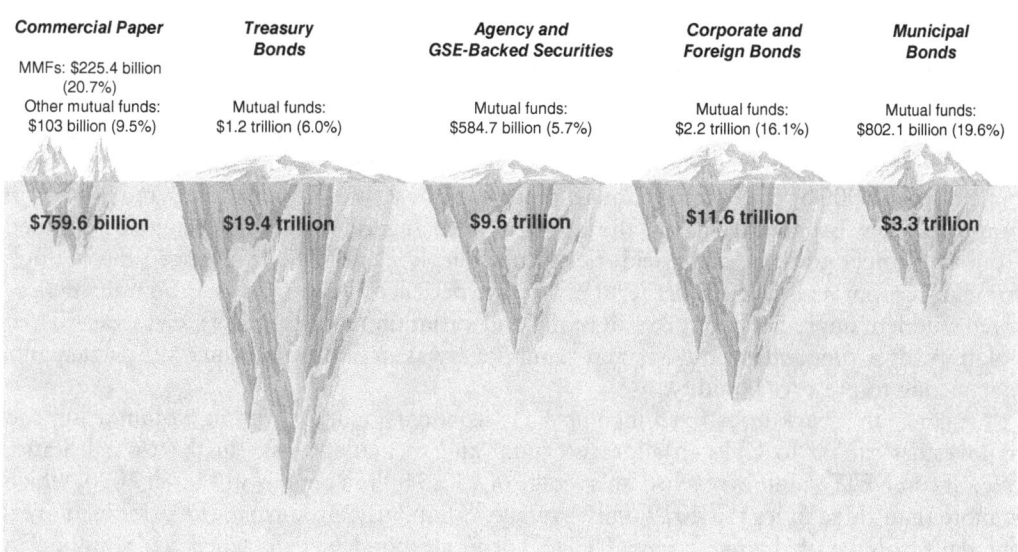

Commercial Paper	Treasury Bonds	Agency and GSE-Backed Securities	Corporate and Foreign Bonds	Municipal Bonds
MMFs: $225.4 billion (20.7%) Other mutual funds: $103 billion (9.5%)	Mutual funds: $1.2 trillion (6.0%)	Mutual funds: $584.7 billion (5.7%)	Mutual funds: $2.2 trillion (16.1%)	Mutual funds: $802.1 billion (19.6%)
$759.6 billion	$19.4 trillion	$9.6 trillion	$11.6 trillion	$3.3 trillion

EXHIBIT 19.1 Mutual Funds in the United States: Just the Tip of the Iceberg
Source: Federal Reserve Z.1 data as of June 2020, available at https://www.federalreserve.gov/releases/z1/20200611/z1.pdf. Graphic not to scale.

trading platforms, asset owners, and asset managers—and policy makers collectively shaped the COVID-19 financial experience. The events in March 2020 demonstrated both market structure strengths and weaknesses. A holistic view of the ecosystem requires ecosystem-wide data. Too often, policy debate tends to overly focus on entities where data are most readily available. The discussion around nonbank finance, for example, often focuses on asset management, where data availability is relatively strong, despite asset managers representing only about a quarter of the entire ecosystem's assets.[6] Mutual funds, for which data are much more readily available, are an even smaller component of the ecosystem. Exhibit 19.1 shows the percentage of debt held by mutual funds relative to other bondholders.

Finally, lessons drawn should include both what worked and what needs to be addressed; both are valuable and should be factored into future reforms. These lessons should be based on a careful differentiation between market risk and systemic risk. For example, credit rating downgrades are a valuable source of market information and not an example of systemic risk. Market risk reflects price volatility that is expected by and disclosed to investors. In contrast, systemic risk is the risk that the failure of one entity will result in a domino effect across firms and markets. There is broad agreement that systemic risk needs to be mitigated, which necessarily requires a close review of the entire ecosystem.

19.4 MARCH 2020: CAPITAL MARKETS HIGHLIGHTS AND OFFICIAL SECTOR INTERVENTION

Several events during March 2020 underscored the extent of financial market stress. The US Treasury market froze and bid–ask spreads for off-the-run US Treasuries peaked at 188 basis points (bp).[7] This reflected the lack of liquidity as banks were disinclined to use their balance sheet capacity for discretionary trading activity, and proprietary trading firms (PTFs) retreated from the market. Bond market volatility reached its highest level for 15 years: the dealer run count (i.e., the number of electronic messages that list the securities that dealers are willing to buy or sell) fell significantly in the United States, limiting the amount of trading information, which in turn increased price uncertainty, and hence transaction costs.[8] The spreads for high-yield bonds had in recent years varied between 300 bp and 600 bp in the United States, but exceeded 1000 bp in March.[9] Similar trends were observed for bank loans and municipal bonds, and new issuance fell across the board. "Fallen angels" (i.e., bonds being downgraded from investment grade to high yield) ticked up sharply as COVID-19 changed the outlook for many corporate issuers. Short-term markets experienced acute strains as liquidity evaporated. Sudden, unpredictable spikes in initial and variation margin across CCPs exacerbated volatility, at a time when liquidity across markets was drying up and market participants were acting to preserve liquidity.

Against this backdrop, fixed-income ETF secondary market trading volumes jumped as investors turned to ETFs to allocate capital and to manage risk. In the United States, fixed-income ETF volumes reached an average of $33.5 billion per day in March 2020, which is more than three times the 2019 daily average.[10] Similarly, in Europe, the combined average daily volume of the five largest UCITS corporate bond ETFs reached $265 million in March, nearly double the 12-month average.[11] The shutdown of short-term markets presented MMFs with challenges: US domiciled Prime MMFs—those investing in corporate commercial paper—saw outflows of approximately 30% in March. In Europe, outflows from sterling and euro MMFs were more muted: assets in Euro Standard MMFs fell 10%, Euro Low Volatility Net Asset Value (LVNAV) MMFs 5%, and Sterling LVNAV MMFs 1% over the month, although the latter two saw outflows of 16% and 11%, respectively, during the most acute 7-day period.[12]

Outflows from investment funds increased across a wide range of asset classes as end investors moved their money to build liquidity or rebalance portfolios. These outflows were generally a small percentage of fund assets but were more elevated for high-yield bond funds, bank loan funds, and municipal bond funds. Outflows from high-yield bond funds averaged 1.8% in the United States in the week to March 18, for example, and outflows from US high-yield municipal bond funds reached $11.6 billion or approximately 9% of assets under management over the entire month of March.[13] To externalize transaction costs to redeeming investors, France and Luxembourg's securities regulators allowed the use of "swing prices" higher than the maximums disclosed in fund prospectuses. Swing pricing is a mechanism that allocates the cost of market liquidity to clients redeeming from or subscribing to investment funds, removing the potential for a first-mover advantage and protecting the remaining investors.

Central bank interventions were effective in calming markets and restoring confidence. Exhibit 19.2 lists the key primary and secondary market facilities designed to maintain funding access for issuers. To the same end, central banks in some regions gave banks relief to temporarily draw down their capital buffers (Countercyclical Capital Buffer and Capital Conservation Buffer) and their liquidity buffers (Liquidity Coverage Ratio).

In the United States, the Federal Reserve released data on the take-up of its programs. Looking at the corporate credit facilities, the Secondary Market Corporate Liquidity program grew since the program's launch, with $12.47 billion deployed for the purchase of corporate debt and bond ETFs on the secondary market as of August 2020 out of an initial $25 billion allocation. In contrast, while the Primary Market Corporate Credit Facility became operational, no transactions were made as of August 2020.[14] The Municipal Liquidity Facility, which became operational in late May 2020, had extended $1.65 billion as

3/12/20	**ECB Asset Purchase Programme** expanded by €120 over 2020
	ECB increases lending volumes and cuts rates for targeted longer-term refinancing operations **(TLTRO III)**
	SSM allows banks to operate below regulatory **capital and liquidity buffers**
3/17/20	**Fed** implements **Primary Dealer Credit Facility**
	Fed implements **Commercial Paper Funding Facility**
3/18/20	**Fed** implements **Money Market Mutual Fund Liquidity Facility**
	ECB Pandemic Emergency Purchase Programme adds €750 billion to Asset Purchase Programme purchases
	ECB expands **Corporate Sector Purchase Programme** eligible assets, including nonfinancial CP
	Bank of England COVID Corporate Financing Facility purchases nonfinancial CP
3/23/20	**Fed** implements **Primary Market Corporate Credit Facility** and **Secondary Market Corporate Credit Facility**
	Fed implements **Term Asset-Backed Securities Loan Facility**
3/25/20	**Bank of England** announced an extra 200 billion in **QE purchases,** split between Gilts and corporate bonds
4/02/20	**Bank of England** confirms 10 billion of 03/25 **QE purchases** will be corporate bonds
4/09/20	**Fed** implements **Municipal Liquidity Facility**

EXHIBIT 19.2   Selected Official Sector Programs Announced in March and April, 2020

of August. Take-up of the Money Market Mutual Fund Liquidity Facility and the Primary Dealer Credit Facility peaked in April 2020, with $51.09 billion and $34.55 billion in outstanding loans, respectively. The facilities' outstanding loans then decreased as markets normalized and collateral came to term. The Commercial Paper Funding Facility's holdings were around $4 billion in May and June 2020, with less than $400 million in loans issued in April and July 2020.[15]

In the Eurozone, the ECB released some data on purchases under the Pandemic Emergency Purchase Programme (PEPP). As of July 31, 2020, cumulative purchases from the PEPP had totaled €440 billion, of which €34.8 billion (8%) were (nonfinancial) commercial paper, €17.6 billion (4%) were corporate bonds, and €3 billion were covered bonds (1%)—the remaining 87% were public sector securities.[16] In the United Kingdom, the Bank of England reported that as of September 9, 2020, gilt purchases totaled £661 billion, of which £18.4 billion were corporate bonds. Under the Corporate Financing Facility, the Bank of England purchased £17.7 billion in commercial paper as of September 9, 2020.[17]

19.5   COVID-19 LESSONS: WHAT WORKED AND WHAT NEEDS TO BE ADDRESSED

The March 2020 financial markets experience illustrated a great deal about performance under stress of different market structures, market participants, asset classes, fund vehicles, and financial services policies. The following represents the most important lessons to date.

Lesson 1: Banks and the banking system entered the COVID-19 crisis in a strong position, with reduced risk-taking, stronger balance sheets, high-quality capital, and ample liquidity. However, post-GFC capital and liquidity requirements left some banks unable or unwilling to use their balance sheets, exacerbating the volatility. In Europe and in the United States,

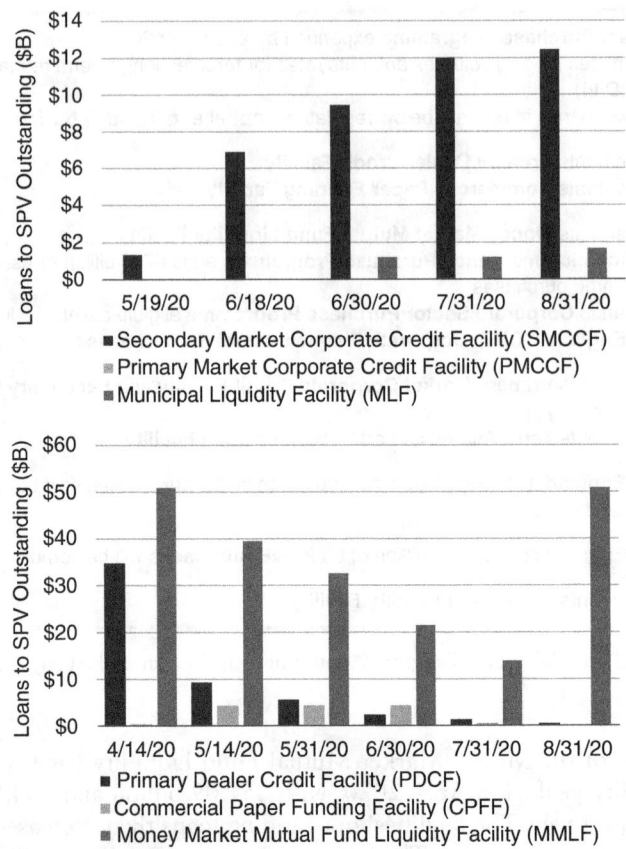

EXHIBIT 19.3 Take-Up of Federal Reserve Facilities
Source: Federal Reserve. Reports to Congress Pursuant to Section 13(3) of the Federal Reserve Act in response to COVID-19.

some banks were hesitant to use prudential buffers or liquidity, even when regulators encouraged them to do so. The use of prudential buffers is complicated by the linkage to dividend distributions, AT1 coupon payments,[18] executive compensation, and potential rating agency actions. When the US Federal Reserve granted dealer banks explicit capital relief for secondary market purchases of commercial paper (CP) from MMFs, banks immediately became willing to intermediate. The absence of similar actions in Europe meant short-term markets remained stressed for several weeks, impacting issuers and investors.

Lesson 2: OTC derivatives' move to central clearing improved transparency and risk management. These reforms proved effective: centrally cleared US futures and options hit an all-time high of 1.43 billion contracts in March.[19] However, margin calls were pro-cyclical, unpredictable, and opaque. Collateral for US futures rose $104 billion (49%) over the month of March. Heightened margin requirements and related cash-raising needs by a wide variety of market participants and corporates added pressure to short-term markets in already challenging conditions.[20]

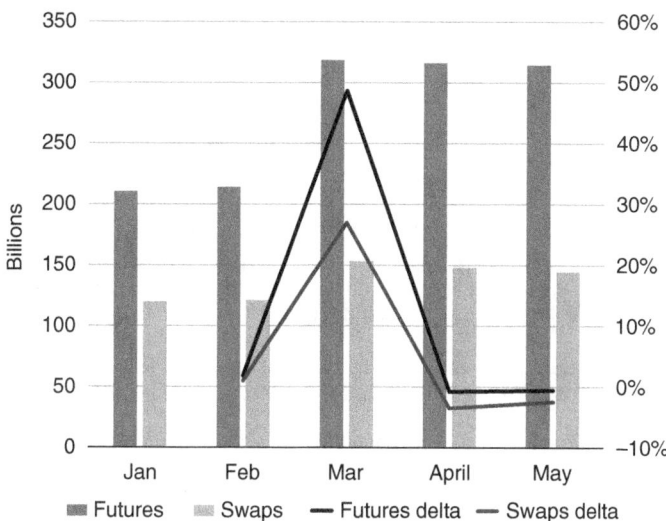

EXHIBIT 19.4 US Futures Commission Merchant (FCM) Required Customer Funds: Futures and Swaps
Source: CFTC.

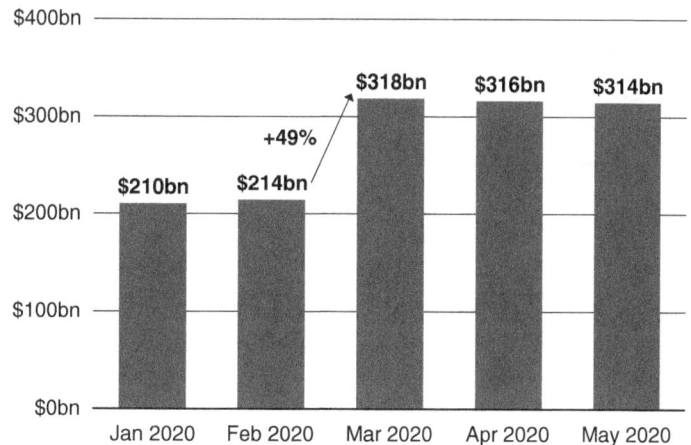

EXHIBIT 19.5 US FCM Required Customer Funds
Source: CFTC, available at: https://cftc.gov/MarketReports/financialfcmdata/index.htm.

Lesson 3: ETFs provided investors access to liquidity and facilitated price discovery. ETFs delivered an incremental layer of liquidity to the bond market because buyers and sellers can easily trade shares of the ETF on exchanges without having to buy or sell the underlying bonds in the primary market. ETFs also provided real-time transparency into bond market prices when cash bond markets were frozen or difficult to trade. This resulted, at times, in ETFs trading at market prices (i.e., the price on exchange) that were lower than (at a discount to) the net asset value (NAV) of the ETF's underlying portfolio, as the NAV is calculated from the day's prices and estimated prices. In many instances, it was cheaper to trade the ETF than the basket of underlying securities. In Europe, for example, credit markets were especially stressed, with bond bid–ask spreads widening by a factor of two or three times compared

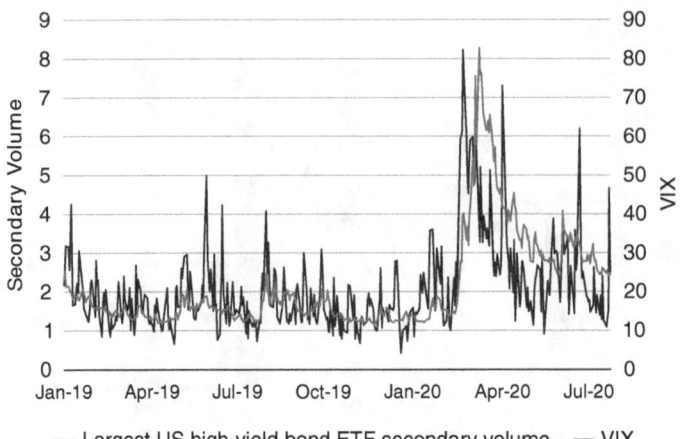

EXHIBIT 19.6 Largest US High-Yield Bond ETF Versus Cboe Volatility Index
Sources: BlackRock, Bloomberg. Cboe Volatility Index® and VIX® are registered trademarks of Cboe Exchange, Inc. Data as of March 24, 2020.

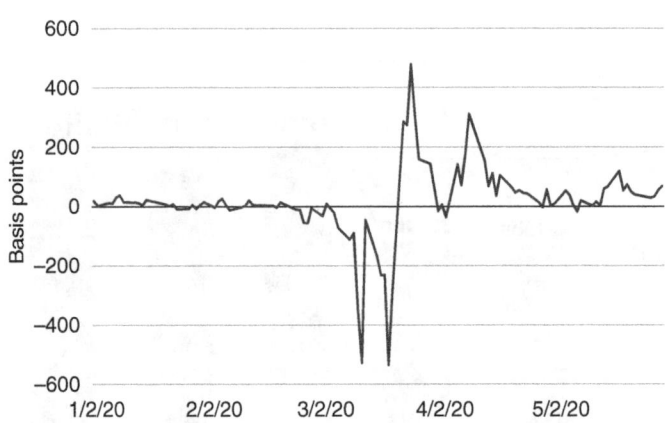

EXHIBIT 19.7 Divergence Between Investment-Grade ETF Price and NAV
Source: Bloomberg. As of June 1, 2020. Data for the largest by assets under management of a US investment-grade corporate bond ETF.

to normal market averages. The cost of trading corporate bonds averaged 55 bp between March 9 and March 20. In comparison, bid–ask spreads in the five largest corporate bond ETFs by assets under management (AUM) averaged 24.4 bp over the same period.[21]

Lesson 4: Equity markets, with a high degree of electronic exchange trading and standardization, were volatile but orderly. Market structure reforms over the past decade improved trading venue resiliency as both Market-Wide Circuit Breakers (implemented four times in two weeks) and Limit-Up-Limit-Down (halts were triggered numerous times) were effective.

Lesson 5: The $18 trillion US Treasury (UST) market experienced unprecedented liquidity challenges. Following post-GFC regulatory changes and technological advances, PTFs and hedge funds have the largest share of USTs market-making; both classes of such entities generally retreated from making markets. Meanwhile, the heightened trading demand for USTs, including selling by non-US investors, overwhelmed the balance sheet capacity of banks given their need to adhere to stricter capital and liquidity requirements. One idea under consideration to address this issue is the expansion of central clearing for USTs, which would reduce reliance on banks and PTFs.

Lesson 6: MMF reform proved beneficial in many areas, including higher quality, shorter maturity, more liquid portfolios, and increased reporting. The United States and European MMF industries have different fund profiles, reflecting different issuer and investor needs, and the profile of fund flows differed during March 2020. However, the crisis highlighted a problem with MMF rules. In both regions, funds that faced the threat of redemption gates and liquidity fees experienced similar problems. Clients regarded the 30% weekly maturing asset buffer as a floor, since breaching it permits fund governance bodies to consider imposing redemption gates and liquidity fees. In contrast, MMFs with a minimum liquid asset buffer that did not have such a link to redemption gates and liquidity fees (such as Standard MMFs in Europe) were able to use their cash buffers in the way policy makers intended.[22]

Lesson 7: Post-GFC mutual fund reforms brought a broader liquidity risk management toolkit with higher standards, more robust fund stress testing and greater transparency to regulators. These proved crucial for handling redemptions: levels of outflows were elevated but remained within a range most asset managers had anticipated. Bond funds, for example, saw high absolute outflows, but these represented a manageable percentage of fund AUM, and even high-yield bond funds were able to navigate flows.

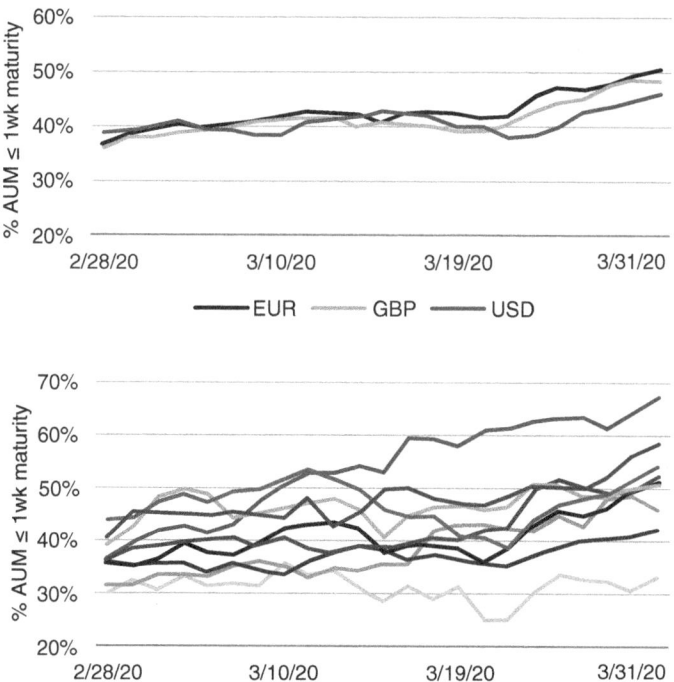

EXHIBIT 19.8 March 2020 Weekly Liquidity Levels in LVNAV MMFs (in Aggregate and for Euro-Denominated MMFs)
Source: iMoneyNet. As of March 31, 2020.
Note: Other gray lines in bottom chart depict individual Euro-denominated MMFs.

While 100% of US bond funds met their redemptions, a small number of funds domiciled outside the United States were forced to suspend redemptions. In nearly all cases, this was not due to the volume of outflows but rather due to "material valuation uncertainty." "Material valuation uncertainty" means that the fund could not be accurately valued, which could put either the redeeming or remaining investors at risk were redemptions done using the best available price. Open-end real estate funds in the United Kingdom were suspended for this reason, as were briefly some Danish fixed-income and equity mutual funds. Although the latter were mutual funds listed on an exchange, their price is not determined by the continuous buying and selling of shares in secondary markets, as is the case with ETFs, but rather by the fund administrator trying to determine their value at least three times daily. Where fund administrators determined they could not accurately value mutual funds, they suspended their redemptions. Some Swedish bond funds suspended redemptions when local managers could not access accurate pricing for some securities—likely attributable to fragmented liquidity and dealers' unwillingness to trade some OTC instruments in particular. Most suspensions lasted between 1 day and 2 weeks, with some funds eventually being liquidated later on.

However, the main difference between the Unites States and Europe was swing pricing, which is permissible *and available* in most (but not all) countries in Europe. Asset managers in Europe increased significantly both the frequency of swing pricing adjustments in March 2020 and the magnitude of the swing factors across a variety of strategies, notably in fixed-income and multi-asset funds. In contrast, for swing pricing, while permissible from a regulatory perspective in the United States, the ecosystem does not support its operationalization.

Lesson 8: Index providers voluntarily delayed all or part of their March 2020 fixed-income rebalance to avoid unnecessary turnover at a time of market uncertainty and limited liquidity. Had the index providers gone ahead by posting the normal formulaic rebalancings, the selling pressure—especially in short-term bonds—had the potential to

EXHIBIT 19.9   High-Yield Bond Flows: Aggregate Outflows and Average Percentage Outflows
Source: EPFR fund flow data. Covers high-yield bond funds domiciled in all jurisdictions globally. This data is representative of funds globally but is not comprehensive. As such the data should be treated as indicative, and absolute-terms dollar outflows should not be taken as exact measures.

Index Provider	March Month-End Rebalancing Status Summary	<1y Securities	Inclusion New Issues	Fallen Angels
Bloomberg	Rebalance proceeded with reduced turnover due to postponement of removal of securities with <1 year to maturity	Delay	Proceed	Proceed
ICE	Postponed rebalance (bond and preferred)	Delay	Delay	Delay
Markit	Postponed majority of rebalance	Delay	Delay	Delay
JPM	Rebalance proceeded, but limiting amount of turnover	Delay	Partial Delay	Delay
FTSE	Postponed rebalance	Delay	Delay	Delay
S&P	Rebalance proceeded	Proceed	Proceed	Proceed

EXHIBIT 19.10 Fixed-Income Index Rebalancing Decisions, Month-End March 2020
Sources: BlackRock, Bloomberg, ICE, Markit, JPM, FTSE, S&P. As of March 26, 2020.

undermine the central banks' actions to add liquidity to the short-term markets. Even with an elevated number of "fallen angels" and robust new issuance, the rebalance at April month-end proved orderly and efficient, justifying the extraordinary decisions made in March.[23]

Lesson 9: Credit downgrades remained high on investors' viewfinders due to the high percentage of BBB bonds in the investment-grade universe and concerns that "fallen angels" could trigger forced selling by mutual funds. While downgrades increased, these are two distinct issues. Concerns about "forced selling upon downgrade" are misplaced as most mutual funds are able to hold "fallen angels," and most investors are motivated to stay invested in them. In many cases, downgrades of higher quality names have represented buying opportunities, especially for opportunistic investors.[24]

Lesson 10: Operational resilience reflected extensive business continuity planning. The work from home (WFH) pivot was quick across the global capital markets ecosystem, including at broker-dealers, custodians, asset managers, and third-party vendors. However, WFH likely contributed to some early market issues with chains of command and decision-making impeded. In addition, outsourcing concentrations have been noted, and specific functionalities needed to be assessed for future improvements.

19.6 RECOMMENDATIONS TO ENHANCE THE RESILIENCE OF CAPITAL MARKETS

The lessons drawn from the experience of financial markets in March 2020 highlighted the need for policy reform and industry enhancements around three pillars: (1) bank regulation, (2) market structure, and (3) certain specific products and activities.

19.6.1 Recommendations Regarding Bank Regulations

Banks were considerably strengthened by the financial reforms following the GFC. They could, however, have played a more impactful role in channeling funding to companies during March 2020 if they had additional regulatory flexibility.

The swift and coordinated response from central banks was decisive and effective. Regulatory relief offered to the banks during this crisis allowed banks in some regions to expand their balance sheets. However, regulatory buffers became an effective floor for some banks, limiting their discretionary activities and restricting their intermediation in markets. More comprehensive relief across regions would have allowed for greater bank intermediation when liquidity was most needed across markets. The following policy reforms are recommended, which seek to achieve a balance between safety (highly constrained bank balance sheets) and smoother market operations through times of market stress. Without such reforms, in future market stress events, there is a risk of a repeat of significant bank balance sheet constraints contributing to a deterioration in secondary market liquidity.

Recommendation 1: Policy makers should incorporate into the regulatory framework guidance on when banks can use their capital and liquidity buffers to provide liquidity to the markets. Ideally, this approach would address bank concerns about potential implications of breaching prudential buffers.

Recommendation 2: Policy makers should make participation in central bank purchase programs balance sheet neutral for banks. The only central bank program that succeeded in unblocking short-term markets was the Fed's MMLF; the capital neutrality encouraged greater bank intermediation in markets.[25]

Recommendation 3: Policy makers should give high-quality CP "High-Quality Liquid Asset" status for the purposes of the Liquidity Coverage Ratio. This would ensure that banks can continue to play a central role in short-term markets, even in times of stress.[26]

19.6.2   Recommendations Regarding Market Structure

Market structure needs modernization. While many elements were resilient and worked well, some must evolve to reduce the reliance on bank balance sheet capacity.[27]

The post-GFC banking system was not designed to have the capacity to cope with the unprecedented supply of long-dated fixed-income securities coming onto the market and the simultaneous unprecedented demand for cash that was experienced during COVID-19. Modernization is especially important for the Treasury, CP, and other fixed-income markets. Enhancements in other asset classes would also be beneficial.

In addition, March 2020 highlighted the importance of high-quality data and well-calibrated electronic trading tools for price discovery and trading. In equity and currency markets, market participants are familiar with data-driven electronic execution, and as a result, liquidity remained in these electronic trading channels, and the equity and currency markets continued to function smoothly throughout March, albeit reflecting higher levels of volatility. In contrast, electronification is still relatively nascent in fixed-income markets.

Even where electronic trading is used, liquidity is fragmented across different venues, preventing the consolidated access to liquidity available in equity markets. In addition, broker algorithms that could not handle the market volatility were turned off, further damaging liquidity. Dealers also turned off algorithms due to a lack of confidence in third-party market data streams. Pricing algorithms rely on transparency in underlying transactional data as a primary input. Centralized, timely, high-quality pricing data in fixed-income markets is needed for algorithms to continue evolving. The lack of data is a serious impediment for market participants and for policy makers in short-term markets. Improved access to data would allow public authorities to more clearly assess the resilience of banks who raise considerable funding in these markets and to better understand how short-term markets transmit monetary policy.

19.6.2.1 Treasuries Recommendation 4: Policy makers should consider the scope of reporting requirements to increase transparency in the UST market. This would allow regulators to more closely examine risk in the system and give more transparency to market participants on Treasury holdings.

Recommendation 5: The expansion of Treasury market clearing merits further study.

19.6.2.2 Short-Term Markets Recommendation 6: Convene an ad hoc group of participants in short-term markets to help advise on how best to modernize the short-term market structure and make it more resilient in times of stress.[28] This group should include issuers (banks, corporates, and public authorities), dealer banks, and different types of investors. It should consider improvements to short-term market structure, with a focus on improving liquidity, price transparency, and, in particular, data quality, as well as potential ways to reduce market reliance on bank balance sheet capacity. Examining market structure adaptations that could more easily match buyers and sellers would be helpful. For example, could all-to-all electronic venues that have become more popular in longer-maturity fixed-income markets be helpful for short-term markets? Could greater standardization of CP issuance improve the market?

Recommendation 7: Policy makers should expand or constitute standing advisory bodies focused on short-term markets, composed of both sell-side and buy-side representatives.[29] We draw inspiration from the ECB's "Bond Market Contact Group," which ensures connectivity in the longer dated primary and secondary bond markets. In normal times, this group meets quarterly, but in times of market stress, it convenes far more regularly to help bridge the information gap between market participants and public authorities. Similarly, the SEC's advisory committees, in particular, the Fixed Income Market Structure Advisory Committee,[30] convenes a variety of market participants to discuss and provide recommendations on key market and regulatory issues. Given the importance of short-term markets to issuers and users, from a "real economy" and financial stability perspective, such a group would be enormously valuable especially in times of market stress.

19.6.2.3 Fixed-Income Markets Recommendation 8: Policy makers should encourage electronic trading venues to offer more comprehensive, equities-style access to liquidity to overcome the fragmentation in fixed-income markets and provide access to pre-trade transparency.

Recommendation 9: The broker community should take steps to improve the resilience of fixed-income market-making algorithms. Had these algorithms been better calibrated and held up in the period of high volatility, they could have had the potential to improve liquidity, relieve system stress, and increase operational capacity, rather than reducing liquidity when they were turned off.

19.6.2.4 Central Clearing Counterparties (CCPs) Recommendation 10: Policy makers should require CCPs to enhance margin modeling to be more conservative and reduce procyclicality.[31] Regulators should ensure that CCPs size initial margin requirements conservatively to cover, with a high degree of confidence, any potential loss that a CCP could incur in liquidating an individual portfolio. This will likely result in higher margin requirements during "peacetime" but should provide the market with more stability during "wartime."

Recommendation 11: MMF units should be approved as collateral under cleared and uncleared bilateral margin rules.[32] In March, many euro and sterling market participants faced significant margin requirements as a result of the stressed markets and central banks' interest rates positioning. This in turn put pressure on short-term markets, including MMFs, to raise cash as collateral. Finding a regulatory and operational solution to allow use of MMF units as collateral would mean that investors in MMFs would not be forced to redeem from the MMF to raise cash for margins, and subsequently, the counterparty would not need to then reinvest the cash elsewhere in short-term markets.

19.6.2.5 Equities Recommendation 12: Market-wide circuit breaker (MWCB) rules should be harmonized and the resumption of trading after a halt should be facilitated.[33] While MWCBs functioned well in March 2020, the experience highlighted that select refinements would further promote market stability, including improving the interaction of single-stock and market-wide guardrails.

19.6.2.6 Indices Recommendation 13: The industry should consider whether guidelines for index providers on addressing potential future rebalancing modifications are necessary.[34] The experience in the financial markets in March was highly unusual in many ways, and it highlighted the importance of indexes as part of the market ecosystem.

19.6.2.7 Data Recommendation 14: Continue to refine TRACE reporting methodology to improve data accuracy for pricing algorithms and to increase transparency for fixed-income market participants. The SEC's Fixed Income Market Advisory Committee's continues to work to improve TRACE.[35]

Recommendation 15: Europe needs a pan-European consolidated tape to establish a single authoritative record of prices and volumes.[36] Post-trade data are an essential input into price discovery, but in Europe it remains fragmented and is generally of low quality. A consolidated tape for fixed-income securities, equities, and ETFs would drive transparency, aiding better investor decision-making and liquidity management and helping to deliver a Capital Markets Union in Europe.

19.6.3 Recommendations Regarding Asset Management

The systemic stability of asset management products and activities has been considerably strengthened by post-GFC reforms, but certain elements of those reforms should be revisited and others further enhanced.

The FSB and US Financial Stability Oversight Council (FSOC) pivoted in 2015 and 2014, respectively, toward a products- and activities-based approach to regulation as the most effective way of mitigating risks in asset management. For asset management, such an approach includes (1) regulators collecting and monitoring extensive data on mutual funds, allowing them to screen outliers and monitor risks, and (2) liquidity risk management, which includes detailed provisions on liquidity and leverage management in investment funds together with the provision of a broad range of tools for fund managers to mitigate risks (e.g., swing pricing, stress testing, gating). Prior to this, policy makers had been considering an entity-based approach that would have focused on designating a small number of large investment funds or asset managers as systemically risky. After analyzing the asset management industry, policy makers recognized that such designations would simply shift rather than mitigate risks—problems in asset management are not correlated to "large firms" or "large funds," as events have demonstrated.[37] In order to address systemic risk in asset management, regulators need to apply the same requirements industry-wide for specific activities and products. As with other instances, during the COVID-19 market turmoil, the funds experiencing issues were not necessarily the largest funds or funds from the largest sponsors.

The preponderance of systemic risk arising from the asset management industry comes from specific activities or products, not from who is engaging in those activities.[38]

Recommendation 16: Decouple the 30% weekly liquid asset requirement of MMFs from the redemption gates and liquidity fee triggers, and provide guidance for the use of buffers during stressed periods.[39] The coupling of these requirements had strong behavioral incentives, as very few MMFs subject to these requirements dipped below the minimum buffer during COVID-19 despite outflow pressures.

Recommendation 17: Make the broadest set of liquidity risk management tools for open-ended funds available to fund managers in all jurisdictions. As set out in Chapter 7, fund managers in many—but not all—jurisdictions were able to use swing pricing and were able to increase the degree of the swing factor where needed to help ensure redeeming clients bore the liquidity cost of their redemption. We recommend that all funds have access to a broader anti-dilution toolkit, such as swing pricing, that assigns transaction costs to the transacting investors. In jurisdictions where swing pricing and other liquidity management tools are available, policy makers should ensure that they can be operationalized with appropriate upgrades to distribution structures and dealing protocols as well as making improvements to underlying market structures. Alternatively, policy makers should consider implementing other anti-dilution measures in jurisdictions where it may not be practical to operationalize swing pricing. Policy makers should consider the trade-offs associated with various ideas, including redemption fees or other measures. As noted in Recommendation 15, centralized, timely, high-quality pricing data in fixed-income markets would further improve risk management and swing pricing models, as would greater data on underlying investor characteristics.

Recommendation 18: Ensure that fund managers stress tested contingency plans and have enhanced data and are fully prepared for crisis situations. Policy makers should ensure that fund managers have contingency plans in place and have tested the underlying procedures on how to use the full range of available liquidity management tools in a crisis situation. Finally, policy makers should act to improve fund manager access to timely granular subscription and redemption data and data analytics to improve the liquidity stress testing models used to predict the liquidity needs to a fund.[40]

Recommendation 19: While ETFs were resilient during March 2020, a few additional enhancements would further add to stability. These include clarification around redemption settlement requirements for US-listed ETFs when underlying markets are closed and greater flexibility in redemption fees for US ETFs in times of extreme volatility.[41] In addition, recent market events have underscored the need for a more descriptive exchange-traded product (ETP) classification system to help end-investors distinguish among different types of ETPs, including the way certain products behave during periods of market volatility and the risks involved.[42] The "ETF" category has become a blanket term for any product that offers exchange-tradability. However, some products use leverage to deliver a return that is a multiple of the index the fund tracks or, in the case of exchange-traded notes, are materially exposed to the creditworthiness of the issuer of the underlying debt. Certain ETPs are tied to commodities, such as oil, which can be quite volatile. A classification framework is needed to distinguish various types of ETPs from ETFs.

Recommendation 20: Policy makers should accelerate efforts to collate better data across the Non-Bank Financial Intermediation (NBFI) ecosystem, as the significant transparency around asset management and investment funds currently provides only a partial view of market activity. The FSB should continue to collate all the data it currently collects and should start to break out market-based finance from shadow banking to better reflect the different risks of each and to focus on the areas that warrant additional focus. Currently, the broad and narrow measures of NBFI aggregate very diverse elements of the financial system and fail to distinguish between positive and negative practices.[43]

Nonbanks are diverse entities with differing investment objectives and constraints. For example, during March 2020, many pension plans sold bonds to make benefit payments and to rebalance into equities given equities had underperformed.

19.7   CONCERNS WITH MACROPRUDENTIAL CONTROLS

Some commentators suggest that there is a mismatch between open-ended funds and their liabilities. They advocate for greater alignment of fund liquidity terms with underlying asset liquidity or call for macroprudential tools to be applied to investment funds.[44] The ECB, for example, has called for mandatory liquidity buffers and a mandatory leverage limit for mutual funds.[45]

We agree that inherently illiquid asset classes, such as direct investments in real estate, should not be offered in daily dealing open-ended funds. The UK Financial Conduct Authority (FCA) has recognized this, recently creating a "Funds Investing in Inherently Illiquid Assets" category.[46] For publicly listed asset classes such as corporate bonds, however, best practice liquidity risk management tools—such as levies, redemption fees and gates, and redemptions in-kind—can be highly effective in aiding investment funds to manage market volatility. Financial stability is best served by ensuring the major fund domiciles allow the broadest set of liquidity risk management tools. More work is needed here to make these tools universally available.

The case for ex ante macroprudential tools fails, on the one hand, to differentiate between bank funding liquidity risk and mutual fund redemption risk and, on the other, conflates market liquidity with fund liquidity. A focus on the funding of activities is needed to understand the source of the different risks in banking and asset management, and in turn the most appropriate way to mitigate them. Bank runs occur because deposits are short-term liabilities, as depositors can demand their money back in short order. The short-term nature of these liabilities embeds a first-mover advantage, as depositors at the front of the queue will receive their cash in full, but depositors at the back of the line could receive nothing.

This potential for run risk is known as *funding liquidity risk* and can lead to insolvency if improperly managed. In contrast, redemption risk in mutual funds is the risk that a fund might have difficulty meeting investor requests to redeem their shares for cash within the time frame required by fund constituent documents or regulation without unduly diluting the interests of remaining shareholders. Because *mutual fund shares reflect equity ownership of the underlying assets*, redemption risk for non-MMFs does not represent an asset-liability mismatch and does not present the same type of systemic risk as a run on the bank.

Fund liquidity should be differentiated from market liquidity. Market liquidity is outside the managers' direct control and can pose challenges for mutual funds as volatility in credit markets in March 2020 demonstrated. In contrast, fund managers have several tools to manage fund liquidity, including deliberately building into funds layers of asset liquidity (e.g., a high-yield bond fund can hold some combination of cash, treasuries, investment-grade bonds, as well as ETFs and potentially derivatives to ensure the fund is able to meet redemptions under stressed conditions), mechanisms to externalize transaction costs (e.g., swing pricing), and mechanisms to avoid becoming a forced seller (e.g., suspensions or gates).[47] Funds were able to use these liquidity management tools to manage redemptions in March 2020, when 100% of US bond funds were able to meet redemptions, and only a small minority of European funds had to suspend redemptions, mainly due to material valuation uncertainty.

Macroprudential tools applied to mutual funds would be at best ineffective and at worst procyclical and are likely to curtail the appetite of investors to invest their capital in markets. For example, some have proposed a cash buffer for mutual funds, under which a fund would hold a "high" proportion of cash in good market conditions to meet redemptions in stressed markets. Such a buffer would, in practice, potentially be ineffective (insufficient to meet redemptions in highly stressed markets), procyclical (liquid assets would need replenishing once the buffer is exhausted), and would disadvantage the end investor by introducing a cash drag on performance.

Some have suggested that central banks provide a liquidity facility for mutual funds via repo. While the presence of a liquidity backstop would likely reduce the inclination of investors to redeem, this approach raises several fundamental issues. The explicit presence of central bank liquidity in a mutual fund creates the potential for significant moral hazard where asset managers might have less incentive to actively manage the liquidity of funds, and asset owners might expect central banks to participate in the downside of their investments. Importantly, a central bank facility for funds would blur the line between bank deposits that government guarantees to ensure return of $1.00 and mutual fund investments where the return of capital is not guaranteed as the net asset value reflects market conditions. Consequently, this approach would socialize risk across the system. Finally, there are questions around the pricing of such a facility, the requirement for capital that would impact the viability of many funds, and the imposition of potentially conflicting regulations. As noted earlier, a better solution is a robust liquidity risk management program that includes the broadest set of liquidity risk tools available.

19.8 CONCLUSION

In the decade since the GFC, wide-ranging policy reforms have been implemented across the capital markets ecosystem, targeting greater financial resilience. The COVID-19 outbreak created serious challenges for healthcare systems, the broader economy, and financial markets. March 2020 provided an extreme stress event that demonstrated the effectiveness of the many improvements that have been made and highlighted across several areas that require further attention. In this chapter, initial lessons from the market turmoil in March were identified. Given COVID-19's impact on the economy, businesses, and individuals, it is important that long-term solutions are identified that will enable companies to access diverse sources of capital to enable them to survive and grow, and individuals are able to achieve personal financial resilience.

19.9 POSTSCRIPT

Much of the resilience exhibited by the financial system during the COVID-19 crisis can be attributed to the many important financial reforms put into place in response to the GFC. As of January 2023, additional reforms are being seriously considered by regulators, such as enhanced monitoring of fund liquidity, additional money market reforms, treasury market structure changes, and renewed attention to the idea of mandating the use of swing pricing for US mutual funds. As laid out in BlackRock's ViewPoint series *Lessons from COVID-19*, additional financial regulatory reforms are needed. That said, there is a wide road to cross between the notion of a market reform and an implemented policy change. This is an area where, most certainly, the "devil is in the details." Optimal rule-making is both enhanced by detailed and thoughtful feedback by market participants while at the same time changes can sometimes be hindered by advocacy of their self-interest. Given the increasing complexity of financial markets and the potential costs of systemic instability, the dialogue between policy makers and market participants has taken on increased urgency. Clearly, the emerging world of "crypto" currencies serves to keep this message current.

NOTES

1. This chapter is an edited version of a *ViewPoint* that was originally published in September 2020, Lessons from COVID-19: Overview of financial stability and non-bank financial institutions.
2. Stephen Fisher, Martin Parkes, Samantha DeZur, Rachel Barry, and Adam Jackson contributed to this chapter.
3. For more information, see BlackRock, 2018, September.
4. For more information, see BlackRock, 2019, February.
5. The *ViewPoint*, The Decade of Financial Regulatory Reform: 2009 to 2019 (January 2020), details the rules that were introduced in the asset management sector and identifies policy areas that warrant continued focus.
6. See McKinsey Performance Lens Global Growth Cube (YE 2017); FSB, 2017; McKinsey & Company, 2013.
7. BlackRock, Bloomberg, NYSE. As of March 31, 2020. A basis point is one hundredth of 1%.
8. "[UST] Bond volatility in particular reached its highest level in the past 15 years for the 5 days ending March 19, and volatility on March 19 was the second highest for a single day over the same period (with March 18, 2009 the highest)." See Liberty Street Economics, 2020.
9. One notable exception to normal high-yield bond spreads was during the commodity crisis of 2016.
10. BlackRock, 2020b.
11. Ibid.
12. BlackRock, 2020f; BlackRock, 2020d.
13. High-yield bond fund flows are an estimate from EPFR data. For municipal bond fund flows, see BlackRock, 2020e.
14. Federal Reserve, "Reports to Congress Pursuant to Section 13(3) of the Federal Reserve Act in response to COVID-19." Available at https://www.federalreserve.gov/publications/reports-to-congress-in-response-to-covid-19.htm.
15. Ibid.
16. ECB, Pandemic Purchase Program (updated September 11, 2020), available at https://www.ecb.europa.eu/mopo/implement/pepp/html/index.en.html.
17. Bank of England, Results and Usage of Facilities (as of September 9, 2020), available at https://www.bankofengland.co.uk/markets/bank-of-england-market-operations- guide/results-and-usage-data.
18. An Additional Tier 1 Contingent Convertible (AT1 or CoCo) bond is a tradable security with a regular coupon payment, issued by a bank. The coupon is the AT1 bond's rate of interest, expressed as a percentage of the face value, and it is paid at a predefined frequency. The coupon is a fixed or a variable rate.
19. FIA, 2020, July 21.
20. CFTC, available at https://cftc.gov/MarketReports/financialfcmdata/index.htm.
21. BlackRock, 2020b.
22. BlackRock, 2020f; BlackRock, 2020d.
23. For more information, see BlackRock, 2020c.

24. BlackRock, 2020g; BlackRock, 2020a.
25. BlackRock, 2020f; BlackRock, 2020d.
26. Ibid.
27. BlackRock, 2019, February; PwC, 2020.
28. BlackRock, 2020f; BlackRock, 2020d.
29. Ibid.
30. See SEC, Spotlight on Fixed Income Market Structure Advisory Committee (FIMSAC) available at https://www.sec.gov/spotlight/fixed-income-advisory-committee.
31. See ABN et al., 2020.
32. For more information, see BlackRock, 2020d.
33. BlackRock, 2019, February.
34. BlackRock, 2020c.
35. FIMSAC Technology and Electronic Trading Subcommittee, 2020. Also see FINRA, 2020.
36. See BlackRock, 2019, February.
37. PwC, 2020.
38. Subsequent problems with Liability-Driven Investment (LDI) products highlight the rationale for focusing primarily on the systemic risks at the product level, not solely on the nature of the institution offering the product.
39. BlackRock, 2019, May. For more information, see BlackRock, 2020f; BlackRock, 2020d.
40. BlackRock, 2016.
41. More recently, the sanctions on Russian securities highlight the need for greater clarity in dealing with such circumstances.
42. See BlackRock et al., 2020.
43. See BlackRock, 2018, February.
44. See Bank of England, 2020.
45. Guindos, 2020.
46. FCA, 2019.
47. On the difference between market and fund liquidity probability, see BlackRock, 2015.

Bibliography

ABN Amro Clearing Bank N.V., Allianz Global Investors, Barclays, BlackRock, Commonwealth Bank of Australia, Citigroup Inc., Credit Suisse, Deutsche Bank AG, Franklin Templeton, Goldman Sachs Group Inc., The Guardian Life Insurance Company, Ivy Investments, Nordea Bank Abp, JPMorgan Chase, Societe Generale, State Street Global Markets, TIAA, T. Rowe Price, UBS AG, and The Vanguard Group. (2020, March 10). *A path forward for CCP resilience, recovery, and resolution* [online]. Available from: https://www.blackrock.com/corporate/literature/whitepaper/path-forward-for-ccp-resilience-recovery-and-resolution.pdf.

Alternative Reference Rates Committee. (2021 March). *Progress report: The transition from US dollar LIBOR*. New York: New York Fed.

Alternative Reference Rates Committee. (2022). *Meeting readout* [online]. https://www.newyorkfed.org/medialibrary/Microsites/arrc/files/2022/ARRC_Readout_November_2022.pdf.

Akerlof, G. and Shiller, R. (2009). *Animal spirits: How human psychology drives the economy, and why it matters for global capitalism*. Princeton, NJ: Princeton University Press.

Almgren, R. and Chriss, N. (2000). *Optimal execution of portfolio transactions* [online]. Available from: https://www.smallake.kr/wp-content/uploads/2016/03/optliq.pdf.

Amihud, Y. and Mendelson, H. (1986). Asset pricing and the bid–ask spread. *Journal of Financial Economics*, 17, pp. 223–249.

Amihud, Y. and Mendelson, H. (1988). Liquidity and asset pricing: Financial management implications. *Financial Management*, 5–15.

Anderson, N., Breedon, F., Deacon, M., Derry, A., and Murphy, G. (1997). *Estimating and interpreting the yield curve*. New York: John Wiley & Sons, Inc.

Ang, A. (2014). *Asset management: A systematic approach to factor based investing*. New York, NY: Oxford University Press.

Bai, X., Scheinberg, K., and Tutuncu, R. (2016). Least-squares approach to risk parity in portfolio selection. *Quantitative Finance*, 16(3), pp. 357–376.

Bank of England. (2020 August). *Financial stability report* [online]. Available from: https://www.bankofengland.co.uk/-/media/boe/files/financial-stability-report/2020/august-2020.pdf.

Barber, J. R. and Copper, M. R. (1996, Fall). Immunization using principal component analysis. *Journal of Portfolio Management*.

Basel Committee on Banking Supervision. (2008). *Principles for sound liquidity risk management and supervision*. Basel, Switzerland: Bank for International Settlements.

Bhaktavatsalam, S. and Wee, G. (2009). Pimco's gross says Harvard, Yale may need to alter investments. *Bloomberg* [online]. Previously available from: http://www.bloomberg.com/apps/news?pid=newsarchive&sid=at0iuIc8_ga0.

Black, F., Derman, E., and Toy, W. (1990). A one-factor model of interest rates and its application to treasury bond options. *Financial Analysts Journal*, pp. 24–32.

Black, F. and Karasinski, P. (1991). Bond and option pricing when short rates are lognormal. *Financial Analysts Journal*, 47(4), pp. 52–59.

Black, F. and Scholes, M. (1973). The pricing of options and corporate liabilities. *Journal of Political Economy*, 81, pp. 637–654.

Bridgewater. (2010). Risk parity is about balance [online]. Bridgewater Associates. Available at: https://www.bridgewater.com/resources/risk-parity-is-about-balance.pdf.

BlackRock. (2013, March). Best practices for better benchmarks. *ViewPoint*. Available from: https://www.blackrock.com/corporate/literature/whitepaper/recommendations-for-financial-benchmark-reform.pdf.

BlackRock. (2015, July). Addressing market liquidity. *ViewPoint*. Available from: https://www.blackrock.com/corporate/literature/whitepaper/viewpoint-addressing-market-liquidity-july-2015.pdf.

BlackRock. (2016, January 13). *Letter to SEC, Open-End Fund Liquidity Risk Management Programs; Swing Pricing; Re-Opening of Comment Period for Investment Company Reporting Modernization Release at* 26-28. Available from: https://www.sec.gov/comments/s7-16-15/s71615-36.pdf.

BlackRock. (2016, October). Resiliency, recovery, and resolution. Revisiting the 3 R's for central clearing counterparties. *ViewPoint*. Available from: https://www.blackrock.com/corporate/literature/whitepaper/viewpoint-ccps-resiliency-recovery-resolution-october-2016.pdf.

BlackRock. (2018, February). Taking market-based finance out of the shadows: Distinguishing market-based finance from shadow banking. *ViewPoint*. Available from: https://www.blackrock.com/corporate/literature/whitepaper/viewpoint-taking-market-based-finance-out-of-the-shadows-february-2018.pdf.

BlackRock. (2018, September). An end-investor perspective on central clearing: Looking back to look forward. *ViewPoint*. Available from: https://www.blackrock.com/corporate/literature/whitepaper/viewpoint-end-investor-perspective-central-clearing-looking-back-to-look-forward.pdf.

BlackRock. (2019, February). Mark-to-Market Structure: An end-investor perspective on the evolution of developed equity markets. *ViewPoint*. Available from: https://www.blackrock.com/corporate/literature/whitepaper/viewpoint-mark-to-market-structure-an-end-investor-perspective-on-the-evolution-of-developed-equity-markets.pdf.

BlackRock. (2019, April). LIBOR the next chapter. *ViewPoint*. Available from: https://www.blackrock.com/corporate/literature/whitepaper/viewpoint-libor-the-next-chapter-april-2018.pdf.

BlackRock. (2019, May 13). *Letter to FSOC re: Comments on proposed interpretive guidance, authority to require supervision and regulation of certain nonbank financial companies*. Available from: https://www.blackrock.com/corporate/literature/publication/fsoc-interpretive-guidance-supervision-regulation-certain-nonbank-financial-companies-051319.pdf.

BlackRock. (2020, January). The decade of financial regulatory reform: 2009 to 2019. Available from: https://www.blackrock.com/corporate/literature/whitepaper/viewpoint-decade-of-financial-regulatory-reform-2009-to-2019.pdf.

BlackRock. (2020, April). BlackRock's guide to LIBOR transition. *ViewPoint*. Available from: https://www.blackrock.com/corporate/literature/whitepaper/viewpoint-blk-guide-libor-transition-april-2020.pdf.

BlackRock. (2020a, July). Lessons from COVID-19: European BBB bonds and fallen angels. *ViewPoint*. Available from: https://www.blackrock.com/corporate/literature/whitepaper/policy-spotlight-lessons-from-covid-19-european-bbb-bonds-and-fallen-angels-july-2020.pdf.

BlackRock. (2020b, July). Lessons from COVID-19: ETFs as a source of stability. *ViewPoint*. Available from: https://www.blackrock.com/corporate/literature/whitepaper/viewpoint-lessons-from-covid-19-etfs-as-a-source-of-stability-july-2020.pdf.

BlackRock. (2020c, July). Lessons from COVID-19: Fixed income index rebalancing. *ViewPoint*. Available from: https://www.blackrock.com/corporate/literature/whitepaper/policy-spotlight-lessons-from-covid-19-fixed-income-index-rebalancing-july-2020.pdf.

BlackRock. (2020d, July). Lessons from COVID-19: The experience of European MMFs in short-term markets. *ViewPoint*. Available from: https://www.blackrock.com/corporate/literature/whitepaper/viewpoint-lessons-from-covid-19-the-experience-of-european-mmfs-in-short-term-markets-july-2020.pdf.

BlackRock. (2020e, July). Lessons from COVID-19: US municipal bond market. *ViewPoint*. Available from: https://www.blackrock.com/corporate/literature/whitepaper/viewpoint-lessons-from-covid-19-us-municipal-bond-market-july-2020.pdf.

BlackRock. (2020f, July). Lessons from COVID-19: US short-term money markets. *ViewPoint*. Available from: https://www.blackrock.com/corporate/literature/whitepaper/viewpoint-lessons-from-covid-19-us-short-term-money-markets-july-2020.pdf.

BlackRock. (2020g, July). Lessons from COVID-19: US BBB bonds and fallen angels. *ViewPoint*. Available from: https://www.blackrock.com/corporate/literature/whitepaper/policy-spotlight-lessons-from-covid-19-us-bbb-bonds-and-fallen-angels-july-2020.pdf.

BlackRock. (2021, June). The endgame: Benchmark reform and transition from IBORs. *ViewPoint*. Available from: https://www.blackrock.com/corporate/literature/whitepaper/libor-viewpoint-benchmark-reform-transition-from-ibors.pdf.

BlackRock, Charles Schwab Investment Management, Fidelity Investments, Invesco, State Street Global Advisors, and Vanguard. (2020, May 13). *Multi-firm letter to Cboe, Nasdaq, and the Intercontinental Exchange re: FTP Classification*. Available from: https://www.blackrock.com/corporate/literature/publication/letters-to-exchanges-regarding-etp-classification-051320.pdf.

Blake C., Petrich, D., and Ulitsky, A. (2003). The right tool for the job. *Institutional Investor, Transition Management*, (1), pp. 33–37.

Bilgili, M., Ferconi, M., and Ulitsky, A. (2017). Stress hedging in portfolio construction. *Risk*, June, pp. 127–132.

Boerse-frankfurt.de. (2023). *Derivatives—a reason to trade for thousands of years* [online]. Available from: https://www.boerse-frankfurt.de/en/know-how/about/geschichte-der-frankfurter-wertpapierboerse/derivatives-a-reason-to-trade-for-thousands-of-years [Accessed 15 Feb. 2023].

Bordia, S., Vaidya, J., Deb, S., Warshawsky, E., and Raghavan, K. (2009). *Mortgage credit tracker*. Barclays Capital.

Brace, A., Gatarek, D., and Musiela, M. (1997). The market model of interest rate dynamics. *Mathematical Finance*, 7(2), 127–154.

Breeden, D. T. (1991). Risk, return, and hedging of fixed rate mortgages. *Journal of Fixed Income*, pp. 85–107.

Breeden, D. T. (1994). Complexities of hedging mortgages. *Journal of Fixed Income*, 4, pp. 6–41.

Brinson, G., Hood L. R., and Beebower G. L. (1986). Determinants of portfolio performance. *Financial Analyst Journal*, 42, (4), pp. 39–44.

Bruce, B. (2016). *Behavioral biases and fixed income*. Brandes Institute white paper.

Bruner, R., and Carr, S. (2007). *The panic of 1907: Lessons learned from the market's perfect storm*. Hoboken, NJ: John Wiley & Sons.

Bullock, N. (2008, September 19). Lehman owes Freddie at least $1.2bn. *Financial Times* [online]. Available from: http://www.ft.com/ cms/s/0/9bbd2a58-85dd-11dd-a1ac-0000779fd18c.html.

Buy Side Risk Managers Forum and Capital Market Risk Advisors. (2008). *Risk principles for asset managers* [online]. Available at https://static1.squarespace.com/static/58d527666a4963244b157400/t/62bdbc7b2f7b7103abca895b/1656601723625/Risk+Principles+for+Asset+Managers.pdf.

Chaves, D., Hsu, J., Li, F., and Shakernia, O. (2012). Efficient algorithms for computing risk parity portfolio weights. *The Journal of Investing*, 21(3), pp.150–163.

Cheng, T., Fagan, S., and Greenberg, D. (2014, June). Hypothetical stress scenario construction. *BlackRock Applied Analytics*.

Cheyette, O. (1997). Chapter 1: Interest rate models. In F. Fabozzi (Ed.). *Advances in fixed income valuation, modeling, and risk management*. New Hope: Frank J. Fabozzi Associates.

Cho, D., Mufson, S., and Tse, T. (2009, September 13). In shift, Wall Street goes to Washington. *Washington Post* [online]. Available from: http://www.washingtonpost.com/wp-dyn/content/article/2009/09/12/AR2009091202932.html.

Clemen, R. T. (1989). Combining forecasts: A review and annotated bibliography. *International Journal of Forecasting*, 5(4), pp. 559–583.

Clemens, R. and Winkler, R. (1999). Combining probability distributions from experts in risk analysis. *Risk Analysis*, 19(2), pp. 187–203.

Committee on Payment and Settlement Systems and Board of the International Organization of Securities Commissions. (2012). *Principles for financial market infrastructures: Disclosure framework and Assessment methodology*. Available from: https://www.bis.org/cpmi/publ/d106.pdf [accessed 15 Feb. 2023].

Committee on Payments and Market Infrastructures and Board of the International Organization of Securities Commissions. (2015). *Public quantitative disclosure standards for central counterparties* [online]. Available from: https://www.bis.org/cpmi/publ/d125.pdf.

Commodity Futures Trading Commission. (n.d.). History of the CFTC | CFTC. [online]. Available from: https://www.cftc.gov/About/HistoryoftheCFTC/history_precftc.html.

Connor, G. (1995). The three types of factor models: A comparison of their explanatory power. *Financial Analysts Journal*, 51(3), pp. 42–46.

Copeland, T. and Galai, D. (1983). Information effects on the bid–ask spread. *Journal of Finance*, 38(5), pp. 1457–1469.

Cornuejols, G. and Tutuncu, R. (2006). *Optimization methods in finance*. Cambridge University Press.

Cotoi, I. and Stamicar, R. (2018). *Reverse stress testing challenges: Toward a systematic framework* (Research Paper No. 116). Axioma.

Countrywide Home Loans Servicing LP. (2007). *CHL mortgage pass-through trust 2007-HY7 prospectus supplement*. Countrywide.

Coval, J., Jurek, J., and Stafford, E. (2008). *The economics of structured finance* (Finance Working Paper No. 09-060). Harvard Business School.

Damasio, A. (1994). *Descartes' error: Emotion, reason, and the human brain*. Putnam.

Davis, B. and Menchero, J. (2011). Risk contribution is exposure times volatility times correlation: Decomposing risk using the x-sigma-rho formula. *The Journal of Portfolio Management*, 37(2), pp. 97–106.

DeLong, J., Shleifer, A., Summers, L., and Waldmann, R. (1990). Noise trader risk in financial markets. *Journal of Political Economy*, 98(4), 703–738.

Dembo, R. (1991). Scenario optimization. *Annals of Operations Research*, 30, pp. 63–80

Desmond, M. (2008, September 17). Lehman ties dim constellation. *Forbes* [online]. Available from: http://www.forbes.com/2008/09/17/constellation-energy-lehman-markets-equity-cx_md_0917markets22.html.

Dor, A., Dynkin, L., Hyman J., Houweling, P., van Leeuwen, E., and Penninga O. (2007). DTS^{SM} (duration times spread). *The Journal of Portfolio Management*. 33(2), pp. 77–100.

Dweck, C. S. (2009). Mindsets: Developing talent through a growth mindset. *Olympic Coach* 21.1, pp. 4–7.

Dynkin, L., Gould, A., Hyman J., Konstantinovsky V., and Phelps, B. (2006). *Quantitative management of bond portfolios*. Princeton University Press.

Engle, R., and Manganelli, S. (1999). *CAViaR: Conditional autoregressive value at risk*. University of California, San Diego.

Fabozzi, F. J. (1988). *Fixed income mathematics*. Probus Publishing Company.

Fabozzi, F. J. and Fabozzi, D. T. (Eds.) (1995a). *The handbook of fixed income securities*. Irwin.

Fabozzi, F. J. (Ed.). (1995b). *The handbook of mortgage-backed securities*. McGraw-Hill.

Fama, E. (1965). The behavior of stock market prices. *Journal of Business*, 38, pp. 34–105.

Fama, E. and French, K. (1993). Common risk factors in the returns on stocks and bonds. *Journal of Financial Economics*, 33(1), pp. 3–56.

Federal Reserve. (n.d.). Reports to Congress Pursuant to Section 13(3) of the Federal Reserve Act in response to COVID-19. Updated February 13, 2022. Available at https://www.federalreserve.gov/publications/reports-to-congress-in-response-to-covid-19.htm.

Feng, Y. and Palomar, D. P. (2015). SCRIP: Successive convex optimization methods for risk parity portfolio design. *IEEE Transactions on Signal Processing*, 63(19), pp. 5285–5300.

Ferson, W. and Harvey, C. (1991). The variation of economic risk premiums. *Journal of Political Economy*, 99(2), pp. 385–415.

Figlewski, S. (1997). Forecasting volatility. *Financial Markets, Institutions & Instruments*, 6(1), pp. 1–88.

Financial Conduct Authority. (2019). *Illiquid assets and open-ended funds and feedback to Consultation Paper CP18/27* (Policy Statement) [online]. Available from: https://www.fca.org.uk/publication/policy/ps19-24.pdf.

Financial Stability Board. (2017, January 12). *Policy recommendations to address structural vulnerabilities from asset management activities* [online]. Available from: https://www.fsb.org/wp-content/uploads/FSB-Policy-Recommendations-on-Asset-Management-Structural-Vulnerabilities.pdf.

FIA. (2020, July 21). *Impact of COVID-19 Pandemic on derivatives clearing*. Presentation to the CFTC Market Risk Advisory Committee.

FIMSAC Technology and Electronic Trading Subcommittee. (2020). *Preliminary recommendation regarding additional TRACE reporting indicators for corporate bond trades*. Presented at FIMSAC meeting.

Financial Accounting Standards Board. (2006). *Original pronouncements as amended Statement of Financial Accounting Standards No. 157*. Author.

Financial Accounting Standards Board. (2008). Determining the fair value of a financial asset when the market for that asset is not active. Author.

Financial Stability Board. (2017). Policy recommendations to address structural vulnerabilities from asset management activities [online]. Available from: https://www.fsb.org/wp-content/uploads/FSB-Policy-Recommendations-on-Asset-Management-Structural-Vulnerabilities.pdf.

FINRA. (2020). *FINRA requests comment on proposed changes to TRACE reporting relating to delayed Treasury Spot and portfolio trades* (Regulatory Notice 20-24).

Finkelstein, B. (2006). *The politics of public fund investing: How to modify Wall Street to fit Main Street*. Simon & Schuster Touchstone.

Fortado, L. and Cahill, T. (2009). Lehman ruling delays return of funds by a decade. *Bloomberg* [online]. Previously available from: http://www.bloomberg.com/apps/news?pid=201601085&sid=as8WvFbLcV00.

Fox, J. (2009). *The myth of the rational market*. Harper-Collins Publishers.

Friedman, M. (1953). *Essays in positive economics*. University of Chicago Press.

Galbraith, J. (1997). *The Great Crash 1929*. Mariner Books.

Glosten, L. and Milgrom, P. (1985). Bid, ask, and transaction prices in a specialist market with heterogeneously informed traders. *Journal of Financial Economics*, 14(1), pp. 71–100.

Glover, J. (2008). Bond insurers may lose AAA Ratings before a bailout. *Bloomberg* [online]. Previously available from: http://www. bloomberg.com/apps/news?pid=20601087&sid=anN9SSjbDU PY& refer=home#.

Goldstein, M. (2008, October 2). Lehman bankruptcy gets ugly. *Business Week* [online]. Available from: https://www.bloomberg.com/news/articles/2008-10-01/lehman-bankruptcy-gets-ugly#xj4y7vzkg.

Golub, B. and Crum C. (2010a). Risk management lessons worth remembering from the credit crisis of 2007–2009. *Journal of Portfolio Management*, 36(3), pp. 21–44.

Golub, B. and Crum, C. (2010b). Reflections on buy-side risk management after (or between) the storms. *Journal of Portfolio Management*, 36(4).

Golub, B., Ferconi, M., Madhavan, A., and Ulitsky, A. (2018a). Factor-based optimisation and the creation/redemption mechanism of fixed income exchange-traded funds. *International Journal of Financial Engineering and Risk Management*, 2(4), pp. 335–350.

Golub, B., Greenberg, D., and Ratcliffe, R. (2018b). Market-driven scenarios: An approach for plausible scenario construction. *Journal of Portfolio Management*, 44(6).

Golub, B. W. and Tilman, L. M. (1997a). Measuring plausibility of hypothetical interest rate shocks. In F. Fabozzi (Ed.). *Managing fixed income portfolios*. Frank J. Fabozzi Associates.

Golub, B. W. and Tilman, L. M. (1997b). Measuring yield curve risk using principal component analysis, value-at-risk, and key rate durations. *Journal of Portfolio Management*, Summer.

Golub, B. W. and Tilman, L. M. (2000). *Risk management: Approaches for fixed income markets*. Wiley, Frontiers in Finance.

Graham, B. and McGowan, B. (2005). *The intelligent investor*. New York: Harper Collins.

Greenberg, D., Babu, A., and Ang, A. (2016). Factors to assets: Mapping factor exposures to asset allocations. *Journal of Portfolio Management*, 42(5), pp. 18–27.

Greenspan, A. (2005, February 16). *Federal Reserve Board's semiannual monetary policy report to the Congress*. Committee on Banking, Housing, and Urban Affairs, U.S. Senate. Available from: https://www.federalreserve.gov/boarddocs/hh/2005/february/testimony.htm.

Grinold, R. and Kahn, R. (1995). *Active portfolio management*. Probus Pub Co.

Grinold, R. and Kahn, R. (1999). *Active portfolio management*. 2nd ed. McGraw-Hill Education.

Griveau-Billion, T., Richard, J. C., and Roncalli, T. (2013). *A fast algorithm for computing high-dimensional risk parity portfolios*. Available from: https://arxiv.org/abs/1311.4057.

Guindos, L. (2020, July 22). *Building the financial system of the 21st century*. Speech given at 18th annual symposium of the European Central Bank. https://www.ecb.europa.eu/press/key/date/2020/html/ecb.sp200722∼338ac4a611.en.html.

Heath, C. and Heath, D. (2008). *Made to stick: Why some ideas take hold and others come unstuck*. Random House.

Heath, D., Jarrow, R., and Morton, A. (1992). Bond pricing and the term structure of interest rates: A new methodology for contingent claims valuation. *Econometrica*, 60(1): 77–105.

Hernandez, R. (2008, March 9). Countrywide said to be subject of federal criminal inquiry. *New York Times* [online]. Available from: http://www.nytimes.com/2008/03/09/business/09lend.html.

Ho, T. S. Y. (1992, September). Key rate durations: Measures of interest rate risks. *Journal of Fixed Income*, pp. 29–44.

Hurtado, P. (2009, July 15). Ex-Bear Stearns hedge fund manager loses bid to dismiss charge. *Bloomberg* [online]. Previously available from: http://www.bloomberg.com/apps/news?pid=20601103&sid=aPXXpmeNWuIc.

Hull, J. and White, A. (1999). Incorporating volatility updating into the historical simulation method for VaR. *Journal of Risk*, 1.

Hyuga, T., Kawamoto, S., and Ito, K. (2008, September 17). Japan banks, insurers have $2.4 billion Lehman risk. *Bloomberg* [online]. Previously available from: http://www.bloomberg.com/apps/news?pid=20601101&sid=a3mSQ9tXT.5w&refer=japan.

Ilmanen, A. (1995/1996). *Understanding the yield curve*. Salomon Brothers.

Ilmanen, A. (1996). When do bond markets reward investors for interest rate risk? *Journal of Portfolio Management* (Winter), pp. 52–63.

Imas, A. (2016). The realization effect: Risk-taking after realized versus paper losses. *American Economic Review*, 106(8), pp. 2086–2109.

Institute of Internal Auditors. (2005). A mindset of strong internal control. *Tone at the Top*, (28).

Javetski, B. and Koller, T. (2018, May). Debiasing the corporation: An interview with Nobel laureate Richard Thaler. *McKinsey Quarterly*.

Jeyapaulraj, J., Desai, D., Chu, P., Mehta, D., Pasquali, S., and Sommer, P. (2022). Supervised similarity learning for corporate bonds using Random Forest proximities. arXiv preprint arXiv:2207.04368.

Johnson, R. and Wichern, D. (1982). *Applied multivariate statistical analysis*. Prentice-Hall.

Jorion, P. (1986). Bayes-Stein estimation for portfolio analysis. *Journal of Financial and Quantitative Analysis*, 21(3), pp. 279–292.

Jorion, P. (1999). *Risk management lessons from long term capital management*. University of California at Irvine.

Kahn, R. N. (1995a). Chapter 14: Fixed income risk modeling. In F. J. Fabozzi (Ed.), *The Handbook of Fixed Income Securities* (5th ed.). Business Ones Irwin.

Kahn, R. N. (1995b). Fixed income risk modeling in the 1990s. *Journal of Portfolio Management*, (Fall), 94–101.

Kahneman, D. (2011). *Thinking, Fast and Slow*. Farrar, Straus and Giroux.

Kahneman, D. and Tversky, A. (1979). Prospect theory. *Econometrica*, 12.

Kahneman, D., Knetsch, J. L., and Thaler, R. H. (1990). Experimental tests of the endowment effect and the Coase theorem. *Journal of Political Economy*, 98(6), pp. 1325–1348.

Kao, D. (1999). *Estimating and pricing credit risk: An overview.* New York: General Motors Investment Management Corporation Publication.

Kaya, H. (2012). *The Bayesian roots of risk parity in a mean risk world* [online]. Available from: https://papers.ssrn.com/sol3/papers.cfm?abstract_id=2109725.

Kelly, B., Pruitt, S., and Su, Y. (2019). Characteristics are covariances: A unified model of risk and return. *Journal of Financial Economics,* 134(3), pp. 501–524.

Keynes, J. M. (1974). The stock market and the beauty contest. *The Journal of Portfolio Management,* 1(1), pp. 88–90.

Khandani, A. and Lo, A. (2008). *What happened to the quants in August 2007? Evidence from Factors and transactions data* [online]. Available from: https://www.nber.org/system/files/working_papers/w14465/w14465.pdf.

Kiel, P. (2008). AIG's spiral downward: A timeline. *ProPublica* [online]. Available from: https://www.propublica.org/article/article-aigs-downward-spiral-1114.

Kim, J. and Finger, C. C. (2000). A stress test to incorporate correlation breakdown. *Journal of Risk,* 2(3) pp. 5–19.

Kindleberger, C. (1978). *Manias, panics, and crashes: A history of financial crises.* Basic Books.

Kinlaw, W. and Turkington, D. (2014). Correlation surprise. *Journal of Asset Management,* 14, pp. 385–399.

Kissell, R. and Glantz, M. (2003). *Optimal trading strategies.* AMACOM.

Kritzman, M. and Yuanzhen, L. (2010). Skulls, financial turbulence, and risk management. *Financial Analysts Journal,* 66(5).

Kuberek, R. C. (1990). *Common factors in bond portfolio returns.* Wilshire Associates.

Kupiec, P. (1999). Stress testing in a value at risk framework. *Journal of Derivatives,* 6(1), pp. 7–24.

LaCapra, L. (2009). Hedge funds find arb opportunity in SPACs. *TheStreet.com* [online]. Available from: https://www.thestreet.com/investing/funds/hedge-funds-find-arb-opportunity-in-spacs-10482888.

Laipply, S., Madhavan, A., Sobczyk, A., and Tucker, M. (2019). *Sources of excess return and implications for active fixed income portfolio construction* (Working Paper). BlackRock.

Lakonishok, J., Shleifer, A., Thaler, R., and Vishny, R. (1991). Window dressing by pension fund managers. *American Economic Review Papers and Proceedings,* 81, pp. 227–231.

Leaders' Statement the Pittsburgh Summit [online]. (2009). Available from: https://www.oecd.org/g20/summits/pittsburgh/G20-Pittsburgh-Leaders-Declaration.pdf [Accessed 15 Feb. 2023].

Ledoit, O. and Wolf, M. (2004). Honey, I shrunk the sample covariance matrix. *Journal of Portfolio Management,* 30(4), pp. 110–119.

Leibowitz, M. L., Kogelman, S., and Bader, L. N. (1993). *Statistical duration—A spread model of rate sensitivity across fixed-income sectors.* Salomon Brothers.

Liberty Street Economics. (2020, April 17). *Treasury market liquidity during the COVID-19 Crisis [blog post].* Federal Reserve Bank of New York. Available from: https://libertystreeteconomics.newyorkfed.org/2020/04/treasury-market-liquidity-during-the-covid-19-crisis.html.

Litterman, R. and Scheinkman, J. (1991, June). Common factors affecting bond returns. *Journal of Fixed Income,* pp. 54–61.

Litzenberger, R. and Modest, D. (2008 July 15). *Crisis and non-crisis risk in financial markets: A unified approach to risk management* (Working Paper) [online]. Available at SSRN: https://ssrn.com/abstract=1160273 or http://dx.doi.org/10.2139/ssrn.1160273.

Lo, A., Petrov, C., and Wierzbicki, M. (2003). It's 11 pm—Do you know where your liquidity is? The mean-variance-liquidity frontier. *Journal of Investment Management,* 1, pp. 55–93.

Lowenstein, R. (2000). *When genius failed: The rise and fall of long-term capital management.* New York: Random House.

Lyashenko, A. and Mercurio, F. (2019). *Looking forward to backward-looking rates: A modeling framework for term rates replacing LIBOR* [online]. Available at http://dx.doi.org/10.2139/ssrn.3330240.

Lynch, S. (2008). Housing Recovery act depends on banks to refinance mortgages. *Bloomberg* [online]. Previously available from: http://www.bloomberg.com/apps/news?pid=20601213& sid=aLOj1Jjg5wbc&refer=home.

Macaulay, F. R. (1938). *Some theoretical problems suggested by the movement of interest rates, bond yields, and stock prices in the United States since 1865.* National Bureau of Economic Research.

Madhavan, A., Pasquali, S., and Sommer, P. (2022). How trading analytics and data science can improve investment outcomes. *The Journal of Investing*, 32(1), pp. 104–114.

Maillard, S., Roncalli, T., and Teïletche, J. (2010). The properties of equally weighted risk contribution portfolios. *Journal of Portfolio Management*, 36(4), pp. 60–70.

Market veterans mourn slow death of historic trading pits. (2021). *Financial Times*. [online]. Available from: https://www.ft.com/content/2e401cd8-12b3-4832-8036-3db5fe4a3ee3 [Accessed 15 Feb. 2023].

Mausser, H. and Rosen, D. (1999). Applying scenario optimization to portfolio credit risk. *Algo Research Quarterly*, 2(2).

McCormack, K. (2006, October 6). Should you invest in these countries? *Business Week* [online]. Available from: http:// www.businessweek.com/investor/content/oct2006/pi20061004_ 368647.htm.

McKinsey & Company. (2013, July). *Strong performance but health still fragile: Global asset management in 2013. Will the goose keep laying golden eggs?* Author.

Menchero, J. and Morozov, A. (2015). Improving risk forecasts through cross-sectional observations. *The Journal of Portfolio Management*, 41(3), pp. 84–96.

Meucci, A. (2009). Managing diversification. *Risk*, pp. 74–79.

Mildenberg, D. and Freifeld, K. (2008). Countrywide's underwriters sued for fraud by New York agencies. *Bloomberg* [online]. Available from: http://www.bloomberg.com/apps/ news? pid= 0601208&sid=axRMZutUG2BQ&refer=finance.

Missal, M. and Richman, L. (2008, October). New century financial: Lessons learned. *Mortgage Banking*.

Mnyanda, L. and Pan. A. (2008). TED Spread at nine-month low, signals credit easing. *Bloomberg* [online]. Previously available from: http://www.bloomberg.com/apps/news?pid=20602007& sid=aFeo78.kipqY.

Mollenkamp, C., Ng, S., Pleven, L., and Smith, R. (2008, October 31). Behind AIG's fall, risk models failed to pass real-world test. *Wall Street Journal*. Available from: http://online.wsj.com/article/ SB122538449722784635.html.

Moses, A. (2008). Bank risk soars on concern bond insurer breakup may fuel losses. *Bloomberg* [online]. Previously available from: http://www.bloomberg.com/apps/news?pid=20601087&sid=acA8ys0 KSTbw&refer=home.

Müller, U. A. (1993). *Statistics of variables observed over overlapping intervals.* Olsen & Associates Research Group discussion.

Newey, W. and West, K. (1987). A simple, positive semidefinite, heteroscedasticity and autocorrelation consistent covariance matrix. *Econometrica*, 55, 703–708.

Park, S., McCormick, J., and Jiltsov, A. (2007). *Introducing our market risk sentiment index.* Global Foreign Exchange Research, Lehman Brothers.

Pastor, L. and Stambaugh, R. (2003). Liquidity risk and expected stock returns. *Journal of Political Economy*, 111(3), pp. 642–685.

Patton, A. J. (2011). Volatility forecast comparison using imperfect volatility proxies. *Journal of Econometrics*, 160(1), 246–256.

Pentland, A. S. (2013). Beyond the echo chamber. *Harvard Business Review* 91.11.

Pittman, M. (2008). Merrill Lynch plans to write off ACA bond insurance. *Bloomberg* [online]. Previously available from: http://www. bloomberg.com/apps/news?pid=20601087&sid=abJ54x Mm7k4Y&refer=home.

Pressman, A. (2009). Yale investing guru Swensen missed problems with his advice. *Business Week* [online]. Available from: https://www.bloomberg.com/news/articles/2009-03-16/yale-investing-guru-swensen-missed-problems-with-his-advice.

Prince, B. (2011). *Risk parity is about balance*. Bridgewater Associates. Available from: https://www .bridgewater.com/resources/risk-parity-is-about-balance.pdf.

PwC. (2020). *ETFs: Unlocking further potential: Developing Europe's ETF trading infrastructure to drive further improvement and growth*. Author.

Qian, E. (2006). On The financial interpretation of risk contribution: Risk budgets do add up. *Journal of Investment Management*, 4(4), pp. 41–51.

Reitano, R. R. (1990). Multivariate duration analysis. *Journal of Portfolio Management*.

Reitano, R. R. (1996). *Non-parallel yield curve shifts and stochastic immunization*. John Hancock Financial Services.

Ronn, E. I. (1996). *The impact of large changes in asset prices on intra-market correlations in the stock and bond markets* (Working Paper). University of Texas, Austin.

Ross, S. (1976). The arbitrage theory of capital asset pricing. *Journal of Economic Theory*, pp. 341–360.

Ruban, O. and Melas, D. (2010). *Stress testing in the investment process*. MSCI Research Report.

Salas, C. (2006). Pfizer's AAA rating is in jeopardy, bond prices show. *Bloomberg* [online]. Previously available from: http://www. bloomberg.com/apps/news?pid=20601103&sid=aV5OnC_qSKs8& refer=news.

Samuelson, P. (1965). Proof that properly anticipated prices fluctuate randomly. *Industrial Management Review*, 6, pp. 41–49.

Satow, J. (2008). Ex-SEC Official Blames Agency for Blow-Up of Broker-Dealers. *New York Sun* [online]. Previously available from: https://www.nysun.com/article/business-ex-sec-official-blames-agency-for-blow-up.

Scherer B. (2015). *Portfolio construction and risk budgeting*. 5th ed. Risk Books.

Securities Industry and Financial Markets Association. (2008). *Restoring confidence in the securitization markets* [online]. Previously available from: http://www.sifma.org/capital_markets/docs/Survey-Restoring-confidence-securitization-markets.pdf.

Sharpe, W. E. (1994). The Sharpe ratio. *Journal of Portfolio Management (Fall)*.

Shiller, R. (1981). Do stock prices move too much to be justified by subsequent changes in dividends? *American Economic Review*, 71, pp. 421–436.

Shleifer, A. and Vishny, R. (1997). The limits of arbitrage. *Journal of Finance*, 52(1), pp. 35–55.

Sicart, F. (2007). *Black swans, the ludic fallacy, and wealth management* [online]. Tocqueville Asset Management. Available from: http://www.tocqueville.com/article/show/204.

Silva, A. and Ural, C. (2011). *Stress testing of portfolios* (Working Paper.) Barclays Capital.

Siu, F. (2014). *Risk parity strategies for equity portfolio management* [online]. ETF.com. Available from: https://www.etf.com/publications/journalofindexes/joi-articles/21890-risk-parity-strategies-for-equity-portfolio-management.html.

Smith, A. (2008). Abu Dhabi: Rising Power. *Time* [online]. Available from: https://content.time.com/time/subscriber/article/0,33009,1825872,00.html.

Sommer, P. and Pasquali, S. (2016). Liquidity—How to capture a multidimensional beast. *Journal of Trading (Spring)*.

Stone, H. (1934). Presentation at the Dedication of the University of Michigan Law School Quadrangle.

Strahilevitz, M. A., and Loewenstein, G. (1998). The effect of ownership history on the valuation of objects. *Journal of Consumer Research*, 25(3), pp. 276–289.

Strang, G. (1980). *Linear algebra and its applications*. Academic Press.

Surowiecki, J. (2004). *The wisdom of crowds: Why the many are smarter than the few and how collective wisdom shapes business, economics, societies and nations*. Doubleday.

Swensen, D. (2009). *Pioneering portfolio management*. Free Press.

Taleb, N. (2007a). *The black swan: The impact of the highly improbable*. Random House,

Taleb, N. (2007b). Black swans and the domain of statistics. *American Statistician*, 61, pp. 1–3.

Tetlock, P. E. and Gardner, D. (2016). *Superforecasting: The art and science of prediction*. Crown.

Thomas, P. and Pearle, L. (2008). Exclusive: WaMu insiders claim execs ignored warnings, encouraged reckless lending. *ABC News* [online]. Available from: https://abcnews.go.com/TheLaw/exclusive-wamu-insiders-claim-execs-warnings-encouraged-reckless/story?id=6021608.

Trowbridge, P. and Mider, Z. (2008). Banks at risk of $203 billion in writedowns, says UBS. *Bloomberg* [online]. Available from: https://www.bloomberg.com/news/articles/2008-02-15/banks-at-risk-of-another-120-billion-in-writedowns-says-ubs.

van Dolder, D. and van den Assem, M. J. (2018). The wisdom of the inner crowd in three large natural experiments. *Nature Human Behaviour*, 2(1), p. 21.

Van and Eck Global. (2009). *The investment case for pre-refunded municipal bonds* [online]. Available from: http://www.vaneck.com/ sld/vaneck/offerings/brochures/PRB_Case_Investment.pdf.

Voreacos, D. and Kary, T. (2008). Bear Stearns faces revised suit over collapse of hedge funds. *Bloomberg* [online]. Previously available from: http://www.bloomberg.com/apps/news?pid=20601103&sid=aCNSu3EEtPRA&refer=us.

Walker, R. (2009). Fortune favours the well-prepared. *Financial Times* [online]. Available from: http://www.ft.com/cms/s/0/ 752d1908-ecd4-11dd-a534-0000779fd2ac.html.

Weil, N. (1973). Macaulay duration: An appreciation. *Journal of Business*, 46, pp. 589–592.

Weir, N. (1996). *Advances in risk management: Applications to portfolio management (Working Paper)*. Goldman Sachs & Co.

Willner, R. (1996, June). A new tool for portfolio managers: Level, Slope, and curvature durations. *Journal of Portfolio Management*.

Wood, D. A. (2008). Return to nuts and bolts. *Risk*, 21(9).

Working Group on Sterling Risk-Free Reference Rates. (2018). *Preparing for 2022: What you need to know about LIBOR transition*. Author.

www.g20.org. (n.d.). About G20. [online] Available from: https://www.g20.org/en/about-g20/.

www.ibm.com. (n.d.). *ILOG CPLEX Optimization Studio—Overview* [online]. Available from: http://www.cplex.com [Accessed 16 Feb. 2023].

www.mosek.com. (n.d.). Mosek ApS [online]. Available from: http://www.mosek.com.

Yale University. (2008). *The Yale endowment* [online]. Available from: https://static1.squarespace.com/static/55db7b87e4b0dca22fba2438/t/578e428de58c629352d75c83/1468940944732/Yale_Endowment_08.pdf.

Yang, S., Keller, F. B., and Zheng, L. (2017). *Social network analysis: Methods and examples*. Thousand Oaks, CA: SAGE. https://dx.doi.org/10.4135/9781071802847.

About the Website

Thank you for purchasing *BlackRock's Guide to Fixed-Income Risk Management*. Additional complementary resources are available at:

www.wiley.com/go/golub/fixedincomemanagment
Password: Golub123

On the website, exhibits from the book are provided in color. The web content is a way to allow those with a paper copy of the book to see the full-color illustrations. Additionally, while the electronic versions of the book are already in color, the web content allows those with an electronic copy to see the illustrations in a larger format.

About the Editor

Bennett W. Golub is one of the eight original founding partners of the firm now known as BlackRock, Inc. Dr. Golub also cofounded BlackRock's risk advisory business, which is BlackRock Solutions. During his 34-year career at BlackRock, Dr. Golub was a member of BlackRock's Global Executive Committee and co-head of its Risk & Quantitative Analysis group. Serving as BlackRock's Chief Risk Officer from 2009–2022, Dr. Golub was responsible for investment, counterparty, technology, operational, regulatory, model, and third-party risk. Additionally, he chaired BlackRock's Enterprise Risk Management Committee. Dr. Golub retired in 2022 and remains a senior advisor to BlackRock.

Dr. Golub is well recognized for his perspectives and experience in risk management. Dr. Golub has authored or coauthored numerous articles on risk management and financial modeling. In 2000, Dr. Golub coauthored *Risk Management: Approaches for Fixed Income Markets*.

In 2016, *Risk* magazine honored Dr. Golub with its Lifetime Achievement award in recognition of his many contributions promoting effective risk management. He was a member of the Financial Research Advisory Committee of the US Treasury's Office of Financial Research and a member of the Financial Advisory Roundtable of the Federal Reserve Bank of New York. He is a board member of the Global Association of Risk Professionals, a member of the MIT Sloan School of Management's North American Executive Board and Finance Group Advisory Board. He also serves as chairman of the advisory board of the MIT Golub Center for Finance and Policy.

Dr. Golub became the president of the Jewish Community Relations Council of New York in July 2022.

Dr. Golub earned an SB and an SM in management and a PhD in applied economics and finance, all from the Massachusetts Institute of Technology Sloan School of Management.

About the Contributors

Nikki Azznara
Vice President, Portfolio Management Group, BlackRock

Tom Booker
Director, Financial Modeling Group, BlackRock

Joe Buehlmeyer
Director, Aladdin Product Group, BlackRock

Christopher Calingo
Director, Risk & Quantitative Analysis, BlackRock

Samara Cohen
Senior Managing Director, ETF and Index Investments, BlackRock

Joanna Cound
Managing Director, Global Public Policy Group, BlackRock

Conan Crum
Former Vice President, Risk & Quantitative Analysis, BlackRock (2013)

Katie Day
Managing Director, Risk & Quantitative Analysis, BlackRock

Amandeep Dhaliwal
Managing Director, Financial Modeling Group, BlackRock

Thomas Donilon
Senior Managing Director, BlackRock Investment Institute, BlackRock

Viola Dunne
Former Managing Director, Risk & Quantitative Analysis, BlackRock (2023)

Ed Fishwick
Chief Risk Officer, BlackRock

Rick Flynn
Managing Director, Risk & Quantitative Analysis, BlackRock

Kate Fulton
Managing Director, Global Public Policy Group, BlackRock

Bennett W. Golub
Senior Advisor, Co-Founder, Former Chief Risk Officer, BlackRock

David Greenberg
Former Managing Director, Technology & Operations—Artificial Intelligence Labs, BlackRock (2022)

Emily Haisley
Managing Director, Risk & Quantitative Analysis, BlackRock

Jack Hattem
Managing Director, Portfolio Management Group, BlackRock

Michael Huang
Managing Director, Risk & Quantitative Analysis, BlackRock

Eileen Kiely
Managing Director, Risk & Quantitative Analysis, BlackRock

Hui Sien Koay
Director, Indexed Fixed Income Portfolio Management Group, BlackRock

Catherine Kress
Director, BlackRock Investment Institute, BlackRock

Yury Krongauz
Managing Director, Financial Modeling Group, BlackRock

Nicky Lai
Director, Risk & Quantitative Analysis, BlackRock

Stephen Laipply
Managing Director, iShares Fixed Income ETFs, BlackRock

Isabelle Mateos y Lago
Managing Director, Official Institutions Group, BlackRock

Barbara Novick
Senior Advisor, Co-Founder, Former Vice Chairman, BlackRock

Vasiliki Pachatouridi
Managing Director, Indexed Fixed Income Portfolio Management Group, BlackRock

Mark Paltrowitz
Managing Director, Risk & Quantitative Analysis, BlackRock

Stefano Pasquali
Managing Director, Liquidity & Trading Research Group, BlackRock

Carl Patchen
Former Vice President, Risk & Quantitative Analysis, BlackRock (2022)

Winnie Pun
Former Managing Director, Global Public Policy Group, BlackRock (2023)

Ronald Ratcliffe
Managing Director, Analytics & Quantitative Solutions, BlackRock

Reade Ryan
Managing Director, Risk & Quantitative Analysis, BlackRock

Philip Sommer
Director, Liquidity & Trading Research Group, BlackRock

Mark Temple-Jones
Former Director, ETF & Index Investments, BlackRock (2023)

Leo M. Tilman
CEO, Tilman & Company
Author of *Agility* (with General Charles H. Jacoby), *Financial Darwinism*, and *Risk Management: Approaches for Fixed Income Markets* (with Bennett W. Golub)
Former Director, Risk & Quantitative Analysis, BlackRock (2001)

Alex Ulitsky
Managing Director, Financial Modeling Group, BlackRock

Eric Van Nostrand
Former Managing Director, BlackRock Sustainable Investment, BlackRock (2022)

Rory van Zwanenberg
Director, Risk & Quantitative Analysis, BlackRock

Daniel Veiner
Managing Director, Global Trading, BlackRock

Kristen Walters
Former Managing Director, Risk & Quantitative Analysis, BlackRock (2020)

Matthew Wang
Managing Director, Fundamental Fixed Income Portfolio Management Group, BlackRock

Carolyn Weinberg
Managing Director, Investment Product Management, BlackRock

Allison White
Director, Risk & Quantitative Analysis, BlackRock

Kemin Yang
Former Associate, BlackRock Investment Institute, BlackRock (2019)

Carol Yu
Former Vice President, Risk & Quantitative Analysis, BlackRock (2022)

Index